The Spirit of Islam

THE SPIRIT OF ISLAM

Within a few centuries after the death of Mohammed (PBUH) in A.D. 632 the Islamic creed had spread across half the world and obtained a permanent and powerful hold over millions of people. In this book the author traces the origins and the history of this religion. He recognizes, almost for the first time in a book in the English Language, its extraordinary effects in uplifting humanity and its true place in the history of religions.

The Spirit of Islam

A HISTORY OF THE EVOLUTION
AND IDEALS OF ISLAM
WITH A LIFE OF THE PROPHET (PBUH)

BY

Syed Ameer Ali

P.C., LL.D., D.L., C.I.E.

سخن كز بهر دين گوئي چه عبراني چه سرياني

مكان كز بهر حق جوئي چه جابلقا چه جابلسا

*What matters it whether the words thou utterest in
prayer are Hebrew or Syrian, or whether the place in
which thou seekest God is Jâbalka or Jâbalsà.*

—SANAI

SANG-E-MEEL PUBLICATIONS
25 - SHAHRA-E-PAKISTAN (LOWER MALL), LAHORE - 2   PAKISTAN

Published by :
NIAZ AHMAD
Sang-e-Meel Publications
Lahore

Printed at :
Combine Printers
Lahore

H.B - ISBN - 969 - 35 - 0612 - X
P.B - ISBN - 969 - 35 - 0613 - 8

TO MY WIFE

PREFACE

IN the following pages I have attempted to give the history of the evolution of Islâm as a world-religion ; of its rapid spread and the remarkable hold it obtained over the conscience and minds of millions of people within a short space of time. The impulse it gave to the intellectual development of the human race is generally recognised. But its great work in the uplifting of humanity is either ignored or not appreciated ; nor are its rationale, its ideals and its aspirations properly understood. It has been my endeavour in the survey of Islâm to elucidate its true place in the history of religions. The review of its rationale and ideals, however feeble, may be of help to wanderers in quest of a constructive faith to steady the human mind after the strain of the recent cataclysm ; it is also hoped that to those who follow the Faith of Islâm it may be of assistance in the understanding and exposition of the foundations of their convictions.

My outline of the life and ministry of the Prophet is based on the *Sîrat-ur-Rasûl* of Ibn Hishâm, who died in 213 A.H. (828-9 A.C.), barely two hundred years after the death of the Prophet, supplemented by, among other works, Ibn ul-Âthîr's monumental history, the Chronicles of Tabari, the *Insân ul-'Uyûn* of al-Halabi (commonly known as *Sîrat-ul-Halabia*). Two new chapters have been added in this edition : one on the *Imâmate* (" The Apostolical Succession "), the other on " The Idealistic and Mystical Spirit in Islâm." Considerable new matter has also been included in the Introduction and

Chapter X., Part II. I take this opportunity of expressing my gratitude to my esteemed friend, Professor E. G. Browne of Cambridge, one of our foremost Orientalists, for his most valuable criticisms on the last chapter, and to Mr. Mohammed Iqbal, Government of India Research Scholar at Cambridge, for his careful revision of the proofs and the compilation of the Index. I also desire to express my acknowledgments to Mr. Abdul Qayum Malik for transcribing for the Printers the Arabic quotations for the new chapters and verifying the Koranic references, and to the Publishers for their unvarying courtesy and patience over a difficult publication.

The work has been carried through the Press under heavy pressure of public duties, and I claim, on that ground, the indulgence of my readers for any mistake that may have passed uncorrected.

N.B.—A few words are necessary to explain the system of transliteration adopted in this work. I have tried to adhere with small modification to the system I have pursued in my previous publications. The letter ث (pronounced by the Arab with a lisp like *th* in thin) to a non-Arab conveys a sound almost identical with *s* in sin, and he accordingly pronounces it as such. Nor, unless an Arabic scholar, does he perceive any difference between ث and *sîn* or ص (*sâd*). He pronounces them all alike. Similarly ذ (*zal*), ز (*Zay*), ض (*Zâd*—pronounced by the Arab something like *dhad*), and ظ (*zoi*), convey to the non-Arab almost identical sounds; certainly he cannot help pronouncing them identically. He also perceives no difference between ت (soft *t*) and ط (*toi*), or between the hard aspirate ح (in Ahmed, Mohammed, Mahmûd, etc.) and the softer used in Hârûn. I have therefore not attempted to differentiate these letters by dots or commas, which, however useful for purposes of translation into Arabic, Persian, Turkish or Urdu, is only bewildering to the general reader unacquainted with the Arabic alphabet and pronunciation. I have given the words as commonly pronounced by non-Arabs. In the case of words spelt with a ث in common use in India and Persia such as *hadîs, masnavi, Isna-'asharia,* etc., I have not considered it necessary to denote the Arabic pronunciation with a *th*.

The ordinary *fatha* I have represented by *a* (pronounced as *u* in ' cut ' or ' but '), excepting in such words as are now commonly written in English with an *e*, as Seljuk (pronounced Saljûk), Merwan (pronounced Marwân), etc. ; the ordinary *zamma* by *u* pronounced like *u* in ' pull,' or in Buldân ; the ordinary *kasra* with the letter *i*, as in Misr. *Aliph* with the *fatha* is represented by *a*, as in ' had ' ; *Aliph* with the *zamma*, by *u* as in Abdul-Muttalib ; with a *kasra* by *i* as in Ibn Abi'l Jawâri. *Waw* (with a *zamma*) by *o* and sometimes by *ô*. Although like Kûfa and several other words, the last syllables in Mahmud, Hârûn and Mâmûn are spelt with a *waw*, to have represented them by an *o* or *ô* would have conveyed a wholly wrong notion of the pronunciation, which is like *oo* ; I have, therefore, used *u* to represent *waw* in such words. *Waw* with a *fatha* I have represented by *au*, as in Maudûd. *Ya* with a *kasra*, when used in the middle of a word, I have represented by *i*, as in Arish. But in Ameer I have kept the classical and time honoured *ee*. *Ya* with a *fatha*, similarly situated by *ai* as in Zaid. *Ya* with a *fatha* at the beginning of a word is represented by *ye*, as in Yezid ; with a *zamma* by *yu*, as in Yusuf. Excepting such names as are commonly known to be spelt with an *'ain* (ع), as *Abd* in Abdul Malik, Abdur Rahman, Arab, Abbas, Aziz, Irâk, etc., I have used the inverted comma to denote that letter.

With regard to names which have become familiar in certain garbs I have made no alteration, such as Kaaba, Omar, Abdullah, Basra, spelt with a *sâd*, etc. *Ghain* (ع) is represented by *gh* ; but I have not attempted to differentiate between ذ and ز, and made no alteration in the time honoured spelling of the Koran. The common *g* (the Persian *gâf*) and *p* have no place in the Arabic alphabet, and therefore the Persian *g* and *p* are transformed in Arabic into *j* or *k* and *b* or *ph* (*f*), as in Atabek and Isfahan. ج is represented by *kh*.

The *l* of *al* when occurring before certain letters (technically called *shamsiêh*) is assimilated with them in sound, as ash-Shams, ad-din, ar-Riza, as-Salât, etc. I have used the word " Moslem " in preference to " Muslim," as most Europeans unacquainted with Arabic pronounce the " u " in " Muslim " as in public.

CONTENTS

INTRODUCTION

PART I

THE LIFE AND MINISTRY OF THE PROPHET

CHAPTER I

MOHAMMED THE PROPHET

CHAPTER II

THE HEGIRA

CONTENTS

CHAPTER IX

FULFILMENT OF THE PROPHET'S WORK

CHAPTER X

THE APOSTOLICAL SUCCESSION

PART II

THE SPIRIT OF ISLÂM

CHAPTER I

THE IDEAL OF ISLÂM

CHAPTER II

THE RELIGIOUS SPIRIT OF ISLÂM

CHAPTER III

THE IDEA OF FUTURE LIFE IN ISLÂM

CONTENTS

CONTENTS

CHAPTER VIII

THE POLITICAL DIVISIONS AND SCHISMS OF ISLÂM

CHAPTER IX

THE LITERARY AND SCIENTIFIC SPIRIT OF ISLÂM

CHAPTER X

THE RATIONALISTIC AND PHILOSOPHICAL SPIRIT OF ISLÂM

CONTENTS

CHAPTER XI

IDEALISTIC AND MYSTICAL SPIRIT IN ISLÂM

INTRODUCTION

ای که در هیـچ جا نداری جا
بو العجب مانده ام که هر جائی
وصا لي
کفر و دیں هر دو در رهت پویاں
وحـــده لا شــریک له گویاں
سنائي

THE continuity of religious progress among mankind
is a subject of enthralling interest to the student
of humanity. The gradual awakening of the human
mind to the recognition of a Personality, of a Supreme Will
overshadowing the universe; the travails through which
individuals and races have passed before they arrived at
the conception of an Universal Soul pervading, regulating,
and guiding all existence,—furnish lessons of the deepest
import. The process by which humanity has been lifted
from the adoration of material objects to the worship of
God, has often been retarded. Masses of mankind and
individuals have broken away from the stream of progress,
have listened to the promptings of their own desires, have
given way to the cravings of their own hearts; they have gone
back to the worship of their passions, symbolised in the idols
of their infancy. But though unheard, the voice of God has
always sounded the call to truth, and when the time has
arrived His servants have risen to proclaim the duties of man to
himself and to his Creator. These men have been the veritable

" messengers of Heaven." They came among their people
as the children of their time ; they represented the burning
aspirations of the human soul for truth, purity, and justice.
Each was an embodiment of the spiritual necessities of his
age ; each came to purify, to reform, to elevate a degraded
race, a corrupted commonwealth. Some came as teachers of
a smaller culture, to influence a smaller sphere ; others came
with a world-wide message—a message not confined to one race
or nation, but intended for all humanity. Such was
Mohammed. His mission was not to the Arabs alone. He
was not sent for one age or clime, but " for all mankind to the
end of the world." The advent of this great Teacher, whose
life from the moment of his Ministry is a verifiable record, was
not a mere accident, an unconnected episode in the history
of the world. The same causes, the same crying evils, the same
earnest demand for an " assured trust " in an all-pervading
Power, which led to the appearance on the shores of Galilee,
in the reign of Augustus Cæsar, of a Prophet whose life is a
tragedy, operated with greater force in the seventh century
of the Christian era. The beginning of the seventh century,
as has been rightly said, was an epoch of disintegration—
national, social, and religious : its phenomena were such as
have always involved a fresh form of positive faith, to recall
all wandering forces to the inevitable track of spiritual evolution
"towards the integration of personal worship." They all pointed
to the necessity of a more organic revelation of divine government than that attained by Judaism or Christianity. The holy
flames kindled by Zoroaster, Moses, and Jesus had been
quenched in the blood of man. A corrupt Zoroastrianism,
battling for centuries with a still more corrupt Christianity,
had stifled the voice of humanity, and converted some of the
happiest portions of the globe into a veritable Aceldama.
Incessant war for supremacy, perpetual internecine strife,
combined with the ceaseless wrangling of creeds and sects,
had sucked the life-blood out of the hearts of nations, and the
people of the earth, trodden under the iron heels of a lifeless
sacerdotalism, were crying to God from the misdeeds of their
masters. Never in the history of the world was the need so
great, the time so ripe, for the appearance of a Deliverer. In

order, therefore, to appreciate thoroughly the achievement of Mohammed in the moral world, it is necessary to take a rapid survey of the religious and social condition of the nations of the earth previous to, and about the time of, the Islâmic Dispensation.

The high table-land of Bactria, appropriately styled by Arab geographers *Umm ul-Bilâd*, or " mother of countries," is supposed to be the cradle of humanity, the original birth-place of creeds and nations. Through the faint and shadowy light, which comparative ethnology throws on the infancy of mankind, we perceive groups of families congregated in this primeval home of the human race, gradually coalescing into clans and tribes, and then forced by the pressure of increasing population, issuing in successive waves to people the face of the globe. The Hamitic branch were apparently the first to leave their ancient habitations. They were followed by the Turanians, or, as they are sometimes called, the Ugro-Finnish tribes, supposed to be an offshot of the Japhetic family. Some of them apparently proceeded northwards, and then spreading themselves in the East, founded the present Mongolian branch of the human race. Another section proceeded westward and settled in Âzarbaijan, Hamadân, and Ghilân, countries to the south and south-west of the Caspian, better known in ancient history as Media. A portion of these descending afterwards into the fertile plains of Babylonia, enslaved the earlier Hamitic colonies, and in course of time amalgamating with them, formed the Accadian nation, the Kushites of the Jewish and Christian Scriptures. This composite race created Babylon, and gave birth to a form of religion which, in its higher phases, was akin to natural pantheism. In its lower phases, with its pan-dæmonism, its worship of the sun-gods and moon-gods, closely associated with the phallic cult and the sexual instincts, the sacrifice of children to Baal and Moloch, of virginity to Beltis and Ashtoreth, it marks an epoch when high material civilisation was allied to gross licentiousness, and cruelty was sanctioned by religion.

The Semites were the next to leave the primeval home. They also, following in the footsteps of the Turanians, migrated towards the West, and apparently settled themselves in the northern part of the Mesopotamian Delta. Increasing in numbers and strength, they soon overthrew the Babylonian kingdom, and founded a far-reaching empire which wielded its sway over all the neighbouring States. In their seat of power between the two great rivers of Western Asia, the Assyrians at times rose to a positive monotheistic conception. Their system of celestial hierarchy furnishes indications of a distinct recognition of one Supreme Personality.

Whilst the main body of the Semitic colony was developing itself in the upper parts of the Delta, a small section had penetrated far into a district called Ur, within the boundaries of the Chaldæan monarchy.[1]   The patriarch of this tribe, whose self-imposed exile and wanderings have passed into the religious legends of more than one creed, became the father of the future makers of history.[2]

The Japhetic family seems to have tarried longest in its ancient habitation. Whilst the other races, which had broken away from the original stock, were forming empires and evolving creeds, the Japhetic branch underwent a development peculiar to itself. But the march of nations once set on foot was never to cease ; actuated by that spirit of unrest which works in barbarous tribes, or influenced by the pressure of population and the scarcity of space in their old haunts for the pursuit of their pastoral avocations, tribe after tribe moved away towards the West. Among the first were the Pelasgians and the Celts. Other tribes followed, until the Aryans proper were left alone in the old haunts. One section apparently had its abode near Badakhshân, the other towards Balkh proper, where for centuries they lived almost isolated from the neighbouring nations, unaffected by their wars or their movements. The light of history which has dawned on the Western races, the founders of kingdoms and civilisations, also falls upon these ancient dwellers of the earth, and reveals, though indistinctly and as through a mist, several clans gathered together on that plateau ; just emerged from

[1] Rawlinson, *Ancient Monarchies*, p. 23.

[2] In the Arabian traditions the father of Abraham is called Âzar, which is evidently the same as Asshur ; and the beautiful idols of Âzar are frequently referred to in Moslem literature. These traditions confirm the belief that Abraham was of Assyrian origin.

savageness into barbarism, they are becoming alive to the sense of an Universal Ideality. Innumerable idealities are taking the place of the natural objects, hitherto worshipped with fear and trembling. With some of them the host of abstractions and personifications of the powers of nature are subordinated to two comprehensive principles—Light and Darkness. The sun, the bright harbinger of life and light, becomes the symbol of a beneficent Divinity, whose power, though held in check, is eventually to conquer the opposing principle of Evil and Darkness. With others, the idealities which they now impress on the fetish they worshipped before, merge in each other ; at one time standing forth as distinct personal entities, at another time resolving themselves into a hylozoic whole. Gradually the clouds lift, and we see the tribal and clan-formations giving way to monarchical institutions ; agriculture taking by slow degrees the place of pastoral avocations ; primitive arts being cultivated ; the use of metals gaining ground, and, above all, the higher conception of a Supreme Personality forcing itself upon the yet unopened mind. Kaiumurs, Hoshang, and the other old kings of whom Firdousi sings with such wondrous power, are types of an advancing civilisation. The introduction of the monarchical institutions among the Aryans proper seems to be coeval with that religious conflict between the two branches of the Aryan family which led to the expulsion of the Eastern branch from their Bactrian home. A powerful religious revolution had been inaugurated among the Western Aryans by a teacher whose name has been preserved in the literature of his religion as Citama Zarathustra. The sharp religious conflict, which resulted from this move-ment, has left its mark in the deep imprecations heaped by the Vedic hymn-singers on the enemy of their race and creed, the Djaradashti of the Vedas. The attitude of the Vedic hymn-singers towards the reformed faith, even more than the extraordinary coincidence in names, furnishes the strongest proof that the religious divergence was the immediate cause of the split between the two branches of the Aryans proper. In this, probably the first religious war waged among man-kind, the Western dualistic clans were successful in driving their half-polytheistic, half-pantheistic brethren across the

Paropamisadæ. The Eastern Aryans burst into India, driving before them the earlier black races, massacring and enslaving them, treating them always as inferior beings, Dasyus and Sudras, slaves and serfs. The difference between the Vedic and the Zoroastrian religions was, however, purely relative. Zoroastrianism substituted for the worship of the phenomena, the adoration of the cause. It converted the gods of the Vedas into demons and the deva-worshippers into infidels ; whilst the Vedic hymn-singer, on his side, called the Ahura of the Avesta an evil god, an Asura, a power hostile to the gods, and heaped burning maledictions on the head of Djaradashti.

Whilst the place and time of the early Zoroaster's birth are enwrapt in mystery, under Darius Hystaspes arose another teacher, who, under the same name, revived, organised, and enlarged the basis of the ancient teachings.

Retracing our steps for a moment, we see the tide of Aryan conquest in India flowing eastward and southward for centuries. The old Aryan religion, which the invaders had brought from their ancient homes, consisted chiefly in the worship of the manes and the adoration of the powers of Nature symbolised in visible phenomena. In the land of the Five Rivers the spiritual conception developed further ; we can read in the Vedas the march of progress until we arrive at the zenith of Hindu religious ideas in the *Upanishads*, which often in the intensity of spiritual yearning approach the highest monotheism. The *Upanishads* dwell not only on the immanence of God, a conception which gave birth in later times to the material pantheism of India ; but also teach that the Supreme Spirit is the protector of all beings and sovereign over all creation, that he dwells in the hearts of men, and finally absorbs the individual soul in infinity " as the ocean absorbs the river " ; when that absorption takes place the human soul loses all consciousness of its experience in the earthly frame. But these interesting records of human progress contained within themselves unquestioned germs of spiritual decadence which soon reversed the process of evolution ; and thus instead of observing a further uplifting, we see a progressive declension. The *Upanishads* make way for the Puranic cults, which again succumb to the power of the Tantric worship.

The idea to which the *Upanishads* frequently give expression that the Supreme Spirit manifests Himself in various forms gave rise to the conception of the *Avatârs* or incarnations. Just as in the Western pagan world philosophy failed to satisfy the craving of the popular mind for a personal God who had dwelt among mankind and held familiar discourse with them, the theistic aspirations of the *Upanishads* did not appeal to the heart or touch the emotions of the masses of India. And a hero-god was soon found in a member of the warrior caste, who came before long to be identified with the Supreme Spirit and to be regarded in his earthly existence as an incarnate god.

The development of the Krishna-cult, like that of its rival, the worship of the " dread Mother," illustrates forcibly not merely the religious welter which prevailed in India in the seventh century of the Christian era, but also the gulf which divided the minds of the philosophers who composed the *Upanishads* and the *Bhagavad-Gita* ; " the Song of Faith," [1] from the thoughts and feelings of the populace. It is abundantly clear that long before they burst into Hindustan proper, the Aryan settlers in the Punjab or their priests and religious teachers made the most stringent rules to prevent the intermixture of the invaders and their descendants with the races they had conquered and enslaved in their steady and prolonged march towards the East. The touch of the latter, who were turned into the lowest and servile caste, was pollution ; all the religious rites peculiar to the three higher castes were strictly forbidden to them.

Among all the flow and ebb of Aryan-Hindu thought in the region of pantheism the worship of the manes has always clung to the Hindu mind as an essential part of his religio-social system. The Sudra was permitted to offer oblations to his dead ancestors, but no Brahman could officiate at the rites without incurring the heaviest penalties. If a Sudra over-heard a Brahman reciting the Vedas, he was to be punished by having molten lead poured into his ears ; if he happened to sit on the same bench with the Brahman he was liable to be

---

[1] A recent writer remarks that the *Bhagavad-Gita* no doubt shows traces of theism, but this theism is blended with other and non-theistic elements.

branded. Whilst unions, legitimate or illegitimate, between the "twice born," as the three superior castes were called, and the Sudras were interdicted under the cruellest penalties. No legislation, however, could prevent their religious ideas and practices being influenced by the primitive beliefs. In course of time the divinities of the pre-Aryan tribes and races were incorporated into the Hindu pantheon, and their worship became part of the Hindu daily ritual. The amalgamations of diverse beliefs of unequal growth and varying tendencies had their inevitable result in the debasement of the complex and abstruse pantheism the philosophers were endeavouring through ages to evolve.

Before the followers of Islâm lifted the veil behind which India had lived enshrouded in mystery for thousands of years, she possessed no history. It is impossible to say when Vasu-deva-Krishna lived, or to judge of his personality. There are innumerable legends which verge on the absurd and puerile, legends evidently manufactured by the priests, who had become the equals, if not the superiors, of the gods ; and whose interest it was to keep the minds of the vulgar fascinated and enthralled. The place which Vasudeva-Krishna occupies in the Hindu pantheon is that of the incarnation of Vishnu, and as such he forms the central figure in the devotional part of the *Bhagavad-Gita*. He is evidently a composite divinity ; one of the man-gods associated with him being the gay hero who lived among the cowherds of Gokul and disported himself in the famous groves of Brindabun with his merry companions.[1]

The cult of Vasudeva-Krishna inculcated absolute *dharma* or faith as the key to salvation ; the believer in this incarnate Vishnu, whatever his conduct in life, was assured of eternal happiness.

The doctrine of perfect faith gave birth to practices and beliefs which are still current in India. As righteousness

---

[1] Krishna is usually called the Gopala-Krishna or Cowherd Krishna ; his female companions are called the *gopis*, the " milkmaids." Many a pretty legend is woven round the adventures of this hero-god of the Ahirs, the cow-herd caste of Upper India. Krishna has been somewhat inaptly called the Apollo of the Hindus, though it is difficult to clothe him with the poetry which generally envelopes the Greek god.

consists in the concentration of the mind in one's self as identical
with the Supreme Spirit represented in Krishna, the gymno-
sophic ascetic practices acquired in the eyes of the people a
superlative merit. To sit for years in the forest with the
eyes fixed on one spot of the human body and the mind on
Krishna ; to stand for years on one leg ; to be swung round by
hooks fixed in the flesh were acts of devotion which cured all
sins. To expiate a sin or to fulfil a vow a man might be
employed to measure by the length of his body the distance
from the abode of the penitent to the temple of the deity.
To read the *Bhagavad-Gita* with true faith or to bathe in the
Ganges or any holy pool, absolved every man or woman from
all breaches of the moral laws.

It is difficult to tell when *Saktism* acquired the predominant
hold it now possesses on large masses of the Hindu population.
The *Sakti* is the female half and active creative side of each
Hindu deity. The *Sakti*, or spouse of Siva, is the dread goddess
known under various names, such as Parbati, Bhavâni,
Kâli, Mâha-Kâli, Durga, Chamunda. The worship of this
goddess, as described in the drama of Bhavabhuti, written
apparently in the seventh century of the Christian era, was
celebrated with human sacrifices and other revolting rites.
There is nothing of the " mater dolorosa " in the spouse of
Siva, by whatever name she is invoked or in whatever form she
is worshipped ; she possesses none of the attributes of human
pity or sympathy with human suffering, the Alexandrian
worshipper associated with Isis " the goddess of myriad names."
This awe-inspiring, not to say, awful concept of a decadent
religious mind, evidently borrowed from the pre-Aryan races,
who delights in human blood and revels in human misery,
has few parallels in the paganism of the world ; for even
Cybele, the *magna mater* of the Romans, was not so merciless
or took so much pleasure in inflicting pain as the *Sakti* of the
" God of destruction " [1] This deity is worshipped according
to the ritual of the *Tantras*, which may be regarded as the
bible of *Saktism*. Many of the *Tantric* hymns are imbued
with considerable devotional spirit, and the invocations addressed to the goddess often appeal to her pity ; but whatever

[1] Siva.

mystical meaning the *Tantras* may possess for the philosopher, the people commonly accept the worship in its most literal sense.[1]

From the two great epics, one of which tells the story of the war between the Pandus and the Kurus, and the other the legend of the abduction of Sita by the king of Ceylon, we can form a fairly accurate idea of the popular creeds of the time. Both represent a developed society and considerable material progress combined with great moral decadence. Thus long before the appearance of Gautama, the founder of Buddhism, religious worship among the masses of India had sunk into mere mechanical performance of sacrifices and oblations at which the ability of the ministering priest, without whose services their observance was not permissible, to perform the " god-compelling " rites with the appropriate incantations, rather than the conduct or piety of the worshipper, supplied the test of merit. The revolt of Gautama and of Mahavira (Mahâbîr) represented the natural uprise of the Hindu mind against a selfish sacerdotalism. Both deny a Creative Principle and the existence of a Supreme Intelligence governing and regulating the universe, both affirm the eventual annihilation of individual life ; both dwell on the merit of work in bringing about this blissful consummation. But whilst Jainism has hung on to the skirts of Brahmanism and is now practically a Brahmanical sect, Buddhism struck out boldly a new path for itself. It placed *Karma* in the forefront of its scheme of salvation ; and its great teacher tried to fulfil its claims in his own life. Its conception of the destiny of man after

[1] There are two chief divisions of *Tantric* worshippers: the *Dakhshina-chari* and *Vamachari*, or right and left hand ritualists ; the worship of the former is public, and not otherwise noticeable than as addressed to other goddesses, such as *Lakshmi* or *Mahalakshini*, the *Sakti* of Vishnu. In the left hand worship, specially called *Tantrika*, the exclusive object of adoration is *Kâli*. This worship is private and is said to be celebrated with impure practices. This particular cult has an enormous number of followers all over India and branches into various subdivisions. In the season of the *Durga Puja*, which is usually celebrated in the month of August, the image of Durga is carried about seated on a throne. In Upper India she is painted as yellow of complexion ; in Bengal she is represented as absolutely black, with four hands, seated on a tiger. In the temple of Kalighat (from which Calcutta derives its name) dripping skulls might be seen hanging from her neck. In one of the temples at Jeypore the goddess may be seen with her head twisted round ; the tradition is that the lady turned her face in disgust when a goat was offered to her in sacrifice instead of a human being.

death was quite opposed to Brahmanical doctrines; and its occult mysticism soon passed into other creeds. But in the land of its birth, after a short but glorious existence Buddhism met with a cruel fate; and the measure of punishment that was meted out to it by a triumphant Brahmanism is depicted on the temples of Southern India. It must be admitted, however, that in its pristine garb Buddhism did not possess the attractions Hinduism offered to its votaries. It never claimed to be a positive religion, and its " rewards " and " sanctions," its promise of bliss in a future existence, its penalties for failure to perform duties in this life, were too shadowy to stir the heart of the masses. It had soon to abandon its contest with the outside world or to arrive at a compromise with the religion it had tried to supplant; and it was not long before the religion that Buddha preached had to allow its lay-votaries to substitute prayer-wheels for pious work, or to take to *Tantrism* to supplement its own barren efforts. Its failure under the most favourable circumstances in the land of its nativity sealed its fate as a rousing religious system, although in some of its mystical aspects it exercised considerable influence on the philosophies of Western Asia and Egypt.

On the expulsion of Buddhism from India, Brahmanism regained its supremacy; the long shadow under which it had lived whilst the religion of Buddha dominated the country had brought no improvement in its spiritual conceptions; and the lifeless formalism against which Buddha had revolted was now re-established on a stronger foundation; the lives of men and women were under the restored Brahmanical regime regulated more closely than ever by a sacrificial cult which appealed to their senses, perhaps to their emotions, rather than to their spiritual instincts. Among the masses religious worship became a daily round of meaningless ritual. For them " the chief objects of worship were the priests, the manes and, for form's sake, the Vedic gods." Fetishism, as a part of the aboriginal belief, was never eradicated from the Indian continent by philosophical Hinduism or by practical Buddhism. It now entered into the inner life of all castes; trees, stones and other natural objects, along with the idols in which the family gods, the household penates and the ancient divinities were symbolised, shared the adoration of the populace. The great Code of Manu, of which Hinduism is justly proud, and which became in later centuries the model for the legal doctrines of other Eastern races, represents a legislation for a state of society where a great advance in material civilisation was combined with the absolute domination of the priestly caste and an astonishing moral decadence amongst the masses. Like the priest the king was now a divinity. In the second century of the Christian era, whilst Manu's Code was still held in reverence and treated as the final authority, its place was taken by the Commentary of Yajnavalkya, " the Contemplative Master." To him caste was as iron-bound as to Manu ; and the Sudra as impure as in early times.

Female infanticide, as among the pagan Arabs, was common. There is no record when widow-burning was first introduced, but it must have been common in the seventh century of the Christian era. To the widow death, however terrible, must have been a welcome release, for unless she was the mother of children her lot was one of dire misery.

A woman was debarred from studying the Vedas or participating in the oblations to the manes, or in the sacrifices to the deities. The wife's religion was to serve her lord ; her eternal happiness depended on the strict performance of that duty. And the faithful wife, who sacrificed herself on the funeral pyre of her dead spouse, found a niche in the hearts of all the votaries of Hinduism as one of the best and noblest of her sex ; and often became herself the object of worship.

Whilst thinking minds saw in the puerile practices of the religion a deeper meaning; whilst their souls floated far above the ceremonialism of the creed they professed, not one philosopher or priest viewed with horror the cruel immolations of the helpless widow, usually no more than a child. Religious associations, generally composed of both sexes and not always remarkable for austerity of life, had already sprung up ; and numerous celibate brotherhoods worshipping different divinities had come into existence. They invariably congregated in monasteries into which women were admitted as lay members. Among them, as among the mendicant fraternities that were established about the same time, the professed celibacy was more nominal than real, honoured in its breach rather than in its observance. Large numbers of the mendicant brotherhoods lived in comfort and ease in temples and muths. Others, like the begging friars of the Middle Ages and the vulgar cynics of the Flavian period, wandered in search of merit from the doles of the devout. Their sole recommendation to the charity of the pious consisted in their matted locks, their unkempt beard, the ochre-coloured shirt that hung over their shoulders, the ash-covered naked bodies and the inevitable beggar's gourd and staff.

As the divinities loved music and dancing, a large number of dancing girls were attached to the temples, who were by no means vestal, and whose services were at the disposal of the ministrants of the cult. Women occupied a very inferior position in early Hindu legislation, and Manu's extreme denunciation of the sex can be compared only to the fanatical pronouncement of the Christian Saint Tertullian, " Women," says Manu, " have impure appetites ; they show weak flexibility and bad conduct. Day and night must they be kept in subjection."

As regards the Sudras, he declared, almost in the words of the Pandects, that the Creator had made them slaves and that a man belonging to that caste, even when he is emancipated by his master, cannot be free ; for bondage being natural to him, who can deliver him from it ?

Such in brief was the religious and social condition among the people of one of the most gifted sections of the Aryan race at the time when the Prophet of Islâm brought his Message to the world.

Let us turn now to Persia—a country which, by its proximity to the birthplace of Islâm, and the powerful influence it has always exercised on Mohammedan thought, not to speak of the character and tone it communicated to Judaism and Christianity, deserves our earnest attention.

Consolidated into a nation and with a new spiritual development, the western Aryans soon burst their ancient bounds, and spread themselves over the regions of modern Persia and Afghanistan. They appear to have conquered or destroyed most of the Hamitic and Kushite races inhabiting those tracts, and gradually reached the confines of the Caspian, where they found the more tenacious and hardy Turanians settled in Media and Susiana. Before, however, they had succeeded in subjugating the Turanians, they themselves fell under the yoke of a foreign invader, Kushite or Assyrian, more probably the latter, under whose iron sway they remained for a considerable time.[1] With the expulsion of the foreigners commenced that conflict between Irân and Turân which lasted with varying fortunes for centuries, and ended with the partial subjugation of the Turanians in Media and Susiana.[2] The frequent contact of the followers of Afrâsiâb and Kai-Kâûs in the field and the hall exercised a lasting effect on the Persic faith. The extreme materialism of the Turanians did not fail to degrade the yet undeveloped idealism of their Iranian rivals and neighbours, who, whilst they succeeded in superimposing themselves on the ancient settlers of Media, had partially to incorporate Turanian worship with their own. And thus, whilst in Persia, Ormuzd alone was adored and Ahriman held up to execration, in Media, the good and the evil principle were both adored at the altars. Naturally, the Turanian population was more inclined to worship their ancient national god than the deity of their Aryan conquerors ; and in the popular worship, Ahriman, or Afrâsiâb, took precedence of Ormuzd.

The Assyrian empire had fallen before a coalition, the first of its kind kr vn in history, of the Medes and the Babylonians, but the religion of Asshur, from its long domination over many of the parts occupied by the Aryans, left an ineffaceable mark on the conceptions of the Zoroastrians. The complex system of celestial co-ordination and the idea prevalent among the Assyrians of a divine hierarchy engrafted itself on Zoroastrianism. Ormuzd was henceforth worshipped as a second Asshur ; and the Persian's symbol of the God of light, the all-beneficent power, became a winged warrior, with bow and lifted hand, enclosed in the world-circle. Their symbol of growth also,

---

[1] According to the Persian traditions, Zahhâk ruled over Irân for over a thousand years, and this is supposed by several scholars to represent the exact period of Assyrian domination. The rise of Farîdûn would, according to this view, be synchronous with the downfall of Nineveh.

[2] Lenormant, *Ancient Hist. of the East*, p. 54.

the tree with the candelabra branches ending upwards in the pine-cone, was converted into the Persian fir-cone. Before the rise of Cyrus in Fârsistân and his consolidating conquests, the symbolic worship in vogue among the early emigrants and settlers became degraded among the masses into pyrolatry, or took the form of Chaldæo-Assyrian Sabæism.

The city of Asshur,—which had ruled Western Asia up to the confines of India for nearly a thousand years, and almost wrested from the Pharaohs the empire of Egypt,—the city of the mighty Sargon and the great Sennacherib, had fallen before the combined forces of the Babylonian and the Mede,[1] never again to raise its head among the nations of the world. Babylon, which after its early rivalry with Nineveh had been reduced to a dependency of Assyria, became again the centre of Asiatic civilisation. She gathered up the arts and sciences of a thousand years of growth, and the product of " interfused races and religions, temples and priesthoods," and supplied the connecting link between the inorganic faiths of antiquity and the modern beliefs. Assyria had, with the civilisation and literature of the early Accadians, also borrowed much of their religion. Babylon, rising into more potent grandeur from the ashes of Nineveh, centred in herself the essence of the Assyrian and Chaldæan cults. Under Nebuchadnezzar the empire of Babylonia attained the zenith of its power ; Judæa fell, and the flower of the nation was carried into captivity to lament by the waters of Babylon the downfall of the kingdom of Jehovah. The mighty conqueror penetrated into Arabia, and overwhelmed and nearly destroyed the Ishmaelites; he smote the Tyrians, and broke the power of the Egyptian Pharaoh. In spite of the maledictions heaped upon her head by the Hebrew patriot, Babylon was by no means such a hard taskmaster as Egypt.[2] The Israelites themselves bear testimony to the generosity of their treatment. Not until the redeemer was nigh with his mighty hosts, marching to the conquest of the doomed city, did the children of Israel raise their voice against Babylon. Then burst forth the storm of imprecations, of predictions of woe, which displayed the characteristics of the race in its pristine savagery. " By the

[1] 606 B.C.   [2] Jer. xlix. 27 to 29.

rivers of Babylon, there we sat down ; yea, we wept when we remembered Zion. O Daughter of Babylon ! happy shall he be who dasheth thy little ones against the stones." [1]

Under Nebuchadnezzar, Babylon was indisputably the centre of all existing civilisations. And the influence wielded by her priesthood did not cease with the empire of Babylonia. The mark of the Babylonian conceptions is traced in unmistakable characters in both the Judaical and Christian systems. The long exile of the Jews among the Chaldæan priesthood, the influence which some of the Hebrews obtained in the court of the Babylonian king, and the unavoidable interfusion of the two peoples, tended to impart a new character to later Judaism. They were carried to Babylon in a state of semi-barbarism ; they returned to Zion after their long probation in the land of exile a new people, advanced in faith and doctrine, with larger aspirations and their political vision extended.

With the conquest of Babylon begins a new era in religious development. Henceforth the religion of dualism holds the empire of Asia. The grand toleration which Cyrus extended towards the Jews naturally led to his exaltation as " the Messiah," " the Redeemer," " the anointed Saviour of the world." The captivity of the Hebraic tribes, and their enforced settlement near the seat of Persian domination, and their subsequent intermixture under Cyrus with the Persians, most probably gave impetus to that religious reform among the Zoroastrians which occurred during the reign of Darius Hystaspes. There was mutual action and reaction. The Israelites impressed on renovated Zoroastrianism a deep and abiding conception of a Divine Personality overshadowing the universe. They received from the Iranians the notion of a celestial hierarchy, and the idea of a duality of principles in the creation of good and evil. Henceforth it is not the Lord who puts a lying spirit into the mouths of evil-doers ; Satan, like Ahriman, from this time takes a prominent part in the religious and moral history of the Hebrews.

The reign of Cyrus was one of conquest, hardly of organisation. The reign of Darius was one of consolidation ; stern worshipper of Ormuzd, to whom he ascribes all his victories, he endeavoured

[1] Ps. cxxxvii.

to purify the faith of Zoroaster of all its foreign excrescences, to stamp out the Magism of the Medes from its stronghold, and to leave Aryan Persia the dominant power of the civilised world. Nothing, however, could arrest the process of decay. Before a hundred years had gone by, Zoroastrianism had imbibed to the full the evils which it had fought against in its infancy. The scourgers of idolatry, the uncompromising iconoclasts, who, in their fiery zeal, had slaughtered the Egyptian Apis and overturned its shrine, soon absorbed into the worship of Ormuzd the Semitic gods of their subject states. The old Magian element-worship was revived, and Artaxerxes Mnemon, one of the immediate successors of Darius, introduced among the Zoroastrians the worship of that androgynous Mythra—the Persian counterpart of the Chaldæan Mylitta or Anaitis, with its concomitant phallic cult. The development of this Mythra-cult into the gorgeous worship of the beautiful Sun-God is one of the marvels of history. The resplendent Sun ascending over the cleft mountains, chasing the Bull into its lair and with its blood atoning human sins, is a conception which has left its ineffaceable mark on one of the dominant religions of the world. This worship of Mythra was carried by the Roman legionaries from the valley of the Euphrates to the furthest corners of Europe, and in the reign of Diocletian it became the state-religion of Rome.

Never was the condition of woman so bad, never was she held under greater subjection,—a slave to the caprice of man,—than under the Mago-Zoroastrians. The laws of Manu imposed certain rules of chastity, and the stringency of primitive exogamy exercised a restraining effect upon human passions. The Persian in the relations of the sexes recognised no law but that of his own will. He could marry his nearest kindred, and divorce his wives at his pleasure. The system of female seclusion was not confined to the Persians alone. Among the Ionic Greeks, women were confined within the *gynaikonitis*, often kept under lock and key, and never allowed to appear in public. But the Greek *gynaikonomoi* were not, until later times, mutilated specimens of humanity. In Persia, the custom of employing eunuchs to guard the women prevailed from the remotest antiquity. As in Greece, concubinage was a recognised social institution, and was interwoven with the foundations of society. The Persian, however, never allowed lewdness to be incorporated with the national worship. He worshipped no Aphrodite Pandemos ; nor was Zoroastrian society tainted with that "moral pestilence," [1] the most degrading of all vices, which was universal in Greece, which spread itself afterwards in Rome, and was not even rooted out by Christianity.

With the downfall of the Achæmenian Empire ended the vitality of Zoroastrianism as a motive power in the growth of the world. The swarms of conquerors, who swept like whirlwinds over the face of Persia, destroyed all social and moral life. The Macedonian conquest, with the motley hordes which followed on its footsteps, the influx of all the dregs of Lesser Asia, Cilicians, Tyrians, Pamphylians, Phrygians, and various others, half Greeks, half Asians, obeying no moral law, the hasty and reckless temper of the conqueror himself,— all led to the debasement of the Zoroastrian faith. The Mobeds, the representatives of the national life, were placed under the ban of persecution by the foreigner, the aim of whose life was to hellenise Asia.

Alexander's career was splendidly meteoric. Shorn of the legends which have surrounded his life and turned it into an epopee, he stands before us a man of gigantic conceptions and masterly purposes, possessed of a towering ambition, a genius which overpowered all opposition, and a personality which enabled him to mould the minds of all around him according to his own will. His was a nature full of contradictions. A disciple of Aristotle, who aimed at the hellenisation of Asia, with himself as the central figure in the adoration of the world, an associate of philosophers and wise men, his life was disgraced by excesses of a revolting type. "The sack of Tyre and the enslavement of its population, the massacres and executions in India and Bactria, the homicide of Clytus, the death warrants of Philotas and the faithful Parmenio, the burning of Persepolis and the conflagration of its splendid library at the instigation of a courtezan, are acts," says an apologist and an admirer, " for which no historian has found

---

[1] Döllinger, *The Gentile and the Jew*, vol. ii. p. 239.

a palliation." With the conquest of Alexander and the extinction of the Achæmenian dynasty, Zoroastrianism gave way to Hellenism and the worst traditions of Chaldæan civilisation. The extreme partiality of the hero of many legends towards Babylon, and his anxious desire to resuscitate that city and make it the centre of a mightier and more complete civilisation, led him to discourage all creeds and faiths, all organisations, religious or political, which militated with his one great desire. Under the Seleucidæ, the process of denationalisation went on apace. Antiochus Epiphanes, the cruel persecutor of the worshippers of Jehovah, won for himself from them as well as the Zoroastrians, the unenviable designation of Ahriman. Even the rise of the Parthian power tended to accelerate the decline and ruin of Zoroastrianism. The Seleucidæ ruled on the Tigris and the Orontes ; the Parthians formed for themselves a kingdom in the middle portion of the Achæmenian empire ; the Græco-Bactrian dynasties were in possession of the eastern tracts, viz. Bactria and the northern part of Afghanistan. The state-religion of the Seleucidæ was a mixture of Chaldæo-Hellenism. The Jews and Zoroastrians were placed under the ban and ostracised. Under the Parthians, Mazdism, though not actually extinguished, was compelled to hide itself from the gaze of the rulers. In quiet and settled parts, Zoroastrianism became mixed with the old Sabæism of the Medes and the Chaldæans ; or, where kept alive in its pristine character, it was confined to the hearts of some of those priests who had taken refuge in the inaccessible recesses of their country. But with Parthia enlarged into an empire, and the Parthian sovereigns aspiring to the title of Shah-in-shah, persecution gave way to toleration, and Mago-Zoroastrianism again raised its head among the religions of the world. And the rise of the Sasanides gave it another spell of power. The founder of the new empire placed the Mobeds at the head of the State. Last sad representatives of a dying faith ! Around them clustered the hopes of a renovated religious existence under the auspices of the Sasanide dynasty. How far the brilliant aspirations of Ardeshir Babekân (Artaxerxes Longimanus), the founder of the new empire, were realised, is a matter of history. The political autonomy of Persia—

its national life—was restored, but the social and religious life
was lost beyond the power of rulers to revive. The teachings
of yore lived perhaps in books, but in the hearts of the people
they were as dead as old Gushtâsp or Rustam.

Under the Sasanides, the Zoroastrians attained the zenith
of their power. For centuries they competed with Rome for
the empire of Asia. Time after time they defeated her armies,
sacked her cities, carried away her Cæsars into captivity,
and despoiled her subjects of their accumulated riches ; but
the fire of Zoroastrianism as a moral factor was extinct. It
burnt upon the high altars of the temples, but it had died out
from the heart of the nation. The worship of the true God had
given place to a Chaldæo-Magian cult, and the fierce intolerance
with which Ardeshir and his successors persecuted rival creeds,
failed to achieve its purpose. The Persian empire, under the
later Sasanides, only rivalled in the turmoil of its sects and
the licentiousness of its sovereigns, in the degeneration of its
aristocracy and the overweening pride of its priesthood, the
empire of the Byzantines. The kings were gods ; they were
absolute masters over the person and property of their subjects,
who possessed no rights, and were virtual serfs. The climax
of depravity was reached when Mazdak, in the beginning
of the sixth century of the Christian era, preached the communism with which modern Europe has now become familiar,
and " bade all men to be partners in riches and women, just as
they are in fire, water, and grass ; private property was not
to exist ; each man was to enjoy or endure the good and bad
lots of this world." [1] The lawfulness of marriages with sisters
and other blood relations had already been recognised by
Mago-Zoroastrianism. The proclamation of this extreme
communism revolted the better minds even among the Persians.
The successor of Zoroaster, as Mazdak styled himself, was put
to death ; but his doctrines had taken root, and from Persia
they spread over the West.

All these evils betokened a complete depravity of moral
life, and foreshadowed the speedy extinction of the nation in
its own iniquities. This doom, though staved off for a time

---

[1] The *Dabistân-i-Mazâhib* of Mohsini Fâni ; see also Shaikh Muhammad
Iqbal's *Development of Metaphysics in Persia*, p. 18.

by the personal character of Kesrâ Anûshirvân, became inevitable after his death.   But a Master had already appeared, destined to change the whole aspect of the world !

Eleven centuries had passed over the Jews since their return from the Babylonian captivity, and witnessed many changes in their fortunes.   The series of disasters which one after another had befallen the doomed nation of Moses, had culminated in the wars of Titus and Hadrian.   Pagan Rome had destroyed their temple, and stamped out in fire and blood their existence as a nation.   Christian Constantinople persecuted them with an equally relentless fury, but the misfortunes of the past had no lessons for them in the future.   Their own sufferings at the hands of ruthless persecutors had failed to teach them the value of humanity and peace.   The atrocious cruelties which they committed in the cities of Egypt, of Cyprus and Cyrene, where they dwelt in treacherous harmony with the unsuspecting natives, take away all sense of pity for their future fate.   The house of Israel was a total wreck ; its members were fugitives on the face of the earth, seeking shelter far and wide, but carrying everywhere their indomitable pride, their rebellious hardness of heart, denounced and reprehended by an endless succession of prophets.   The Jews, in their safe retreats in foreign lands, re-enacted the scenes of past times.   The nation lived in hope, but the hope was mixed with rigid uncompromising bigotry on the one hand, and a voluptuous epicureanism on the other.   Jesus had come and gone, without producing any visible effect upon them. The child of his age, he was imbued with the Messianic ideas floating in the atmosphere in which he lived and moved. The Book of Daniel, written during one of the greatest travails of the nation, with its hopes and aspirations, could not but make a deep impression on the mind of the Teacher mourning over the sight of his stricken people.   The fierce intolerance of the Zealots seated in their mountain homes, the lifeless ceremonialism of the Sadducees, the half-hearted liberalism of the Pharisees, the dreamy hopefulness of the Essenes, with one hand extended towards Alexandria and the other towards Buddhistic India, the preachings and denunciations of the wild Dervish, whose life became a sacrifice to the depravity

of the Herodian court, all appealed to the heart of Jesus. But
the Eagle's talons were clutched on the heart of Judæa and its
legions crushed out all hope of a violent change. The quietism
of Jesus, and his earnest anticipation of a kingdom of heaven,
to be ushered in by the direct instrumentality of God, were the
outcome of his age. Among a nation of furious and relentless
bigots, he had come as the messenger of universal brotherhood
and love. In the midst of a proud and exclusive race, he trod
the path of humility and meekness ; kind and gentle to his
immediate followers, devoted to the cause of all, he left behind
him the impress of an elevated, self-denying spirit. Among
the powerful, the rich, and the ruling classes, he had roused
only feelings of hatred, fear, and opposition ; among the
poor, the despised, the ignorant and the oppressed, the deep
compassion of the great Teacher had awakened sentiments of
gratitude and love. One bright sunny morning he had entered
the stronghold of Jewish fanaticism full of hope in his ministry
as the promised Messiah ; before a fortnight had run out, he
was sacrificed to the vested interests of his day.

Amidst the legends which surround his life, so much at least
is clear. Born among the poor, his preachings were addressed
to the poor. Deeply versed in the Rabbinical lore, his short
ministry was devoted almost exclusively to the humble denizens
of the country side—the poverty-stricken peasantry and the
fishermen of Galilee. His disciples were poor, ignorant folk.
In spite of their credulous natures, and the vivid—not to say
weird—effect exercised on their imaginations by the untimely
disappearance of the Master, they never regarded him as
anything more than a man. It was not until Paul adopted
the creed of him whose execution he had witnessed, that the
idea of an incarnate God or angel was introduced into Christianity. In spite of the promise attached to the " effusion of
the Holy Ghost," " it was found necessary," says the historian
of Ecclesiasticism, " that there should be some one defender
of the gospel who, versed in the learned arts, might be
able to combat the Jewish doctors and the pagan philosophers
with their own arms. For this purpose Jesus himself, by an
extraordinary voice from heaven, had called to his service a
thirteenth apostle, whose name was Saul (afterwards Paul),

and whose acquaintance both with Jewish and Grecian learning
was very considerable." [1]

The Mago-Zoroastrian believed in an angel-deliverer, in the
Surûsh who was to appear from the East ; the Buddhist, in
an incarnate god born of a virgin ; the Alexandrian mystic
inculcated the doctrine of the Logos and the Demiurge. The
esoteric conceptions regarding the birth, death, and resurrection of Osiris, the idea of the Isis-Ceres, the virgin mother
" holding in her arms the new-born sun-god Horus," [2] were
in vogue both in Egypt and Syria. And Paul, the Pharisee
and the scholar, was deeply imbued with these half-mystical,
half-philosophical notions of his time. A visionary and
enthusiast by nature, not free from physical ailments, as
Strauss suggests, he, who had never come in actual contact
with the Master, was easily inclined to attach to him the
attributes of a Divinity—of an Angel Incarnate. He infused
into the simple teachings of Jesus the most mysterious
principles of Neo-Pythagoreanism, with its doctrine of intelli-
gences and its notion of the triad, borrowed from the far East.

The jealousy between the home and the foreign, the Judaical
and the anti-Judaical party, was shown in the curious though
well-known antipathy of the two apostles, Peter and Paul. [3]
The Ebionites most probably represented the beliefs of the
original companions of the Prophet of Nazareth. He had
conversed with them familiarly, and " in all the actions of
rational and animal life " had appeared to them as of the same
nature as themselves. They had marked him grow from
infancy to youth and from youth to manhood ; they had
seen him increase in stature and wisdom. Their belief was
tempered by their knowledge of him as a man. The depravation of ideas from this original faith, through various intermediate phases like those of the Docetes, the Marcionites, the
Patripassians, [4] and various others down to the decisions of the

---

[1] Mosheim, *Ecclesiastical History*, vol. ii. p. 63.

[2] Comp. Mr. Ernest de Bunsen's Essay on Mohammed's Place in the
Church, *Asiatic Quarterly Review*, April 1889.

[3] Milner, *Hist. of the Church of Christ*, vol. i. pp. 26, 27.

[4] The Docetes believed Jesus to be a pure God. The Marcionites regarded
him as a being " most like unto God, even his Son Jesus Christ, clothed with
a certain shadowy resemblance of a body, that he might thus be visible to

Council of Nice in 328, forms a continuous chain. The prevalent belief in æons and emanations predisposed all classes of people, especially those who had never beheld the Prophet, observed his humanity, or noted his everyday life, to accept his divinity without any question.

At the time Jesus began his preaching the Empire of Rome stretched over more than half Europe, and included almost the whole of Northern Africa and a large part of Western Asia. This vast area by an accident became, in the coming centuries, the seed-ground of Christianity and the battlefield of contending sects.

Exactly a century before the Phrygian Cybele [1] was brought to Rome, Ptolemy Soter, the most fortunate and probably the most far-sighted of Alexander's generals, had become master of Egypt. With the object of fusing the Egyptians and Greeks into a homogeneous nation by the unifying bond of a common religion he conceived the design of establishing a worship in the practice of which the two peoples would join hands. The same idea occurred to Akbar some two thousand years later; but where the great Akbar failed, Ptolemy succeeded, for all the conditions were in his favour. The Greeks worshipped Zeus, Demeter and Apollo or Dionysus; the Egyptians, Osiris, Isis and Horús; the trinitarian belief was common to both. The Egyptian faith revolved round the Passion and Resurrection of Horus, the Son; the Greek in the Passion and Resurrection of Dionysus. The Greek had his Eleusinian mysteries with all the mystic rites of initiation and communion; the Egyptian hierophant, the mysteries of Isis with similar rites and similar significance. To neither it mattered under what names the gods were worshipped or the rituals were conducted. So long as the main idea was maintained they were indifferent to mere names. Thus was born the great cult of the Serapeum. Serapis took the place of Zeus among the Greeks, of Osiris among the Egyptians; Isis who became the " mater dolorosa " of the votaries of the

mortal eyes." The Patripassians believed that the Father suffered with the Son on the cross (Mosheim and Gibbon, *in loco*; and Neander, vol. ii. pp. 150, 301 *et seq*.).

[1] The worship of Cybele has a very close analogy to the cult of the famous Hindu goddess Durga or Kâli.

Alexandrian cult, displaced Demeter ; and Horus Happocrates absorbed the adoration hitherto rendered to Dionysus.   This deity does not seem, however, to have lost his hold among the inhabitants of the sea-board of Asia Minor ; and the prevailing belief that a god had lived among mankind, had suffered and died and risen again made easy in later centuries the spread of Christianity.

The worship of Isis, whose glory had overshadowed the personality of her consort, was brought to Rome, it is said, some eighty years before the birth of Jesus.   It seized at once the fancy both of the populace and of the cultivated classes. Its gorgeous ritual, its tonsured, clean-shaven priests, the young acolytes in white, carrying lighted tapers, the solemn processions in which nothing was wanting to stimulate the emotions, the passionate grief at the suffering and death of Osiris-Horus, the frenzied joy at his resurrection, the mysteries with all their mystical meanings, the initiation, above all the promise of immortality, appealed vividly to a world whose old gods were mute and which yearned for a closer touch with the eternal problem of the Universe.   It is not surprising that Isis took a strong hold on the heart of the Roman people.[1]

Although the worship of Isis, " the bestower on the wretched the sweet-affection of a mother " never lost its power on their emotions, the more virile cult of Mythra the beautiful sun-god, with all its mystic rites, its doctrine of atonement, its insistence on the direct touch òf its god with humanity, was held in special favour among the Roman soldiers ; and wherever the legionaries were quartered they appear to have left the memorials of their worship.

To form a just estimate of the superlative and exclusive claim advanced by Christianity to enrol under her banner and to dominate the conscience of all mankind, it is necessary to bear in mind the causes that helped in the diffusion of the Galilean faith before the ascension of Constantine to the throne. The promise of the second advent of Jesus with the immediate ushering in of " the Kingdom of God," when the poor would

---

[1] Dill's *Roman Society from Nero to Marcus Aurelius*, chapter v.; Legge's *Forerunners and Rivals of Christianity*, vol. ii. p. 87.

be exalted, and Lazarus would take the place of Dives in the
enjoyment of heavenly gifts, created among the humble folk
a wild excitement. The fervent anticipations of the immediate
disciples and followers of Jesus naturally communicated themselves to the neighbouring peoples ; and as the missionaries
of the faith multiplied they carried this vivid belief far and
wide. The religion that held forth the promise of an early
adjustment of inequalities and redress of wrongs and injustice
received a ready acceptance among the masses. So strong
a hold did the belief in the establishment of the kingdom of
God with the second ádvent acquire among the populace, that
although the fulfilment of the promise, which was assured to
take place within the lifetime of the early disciples, receded as
decades went by into dim futurity, the anticipations and hopes
to which it gave birth did not lose their force until the final
collapse of the Crusades. After a thousand years, first of
travail and later of success, the warriors of Christianity
went forth to destroy the professors of another faith in the
full belief that the second coming of their Lord was nigh.

Besides this there were other causes equally potent which
helped the diffusion of Christianity in the shape it assumed
after the death or, according to Ebionite and Moslem belief,
the disappearance of the Master.

As already observed, among all the peoples of Asia Minor,
Syria and the Mediterranean littoral, excepting the Jews,
the idea of a god who had died and risen again, and of a divine
Trinity, was universal. It was an essential part of the
Serapean cult ; and with the spread of Isis-worship every
part of the Roman world was permeated by the trinitarian
conception ; there was no difficulty arising from sentiment
or religious predilection to the acceptance of the principal
doctrines of post-Jesus Christianity.

The philosophers at the same time, albeit unconsciously
and without the intention of helping Christianity, even without
any knowledge of its tenets, furthered its cause. Their
speculations with regard to the nature of God and of a life after
death undermined the faith of many thinking pagans in the
mysteries of Isis and Mythra, and in the rites and practices of
the old cults. And yet the hold of the Alexandrian divinities

and of the Sun-god on the hearts of the cultivated classes, who looked askance at the revolutionary doctrines of the new cult, was so strong that for nearly three centuries the spread of Christianity was confined to the ignorant and uneducated. Not until the Christian Church had incorporated with its theology and ecclesiastical system many dogmas borrowed from its great and fascinating rivals, and almost all their rités and ceremonialism, and practices and institutions, did it make any headway among people of culture. And when these, under the stress of religious persecution or imperial pressure, began entering the fold they brought with them all the elements that have gone to mould modern Christianity with its multitudinous sects.[1] Relentless persecution lasting for centuries secured, however, in the early period of its growth a certain uniformity of faith and doctrines.

Among the masses Isis-worship was transformed into Mariolatry; and Mary the mother of Jesus became, instead of the Egyptian goddess, " the haven of peace," and " the altar of pity." Thenceforth she was worshipped, as she still is among the Latin races, as the " madre de dios."

Asceticism was a favoured institution among the votaries of the Alexandrian divinities; it was practised by the Pythagoreans and Orphics, who had derived much of their inspiration from the hierophants of the Gangetic Delta, among whom it was a common practice; the Christian Church adopted and sanctified this institution for both sexes. From the simple immersion used by John the Baptist, baptism under the influence of the cult of Isis grew into a mystical and cumbrous rite. Communion took the place of initiation; and even the dogma connected with the mysteries of Isis regarding the change of wine into the blood of the mourned god was absorbed into the Christian system. In the tonsured clean-shaven, pale-clad priests, the white robed acolytes, in the gorgeous rituals, " in the form of the sacraments, in the periods of the fasts and festivals "[2] of the Christian Church, looking back through the vista of ages, one is forcibly reminded of the older cults; and the religions which Christianity displaced rise

---

[1] Dill's *Roman Society from Nero to Marcus Aurelius*, chapter v.
[2] Legge, *Forerunners and Rivals of Christianity*, *in loco*.

before us in all their pomp and pageantry. We seem to hear
once more in the litanies of the Church the beautiful touching
hymns sung to the Alexandrian goddess (the *Mater dolorosa*
of the Western pagan world), by a thousand white-robed boys
and girls, and it requires but little effort of fancy to carry
back the imagination from St. Peter's or St. Paul's to the
Serapeum.

The religion of Jesus, as taught by his chief disciples, had,
besides these borrowed and adventitious recommendations,
distinct and independent claims to draw to itself the homage
of those who, in the welter of spiritual conceptions and religious
beliefs, were groping in semi-darkness for a resting place where
high and low, ignorant and educated, should stand on the
same plane. In its higher phases, it appealed to the nobler
instincts of mankind if not more forcibly than the Isiac or
Mythraic creeds, certainly with greater assurance. Its promise
of a life after death was less veiled in mysteries ; its doctrines
were more positive and concrete than the abstract speculations
of the philosophers. It brought solace and comfort to the
down-trodden and held forth a promise—not yet fulfilled—of
equality and brotherhood among mankind, with an assured
trust in future salvation to rich and poor alike among those who
accepted its doctrines. Whilst the dogmatism of its preachers
often assisted by secular force silenced questioning minds,
it satisfied the yearnings of those who, turning from the
mysticism of the older cults or fleeing from the hidden inde-
cencies associated with Nature-worship, hungered for an assurance that the existence on earth was but part of a larger life.
The whole of the Western pagan world was in short in an
expectant mood, waiting for a positive and direct revelation ;
and all the teachings of the past had attuned its mind to the
reception of a call. The Galilean faith seized the opportunity,
and after appropriating and absorbing the ritual and doctrinal
legacies left by its " Forerunners and Rivals," gradually
monopolised the homage of the peoples who had been subjected
by Rome. Whether this adaptation of the simple teachings
of Jesus, to make them more readily acceptable, was a development or the reverse must remain for the present unanswered.
But the charge the Moslems make against his followers that

they corrupted his faith can hardly be said to be altogether unwarranted.

The early cessation of the ministry of Jesus and the absence of any organic teaching, whilst it allowed a freer scope to imagination, perhaps " a freer latitude of faith and practice," [1] as shown in the lives of even the early Christians, furnished an open ground for contending factions to dispute not only about doctrines and discipline, but also as to the nature of their Teacher. The expulsion of the Jews and the Christians from Jerusalem, which abounded in so many traditions relating to Jesus as a man ; the intermixture of his followers with the non-Judaic people who surrounded them on all sides, and among whom the Neo-Pythagorean or Platonic ideas as to the government of the universe were more or less prevalent ; the very vagueness which surrounded the figure of Jesus in the conception of his followers—soon gave birth to an infinite variety of doctrines and sects. And age after age everything human, " everything not purely ideal, was smoothed away from the adored image of an incarnate God," the essentially pathetic history of Jesus was converted into a " fairy tale," and his life so surrounded with myths that it is now impossible for us to know " what he really was and did."

The fantastic shapes assumed by Christianity in the centuries which preceded the advent of Mohammed are alike interesting and instructive.

The Gnostic doctrines, which were wholly in conflict with the notions of the Judaic Christians, are supposed to have been promulgated towards the end of the first century, almost simultaneously with the capture and destruction of Jerusalem by Hadrian. Cerinthus, the most prominent of the Gnostic teachers in this century, inculcated among his followers the dual worship of the Father and the Son, whom he supposed to be totally distinct from the man Jesus, " the creator of the world."

The narrowness of Pauline Christianity, and its futile endeavours to reconcile its doctrines with the philosophy of the Alexandrian schools, gave birth about the same time to the Neo-Platonic eclecticism of Ammonius Saccas, adopted after-

[1] Mosheim, p. 121.

THE SPIRIT OF ISLÂM

wards by Origen and other leading Christians. This versatile writer, whose impress is visible in the writings of almost all the prominent thinkers of Christendom in the earlier centuries, endeavoured to bring about a general concordance among all the existing creeds and sects. In some respects, Ammonius was the prototype of Mâni, or Manes, and was undoubtedly above the level of his contemporaries. He succeeded in forming a school, but his teachings never regulated the morals or influenced the faith of a community.

The second century of the Christian era was ushered in in strife and disorder. Divisions and heresies were rife throughout the Christian Church. Gnosticism was in great force, and left its character indelibly impressed on Christianity. Some of the sects which came into prominence in this century deserve a passing notice, as they show not only the evils which flowed from the teachings of the Church, but also the influence exercised upon Christianity by Zoroastrianism, Neo-Pythagoreanism, and the ancient Sabæism of the Chaldæans.

The Marcionites, who were perhaps the most important of the early Gnostics, believed in the existence of two principles, the one perfectly good and the other perfectly evil. Between these there existed the Demiurge, an intermediate kind of deity, neither perfectly good nor perfectly evil, but of a mixed nature, who administered rewards and inflicted punishments. The Demiurge was, according to the Marcionite doctrines, the creator of this inferior world, and engaged in perpetual conflict with the Principle of Evil,—mark the impress of the Zoroastrian ideas ! The Supreme Principle, in order to terminate this warfare and to deliver from their bondage the human souls, whose origin is celestial and divine, sent to the Jews, " a being most like unto Himself, even His Son Jesus Christ," clothed with a certain shadowy resemblance of a body, that thus he might be visible to mortal eyes. The commission to this celestial messenger was to destroy the empire, both of the Evil Principle and of the Author of this world, and to bring back wandering souls to God. "On this account he was attacked with inexpressible violence and fury by the Principle of Evil " and by the Demiurge, but without effect, since, having a body only in appearance, he was thereby rendered incapable of suffering.

The Valentinians, whose influence was more lasting, taught that " the supreme God permitted Jesus, His Son, to descend from the upper regions to purge mankind of all the evils into which they had fallen, clothed, not with a real, but with a celestial and aerial body." The Valentinians believed Jesus to be an emanation from the Divine Essence come upon earth to destroy the dominion of the Prince of Darkness.

The Ophites, who flourished in Egypt, entertained the same notions as the other Egyptian Gnostics concerning the æons, the eternity of matter, the creation of the world in opposition to the will of God, the tyranny of the Demiurge, and " the divine Christ united to the man Jesus in order to destroy the empire of this usurper." They also maintained that the serpent, by which Adam and Eve were deceived, was either Christ himself, or Sophia, disguised as a serpent.

Whilst the Gnostic creeds were springing into existence under the influence of Chaldæan philosophy, the Greeks on their side endeavoured to bring about a certain harmony between the Pauline doctrine concerning " the Father, Son, and the Holy Ghost, and the two natures united in Christ," and their own philosophical views as to the government of the world. Praxeus was the first of these sophistical preachers of Christianity, and he set the ball rolling by denying any real distinction between the " Father, Son, and Holy Ghost," and maintained that the Father was so intimately united with the man Christ, His Son, that He suffered with him the anguish of an afflicted life, and the torments of an ignominious death !

" These sects," says Mosheim, " were the offspring of philosophy. A worse evil was to befall the Christian Church in the person of Montanus, a native of Phrygia." This man, who disdained all knowledge and learning, proclaimed himself the Paraclete promised by Jesus. He soon succeeded in attaching to himself a large body of followers, the most famous of whom were Priscilla and Maximilla, the prophetesses, " ladies more remarkable for their opulence than for their virtue." They turned Northern Asia into a slaughter-house, and by their insensate fury inflicted terrible sufferings on the human race.

Whilst the Marcionites, Valentinians, Montanists, and the

other Gnostic sects were endeavouring to spread their doctrines throughout the empire of Rome, there arose in Persia a man whose individuality has impressed itself in ineffaceable characters on the philosophy of two continents. Mâni was, to all accounts, the most perfect embodiment of the culture of his age. He was an astronomer, a physicist, a musician, and an artist of eminence. The stories relating to his art-gallery [1] have passed into a proverb.

Thoroughly acquainted with the Jewish Cabbala and the teachings of the Gnostic masters, imbued with the ancient philosophy and mysticism of the East, a Magi by birth and Christian by education, he rose in revolt against the jarring discord which surrounded him on all sides, and set himself to the task of creating, from the chaos of beliefs, an eclectic faith which would satisfy all demands, the aspirations of all hearts. The audacity with which Mâni applied himself to undermine the current faiths by an outward profession, joined to a subtle criticism, which destroyed all foundations of belief in the neophyte—a process afterwards imitated by his congeners, the Ismâ'ilias, [2]—and his assertion, like the Bâtinis, of an esoteric insight into all religious doctrines, armed against him every creed and sect ; and naturally, wherever he or his disciples appeared, they were persecuted with unparalleled ferocity.

The doctrine of Mâni was a fantastic mixture of the tenets of Christianity with the ancient philosophy of the Persians and the Chaldæans. According to him, Matter and Mind are engaged in perpetual strife with each other. In the course of this conflict human beings were created by the Principle of Matter endowed with two natures, one divine, the other material, the former being a part of the light or spirit which had been filched from heaven. In order to release the struggling divine soul from the prison in which it was confined, the Supreme God sent from the solar regions an Entity created from His own substance—which was called Christ. Christ accordingly appeared among the Jews clothed with the shadowy form of a human body, and during his ministry taught mortals how to disengage the rational soul from the corrupt body—

---

[1] *Arzang-i-Mâni.*   [2] See *post*, part ii. chap. x.

to conquer the violence of malignant matter. The Prince of Darkness having incited the Jews to put him to death, he was apparently, but not in reality, crucified. On the contrary, having fulfilled his mission, he returned to his throne in the sun.

The Manichæan Christ thus could neither eat, drink, suffer, nor die ; he was not even an incarnate God, but an illusory phantasm—" the all-pervading light-element imprisoned in nature, striving to escape matter, without assuming its forms." However blasphemous and irrational these doctrines may seem, they appear hardly more so to Moslems than the doctrine of transubstantiation, the changing of the eucharistic elements into the actual flesh and blood of the Deity.

Manes divided his disciples into two classes ; one, the " elect," and the other, the " hearers." The " elect " were compelled to submit to a rigorous abstinence from all animal food and intoxicating drink, to abjure wedlock and all gratifications of the senses. The discipline appointed for the " hearers " was of a milder kind. They were allowed to possess houses, lands, and wealth, to feed upon flesh, to enter into the bonds of conjugal relationship ; but this liberty was granted them with many limitations, and under the strictest conditions of moderation and temperance.

Manes, or Mâni, was put to death by Bahrâm-Gôr, but his doctrines passed into Christianity and were visible in all the struggles which rent the Church in later times.

About the middle of the third century arose the sect of the Sabellians, which marked a new departure in the religion of Jesus. They regarded Jesus as only a man, and believed that a certain energy proceeding from the Supreme Father had united itself with the man Jesus, thus constituting him the son of God. This peculiar doctrine, which Gibbon regards as an approach to Unitarianism, was the cause of serious disorders in the Christian Church, and led to the promulgation in the early part of the fourth century, by Origen, of the doctrine of three distinct personalities in the Godhead. Tritheism was only a modification of the ancient paganism suited to the character of the people who had adopted the creed of Jesus. Polytheism was ingrained in their nature, and tritheism was a compromise between the teachings of Jesus and the ancient worship of a number of personalities. In the course of time, tritheism merged into the doctrine of the trinity, but not before it had given birth to the most philosophic sect of Christianity.[1]

The rise of Arianism is due principally to the revolt of the human intellect from the irrational teachings of the Church. In Alexandria, which was at that time the most fanatical of Christian cities, Arius had the boldness to preach, in opposition to his own bishop, that Christ was not of the same essence with God. Arianism soon spread itself in Egypt and Northern Africa, and in spite of violent and frequent persecution, kept its hold in these parts as well as Spain until his followers were taken into the fold of Islâm.[2]

The troubles generated by the schism of Arius induced Constantine, in A.C. 325, to assemble the Council of Nice, in Bithynia. In this general council, after many violent efforts on both sides, the doctrine of Arius was condemned, and " Christ was declared consubstantial with the Father." [3] Whatever may have been the condition of the Christian Church before, henceforth its history presents a constant and deplorable record of trouble and violence, of internecine strife and wrangling, of fearful and cruel persecutions, of bitter hatred and a perpetual endeavour to crush out reason and justice from the minds of men. The vices of the regular clergy assumed monstrous proportions, and the luxury, arrogance, and voluptuousness of the sacerdotal order became the subject of complaint on all sides. The asceticism of the early times had given place to monasticism, and the licentiousness of the monks became a byword. They were the free lance of the Church,—always foremost in fomenting tumults and seditions, and the streets of Constantinople, Alexandria, and Rome frequently ran with blood in consequence of their unruliness and turbulence.

---

[1] Mosheim, p. 411.

[2] In the latter part of the sixteenth century of the Christian era Socinus of Sienna (in Italy) revived and amplified the doctrines of Arius. The unitarians of the present day are the direct spiritual descendants of the Socinians, who denied the divinity of Jesus. They also repudiated the doctrine of original sin and atonement. To them God alone was the object of adoration.

[3] Gibbon, vol. iv. 307.

The disputes of Nestorius with Cyril, the murderer of Hypatia, forms a prominent chapter in the history of Christianity. The second Council of Ephesus was convoked partly with the object of conciliating the various parties which had sprung up in the Church; but " the despotism of the Alexandrian Patriarch," says Gibbon, " again oppressed the freedom of debate. The heresy of the two natures was formally condemned. 'May those who divide Christ, be divided with the sword.' 'May they be hewn in pieces.' 'May they be burned alive!' were the charitable wishes of a Christian synod."

At the Council of Chalcedon, which was convened at the instance of the Bishop of Rome, the doctrine of the incarnation of Christ in one person but in two natures was definitely settled.

The Monophysites and Nestorians, revolting from the doctrine of incarnation, endeavoured to make a stand against the decree of Chalcedon. But they succumbed under the furious onslaught of the orthodox, who had succeeded in solving the mystery of their Teacher's nature. Jerusalem was occupied by an army of monks; in the name of one incarnate nature they pillaged, they murdered; the sepulchre of Christ was defiled with blood. The Alexandrian Christians, who had murdered a woman, did not hesitate to massacre their Patriarch in the baptistery, committing his mangled corpse to the flames and his ashes to the wind.

About the middle of the sixth century the drooping fortunes of the Monophysites revived under the guidance of one of their leaders, Jacob, bishop of Edessa. Under him and his successor they acquired overwhelming predominance in the Eastern empire, and by their unrelenting persecution of the Nestorians and their bitter quarrels with the orthodox or the Chalcedonians, plunged the Christian Church into internecine warfare and bloodshed. To a non-Christian, the doctrines of the Monophysites, who taught that " the divine and human nature of Christ were so founded as to form only one nature, yet without any change, confusion, or mixture of the two natures," seem to be in no way different from those laid down by the Council of Chalcedon. And yet this distinction without a difference was the cause of untold misery to a large number of the human

race. At last, in 630 A.C., Heraclius tried to allay the disorders
by starting a new sect, that of the Monothelites, whose doctrines
were no less monstrous and fantastical. The Monothelites
maintained that " Christ was both perfect God and perfect
man, and that in him were two distinct natures so united as to
cause no mixture or confusion, but to form by their union
only one person." Instead, however, of bringing peace into
the bosom of the Church of Jesus, the rise of this sect intensified the evil ; and Western Asia, Northern Africa, and various
parts of Europe continued to be the scene of massacres and
murders and every kind of outrage in the name of Christ.

Such was the religious condition of Christendom during the
centuries which preceded the advent of Islâm.

With the apparent conversion of Constantine, Christianity
became the dominant power in the Roman empire. The fate
of paganism was sealed. Its downfall, though staved off for
a time by the greatest and most sincere of the Roman emperors,
had become inevitable. " After the extinction of paganism,"
says Gibbon, " the Christians, in peace and piety, might have
enjoyed their solitary triumph. But the principle of discord
was alive in their bosom, and they were more solicitous to
explore the nature than to practise the laws of their founder." [1]
The whole of Christian Europe was immersed in absolute
darkness, and the Church of Jesus was rent with schisms and
heresies. The religious conception of the masses had not
advanced beyond the pagan stage ; the souls of the dead were
worshipped in numbers, and the images of those who were
honoured in life were objects of adoration. Relic and saint
worship had become universal ; Christianity had reverted to
heathenism.

The social and political condition of the nations subject to
the sway of Christianity was equally deplorable. Liberty of
thought and freedom of judgment were crushed out from
among mankind. And the reign of Christ was celebrated by
the sacrifice of heretics who ventured to differ from any idea
which predominated for the time.

---

[1] The Emperor Julian (the so-called Apostate) is reported to have said :
" No wild beasts are so hostile to man as Christian sects in general are to one
another."

In the streets of Alexandria, before the eyes of the civilised world, the noblest woman of antiquity was slaughtered with nameless horrors by a Christian who bears the title of saint in the annals of Christendom, and who, in modern times, has found an apologist. The eloquent pages of Draper furnish a vivid account of the atrocious crime which will always remain one of the greatest blots on Christianity. A beautiful, wise, and virtuous woman, whose lecture-room was full to overflowing with the wealth and fashion of Alexandria, was attacked as she was coming out of her academy by a mob of the zealous professors of Christianity. Amidst the fearful yelling of these defenders of the faith she was dragged from her chariot, and in the public street stripped naked. Paralysed with fear, she was haled into an adjoining church, and there killed by the club of a " saint." The poor naked corpse was outraged and then dismembered ; but the diabolical crime was not completed until they had scraped the flesh from the bones with oyster shells and cast the remnants into the fire. Christendom honoured with canonisation the fiend who instigated this terrible and revolting atrocity, and the blood of martyred Hypatia was avenged only by the sword of Amru ! [1]

The condition of Constantinople under Justinian, the Christian and the glorified legislator, is the best index to the demoralised and degraded state of society all over Christendom. Public or private virtue had no recognition in the social conceptions ; a harlot sat on the throne of the Cæsars, and shared with the emperor the honours of the State. Theodora had publicly plied her trade in the city of Constantine, and her name was a byword among its dissolute inhabitants. And now she was adored as a queen in the same city by " grave magistrates, orthodox bishops, victorious generals, and captive monarchs." The empire was disgraced by her cruelties, which recognised no religious or moral restraint. Seditions, outbreaks, and sanguinary tumults, in which the priesthood always took the most prominent part, were the order of the day. On these occasions every law, human or divine, was trampled under foot ; churches and altars were polluted by atrocious murders ; no place was safe or sacred from depredations ;

[1] 'Amr(u) ibn al-'Asi or 'As of Arabian history.

the bonds of society were rent asunder, and revolting outrages were perpetrated in broad daylight. Nothing, however, can equal the horrors which were inflicted upon this unholy city during the Nika riots in the fifth year of Justinian's reign. The horrible anarchy of the circus, with its incessant bloodshed and sensuality, stimulated to its worst excesses by the support and encouragement which the imperial champions of orthodoxy extended to the most barbarous of the factions, was unparalleled in any heathen land.

As compared with Constantinople at this period, Persia was a country of order and law.

Humanity revolts from the accounts of the crimes which sully the annals of Christian Constantinople. Whilst the Prophet of Islâm was yet an infant, one of the most virtuous emperors who ever ascended the throne of Byzantium was massacred, with his children and wife, with fearful tortures at the instance of a Christian monarch. The emperor was dragged from his sanctuary, and his five sons were successively murdered before his eyes ; and this tragic scene closed with the execution of the emperor himself. The empress and her daughters were subjected to nameless cruelties and then beheaded on the very ground which had been stained with the blood of the poor Emperor Maurice. The ruthless treatment meted out to the friends, companions and partisans of the imperial victim, serves as an index to the morality of the Byzantine Christians. Their eyes were pierced, their tongues were torn from the root, their hands and feet were amputated ; some expired under the lash, others in the flames, others again were transfixed with arrows. "A simple, speedy death," says Gibbon, "was a mercy which they could rarely obtain."

The Byzantine empire, slowly bleeding unto death, torn by political and religious factions, distracted with theological wranglings, and "crazed by an insane desire to enforce uniformity of religious belief," offered a wretched spectacle of assassinations, dissoluteness, and brutality.[1]

---

[1] Milman thus describes the Christianity of those days : " The Bishop of Constantinople was the passive victim, the humble slave, or the factious adversary of the Byzantine emperor ; rarely exercised a lofty moral control upon his despotism. The lower clergy, whatever their more secret beneficent or sanctifying workings on society, had sufficient power, wealth, and rank

The countries included in Asiatic Turkey westward of the Euphrates, devastated alternately by the Parthians and the Romans, and then by the Persians and the Byzantines, presented a picture of utter hopelessness. The moral misery of the people was surpassed by their material ruin. The followers of Jesus, instead of alleviating, intensified the evil. Mago-Zoroastrianism combating with a degraded Christianity in Mesopotamia, the Nestorians engaged in deadly conflict with the orthodox party, the earlier contests of Montanus and the prophetesses, had converted Western Asia into a wilderness of despair and desolation.

The whirlwinds of conquest which had passed over Africa, the massacres, the murders, the lawlessness of the professors and teachers of the Christian religion, had destroyed every spark of moral life in Egypt and in the African provinces of the decaying empire. In Europe the condition of the people was, if possible, still more miserable. In the open day, in the presence of the ministers of religion and the people, Narses, the benefactor of his country, was burnt alive in the market-place of Constantinople. In the streets of Rome, under the eyes of the Exarch, the partisans of rival bishops waged war, and deluged churches with the blood of Christians. Spain exhibited a heart-rending scene of anarchy and ruin. The rich, the privileged few, who held the principal magistracies of the province under the emperors, or who were dignified with the title of magistrates, were exempt from all burdens. They lived in extreme luxury in beautiful villas, surrounded by slaves of both sexes ; spending their time in the baths, which were so many haunts of immorality ; or at the gaming

to tempt ambition or to degrade to intrigue ; not enough to command the public mind for any great salutary purpose, to repress the inveterate immorality of an effete age, to reconcile jarring interests, to mould together hostile races ; in general they ruled, when they did rule, by the superstitious fears, rather than by the reverence and attachment of a grateful people. They sank downward into the common ignorance, and yielded to the worst barbarism—a worn-out civilisation. Monasticism withdrew a great number of those who might have been energetic and useful citizens into barren seclusion and religious indolence ; but except when the monks formed themselves, as they frequently did, into fierce political or polemic factions, they had little effect on the conditions of society. They stood aloof from the world—the anchorites in their desert wildernesses, the monks in their jealously-barred convents ; and secure, as they supposed, of their own salvation, left the rest of mankind to inevitable perdition."—Milman, *Latin Christianity*, vol. i. *Introd.* p. 4.

table, when not engaged in eating and drinking. The sight of this luxury and opulence offered a terrible contrast to the miseries of the masses. The middle class, the free population of the cities and the villages, were ground to the earth by the tyranny of the Romans. Agrarian slavery had disappeared ; its place was taken by the colonists, occupying an intermediate position between freedom and slavery. They were in some respects happier than the slaves. They could contract valid marriages ; they obtained a limited share of the produce of the lands they cultivated ; and their patrons could not take their goods and chattels from them. But in all other respects they were the slaves of the soil. Their personal services were at the disposal of the State. They were liable to corporal chastisement, like the domestic slaves ; [1] slaves, not of an individual, but of the soil, they remained attached to the lands they cultivated by an indissoluble and hereditary tie. The condition of the slaves, who formed the bulk of the population, was miserable beyond description. They were treated with pitiless cruelty, worse than cattle. The invasion of the barbarians brought with it a dire punishment upon the ill-fated land. In their wake followed desolation, terrible and absolute ; they ravaged, they massacred, they reduced into slavery the women, children, and the clergy.

A vast number of Jews were settled in the peninsula for centuries. The terrible persecutions which they suffered at the hands of the ecclesiastics in the reign of the Visigoth Sisebut in the year 616 A.C., lasted until Islâm brought emancipation to the wretched victims of ignorance and fanaticism. It was Islâm which rendered possible for Judaism to produce such men as Maimonides or Ibn Gebrol.

Let us turn now to Arabia, that land of mystery and romance, which has hitherto lain enwrapt in silence and solitude, isolated from the great nations of the world, unaffected by their wars or their polity. The armies of the Chosroes and the Cæsars had for centuries marched and re-marched by her frontiers without disturbing her sleep of ages. And though the mutterings of the distant thunder, which so frequently rolled across

---

[1] Three hundred lashes was the usual allowance for trivial faults. See Dozy, *Hist. des Musulmans d'Espagne*, vol. ii. p. 87.

the dominions of the Byzantine and the Persian, often reached her ears, they failed to rouse her from her slumber. Her turn, however, was come, and she found her voice in that of the noblest of her sons.

The chain of mountains which, descending from Palestine towards the Isthmus of Suez, runs almost parallel to the Red Sea down to the southern extremity of the Arabian peninsula, is designated in the Arabic language, Hijâz, or Barrier, and gives its name to all the country it traverses until it reaches the province of Yemen. At times the mountains run close to the sea, at times they draw far away from the coast, leaving long stretches of lowland, barren, desolate, and inhospitable, with occasional green valleys and rich oases formed in the track of the periodical rain-torrents. Beyond this range, and eastward, stretches the steppe of Najd—the " highland " of Arabia—a vast plateau, with deserts, mountain gorges, and here and there green plantations refreshing to the eye. In Hijâz, the barrier-land, lie the holy cities, Mecca and Medîna, the birthplace and cradle of Islâm.

This vast region is divided into four tolerably well-defined countries. First, to the north lies Arabia Petræa, including the countries of the ancient Edomites and the Midianites. Then comes Hijâz proper, containing the famous city of Yathrib, known afterwards in history as the City of the Prophet,—Medîna't un-Nabi, or Medîna. South of Hijâz proper lies the province of Tihâma, where are situated Mecca and the port of Jeddah,—the landing-place of the pilgrims of Islâm. The fourth and the southernmost part is called Asyr, bordering on Yemen. Yemen, properly so called, is the country forming the south-western extremity of the Arabian Peninsula, bounded on the west by the Red Sea, on the south by the Indian Ocean, on the north by Hijâz, and on the east by Hazramaut (Hadhramaut). The name of Yemen is often applied to southern Arabia generally. It then includes, besides Yemen proper, Hazramaut and the district of Mahra to the east of Hazramaut. Beyond Mahra, at the south-east corner of the peninsula, is Oman, and to the north of this al-Bahrain, or al-Ahsa, on the Persian Gulf. This latter country is also called Hijr, from the name of its principal province.

Najd, the highland, is the large plateau which, commencing
westward on the eastern side of the mountains of Hijâz,
occupies the whole of Central Arabia. That portion of Najd,
which borders on Yemen, is called the Najd of Yemen, and the
northern part simply Najd. These two divisions are separated
by a mountainous province called Yemâma, famous in the
history of Islâm. North of Najd, stretches the Syrian desert,
not really a part of Arabia, but where the Arab tribes now roam,
free and wild, leading a nomadic life like their ancient Aramæan
predecessors. North-east are the deserts of Irâk (Barriyat
ul-Irâk), bordering the fertile territory of Chaldæa on the right
bank of the Euphrates, and separating it from the cultivated
portions of Arabia. Eastward, Najd is separated from al-Ahsa
by one of those strips of desert called *Nafûd* by the Arabs.
Towards the south lies the vast desert of Dahna. It separates
Najd from Hazramaut and Mahra.

This vast region, which embraces an area twice the size of
France in the height of its power, was then as now inhabited
by two different types of people, " the people of the town "
and " the dwellers of the desert." The virtues and the defects
of the Bedawee, his devotion to his clan, his quixotic sense of
honour, with his recklessness and thirst for revenge, and his
disregard for human life, have been portrayed in vivid and
sympathetic colours by eminent writers like Burton and
Poole. But whatever the difference between the Bedouin
and the citizen, the Arab is peculiarly the child of the desert.
His passionate love of freedom and his spiritual exaltation
are the outcome of the free air which he breathes and of the
wide expanse which he treads,—conscious of his own dignity
and independence. In spite of the annual gatherings at Mecca
and 'Ukâz, the tribes and nationalities which inhabited
the soil of Arabia were far from homogeneous. Each was
more or less distinct from the other in development and
religion. This diversity was mainly due to the diversity
of their origin. Various races had peopled the peninsula
at various times. Many of them had passed away, but
their misdeeds or their prowess were fresh in the memory
of successive generations, and these traditions formed the
history of the nation. The Arabs themselves divide the

races who have peopled the peninsula into three grand subdivisions, viz. : (1) the *Arab ul-Bâidah*, the extinct Arabs,
under which are included the Hamitic colonies (Kushites),
which preceded the Semites in the work of colonisation, as also
the Aramæan populations of Syria, Phœnicia, and other parts ;
(2) the *'Arab ul-'Âriba*, or *Mut'ariba*, original Arabs, true
Semites, whom tradition represents to be descended from
Kahtân, or Joktan, and who, in their progress towards the
south, destroyed the aboriginal settlers. The Joktanite
Arabs, nomads by nature, super-imposed themselves in those
countries on the primitive inhabitants, the Hamitic astral-
worshippers. Their original cradle was the region whence also
came the Abrahamites, and is precisely indicated by the
significant names of two of the direct ancestors of Joktan,
Arphaxad, " border of the Chaldæan," and Eber, " the man
from beyond (the river)," in reference to Babylon, or the
district now called Irâk-Araby, on the right bank of the
Euphrates.[1] (3) The *'Arab ul-Must'ariba*, " or naturalised
Arabs," Abrahamitic Semites, who, either as peaceful immi-
grants or as military colonists, introduced themselves into the
peninsula, and who intermarried and settled among the
Joktanite Arabs.[2] These three names, *'Âriba, Mut'ariba*,
and *Must'ariba*, are derived from the same root, and by the
modification of their grammatical form indicate the periods
when these races were naturalised in the country.[3]

Among the *'Arab ul-'Âriba*, the races which require special
mention in connection with the history of Islâm are the Banî-
'Âd,[4] the 'Amâlika, the Banî-Thamûd,[5] and Banî-Jadîs (the
Thamudiens and Jodicites of Diodorus Siculus and Ptolemy).
The Banî-'Âd, Hamitic in their origin, were the first settlers
and colonists in the peninsula, and they were established

[1] Lenormant, *Ancient History of the East*, vol. ii. p. 293.

[2] Ibn-ul-Athîr, vol. i. pp. 55-58.

[3] Caussin de Perceval regards the *Bâidah* as the same as *'Ariba*, and puts the *Mut'ariba* as forming the second group. In the following pages I adopt his classification.

[4] The 'Âdites are said to have been overwhelmed, conquered, and destroyed by the Joktanite Arabs ; the Thamûdites, " that strange race of troglodytes," by the Assyrians under Chedorlaomer (Khozâr al-Ahmar).

[5] With a ث.

principally in that region of Central Arabia, which is called by
Arab historians and geographers, the *Ahsâf ur-ramal*, contiguous to Yemen, Hazramaut, and Oman. They appear during
one period of their existence to have formed a powerful and
conquering nation. One of the sovereigns of this race, Shaddâd,
whose name is preserved in the Koran, seems to have extended
his power even beyond the confines of the Arabian peninsula.
He is said to have conquered Irâk, and even approached the
borders of India. This tradition probably points to the
invasion of Babylonia or Chaldæa by the Arabs more than
2000 years before Christ, and possibly might be referred to
the same event which, in Persian traditions, is called the
invasion of Zahhâk. The same Shaddâd, or one of his successors
bearing the same name, carried his arms into Egypt and farther
west. This invasion of Egypt by the Arabs has been identified
with the irruption of the Hyksos into that country. And the
way in which the nomadic invaders were ultimately driven
out of Africa by a combination of the princes of the Thebaid,
with the assistance of their Ethiopian or Kushite neighbours
towards the south, gives some degree of corroboration to the
theory.

The bulk of the ‘Âdites are said to have been destroyed by a
great drought which afflicted their country. A small remnant
escaped and formed the second ‘Âdite nation, which attained
considerable prosperity in Yemen. These later ‘Âdites,
however, were engulfed in the Joktanide wave.

The Bani-‘Amâlika, supposed by Lenormant to be of
Aramæan origin, who are undoubtedly the same as the Amalekites of the Jewish and the Christian Scriptures—the Shashu
of the Egyptian monuments—expelled from Babylonia by the
early Assyrian sovereigns, entered Arabia, and gradually
spread themselves in Yemen and Hijâz, as well as Palestine
and Syria. They appear to have penetrated into Egypt, and
gave her several of her Pharaohs. The ‘Amâlika of Hijâz
were either destroyed or driven out by the Banî-Jurhum, a
branch of the Banî-Kahtân, who had originally settled in the
south, and subsequently moving northwards, overwhelmed the
Amâlika.

The Banî-Thamûd, who, like the Bani-‘Âd, were Kushite

or Hamitic, inhabited the borders of Edom and afterwards the country named Hijr, situated to the east of Arabia Petræa, and between Hijâz and Syria. These people were troglodytes, and lived in houses carved in the side of rocks. Sir Henry Layard, in his *Early Travels*, has described the ruins of these rocky habitations, and one can fix the exact location of the Thamudites by comparing the Arabian traditions with the accounts of modern travellers and the results of recent discoveries. As the " indispensable middlemen " of the commerce between Syria and Najd or Hijâz, the Thamudites attained a high degree of prosperity. They were, ultimately, in great part exterminated by Chedorlaomer (Khuzâr al-Ahmar), the great Elamite conqueror, in the course of his victorious campaigns in Syria and Arabia. The terrible fate which overtook these ancient cave-dwellers, who, in their solid habitations, considered themselves safe from divine wrath, is often referred to in the Koran as a warning to the Koreishites.

After this disaster, the rest of the Banî-Thamûd retreated to Mount Seir, on the north of the Elamitic Gulf, where they lived in the times of Isaac and Jacob. But they soon disappeared, doubtless absorbed by the neighbouring tribes, and their place was taken by the Edomites who held Mount Seir for a time.[1] These Edomites were apparently succeeded in their possessions by a body of Arabs driven from Yemen by the Banî-Kahtân. In the days of Diodorus Siculus, under the same name as their predecessors they furnished contingents to the Roman armies.

Leaving the Tasm and Jadîs and other smaller tribes, as too unimportant to require any specific mention, we come to the Banî-Jurhum, who, also, are classed under the head of *'Arab ul-'Âriba*, and who appear to have overwhelmed, destroyed, and replaced the 'Amâlika in Hijâz. There seem to have been two tribes of that name, one of them, the most ancient, and contemporaneous with the 'Âdites, and probably Kushite in their origin ; the other, descendants of Kahtân, who, issuing from the valley of Yemen in a season of great sterility, drove out the 'Amalekite tribes of Hijâz, and established themselves in their possessions. The irruption of the

---

[1] Gen. xiv. 4, 6.

Banî-Jurhum, of Kahtanite origin, is said to have taken place at a time when the Ishmaelitic Arabs were acquiring prominence among the 'Amâlika, in whose country they had been long settled. The Ishmaelites entered into amicable relations with the invading hordes, and lived side by side with them for a period. Before the advancing tide of the descendants of Ishmael, the Jurhumites began gradually to lose their hold over the valley, and before a century was well over the dominion of Hijâz and Tihâma passed into the hands of the Abrahamitic Arabs. The development of the *Must'ariba* Arabs suffered a temporary check from the inroad of the Babylonian monarch, but, as we shall see later, they soon recovered their vitality, and spread themselves over Hijâz, Najd, and the deserts of Irâk and Mesopotamia, where they finally absorbed the descendants of Kahtân, their predecessors.

The *'Arab ul-Mut'ariba* were tribes sprung from Kahtân, son of Eber,[1] and were chiefly concentrated in Yemen. The descendants of Kahtân had burst into Arabia from its northeast corner, and had penetrated down into the south, where they lived for a time along with the 'Âdites of the race of Kush, subject to their political supremacy, and at last became the governing power. The population sprung from Kahtân was not, however, exclusively confined to Southern Arabia. Their primitive cradle lay in Mesopotamia. In moving southward from that locality to Yemen, the Kahtanite tribes must have passed through the whole length of the Arabian peninsula, and no doubt left some settlements behind them along their route.

According to the Arab historians, the wave which entered the peninsula at this period was headed by two brothers, Kahtân and Yaktân, the sons of Eber or Heber. And it was the son of Kahtân, Yareb, whom they regard as the first prince of Yemen, who gave his name to all his descendants and to the whole of the peninsula. Yareb is said to have been succeeded by his son Yeshhad, founder of Mareb, the ancient capital of the realm, and father of the famous Abd ush-Shams, surnamed *Saba*. This surname, which means Capturer, was given to him on account of his victories. The posterity of

---

[1] Ibn ul-Athîr calls him *Ghâbir or 'Âbir*.

Saba became the progenitors of the various tribes of Kahtanite descent, famous in Arab traditions. Saba left two sons, Himyar (which means red) [1] and Kuhlân. The former succeeded to his father's throne, and it was after him that the dynasty of Saba were called Himyary' or Himyarite.[2] His descendants and those of Kuhlân, his brother and successor, alternately ruled Yemen until the century before Mohammed. To this dynasty belonged the great Zu'lkarnain, and the celebrated Bilkîs, who went to Jerusalem in the time of Solomon.[3]

---

[1] From the red mantle which he used to wear in imitation of the Pharaohs.

[2] The Himyarite sovereigns of Yemen, who were styled Tobbas, seem to have been from the earliest times in communication both with Persia and Byzantium.

[3] There is considerable doubt as to the identity of Zu'lkarnain. Several Mohammedan historians have thought that the Zu'lkarnain referred to in the Koran is identical with Alexander of Macedon. This opinion, however, is open to question. Zu'lkarnain in its primitive sense means " the lord of two horns." When we remember the head-dress worn by the ancient Sabæan sovereigns, the crescent-shaped moon with its two horns, borrowed probably from Egypt about the period of this king, there can be little room for doubt that the reference in the Koran is to some sovereign of native origin, whose extensive conquests became magnified in the imagination of posterity into a world-wide dominion.

Lenormant thinks that Shaddâd, Zu'lkarnain, and Balkîs were all Kushites.

Judaism was strongly represented among the subjects of the Himyarite sovereigns, and in the year 343 A.C., at the instance of an ambassador sent to Yemen by the Emperor Constantine, several Christian churches were erected in their dominions. But the bulk of the nation adhered to the primitive Semitic cult.

Towards the end of the fifth century, Zu-Nawâs, known to the Byzantines as Dimion, made himself the master of Yemen and its dependencies, after slaying the ferocious usurper, Zu-Shinâtir. His cruel persecution of the Christians, under the instigation of the Jews, whose creed he had adopted, drew upon him the vengeance of the Byzantine emperor. Instigated from Constantinople, an Abyssinian army, under the command of Hârith or Aryât, landed on the shores of Yemen, defeated and killed Zu-Nawâs, and made themselves masters of Yemen. This occurred about 525 A.C.

Shortly afterwards (537 A.C.) Aryât was killed by Abraha al-Ashram, who subsequently became the Abyssinian viceroy. It was under Abraha that the Christian Abyssinians made their abortive attempt to conquer Hijâz. Yemen remained under the Abyssinian domination for nearly half a century, when M'adi Karib, the son of the famous Saif zu'l Yezen, whose heroic deeds are sung up to the present day by the Arabs of the desert, restored the Himyarite dynasty (573 A.C.) with the help of an army furnished by Kesrâ Anûshirvân. On M'adi Karib's assassination by the Christians in 597, Yemen came under the direct domination of Persia, and was ruled by viceroys appointed by the court of Ctesiphon. Wahraz was the first Marzbân. Under him Yemen, Hazramaut, Mahra, and Oman were added to the Persian empire. The last of these viceroys was Bâzân, who became Marzbân under Khusru Parvîz towards the year 606. It was during the viceroyalty of Bâzân that Islâm was introduced into Yemen, and he himself accepted the Faith. The Persian

The traditions respecting the early Ishmaelite settlement in Arabia relate back to the time of Abraham and his expulsion or expatriation from Chaldæa. The descendants of Ishmael prospered and multiplied in Hijâz until they, with their allies the Jurhumites, were overwhelmed and almost destroyed by the formidable king of Babylonia, Nebuchadnezzar, who, of all the monarchs that endeavoured to attack the heart of Arabia, was alone successful in wounding it seriously. The foundation of Mecca was apparently co-eval with the establishment of the Abrahamitic Arabs in the peninsula, for according to the Arab traditions a Jurhumite chief named Meghass ibn-Amr, whose daughter was married to the progenitor of the *Mustʻariba Arabs*, Ishmael or Ismâʻil, was the founder of the city. About the same time was built the temple which gave Mecca an overwhelming predominance over the other cities of Arabia. Built by Abraham, that " Saturnian father of the tribes," in the remotest antiquity, the Kaaba ever remained the holiest and most sacred of the temples of the nation. Here were ranged the three hundred and sixty idols, one for each day, round the great god Hobal, carved of red agate, the two *ghazâlas*, gazelles of gold and silver, and the image of Abraham and of his son. Here the tribes came, year after year, " to kiss the black stone which had fallen from heaven in the primeval days of Adam, and to make the seven circuits of the temple naked." Mecca was thus from the earliest times the centre, not only of the religious associations of the Arabs, but also of their commercial enterprises. Standing on the highway of the commerce of antiquity, it gathered to itself the wealth and culture of the neighbouring countries. Not even the Babylonian monarch could touch her mercantile prosperity ; for, from the necessity of their situation, the Arabs of Hijâz became the carriers of the nations of the world.

Mecca was the centre of the commercial activity which has distinguished the Arabs at all times from the other nations of the East. From Mecca eradiated the caravans which carried to the Byzantine dominions and to Persia the rich products of

domination of Yemen was extremely mild. All religions enjoyed equal toleration, and the chiefs of the different tribes exercised their authority in their different tracts, subject to the control of the Marzbân.

Yemen and the far-famed Ind, and brought from Syria the silks and stuffs of the Persian cities. But they brought with them more than articles of trade ; in the train of these caravans came all the luxurious habits and vices which had corroded the very heart of the neighbouring empires. Grecian and Persian slave girls, imported from Syria and Irâk, beguiled the idle hours of the rich with their dancing and singing, or ministered to their vices. The poet, whose poems formed the pride of the nation, sung only of the joys of the present life, and encouraged the immorality of the people. And no one bethought himself of the morrow.

The Arabs, and especially the Meccans, were passionately addicted to drinking, gambling, and music. Dancing and singing, as in other Eastern countries, were practised by a class of women occupying a servile position, who were called *Kiyân*, or, in the singular, *Kayna*, and whose immorality was proverbial. And yet they were held in the highest estimation, and the greatest chiefs paid public court to them.[1] As among the Hindus, polygamy was practised to an unlimited extent. A widow (other than the mother) was considered an integral part of her deceased husband's patrimony, and passed into the use of the son ; and the atrocious and inhuman practice of burying female infants was universal.

The Jews, chased successively from their native homes by the Assyrians, the Greeks, and the Romans, had found among the Arabs safety and protection. But they had brought with their religion that bitter spirit of strife which was perhaps the cause of the greater portion of their misfortunes. They had succeeded, however, in gaining in Arabia a considerable body of proselytes ; and at the time when Mohammed proceeded to announce his mission, Judaism was professed in Yemen by a notable fraction of the descendants of Himyar

---

[1] The moral depravity of the people is evidenced by the fact that these women used to give receptions, which were attended by all the men of light and leading in the city.

The town Arab was so passionately addicted to dice that he would frequently, like the Germans of Tacitus, stake away his own liberty. It was on account of these evils, and the immoralities associated with their practice, that Mohammed wisely prohibited to his followers gambling, dancing, and drinking of wine. The Ommeyyades revived all the three evils ; they represented, in fact, the uprise of the old paganism, which had been stamped out with such labour by the great Prophet.

and Kinda, issue of Kuhlân ; at Khaibar and at Yathrîb,
by the Kuraizha and the Nazîr, tribes of Ishmaelite origin,
but naturalised as Arabs from very ancient times. The
Nestorians and the Jacobite Christians had also founded
colonies in Arabia. The deadly rivalry between these two
creeds to dominate over Arabia occasioned sanguinary wars
in the most fertile provinces.[1] Christianity had commenced
to introduce itself among some families of the race of Rabî'a
son of Nizâr, such as the Taglibites established in Mesopotamia,
and the Banî Abd ul-Kais who were settled in al-Bahrain.
It flourished at Najrân among the Bani-l-Hârith ibn Ka'b ;
in Irâk, among the Ibâd ; in Syria, among the Ghassanides
and some Khuzaite families ; at Dûmat ul-Jandal, among the
Saconi and Bani-Kalb. And some of the tribes who roamed
over the desert that lay between Palestine and Egypt were also
Christians. Magism and Sabæism had also their representatives
among the Arabs, and specially among the Himyarites : the
Bani-Asad worshipped Mercury ; the Jodhâm, Jupiter ;
the Bani-Tay, Canopus ; the descendants of Kais-Aylan,
Sirius ;[2] a portion of the Koreish, the three moon-goddesses—
al-Lât, the bright moon, al-Manât the dark, and al-'Uzza, the
union of the two,—who were regarded as the daughters of the
high god (*Banât-ullâh*). Mecca was, at this time, the centre
of a far-reaching idolatry, ramifications of which extended
throughout the tribes of the peninsula. The Kinâna, closely
allied to the Koreish politically and by blood, besides the star
Aldobaran, served the goddess 'Uzza, represented by a tree
at a place called Nakhla, a day and a half's journey from
Mecca. The Hawâzin, who roamed towards the south-east
of Mecca, had for their favourite idol the goddess Lât, located
at Tâyef. Manât was represented by a rock on the caravan
road between Mecca and Syria. The worship of these idols
was chiefly phallic, similar in character to that which prevailed
among the ancient Semites, the Phœnicians and the Babylonians. But the majority of the nation, especially the tribes

[1] Ibn ul-Athîr, vol. i. p. 308 *et seq.* ; Gibbon, *Decline and Fall of the Roman Empire*, vol. vi. pp. 114, 115 ; Caussin de Perceval, *Hist. des Arabes*, vol. i. pp. 128-131.

[2] Koran, sura xli. 37.

belonging to the race of Mozar, were addicted to fetishism of a very low type. Animals and plants, the gazelle, the horse, the camel, the palm-tree, inorganic matter like pieces of rock, stones, etc., formed the principal objects of adoration. The idea of a Supreme Divinity, however, was not unrecognised ; but its influence was confined to an inappreciable few, who, escaping from the bondage of idolatry, betook themselves to a philosophical scepticism, more or less tinged with the legendary notions, religious and secular, of their neighbours, the Sabæans, the Jews, or the Christians. Among these some distinctly recognised the conception of the supreme Godhead, and, revolting at the obscenities and gross materialism of their day, waited patiently for the appearance of a Deliverer who, they felt in their hearts, would soon appear.

Among some tribes, in the case of a death, a camel was sacrificed on the tomb, or allowed to die from starvation, in the belief that it would serve as a conveyance for the deceased in a future existence. Some believed that when the soul separated itself from the body, it took the shape of a bird called *Hama* or *Sada*. If the deceased was the victim of a violent death, the bird hovered over the grave, crying *askuni*, " Give me drink," until the murder was avenged. Belief in *Jins*, *ghouls*, and oracles rendered by their idols, whom they consulted by means of pointless arrows, called *Azlâm* or *Kidâh*, was universal. Each tribe had its particular idols and particular temples. The priests and hierophants attached to these temples received rich offerings from the devotees. And often, there arose sanguinary conflicts between the followers or the worshippers of rival temples.[1]

But the prestige of the Kaaba, the chapel of Abraham and Ishmael, stood unimpeached among all. Even the Jews and the Sabæans sent offerings there. The custody of this temple was an object of great jealousy among the tribes, as it conferred on the custodians the most honourable functions and privileges in the sight of the Arabs. At the time of Mohammed's birth

---

[1] Among others, the temple of Zu'l-Khulâsa in Yemen, belonging to the tribe of Bani-Khathâm ; the temple of Rodha in Najd, belonging to the Banî-Rabî'a ; the temple of Zu Sabât in Irâk ; and that of Manât at Kodayd, not far from the sea, belonging to the tribe of Aus and Khazraj, domiciled at Yathrib—were the most famous.

this honour was possessed by his family ; and his grandfather was the venerable chief of the theocratic commonwealth which was constituted round the Kaaba. Human sacrifices were frequent. Besides special idols located in the temples each family had household penates which exacted rigorous observances.

Such was the moral and religious condition of the Arabs. Neither Christianity nor Judaism had succeeded in raising them in the scale of humanity. " After five centuries of Christian evangelization," says Muir, " we can point to but a sprinkling here and there of Christians ;—the Baní Hârith of Najran ; the Baní Hanifa of Yemâma ; some of the Baní Tay at Tayma, and hardly any more. Judaism, vastly more powerful, had exhibited a spasmodic effort of proselytism under Zu Nawâs ; but, as an active and converting agent the Jewish faith was no longer operative. In fine, viewed thus in a religious aspect, the surface of Arabia had been now and then gently rippled by the feeble efforts of Christianity ; the sterner influences of Judaism had been occasionally visible in a deeper and more troubled current ; but the tide of indigenous idolatry and of Ishmaelite superstition, setting from every quarter with an unbroken and unebbing surge towards the Kaaba, gave ample evidence that the faith and worship of Mecca held the Arab mind in a thraldom, rigorous and undisputed." [1]

The divisions and jealousies of the tribes,[2] combined with the antagonistic feelings which actuated one against the other from religious and racial differences, had enabled the Assyrians, the Babylonians, the Greeks, the Persians, and Abyssinians, to become masters of various provinces in the north, in the east, and in the south-west. The Abyssinians had even gone so far as to invade Hijâz, with the intention of destroying the national temple. But their power was broken before Mecca by the sturdy patriotism of Abd ul-Muttalib. After twenty years' oppression, they were driven out of Yemen with the assistance of Persia, by a native prince, the son of the celebrated Saif zu'l-Yezen. On his assassination by the Christians, the

[1] Muir, vol i. Introd. p. ccxxxix.
[2] These tribal jealousies and family feuds, which I shall have to describe later, were the causes which led to the ruin of the Arab empire.

sovereignty he had enjoyed under the auspices of the great Anûshirvân passed entirely into Persian hands, and Yemen became tributary to Persia.[1]

Besides the direct domination which the rival empires of Constantinople and Ctesiphon exercised over the various provinces of Arabia, two of the greatest chieftains, the kings of Ghassân and of Hîra, divided their allegiance between the Cæsars and the Chosroes ; and in the deadly wars, profitless and aimless, which Persian and Byzantine waged against each other, sucking out the lifeblood of their people from mere lust of destruction, though oftener the right was on the side of the Zoroastrian than the Christian, the Ghassanide and Hirite stood face to face in hostile array, or locked in mortal combat.[2]

The heterogeneous elements of which the Arabian peninsula was thus composed gave an extremely varied character to the folklore of the country. Among uncultured nations, the tendency is always to dress facts in the garb of legends. Imagination among them not only colours with a roseate hue, but magnifies distant objects. And the variety of culture multiplies legends, more or less based on facts. The Hamitic colonies of Yemen and of the south-west generally ; the true Semites who followed in their footsteps, like the Aryans in the East; the Jews, the Christians,—all brought their traditions, their myths, their legends with them. In the course of ages, these relics of the past acquired a consistency and character, but however unsubstantial in appearance, on analysis there is always to be found underlying them a stratum of fact. In the legend of Shaddâd and his garden of Irem, we see in the hazy past the reflection of a mighty empire, which even conquered Egypt—" of a wealthy nation, constructors of great buildings, with an advanced civilisation analogous to that of

---

[1] Ibn ul-Athîr, vol. i. pp. 324, 327 ; Caussin de Perceval, vol. i. p. 138 et seq. ; Tabari (Zotenberg's transl.), vol. ii. pp. 217, 218.

[2] The sedentary portion of the Arab population of Yemen, of Bahrain and Irâk, obeyed the Persians. The Bedouins of these countries were in reality free from all yoke. The Arabs of Syria were subject to the Romans ; those of Mesopotamia recognised alternately the Roman and Persian rule. The Bedouins of Central Arabia and of Hijâz, over whom the Himyarite kings had exercised a more or less effective sovereignty, had nominally passed under Persian rule, but they enjoyed virtual independence.

Chaldæa, professing a religion similar to the Babylonian ;
a nation, in short, with whom material progress was allied to
great moral depravity and obscene rites." [1]   In the traditional,
half-legendary, half-historic destruction of the 'Âdites and the
Thamudites, we see the destructive fate which overwhelmed
these Hamitic races before the Semitic tide, Assyrian and
Arab.[2]

The children of Jacob, flying from their ruthless enemies,
brought their legends and traditions with them, and thus
contributed their quota to the folklore of the Peninsula. The
last of the Semitic colonies that entered Arabia was acknowledged by themselves as well as their neighbours to be descended
from Abraham ; and tradition had handed down this belief,
and given it a shape and character.

Manicheism, stamped out from Persia and the Byzantine
dominions, had betaken itself to Arabia.[3]   The early Docetes,
the Marcionites, the Valentinians, all had their representatives
in this land of freedom.   They all disseminated their views and
traditions, which in course of time became intermixed with
the traditions of the country.   These Christians, more consistent in their views than their orthodox persecutors, believed
that the God incarnate, or at least the Son of God, His Word,
born in the bosom of eternity, an Æon, an Emanation issuing
from the Throne of Light, could not, did not, die on the cross ;
that the words of agony which orthodox Christian traditions
put into the mouth of Jesus did not, and could not, escape
from his lips ; in short, that the man who suffered on the cross
was a different person from the Divine Christ, who escaped
from the hands of his persecutors and went away to the regions
whence he had come.[4]   This doctrine, however fanciful, was
more consistent with the idea of the sonship of Jesus, and in
itself appears to have been based on some strong probabilities.
The intense desire of Pilate, whom Tertullian calls a Christian
at heart, to save Jesus ; [5]   even the unwillingness of Herod

[1] Lenormant, *Ancient History of the East*, vol. ii. p. 296.
[2] Ibn ul-Athîr, vol. i. pp. 55-58.
[3] Beausobre, *Hist. du Manicheisme*, pt. i. l. ii. chap. iv.
[4] Mosheim and Gibbon, *in loco*.
[5] Blunt, *History of the Christian Church*, p. 138.

to incur more odium by the murder of the Prophet of Nazareth; the darkness of the short hours when that great benefactor of humanity was led forth for the consummation of the frightful scenes which had continued throughout the night; the preternatural gloom which overshadowed the earth at the most awful part of this drama;[1] all these coincident circumstances lend a strong probability to the belief that the innocent escaped and the guilty suffered.[2]

Before the Advent of Mohammed, all these traditions, based on fact though tinged by the colourings of imagination, must have become firmly imbedded in the convictions of the people, and formed essential parts of the folklore of the country. Mohammed, when promulgating his faith and his laws, found these traditions current among his people; he took them up and adopted them as the lever for raising the Arabs and the surrounding nations from the depths of social and moral degradation into which they had fallen.

The light that shone on Sinai, the light that brightened the lives of the peasants and fishermen of Galilee, is now aflame on the heights of Fârân![3]

[1] Comp. Milman, *History of Christianity*, vol. i. pp. 348-362.

[2] If anything could lend stronger probability to this curious belief, it ought to be the circumstantial account of Luke xxiv. 36 *et seq.*, about Jesus allowing himself to be touched and felt (after the resurrection) in order to calm his affrighted disciples, who believed him to be a spirit; and his asking for " meat," and partaking of " a broiled fish and of a honey-comb."

[3] The tradition which I have paraphrased into English is as follows:—

جاء الله من سيناء و اشرق من ساعير او استعلن من فا ران

" Sâ'îr," says Yâkût in his Geographical Encyclopædia, " is a hill in Palestine and Fârân is the hill of Mecca;" *Mu'jam ul-Buldân*, vol. iii. p. 834.

PART I.

THE LIFE AND MINISTRY OF THE PROPHET

CHAPTER I

MOHAMMED THE PROPHET

بَلَـغَ الْعُلــى بِكَمَالِـهِ

كَشَفَ الدُّجى بِجَمَـالِه

حَسُنَتْ جَمِيعُ خِصَالِهِ

صَلُّو عَلَيـهِ وَ آلِــهِ

THESE lines, untranslatable in their beauty, do not in
the least exaggerate the gentleness of disposition,
the nobility of character, of the man whose life,
career, and teachings we propose to describe in the following
pages. At the dawn of the seventh century of the Christian
era, in the streets of Mecca might often be seen a quiet
thoughtful man, past the meridian of life, his Arab mantle
thrown across his shoulders, his *tailasân* [1] drawn low over
his face ; sometimes gently sauntering, sometimes hurrying
along, heedless of the passers-by, heedless of the gay scenes
around him, deeply absorbed in his own thoughts—yet withal
never forgetful to return the salutation of the lowliest, or
to speak a kindly word to the children who loved to throng
around him. This is *al-Amin*, " the Trusty." He has so
honourably and industriously walked through life, that he
has won for himself from his compatriots the noble designation of the true and trusty. But now, owing to his strange

[1] A scarf thrown over the head usually covering the turban, and brought
round under the chin and passed over the left shoulder.

preaching, his fellow-townsmen are beginning to look suspiciously upon him as a wild visionary, a crazed revolutionist, desirous of levelling the old landmarks of society, of doing away with their ancient privileges, of making them abandon their old creeds and customs.

Mecca was, at this time, a city of considerable importance and note among the townships of Arabia, both from its associations and its position. Situated in a low-lying valley stretching north to south, bordered on the west by a range of hills, on the east by high granite rocks—the Kaaba in its centre, its regular and paved streets, its fortified houses, its public hall opening on to the platform of the temple, the city presented an unusual appearance of prosperity and strength. The guardianship of the Kaaba, originally an appanage of the children of Ishmael, had in consequence of the Babylonian attack, passed into the hands of the Jurhumites. The combination of the secular and religious power enabled the chiefs of the Banî-Jurhum to assume the title of *malik* or king. In the early part of the third century the Jurhumites were overwhelmed by the irruption of a Kahtanite tribe, called the Banî-Khuzâ'a, who, issuing from Yemen, possessed themselves of Mecca and the southern parts of Hijâz. In the meantime, the race of Ishmael, which had suffered so terribly at the hands of the Babylonian king, was gradually regaining its former strength. 'Adnân, one of the descendants of Ishmael, who flourished about the first century before Christ, had, like his ancestor, married the daughter of the Jurhumite chief, and established himself at Mecca, and his son Ma'add became the real progenitor of the Ishmaelites inhabiting Hijâz and Najd. FIHR, surnamed Koreish, a descendant of Ma'add, who flourished in the third century, was the ancestor of the tribe which gave to Arabia her Prophet and Legislator.

The Khuzâites remained in possession of the temple, and of all the pre-eminence it conferred on them, for more than two centuries. Upon the death of Holayl, the last of the Khuzâite chiefs, Kossay, a descendant of Fihr,[1] who had married Holayl's daughter, drove the Khuzâites out of Mecca, and possessed

---

[1] Kossay was the fifth in descent from Fihr, and was born about 398 A.C. The word Koreish is derived from *Karash*, to trade, as Fihr and his descendants were addicted to commerce.

himself of the entire power, both secular and religious, in the city, and thus became the virtual ruler of Hijâz.[1] We now arrive on absolutely historical grounds.

Kossay appears to have made himself the master of Mecca about the middle of the fifth century of the Christian era, and he at once set himself to the task of placing the administration of the city upon an organised basis.   Until Kossay's time, the different Koreishite families had lived dispersed in separate quarters, at considerable distances from the Kaaba, and the extreme sanctity they attached to the temple had prevented their erecting any habitation in its neighbourhood.   Perceiving the dangers to which the national pantheon was exposed from its unprotected condition, he induced the Koreish to settle in its vicinity, leaving a sufficient space free on the four sides of the temple for the *tawâf* (circumambulation).   The families, to whom the lands were allotted, dwelt in strongly fortified quarters.

Kossay built for himself a palace, the door of which opened on the platform of the temple.   This palace was called the *Dâr un-Nadwâ*,[2] " the council hall," where, under the presidency of Kossay, public affairs were discussed and transacted.   To this hall, no man under the age of forty, unless a descendant of Kossay, could gain admission.   Here also were performed all civil functions.   At the *Dâr un-Nadwâ*, the Koreishites, when about to engage in a war, received from the hands of Kossay the standard, *liwa*.   Kossay himself attached to the end of a lance a piece of white stuff, and handed it, or sent it by one of his sons, to the Koreishite chiefs.   This ceremony, called the *Akd ul-liwa*, continued in vogue from the time of its inauguration by Kossay until the very end of the Arab empire.   Another of Kossay's institutions endured much longer.   By representing to the Koreish the necessity of providing food for the poor pilgrims who annually visited Mecca, and by impressing on them the duties of hospitality, Kossay succeeded in making them submit to the payment of an annual poor-tax, called the *Rifâda*, which he applied in feeding the poorer pilgrims during

[1] The next we hear of the Khuzâites is when the Koreish invoked their assistance against the Prophet.

[2] This building, after having been renewed several times, was ultimately converted into a mosque, under Abdul Malik II. (one of the Ommeyyades).

the *Ayyâm ul-Minâ* [1]—the day of the sacrificial feast, and the two following days which they passed at Minâ. This usage continued after the establishment of Islâm, and was the origin of the distribution of food which was made at Minâ each year during the pilgrimage, in the name of the Caliphs and the Sultans, their successors. The words *nadwa, liwa* and *rifâda* denote the functions exercised by Kossay, being the right of convoking and presiding at the council of the nation, of bestowing the standard,—the symbol of military command,—and of levying imposts, raised for the purpose of supplying food to the pilgrims. With these dignities, Kossay also held the administration of the water supplied by the wells in Mecca and its neighbourhood (*sikâya*) and the custody of the keys of the Kaaba (*hijâba*), with the ministration to the worship of the gods.

Kossay thus united in his own person all the principal religious, civil, and political functions. He was king, magistrate and chief pontiff. His power, which was almost royal, threw great lustre on the tribe of Koreish, of whom he was the acknowledged chief, and from his time the Koreish acquired a marked preponderance among the other descendants of Ishmael.

Kossay died at an advanced age, about the year 480 A.C.

He had in his lifetime designated his eldest son Abd ud-Dâr as his successor, and after his death the son succeeded quietly, and without dispute, to the high position of the father. Upon the death of Abd ud-Dâr, serious disputes broke out between his grandchildren and the sons of Abd(u)Manâf, his brother. The various clans and their allies and neighbours ranged themselves on opposite sides. The dispute, however, was amicably settled for the time. By the compromise thus effected, the *sikâya* and the *rifâda* were intrusted to Abd us-Shams, the son of Abd(u)Manâf, whilst the *hijâba, nadwa,* and *liwa* remained in the hands of the children of Abd ud-Dâr. Abd us-Shams, who was comparatively a poor man, transferred the duties which had been intrusted to him to his brother Hâshim, a man of great consequence as well as riches among the Koreish. HÂSHIM was the receiver of the tax imposed on the Koreishites by Kossay for the support of the pilgrims,

[1] Minâ (the ' i ' is pronounced very short) is a suburb of Mecca.

and the income derived from their contributions joined to his own resources, was employed in providing food to the strangers who congregated at Mecca during the season of the pilgrimage.

Like the majority of the Meccans, Hâshim was engaged in commerce.   It was he who founded among the Koreishites the custom of sending out regularly from Mecca two caravans, one in winter to Yemen, and the other in summer to Syria.   Hâshim died in the course of one of his expeditions into Syria, in the city of Ghazza, about the year 510 A.C., leaving an only son, named Shayba, by an Yathribite lady of the name of Salma. The charge of the *rifâda* and the *sikâya* passed, upon his death, to his younger brother Muttalib, who had won for himself a high place in the estimation of his compatriots, and the noble designation of *al-Faiz* (the Generous) by his worth and munificence.   Muttalib brought Shayba, the white-haired youth, from Yathrib, to Mecca.   Mistaking Shayba for a slave of Muttalib, the Meccans called him ABD UL-MUTTALIB and history recognises the grandfather of the Prophet under no other name than that of *Abd ul-Muttalib*, " the slave of Muttalib." [1]

Muttalib died at Kazwân, in Yemen, towards the end of 520 A.C., and was succeeded by his nephew, Abd ul-Muttalib, as the virtual head of the Meccan commonwealth.   The government of Mecca was at this time vested in the hands of an oligarchy composed of the leading members of the house of Kossay. After the discovery of the sacred well of Zemzem by Abd ul-Muttalib, and the settlement of the disputes regarding its superintendence, the governing body consisted of ten senators, who were styled *Sharîfs*.   These decemvirs occupied the first place in the State, and their offices were hereditary in favour of the eldest member, or chief, of each family.   These dignities were—

(1). The *Hijâba*, the guardianship of the keys of the Kaaba, a sacerdotal office of considerable rank.   It had been allotted to the house of Abd ud-Dâr, and at the time when Mecca was converted to Islâm, it was held by Osmân, the son of Talha.

---

[1] Of the sons of Abd(u)Manâf, Hâshim died first, at Ghazza ; then died Abd ush-Shams at Mecca ; then Muttalib at Kazwân ; and lastly, Naufâl, some time after Muttalib, at Silmân, in Irâk.

(2). The *Sikâya*, or the intendance of the sacred wells of Zemzem, and of all the water destined for the use of the pilgrims. This dignity belonged to the house of Hâshim, and was held at the time of the conquest of Mecca, by Abbâs, the uncle of the Prophet.

(3). The *Diyat*, or the civil and criminal magistracy, which had, for a long time, belonged to the house of Taym ibn-Murra, and, at the time of the Prophet's advent, was held by Abdullah ibn-Kuhâfa, surnamed Abû Bakr.

(4). The *Sifârah*, or legation. The person to whom this office belonged was the plenipotentiary of the State, authorised to discuss and settle the differences which arose between the Koreish and the other Arab tribes, as also with strangers. This office was held by Omar.

(5). The *Liwa*, or the custody of the standard under which the nation marched against its enemies. The guardian of this standard was the general-in-chief of all the forces of the State. This military charge appertained to the house of Ommeyya, and was held by Abû Sufiân, the son of Harb, the most implacable enemy of Mohammed.

(6). The *Rifâda*, or the administration of the poor tax. Formed with the alms of the nation, it was employed to provide food for the poor pilgrims, whether travellers or residents, whom the State regarded as the guests of God. This duty, after the death of Abû Tâlib, upon whom it had devolved after Abd ul-Muttalib, was transferred to the house of Naufal, son of Abd(u)Manâf, and was held at the time of the Prophet by Hârith, son of Amr.

(7). The *Nadwa*, the presidency of the national assembly. The holder of this office was the first councillor of the State, and under his advice all public acts were transacted. Aswad, of the house of Abd ul-'Uzza, son of Kossay, held this dignity at the time of the Prophet.

(8). The *Khaïmmeh*, the guardianship of the council chamber. This function, which conferred upon the incumbent the right of convoking the assembly, and even of calling to arms the troops, was held by Khâlid, son of Walîd, of the house of Yakhzûm, son of Marra.

(9) *Khâzina*, or the administration of the public finances,

belonged to the house of Hasan, son of Kaab, and was held by
Hârith, son of Kais.

(10). The *Azlâm*,[1] the guardianship of the divining arrows by
which the judgment of the gods and goddesses was obtained.
Safwân, brother of Abû Sufiân, held this dignity. At the same
time it was an established custom that the oldest member
exercised the greatest influence, and bore the title of Rais or
Syed, chief and lord *par excellence*. Abbâs was at the time
of the Prophet the first of these senators.

In spite, however, of this distribution of privilege and power,
the personal character and influence of Abd ul-Muttalib gave
him an undoubted pre-eminence. The venerable patriarch,
who had, in accordance with the custom of his nation, vowed
to the deities of the Kaaba the sacrifice of one of his male
children, was blessed with a numerous progeny.[2] And in
fulfilment of his vow he proceeded to offer up to the inexorable
gods of his temple the life of his best beloved son, Abdullah.
But this was not to be. The sacrifice of the human life was
commuted, by the voice of the Pythia attached to the temple,
to a hundred camels—thenceforth the fixed *Wehrgeld*, or price
of blood.

Abdullah was married to Âmina, a daughter of Wahb, the
chief of the family of Zuhri. The year following the marriage
of Abdullah was full of momentous events. At the beginning
of the year the whole of Arabia was startled by an event which
sent a thrill through the nation. Abraha al-Ashram, the
Abyssinian viceroy of Yemen, had built a church at San'â, and
was anxious to divert into his own city the wealth which the
sanctity of the Kaaba attracted to Mecca. The desecration
of the church by a Meccan furnished him with an ostensible

---

[1] With a ﺯ (*zay*), plural of *zalam*.

[2] Abd ul-Muttalib had twelve sons and six daughters. Of the sons, Hârith,
born towards A.C. 538, was the eldest ; the others were Abd ul-'Uzza, *alias Abû
Lahab*, the persecutor of the Prophet ; Abd(u) Manâf, better known as *Abû
Tâlib* (born in A.C. 540, died in 620 A.C.) ; Zubair and ABDULLAH (545), born
of Fâtima, the daughter of 'Amr, the Makhzumi ; Dhirâr and Abbâs (566-652),
born of Nutayla ; Mukawwim, Jahm, surnamed al-Ghaydâk (the liberal), and
Hamzah, born of Hâla. The daughters were Atika, Omayma, Arwa, Barra,
and Umm-i-Hakîm, surnamed al-Bayza (the fair), by Fâtima, and Safiya, born
of Hâla, who married Awwâm, the grandfather of the famous Abdullah ibn-
Zubair, who played such an important part in the history of Islâm. The
names of the other two sons of Abd ul-Muttalib are not known, probably
because they left no posterity.

motive, and he marched a large army to the destruction of the temple, himself riding at the head of his troops on a magnificently caparisoned elephant. The sight of the huge animal striding solemnly in the midst of the vast force so struck the imagination of the Arabian tribes, that they dated an era from this event, and named it as the Era of the Elephant (570 A.C.). On the approach of the Abyssinians, the Koreish, with their women and children, retired to the neighbouring mountains, and from there watched the course of affairs, hoping all the while that the deities of the Kaaba would defend their dwelling place. The morning dawned brightly as the Abyssinians advanced towards Mecca, when, lo and behold, say the traditionists, the sky was suddenly overcast by an enormous flight of small birds, swallows, which poured small stones over the ill-fated army. These stones, penetrating through the armour of men and horses, created terrible havoc among the invaders. At the same time the flood-gates of heaven were opened, and there burst forth torrents of rain, carrying away the dead and dying towards the sea.

Abraha fled to San'â covered with wounds, and died there soon after his arrival. Ibn-Hishâm, after narrating this prodigy, adds, " it was in the same year that small-pox manifested itself for the first time in Arabia." " This indication explains the miracle," says Caussin de Perceval. One can well understand the annihilation of Abraha's army by some terrible epidemic, similar to the fate which overtook Sennacherib, to which was joined perhaps one of those grand downpours of rain which often produce terrible inundations in the valley of Mecca.

Shortly after this event, Abdullah died in the course of a journey to Yathrib, in the twenty-fifth year of his age.[1] And, a few days after, the afflicted wife gave birth to a son who was named MOHAMMED. Mohammed was born on the 12th of Rabi I., in the year of the Elephant, a little more than fifty days after the destruction of the Abyssinian army, or the 29th of August 570.[2] His birth, they say, was attended with signs

---

[1] He was buried in the quarter occupied by the sons of 'Adi, his maternal uncles.

[2] Towards the end of the fortieth year of the reign of Kesrâ Anûshirvûn, and the end of the year 880 of the era of the Seleucidæ.

and portents from which the nations of the earth could know
that the Deliverer had appeared. The rationalistic historian
smiles, the religious controversialist, who, upon *a priori* reasoning, accepts without comment the accounts of the wise men
following the star, scoffs at these marvels. To the critical
student, whose heart is not devoid of sympathy with earlier
modes of thought, and who is not biased with pre-conceived
notions, " the portents and signs " which the Moslem says
attended the birth of his Prophet are facts deserving of historical
analysis. We, moderns, perceive, in the ordinary incidents
in the lives of nations and individuals, the current of an
irresistible law ; what wonder then that 1400 years ago they
perceived in the fall of a nation's memorial the finger of God,
pointing to the inevitable destiny, which was to overtake it
in its iniquity. In accordance with the custom of the Arabs,
the child was confided during his early infancy to a Bedouin
woman [1] of the tribe of Banî-Sa'd, a branch of the Hawâzin,
and upon being returned by her to his mother, was brought
up by Âmina with the tenderest care. But she died not long
after, and the doubly-orphaned child was thus thrown upon
the care of his grandfather, Abd ul-Muttalib, who, during the
few years that he survived the mother, watched his grandson
with the utmost tenderness. But nothing could make up for
the loss of that parental care and love which are the blessings
of childhood. His father had died before he was born. He
was bereft of his mother when only six years of age, and this
irreparable loss made a deep impression on the mind of the
sensitive child. Three or four years later he lost his grandfather also. Abd ul-Muttalib died towards the year 579
A.C.,[2] shortly after his return from a journey to San'â, where he
had gone as the representative of the Koreish to congratulate

[1] In after life, when this poor Bedouin woman was brought by the Koreish
as a captive to Mecca, Mohammed recognised her with tears of joy, and
obtained for her from his rich wife an ample provision for her life.

[2] Of the two duties of the *Sikâya* and *Rifâda* held by Abd ul-Muttalib, the
Sikâya, with the custody of the Zemzem, passed to his son Abbâs. The
second devolved on Abû Tâlib, who enjoyed at Mecca great authority and
consideration. Abû Tâlib, however, did not transmit the *Rifâda* to his
children. This dignity was transferred, upon his death, to the branch of
Naufal, son of Abd(u) Manâf ; and at the time Mecca surrendered to the
Prophet, Hârith, the son of 'Amr, and the grandson of Naufal, exercised, as
we have said before, the functions of the *Rifâda* ; Zaini, vol. i. p. 14.

Saif the son of Zu'l Yezen on his accession to the throne of the Tobbas, with the help of the Persians.

With the death of Abd ul-Muttalib opens another epoch in the life of the orphan. On his death-bed the old grandfather had confided to Abû Tâlib the charge of his brother's child, and in the house of Abû Tâlib Mohammed passed his early life. We can almost see the lad with his deep wistful eyes, earnest and thoughtful, looking, as it were, into futurity, moving about in the humble unpretentious household of his uncle, or going often into the desert to gaze upon the beauteous face of nature ; sweet and gentle of disposition, painfully sensitive to human suffering, this pure-hearted child of the desert was the beloved of his small circle, and there ever existed the warmest attachment between uncle and nephew. " The angels of God had opened out his heart, and filled it with light." His early life was not free from the burden of labour. He had often to go into the desert to watch the flocks of his uncle. The princely munificence of Hâshim and Abd ul-Muttalib had told upon the fortunes of their heirs, and the Hâshimites, owing to the lack of means, were fast losing their commanding position. The duty of providing the pilgrims with food was given up to the rival branch of Ommeyya, who had always entertained the bitterest jealousy towards the children of Hâshim.

Mohammed was but a child when the " Sacrilegious Wars " —the Ghazwat ul-Fijâr, which continued with varying fortunes and considerable loss of human life for a number of years— broke out at 'Ukâz between the Koreish and the Banî-Kinâna on one side, and the Kais-Aylân on the other. 'Ukâz lies between Tâyef and Nakhla, three short journeys from Mecca. At this place, famous in Arab history, was held a great annual fair in the sacred month of Zu'l-ka'da, when it was forbidden to engage in war or shed human blood in anger—" a sort of God's truce." Other fairs were held at Majna near Marr uz-Zuhrân, not far from Mecca, and at Zu'l Majâz at the foot of Mount 'Arafât ; but the gathering at 'Ukâz was a great national affair. Here, in the sacred month, when all enmity and tribal vendetta was supposed to lie buried for the time, flowed from all parts of Arabia and even more distant lands, the commerce of the world. Here came the merchants of " Araby the blest," of

Hijâz, of Najd ; the poet-heroes of the desert ; and the actors, often disguised from the avengers of blood, in masks or veils, to recite their poems and win the applause of the nations gathered there. 'Ukâz was " the Olympia of Arabia " ; here they came, not for trade only, but to sing of their prowess, of their glory—to display their poetical and literary talents. The *Kasîdas*, which won the admiration of the assembled multitude, were inscribed in letters of gold (*Muzahhabât*, golden), and hung up in the national pantheon as a memorial to posterity.[1] During these weeks, 'Ukâz presented a gay scene of pleasure and excitement. But there was also another side to the picture. The dancing women, like their modern representatives the *almas* and *ghawâzin* of Egypt, moving from tent to tent, exciting the impetuous son of the desert by their songs and their merriment ; the congregation of Corinthians, who did not even pretend to the calling of music ; the drunken orgies, frequently ending in brawls and bloodshed ; the gaming-tables, at which the Meccan gambled from night till morning ; the bitter hatred and ill-feeling evoked by the pointed personalities of rival poets, leading to sudden affrays and permanent and disastrous quarrels, deepened the shadows of the picture, and made a vivid impression on the orphan child of Âmina.

During the interval between the first and second of those fratricidal wars, named *sacrilegious* from the violation of the sanctity of the month in which all quarrel was forbidden, Mohammed accompanied his uncle and guardian on one of his mercantile journeys to Syria.[2] Here was opened before him a scene of social misery and religious degradation, the sight of which never faded from his memory. Silently and humbly, with many thoughts in his mind, the solitary orphan boy grew from childhood to youth and from youth to manhood.

Deeply versed in the legendary lore of his nation, education in the modern sense of the term he had none. With all his affection for his people, in his ways and mode of thought he seemed far removed from them, isolated in the midst of a

---

[1] Hence also called the *Mu'allakât*, or " suspended poems."

[2] Abû Tâlib, like his father and grandfather, carried on a considerable trade with Syria and Yemen. He transported to Damascus, to Basra, and other places in Syria the dates of Hijâz and Hijr and the perfumes of Yemen, and in return brought back with him the products of the Byzantine empire.

chaotic society with his eyes fixed intently on the moving
panorama of an effete and depraved age. The lawlessness
rife among the Meccans, the sudden outbursts of causeless
and sanguinary quarrels among the tribes frequenting the
fairs of 'Ukâz, the immorality and scepticism of the Koreish,
naturally caused feelings of intense horror and disgust in the
mind of the sensitive youth.

In the twenty-fifth year of his age, Mohammed travelled
once more into Syria as the factor or steward of a noble
Koreishite lady named Khadîja, a kinswoman of his. The
prudence with which he discharged his duties made a favourable
impression on Khadîja, which gradually deepened into attachment. A marriage, which proved a singularly happy one, was
soon after arranged between Mohammed and his noble kinswoman, and was solemnised amidst universal rejoicings. In
spite of the disparity of age between Mohammed and his wife,
who was much the senior of her husband, there always existed
the tenderest devotion on both sides. This marriage " brought
him that repose and exemption from daily toil which he needed
in order to prepare his mind for his great work. But beyond
that it gave him a loving woman's heart, that was the first to
believe in his mission, that was ever ready to console him in his
despair, and to keep alive within him the thin flickering flame
of hope when no man believed in him—not even himself—and
the world was black before his eyes."

Khadîja is a notable figure, an exemplar among the womanhood of Islâm. The calumny which is levelled at Mohammed's
system, that it has degraded the female sex, is sufficiently
refuted by the high position which his wife and youngest daughter,
our " Lady of Light," occupy in the estimation of the Moslem.
Khadîja bore Mohammed several children—three sons and
four daughters ; but the sons all died in infancy, and their loss,
which wrung the heart of the bereaved father so tenderly and
devotedly attached to them, supplied the hostile Koreish later
with an abusive epithet to apply to the Prophet.[1] The
daughters long survived the new Dispensation. With the
exception of an occasional appearance in public when the
exigencies of his position or the necessities of the city of his

---

[1] *Al-abtar*, literally without a tail ; in its secondary sense, one without issue.

birth demanded it, the next fifteen years after his marriage is a silent record of introspection, preparation, and spiritual communion. Since the death of Abd ul-Muttalib authority in Mecca had become more or less divided. Each of the senators enjoyed a somewhat limited authority, and among the different functions there was no such institution as a magistracy to insure the peaceable enjoyment by individuals of their rights and property. The ties of blood and family *esprit de corps* afforded some degree of protection to every citizen against injustice and spoliation, but strangers were exposed to all kinds of oppression. They would often find themselves robbed, not only of their goods and chattels, but also of their wives and daughters. A famous poet of the name of Hanzala of the tribe of Bani'l Kayn, better known as Abû Tamahân, was publicly robbed in the streets of Mecca, notwithstanding that he had entered the city as a client of a Koreishite notable, Abdullah ibn Juda'ân. Another similar act of lawlessness brought matters to a crisis. At the instance of Mohammed, the descendants of Hâshim and of Muttalib and the principal members of the family of Zuhra and Taym bound themselves by a solemn oath to defend every individual, whether Meccan or stranger, free or slave, from any wrong or injustice to which he might be subjected in Meccan territories, and to obtain redress for him from the oppressor. This chivalrous league received the name of the *Hilf ul-Fuzûl*, or the Federation of the Fuzûl, in memory of an ancient society instituted with a similar object among the Jurhum, and composed of four personages, named Fazl, Fazâl, Muffazzal, and Fuzail, collectively Fuzûl. Mohammed was the principal member of this new association, which was founded about 595 A.C., shortly after his marriage. "The League of the Fuzûl" exercised efficient protection over the weak and oppressed, and during the first year of its institution the simple threat of its intervention was sufficient to repress the lawlessness of the strong, and to afford redress to the helpless. The League continued to exist in full force for the first half-century of Islâm. It was some years after the establishment of the *Hilf ul-Fuzûl*, and towards the commencement of the seventh century of the Christian era, that an attempt was made by Osmân, son of Huwairith, backed

by Byzantine gold, to convert Hijâz into a Roman dependency.
His attempt failed chiefly through the instrumentality of
Mohammed, and Osmân was obliged to fly into Syria, where
he was subsequently poisoned by 'Amr, the Ghassanide prince.
In 605 A.C., when Mohammed was thirty-five, the Koreish took
in hand the reconstruction of the Kaaba. In the course of this
work a dispute among the different families engaged in the
building of the temple, which at one time seemed likely to
lead to great bloodshed, was happily settled by the ready
intervention of Mohammed. These are all we know of his
public acts within these fifteen years. His gentle disposition, his
austerity of conduct, the severe purity of his life, his scrupulous refinement, his ever-ready helpfulness towards the poor and
the weak, his noble sense of honour, his unflinching fidelity,
his stern sense of duty had won him, among his compatriots,
the high and enviable designation of al-Amîn, the Trusty.

It was at this period that he tried to discharge some portion
of the debt of gratitude and obligation he owed his uncle Abû
Tâlib, by charging himself with the education of Ali, one of
his sons. Abû Tâlib's endeavour to maintain the old position
of his family had considerably straitened his circumstances.
Mohammed, rich by his alliance with Khadîja, and Abbâs,
the brother of Abû Tâlib, were the most opulent citizens of
Mecca. During a severe famine which afflicted the country,
Mohammed persuaded his uncle Abbâs, to adopt one of the sons
of Abû Tâlib, whilst he adopted another. Thus Abbâs took
Ja'far ; Mohammed, Ali, and 'Akîl remained with his father.[1]
Mohammed had lost all his sons in early infancy. In the
love of Ali he found some consolation for their loss ; and the
future marriage of the son of Abû Tâlib with the youngest
daughter of Mohammed, Fâtima,[2] sealed the bond of love
and devotedness.

Mohammed about this time set an example to his fellow-
citizens by an act of humanity which created a salutary effect
upon his people. A young Arab of the name of Zaid, son of
Hârith, was brought as a captive to Mecca by a hostile tribe,

[1] Ibn-Hishâm, p. 109 ; al-Halabi, *Insân-ul-'Uyûn*, vol. 212 ; Ibn ul-Athír,
vol. ii. p. 42.
[2] Born in 606 A.C.

and sold to a nephew of Khadîja, who presented the young lad to her. Mohammed obtained Zaid as a gift from Khadîja, and immediately enfranchised him. This kindness on the one side gave rise to absolute devotion on the other, and the Arab boy could not be induced, even by his own father, to return to his tribe or forsake Mohammed.

Thus passed the fifteen years of trial and probation, years marked by many afflictions and yet full of sympathy with human suffering and sorrow.

Before him lay his country, bleeding and torn by fratricidal wars and inter-tribal dissensions, his people sunk in ignorance, addicted to obscene rites and superstitions, and, with all their desert virtues, lawless and cruel. His two visits to Syria had opened to him a scene of unutterable moral and social desolation ; rival creeds and sects tearing each other to pieces, wrangling over the body of the God they pretended to worship, carrying their hatred to the valleys and deserts of Hijâz, and rending the townships of Arabia with their quarrels and bitterness. The picture before him was one of dreary hopelessness. The few who, abandoning their ancient beliefs, were groping in the dark for some resting-place, represented a general feeling of unrest.[1] In their minds there was nothing capable of appealing to the humanity beyond themselves. Mohammed's soul was soaring aloft, trying to peer into the mysteries of creation, of life and death, of good and evil, to find order out of chaos. And God's words uttered to his soul became at last the life-giving power of the world. For years after his marriage it had been his wont to betake himself, sometimes with his family, at other times alone, for prayer and meditation to a cave on the Mount Hira,[2] " a huge barren

[1] Four men, Zaid, Waraka, son of Naufal and a cousin of Khadîja, and two others (Obaidullah and Osmân), abandoning the fetishism of their countrymen, had betaken themselves to a search for the true faith. Zaid was the principal person among them. Before the Prophet retired into the wilderness, like Jesus, to commune with God, he had come in contact with Zaid, and learnt to esteem his abhorrence of idolatry. When Zaid's cousin asked the Prophet in later times to supplicate divine mercy for him, Mohammed, who would not pray for his own grandfather, as he had died in idolatry, willingly did so for Zaid.—Ibn-Hishâm, p. 145.

[2] Now called the Mount of Light. Ibn-Hishâm, Ibn ul-Athîr, and Abulfedâ mention the month of Ramazân as the month which Mohammed usually spent at Hira in prayer and the succour of the poor and famished wayfarers of the desert. Tabari mentions Rajab.

rock, torn by cleft and hollow ravine, standing out solitary
in the full white glare of the desert sun, shadowless, flowerless,
without well or rill." Solitude had indeed become a passion
with him. Here in this cave he often remained whole nights

plunged in profoundest thought, deep in communion (التَّحَنُّث)
with the unseen yet all-pervading God of the Universe. Slowly
the heaven and earth fill with pre-destined vision and command.
A voice seems to issue even from the inanimate objects around
him, the stones and rocks and trees, calling on him to fulfil
the task an Almighty Power was directing him to undertake.[1]
Can the poetry of the soul go further? The mental visions
and the apparitions of angels at these moments were the bright,
though gradual, dawnings of those truths with which he was
to quicken the world into life. Often in the dark and benighted
pathways of concrete existence, the soul of every great man has
been conscious of unrealised yet not unseen influences, which
have led to some of the happiest achievements of humanity.
From Samuel, that ancient Seer, wild and awful as he stands,
deep in the misty horizon of the Past, to Jesus in the wilderness,
pondering over the darksome fate of his people and the magnitude of his work, listening to the gentle accents of the God of
Truth,—from Jesus to Mohammed in the solitude of his
mountain retreat, there is no break in the action of these
influences.[2] In the still hours of the night, in the calmness of the early dawn, in the depth of solitude, when no
human sympathy is near, a Voice comes to him from heaven,
softly as the sough of the morning breeze: "Thou art the
man, Thou art the Prophet of God"; or, when wrapt in
thought it comes in mighty waves: "Cry in the name of thy
Lord."[3] The over-wrought mind at these moments raises a
vision before the eye, a vision of the celestial ministrants who
are believed to form the medium of inter-communication
between the God of Heaven and the man on earth. "The
Father of Truth chooses His own prophets, and He speaks to
them in a voice stronger than the voice of thunder. It is the

[1] Ibn-Hishâm, p. 151.

[2] Koran, sura xcvi. 2; Ibn-Hishâm, p. 153; Al-Halabi, *Insân-ul-ʿUyún*,
vol. i. p. 249; Ibn ul-Athîr, vol. ii. p. 34.

[3] Comp. Isa. xl. 6.

same inner voice through which God speaks·to all of us. That voice may dwindle away, and become hardly audible ; it may lose its divine accent, and sink into the language of worldly prudence ; but it may also from time to time assume its real nature with the chosen of God, and sound in their ears as a voice from heaven."[1]

" The natural relations of Mahomet's vast conception of the personality of God with the atmosphere of his age," says a great writer,[2] " is the only explanation of that amazing soberness and self-command with which he entertained his all-absorbing visions " ; and then adds, " it could not have been accidental that the one supreme force of the epoch issued from the solitudes of that vast peninsula round which the tides of empire rose and fell. Every exclusive prophetic claim in the name of a sovereign Will has been a cry from the desert. The symbolic meaning given to Arabia by the withdrawal of the Christian apostle to commune with a power above flesh and blood, in Mahomet became more than a symbol. Arabia was itself the man of the hour, the prophet of Islâm its concentrated word. To the child of her exalted traditions, driven by secret compulsion out into the lonely places of the starry night, his mouth in the dust, the desert spoke without reserve."

One night—" the Night of Power and Excellence "—when a divine peace rests on creation, and all nature is lifted up towards its Lord—in the middle of that night the Book was opened to the thirsting soul. Whilst lying self-absorbed, he is called by a mighty Voice, surging like the waves of the ocean, to cry. Twice the Voice called, and twice he struggled and waived its call. But a fearful weight was laid on him, and an answer was wrung out of his heart. " Cry ! " called out the Voice for the third time.

And he said, " What shall I cry ? " Came the answer : " Cry—in the name of thy Lord ! "

When the Voice had ceased to speak, telling him how from minutest beginnings man had been called into existence and lifted up by understanding and knowledge of the Lord, who is

---

[1] Professor Muller, quoted from Dean Stanley's *Lectures on the History of the Jewish Church*, Part i. Lect. xviii. p. 394.

[2] Johnson, *Oriental Religions*, p. 561.

most beneficent, and who *by the Pen* had revealed that which
men did not know,[1] Mohammed woke from his trance, and felt
as if the words spoken to his soul had been written on his heart.
A great trembling came upon him, and he hastened home to
his wife, and said, " O Khadîja ! What has happened to me ? "
He lay down, and she watched by him. When he recovered
from his paroxysm he said, " O Khadîja ! he of whom one
would not have believed it (meaning himself) has become either
a soothsayer [2] (*Kâhin*) or one possessed—mad." She replied,
" God is my protection, O Abu'l-Kâsim ! (a name of Mohammed,
derived from one of his boys), He will surely not let such a
thing happen unto thee ; for thou speakest the truth, dost not
return evil for evil, keepest faith, art of a good life, and kind to
thy relations and friends. And neither art thou a babbler
in the market-places. What has befallen thee ? Hast thou
seen aught terrible ? " Mohammed replied, " Yes." And he
told her what he had seen. Whereupon she answered and
said, " Rejoice, O dear husband, and be of good cheer. He,
in whose hands stands Khadîja's life, is my witness that thou
wilt be the Prophet of this people." Then she arose and went
to her cousin Waraka, son of Naufal, who was old and blind,
and " knew the Scriptures of the Jews and Christians." When
she told him what she had heard, he cried out, " *Kuddûsun,
Kuddûsun* ! Holy, holy ! Verily this is the *Nâmûs al-akbar* [3]
who came to Moses and Jesus. He will be the Prophet of
his people. Tell him this. Bid him be of brave heart."

In the midst of the wreck of empires and nations, in the wild
turmoil of tribes and clans, there was a voice in the air—east
and west, north and south—that God's message was close
at hand : the shepherd was nigh who was to call back the

---

[1] Sura xcvi. vers. 1-5. " Ikrâ " is usually rendered into " read " ; but I
have preferred to follow the rendering suggested by Deutsch, as more in
accordance with the call to the Prophet ; see Rodwell also, and compare
Zamakhshari (the *Kashshâf*).

[2] Diviners and soothsayers were his particular aversions ; most of them
were attached to the temples.

[3] The primary signification of the word *Nâmûs* in Arabic is a messenger,
one who communicates a secret message. It also means law, as the Greek
νομος. " In Talmudical phraseology," says Deutsch, " it signifies the revealed
law. In Waraka's mind these different significations were combined ; the
messenger and the message, both divine, had come to Mohammed even as
they had come to Moses and Jesus."

erring flock into the Master's fold. It had spoken to the heart of Waraka.

And when the two men met subsequently in the streets, the blind old reader of the Jewish and Christian Scriptures, who had searched in them for consolation and found none, but who knew of the promise held out to mankind of a Deliverer, spoke of his faith and trust. " I swear by Him in whose hand Waraka's life is," said the old man, " God has chosen thee to be the prophet of this people ; the *Nâmûs al-akbar* has come to thee. They will call thee a liar, they will persecute thee, they will banish thee, they will fight against thee. Oh, that I could live to those days ! I would fight for thee." [1] And he kissed him on his forehead. These words of hope and trust brought comfort to the troubled soul.[2] And then followed a period of waiting for the Voice to come again—the inspiration of Heaven to fall once more on the anxious mind.

We can appreciate the spiritual throes, the severe mental conflicts, the doubts, hopes, and misgivings which alternately wrung the heart of Mohammed, when we are told that before he had himself realised his Mission he was driven to the verge of self-destruction, when the angel of God recalled him to his duty to mankind.[3] It spoke to the poor grieved heart, agitated by doubt and fear,—of hope and trust, of the bright future when he should see the people of the earth crowding into the one true Faith.

Saved by the gracious monition, he hurries home from the desert, exhausted in mind and body, to the bosom of his devoted wife, praying only to be covered from the overwhelming Presence.

His was not the communion with God of those egoists who bury themselves in deserts or forests, and live a life of quietude for themselves alone. His was the hard struggle of the man who is led onwards by a nobler destiny towards the liberation of his race from the bondage of idolatry. His destiny was unfolded to him when, wrapt in profound meditation, melancholy and sad, he felt himself called by that Voice from heaven

---

[1] Ibn-Hishâm, p. 103; al-Halabi, *Insân-ul-'Uyûn,* vol. i. p. 256.

[2] Waraka died soon after this event.—Ibn-Hishâm, p. 104.

[3] Ibn ul-Athîr, vol. ii. pp. 35, 36 ; Tibri (Zotenberg's transl.), vol. ii. p. 392.

which had called those who had gone before him, to arise and preach. " O thou, enwrapped in thy mantle, arise and warn, and glorify thy Lord." [1] And he arose and girded himself for the work to which he was called. Thenceforth his life is devoted to humanity. Preaching with unswerving purpose amidst unremitting persecution, insulted and outraged, he held on in his path of reproof and reform.

Khadîja was the first to accept his Mission. She was the first to believe in the revelation, to abandon the idolatry of her people, and to join with him in purity of heart in offering up prayers to the All-Merciful. Not only was she the first to believe in him and his divine message, but in the struggle which was to follow she was his true consoler ; and " God," says tradition, " comforted him through her when he returned to her, for she roused him up again and made his burden more light to him, assuring him of her own faith in him, and representing to him the futility of men's babble."

In the beginning Mohammed opened his soul only to those who were attached to him, and tried to wean them from the gross practices of their forefathers. After Khadîja, Ali was the next disciple. [2] Often did the Prophet go into the depths of the solitary desert around Mecca, with his wife and young cousin, that they might together offer up their heartfelt thanks to the God of all nations for His manifold blessings. Once they were surprised in the attitude of prayer by Abû Tâlib, the father of Ali. And he said to Mohammed, " O son of my brother, what is this religion that thou art following ? " " It is the religion of God, of His angels, of His prophets, and of our ancestor Abraham," answered the Prophet. " God has sent me to His servants to direct them towards the truth ; and thou, O my uncle, art the most worthy of all. It is meet that I should thus call upon thee, and it is meet that thou shouldst accept the truth and help in spreading it." " Son of my brother," replied Abû Tâlib, in the true spirit of the sturdy old Semite, " I cannot abjure the religion of my fathers ; but by the Supreme God, whilst I am alive none shall dare to injure

---

[1] Koran, sura lxxiv.

[2] Ibn-Hishâm, p. 155 ; al-Halabi, *Insân-ul-'Uyún*, vol. i. p. 285.

thee." Then turning towards Ali, his son, the venerable patriarch inquired what religion was his. " O father," answered Ali, " I believe in God and His Prophet, and go with him." " Well, my son," said Abû Tâlib, " he will not call thee to aught save what is good, wherefore thou art free to cleave unto him." [1]

Soon after Zaid, the son of Hârith, who notwithstanding his freedom had cast in his lot with Mohammed, became a convert to the new faith. He was followed by a leading member of the Koreishite community of the name of Abdullah, son of Abû Kuhâfa, who afterwards became famous in history as Abû Bakr. [2] A member of the important family of Taym ibni-Murra, a wealthy merchant, a man of clear, calm judgment, at the same time energetic, prudent, honest, and amiable, he enjoyed great consideration among his compatriots. He was but two years younger than the Prophet, and his unhesitating adoption of the new faith was of great moral effect. Five notables followed in his footsteps, among them Osmân, son of Affân, of the family of Ommeyya, who afterwards became the third caliph ; Abdur Rahmân, son of 'Auf ; Sa'd, son of Abî Wakkâs, afterwards the conqueror of Persia ; Zubair, son of Awwâm and nephew of Khadîja, presented themselves before the Prophet and accepted Islâm at his hands. Several proselytes also came from the humbler walks of life. It is a noble feature in the history of the Prophet of Arabia, and one which strongly attests the sincerity of his character, the purity of his teachings and the intensity of his faith and trust in God, that his nearest relations, his wife, his beloved cousin, and intimate friends, were most thoroughly imbued with the truth of his Mission and convinced of his inspiration. Those who knew him best, closest relations and dearest friends, people who lived with him and noted all his movements, were his sincere and most devoted followers. If these men and women, noble, intelligent, and certainly not less educated than the fishermen of Galilee, had perceived the slightest sign of

---

[1] The above is a praraphrase of the account given by Ibn Hishâm, pp. 159, 160 ; and Ibn ul-Athîr, vol. ii. pp. 42, 43.

[2] Desvergers in a note (p. 108) mentions that before his conversion to Islâm, he was called Abd ul-Kaaba, " servant of the Kaaba."

earthliness, deception, or want of faith in the Teacher himself,
Mohammed's hopes of moral regeneration and social reform
would all have been crumbled to dust in a moment.   They
braved for him persecution and dangers ; they bore up against
physical tortures and mental agony, caused by social excom-
munication, even unto death.   Would this have been so had
they perceived the least backsliding in their master ?   But
even had these people not believed in Mohammed with such
earnest faith and trust, it would furnish no reason for doubting
the greatness of his work or the depth of his sincerity.   For the
influence of Jesus himself was least among his nearest relations.
His brothers never believed in him,[1] and they even went so
far as once to endeavour to obtain possession of his person,
believing him to be out of his mind.[2]   Even his immediate
disciples were not firm in their convictions.[3]

Perhaps this unsteadiness may have arisen from weakness
of character, or it may have resulted, as Milman thinks,[4] from
the varying tone of Jesus himself ; but the fact is undeniable.[5]
The intense faith and conviction on the part of the immediate
followers of Mohammed is the noblest testimony to his sincerity
and his utter self-absorption in his appointed task.

For three weary long years he laboured quietly to wean his
people from the worship of idols.   But polytheism was deeply
rooted among them ; the ancient cult offered attractions, which
the new Faith in its purity, did not possess.   The Koreish
had vested interests in the old worship ; and their prestige was
involved in its maintenance.   Mohammed had thus to contend,
not only with the heathenism of his city sanctified by ages of
observance and belief but also with the opposition of the
oligarchy which ruled its destinies, and with whom like the
generality of their people, superstition was allied to great
scepticism.   With these forces fighting against him, little
wonder that the life and death-struggle of the three years drew

[1] John vii. 5.   [2] Mark iii. 21.

[3] And these were the men whom Jesus called " his mother and brethren,"
in preference to his *own* mother and brothers, Matt. xii. 45-48 ;   Mark iii. 32, 33.

[4] Milman, *History of Christianity*, vol. i. pp. 254, 255.

[5] Sir W. Muir admits this in the most positive terms (vol. ii. p. 274) ;
he says, " the apostles fled at the first sound of danger."

only thirty followers. But the heart of the great Teacher
never failed. Steadfast in his trust in the Almighty Master
whose behests he was carrying out, he held on. Hitherto he
had preached quietly and unobtrusively. His compatriots
had looked askance at him, had begun to doubt the sanity of
al-Amîn, thought him crazed or "possessed," but had not
interfered with his isolated exhortations. He now determined
to appeal publicly to the Koreish to abandon their idolatry.
With this object he convened an assembly on the hill of Safa,
and there spoke to them of the enormities of their crimes in
the sight of the Lord, their folly in offering adoration to carved
idols. He warned them of the fate that had overtaken the
races which had passed unheeded the words of the preachers
of bygone days, and invited them to abjure their old impious
worship, and adopt the faith of love and truth and purity.
But the mockers mocked his words, laughed at the enthusiasm
of young Ali, and departed with taunts and scoffs on their
lips, and fear in their hearts at the spirit of revolution which
had risen in their midst. Having thus failed to induce the
Koreish to listen to the warnings of Heaven, he turned his
attention to the strangers visiting the city for trade or pilgrimage. To them he endeavoured to convey God's words. But
here again his efforts were frustrated by the Koreish. When
the pilgrims began to arrive on the environs of the city, the
Koreishites posted themselves on the different routes and
warned the strangers against holding any communication with
Mohammed, whom they represented as a dangerous magician.
This machination led, however, to a result little expected by
the Meccans. As the pilgrims and traders dispersed to their
distant homes, they carried with them the news of the advent
of the strange, enthusiastic preacher, who, at the risk of his
own life, was calling aloud to the nations of Arabia to give up
the worship of their fathers.

If the Koreish were under the impression that Mohammed
would be abandoned by his own kith and kin, they were soon
undeceived by a scathing denunciation hurled at them by
Abû Tâlib. The old patriarch, who had refused, with characteristic persistency, to abandon his ancient creed, or to adopt
the new faith rebelled at the injustice and intolerance of his

compatriots towards the reformer, and with true desert chivalry
he deplored, in a poem which lies embalmed in history, the
enormities of the Koreish towards one who was the benefactor
of the orphan and the widow—*al-Amîn*, who never failed in
word or deed ; and declared that the children of Hâshim and
of Muttalib would defend the innocent with their lives. About
the same time an Yathribite chief wrote to the Koreish of
Mecca, and, holding up the examples of bygone ages, exhorted
them not to embroil themselves with civil dissensions and
warfare. He advised them to give a hearing to the new
preacher : " An honourable man has adopted a certain religion,
why persecute him ? for it is only the Lord of the Heaven who
can read the heart of man ! " His counsel had some effect,
and occasioned a change of tactics among the Koreish. For
a time accordingly, calumnies and vilifications, exasperating
contumelies and petty outrages were substituted for open
and violent persecution. The hostile Koreish stopped the
Prophet from offering his prayers at the Kaaba ; they pursued
him wherever he went ; they covered him and his disciples
with dirt and filth when engaged in their devotions. They
incited the children and the bad characters of the town to follow
and insult him. They scattered thorns in the places which
he frequented for devotion and meditation. In this act of
refined cruelty the lead was always taken by Umm ul-Jamîl,
the wife of Abû Lahab, one of Mohammed's uncles. She was
the most inveterate of his persecutors. Every place which he
or his disciples frequented for devotion she covered with thorns.
This exasperating conduct brought down upon her the designation of being " the bearer of faggots " (*hammâlat ul-hatab*)
[to hell].

Amidst all these trials Mohammed never wavered. Full of
the intensest confidence in his Mission, he worked steadily on.
Several times he was in imminent danger of his life at the
hands of the Koreish. On one occasion he disarmed their
murderous fury by his gentle and calm self-control. But
persecution only added to the strength of the new faith. " The
blood of the martyrs is the seed of the Church," is a truth not
confined to one creed. The violence of the Koreish towards
Mohammed, their burning and bitter intolerance, led to the

conversion of the redoubtable Hamza, the youngest son of Abd ul-Muttalib. This intrepid warrior, brave, generous, and true, whose doughty sword was held in dread by all the Koreish, about this time came to the Prophet, adopted his faith, and became thenceforth a devoted adherent of Islâm, and finally laid down his life in the cause.

Amidst all this persecution Mohammed never ceased calling to the nation so wedded to iniquity to abandon their evil ways and abominations. He threw his heart and soul into his preachings. He told them in burning words that seared into the hearts of the listeners, the punishment which had alighted on the tribes of 'Âd and Thamûd who had heeded not the warnings of God's messengers, of the outpouring of Heaven's wrath at the iniquities of Noah's people. He adjured them by the wonderful sights of nature, by the noon-day brightness, by the night when she spreadeth her veil, by the day when it appeareth in glory, to listen to the warning before a like destruction came upon them. He told them of the day of reckoning, when the deeds done by man in this world shall be weighed before the Eternal Judge, when the children who had been buried alive shall be asked for what crime they had been put to death, and when heaven and earth shall be folded up and none be near but God. He spoke to them of the rewards and punishments of the Hereafter, describing to his materialistic people the joys of Paradise and the pains of hell " with all the glow of Eastern imagery." He told them what the unbelievers were like—" They are like unto one who kindleth a fire, and when it hath thrown its light on all around him, God taketh away the light and leaveth him in darkness and they cannot see."

" Deaf, dumb, blind, therefore they shall not retrace their steps."

" They are like those who, when there cometh a storm-cloud of heaven big with darkness, thunder, and lightning, thrust their fingers into their ears because of the thunder-clap for fear of death. God is round about the infidels."

" The lightning almost snatcheth away their eyes ; so oft as it gleameth on them, they walk on in it ; but when darkness closeth upon them, they stop ; and if God pleased, of their ears and of their eyes would He surely deprive them : verily God is Almighty." [1]

" As to the infidels, their works are like the *Saráb* on the plain,[2] which the thirsty [traveller] thinketh to be water, and then when he cometh thereto, he findeth it [to be] nothing ; but he findeth God round about him, and He will fully pay him his account ; for swift in taking an account is God."

" Or, as the darkness over a deep sea, billows riding upon billows below, and clouds above ; one darkness over another darkness ; when a man stretcheth forth his hand he is far from seeing it ; he to whom God doth not grant light, no light at all hath he." [3]

The people were awestruck, and conversions grew frequent.

The Koreish were now thoroughly alarmed ; Mohammed's preaching betokened a serious revolutionary movement. Their power and prestige were at stake. They were the custodians of the idols whom Mohammed threatened with destruction ; they were the ministers of the worship which Mohammed denounced—their very existence depended upon their maintaining the old institutions intact. If his predictions were fulfilled, they would have to efface themselves as a nation pre-eminent among the nationalities of Arabia. The new preacher's tone was intensely democratic ; in the sight of his Lord all human beings were equal. This levelling of old distinctions was contrary to all their traditions. They would have none of it, for it boded no good to their exclusive privileges. Urgent measures were needed to stifle the movement before it gained further strength.

They accordingly decided upon an organised system of persecution. In order, however, not to violate their laws of vendetta, each family took upon itself the task of strangling the new religion within its own circle. Each household tortured its own members, or clients, or slaves, who were supposed to have attached themselves to the new faith. Mohammed, owing to the protection of Abû Tâlib and his kinsmen, Abû Bakr and a few others, who were either distinguished by their rank or possessed some influential friend or protector among the Koreish, were, for the time, exempt from immediate

[1] Sura ii. [2] *i.e.* the mirage of the desert. [3] Sura xxiv. 39, 40.

violence. The others were thrown into prison, starved, and then beaten with sticks. The hill of Ramdhâ and the place called Bathâ became thus the scenes of cruel tortures.[1] The men or women whom the Koreish found abandoning the worship of the idol-gods, were exposed to the burning heat of the desert on the scorching sand, where, when reduced to the last extremity by thirst, they were offered the alternative of adoring the idols or death. Some recanted only to profess Islâm once more when released from their torments ; but the majority held firmly to their faith. Such a one was Bilâl, the first Muezzin of Islâm. His master, Ommeyya, son of Khalaf, conducted him each day to Bathâ when the heat of the sun was at its greatest, and there exposed him bare-backed with his face to the burning sun, and placed on his chest a large block of stone with the words, " There shalt thou remain until thou art dead or thou hast abjured Islâm." As he lay half-stifled under his heavy weight, dying with thirst, he would only answer, " *Ahadun, ahadun,*" " one [God], one." This lasted for days, until the poor sufferer was reduced to the verge of death, when he was ransomed by Abû Bakr, who had in like manner purchased the liberty of six other slaves. They killed with excruciating torments Yâsar and Samiya his wife ; they inflicted fearful tortures on 'Ammâr their son. Mohammed was often an eye-witness to the sufferings of his disciples—sufferings borne with patience and fortitude as became martyrs in the cause of truth. And these were not the only martyrs in the early history of Islâm.[2]

Like the Pharisees tempting Jesus, the Koreish came to Mohammed with temptations of worldly honour and aggrandisement, to draw him from the path of duty. One day, says the chronicler, he was sitting in the Kaaba, at a little distance from an assembly of the antagonistic chiefs, when one of them, 'Otba, son of Rab'ïa, a man of moderate views came to him

---

[1] Ibn ul-Athír, vol. ii. p. 50 ; Ibn-Hishâm, pp. 205-209.

[2] *E.g.* Khobaib bin 'Adi, who, being perfidiously sold to the Koreish, was by them put to death in a cruel manner by mutilation and cutting off his flesh piece-meal. In the midst of his tortures, being asked whether he did not wish Mohammed in his place, answered, " *I would not wish to be with my family, my substance, and my children on condition that Mohammed was only to be pricked with a thorn.*"

and said, " O son of my brother, thou art distinguished by thy qualities and thy descent. Now thou hast sown division among our people, and cast dissension in our families ; thou denouncest our gods and goddesses ; thou dost tax our ancestors with impiety. We have a proposition to make to thee ; think well if it will not suit thee to accept it." " Speak, O father of Walîd," [1] said the Prophet, " I listen, O son of my brother." Commenced 'Otba : " If thou wishest to acquire riches by this affair, we will collect a fortune larger than is possessed by any of us ; if thou desirest honours and dignity, we shall make thee our chief, and shall not do a thing without thee ; if thou desirest dominion, we shall make thee our king ; and if the spirit (demon) which possesses thee cannot be over-powered, we will bring thee doctors and give them riches till they cure thee." And when he had done, " Hast thou finished, O father of Walîd ? " asked the Prophet. " Yes," replied he. " Then listen to me." " I listen," he said. " In the name of the most merciful God," commenced the Warner, " this is a revelation from the most Merciful : a book, the verses whereof are distinctly explained, an Arabic Koran, for the instruction of people who understand ; bearing good tidings, and denouncing threats : but the greater part of them turn aside, and hearken not thereto. And they say, ' Our hearts are veiled from the doctrine to which thou invitest us ; and there is a deafness in our ears, and a curtain between us and thee : wherefore act thou as thou shalt think fit ; for we shall act according to our own sentiments.' Say ' verily I am only a man like you. It is revealed unto me that your God is one God : wherefore direct your way straight unto Him ; and ask pardon of Him for what is past.' And woe be to the idolaters, who give not the appointed alms, and believe not in the life to come ! [2] But as to those who believe and work righteous-ness, they shall receive an everlasting reward." [3] When the Prophet finished this recitation, he said to 'Otba, " Thou

---

[1] Walîd being a son of 'Otba. It was usual, and is so even now, among the Arabs to call a man as the father of so-and-so, instead of using his own name, as a mark of consideration.

[2] Whilst hospitality was regarded as a great virtue, charity was considered a weakness among the Arabs ; and a future life, an old woman's fable.

[3] Koran, Sura xli.

hast heard, now take the course which seemeth best to thee." [1]

Profoundly afflicted by the sufferings of his disciples, whose position, as time went on, became more and more unbearable, he advised them to seek a refuge in the neighbouring Christian kingdom of Abyssinia, where ruled a pious sovereign, till God in His mercy wrought a change in the feelings of the Koreish. He had heard of the righteousness of this Christian king, of his tolerance and hospitality, and was certain of a welcome for his followers.

Some immediately availed themselves of the advice, and sailed, to the number of fifteen, to the hospitable shores of the Negus (Najâshi). This is called the first Exile (*muhájarat*) in the history of Islâm, and occurred in the fifth year of Mohammed's Mission (615 A.C.). These emigrants were soon joined by many more of their fellow-sufferers and labourers in the cause of truth, until their number amounted to eighty-three men and eighteen women.[2] But the untiring hostility of the Koreish pursued them even here. They were furious at the escape of their victims, and sent deputies to the king to demand the delivery of these refugees that they might be put to death. They stated the chief charges against the poor fugitives to be the abjuration of their old religion, and the adoption of a new one. The Negus sent for the exiles, and inquired of them whether what their enemies had stated was true. "What is this religion for which you have abandoned your former faith," asked the king, "and adopted neither mine nor that of any other people ? " Ja'far, son of Abû Tâlib, and brother of Ali, acting as spokesman for the fugitives, spoke thus : " O king, we were plunged in the depth of ignorance and barbarism ; we adored idols, we lived in unchastity ; we ate dead bodies, and we spoke abominations ; we disregarded every feeling of humanity, and the duties of hospitality and neighbourhood ; we knew no law but that of the strong, when God raised among us a man, of whose birth, truthfulness, honesty, and purity we were aware ; and he called us to the unity of God, and taught us not to associate anything with

[1] Ibn-Hishâm, pp. 185, 186.
[2] Ibn-Hishâm, p. 208 *et seq.*; Ibn ul-Athîr, vol. ii. p. 58 ; Abulfedâ, p. 20.

Him ; [1] he forbade us the worship of idols ; and enjoined us
to speak the truth, to be faithful to our trusts, to be merciful,
and to regard the rights of neighbours ; he forbade us to speak
evil of women, or to eat the substance of orphans ; he ordered
us to fly from vices, and to abstain from evil; to offer prayers,
to render alms, to observe the fast.   We have believed in him,
we have accepted his teachings and his injunctions to worship
God, and not to associate anything with Him.   For this
reason our people have risen against us, have persecuted us
in order to make us forego the worship of God and return to
the worship of idols of wood and stone and other abominations.
They have tortured us and injured us, until finding no safety
among them, we have come to thy country, and hope thou
wilt protect us from their oppression." [2]

The demands of the Koreish were scouted by the king, and
the deputies returned in confusion to Mecca.

Whilst the disciples of Mohammed were seeking safety in
other lands from the persecution of their enemies, he himself
stood bravely at his post, and amidst every insult and outrage
pursued his mission.   Again they came to him with promises
of honour and riches, to seduce him from his duty ; the reply
was as before, full of life, full of faith : " I am neither desirous
of riches nor ambitious of dignity nor of dominion ; I am sent
by God, who has ordained me to announce glad tidings unto
you.   I give you the words of my Lord ; I admonish you.
If you accept the message I bring you, God will be favourable
to you both in this world and in the next ; if you reject my
admonitions, I shall be patient, and leave God to judge between
you and me."   They mocked him, scoffed at him, tried by
insidious questions to expose the fallacy of his teachings. [3]
His simple trust and sublime faith in his Master rose superior
to all their materialistic scepticism.   They asked him to
cause wells and rivers to gush forth, to bring down the heaven

---

[1] The idolaters are almost always called " Associaters," *Mushrikîn*, in the
Koran, or men who associate other beings with God.

[2] Can there be a better summary of Mohammed's work or of his teachings ?
Ibn ul-Athîr, vol. ii. p. 61 ; and Ibn-Hishâm, pp. 219, 220.

[3] Ibn-Hishâm. p. 188.   A Christian historian goes into raptures at the
subtlety of the idolaters ; see Osborn, *Islam under the Arabs.*

in pieces, to remove mountains, to have a house of gold erected,
to ascend to heaven by a ladder.[1]   It was a repetition of the
old story, with this difference, that in the case of Jesus his own
followers insisted upon his performing miracles to satisfy
them of the truth of his mission.   " His immediate disciples,"
says Professor Momerie, " were always misunderstanding him
and his work : wanting him to call down fire from heaven ;
wanting him to declare himself king of the Jews ; wanting to
sit on his right hand and on his left hand in his kingdom ;
wanting him to show them the Father, to make God visible
to their bodily eyes ; wanting him to do, and wanting to do
themselves, anything and everything that was incompatible
with his great plan.   This was how they treated him until
the end.   When that came, they all forsook him, and
fled."

To these unsatisfied, lukewarm spirits, whose craving for
wonders was no less strong than that of the Koreish, and who
afterwards clothed the revered figure of Jesus in a mist, a legacy
which even modern idealistic Christianity cannot shake off,
the Master was wont to reply, at times angrily, that it was an
evil and adulterous age which sought after a sign, and that no
sign should be given to it ; and that if a man believed not in
Moses and the prophets, he would not repent even though one
rose from the dead.[2]

It must be said to the credit of the disciples of the Arabian
Teacher, that they never called for a miracle from *their* Master.
They—scholars, merchants, and soldiers—looked to the moral
evidences of his mission.   They ranged themselves round the
friendless preacher at the sacrifice of all their worldly interests
and worldly hopes, and adhered to him through life and death
with a devotion to his human personality to which there is
scarcely a parallel in the history of the world.

In an age when miracles were supposed to be ordinary
occurrences at the beck of the commonest saint, when the

---

[1] Sura xvii. 92-96.

[2] Patristic Christianity has held, and still holds, to the miracles as a proof
of the divinity of Jesus ; modern Christianity calls them *Aberglaube*.   It may
well be, as the author of *Literature and Dogma* says, that the miracles are
doomed, and that the miracle-saga of Christianity must, sooner or later, go
with all legends, Eastern or Western.

whole atmosphere was surcharged with supernaturalism, not only in Arabia, but in the neighbouring countries where civilisation had made far greater progress, the great Pioneer of rationalism unhesitatingly replies to the miracle-seeking heathens—" God has not sent me to work wonders ; He has sent me to preach to you. My Lord be praised ! Am I more than a man sent as an apostle ? . . . Angels do not commonly walk the earth, or God would have despatched an angel to preach His truth to you.[1] I never said that Allah's treasures are in my hand, that I knew the hidden things, or that I was an angel. . . . I who cannot even help or trust myself, unless God pleaseth." . . . No extraordinary pretensions, no indulgence in hyperbolical language, no endeavour to cast a glamour round his character or personality. " I am only a preacher of God's words, the bringer of God's message to mankind," repeats he always. From first to last no expression escapes him " which could be construed into a request for human worship " ;[2] from first to last there is unvarying soberness of expression, which, considering the age and surrounding, is more marvellous ; from first to last the tone is one of simple, deep humility before the Creator. And in the moment of his greatest exaltation the feeling is one of humble, sweet thankfulness :—

" In the name of God, the Merciful, the Compassionate ! Whatsoever is in heaven and on earth praises God the King, the Holy One, the Almighty, the All-wise. It is He who out of the midst of the illiterate Arabs has raised an apostle to show unto them His signs, and to sanctify them, and to teach them the Scripture and the Wisdom, them who before had been in great darkness. . . . This is God's free grace, which He giveth unto whomsoever He wills. God is of great mercy ! "[3]

Disclaiming every power of wonder-working, the Prophet of Islâm ever rests the truth of his divine commission entirely upon his Teachings. He never resorts to the miraculous to assert his influence or to enforce his warnings. He invariably appeals to the familiar phenomena of nature as signs of the

---

[1] Sura xvii. 95-98 ; sura lxxii. 21-24.   [2] Professor Momerie.
[3] Sura lxii. vv. 1-10.

divine presence.[1]   He unswervingly addresses himself to the
inner consciousness of man, to his reason, and not to his weakness or his credulity.   Look round yourself : is this wonderful
world, the sun, the moon, and the stars, holding their swift silent
course in the blue vault of heaven, the law and system prevailing
in the universe ; the rain-drops falling to revive the parched
earth into life ; the ships moving across the ocean, beladen
with what is profitable to mankind ; the beautiful palm
covered with its golden fruit—are these the handiwork of your
wooden or stone gods ? [2]

Fools ! do you want a sign, when the whole creation is full
of the signs of God ?   The structure of your body, how wonderfully complex, how beautifully regulated ; the alternations
of night and day, of life and death ; your sleeping and awaking ;
your desire to accumulate from the abundance of God ; the
winds driving abroad the pregnant clouds as the forerunners
of the Creator's mercy ; the harmony and order in the midst
of diversity ; the variety of the human race, and yet their
close affinity ; fruits, flowers, animals, human beings themselves—are these not signs enough of the presence of a Master-
Mind ? [3]

To the Prophet of Islâm, nature in itself is a revelation and
a miracle.

> " There is a tongue in every leaf,
>   A voice in every rill,
> A voice that speaketh everywhere,
> In flood and fair, through earth and air,
>   A voice that's never still." [4]

The Prophet of Monotheism is pre-eminently the Prophet of
Nature.   His ethical appeal and his earnest assertion of divine

---

[1] The passage of Sir W. Muir on this point is, to say the least, remarkable.
He says : " Whether the idolatry of Mecca would not have succumbed without a struggle before such preaching as Mahomet's, *sustained by reasonable
evidence*, may be matter for speculation " (the italics are his own), vol. ii. p.
144.   Like the Koreish, Sir W. Muir is not satisfied with the teachings, unless
supported by wonder-workings.

[2] Sura xxv. 49-59 ; sura l. 9, etc.

[3] Sura vi. 96-99, li. 20, xv. 20, xx. 50-57, xxxiv. 20-28, 39, etc.

[4] Comp.   هر گیاهے که از زمین روید ٭ وحده لا شریک له کبد
" Every blade that springs from the earth bears testimony to the unity of
God."

Unity are founded upon the rational and intellectual recognition of all-pervading order, of the visible presence of one Mind, one Will, regulating, guiding, and governing the Universe. His grandest miracle is the Book in which he has poured forth with an inspired tongue all the " revelations of nature, conscience, and prophecy." Ask you a greater miracle than this, O unbelieving people ! than to have your vulgar tongue chosen as the language of that incomparable Book, one piece of which puts to shame all your golden poesy and suspended songs—to convey the tidings of universal mercy, the warnings to pride and tyranny !

But to all his exhortations the Koreish turned a deaf ear. They were blind to the signs of God, blind to the presence of a Divine Personality in nature, deaf to the call of the Seer to come back to righteousness, to forego the crimes and abominations of antiquity. Their answer to him breathes a fierce animosity paralleled only by the darkest days of Arian or Pelagian persecution in Christendom. " Know this, O Mohammed," said they, " we shall never cease to stop thee from preaching till either thou or we perish."

During this interval occurred an incident which has been differently construed by the Moslem historians and the Christian biographers of the Prophet. One day, in one of his prophetic trances, Mohammed was reciting within the Kaaba some verses which now form part of the fifty-third chapter of the Koran. When he came to the words, " What think ye of al-Lât, al-'Uzza, and Manât ? the third besides," an idolater who was present on the occasion, and whom tradition has converted into the devil, anxious to avert the threatened denunciation called out, " They are exalted damsels, and their intercession with God may be hoped for." These words were supposed to form part of the Prophet's revelation. And the Koreish, overjoyed either at the trick or at Mohammed's supposed concession, hastened to express their willingness to come to terms. When Mohammed learnt what had happened, he immediately proclaimed the words, " They are nought but empty names, which you and your fathers have invented." This is the version given by Mohammedan historians and traditionists. According to the Christian biographers, the incident is supposed to indicate a momentary desire on the part of the Prophet to end the strife with the Koreish by some compromise. The bigot calls it " a lapse " and " a fall "; but the generous and unbiased historian considers the episode as throwing additional lustre on the Prophet of Arabia. Persecution was becoming fiercer and fiercer every day, the sufferings of his followers were increasing, and the whole city was up in arms against them. The sight of his poor disciples afflicted him deeply ; his weary struggle with the Arabian idolatry filled him with grief. What wonder that a momentary thought crossed his mind to end the conflict by making a slight concession to the bigotry of his enemies. " And so Mohammed made his first and last concession. He recited a revelation to the Koreish, in which he spoke respectfully of the three moon-goddesses, and asserted that their intercession with God might be hoped for : ' Wherefore bow down before God and serve Him ' ; and the whole audience, overjoyed at the compromise, bowed down and worshipped at the name of the God of Mohammed—the whole city was reconciled to the double religion. But this dreamer of the desert was not the man to rest upon a lie. At the price of the whole city of Mecca he would not remain untrue to himself. He came forward and said he had done wrong—the devil had tempted him. He openly and frankly retracted what he had said ; and ' as for their idols, they were but empty names which they and their fathers had invented.' "

" Western biographers have rejoiced greatly over ' Mohammed's fall.' Yet it was a tempting compromise, and few would have withstood it. And the life of Mohammed is not the life of a god, but of a man ; from first to last it is intensely human. But if for once he was not superior to the temptation of gaining over the whole city, and obtaining peace where before had been only bitter persecution, what can we say of his manfully thrusting back the rich prize he had gained, freely confessing his fault, and resolutely giving himself over again to the old indignities and insults ? If he was once insincere—and who is not ?—how intrepid was his after sincerity ! He was untrue to himself for a while, and he is ever referring to it in his public preaching with shame and remorse ; but the false step was more than atoned for by his magnificent recantation." [1]

Upon the promulgation that Lât, ʻUzza, and Manât were but empty names, the persecution burst out anew with re-doubled fury.

Supported, however, by a firm conviction of divine assistance, and upheld by the admonitions of the heavenly voice within, conveyed to him by the ministrators of heavenly mercy, he continued his preaching undeterred by the hostility of his enemies, or by the injuries they inflicted upon him. In spite of all opposition, however, slowly but surely the new teachings gained ground. The seeds of truth thus scattered could not fail to fructify. The wild Arab of the desert, the trading citizen of distant townships who came to the national fair, heard the words of the strange man whom his enemies thought possessed, listened to the admonitions in which he poured forth his soul, listened with awe and wonder to his denunciations of their divinities and of their superstitions, of their unright-eousness, of their evil ways, and carried back to their far-off homes new light and new life, even unconsciously to themselves. And the satires, the ill-names his enemies heaped upon Mohammed, only tended to make his words more extensively known.

The Meccans, on their side, were by no means quiet. Several times the Koreish sent deputations to Abû Tâlib, asking him to stop his nephew from preaching against their religion. At first Abû Tâlib turned them away with soft and courteous words. But as Mohammed persisted in his fiery denunciations against their godlessness and impiety, they expelled him from the Kaaba where he had been wont to preach, and then came in a body to his uncle.[2] " We respect thy age and thy rank," said they, " but our respect for thee has bounds, and verily we can have no further patience with thy nephew's abuse of our gods, and his ill words against our ancestors ; wherefore do thou either prevent him from so doing, or thyself take part with him, so that we may settle the matter by fight

---

[1] Stanley Lane-Poole, *Introd. to the Selections from the Koran*, p. xlix.

[2] Tabari, vol. ii. p. 406 ; according to this author's authorities, ver. 214 of chap. xxi. of the Koran was revealed about this period.

until one of the two parties is exterminated." [1]   Having thus
spoken, they departed.   Abû Tâlib was unwilling to separate
himself from his people, neither did he like abandoning his
nephew to the idolaters.   Sending for Mohammed, he informed
him of the speech of the Koreish, and begged him to renounce
his task.   Mohammed thought his uncle wished to withdraw
his protection ; but his high resolve did not fail him even at
this moment.   Firmly he replied : " O my uncle, if they
placed the sun on my right hand and the moon on my left, to
force me to renounce my work, verily I would not desist therefrom until God made manifest His cause, or I perished in the
attempt."   But overcome by the thought of desertion by his
kind protector, he turned to depart.   Then Abû Tâlib called
aloud : " Son of my brother, come back " ;   and he came.
And Abû Tâlib said : " Say whatsoever thou pleasest ;   for
by the Lord, I shall not abandon thee, nay, never." [2]   The
Koreish made another attempt to persuade Abû Tâlib to deliver
up his nephew to them.   They offered in exchange a young
man of the family of Makhzûm, but it was of no avail. [3]   The
declared intention of Abû Tâlib to support his nephew excited
their fury, and they renewed their menaces of violence.   The
venerable patriarch appealed to the sense of honour of the
Banî-Hâshim and Banî-Muttalib, the kinsmen of Mohammed,
to protect a distinguished member of their family from falling
a victim to the hatred of rival clans.   And the appeal was
nobly responded to, with the solitary exception of the squint-
eyed Abû Lahab, " the Father of the Flame," as the sequel
will show.

At this time the new Faith gained a valuable adherent in
Omar, whose energy of character made him an important
factor in the future commonwealth of Islâm.   His services to
the religion of Mohammed have engraved his name on the
pages of history.   A distinguished member of the family of
'Adi ibn-Ka'b, and the son of Khattâb, notorious for the
persecution of the Moslems, he was hitherto a violent opponent
of Islâm, and a bitter adversary of the Prophet.   His

---

[1] Ibn ul-Athîr, vol. ii. p. 47 ; Ibn-Hishâm, pp. 167, 168.
[2] Ibn-Hishâm, p. 168 ; Ibn ul-Athîr, vol. ii. p. 48 ; Abulfedâ, p. 17.
[3] Ibn-Hishâm, p. 169 ; Ibn ul-Athîr, vol. ii. p. 48.

conversion is said to have been worked by the magic effect on his mind of a chapter of the Koran which he heard recited in his sister's house, where he had gone in a furious rage and with murderous intent.

Struck with the words which he had heard, he went straight to the Prophet with the naked sword in his hand with which he had meant to slay Mohammed and his disciples, causing considerable consternation among the assembly of the Faithful listening to the Preacher. He kissed the Master's hand, and then demanded to be taken into the fold of God ; and heartfelt thanks went up to heaven from the Moslems for the grace that had fallen on Omar. After his conversion he became one of the bulwarks of the Faith.

Islâm need no more hide its head in byways and corners, go about in concealment, or offer its prayers to God in secret and trepidation. Besides a large following taken from the humbler walks of life, there were now gathered round the Prophet a chosen band of apostles, consisting, not of ignorant folk, but of men of energy, talent, and worth, like Hamza, Abû Bakr, and Omar. And though Ali was in his youth, he was fast rising into prominence.

These important adhesions gave heart to the Moslems, and they now ventured to perform their devotions in public. The Koreish, who were at first thunderstruck at the conversion of Omar, saw the gravity of the situation. And yet they waited to strike the decisive blow.

The return of the deputies, however, from Abyssinia, and the announcement of their unsuccessful mission, roused them to frenzy. They determined at last to exterminate with one stroke the entire clan of Hâshim and Muttalib. With that purpose they, in the 7th year of the Mission, towards the end of 616 A.C., formed a league against the descendants of Hâshim and Muttalib. They bound themselves by a solemn document, which was deposited in the Kaaba, not to enter into any contract of marriage with the Hâshimites, or to buy and sell with them. The Hâshimites and Muttalibites, Musulmans as well as idolaters, were struck with dismay, and fearful that this might be the prelude to some other attack, judged it safer to abandon their houses dispersed in the city,

and concentrate themselves at one point. They betook
themselves accordingly to the *Shi‘b* (or quarter) of Abû Tâlib
—a long, narrow mountain defile on the eastern skirts of
Mecca, cut off by rocks or walls from the city, except for one
narrow gateway. Abû Lahab alone remained aloof, and
ranged himself on the side of the enemy.

They lived in this defensive position with Mohammed in
their midst for nearly three years, beleaguered by the Koreish,
and subjected to every privation. The provisions which they
had carried with them were soon exhausted, and the cries of
the starving children could be heard outside. Probably they
would have entirely perished but for the occasional help they
received surreptitiously from less bigoted compatriots. Some
of the chiefs, however, were beginning to be ashamed of their
injustice. Towards the tenth year of the Mission (619 A.C.),
Hishâm, son of ‘Amr, who took a lively interest in the Hâshimites, tried to bring about a reconciliation between the
Koreishites and the two families of Hâshim and Muttalib.
He succeeded in winning over Zubair, son of Abû Ommeyya,
to his side ; and, seconded by him and others, the pact was
annulled, and the two families were taken back to the enjoyment of the communal rights, and were allowed to return to
Mecca.

During the period Mohammed was shut up in the *Shi‘b* with
his kinspeople, Islâm made no progress outside. In the
sacred months, when violence was considered a sacrilege, the
Teacher would come out of his prison and endeavour to obtain
hearers among the pilgrims ; but the squint-eyed " Father of
the Flame " followed him about, and made his words nought
by calling him " a liar and a Sabean."

The year which followed is called in the history of Islâm
" the Year of Mourning " for the loss of Abû Tâlib and Khadîja,
who followed each other to the grave within a short interval.
In Abû Tâlib, Mohammed lost the guardian of his youth, who
had hitherto stood between him and his enemies. The death
of Khadîja was a severe blow. When none believed in him,
when he himself had not yet awakened to the full consciousness
of his mission, and his heart was full of doubts, when all around
him was dark and despairing, her love, her faith had stood by

him. " She was ever his angel of hope and consolation."
To the end of his life he retained the tenderest recollection of
her love and devotion.

Note to Chapter I.

Sir W. Muir thinks M. Caussin de Perceval has made a
mistake in supposing Bathâ to be the name of a place. He
thinks it signifies the nature of the soil over which these
people were tortured ; vol. ii. p. 128. To corroborate M.
Caussin de Perceval and myself, I have only to add that the
existence of this place is an undoubted fact ; and Bathâ
especially has been frequently referred to by Mohammedan
authors as a place in the immediate vicinity of Mecca. For
example, the celebrated Hakîm Sanâi says :

> Cho 'ilmat hast khidmat kun cho
> bi-'ilman, ke zisht âid,
> Girifta Chînian ihrâm, wa Mekki
> khufta dar Bathâ.

" If thou possessest knowledge, serve like those who are
ignorant ; for it is unseemly that people from China should
adopt the Ihrâm (that is to say, come on a pilgrimage to
Mecca), and the native of Mecca should lie sleeping at Bathâ."

CHAPTER II

THE HEGIRA

مُحَمَّدٌ سَيِّدُ الْكَوْنَيْنِ وَ الثَّقَلَيْنِ • وَالْفَرِيقَيْنِ مِنْ عُرْبٍ وَ مِّنْ عَجَمِ

THE children of Ommeyya and other hostile clans, actuated as much by their attachment to the old cult as by their jealousy of, and hatred towards, the Hâshimites, considered this a favourable opportunity to crush out Islâm in Mecca; and the death of Abû Tâlib, whose personal influence and character had restrained their fury within some limits, became the signal for the Koreish to redouble their persecutions.[1]

Weighed down by the loss of his venerable protector and of his cherished wife, hopeless of turning the Koreish from idolatry, with a saddened heart, and yet full of trust, he determined to turn to some other field for the exercise of his ministry. Mecca had rejected the words of God, hapless Tâyef may listen to them. Accompanied by his faithful servant Zaid, he arrived among the Thakîf.[2] He spoke to them about his Mission; told them about their iniquities, and called them to the worship of God. His words caused a storm of indignation. Who was this crazy man, said they, who invited them to abandon the beautiful divinities they worshipped with such lightness of heart and such freedom of morals? They drove him from the city; and the rabble and the slaves followed, hooting and pelting him with stones until the evening, when they left him to pursue his way alone. Wounded and bleeding, footsore and weary, he betook himself

---

[1] Ibn ul-Athîr, vol. ii. p. 69.　　　[2] The people of Tâyef.

to prayer under the shade of some palm trees, which afforded a welcome shelter to the thirsty and famished wayfarer. Raising his hands towards heaven, he cried : " O Lord ! I make my complaint unto Thee, out of my feebleness, and the vanity of my wishes, I am insignificant in the sight of men. O Thou most merciful ! Lord of the weak ! Thou art my Lord ! Do not forsake me. Leave me not a prey to strangers, nor to mine enemies. If Thou art not offended, I am safe. I seek refuge in the light of Thy countenance, by which all darkness is dispersed, and peace comes here and hereafter. Let not Thy anger descend on me ; solve my difficulties as it pleaseth Thee. There is no power, no help, but in Thee." [1]

Mohammed returned to Mecca sorely stricken in heart. He lived here for some time, retired from his people, preaching occasionally, but confining his efforts mainly to the strangers who congregated in Mecca and its vicinity during the season of the annual pilgrimage, hoping, as Tabari expresses it, to find among them some who would believe in him, and carry the truth to their people.

One day, whilst thus sadly but yet hopefully working among these half-traders, half-pilgrims, he came upon a group of six men from the distant city of Yathrib conversing together. He asked them to sit down and listen to him ; and they sat down and listened. Struck by his earnestness and the truth of his words, they became his proselytes (620 A.C.) ; [2] and returning to their city, they spread the news, with lightning rapidity, that a Prophet had risen among the Arabs who was to call them to God, and put an end to their dissensions, which had lasted for centuries.

The next year these Yathribites returned, and brought six more of their fellow-citizens as deputies from the two principal tribes who occupied that city.[3]

On the self-same spot which had witnessed the conversion of the former six, the new-comers gave in their adhesion to

[1] Ibn-Hishâm, pp. 279, 280 ; Ibn ul-Athîr, vol. ii. pp. 70, 71.

[2] Ibn-Hishâm, pp. 286, 287 ; Tabari (Zotenberg's transl.), vol. ii. p. 438.

[3] Aus and Khazraj.

Mohammed.   This is called the first Pledge of 'Akaba, from the name of the hill on which the conference was held.[1]

The pledge they took was as follows : " We will not associate anything with God ; we will not steal, nor commit adultery, nor fornication ; we will not kill our children ; we will abstain from calumny and slander ; we will obey the Prophet in everything that is right ; and we will be faithful to him in weal and in sorrow." [2]

After the pledge, they returned home with a disciple of Mohammed to teach them the fundamental doctrines of the new religion, which rapidly spread among the inhabitants of Yathrib.

The interval which elapsed between the first and second pledge is remarkable as one of the most critical periods of Mohammed's Mission. The sublime trust of Mohammed in God, and the grandeur of his character, never stand forth more prominently than at this period. He was sad at the sight of his people so sternly wedded to idolatry ;[3] but his sorrow was assuaged by the hope that the truth would in the end prevail.[4] He might not live to see it ;[5] but as surely as darkness flies before the rays of the sun, so surely falsehood will vanish before truth.[6] Regarding this epoch, a few words of unconscious admiration escape even the lips of Muir : " Mahomet, thus holding his people at bay, waiting, in the still expectation of victory, to outward appearance defenceless, and with his little band, as it were, in the lion's mouth, yet trusting in His Almighty power whose messenger he believed himself to be, resolute and unmoved—presents a spectacle of sublimity paralleled only in the sacred records by such scenes as that of the prophet of Israel, when he complained to his Master, ' I, even I only, am left.' "[7]

---

[1] In the history of Islâm, this pledge is also called the " Pledge of Women," in contradistinction to the second pledge, in which the deputies of Yathrib took an oath to assist the Moslems, *even by arms* against the attacks and outrages of their enemies.

[2] Ibn-Hishâm, p. 289 ; Ibn ul-Athîr, vol ii. pp. 73, 74.

[3] Koran, sura vi. ver. 107.

[4] Koran, sura xl. ver. 78, xliii. ver. 40, etc.

[5] Koran, sura xxi. ver. 18.

[6] Koran, sura xvii. ver. 18.   [7] *Life of Mahomet*, vol. ii. p. 228.

This period of anxious waiting is also remarkable for that notable Vision of the Ascension which has furnished worlds of golden dreams for the imaginative genius of poets and traditionists. They have woven beautiful and gorgeous legends round the simple words of the Koran : " Praise be to Him who carried His servant by night from the sacred temple to the temple that is more remote, whose precincts We have blessed, that We might show him some of our signs ! for He is the Hearer, the Seer." [1] And again : " And remember we said to thee, Verily, thy Lord is round about mankind ; We ordained the Vision which We showed thee." [1] In spite of the beautiful garb in which the traditionists have dressed this incident, " it is still a grand vision full of glorious imagery, fraught with deep meaning." [2]

The following year (622 A.C.), the Yathribites who had adopted the new religion repaired to Mecca, to the number of seventy-five, in company with their idolatrous brethren, to invite the Prophet to their city ; [3] but the idolaters had no knowledge of the intention of their companions.

In the stillness of night,[4] when all hostile elements appeared slumbering, these pioneers of the new faith met under the hill which had witnessed the first pledge. Mohammed appeared among them, accompanied by his uncle Abbâs, who, though not a convert, yet took a warm interest in the progress of Islâm. He opened the conference, and vividly described to the Yathribites the risk they incurred by adopting Islâm and inviting its Teacher to their city. They replied with one

[1] Koran, chap. xvii. ver. 1. " All that Mohammedans *must* believe respecting the Merâj is, that *the Prophet saw himself*, in a vision, transported from Mecca to Jerusalem, and that in such vision he really beheld some of the greatest signs of his Lord. It must be evident to the reader that the visions also of a prophet are a mode of divine inspiration."—Syed Ahmed Khan, *Ess.* xi. p. 34. Muir says that " the earliest authorities point only to a vision, not to a real bodily journey," vol. ii. p. 221, note. Compare the early traditions given by Ibn-Hishâm, p. 267, which support this view. It may, I think, be fairly asked why Christians, who believe in the bodily resurrection and bodily ascension of Jesus and of Elijah, should look upon those Moslems who believe in the bodily ascension of Mohammed as less rational than themselves ?

[2] Stanley Lane-Poole, *Introd. to the Selections from the Koran*, p. lvi.

[3] Ibn-Hishâm, p. 296 ; al-Halabi, *Insân ul-'Uyûn*, vol. i. p. 389.

[4] In the night of the first and second day of the *Tashrîk*, the period of three days which follow immediately the celebration of the rites of the pilgrimage.

voice, that they adopted the religion fully conscious of the dangers that surrounded them. " Speak, O Prophet of God," said they, " and exact any pledge for thyself and thy Lord." The Prophet began, as was his wont, by reciting several passages of the Koran ; he then invited all present to the service of God, and dwelt upon the blessings of the new dispensation.[1] The former pledge was repeated, that they would worship none but God ; that they would observe the precepts of Islâm ; that they would obey Mohammed in all that was right, and defend him and his, even as they would their women and children.[2] " And," said they, " if we die in the cause of God, what shall be our return ? "   " Happiness hereafter," was the reply.[3] " But," said they, " thou wilt not leave us in the hour of prosperity to return to thy people ? "   The Prophet smiled and said : " Nay never ; your blood is my blood ; I am yours, you are mine."   " Give us then thy hand " ; and each one placing his hand on that of the Prophet, swore allegiance to him and his God.   Scarcely had the compact been concluded, when the voice of a Meccan, who had been watching this scene from a distance, came floating on the night air, striking a sudden panic into the self-denying hearts there assembled. The firm words of Mohammed restored their presence of mind.

Mohammed then selected twelve men from among them— men of position, pointed out to him by the voice of the people —as his delegates (Nakîbs).[4]   Thus was concluded the second Pledge of 'Akaba.

The Meccan spy had already spread the news of this conference through the city.   Astounded at the temerity of Mohammed and his followers, the Koreish proceeded in a body to the caravan of the Yathribites to demand the men who had entered into the pledge with him.   Finding no clue, however, as to the persons who had taken part at the meeting, they allowed the caravan to depart unmolested.   But this apparent modera-

---

[1] Ibn-Hishâm, p. 296 ; Ibn ul-Athîr, vol. ii. p. 76.   [2] Ibid.

[3] Ibn ul-Athîr, vol. ii. p. 77.

[4] Ibn Hishâm, pp. 297-300.   Seventy-five people, men and women, took part in this Pledge.   This event occurred in the month of Zu'l-Hijja, and the Prophet stopped at Mecca throughout the remainder of this month, and Muharram and Safar.   In Rabi I. he left for Medina ; Ibn ul-Athîr, vol. ii. p. 78.

tion on the part of the Koreish formed only a prelude to a furious persecution of Mohammed and his disciples. The position of the latter became every day more and more perilous. The Prophet, fearing a general massacre, advised his followers to seek immediate safety at Yathrib ; whereupon about one hundred families silently disappeared by twos and threes from Mecca and proceeded to Yathrib, where they were received with enthusiasm. Entire quarters of the city thus became deserted ; and 'Otba, the son of Rab'îa, at the sight of these vacant abodes, once so full of life, " sighed heavily," and recited the old verse : " Every dwelling-place, even if it has been blessed ever so long, will one day become a prey to unhappiness and bitter wind " ; " And," he sorrowfully added, " all this is the work of the son of our brother, who has scattered our assemblies, ruined our affairs, and created dissension amongst us." [1]

As it was with Jesus, so it was with Mohammed ; only with this difference, that in one case the Teacher himself says : " Think not that I came to send peace on earth ; I came not to send peace, but a sword : for I am come to set a man at variance against his father, and the daughter against her mother, and the daughter-in-law against her mother-in-law." [2] In Mohammed's case it was one of his most persevering opponents who accused him of creating dissension in families.

Throughout this period, when the storm was at its height and might at any moment have burst over his head, Mohammed never quailed. All his disciples had left for Yathrib ; alone he remained bravely at his post, with the devoted Ali and the venerable Abû Bakr.

Meanwhile the clouds were gathering fast. Fearful of the escape of the Prophet, an assembly of the Koreish met in all despatch in the town-hall (Dâr un-Nadwâ), and some chiefs of other clans were invited to attend. The matter had become one of life and death. Stormy was the meeting, for fear had entered their hearts. Imprisonment for life, expulsion from the city, each was debated in turn. Assassination was then proposed ; but assassination by one man would have exposed him and his family to the vengeance of blood. The difficulty

[1] Ibn-Hishâm, p. 316.   [2] Matt. x. 34, 35.

was at last solved by Abû Jahl,[1] who suggested that a number
of courageous men, chosen from different families, should
sheathe their swords simultaneously in Mohammed's bosom, in
order that the responsibility of the deed might rest upon all,
and the relations of Mohammed might consequently be unable
to avenge it.   This proposal was accepted, and a number of
noble youths were selected for the sanguinary deed. As the
night advanced, the assassins posted themselves round the
Prophet's dwelling.   Thus they watched all night long, waiting
to murder him when he should leave his house in the early
dawn, peeping now and then through a hole in the door to
make sure that he still lay on his bed.   But, meanwhile, the
instinct of self-preservation, the instinct which had often led
the great Prophet of Nazareth to evade his enemies,[2] had
warned Mohammed of the danger. In order to keep the
attention of the assassins fixed upon the bed, he put his own
green garment upon the devoted and faithful Ali, bade him
lie on his bed,[3] " and escaped, as David had escaped, through
the windows." He repaired to the house of Abû Bakr, and
they fled together unobserved from the inhospitable city of
their birth. They lay hid for several days in a cavern of
Mount Thaur, a hill to the south of Mecca.[4]

The fury of the Koreish was now unbounded. The news
that the would-be assassins had returned unsuccessful, and
Mohammed had escaped, aroused their whole energy. Horsemen

---

[1] Ibn-Hishâm, pp. 323-325 ; Ibn ul-Athîr, vol. ii. p. 79 ; the Koran, sura
viii. ver. 30.   According to Ibn-Hishâm, this proposal of Abû Jahl, one of
the Koreish, was seconded by a stranger, in the guise of a venerable Sheikh
from Najd whom tradition has resolved into Satan himself. Abû Jahl was
one of the bitterest enemies of the Prophet.   His real name was 'Amr and he
was surnamed, for his sagacity, Abu'l Hikam (" father of wisdom," in the
plural).   Owing to his fanaticism and bigotry, which prevented his perceiving
any good in the new Teachings, Mohammed called him instead Abû Jahl
(" father of ignorance ").   Ignorance has in all ages posed as the champion
of orthodoxy. Abû Jahl has thus become a type.   It is to this fact Hakîm
Sanâî, the great mystical poet, refers in the following couplet :—

" Ahmed-i-Mursal nishista kai rawâ dârad Khirad.
" Dil asîr-i-sîrat-i-Bû Jahl-i-Kâfir dâshtan."

" Ahmed the Prophet is sitting (in your midst), how can reason allow
" The heart to become captive of the qualities of Bû-Jahl the unbeliever."

[2] Comp. Milman, Hist. of Christianity, vol. i. p. 253.

[3] Ibn-Hishâm, p. 325 ; Ibn ul-Athîr, vol. ii. p. 80.

[4] See Desvergers' note (57) to his Abulfedâ, p. 116.

scoured the country. A price was set upon Mohammed's head.[1] Once or twice the danger approached so near that the heart of old Abû Bakr quaked with fear. " We are but two," said he. " Nay," said Mohammed, " we are three, God is with us ; " and He was with them. After three days the Koreish slackened their efforts. All this time Mohammed and his companion were sustained by food brought to them at night by a daughter of Abû Bakr.[2] On the evening of the third day the fugitives left the cavern, and, procuring with great difficulty two camels, endeavoured to reach Yathrib by unfrequented paths. But even here the way was full of danger. The heavy price set upon Mohammed's head had brought out many horsemen from Mecca, and they were still diligently seeking for the helpless wanderer. One, a wild and fierce warrior, actually caught sight of the fugitives and pursued them. Again the heart of Abû Bakr misgave him, and he cried, " We are lost." " Be not afraid," said the Prophet, " God will protect us." As the idolater overtook Mohammed, his horse reared and fell. Struck with sudden awe, he entreated the forgiveness of the man whom he was pursuing and asked for an attestation of his pardon. This was given to him on a piece of bone by Abû Bakr.[3]

The fugitives continued their journey without further molestation and after three days' journeying reached the territories of Yathrib. It was a hot day in June, 622 of the Christian era, when Mohammed alighted from his camel upon the soil which was thenceforth to become his home and his refuge. A Jew watching on a tower first espied him,[4] and thus were the words of the Koran fulfilled : " They, to whom the Scriptures have been given, recognise him as they do their own children." [5] Mohammed and his companion rested for a few days [6] at a village called Koba,[7] situated only two miles to the south of Yathrib, and remarkable for its beauty and

---

[1] Of a hundred camels, Ibn-Hishâm, p. 328 ; Ibn ul-Athîr, vol. ii. p. 81.

[2] Ibn ul-Athîr, vol. ii. p. 81.

[3] Ibn-Hishâm, pp. 331, 332 ; Ibn ul-Athîr, *ibid.*

[4] Ibn-Hishâm, p. 330.   [5] Koran, sura vi. ver. 20.

[6] Monday, Tuesday, Wednesday and Thursday, Ibn-Hishâm, p. 335 ; Ibn ul-Athîr, vol. ii. p. 83.

[7] See Desvergers' Abulfedâ, p. 116, note 59.

fertility. Here he was joined by Ali, who had been severely maltreated by the idolaters after their disappointment at Mohammed's escape.[1] Ali fled from Mecca and journeyed on foot, hiding himself in the daytime and travelling only at night, lest he should fall into the hands of the Koreish.[2]

The Banî 'Amr bin-'Auf, to whom the village belonged, invited the Prophet to prolong his stay amongst them. But his duty lay before him ; and he proceeded towards Yathrib, attended by a numerous body of his disciples. He entered the city on the morning of a Friday, 16th of Rabi I., corresponding (according to M. Caussin de Perceval) with the 2nd of July 622.[3]

Thus was accomplished the Hijrat, called in European annals " the flight of Mohammed," from which dates the Mohammedan calendar.

NOTE I TO CHAPTER II

The " Hegira," or the era of the *Hijrat*, was instituted seventeen years later by the second Caliph. The commencement, however, is not laid at the real time of the departure from Mecca, which happened on the 4th of Rabi I., but on the first day of the first lunar month of the year, viz. Muharram —which day, in the year when the era was established, fell on the 15th of July.

But though Omar instituted the official era, the custom of referring to events as happening before or after the *Hijrat* originated, according to some traditions, with the Prophet himself ; this event naturally marking the greatest crisis in the history of his Mission.—Comp. al-Halabi, *Insân-ul-'Uyûn, in loco*.

NOTE 2 TO CHAPTER II

The twelve Moslem months are ; Muharram (the sacred month), Safar (the month of departure), Rabi I. (first month

[1] Ibn ul-Athîr, vol. ii. p. 80.
[2] *Ibid.* vol. ii. 82.
[3] Caussin de Perceval, vol. iii. pp. 17-20 ; Ibn-Hishâm, p. 335.

of the spring), Rabi II. (second month of the spring), Jumâdî I. (first dry month), Jumâdî II. (second dry month), Rajab (*respected*, called often Rajab *ul-Murajjab*), Sha'bân (the month of the budding of trees), Ramazân (month of heat), Shawwâl (month of junction), Zu'l-Ka'da (month of truce, rest, or relaxation), Zu'l Hijja (month of pilgrimage). The ancient Arabs observed the lunar year of 354 days, 8 hours, 48 seconds, divided into twelve months of 29 and 30 days alternately. In order to make them agree with the solar year of their neighbours, the Greeks and the Romans, and also in order to make the months fall in the right season, they added a month every third year. This intercalation was called *Nasî*; and although it was not perfectly exact, it served to maintain a sort of correlation between the denomination of the months and the seasons. Since the suppression of the *Nasî*, on account of the orgies and various heathen rites observed in the intercalary years, the names of the months have no relation to the seasons.

CHAPTER III

THE PROPHET AT MEDINA

پیش از همه شاهان غیور آمدهٔ
هرچند که آخر بظهور آمدهٔ
اے ختم رسل قرب تو معلومم شد
دیر آمدهٔ ز راه دور آمدهٔ

FEW Musulmans of the present day understand the full import of the mystical verses quoted at the head of this chapter, but all appreciate the deep devotion to the grand Seer implied in those words. And this devotion is not one which has twined itself round a mythical ideal, or has grown with the lapse of time. From the moment of his advent into Yathrib he stands in the full blaze of day—the grandest of figures upon whom the light of history has ever shone. The minutest details of his life are carefully noted and handed down to posterity, to become crystallised, often against the spirit of his own Teachings, which aimed at the perpetual growth of the human race. We have seen this wonderful man as an orphan child who had never known a father's love, bereft in infancy of a mother's care, his early life so full of pathos, growing up from a thoughtful childhood to a still more thoughtful youth. His youth as pure and true as his boyhood ; his manhood as austere and devout as his youth. His ear ever open to the sorrows and sufferings of the weak and the poor ; his heart ever full of sympathy and tenderness towards all God's creatures. He walks so humbly and so purely, that men turn round and point, there goes al-Amîn, the true, the upright, the trusty. A faithful friend, a devoted husband ; a thinker intent on the mysteries of life and death, on the responsibilities of human actions, the end and aim of human existence,—he sets himself to the task of reclaiming and reforming a nation, nay, a world, with only one loving heart to comfort and solace him. Baffled, he never falters ; beaten, he never despairs. He struggles on with indomitable spirit to achieve the work assigned to him. His purity and nobleness of character, his intense and earnest belief in God's mercy, bring round him ultimately many a devoted heart ; and when the moment of the severest trial comes, like the faithful mariner, he remains steadfast at his post until all his followers are safe, and then betakes himself to the hospitable shore : such we have seen him. We shall see him now the king of men, the ruler of human hearts, chief, lawyer, and supreme magistrate, and yet without any self-exaltation, lowly and humble. His history henceforth is merged in the history of the commonwealth of which he was the centre. Henceforth the Preacher who with his own hands mended his clothes, and often went without bread, was mightier than the mightiest sovereigns of the earth.

" Mohammed had shown men what he was ; the nobility of his character, his strong friendship, his endurance and courage, above all, his earnestness and fiery enthusiasm for the truth he came to preach—these things had revealed the hero ; the master whom it was alike impossible to disobey and impossible not to love. Henceforward it is only a question of time. As the men of Medîna come to know Mohammed, they too will devote themselves to him body and soul ; and the enthusiasm will catch fire and spread among the tribes, till all Arabia is at the feet of the Prophet of the one God. ' No emperor with his tiaras was obeyed as this man in a cloak of his own clouting.' He had the gift of influencing men, and he had the nobility only to influence them for good."

Medîna, the " illuminated " [1]—the city of many names—is situated about eleven days' journey to the north of Mecca. Now a walled city of considerable strength, in those days it was completely open and exposed to outside attacks until the

[1] *Munawwarêh.*

Prophet made the famous moat as a defence against the Koreishites. The city is said to have been established by an 'Amalekite chief, whose name it bore until the advent of the Prophet. In early times Yathrib [1] and its environs were inhabited by the 'Amalekites ; these are said to have been overwhelmed and destroyed by successive colonies of Jews, who, flying before Babylonian and Greek and Roman persecutors or avengers, entered Arabia and established themselves in the northern part of Hijâz. The most important of these colonies were the Banî-Nazîr at Khaibar, the Banî-Kuraizha at Fidak, the Banî-Kainukâ'a near Medîna itself. Living in fortified cantons, they had domineered over the neighbouring Arab tribes, until the establishment of two Kahtanite tribes, Aus and Khazraj at Yathrib. These two tribes, who yielded at first some sort of obedience to the Jews, were able to reduce them to a state of clientage. Before long, however, they commenced quarrelling among themselves, and it was only about the time when the Prophet announced his Mission at Mecca that, after long years of decimating warfare, they had succeeded in patching up a peace.

Such was the political condition of Yathrib when the Prophet made his appearance among the Yathribites. With his advent a new era dawned upon the city.

The two tribes of Aus and Khazraj, forgetting their inveterate and mortal feuds in the brotherhood of the Faith, rallied round the standard of Islâm and formed the nucleus of the Moslem commonwealth. The old divisions were effaced, and the honorable designation of *Ansâr* (Helpers) became the common title of all who had helped Islâm in its hour of trial. The faithful band who had forsaken their beloved birthplace, and every tie of home, received the name of *Muhâjirîn* (Emigrants or Exiles).

In order to unite the *Ansâr* and the *Muhâjirîn* in closer bonds, the Prophet established a brotherhood between them, which linked them together in sorrow and in happiness.

Yathrib changed its ancient name, and was henceforth styled *Medînat un-Nabî*, the City of the Prophet, or shortly, Medîna, the city *par excellence*.

---

[1] With a ث (pronounced by the Arabs like *th* in *thin*, by all non-Arabs like *s*).

A mosque was soon built, in the erection of which Mohammed assisted with his own hands ; and houses for the accommodation of the exiles rose apace. Two brothers, who owned the land on which it was proposed to build the mosque, had offered it as a free gift ; but as they were orphans, the Prophet paid them its value.

The building was simple in form and structure, suited to the unostentatious religion he taught. The walls were of brick and earth, and the roof of palm leaves. A portion of the mosque was set apart as a habitation for those who had no home of their own.

Everything in this humble place of worship was conducted with the greatest simplicity. Mohammed preached and prayed standing on the bare ground or leaning against a palm tree, and the devoted hearts around him beat in unison with his soul-stirring words.

" He who is not affectionate to God's creatures and to his own children," he would say, " God will not be affectionate to him. Every Moslem who clothes the naked will be clothed by God in the green robes of Paradise." [1]

In one of his sermons he thus dwelt on the subject of charity : " When God created the earth, it shook and trembled, until He put mountains upon it to make it firm. Then the angels asked, ' O God, is there anything in Thy creation stronger than these mountains ? ' And God replied, ' Iron is stronger than the mountains, for it breaks them.' ' And is there anything in Thy creation stronger than iron ? ' ' Yes ; fire is stronger than iron, for it melts it.' ' Is there anything in Thy creation stronger than fire ? ' ' Yes, water, for it quenches fire.' ' O Lord, is there anything in Thy creation stronger than water ? ' ' Yes ; wind, for it overcomes water and puts it in motion.' ' Oh, our Sustainer, is there anything in Thy creation stronger than wind ? ' ' Yes ; a good man giving alms ; if he give with his right hand and conceal it from his left, he overcomes all things.' "

His definition of charity embraced the wide circle of kindness : " Every good act," he would say, " is charity. Your smiling in your brother's face is charity ; an exhortation addressed to

[1] From Abû Huraira, *Mishkât*, book xii. chap. iii. part i.

THE PROPHET AT MEDINA

your fellow-men to do virtuous deeds is equal to alms-giving.
Putting a wanderer in the right path is charity; assisting the
blind is charity; removing stones and thorns and other
obstructions from the road is charity; giving water to the
thirsty is charity." [1] " A man's true wealth hereafter is the
good he does in this world to his fellow-men. When he dies,
people will ask, What property has he left behind him ? But
the angels, who examine him in the grave,[2] will ask, What good
deeds hast thou sent before thee ? "

" Oh Prophet ! " said one of his disciples, " my mother,
Umm Sa'd, is dead ; what is the best alms I can give away
for the good of her soul ? " " Water ! " replied Mohammed,
bethinking himself of the panting heat of the desert. " Dig
a well for her, and give water to the thirsty." The man
dug a well in his mother's name, and said, " This is for my
mother, that its blessings may reach her soul."

" Charity of the tongue," says Irving, " that most important
and least cultivated of charities, was likewise earnestly inculcated by Mahomet." Abû Jariya, an inhabitant of Basra,
coming to Medîna, and being convinced of the apostolic office
of Mohammed, begged of him some great rule of conduct.
" Speak evil of no one," answered the Prophet. " From that
time," says Abû Jariya, " I never abused any one, whether
freeman or slave."

The teachings of Islâm extended to the courtesies of life.
Make a salutation to the dwellers of a house on entering and
leaving it.[3] Return the salute of friends and acquaintances,
and wayfarers on the road. He who rides must be the first to
make the salute to him who walks ; he who walks to him
who is sitting ; a small party to a large party, and the young
to the old." [4]

---

[1] From Abû Sa'îd Khazrî.   [2] See *post*, pt. ii. chap. x.

[3] Compare Koran, chap. xxiv. vers. 27, 28, 61 and 62.

[4] From Abû Hurairah, *Mishkât*, Bk. xxii. chap. i. part 1. Besides the
references already given, consult the *Kitâb ul-Mustatraf*, chaps. iv. v. x. xiii.
xix. xxii. xxiii. and xxv. The *Mustatraf* gives fully the references to Tirmizi,
Muslim, and Bukhârî. Consult also the *Majâlis ul-Abrâr*, *Majlis* (seance), 84.

CHAPTER IV

THE HOSTILITY OF THE KOREISH AND THE JEWS

1 A.H. = 19th April 622-7th May 623 A.C.

بلغ الله صلاتي و سلامي ابدًا
لنبي عربي, مدني, حرمي

شمس فضل و ضياء و سناء اسفلى
نور بدر و بهاء و سماء الكرم

اكرم الخلق ركوعًا و سجودًا و هجودًا
احسن الناس سخاءً بعطاء النعَم

A T this time there were three distinct parties in Medîna. The Muhâjirîn (the Exiles) and the Ansâr (the Helpers) formed the kernel of Islâm. Their devotion to the Prophet was unbounded. The Exiles had forsaken their homes, and abandoned, contrary to all Arab traditions, the ties of kith and kin, in the cause of the Faith. They had braved all sufferings, withstood all temptations in the service of the Lord. Many of them had come to the City of Safety without means. They had been received with open arms by the Medinite converts, who in many cases shared their worldly goods with the poorer of the new-comers. The brotherhood of Faith, so wisely established by the Prophet, whilst it prevented the growth of jealousy, gave rise to a.

1 A.H. = 19th April 622 to 7th May 623 A.C.

generous emulation, both among the Ansâr and the Muhâjirîn, as to who would bring the greatest sacrifice in the service of God and His Prophet. The enthusiasm and earnestness with which these men and women devoted themselves to the new awakening, the zeal with which they laid down their lives, was a manifestation such as had not been seen since the best days of the Christian phase of religious development. The second, and at first by no means an unimportant party, was composed principally of lukewarm converts to the Faith, who retained an ill-concealed predilection for idolatry ; and was headed by Abdullah ibn-Ubayy, a chief of some position in the city, who aspired to the kinghood of Medîna. With this object he had gathered round him, like Abû Sufiân at Mecca, a strong body of partizans. Everything was ripe for him to seize the reins of power, when the arrival of the Prophet upset his designs. The popular enthusiasm compelled him and his followers to make a nominal profession of Islâm ; but, ever ready as they were to turn against the Moslems at the least opportunity, they were a source of considerable danger to the new-born commonwealth, and required unceasing watchfulness on the part of the Prophet. Towards them he always showed the greatest patience and forbearance, hoping in the end to win them over to the Faith. And this expectation was fully justified by the result. With the death of Abdullah ibn-Ubayy his party, which has been stigmatised [1] as the party of the *Munâfikîn* (the Disaffected), disappeared for a time from view.

But the Jews, who may be said to have formed the third party, constituted the most serious element of danger. They had close business relations with the Koreish, and their ramifications extended into various parts hostile to the Faith. At first they were inclined to look with some favour on the preachings of Mohammed. He could not, of course, be their promised Messiah, but perhaps a weak dreamer, a humble preacher, dependent upon the hospitality of their old enemies,

---

[1] Koran, sura xlii. ; Ibn-Hishâm, pp. 363, 411. The *Munâfikîn* or the *Irreconcilables* have never disappeared completely from the Islâmic body politic. Ever and anon they have exercised the most disastrous effects in Islâm. In later times they posed as the champions of orthodoxy ; note for example, the *Khârijis* of Africa.

now their patrons, the Aus and the Khazraj, might become their avenger, help them in conquering the Arabs, and found for them a new kingdom of Judah. With this aim in view, they had joined with the Medinites in a half-hearted welcome to the Prophet. And for a time they maintained a pacific attitude. But it was only for a time ; for barely a month had gone by before the old spirit of rebellion, which had led them to crucify their prophets, found vent in open seditions and secret treachery. One of the first acts of Mohammed after his arrival in Medîna was to weld together the heterogeneous and conflicting elements of which the city and its suburbs were composed, into an orderly confederation. With this object he had granted a charter to the people, by which the rights and obligations of the Moslems *inter se*, and of the Moslems and Jews, were clearly defined. And the Jews, borne down for the moment by the irresistible character of the movement, had gladly accepted the Pact. This document, which has been carefully preserved in the pages of Ibn-Hishâm, reveals the Man in his real greatness—a master-mind, not only of his own age, as Muir calls him, but of all ages. No wild dreamer he, bent upon pulling down the existing fabrics of society, but a statesman of unrivalled powers, who in an age of utter and hopeless disintegration, with such materials and such polity as God put ready to his hands, set himself to the task of reconstructing a State, a commonwealth, a society, upon the basis of universal humanity. " In the name of the most merciful and compassionate God," says this first charter of freedom of conscience, " given by Mohammed, the Prophet, to the Believers, whether of the Koreish or of Yathrib, and all individuals of whatever origin who have made common cause with them, all these shall constitute one nation." Then, after regulating the payment of the *Diyat*[1] by the various clans, and fixing some wise rules regarding the private duties of Moslems as between themselves, the document proceeds thus : " The state of peace and war shall be common to all Moslems ; no one among them shall have the right of concluding peace with, or declaring war against, the enemies of his co-religionists.

[1] Diyat, *Wehrgeld*, price which a homicide had to pay to the family of the victim, if they consented to it.

The Jews who attach themselves to our commonwealth shall be protected from all insults and vexations ; they shall have an equal right with our own people to our assistance and good offices : the Jews of the various branches of 'Auf, Najjâr, Hârith, Jashm, Th'alaba, Aus, and all others domiciled in Yathrib, shall form with the Moslems one composite nation ; they shall practise their religion as freely as the Moslems ; the *clients* [1] and allies of the Jews shall enjoy the same security and freedom ; *the guilty shall be pursued and punished* ; the Jews shall join the Moslems in defending Yathrib (Medîna) against all enemies ; the interior of Yathrib shall be a sacred place for all who accept this Charter ; the *clients* and allies of the Moslems and the Jews shall be as respected as the *patrons* ; all true Moslems shall hold in abhorrence every man guilty of crime, injustice, or disorder : no one shall uphold the culpable, though he were his nearest kin." Then, after some other provisions regarding the internal management of the State, this extraordinary document concluded thus : " All future disputes between those who accept this Charter shall be referred, under God, to the Prophet." [2]

A death-blow was thus given to that anarchic custom of the Arabs, which had hitherto obliged the aggrieved and the injured to rely upon his own or his kinsmen's power in order to exact vengeance, or satisfy the requirements of justice. It constituted Mohammed the chief magistrate of the nation, as much by his prophetic function as by a virtual compact between himself and the people.

The Jewish tribes of the Banî-un-Nazîr, [3] Banî-Kuraizha, and Banî-Kainukâ'a settled in the vicinity of Medîna, were not at first included in this Charter ; but after a short time they, too, gratefully accepted its terms.

2 A.H. 7th May 623 to 26th April 624 A.C.

No kindness or generosity, however, on the part of the Prophet would satisfy the Jews ; nothing could conciliate the bitter feelings with which they were animated. Enraged that they could not use him as their instrument for the conversion

[1] *I.e.* the protected.

[2] Ibn-Hishâm, pp. 341-343. This is a paraphrase of an important historical document.

[3] With a *zâd*.

of Arabia to Judaism, and that his belief was so much simpler
than their Talmudic legends, they soon broke off, and ranged
themselves on the side of the enemies of the new Faith. And
when asked which they preferred, idolatry or Islâm, they,
like many Christian controversialists, declared they preferred
idolatry, with all its attendant evils, to the creed of Mohammed.
They reviled him ; they " twisted their tongues " and mis-
pronounced the Koranic words and the daily prayers and
formulæ of Islâm, rendering them meaningless, absurd, or
blasphemous ; and the Jewish poets and poetesses, of whom
there existed many at the time, outraged all common decency
and the recognised code of Arab honour and chivalry by
lampooning in obscene verse the Moslem women. But these
were minor offences. Not satisfied with insulting the women
of the Believers and reviling the Prophet, they sent out
emissaries to the enemies of the State, the protection of which
they had formally accepted. The Koreish, who had sworn
Mohammed's death, were well acquainted, thanks to the
party of Abdullah-ibn-Ubayy and the faithless Israelites, with
the exact strength of the Moslems. They also knew that the
Jews had accepted Mohammed's alliance only from motives
of temporary expediency, and that the moment they showed
themselves in the vicinity of Medîna the worshippers of
Jehovah would break away from him and join the idolaters.

And now came the moment of severest trial to Islâm.
Barely had the Prophet time to put the city in a state of
defence and organise the Believers, before the blow descended
upon him.[1] Medîna itself was honeycombed by sedition
and treachery. And it became the duty of Mohammed to
take serious measures to guard against that dreaded catastrophe
which a rising within, or a sudden attack from without, would
have entailed upon his followers. He was not simply a preacher
of Islâm ; he was also the guardian of the lives and liberties
of his people. As a Prophet, he could afford to ignore the
revilings and the gibes of his enemies ; but as the head of the
State, " the general in a time of almost continual warfare,"
when Medîna was kept in a state of military defence and under

---

[1] Koran, sura ix. ver. 13 ; Zamakhshari (the *Kashshâf*), Egypt. ed., pp.
314, 315 ; al-Halabi, *Insân-ul-'Uyûn*, vol. ii.

a sort of military discipline, he could not overlook treachery. He was bound by his duty to his subjects to suppress a party that might have led, and almost did lead to the sack of the city by investing armies.   The safety of the State required the proscription of the traitors, who were either sowing the seeds of sedition within Medîna or carrying information to the common enemy.   Some half a dozen were placed under the ban, outlawed, and executed.   We are, however, anticipating the course of events in referring to these executions.

The Koreish army was afield before Mohammed received God's command to do battle to His enemies.

He who never in his life had wielded a weapon, to whom the sight of human suffering caused intense pain and pity, and who, against all the canons of Arab manliness, wept bitterly at the loss of his children or disciples, whose character ever remained so tender and so pathetic as to cause his enemies to call him womanish,[1]—this man was now compelled, from the necessities of the situation, and against his own inclination, to repel the attacks of the enemy by force of arms, to organise his followers for purposes of self-defence, and often to send out expeditions to anticipate treacherous and sudden onslaughts.   Hitherto, Arab warfare consisted of sudden and murderous forays, often made in the night or in the early morn ; isolated combats or a general melée, when the attacked were aware of the designs of the attacking party.   Mohammed, with a thorough knowledge of the habits of his people, had frequently to guard against these sudden onslaughts by sending forth reconnoitring parties.

The Meccans and their allies commenced raiding up to the very vicinity of Medîna, destroying the fruit-trees of the Moslems, and carrying away their flocks.   A force, consisting of a thousand well-equipped men, marched under the noted Abû Jahl, "the Father of Ignorance," towards Medîna to destroy the Moslems, and to protect one of their caravans bringing munitions of war.   The Moslems received timely notice of the movement, and a body of three hundred disciples proceeded at once to forestall the heathens by occupying the valley of Badr, upon which Abû Jahl was moving.   When

[1] Compare Dozy, *Histoire des Musulmans d'Espagne*, vol. i. p. 32.

Mohammed saw the infidel army arrogantly advancing into the valley, raising his hands towards heaven, like the prophets of Israel, he prayed that the little band of the Faithful might not be destroyed : " O Lord, forget not Thy promise of assistance. O Lord, if this little band were to perish, there will be none to offer unto Thee pure worship." [1]

Three of the Koreish advanced into the open space which divided the Moslems from the idolaters, and, according to Arab usage, challenged three champions from the Moslem ranks to single combat. Hamza, Ali, and Obaidah accepted the challenge, and came out conquerors. The engagement then became general. At one time the fortunes of the field wavered, but Mohammed's appeal to his people decided the fate of the battle. " It was a stormy winter day. A piercing blast swept across the valley." It seemed as if the angels of heaven were warring for the Moslems. Indeed, to the earnest minds of Mohammed and his followers, who, like the early Christians, saw God's providence " in all the gifts of nature, in every relation of life, at each turn of their affairs, individual or public,"—to them those blasts of wind and sand, the elements warring against the enemies of God, at that critical moment appeared veritable succour sent from heaven ; as angels riding on the wings of the wind, and driving the faithless idolaters before them in confusion.[2] The Meccans were driven back with great loss ; many of their chiefs were slain ; and Abû Jahl fell a victim to his unruly pride.[3]

A large number remained prisoners in the hands of the Moslems, but only two of them were executed. They had been noted for their virulent animosity towards the followers of the new Faith, and by the laws of war among the Arabs they now paid the penalty of their conduct.[4]

[1] Ibn-Hishâm, p. 444 ; Ibn ul-Athîr, vol. ii. p. 97.

[2] Koran, Sura viii. ver. 9, and Sura iii. vers. 11, 121-128.   Comp. also Muir, vol. iii. p. 106.

[3] Ibn-Hishâm, p. 443 et seq. ; Ibn ul-Athîr, vol. ii. p. 26 et seq.   Sir W. Muir mentions that when the head of Abû Jahl was brought to Mohammed, he said, " It is more acceptable to me than the choicest camel in Arabia." This passage, which is not to be found either in Ibn-Hishâm, Ibn ul-Athîr, Abulfedâ or Tabari, is apocryphal.

[4] Nazr, son of Hârith, referred to in ver. 32 of Sura viii. of the Koran, was one of these men.

The rest of the prisoners, contrary to all the usages and traditions of the Arabs, were treated with the greatest humanity. The Prophet gave strict orders that respect should be paid to their misfortunes, and that they should be treated with kindness. The Moslems, to whose care he confided them, faithfully obeyed his instructions. They shared their own food with the prisoners, giving them the bread which forms the best part of their repast, and contenting themselves with dates alone.[1]

The division of the spoil gave rise to sharp dissensions among the Moslem soldiery. For the present, Mohammed calmed their disputes by dividing it equally amongst all.[2] But as such dissensions among an unruly people were likely to lead to mischief, the Prophet, with a view to prevent all future quarrels over spoil acquired in war, promulgated a special ordinance, which is incorporated in the chapter of the Koran entitled al-Anfál (the Spoils). By this law the division of the spoils was left to the discretion of the chief of the commonwealth ; a fifth being reserved for the public treasury for the support of the poor and indigent.[3]

The remarkable circumstances which led to the victory of Badr, and the results which followed from it, made a deep impression on the minds of the Moslems. They firmly believed that the angels of heaven had battled on their side against the unbelieving host.

[1] Ibn-Hishâm, pp. 459, 460 ; Caussin de Perceval, vol. iii. p. 79. Muir speaks thus : " In pursuance of Mahomet's commands, the citizens of Medína, and such of the refugees as possessed houses, received the prisoners, and treated them with much consideration. ' Blessings be on the men of Medína ! ' said one of these prisoners in later days ; ' they made us ride, while they themselves walked ; they gave us wheaten bread to eat when there was little of it ; contenting themselves with dates,' " vol. iii. p. 122.

[2] " It is remarkable," says Sale, " that the dispute among Mohammed's men about sharing the booty at Badr arose on the same occasion as did that among David's soldiers in relation to the spoils taken from the Amalekites ; those who had been in the action insisting that they who tarried by the stuff should have no part of the spoil ; and that the same decision was given in both cases, which became a law for the future, to wit, that they should part alike." Prel. Disc. sec. vi.

[3] Koran, chap. viii. ver. 41. Though the distribution was left to the discretion of the chief of the State, certain customs were invariably observed which under the Caliphs became precedents, and thus gave a more definite shape to the law. Compare M. Querry's splendid work, entitled Droit Mussulman (Paris 1871), tome i. p. 335.

The few simple touches in the Koran which bring into vivid prominence the poetic element involved in the conception of the angels fighting the battle of the Lord, will not yield in beauty or sublimity to the most eloquent words of the Psalmist. Indeed, the same poetic character is perceptible in both.[1]

Probably Mohammed, like Jesus and other teachers, believed in the existence of intermediate beings, celestial messengers from God to man. The modern disbelief in angels furnishes no reason for ridiculing the notions of our forefathers. Our disbelief is as much open to the name of superstition as their belief ; only one is negative, the other positive. What we, in modern times, look upon as the principles of nature, they looked upon as angels, ministrants of heaven. Whether there exist intermediate beings, as Locke thinks, between God and man, just as there are intermediate beings between man and the lowest form of animal creation, is a question too deep to be fathomed by the reason of man.

Mohammed also, like Jesus, probably believed in the existence of the Principle of Evil as a personal entity. But an analysis of his words reveals a more rationalistic element, a subjective conception clothed in language suited for the apprehension of his followers. When somebody asked him where Satan lived, he replied " In the heart of man," whilst Christian tradition converts the Pharisee who tempted Jesus, into the veritable Prince of Hell.[2]

The belief in angels and devils has given rise to an extraordinary number of legends both in Islâm and in Christianity. The saints of heaven and angels fight for the Christian. The Moslem only accepts the assistance of angels in the battles of life.

---

[1] Ps. xviii.

[2] All the Schleiermacher school believe the tempter to have been the head priest. Milman mentions this view as well as the patristic and orthodox one, but dexterously leaves for the reader to choose which he likes. The chapter of Reuss on Angels (*History of Christian Theology in the Apostolic Age*, English translation, note 1, pp. 401-404), with the mass of references arrayed therein, distinctly proves that the early Christians, the immediate disciples of Jesus, firmly believed the angels and devils to be personal entities, beings slightly ethereal, but in every way human-like ; and this belief those disciples of Jesus must have received from the Master himself, who, indeed, as Renan says, could not have been, in these respects, intellectually different from the people of his age ; *Vie de Jesus*, 3rd ed. 1867, p. 267.

NOTE TO CHAPTER IV

THE story of Mohammed's inhuman reply to the appeal of 'Okba, son of Abû Mu'ait, when he was being led forward to execution, is utterly false ; it is said that on 'Okba's asking, " Who will take care of my little children ? " Mohammed answered, " Hell fire." This story is so preposterous in itself, so opposed to Mohammed's true character (one of whose noblest traits was his love for children, and who always inculcated love and protection of orphans as an absolute duty, and an act most acceptable to God), that it is hardly necessary to search for its true origin. Christian writers, however, seem to gloat over it, and hence it becomes needful to examine how the story arose.

It originated most probably from the sobriquet of *Sibyat un-Nâr* (children of fire), applied to the children of 'Okba. 'Okba himself belonged to the tribe of 'Ajlan,[1] a branch of which inhabited certain valleys near Safra, and were known by the name of Banî un-Nâr (children or descendants of fire). The sobriquet was probably derived from this circumstance ; and the story of Mohammed's reply from the nickname.

Another story of Mohammed's having bitterly apostrophised the dead of the idolaters on their burial is, to say the least, distorted. Tabari thus narrates the circumstances which have given rise to this calumny : " The Prophet placed himself by the side of the large grave or pit which had been prepared for the corpses ; and as the bodies were lowered, the names were called out, and Mohammed then uttered these words, ' You, my kindred, you accused me of lying, when others believed in me ; you drove me from my home, when others received me ; what destiny has been yours ! Alas ! all that God threatened is fulfilled.' " These words, which were palpably meant to express pity, have been distorted to imply bitterness.

---

[1] Aghâni, according to C. de Perceval, vol. iii. p. 79.

CHAPTER V

THE INVASION OF MEDINA BY THE KOREISH

2 A.H. = 624 A.C.

كالزَّهرِ في تَرَفٍ وَّالبَدرِ في شَرَفٍ

وِ البَحرِ في كرمٍ وِّ الدَّهرِ في هِمَمٍ

SUCCESS is always one of the greatest criterions of truth. Even in the early days of Christianity, the good Pharisee said, " Let them alone ; if these men be false, they will come to nought, or else you yourselves shall perish."

If Constantine had not seen, or fancied he had seen, the notable cross in the heavens ; if he had not marched to success under its auspices ; if it had not led him on to victory and to the throne—we can hardly conceive what would have been the fate of Christianity. What the victory of Badr was for Islâm, the victory of the Milvian Bridge was for Christianity.[1] It thenceforth ruled from the throne of the Cæsars.

For the Moslems the victory of Badr was indeed most auspicious. It was not surprising that they, like the Israelites or Christians of yore, saw the hand of Providence in their success over the idolaters. Had the Moslems failed, we can imagine what their fate would have been—a universal massacre.

Whilst Mohammed was engaged in this expedition, he lost

---

[1] The Christians themselves look upon the defeat of Maxentius by Constantine (312 A.C.) as the greatest triumph of their faith. The chapter of Gibbon, vol. iii. chap. xx., mingled satire and history, shows how the success of Christianity dates from that event.

one of his favourite daughters, Rukaiya, married to Osmân, who had only recently returned from the Abyssinian exile. But the desire for revenge with which the idolaters were burning allowed him no time to indulge in domestic sorrow. As soon as all the Koreishite prisoners had returned home, Abû Sufiân issued forth from Mecca with two hundred horsemen, vowing solemnly never to return until he had avenged himself on Mohammed and his followers. Scouring the country to within a few miles of Medîna, he came down with a fell swoop on the unprepared Moslems, slaying the people, and ravaging date-groves which furnished the staple food of the Arabs. The Meccans had provided themselves with bags of " sawîk " [1] for the foray. As soon, however, as the Moslems sallied forth from Medîna to avenge the murders, the Meccans turned bridle and fled, dropping the bags in order to lighten their beasts : whence this affair was derisively called by the Moslems, Ghazwat us-sawîk, " the battle of the meal-bags." [2]

It was on this occasion that an incident happened to the Prophet, which has been exceedingly well told by Washington Irving. Mohammed was sleep- 5th Zi'l-Hijja ing one day alone at the foot of a tree, at a = 1st April 624. distance from his camp, when he was awakened by a noise, and beheld Durthur, a hostile warrior, standing over him with a drawn sword. " O Mohammed," cried he, " who is there now to save thee ? " " God ! " replied the Prophet. The wild Bedouin was suddenly awed, and dropped his sword, which was instantly seized upon by Mohammed. Brandishing the weapon, he exclaimed in turn, " Who is there now to save thee, O Durthur ? " " Alas, no one ! " replied the soldier. " Then learn from me to be merciful." So saying, he returned the sword. The Arab's heart was overcome ; and in after years he proved one of the staunchest adherents of the Prophet.[3]

---

[1] Sawîk is the old and modern Arabic name for a dish of green grain, toasted, pounded, mixed with dates or sugar, and eaten on journeys when it is found difficult to cook.

[2] The place where the affair took place bears now the name of Suwayka—a few hours' journey to the south-west of Medîna.

[3] The last month of this year was marked by the death of Osmân, son of Mahzûn, and the marriage of Ali, son of Abû Tâlib, to Fâtima, Mohammed's daughter.

Osmân was one of the earliest believers, and he was the first of the

But this skirmish, between the idolaters and the Moslems, like others which followed, proved only a prelude to the great drama that was about to be enacted.

The idolaters were burning for revenge.   They made formidable preparations for another war upon the
Moslems.   Their emissaries succeeded in obtaining the assistance of the tribes of Tihâma
and Kinâna, and their united forces soon
amounted to three thousand well-equipped soldiers (of whom seven hundred were mailed warriors), animated with but one desire, that of revenge.   This army was as formidable to the petty tribes of Arabia as the multitudinous hordes of Xerxes to the Grecian States.

3 A.H. = 26th April 624 to 15th April 625 A.C.

Marching under the command of the relentless Abû Sufiân, and meeting with no opposition from any side, they took up a well-chosen position to the north-east of Medîna, where only the hill of Ohod and a valley separated them from the devoted city.   From this safe vantage-ground they ravaged the fields and fruit groves of the Medinites.

Forced by the enthusiasm of his followers, and by their fury at the destruction of their property, Mohammed marched out of Medîna with a thousand men.   The ill-concealed enmity of the Jews led to the defection of Abdullah ibn-Ubayy, the leader of the Munâfikîn (the Disaffected), with three hundred of his followers.   This desertion reduced the strength of Mohammed's small force to seven hundred men, who only possessed two horses amongst them.   But still this gallant band marched steadily forward.   Advancing quietly through groves of fruit trees, they soon gained the hill of Ohod.   They passed the night in the defile, and in the morning, after offering prayers as they stood to arms, they debouched into the plain.   Mohammed now took up his position immediately under the hill.[1]   Posting

Muhâjirîn who died at Medîna, and was interred at Bâki, a suburb of Medîna, where lie buried a number of illustrious and saintly people, whose tombs are up to the present day venerated by the Moslems.

Ali had been betrothed to Fâtima several days before the expedition to Badr, but the marriage was only celebrated three months later, Ali being in his twenty-first, and Fâtima in her fifteenth year.

[1] Burton thus describes the spot : " This spot, so celebrated in the annals of El Islam, is a shelving strip of land, close to the southern base of Mount Ohod.   The army of the infidels advanced from the fiumara in crescent shape,

a few archers on a height behind the troops, he gave them strict injunctions not to abandon their place whatever happened but to harass the cavalry of the enemy and protect the flanks of the Moslems. The idolaters, confident in their numbers, marched down into the plain with their idols in the centre of their army, and the wives of the chiefs chanting their war-songs and beating their timbrels.[1] The first violent onslaught of the Koreish was bravely repulsed by the Moslems, led by Hamza, who, taking advantage of the confusion of the enemy, dashed into the midst of the Koreishites, dealing havoc on all sides. Victory had almost declared for the Moslems, when the archers, forgetting the injunctions of the Prophet, and seeing the enemy in flight, dispersed in search of plunder.[2] And what happened in later days at Tours happened at Ohod. Khâlid bin Walîd, one of the Koreish, at once perceived their error, and rallying his horse, fell on the rear of the Moslems.[3] The infantry of the Koreish also turned, and the Moslem troops, taken both in rear and front, had to renew the battle at fearful odds. Some of the bravest chiefs in the Moslem army fell fighting. The intrepid Hamza, with several others, was killed ; Ali, who had chivalrously answered the first call of defiance (Rajz) of the idolaters,[4] and Omar and Abû Bakr were severely wounded.

with Abû Sufiyan, the general, and his idols in the centre. It is distant about three miles from El Medinah in a northerly direction. All the visitor sees is hard gravelly ground, covered with little heaps of various coloured granite, red sandstone, and bits of porphyry, to denote the different places where the martyrs fell and were buried. Seen from this point, there is something appalling in the look of the holy mountain. Its seared and jagged flanks rise like masses of iron from the plain, and the crevice into which the Moslem host retired, when the disobedience of the archers in hastening to plunder enabled Khalid ben Walid to fall upon Mohammed's rear, is the only break in the grim wall. Reeking with heat, its surface produces not one green shrub or stunted tree ; not a bird or beast appeared upon its inhospitable sides, and the bright blue sky glaring above its bald and sullen brow made it look only the more repulsive."—Burton's *Pilgrimage to Mecca*, vol. ii. pp. 236, 237.

[1] Extracts from their war-songs are given by Ibn ul-Athîr, vol. ii. p. 118. " Courage ! Ye sons of Abd ud-Dâr ; courage ! defenders of women ! strike home with the edges of your swords." Another runs thus : " We are daughters of the Star of the Morn (Târik) ; we tread softly on silken cushions (*namârik*) ; face the enemy boldly, and we shall press you in our arms ; fly, and we shall shun you, shun you with disgust."

[2] This disobedience is referred to in the Koran, sura iii. ver. 146.

[3] Ibn ul-Athîr, vol. ii. 119 ; al-Halabi, *Insân ul-'Uyûn*, vol. ii. p. 239.

[4] Tabari says that Talha, the standard-bearer of the idolaters, a man of heroic bravery, placed himself before Ali, and brandishing his sabre, defied

The efforts of the idolaters were, however, principally directed towards Mohammed, who, surrounded by a few disciples and separated from the main body of his people, became now the chief object of their assaults. His friends fell fast around him. Though wounded and bleeding he did not forget their loving hearts, and blessed the hand that tried to stanch the blood which flowed from his forehead.[1] But rescue was nigh. The brave warriors who under Ali had been fighting in the centre with the energy of despair, succeeded in retreating to a point on the hill, where they were secure from the attacks of the enemy, but full of consternation at the loss, as they supposed, of their great Master. Seeing, however, their brethren still fighting in another part of the field, they rushed down into the midst of the idolaters. Penetrating to the place where the small group of Moslems yet defended the Prophet, and finding that he still lived, they succeeded, after great exertions, in retreating with him to the heights of Mount Ohod, where they breathed again. Ali fetched water in his shield from the hollow of a rock. With this he bathed Mohammed's face and wounds, and with his companions offered up the mid-day prayers sitting.

The Koreish were too exhausted to follow up their advantage, either by attacking Medîna or driving the Moslems from the heights of Ohod. They retreated from the Medinite territories after barbarously mutilating their slain enemies. The wife of Abû Sufiân, Hind, the daughter of 'Otba, with the other Koreishite women, showed the greatest ferocity in this savage work of vengeance, tearing out the heart of Hamza, and making bracelets and necklaces of the ears and noses of the dead.

The barbarities practised by the Koreish on the slain created among the Moslems a feeling of bitter exasperation. Even Mohammed was at first so moved by indignation as to

him, crying, " You Moslems say that our dead will go to hell, and yours to heaven ; let me see whether I cannot send thee to heaven." Upon this Ali replied, " Be it so ! " and they fought, and Talha was struck to the ground. " Mercy, O son of my uncle," cried he. Ali replied, " Mercy be it ; thou dost not deserve the fire."—Vol. iii. p. 25.

[1] Ibn ul-Athîr, vol. ii. p. 114, and Abulfedâ, p. 44, mention the date of the battle of Ohod as the 7th of Shawwâl ; Tabari, vol. iii. p. 21, mentions the 8th ; Ibn-Hishâm, the 5th ; and several others the 11th. C. de Perceval, however, calculates the 11th to have been the real date of the battle, as according to all the chroniclers the day was a Saturday, and the 11th of Shawwâl (26th of January) fell on a Saturday.—*Hist. des Arabes*, vol. iii. p. 96, note.

declare that the dead of the Koreish should in future be treated in like manner.[1] But the gentleness of his nature conquered the bitterness of his heart. " Bear wrong patiently," he preached ; " verily, best it will be for the patiently enduring." [2] And from that day the horrible practice of mutilation which prevailed among all the nations of antiquity was inexorably forbidden to the Moslems.[3]

On his return to Medîna the Prophet directed a small body of the disciples to pursue the retreating enemy, and to impress on them that the Moslems, though worsted in battle, were yet unbroken in spirit, and too strong to be attacked again with impunity. Abû Sufiân, hearing of the pursuit, hastened back to Mecca, having first murdered two Medinites whom he met on his route. He, however, sent a message to the Prophet, saying that he would soon return to exterminate him and his people. The reply as before was full of trust and faith—" God is enough for us, a good guardian is He ! " [4]

The moral effect of this disastrous battle was at once visible in the forays which the neighbouring nomads prepared to make on the Medinite territories. Most of them, however, were repressed by the energetic action of Mohammed, though some of the hostile tribes succeeded in enticing Moslem missionaries into their midst, under the pretence of embracing Islâm, and then massacred them. On one such occasion seventy Moslems were treacherously murdered near a brook called Bîr-Ma'ûna, within the territories of two tribes, the Banî-'Âmir and the Banî-Sulaim, chiefly through the instrumentality of the latter. One of the two survivors of the slaughter escaped towards Medîna. Meeting on the way two unarmed Arabs belonging to the Banî-'Âmir who were travelling under a safe-conduct of the Prophet, and mistaking

---

[1] Ibn-Hishâm, p. 580 *et seq.* ; Ibn ul-Athîr, vol. ii. pp. 115-126 ; Tabari, vol. iii. p. 16 *et seq.* ; al-Halabi, *Insân ul-'Uyûn*, vol. ii. p. 242.

[2] Koran, sura xvii. ver. 127 ; Ibn-Hishâm, pp. 584, 585 ; Zamakhsharî (the *Kashshâf*), Egypt. ed., p. 446.

[3] The Jews used to burn their prisoners alive, and most barbarously mutilate the slain. The Greeks, the Romans, and the Persians all practised similar barbarities. Christianity effected no improvement in these frightful customs, for as late as the sixteenth century we read of the most horrible mutilations.

[4] Ibn-Hishâm, p. 590 ; Koran, sura iii. ver. 167.

them for enemies, he killed them. When Mohammed heard of
this he was deeply grieved. A wrong had been committed by
one of his followers, though under a mistake, and the relatives
of the men that were killed were entitled to redress. Accordingly orders were issued for collecting the *diyat* (the *Wehrgeld*)
from the Moslems and the people who had accepted the Charter.[1]
The Jewish tribes of the Banî un-Nazîr, the Kuraizha, and
others were bound equally with the Moslems to contribute
towards this payment.[2] Mohammed himself, accompanied by
a few disciples, proceeded to the Banî un-Nazîr, and asked
from them their contribution. They seemingly agreed to the
demand, and requested him to wait awhile. Whilst sitting
with his back to the wall of a house, he observed sinister movements amongst the inhabitants, which led him to divine their
intention of murdering him.

But to explain the hostility of the Jews we must trace back
the course of events. We have seen with what bitter animosity
they dogged Mohammed's footsteps from the moment of his
arrival at Medîna. They tried to sow disaffection among his
people. They libelled him and his followers. They mis-
pronounced the words of the Koran so as to give them an
offensive meaning. But this was not all. By their superior
education and intelligence, by their union with the party of
the Munâfikîn (the Disaffected), and by the general unanimity
which prevailed among them (so different from the disunion
of the Arabs), the Jews formed a most dangerous element
within the federated State which had risen under the Teacher
of Islâm. Among unadvanced nations poets occupy the
position and exercise the influence of the press in modern
times.[3] The Jewish poets by their superior culture naturally

---

[1] See *ante*, pp. 58-59.

[2] Ibn ul-Athîr, vol. iii. p. 133 ; Tabari, vol. iv. p. 50. Muir and Sprenger
have strangely garbled this part of the affair. Sir W. Muir does not find
any authority for M. C. de Perceval's saying, that the Jews were bound by
treaty to contribute towards the *Diyat*. If he had referred to Tabari he would
have seen the following statement: "En suite il ordonna de réunir cette
somme, ou la répartissant sur la ville de Medine, et d'y faire contribuer égale-
ment les Juifs, tels que les Beni-Nadhîr, les Koraizha et ceux de Fadak, qu'y
étaient obligés par le traité."—Zotenberg's transl. vol. iii. p. 50. So also
Ibn ul-Athîr, vol. ii. p. 133.

[3] An example of the influence which poets and rhapsodists exercise among
unprogressed nations is afforded by one of the episodes connected with the

exercised a vast influence among the Medinites; and this influence was chiefly directed towards sowing sedition among the Moslems, and widening the breach between them and the opposing faction. The defeat of the idolaters at Badr was felt as keenly by the Jews as by the Meccans. Immediately after this battle a distinguished member of their race, called Ka'b, the son of Ashraf, belonging to the tribe of Nazîr, publicly deploring the ill-success of the idolaters, proceeded towards Mecca. Finding the people there plunged in grief, he spared no exertion to revive their courage. By his satires against the Prophet and his disciples, by his elegies on the Meccans who had fallen at Badr, he succeeded in exciting the Koreish to that frenzy of vengeance which found vent on the plains of Ohod. Having attained his object, he returned to his home near Medîna in the canton of Nazîr, where he continued to attack Mohammed and the Musulmans in ironical and obscene verses, not sparing even the women of the Believers, whom he addressed in terms of the grossest character. His acts were openly directed against the commonwealth of which he was a member. He belonged to a tribe which had entered into the Compact [1] with the Moslems, and pledged itself for the internal as well as the external safety of the State. Another Jew of the Nazîr, Abû Râf'e Sallâm, son of Abu'l Hukaik, was equally wild and bitter against the Musulmans. He inhabited, with a fraction of his tribe, the territories of Khaibar, four or five days' journey to the north-west of Medîna. Detesting Mohammed and the Musulmans, he made use of every endeavour to excite the neighbouring Arab tribes, such as the Sulaim and the Ghatafân, against them. It was impossible for the Musulman Commonwealth to tolerate this open treachery on the part of those to

war of Ohod. Whilst preparing for this eventful campaign, the Koreish requested a poet of the name of Abû 'Uzza to go round the tribes of the desert, and excite them by his songs and poetry against the Moslems, and persuade them to join the confederacy, formed under the auspices of the Meccans, for the destruction of Mohammed and his followers. This man had been taken prisoner by the Moslems in the battle of Badr, but was released by the Prophet, without ransom, on pledging himself never again to take up arms against the Medinites. In spite of this, he was tempted to break his word, and went round the tribes, rousing them to arms by his poetry; and it is said he was eminently successful in his work. After Ohod he was again taken prisoner and executed by the Moslems; Ibn-Hishâm, p. 591.

[1] See *ante*, p. 58.

whom every consideration had been shown, with the object of
securing their neutrality, if not their support. The very
existence of the Moslem community was at stake ; and every
principle of safety required that these traitorous designs
should be quietly frustrated. The sentence of outlawry was
executed upon them by the Medinites themselves—in one
case by a member of the tribe of Aus, in the other by a
Khazrajite.

Christian controversialists have stigmatised these executions
as "assassinations." And because a Moslem was sent secretly to
kill each of the criminals, in their prejudice against the Prophet,
they shut their eyes to the justice of the sentence, and the
necessity of a swift and secret execution. There existed then
no police court, no judicial tribunal, nor even a court-martial,
to take cognisance of individual crimes. In the absence of a
State executioner any individual might become the executioner
of the law. These men had broken their formal pact ; it was
impossible to arrest them in public, or execute the sentence in
the open before their clans, without causing unnecessary bloodshed, and giving rise to the feud of blood, and everlasting
vendetta. The exigencies of the State required that whatever
should be done should be done swiftly and noiselessly upon
those whom public opinion had arraigned and condemned.[1]
The existence of the republic, and the maintenance of peace
and order within the city, depended upon the prompt execution
of the sentence passed upon the culprits before they could rally
their clansmen round them.

The fate of these two traitors, and the expulsion of their
brethren the Banî-Kainuka from the Medinite
territories, had given rise to a bitter feeling of
animosity among the Nazîr against the
Prophet. The circumstances connected with the banishment
of the Kainukâ' require a brief notice. Whilst the other
Jewish tribes were chiefly agricultural, the Banû-Kainukâ'
hardly possessed a single field or date plantation. They were

2 A.H. Shaw-
wâl, February
624 A.C.

[1] Our Christian historians forget that the " wise " Solon himself, for the
safety of his small city, made it obligatory on the Athenians to become
executioners of the law, by pursuing the factious, or taking one or two sides
in a public riot. They also forget that even the laws of Christian England
allow any person to pursue and kill " an outlaw."

for the most part artisans employed in handicraft of all kinds.[1]
Seditious and unruly, always ready for a broil like their co-
religionists of Alexandria, the Banû-Kainukâ' were also noted
for the extreme laxity of their morals. One day a young girl
from the country came to their bazaar or market (Sûk) to sell
milk. The Jewish youths insulted her grossly. A Moslem
passer-by took the part of the girl, and in the fray which ensued
the author of the outrage was killed ; whereupon the entire
body of the Jews present rose and slaughtered the Moslem. A
wild scene then followed. The Moslems, enraged at the murder
of their compatriot, flew to arms, blood flowed fast, and many
were killed on both sides. At the first news of the riots,
Mohammed hastened to the spot, and, by his presence, succeeded in restraining the fury of his followers. He at once
perceived what the end would be of these seditions and disorders
if allowed to take their course. Medîna would be turned into
an amphitheatre, in which members of hostile factions might
murder one another with impunity. The Jews had openly and
knowingly infringed the terms of their compact. It was
necessary to put a stop to this with a firm hand, or farewell to
all hope of peace and security. Consequently Mohammed
proceeded at once to the quarter of the Banî-Kainukâ', and
required them to enter definitely into the Moslem Commonwealth by embracing Islâm, or to vacate Medîna. The reply
of the Jews was couched in the most offensive terms. " O,
Mohammed, do not be elated with the victory over thy
people (the Koreish). Thou hast had an affair with men
ignorant of the art of war. If thou art desirous of
having any dealings with us, we shall show thee that
we are men." [2] They then shut themselves up in their fortress,
and set Mohammed's authority at defiance. But their reduction was an absolute duty, and siege was accordingly laid to
their stronghold without loss of time. After fifteen days they
surrendered. At first it was intended to inflict some severe
punishment on them, but the clemency of Mohammed's nature

[1] Tabari, vol. iii. p. 8.
[2] Ibn-Ḥishâm, p. 545. Tabari gives the speech of the Kainukâ' with a
slight variation. But all historians agree in its being defiant and offensive.
I cannot understand whence Gibbon obtained the excessively meek reply he
puts into the mouth of these people.

overcame the dictates of justice, and the Banî-Kainukâ' were simply banished.

All these circumstances were rankling within the breasts of the Banî un-Nazîr. They only waited for a favourable opportunity to rid themselves of Mohammed, and therefore looked upon his arrival amongst them as providential. But their sinister designs, as we have before said, did not escape the eye of the Prophet. He immediately left the place without raising the suspicions of the Jews, and thus saved himself and his disciples from almost certain destruction.[1]

The Banî un-Nazîr had now placed themselves in exactly the same position as the Banî-Kainukâ' had previously done. They had by their own act put themselves outside the pale of the Charter ; and therefore on his arrival at Medîna, Mohammed sent them a message of the same import as that which was sent to the Kainukâ'. Relying on the support of the Munâfikîn and Abdullah ibn-Ubayy, the Banî un-Nazîr returned a defiant answer. Disappointed, however, in the promised assistance of Abdullah, and of their brethren, the Banî-Kuraizha, after a siege of fifteen days [2] they sued for terms. The previous offer was renewed, and they agreed to evacuate their territories. They were allowed to take all their movables with them, with the exception of arms.[3] In order to prevent the Moslems from occupying their dwellings, they destroyed these before leaving.[4]

Their lands, warlike materials, etc., which they could not carry away, were distributed by the Prophet with the consent and cordial approval of the Ansâr, among the Muhâjirîn, who, up to this time had been entirely dependent for support on the generosity of the Medinites. Notwithstanding the strong brotherly love which existed between the " Refugees " and the " Helpers," [5] Mohammed knew that the assistance of the Medinites afforded

Rabi I. 4 A.H.
= June to July
625 A.C.

---

[1] As any betrayal of suspicion by Mohammed or his disciples of the intents of the Jews would have made these people desperate, and precipitated matters, the Prophet went away by himself, leaving his followers behind, which led the Jews to suppose he was not gone far, and would quickly return.

[2] Tabari says eleven days (vol. iii p. 54).

[3] Ibn-Hishâm, pp. 652, 653 ; Ibn ul-Athîr, vol. ii. p. 133 ; Abulfedâ, p. 49.

[4] Koran, sura lix. ver. 5.   [5] See ante, p. 53.

but a precarious means of subsistence. He accordingly assembled the principal men from among the Ansâr, and asked them whether they had any objection to his distributing among their poor brethren who had followed him from Mecca the goods left behind by the Jews. With one voice they answered, " Give to our brothers the goods of the Jews ; assign to them even a portion of ours : we willingly consent." Upon this the Prophet divided the property among the Muhâjirîn and two of the Ansâr who were extremely poor.[1]

The expulsion of the Banî un-Nazîr took place in the month of Rabi I. of the fourth year.[2] The remaining portion of this year and the early part of the next were passed in repressing the spasmodic hostile attempts of the nomadic tribes against the Moslems, and in inflicting punishments for various murderous forays on the Medinite territories.[3]

Meanwhile the enemies of the Faith were by no means idle. Far and wide the idolaters had sent their emissaries to stir up the tribes against the Moslems. The Jews were the most active in these efforts. Some of the Banî-Nazîr had remained behind with their brethren settled near Khaibar, and there, fired with the hope of vengeance, had set themselves to the work of forming another league for the destruction of the Believers.[4] Their efforts were successful beyond their utmost hopes. A formidable coalition was soon formed ; and an army, consisting of ten thousand well-appointed men, marched upon

5 A.H. =3rd
May 626 to 23rd
April 627 A.C.

---

[1] Ibn-Hishâm, p. 654 ; Ibn ul-Athîr, vol. ii. p. 133 ; Tabari, vol. iii. p. 54. A principle was henceforth established that any acquisition, not made in actual warfare, should belong to the State, or the chief of the State ; and that its application should depend upon his discretion (vide *Droit Musulman* by M. Querry, p. 337). Sura lix. of the Koran treats almost entirely of the circumstances connected with the banishment of the Banî un-Nazîr.

[2] According to Ibn-Hishâm, p. 653, and Abulfedâ, p. 49 ; Tabari, vol. iii. p. 55, says it was the month of Safar.

[3] Of this nature was the expedition against the Christian Arabs of Dûmat ul-Jandal (a place according to Abulfedâ, about seven days' journey to the south of Damascus), who had stopped the Medinite traffic with Syria and even threatened a raid upon Medîna ; these marauders, however, fled on the approach of the Moslems, and Mohammed returned to Medîna, after concluding a treaty with a neighbouring chief, to whom he granted permission of pasturage on the Medinite territories.—C. de Perceval, vol. iii. p. 129 ; Tabari, vol. iii. p. 60.

[4] Ibn-Ishâm, p. 963 ; Ibn ul-Athîr, vol. ii. p. 639 ; Tabari, vol. iii. pp. 60, 61.

Medîna, under the command of the relentless Abû Sufiân. Meeting no opposition on their way, they soon encamped within a few miles of Medîna, on its most vulnerable side, towards Ohod. To oppose this host the Moslems could only muster a body of three thousand men.[1] Forced thus by their inferiority in numbers, as well as by the factious opposition of the *Munâfikîn* within the city,[2] to remain on the defensive, they dug a deep trench round the unprotected quarters of Medîna, and, leaving their women and children for safety in their fortified houses, they encamped outside the city, with the moat in front of them. In the meantime they relied for the safety of the other side, if not upon the active assistance, at least upon the neutrality of the Banî-Kuraizha, who possessed several fortresses at a short distance, towards the south-east, and were bound by the Compact to assist the Moslems against every assailant. These Jews, however, were persuaded by the idolaters to violate their pledged faith, and to join the Koreish. As soon as the news of their defection reached Mohammed, he deputed " the two Saʿds," Saʿd ibn-Muʿâz and Saʿd ibn-ʿUbâda, to entreat them to return to their duty. The reply was defiant and sullen : " Who is Mohammed, and who is the Apostle of God that we should obey him ? There is no bond or compact betwixt us and him." [3]

As these Jews were well acquainted with the locality, and could materially assist the besiegers by showing them the weak points of the city, the consternation among the Moslems became great, whilst the disaffected body within the walls increased the elements of danger.[4]

The idolaters and the Jews, failing in all their attempts to

Shawwâl, 5 A.H. =2 February 627.

---

[1] Ibn-Hishâm, p. 678.

[2] Referred to in the Koran, sura xxxiii. vers. 12, 13, 14, etc.

[3] Ibn-Hishâm, p. 675 ; Muir, vol. iii. p. 259.

[4] The whole scene is so beautifully painted in the Koran, sura xxxiii. (Surat ul-Ahzâb, " The Confederates "), that I cannot resist quoting a few verses here : " When they assailed you from above you and from below you, and when your eyes became distracted, and your hearts came up into your throats, and ye thought divers thoughts of God, then were the Faithful tried, and with strong quaking did they quake ; and when the disaffected and diseased of heart (with infidelity) said, ' God and His Apostle have made us but a cheating promise.' "

draw the Moslems into the open field, or to surprise the city under the direction of Jewish guides, determined upon a regular assault. The siege had already lasted twenty days. The restless tribes of the desert, who had made common cause with the Koreish and their Jewish allies, and who had expected an easy prey, were becoming weary of this protracted campaign. Great efforts were made at this critical moment by the leaders of the beleaguering host to cross the trench and fall upon the small Moslem force. Every attempt was, however, repulsed by untiring vigilance on the part of the Prophet. The elements now seemed to combine against the besieging army; their horses were perishing fast, and provisions were becoming scanty. Disunion was rife in their midst, and the far-seeing chief of the Moslems, with matchless prudence, fomented it into actual division. Suddenly this vast coalition, which had seemed to menace the Moslems with inevitable destruction, vanished into thin air. In the darkness of night, amidst a storm of wind and rain, their tents overthrown, their lights put out, Abû Sufiân and the majority of his formidable army fled, the rest took refuge with the Banî-Kuraizha.[1] Mohammed had in the night foretold to his followers the dispersion of their enemies. Daybreak saw his prognostications fulfilled, and the Moslems returned in joy to the city.[2]

But the victory was hardly achieved in the opinion of the Moslems as long as the Banî-Kuraizha remained so near, and in such dangerous proximity to the city of Islâm. They had proved themselves traitors in spite of their sworn alliance, and had at one time almost surprised Medîna from their side,—an event which, if successful, would have involved the general massacre of the faithful. The Moslems therefore felt it their duty to demand an explanation of the treachery. This was doggedly refused. The consequence was that the Jews were besieged, and compelled to surrender at discretion. They made only one condition, that their punishment should be left to the judgment of the Ausite chief, Sa'd ibn-Mu'âz. This man, a fierce soldier who had been

5 A.H. = 28th February 626 to 24 March 627 A.C.

[1] Ibn-Hishâm, p. 683; Ibn ul-Athîr, vol. ii. p. 140.
[2] In Moslem annals this war is called the " War of the Trench."

wounded in the attack, and indeed died from his wounds the
next day, infuriated by their treacherous conduct, gave
sentence that the fighting men should be put to death, and that
the women and children should become the slaves of the
Moslems ; and this sentence was carried into execution.[1] " It
was a harsh, bloody sentence," says Lane-Poole, " worthy of
the episcopal generals of the army against the Albigenses, or
of the deeds of the Augustan age of Puritanism ; but it must
be remembered that the crime of these men was high treason
against the State during a time of siege ; and those who have
read how Wellington's march could be traced by the bodies
of deserters and pillagers hanging from the trees, need not be
surprised at the summary execution of a traitorous clan." [2]

The punishment inflicted on the various Jewish tribes has
furnished to the Christian biographers of the Prophet, like
Muir, Sprenger, Weil and Osborn, a ground for attack. The
punishment meted out to the Banî-Kainukâ' and Banî un-
Nazîr was far below their deserts. The Banî-Kuraizha alone
were treated with severity.

Human nature is so constituted that, however criminal the
acts of an individual may be, the moment he is treated with a
severity which to our mind seems harsh or cruel, a natural
revulsion of feeling occurs, and the sentiment of justice gives
place to pity within our hearts. No doubt the sentence on the
Banî-Kuraizha, from our point of view, was severe. But,
however much we may regret that the fate of these poor people
should have been, though at their own special request, left in
the hands of an infuriated soldier—however much we may
regret that the sentence of this man should have been so carried
into effect—we must not, in the sentiment of pity, overlook
the stern question of justice and culpability. We must bear
in mind the crimes of which they were guilty—their treachery,
their open hostility, their defection from an alliance to which
they were bound by every sacred tie. Nor must we altogether
forget the temptations which they, the worshippers of the
pure Jehovah, held out to the heathen Arabs to continue in the

[1] Ibn-Hishâm, pp. 686-690 ; Ibn ul-Athîr, vol. ii. p. 141 *et seq.* ; Tabari,
vol. iii. p. 68 *et seq.*
[2] *Selections from the Koran,* Introd. p. lxv.

practice of idolatry. Some Moslems might naturally be inclined to say, with the Christian moralist : " It is better that the wicked should be destroyed a hundred times over than that they should tempt those who are yet innocent to join their company." [1]

These Moslems might say with him, with only the variation of a word : " Let us but think what might have been our fate, and the fate of every other nation under heaven at this hour, had the sword of the *Arab* [2] done its work more sparingly. The *Arab's* sword, in its bloodiest executions, wrought a work of mercy for all the countries of the earth to the very end of the world." If the Christian's argument is correct and not inhuman, certainly the Moslem's argument cannot be otherwise. Other Moslems, however, might look upon this fearful sentence on the Banî-Kuraizha in the same light as Carlyle looks upon the order of Cromwell for the promiscuous massacre of the Irish inhabitants of Drogheda : " An armed soldier solemnly conscious of himself that he is the soldier of God the Just,—a consciousness which it well beseems all soldiers and all men to have always,—armed soldier, terrible as death, relentless as doom ; doing God's judgment on the enemies of God."

We, however, are not disposed to look at the punishment of these Jews from either of these points of view. We simply look upon it as an act done in complete accordance with the laws of war as then understood by the nations of the world : " a strict application of admitted customs of war in those days." [3] These people brought their fate upon themselves. If they had been put to death, even without the judgment of Sa'd, it would have been in consonance with the principles which then prevailed. But they had themselves chosen Sa'd as the sole arbiter and judge of their fate ; they knew that his judgment was not at all contrary to the received notions, and accordingly never murmured. They knew that if they had succeeded they would have massacred their enemies without compunction. People judge of the massacres of King David according to the

[1] Arnold's *Sermons*, 4th Sermon, " Wars of the Israelites," pp. 35, 36.
[2] In the original, of course, Israelites.
[3] An observation of Grote, *Hist. of Greece*, vol. vi. p. 499.

" lights of his time." [1] Even the fearful slaughters committed by the Christians in primitive times are judged according to certain " lights." Why should not the defensive wars of the early Moslems be looked at from the same standpoint ? But, whatever the point of view, an unprejudiced mind [2] will perceive that no blame can possibly attach to the Prophet in the execution of the Banî-Kuraizha.

The number of men executed could not have been more than 200 or 250.

In the distribution of the surviving people, it is said, a young Jewess of the name of Raihâna was allotted to the Prophet. Some say she was previously set apart. The Christian historians, always ready to seize upon any point which to their mind offers a plausible ground for attacking Mohammed, have not failed to make capital of this story. Leaving the examination of the question of slavery to a later chapter, we will here only observe that the allotment of Raihâna, even if true, furnishes no ground for modern attack, as it was perfectly consonant with the customs of war recognised in those days. The story about Raihâna becoming a wife of the Prophet is a fabrication, for, after this event, she disappears from history and we hear no more of her, whilst of others we have full and circumstantial accounts.

[1] 2 Sam. viii. 2 : " The conquered Ammonites he treated with even greater ferocity, tearing and hewing some of them in pieces with harrows, axes, and saws ; and roasting others in brick-kilns " (xii. 31) ; Maitland, *Jewish Literature and Modern Education*, p. 21. Compare also Stanley's *Lectures on the Jewish Church*, vol. ii. p. 99.

[2] I can only remember M. Barthélemy St. Hilaire, Mr. Johnson, and Mr. Stanley Lane-Poole among Europeans who have not been carried away by prejudice.

CHAPTER VI

MOHAMMED'S CLEMENCY

دَعَا الِى اللَّهِ فَالْمُسْتَمْسِكُونَ بِهِ - مُسْتَمْسِكُونَ بِحَبْلٍ غَيْرِ مُنْقَصِمٍ

T HE formidable coalition formed by the Jews and the idolaters to compass the destruction of the new commonwealth of Medîna had utterly failed, well might the Moslems say, miraculously.[1] But the surrounding tribes of the desert, wild and fierce, were committing depredations, accompanied with murders, on the Medinite territories : and the existence of the State required the employment of stern measures for their repression. Several expeditions were despatched against these marauders, but the slippery sons of the desert generally evaded the approach of the Moslems. The Banî-Lihyân, who had requested Mohammed to send a few of his disciples among them to teach the precepts of Islâm, and who, on the arrival of the missionaries, had killed some and sold the rest to the Meccans,—had, up to this period, remained unpunished. But the time had come when this crime should be avenged. In the month of Jumâdî I. of this year, a body of troops, under the personal command of the Prophet, marched against the Banî-Lihyân. The marauders, however, receiving timely notice of the Prophet's approach, fled into the mountains, and the Moslems returned to Medîna without having accomplished their purpose.[2]

6 A.H. =23rd April 627 to 12th April 628 A.C.

---

[1] Comp. Koran, sura xxxiii. ver. 9.

[2] Ibn-Hishâm, p. 718; Ibn ul-Athîr, vol. ii. p. 143; Tabari, vol. iii. p. 72.

A few days had only elapsed when a chief of the Banî-Fizâra, a branch of the nomad horde of Ghatafân (Khail-Ghatafân), suddenly fell upon the open suburbs of the city, and drove off a large herd of camels, murdering the man who had charge of them, and carrying off his wife. The Moslems were immediately on their track, and a few of the animals were recovered ; but the Bedouins escaped into the desert with the larger portion of their booty.

It was about this time that the Prophet granted to the monks of the monastery of St. Catherine, near Mount Sinai, and to all Christians, a Charter which has been justly designated as one of the noblest monuments of enlightened tolerance that the history of the world can produce. This remarkable document, which has been faithfully preserved by the annalists of Islâm, displays a marvellous breadth of view and liberality of conception. By it the Prophet secured to the Christians privileges and immunities which they did not possess even under sovereigns of their own creed ; and declared that any Moslem violating and abusing what was therein ordered, should be regarded as a violater of God's testament, a transgressor of His commandments, and a slighter of His faith. He undertook himself, and enjoined on his followers, to protect the Christians, to defend their churches, the residences of their priests, and to guard them from all injuries. They were not to be unfairly taxed ; no bishop was to be driven out of his bishopric ; no Christian was to be forced to reject his religion ; no monk was to be expelled from his monastery ; no pilgrim was to be detained from his pilgrimage. Nor were the Christian churches to be pulled down for the sake of building mosques or houses for the Moslems. Christian women married to Moslems were to enjoy their own religion, and not to be subjected to compulsion or annoyance of any kind on that account. If Christians should stand in need of assistance for the repair of their churches or monasteries, or any other matter pertaining to their religion, the Moslems were to assist them. This was not to be considered as taking part in their religion, but as merely rendering them assistance in their need, and complying with the ordinances of the Prophet which were made in their favour by the authority of God and of His Apostle.

Should the Moslems be engaged in hostilities with outside Christians, no Christian resident among the Moslems should be treated with contempt on account of his creed. Any Moslem so treating a Christian should be accounted recalcitrant to the Prophet.

Man always attaches an idea of greatness to the character of a person who, whilst possessing the power of returning evil for evil, not only preaches but *practises* the divine principle of forgiveness. Mohammed, as the chief of the State and guardian of the life and liberty of the people, in the exercise of justice sternly punished every individual guilty of crime. Mohammed the Prophet, the Teacher, was gentle and merciful even to his greatest enemies. In him were combined the highest attributes that the human mind can conceive—justice and mercy.

A chief of the tribe of Hanifa, named Thumâma, son of Uthâl, was taken prisoner by the Moslems in one of their expeditions against the unruly Arabs of the desert. He was brought to Medîna, where he was so affected by the kindness of the Prophet, that from an enemy he soon became the most devoted follower. Returning to his people he stopped the transport to Mecca of provisions from Yemâma, and this stoppage by Thumâma reduced the Meccans to the direst straits. Failing to move the Hanafites, they at last addressed themselves to Mohammed, and besought him to intercede for them. The Prophet's heart was touched with pity, and he requested Thumâma to allow them to have whatever they wanted ; and at his word the convoys were again permitted to reach Mecca.

Endless instances might be cited of Mohammed's merciful nature. We will, however, only instance two. A daughter of his—a beloved child—was, after the treaty of Hudaibiya, fleeing from Mecca. She was far advanced in pregnancy, and as she was mounting her camel, a Koreish named Habrâr, with characteristic ferocity, drove the butt end of his lance against her, throwing her to the ground, and eventually causing her death. On the conquest of Mecca the murderer was proscribed. After hiding for some time he presented himself before the Prophet, and threw himself on the mercy of the bereaved father. The wrong was great ; the crime was

atrocious—but the injury was personal. The man was to all
appearance sincere in his penitence and the profession of the
Faith. Pardon was unconditionally granted. The Jewess who
attempted his life at Khaibar, and Ikrima, the son of Abû Jahl,
who was bitterly personal in his animosity towards the Prophet,
were freely forgiven.

A tribe of Christian Bedouins (the Banî-Kalb), settled about
Dûmat ul-Jandal, had, in their depredations, appeared on the
Medinite territories. An expedition was now despatched to
summon them to embrace Islâm and forego their lawless
practices. Whilst delivering his injunctions to the captain who
headed this small force, Mohammed used the memorable words,
" In no case shalt thou use deceit or perfidy, nor shalt thou kill
any child." [1]

In his instructions to the leaders of the expeditions against
marauding and hostile tribes and people, he invariably enjoined
them in peremptory terms never to injure the weak. " In
avenging the injuries inflicted upon us,," he said to his troops,
whom he despatched against the Byzantines, " molest not the
harmless inmates of domestic seclusion ; spare the weakness
of the female sex ; injure not the infant at the breast, or those
who are ill in bed. Abstain from demolishing the dwellings of
the unresisting inhabitants ; destroy not the means of their
subsistence, nor their fruit trees ; and touch not the palm."
Abû Bakr, following his master, thus enjoined his captain :
" O Yezîd ! be sure you do not oppress your own people, nor
make them uneasy, but advise with them in all your affairs,
and take care to do that which is right and just ; for those that
do otherwise shall not prosper. When you meet your enemies
quit yourselves like men, and do not turn your backs ; and if
you gain the victory, kill not little children, nor old people, nor
women. Destroy no palm trees, nor burn any fields of corn.
Cut down no fruit trees, nor do any mischief to cattle, only such

[1] Ibn-Hishâm, p. 992. Compare these injunctions of the Arabian Prophet
as also the historic words of Abû Bakr (the first Caliph) to Yezîd bin Abû
Sufiân, when despatching him against the Byzantines, with the commands of
the Israelite Prophet : " Thus saith the Lord of Hosts ... Now go and
smite Amalek, and utterly destroy all that they have, and spare them not ;
but slay both man and woman, infant and suckling, ox and sheep, camel and
ass." I. Sam. xv. 3 ; " Slay utterly old and young, both maids, and little
children, and women." Ezek. ix. 6.

as you kill for the necessity of subsistence. When you make any covenant or article, stand to it, and be as good as your word. As you go on, you will find some religious persons that live retired in monasteries, who propose to themselves to serve God that way. Let them alone, and neither kill them nor destroy their monasteries." [1] These injunctions contrast strangely with the fearful denunciations of the Christians, Catholic, Protestant and Greek, from the days of St. Lactantius to those of the Covenanters.[2] The followers of the " Prince of Peace " burnt and ravished, pillaged and murdered promiscuously, old and young, male and female, without compunction, up to recent times. And his vicegerents on earth, popes and patriarchs, bishops, priests, and presbyters, approved of their crimes, and frequently granted plenary absolution for the most heinous offences.

In the month of Sha'bân of this year (November-December, 627) an expedition was directed against the Banî-Mustalik. These people had up to this time been on friendly terms with the Moslems. But, recently, instigated by their chief Hârith, the son of Abû Zirâr,[3] they had thrown off their allegiance, and committed forays on the suburbs of Medîna. The expedition was entirely successful, and several prisoners were taken, amongst whom was a daughter of Hârith, called Juwairiya.

Six years had now passed since the exiles of Mecca had left their homes and their country for the sake of their faith, and of him who had infused into them a new consciousness such as they had never felt before, awakening in them the spirit of union, love, and brotherhood. People flocked from every part of Arabia to listen to the words of the wondrous man who had achieved all this ; to ask his counsel in the affairs of everyday life, even as the sons of Israel consulted of old the prophet Samuel.[4]

[1] Compare Mill's *History of Muhammedanism*, pp. 45, 46 ; and Gagnier, *Vie de Mahomet*, *in loco*.

[2] The massacre of 5000 Chinese men, women and children at Blagovestchenk in Manchuria in the twentieth century by the troops of a great Christian power needs no mention.

[3] With a *zâd* ; Ibn-Hishâm, p. 725 ; Ibn ul-Athîr, vol. ii. p. 146.

[4] Stanley's *Lectures on the Jewish Church*, vol. i. *in loco*.

But the hearts of these exiles still yearned sadly for the place of their birth. Driven from their homes, they had found refuge in a rival city ; expelled from the precincts of the sacred Kaaba, which formed the glorious centre of all their associations,—the one spot round which gathered the history of their nation,—for six years had they been denied the pilgrimage of the holy shrine, a custom round which time, with its hoary traditions, had cast the halo of sanctity. The Teacher himself longed to see the place of his nativity with as great a yearning. The temple of the Kaaba belonged to the whole Arab nation. The Koreish were merely the custodians of this shrine, and were not authorised by the public law of the country to interdict the approach even of an enemy, if he presented himself without any hostile design, and with the avowed object of fulfilling a religious duty.[1]

The season of the pilgrimage had approached ; the Prophet accordingly announced his intention of visiting the holy places. At once a thousand voices responded to the call. Preparations were rapidly made, and, accompanied by seven hundred Moslems, Ansâr and Muhâjirîn, all perfectly unarmed, he set out on the pilgrimage.[2] The animosity of the Koreish, however, was not yet extinguished. They posted themselves, with a large army, some miles in advance of Mecca, to bar the way, but soon after fell back on the city, in order to keep every point of access closed to the Moslems. They swore solemnly not to allow the followers of the Prophet to enter the shrine, and maltreated the envoy who was sent to them to solicit permission to visit the Kaaba. A body of the Meccans went round the Prophet's encampment with the avowed object of killing any unwary Moslem who might leave the camp. They even attacked the Prophet with stones and arrows.[3] Finding

[1] Tabari, vol. iii. p. 84 ; Caussin de Perceval, vol. iii. pp. 174, 175 *et seq.*

[2] Ibn-Hishâm, p. 740 ; Tabari, vol. iii. p. 84 ; Ibn ul-Athîr, vol. ii. p. 152. Abulfedâ, p. 60, mentions the number as 1400.

[3] When some of these men were seized and brought before the Prophet, he pardoned and released them, Ibn-Hishâm, p. 745. It was on this occasion that the Moslems took the pledge, called " The Agreeable Pledge " (*Bai at-ur-Rizwân*), or " The Pledge of the Tree " (*Bai'at-ush-Shajara*). Osmân being sent to the Koreish to repeat the request for permission, they seized and detained him. The Moslems, fearful of his murder, flocked round Mohammed, and solemnly swore to avenge his death. Ibn-Hishâm, p. 746 ; Koran, sura xlviii. ver. 17 ; comp. also Muir, vol. iv. p. 32.

the idolaters immovable, and wishful himself to end the state
of warfare between the Moslems and the Koreish, Mohammed
expressed himself willing to agree to any terms the Meccans
might feel inclined to impose.　After much difficulty a treaty
was concluded, by which it was agreed that all hostilities
should cease for ten years ; that anyone coming from the
Koreish to the Prophet without the permission of the guardian
or chief, should be re-delivered to the idolaters ; that any
individual from among the Moslems going over to the Meccans
should not be surrendered ; that any tribe desirous of entering
into alliance, either with the Koreish or with the Moslems,
should be at liberty to do so without hindrance ; that the
Moslems should retrace their steps on this occasion, without
advancing farther ; that they should be permitted in the
following year to visit Mecca and to remain there for three
days with their travelling arms, namely, their " scimitars in
sheaths." [1]

The moderation and magnanimity displayed by Mohammed
in concluding this treaty caused some discontent among the
more impulsive of his followers, in whose hearts the injuries
and cruelties inflicted by the Koreish yet rankled.　In virtue
of the third stipulation of the treaty, by which the Moslems
bound themselves to surrender every idolater who came over
to their cause without the permission of their patron or chief,
the Koreish demanded the surrender of several of the Prophet's
disciples ; and their demand was immediately complied with
by Mohammed, in spite of the murmurs of some of the
Moslems.[2]

On his return to Medîna, Mohammed, in pursuance of the
catholic wish by which he was inspired, that his religion should

---

[1] *I.e.* the *Silâh-ur-râkib* ;　Ibn-Hishâm, p. 747 ;　Ibn ul-Athîr, vol. ii. p.
156 ;　*Mishkât*, bk. xvii. chap. 10, part i.　It was on the occasion of this peace
that a Koreishite envoy who was sent to the Moslem encampment, struck with
the profound reverence and love shown to the Prophet by his followers, on
his return to the Koreish, told them he had seen sovereigns like the Chosroes
(Kesrâ), the Cæsar (Kaiser), and the Negus (Najâshi), surrounded with all the
pomp and circumstance of royalty ; but he had never witnessed a sovereign
in the midst of his subjects receiving such veneration and obedience as was
paid to Mohammed by his people ; Ibn-Hishâm, p. 745 ; Ibn ul-Athîr, vol. ii.
p. 154 ; Tabari, vol. iii. p. 87 ; and Abulfedâ, p. 61.

[2] As women were not included in the treaty, the demand of the idolaters
for the surrender of the female Moslems was peremptorily declined.

embrace all humanity,[1] despatched several envoys to invite the neighbouring sovereigns and their subjects to drink of the cup of life offered to them by the Preacher of Islâm. Two of the most noted embassies were to Heraclius, the Emperor of the Greeks, and to Khusru Parvîz, the Kesrâ of Persia. The King of Kings was amazed at the audacity of the fugitive of Mecca in addressing him, the great Chosroes, on terms of equality, and enraged at what he considered the insolence of the letter, tore it to pieces, and drove the envoy from his presence with contumely. When the news of this treatment was brought to the Prophet, he quietly observed, " Thus will the empire of Kesrâ be torn to pieces." [2] The fulfilment of the prophecy is engraved on the pages of history. Heraclius, more polite or more reverential, treated the messenger with great respect, and returned a gracious and careful reply. Before, however, leaving Syria he tried to acquaint himself better with the character of the man who had sent him the message. With this object he is said to have summoned to his presence some Arab merchants who had arrived at Gaza with a caravan from Arabia. Among them was the notorious Abû Sufiân, still one of the bitterest enemies of the Prophet. The Greek emperor appears to have questioned him with regard to Mohammed, and his replies, as preserved in the traditions, are almost identical with the summary which Ja'far gave to the Negus of the teachings of Mohammed. " What are the doctrines Mohammed advances ? " asked Heraclius of Abû Sufiân. " He bids us abandon the worship of our ancient idols and to adore one God ; to bestow alms ; to observe truth and purity ; to abstain from fornication and vice, and to flee abominations." Asked if his followers were increasing in number, or if they were falling off, the reply was, " his adherents are increasing incessantly, and there has not been one who has forsaken him."

Another ambassador sent soon afterwards to the Ghassanide prince, a feudatory of Heraclius, residing at Busra, near Damascus, instead of receiving the reverence and respect due to an envoy, was cruelly murdered by another chief of the

[1] Koran, sura vii. vers. 157, 158.
[2] Ibn ul-Athîr, vol. ii. pp. 163, 164.

same family, and *Ameer* of a Christian tribe subject to Byzantium. This wanton outrage on international obligations became eventually the cause of that war which placed Islâm in conflict with the whole of Christendom. But of this we shall treat later.

CHAPTER VII

THE DIFFUSION OF THE FAITH

فَمَا تَطَاوَلُ آمَالُ الْمَدِيحِ اِلَى - مَا فِيهِ مِن كَرَمِ الاخْلاقِ وَ الشِّيمِ

THE Jewish tribes, in spite of the reverses they had already suffered were still formidable,—still busy with their machinations to work the destruction of the Moslems. They possessed, at the distance of three or four days' journey to the north-east of Medîna, a strongly fortified territory, studded with castles, the principal of which, called al-Kamûs, was situated on an almost inaccessible hill. This group of fortresses was called *Khaibar*, a word signifying a fortified place. The population of Khaibar included several branches of the Banî-Nazîr and the Kuraizha, who had taken refuge there. The Jews of Khaibar had shown an active and implacable hatred towards Mohammed and his followers, and since the arrival of their brethren among them, this feeling had acquired greater force. The Jews of Khaibar united by an ancient alliance with the Bedouin horde of the Banî-Ghatafân, and other cognate tribes, worked incessantly for the formation of another coalition against the Moslems.[1] These latter were alive to the power possessed by the desert-races to injure them, and prompt measures were needed to avert the evils of another league against Medîna. Accordingly, early in the month of Muharram of this year, an expedition, consisting of about 1400 men, was despatched against Khaibar. The Jews now solicited the assistance of their allies. The Banî-Fizâra hastened to their

7 A.H. = 12th April 628 to 1st May 629 A.C.

[1] Caussin de Perceval, vol. iii. pp. 193, 194.

support, but afraid of the Moslems turning their flank, and surprising their flocks and herds in their absence, speedily retreated. The Jews were thus left alone to bear the brunt of the war. Terms were offered to them by the Moslems, but were refused. In spite of the most determined resistance on the part of the Jews, fortress after fortress opened its gate. At last came the turn of the most formidable castle, al-Kamûs. After a spirited defence, it also fell into the hands of the Moslems. The fate of this, their principal fortress, brought the remaining Jewish townships to see the utter futility of further resistance. They sued for forgiveness, which was accorded. Their lands and immovable property were guaranteed to them (on condition of good conduct), together with the free practice of their religion ; and, as they were exempt from the regular taxes, the Prophet imposed upon them the duty of paying to the Common-wealth, in return for the protection they would thenceforth enjoy, half the produce of their lands. The movable property found in the fortress which the Moslems reduced by regular sieges and battles, was forfeited to the army, and distributed among the men according to the character of their arms ; thus, for instance, three shares were given to a horseman, whilst a foot-soldier received only one.[1]

Towards the end of the seventh year of the Hegira, Moham-med and his disciples availed themselves of their truce with the Koreish to accomplish the desire of their hearts [2]—the pilgrimage to the holy places. This journey, in Moslem history, is reverently styled " the Pilgrimage, or Visit of Accomplish-ment." [3] It was in March 629 that the Prophet, accompanied by 2000 Moslems, proceeded to Mecca to perform the rites of the

---

[1] Ibn-Hishâm, pp. 764 and 773 ; Ibn ul-Athîr, vol. ii. p. 169. The story of Kinâna being tortured for the sake of disclosing the concealed treasures is false.

Frequent attempts were made about this time to assassinate the Prophet. On his entry into Khaibar, a Jewess, animated with the same vengeful feeling as the Judith of old, spread a poisoned repast for him and some of his followers. One of them died immediately after he had taken a few mouthfuls. The life of the Prophet was saved, but the poison permeated his system, and in after-life he suffered severely from its effects, and eventually died thereof. In spite of this crime, Mohammed forgave the woman, and she was allowed to remain among her people unharmed ; Tabari, vol. iii. p. 104 ; Ibn ul-Athîr, vol. ii. p. 170.

[2] See Koran, sura xlviii. ver. 27.   [3] *Umrat-ul-Kazâ.*

Lesser Pilgrimage—rites which every pilgrim of Islâm has now
to observe.   The Koreish would, however, have nothing to say
to the pilgrims, and hold no converse with them.   For the three
days during which the ceremonies lasted, they evacuated the
city, and from the summits of the neighbouring heights watched
the Moslems performing the rites.   " It was surely a strange
sight," says Muir, with an unconscious thrill, " which at this
time presented itself in the vale of Mekka,—a sight unique in
the history of the world.   The ancient city is for three .days
evacuated by all its inhabitants, high and low, every house
deserted ; and, as they retire, the exiled converts, many years
banished from their birthplace, approach in a great body,
accompanied by their allies, revisit the empty homes of their
childhood, and within the short allotted space, fulfil the rites
of pilgrimage.   The outside inhabitants, climbing the heights
around, take refuge under tents, or other shelter among the
hills and glens ; and, clustering on the overhanging peak of
Aboo-Kubeys, thence watch the movements of the visitors
beneath, as with the Prophet at their head they make the
circuit of the Kaabeh, and the rapid procession between
Es-Safá and Marwah ; and anxiously scan every figure if
perchance they may recognise among the worshippers some
long-lost friend or relative.   It was a scene rendered possible
only by the throes which gave birth to Islâm." [1]   In strict
conformity with the terms of the treaty, they left Mecca after
a sojourn of three days.   This peaceful fulfilment of the day-
dream of the Moslems was followed by important conversions
among the Koreish.   The self-restraint and scrupulous
regard for their pledged word displayed by the Believers
created a visible impression among the enemies of Islâm.
Many of those who were most violent among the Koreish
in their opposition to the Prophet, men of position and
influence, who had warred against him, and reviled him,
struck by Mohammed's kindness of heart and nobility of
nature, which overlooked all crimes against himself, adopted
the Faith. [2]

[1] Muir, *Life of Mohammed*, vol. iii. 402.

[2] For instance, Khâlid bin-Walîd, who commanded the Koreish cavalry at
Ohod, and 'Amr(u) ibn al-'Âsi, famous as Amru.

The murder of the Moslem envoy by a feudatory [1] of the
Greek emperor was an outrage which could not be passed over
in silence, and unpunished.   An expedition, consisting of three
thousand men, was despatched to exact reparation from the
Ghassanide prince.   The lieutenants of the Byzantine emperor,
instead of disavowing the crime, adopted it, and thus made the
quarrel an imperial one.   Uniting their forces, they attacked
the Moslems near Múta, a village not far from Balkâ in Syria,
the scene of the murder.   The Byzantines and their allies were
repulsed, but the disparity of numbers was too great, and the
Moslems retreated to Medîna. [2]

It was about this time that the Koreish and their allies the
Banî-Bakr, in violation of the terms of peace concluded at
Hudaibiya, attacked the Banî-Khuzâ'a, who were under the
protection of, and in alliance with, the Moslems.   They
massacred a number of the Khuzâ'a, and dispersed the rest.
The Banû-Khuzâ'a brought their complaints to Mohammed,
and asked for justice.   The reign of iniquity and oppression
had lasted long at Mecca.   The Meccans had themselves
violated the peace, and some of their chief men had taken part
in the massacre of the Khuzâ'a.   The Prophet immediately
marched ten thousand men against the idolaters.   With the
exception of a slight resistance by Ikrima, [3] and Safwân [4] at
the head of their respective clans, in which several Moslems
were killed, Mohammed entered Mecca almost unopposed.

Thus, at length, Mohammed entered Mecca as a conqueror.
He, who was once a fugitive and persecuted, now came to prove
his mission by deeds of mercy.   The city which had treated
him so cruelly, driven him and his faithful band for refuge
amongst strangers, which had sworn his life and the lives of his
devoted disciples, lay at his feet.   His old persecuters, relentless
and ruthless, who had disgraced humanity by inflicting cruel

[1] According to Caussin de Perceval, the name of this chieftain was
Shurâhbîl, son of 'Amr (and not, as Abulfedâ mentions it, 'Amr, son of
Shurâhbîl).—Vol. ii. p. 253, and vol. iii. p. 211.

[2] Caussin de Perceval, vol. iii. p. 211 *et seq.* ; Ibn ul-Athîr, vol. ii. pp. 178-
180.   In this battle, Zaid, the son of Hârith, who commanded the Moslem
troops, Ja'far, the cousin of Mohammed, and several other notables were killed.

[3] The son of Abû Jahl, who fell at Badr.

[4] The son of Ommeyya.

outrages upon inoffensive men and women, and even upon the lifeless dead, were now completely at his mercy. But in the hour of triumph every evil suffered was forgotten, every injury inflicted was forgiven, and a general amnesty was extended to the population of Mecca. Only four criminals, "whom justice condemned," made up Mohammed's proscription list when he entered as a conqueror the city of his bitterest enemies. The army followed his example, and entered gently and peaceably ; no house was robbed, no woman was insulted. Most truly has it been said that through all the annals of conquest, there has been no triumphant entry like unto this one. But the idols of the nation were unrelentingly struck down. Sorrowfully the idolaters stood round and watched the downfall of the images they worshipped. And then dawned upon them the truth, when they heard the old voice, at which they were wont to scoff and jeer, cry, as he struck down the idols, " Truth has come, and falsehood vanisheth ; verily falsehood is evanescent," [1] how utterly powerless were their gods !

After destroying these ancient idols and abolishing every pagan rite, Mohammed delivered a sermon to the assembled people. He dwelt first upon the natural equality and brotherhood of mankind, in the words of the Koran,[2] and then proceeded as follows : " Descendants of Koreish, how do you think I should act towards you ? " " With kindness and pity, gracious brother and nephew," replied they.[3] At these words, says Tabari, tears came into the eyes of the Prophet, and he said, " I shall speak to you as Joseph spake unto his brothers, ' I shall not reproach you to-day ; God will forgive,' He is the most merciful and compassionate." [4]

And now was enacted a scene of which there is no parallel in the history of the world. Hosts upon hosts came and adopted the religion of Mohammed. Seated on the hill of Safâ, he received the old pledge, exacted before from the Medinites : " They would not adore anything ; they would not

[1] Koran, sura xvii. ver. 83 ; Ibn ul-Athîr, vol. ii. p. 192.
[2] Koran, sura xlix. ver. 10.
[3] Ibn-Hishâm, p. 821 ; Tabari, vol. iii. p. 134.
[4] Koran, sura xii. ver. 31.

commit larceny, adultery, or infanticide ; they would not utter falsehood, nor speak evil of women." [1]

Thus were the words of the Koranic prophecy fulfilled, " When arrives victory and assistance from God, and seest thou men enter in hosts the religion of God, then utter the praise of thy Lord, and implore His pardon ; for He loveth to turn in mercy (to those who seek Him)." [2] Mohammed now saw his Mission all but completed. His principal disciples were despatched in every direction to call the wild tribes of the desert to Islâm, and with strict injunctions to preach peace and good-will. Only in case of violence were they to defend themselves. These injunctions were loyally obeyed with one exception. The men of Khâlid bin-Walîd, under the orders of this fierce and newly-converted warrior, killed a few of the Banî Jazîma [3] Bedouins, apparently mistaking them for hostile soldiers ; but the other Moslems interfering, prevented further massacre. The news of this wanton bloodshed deeply grieved the Prophet, and he cried, raising his hands towards heaven, " O Lord ! I am innocent of what Khâlid has done." He immediately despatched Ali to make every possible reparation to the Banî Jazîma for the outrage committed on them. This was a mission congenial to Ali's nature, and he executed it faithfully. He made careful inquiries as to the number of persons killed by Khâlid, their status, and the losses incurred by their families, and paid the *Diyat* strictly. When every loss was made good, he distributed the remainder of the money he had brought among the kinsmen of the victims and other members of the tribe, gladdening every heart, says the chronicler, by his gentleness and benevolence. Carrying with him the blessings of the whole people, he returned to the Prophet, who overwhelmed him with thanks and praises. [4]

The formidable Bedouin tribes, the Hawâzin, the Thakîf, [5] and various others who pastured their flocks on the territories

---

[1] Ibn ul-Athîr, vol. ii. p. 292 ; Caussin de Perceval, vol. iii. p. 234.

[2] Koran, sura cx.; comp. Zamakhshari (the *Kashshâf*), Egypt. ed., pt. ii. pp. 490, 491. The verse is given at the head of Chapter IX. *post.*

[3] With a ذ (*zâl*).

[4] Ibn-Hishâm, pp. 834, 835 ; Ibn ul-Athîr, vol. ii. p. 195 ; Tabari, vol. iii. p. 141.

[5] With a ث

bordering Mecca, and some of whom possessed strongly-fortified towns like Tâyef, unwilling to render obedience to the Moslems without resistance, formed a league, with the intention of overwhelming Mohammed before he could make preparations to repulse their attack. His vigilance, however, disappointed them. After a well-contested battle fought near Hunain, a deep and narrow defile about ten miles to the north-east of Mecca,[1] the idolaters were defeated with great loss.[2] Separating their forces, one body of the enemy, consisting principally of the Thakîf, took refuge in their city of Tâyef, which only eight or nine years before had driven the Prophet from within its walls with insults ; the rest fled to a fortified camp in the valley of the Autâs. This was forced, and the families of the Hawâzin, with all their worldly effects,—their flocks and herds,—fell into the hands of the Moslems. Tâyef was then besieged, but after a few days Mohammed raised the siege, well knowing that the pressure of circumstances would soon force the Tâyefites to submit without bloodshed. Returning to the place where the captured Hawâzin were left for safety, he found a deputation from this powerful tribe awaiting his return to solicit the restoration of their families. Aware of the sensitiveness of the Arab nature regarding their rights, Mohammed replied to the Bedouin deputies that he could not force his people to abandon all the fruits of their victory, and that they must at least forfeit their effects if they would regain their families. To this they consented, and the following day, when Mohammed was offering the mid-day prayers,[3] with his disciples ranged behind him, they came and repeated the request : " We supplicate the Prophet to intercede with the Moslems, and the Moslems to intercede with the Prophet, to restore us our women and children." Mohammed replied to the deputies, " My own share in the captives, and that of the children of Abd ul-

---

[1] Caussin de Perceval, vol. iii. p. 248 ; in the *Kâmûs*, Hunain is merely said to be on the road from Mecca to Tâyef. In the *Mu'jam ul-Buldân* the distance between Mecca and Hunain (lying to the south of Zu'l Majâz) is given as three nights' journey; vol. ii. p. 35.

[2] This battle is referred to in the Koran, sura ix. vers. 25, 26 ; Ibn-Hishâm, p. 840 ; Ibn ul-Athîr, vol. ii. pp. 200, 201.

[3] Tabari says morning prayer, vol. iii. p. 155.

Muttalib, I give you back at once." His disciples, catching his spirit, instantaneously followed his example, and six thousand people were in a moment set free.[1] This generosity won the hearts of many of the Thakîf,[2] who tendered their allegiance, and became earnest Moslems. The incident which followed after the distribution of the forfeited flocks and herds of the Hawâzin, shows not only the hold the Prophet had over the hearts of the Medinites, and the devotion he inspired them with, but it also proves that at no period of his career had he any material reward to offer to his disciples. In the division of the spoil a larger proportion fell to the share of the newly-converted Meccans than to the people of Medîna. Some of the Ansâr looked upon this as an act of partiality, and their discontent reaching the ear of the Prophet, he ordered them to be assembled. He then addressed them in these words : " Ye Ansâr, I have learnt the discourse ye hold among yourselves. When I came amongst you, you were wandering in darkness, and the Lord gave you the right direction ; you were suffering, and He made you happy ; at enmity amongst yourselves, and He has filled your hearts with brotherly love and concord. Was it not so, tell me ? " " Indeed, it is even as thou sayest," was the reply ; " to the Lord and His Prophet belong benevolence and grace." " Nay, by the Lord," continued the Prophet, " but ye might have answered, and answered truly, for I would have testified to its truth myself. ' *Thou camest to us rejected as an impostor, and we believed in thee* ; *thou camest as a helpless fugitive, and we assisted thee* : *poor, and an outcast, and we gave thee an asylum* ; *comfortless, and we solaced thee.*' Ye Ansâr, why disturb your hearts because of the things of this life ? Are ye not satisfied that others should obtain the flocks and the camels, while ye go back unto your homes with me in your midst ? By Him who holds my life in His hands, I shall never abandon you. If all mankind went one way and the

---

[1] Ibn-Hishâm, p. 876 ; Ibn ul-Athîr, vol. ii. p. 206 ; Tabari, vol. iii. p. 155.

[2] The people of Tâyef were so called. The story told by Muir (vol. iv. p. 149), as a curious illustration of the Prophet's mode of life, is apocryphal. It must be remembered, firstly, that the division of the booty had not taken place, and consequently the Prophet could not have given away as gift part of his own share ; but this he had promised to the deputies before the division to restore to the Hawâzin. The story is a fabrication, and utterly worthless.

Ansâr another, verily I would join the Ansâr. The Lord be favourable unto them, and bless them, and their children, and their children's children!" At these words, says the chronicler, they all wept until the tears ran down upon their beards. And they all cried with one voice, " Yea, Prophet of God, we are well satisfied with our share." Thereupon they retired happy and contented.[1]

Mohammed soon after returned to Medîna.

[1] Ibn-Hishâm, p. 886 ; Ibn ul-Athîr, vol. ii. p. 208 ; Abulfedâ, p. 82.

CHAPTER VIII

THE YEAR OF DEPUTATIONS

ٱتَى الدَّبِيِّينَ فِيْ خُلُقٍ وَّ فِيْ خُلُقٍ

وَ لَمْ يُدَانُـوْ فِيْ عِلْـمٍ وَّلَا كَـرَمِ

دَعْ مَا ادَّعَتْهُ النَّصَارَى فِيْ نَبِيِّهِمْ

وَ احْكُمْ بِمَا شِئْتَ مَدْحاً فِيْهِ وَ احْتَكِمْ

KASÎDAT-UL-BURDA.

إِنَّ الرَّسُوْلَ لَنُـوْرٌ يُسْتَضَـاءُ بِه

وَ طَارِمٌ مِنْ سُيُوْفِ اللهِ مَسْلُوْلُ

BÂNAT SUÂD.

THE ninth year of the Hegira was noted for the embassies which flocked into Medîna to render homage to the Prophet of Islâm. The cloud which so long had rested over this land, with its wild chivalry, its blood-feuds, and its heathenism, is now lifted for ever. The age of barbarism is past.

The conquest of Mecca decided the fate of idolatry in Arabia. The people, who still regarded with veneration those beautiful moon-goddesses, Manât, Lât, and ʿUzzâ, and their peculiar cult, were painfully awakened by the fall of its stronghold. Among the wild denizens of the desert the moral effect of the submission of the Meccans was great. Deputations began to arrive

9 A.H. 20th
April 630 to 9th
April 631 A.C.

from all sides to tender the allegiance and adherence of tribes hitherto most inimical to the Moslems.[1] The principal companions of the Prophet, and the leading citizens of Medîna, at his request, received these envoys in their houses, and entertained them with the time-honoured hospitality of the Arabs. On departure, they always received an ample sum for the expenses of the road, with some additional presents, corresponding to their rank. A written treaty, guaranteeing the privileges of the tribe, was often granted, and a teacher invariably accompanied the departing guests to instruct the newly-converted people in the duties of Islâm, and to see that every remnant of idolatry was obliterated from their midst.

Whilst thus engaged in consolidating the tribes of Arabia under the new gospel, the great Seer was alive to the dangers which threatened the new confederation from outside.

The Byzantines seem about this time to have indulged in those dreams of Arabian conquests which had, once before, induced the founder of the Roman Empire to despatch expeditions into that country.[2] Heraclius had returned to his dominions elated by his victories over the Persians. His political vision could not have been blind to the strange events which were taking place in Arabia, and he had probably not forgotten the repulse of his lieutenants, at the head of a large army, by a handful of Arabs. During his stay in Syria he had directed his feudatories to collect an overwhelming force for the invasion of Arabia. The news of these preparations was soon brought to Medîna, and caused some consternation among the Moslems. If the report was true it meant a serious danger to the Islâmic commonwealth. Volunteers were summoned from all quarters to repel the threatened attack. Unfortunately, a severe drought had lately afflicted Hijâz and Najd ; the date crops had been ruined, and the beasts of burden had died in large numbers ; and the country people at large were unwilling to engage at this juncture on an expedition far from their homes. To some, the time of the year seemed unseasonable ; whilst the intensity of the heat, the hardships of the journey and the marvellous stories regarding the power of the

[1] Ibn-Hishâm, p. 934 *et seq.* ; Ibn ul-Athîr, vol. ii. p. 219.
[2] I allude to the expedition of Ælius Gallus under Augustus.

Byzantine empire added largely to the fears of the timorous.
Many applied to be exempted from service ; and the Prophet
acceded to the prayers of those who were either too weak or
too poor to take up arms or leave their homes, and such others
as had no one besides themselves to look after their families.[1]

The unwillingness of the lukewarm was aggravated by the
machinations of the *Munâfikîn*, who spared no endeavours to
fan it into discontent.[2]   The example, however, of the principal
disciples and other sincere followers of the Faith, infused
vitality into the hearts of the timorous, and shamed the back-
sliders into enthusiasm which soon spread among the people.
Contributions poured in from all sides.   Abû Bakr offered all he
possessed towards the expenses of the expedition ;   Osmân
equipped and supplied at his own expense a large body of
volunteers, and the other prominent and affluent Moslems were
equally generous.   The women brought their ornaments and
jewelleries and besought the Prophet to accept the same for
the needs of the State.   A sufficient force was eventually
collected,[3] and accompanied by the Prophet the volunteers
marched towards the frontier.

During his absence from Medîna the Prophet left Ali in
charge of the city.   The *Munâfikîn*, with Abdullah ibn-Ubayy,
had proceeded with the army as far as "the Mount of Farewell,"[4]
but they quietly fell back from there and returned to the city.
Here they spread the report that the Prophet had not taken
his cousin with him as he was apprehensive of the dangers of
the expedition.   Stung by the malicious rumour, Ali seized his
arms and hastened after the army.   Overtaking the troops, he
told the Prophet what he had heard.   Mohammed pronounced

[1] These were called the *al-Bakkâûn*, the *Weepers*, as they were distressed
by their inability to join in the sacred enterprise of repelling a dangerous
enemy.—Ibn-Hishâm, p. 791 ; al-Halabi, *Insân ul-'Uyûn*, vol. iii. p. 75.

[2] The machinations of the Disaffected are censured in Sura IX, v. 82.   These
secret conspirators had for their rendezvous the house of a Jew named
Suwailim near the suburb of Jâsûm.   This house was ultimately rased to
the ground.   It was at this time that the great Teacher made the prophecy
that there will always be *Munâfikîn* in Islâm to thwart the endeavours of the
true followers of the Faith to do good to their people.

[3] It was called the *Jaish-ul-'usra*, "the army of distress," owing to the
difficulties with which it was collected ; Ibn-Hishâm, p. 795.

[4] *Thiniat-ul-Wadâ'* with a ث., *Mu'jam ul-Buldân*, vol. i. p. 937.

it to be a base calumny. " I have appointed thee my Vice-
gerent (*Khalîfa*) and left thee in my stead. Return then to
thy post, and be my deputy over my people and thine. O Ali,
art thou not content that thou art to me what Aaron was to
Moses." [1]   Ali accordingly returned to Medîna.

The sufferings of the troops from heat and thirst were
intense. After a long and painful march they reached Tabûk,
a place situated midway between Medîna and Damascus,[2]
where they halted. Here they learnt to their amazement, and
perhaps to their relief, that the apprehended attack was a
Grecian dream, and that the emperor had his hands full at
home. Finding, therefore, nothing at the moment to threaten
the safety of the Medinite commonwealth, the Prophet ordered
the Moslems to retrace their steps.[3] After a sojourn of twenty
days at Tabûk, where they found abundance of water for themselves and forage for their famished beasts of burden, the
Moslems returned to Medîna in the month of Ramazân.[4]

The Prophet's return to Medîna was signalised by the arrival
of a deputation from the refractory and hard-hearted idolaters
of Tâyef, the very people who had driven the poor Preacher
from their midst with insults and violence. 'Orwa, the Tâyefite
chief, who had been to Mecca after the Hudaibiya incident as
the Koreishite envoy, was so impressed with the words of the
Teacher and his kindness, that shortly after the accomplish-
ment of his mission he had come to the Prophet and embraced
his religion. Though repeatedly warned by Mohammed of the
dangers he ran among the bigoted of his city, he hastened back
to Tâyef to proclaim his abjuration of idolatry, and to invite

[1] قتال كذبوا ولكني خلقتك لما تركت و راءي فارجع فاخلفني في اهلي و اهلك

أفلا ترضى يا علي ان تكون مني بمنزلة هارون من موسى *

Ibn-Hishâm
p. 897.

According to the Shiahs, the Prophet distinctly indicated in these words
that Ali should be his successor.

[2] Caussin de Perceval, vol. iii. pp. 285, 286.

[3] Ibn-Hishâm, p. 904 ; Ibn ul-Athîr, vol. ii. p. 215 ; Abulfedâ, p. 85.

[4] According to C. de Perceval, middle of December 630 A.C. Chapter iv.
of the Koran treats vividly of these events. At Tabûk Mohammed received
the submission of many of the neighbouring chiefs ; Ibn ul-Athîr, vol. ii.
p. 215.

his fellow-citizens to share in the blessings imparted by the new Faith. Arriving in the evening, he made public his conversion and called upon the people to join him. The following morning he again addressed them ; but his words roused the priests and worshippers of 'Uzzâ into frenzy, and they literally stoned him to death. With his dying breath he said he had offered up his blood unto his Master for the good of his people, and he thanked God for the honour of martyrdom, and as a last wish prayed his friends to bury him by the side of the Moslems who had fallen at Hunain.[1] The dying words of 'Orwa had a greater effect upon his compatriots than all his endeavours whilst living. The martyr's blood blossomed into faith in the hearts of his murderers. Seized with sudden compunction, perhaps also wearying of their hostility with the tribes of the desert, the Tâyefites sent the deputation to which we have referred above, to pray for forgiveness and permission to enter the circle of Islâm. They begged, however, for a short respite for their idols. First they asked two years, then one year, and then six months, but all to no purpose. The grace of one month might surely be conceded, they argued as a last appeal. Mohammed was immovable. Islâm and the idols could not exist together. They then begged for exemption from the daily prayers. Mohammed replied that without devotion religion could be nothing.[2] Sorrowfully, at last, they submitted to all that was required of them. They were excused, however, from destroying the idols with their own hands, and the notorious Abû Sufiân, the son of Harb, the father of the well-known Mu'âwiyah, the Judas Iscariot of Islâm, one of those who have been stigmatised as the *Muallafat ul-Kulûb* (the nominal believers)—for they had adopted the Faith from policy,—and Mughîra, the nephew of 'Orwa, were selected for that work. They executed their commission amidst uproarious cries of despair and grief from the women of Tâyef.[3]

[1] Ibn-Hishâm, pp. 914, 915 ; Ibn ul-Athîr, vol. ii. p. 216.

[2] Ibn ul-Athîr, vol. ii. p. 217.

[3] Ibn-Hishâm, pp. 917, 918 ; Tabari, vol. iii. pp. 161-163. The great number of deputations received by Mohammed in the ninth year has led to its being called the " Year of Deputations " ; (*wufûd*, pl. of *wafad*). The principal adhesions which followed immediately upon the conversion of the Thakîf

The tribe of Tay had about this time proved recalcitrant, and their disaffection was fostered by the idolatrous priesthood. A small force was despatched under Ali to reduce them to obedience and to destroy their idols. 'Adi, the son of the famous Hâtim, whose generosity and munificence have been sung by poets and minstrels throughout the Eastern world, was the chief of his tribe. On the approach of Ali he fled to Syria ; but his sister, with some of his principal clansmen, fell into the hands of the Moslems. They were conducted, with every mark of respect and sympathy, to Medîna. Mohammed at once set the daughter of Hâtim and her people at liberty, and bestowed on them many valuable gifts. She proceeded to Syria, and told her brother of the nobleness of Mohammed. Touched by gratitude, 'Adi hastened to Medîna to throw himself at the feet of the Prophet, and eventually embraced Islâm. Returning to his people, he persuaded them to abjure idolatry ; and the Banî-Tay, once so wedded to fetishism, became thenceforth devoted followers of the religion of Mohammed.[1]

Another notable conversion which took place about the same time as that of the Banî-Tay is deserving of more than passing notice. Ka'b ibn-Zuhair, a distinguished poet of the tribe of Mozayna, had placed himself under the ban by trying to incite hostilities against the Moslems. His brother was a Moslem

were of the Himyarite princes of Yemen, of Mahra, of Oman, of the country of the Bahrain, and of the tribes domiciled in Yemâma.

[1] Ibn-Hishâm, pp. 948, 949 ; Ibn ul-Athîr, vol. ii. p. 218 ; *Insân ul-'Uyûn*, vol. iii. p. 234. The conversion of 'Adi occurred in Rabi II. of the ninth year (July-August, 630 A.C.), and accordingly, ought to have been placed before the expedition to Tabûk. But I have followed the order of the Arab historians. When the daughter of Hâtim, whose name was Sufâna, came before the Prophet, she addressed him in the following words : " Apostle of God, my father is dead ; my brother, my only relation, fled into the mountains on the approach of the Moslems. I cannot ransom myself ; it is thy generosity which I implore for my deliverance. My father was an illustrious man, the prince of his tribe, a man who ransomed prisoners, protected the honour of women, nourished the poor, consoled the afflicted, never rejected any demand. I am Sufâna, daughter of Hâtim." " Thy father," answered Mohammed, "had the virtues of a Musulman ; if it were permitted to me to invoke the mercy of God on any one whose life was passed in idolatry, I would pray to God for mercy for the soul of Hâtim." Then addressing the Moslems around him, he said : " The daughter of Hâtim is free, her father was a generous and humane man ; God loves and rewards the merciful." And with Sufâna, all her people were set at liberty. The Persian poet Sa'di has some beautiful lines in the *Bostân* concerning this touching episode.

and had counselled him strongly to renounce idolatry and
embrace Islâm. Ka'b, following the advice of his brother,
came secretly to Medîna, and proceeded to the mosque where
Mohammed was wont to preach. There he saw a man surrounded by Arabs listening to his words with the greatest
veneration. He at once recognised the Prophet, and penetrating into the circle, said aloud, " Apostle of God, if I should
bring before thee Ka'b as a Musulman, would you pardon
him ? " " Yes," answered Mohammed. " It is I who am
Ka'b, the son of Zuhair." Several people around the Prophet
wanted leave to put him to death. " No," said the Prophet,
" I have given him grace." Ka'b then begged permission to
recite a *Kasîda* [1] (poem) which has always been considered a
masterpiece of Arabic poetry. When he came to the lines [2]
quoted at the head of this chapter, the Prophet bestowed on
the poet his own mantle, which was afterwards sold by his
family to Mu'âwiyah for 40,000 dirhems, and, after passing into
the hands of the Ommeyades and Abbasides, is now in the
possession of the Ottoman Caliphs. [3]

Hitherto no prohibition had issued against the heathens
entering the Kaaba, or performing their old idolatrous rites
within its sacred precincts. It was now decided to put an end
to this anomalous state, and remove once for all any possibility

---

[1] Called the *Kasîda of Bânat Su'âd* from the opening words of the poem,
which begins with the prologue usual in Arabic *Kasîdas*. The poet tells
his grief at the departure of Su'âd (his beloved) ; she has left him, his heart
is drooping, distracted and unhappy, following her train like a captive in
chains. He praises her beauty, her sweet soft voice, her bright laughter, her
winsome smile. The theme suddenly changes, and the poet reaches the
climax when he bursts forth into a song of praise of his great subject. The
language throughout is sonorous and virile—a quality often wanting in the
poems of later times, and the rhythmical swing and cadence are maintained,
with extraordinary evenness, up to the last.

[2] " The Prophet is the torch which has lighted up the world ; he is the
sword of God for destroying ungodliness."

[3] Called the *Khirkai-sharîf* (the Holy Mantle) which is taken out as the
national standard in times of great emergency. The *Kasîda of Bânat Su'âd*,
which is sometimes also called the *Kasîdat-ul-Burda* (the Kasîda of the
Mantle), is different from the *Kasîdat-ul-Burda* of Abû Abdullah Mohammed
ibn-Sa'îd, who flourished in the reign of Malik Zâhir, which opens with the
following lines :—

امن تذكر جيران بذى سَلم ۰ مَزجتَ دمعاً جري من مقلة بدم

For translation see Appendix.

of a relapse into idolatry on the part of those upon whom the new and pure creed hung somewhat lightly. Accordingly, towards the end of this year, during the month of pilgrimage, Ali was commissioned to read a proclamation to the assembled multitudes, on the day of the great Sacrifice (*Yeum-un-Nahr*), which should strike straight at the heart of idolatry and the immoralities attendant upon it : " No idolater shall, after this year, perform the pilgrimage ; no one shall make the circuit (of the temple) naked ; [1] whoever hath a treaty with the Prophet, it shall continue binding till its termination ; for the rest, four months are allowed to every man to return to his territories ; after that there will exist no obligation on the Prophet, except towards those with whom treaties have been concluded." [2]

This " Declaration of Discharge," as it is styled by Moslem writers, was a manifestation of far-sighted wisdom on the part of the Prophet. It was impossible for the state of society and morals which then existed to continue ; the idolaters mixing year after year with the Moslem pilgrims, if allowed to perform the lascivious and degrading ceremonies of their cult, would soon have undone what Mohammed had so laboriously accomplished. History had already seen another gifted, yet uncultured, branch of the same stock as the Arabs, settling amongst idolaters ; their leaders had tried to preserve the worship of Jehovah by wholesale butcheries of the worshippers of Baal. They had failed miserably. The Israelites had not only succumbed under the evil influences which surrounded them, but had even surpassed those whom they at first despised in the practice of nameless abominations. Mohammed felt that any compromise with heathenism would nullify all his work. He accordingly adopted means seemingly harsh, but yet benignant in their ultimate tendency. The vast concourse who had listened to Ali returned to their homes, and before the following year was over the majority of them were Moslems.

[1] Alluding to a disgraceful custom of the idolatrous Arabs.
[2] Ibn-Hishâm, pp. 921, 922 ; Ibn ul-Athîr, vol. ii. p. 222 ; Abulfedâ, p. 87.

CHAPTER IX

THE FULFILMENT OF MOHAMMED'S MISSION

إِذَا جَآءَ نَصْرُ اللَّهِ وَٱلْفَتْحُ • وَرَأَيْتَ ٱلنَّاسَ يَدْخُلُونَ فِيْ دِيْنِ

اللَّهِ أَفْوَاجًا • فَسَبِّحْ بِحَمْدِ رَبِّكَ وَٱسْتَغْفِرْهُ إِنَّهُ كَانَ تَوَّابًا

DURING this year,[1] as in the preceding, numerous embassies poured into Medîna from every part of Arabia to testify to the adhesion of their chiefs and their tribes. To the teachers, whom Mohammed sent into the different provinces, he invariably gave the following injunctions : " Deal gently with the people, and be not harsh ; cheer them, and contemn them not. And ye will meet

10 A.H. 9th
April 631 to 29th
March 632 A.C.

with many people of the books [2] who will question thee, what is the key to heaven ? Reply to them (the key to heaven is) to testify to the truth of God, and to do good work." [3]

The mission of Mohammed was now achieved. In the midst of a nation steeped in barbarism a Prophet had arisen " to rehearse unto them the signs of God to sanctify them, to teach them the scriptures and knowledge,—them who before had been in utter darkness." [4] He found them sunk in a degrading and sanguinary superstition ; he inspired them with the belief in one sole God of truth and love. He saw them disunited,

---

[1] In the tenth year of the Hegira took place the conversions of the remaining tribes of Yemen and of Hijâz. Then followed the conversions of the tribes of Hazramût and Kinda.

[2] Christians, Jews, and Zoroastrians.   [3] Ibn-Hishâm, p. 907.

[4] Koran, sura lxii. vers. 2-5.

and engaged in perpetual war with each other ; he united them
by the ties of brotherhood and charity.   From time immemorial
the Peninsula had been wrapped in absolute moral darkness.
Spiritual life was utterly unknown.   Neither Judaism nor
Christianity had made any lasting impression on the Arab
mind.   The people were sunk in superstition, cruelty, and
vice.   Incest and the diabolical custom of female infanticide
were common.   The eldest son inherited his father's widows,
as property, with the rest of the estate.   The worse than
inhuman fathers buried alive their infant daughters ; and this
crime, which was most rife among the tribes of Koreish and
Kinda, was regarded, as among the Hindu Rajpoots, a mark
of pride.   The idea of a future existence, and of retribution of
good and evil, were, as motives of human action, practically
unknown.   Only a few years before, such was the condition
of Arabia.   What a change had these few years witnessed !
The angel of heaven had veritably passed over the land, and
breathed harmony and love into the hearts of those who had
hitherto been engrossed in the most revolting practices of semi-
barbarism.   What had once been a moral desert, where all
laws, human and divine, were contemned and infringed without remorse, was now transformed into a garden.   Idolatry,
with its nameless abominations, was utterly destroyed.   Islâm
furnishes the only solitary example of a great religion which
though preached among a nation and reigning for the most part
among a people not yet emerged from the dawn of an early
civilisation, had succeeded in effectually restraining its votaries
from idolatry.   This phenomenon has been justly acknowledged as the pre-eminent glory of Islâm, and the most remarkable evidence of the genius of its Founder.   Long had
Christianity and Judaism tried to wean the Arab tribes from
their gross superstition, their inhuman practices, and their
licentious immorality.   But it was not till they heard " the
spirit-stirring strains " of the " Appointed of God " that they
became conscious of the God of Truth, overshadowing the
universe with His power and love.   Henceforth their aims are
not of this earth alone ; there is something beyond the grave—
higher, purer, and diviner—calling them to the practice of
charity, goodness, justice, and universal love.   God is not

merely the God of to-day or of to-morrow, carved out of wood or stone, but the mighty, loving, merciful Creator of the world. Mohammed was the source, under Providence, of this new awakening,—the bright fountain from which flowed the stream of their hopes of eternity ; and to him they paid a fitting obedience and reverence. They were all animated with one desire, namely, to serve God in truth and purity ; to obey His laws reverently in all the affairs of life. The truths and maxims, the precepts which, from time to time during the past twenty years, Mohammed had delivered to his followers, were embalmed in their hearts, and had become the ruling principles of every action. Law and morality were united. " Never, since the days when primitive Christianity startled the world from its sleep, and waged a mortal conflict with heathenism, had men seen the like arousing of spiritual life,—the like faith that suffered sacrifices, and took joyfully the spoiling of goods for conscience' sake." [1]

The Mission of Mohammed was now accomplished. And in this fact—the fact of the whole work being achieved in his lifetime—lies his distinctive superiority over the prophets, sages, and philosophers of other times and other countries. Jesus, Moses, Zoroaster, Sakya-Muni, Plato, all had their notions of realms of God, their republics, their ideas, through which degraded humanity was to be elevated into a new moral life ; all had departed from this world with their aspirations unfulfilled, their bright visions unrealised ; or had bequeathed the task of elevating their fellow-men to sanguinary disciples or monarch pupils. [2] It was reserved for Mohammed to fulfil his mission, and that of his predecessors. It was reserved for him alone to see accomplished the work of amelioration—no royal disciple came to his assistance with edicts to enforce the new teachings. May not the Moslems justly say, the entire work was the work of God ?

The humble preacher, who had only the other day been hunted out of the city of his birth, and been stoned out of the

[1] Muir, vol. ii. p. 269. Coming from an avowed enemy of Islâm, this observation is of the utmost value.

[2] A Joshua among the Israelites ; an Asoka among the Buddhists ; a Darius among the Zoroastrians ; a Constantine among the Christians.

place where he had betaken himself to preach God's words, had, within the short space of nine years, lifted up his people from the abysmal depths of moral and spiritual degradation to a conception of purity and justice.

His life is the noblest record of a work nobly and faithfully performed. He infused vitality into a dormant people ; he consolidated a congeries of warring tribes into a nation inspired into action with the hope of everlasting life ; he concentrated into a focus all the fragmentary and broken lights which had ever fallen on the heart of man. Such was his work, and he performed it with an enthusiasm and fervour which admitted no compromise, conceived no halting ; with indomitable courage which brooked no resistance, and allowed no fear of consequences ; with a singleness of purpose which thought of no self. The religion of divine unity preached on the shores of Galilee had given place to the worship of an incarnate God ; the old worship of a female deity had revived among those who professed the creed of the Master of Nazareth. The Recluse of Hirâ, the unlettered philosopher—born among a nation of unyielding idolaters—impressed ineffaceably the unity of God and the equality of men upon the minds of the nations who once heard his voice. His " democratic thunder " was the signal for the uprise of the human intellect against the tyranny of priests and rulers. In " that world of wrangling creeds and oppressive institutions," when the human soul was crushed under the weight of unintelligible dogmas, and the human body trampled under the tyranny of vested interests, he broke down the barriers of caste and exclusive privileges. He swept away with his breath the cobwebs which self-interest had woven in the path of man to God. He abolished all exclusiveness in man's relations to his Creator. This unlettered Prophet, whose message was for the masses, proclaimed the value of knowledge and learning. By the Pen, man's works are recorded. By the Pen, man is to be judged. The Pen is the ultimate arbiter of human actions in the sight of the Lord. His persistent and unvarying appeal to reason and to the ethical faculty of man-kind, his rejection of miracles, " his thoroughly democratic conception of divine government, the universality of his religious ideal, his simple humanity,"—all serve to differentiate him from his predecessors, " all affiliate him," says the author of *Oriental Religions*, " with the modern world." His life and work are not wrapt in mystery. No fairy tale has been woven round his personality.

When the hosts of Arabia came flocking to join his faith, the Prophet felt that his work was accomplished,[1] and under the impression of his approaching end, he determined to make a farewell pilgrimage to Mecca. On the 25th of Zu'l-Ka'da (23rd February 632), the Prophet left Medîna with an immense concourse of Moslems.[2] On his arrival at Mecca, and before completing all the rites of the pilgrimage, he addressed the assembled multitude from the top of the *Jabal ul-'Arafât* (8th Zu'l-Hijja, 7th March), in words which should ever live in the hearts of all Moslems.

" Ye people ! listen to my words, for I know not whether another year will be vouchsafed to me after this year to find myself amongst you at this place."

" Your lives and property are sacred and inviolable amongst one another until ye appear before the Lord, as this day and this month is sacred for all ; and (remember) ye shall have to appear before your Lord, who shall demand from you an account of all your actions. . . . Ye people, ye have rights over your wives, and your wives have rights over you. . . . Treat your wives with kindness and love. Verily ye have taken them on the security of God, and have made their persons lawful unto you by the words of God." " Keep always faithful to the trust reposed in you, and avoid sins." " Usury is forbidden.[3] The debtor shall return only the principal ; and the beginning will be made with (the loans of) my uncle Abbâs,

---

[1] Koran, sura cx.

[2] Ibn-Hishâm, p. 966 ; Ibn ul-Athîr, vol. ii. p. 230. It is said that from 90,000 to 140,000 people accompanied the Prophet. This pilgrimage is called the *Hajjat-al-Balâgh*, the Great *Hajj*, or *Hajjat-ul-Islâm*, the Hajj of Islâm, and sometimes *Hajjat-ul-Wadâ'a*, Pilgrimage of Farewell.

[3] *Ribâ* or interest in kind was prohibited but not legitimate profit on advances or loans for purposes of business or trade. No one who realises the economic condition of Arabia can fail to appreciate the wisdom of this rule. In fact the same reasons which impelled the great Prophet to forbid usury in his country, induced the Christian divines, up to nearly the end of the seventeenth century of the Christian era, to anathematise against usury. The elder Disraeli's chapter on this subject in his *Curiosities of Literature* is most interesting.

son of Abd ul-Muttalib.[1] . . . Henceforth the vengeance of blood practised in the days of paganism (*Jáhilyat*) is prohibited; and all blood-feud abolished, commencing with the murder of Ibn Rabí'a [2] son of Hârith son of Abd ul-Muttalib . . .

" And your slaves! See that ye feed them with such food as ye eat yourselves, and clothe them with the stuff ye wear; and if they commit a fault which ye are not inclined to forgive, then part from them, for they are the servants of the Lord, and are not to be harshly treated."

" Ye people! listen to my words and understand the same. Know *that all Moslems are brothers unto one another.* Ye are one brotherhood. Nothing which belongs to another is lawful unto his brother, unless freely given out of good-will. Guard yourselves from committing injustice."

" Let him that is present tell it unto him that is absent. Haply he that shall be told may remember better than he who hath heard it." [3]

This Sermon on the Mount, less poetically beautiful, certainly less mystical, than the other, appeals by its practicality and strong common-sense to higher minds, and is also adapted to the capacity and demands of inferior natures which require positive and comprehensible directions for moral guidance.

Towards the conclusion of the sermon, the Prophet, overcome by the sight of the intense enthusiasm of the people as they drank in his words, exclaimed, " O Lord! I have delivered my message and accomplished my work." The assembled host below with one voice cried, " Yea, verily thou hast." " O Lord, I beseech Thee, bear Thou witness unto it."

With these words the Prophet finished his address, which, according to the traditions, was remarkable for its length, its eloquence, and enthusiasm. Soon after, the necessary rites of

[1] This shows that Abbâs must have been a rich man. In the application of the rule against *Ribá* and blood-feud, the Prophet set to his fiery people the example of self-denial in his own family.

[2] Ibn Rabí'a, a cousin of the Prophet. He was confided, in his infancy, to the care of a family of the Banî Laith. This child was cruelly murdered by members of the tribe of Huzail, but the murder was not yet avenged.

[3] After each sentence the Prophet stopped and his words were repeated in a stentorian voice by Rabí'a, the son of Ommeyya, son of Khalaf, who stood below, so that whatever was said was heard by the entire assembled host.

the pilgrimage being finished, the Prophet returned with his followers to Medîna.[1]

The last year of Mohammed's life was spent in that city.   He settled the organisation of the provinces and tribal communities which had adopted Islâm and become the component parts of the Moslem federation.   In fact, though the Faith had not penetrated among the Arab races settled in Syria and Mesopotamia, most of whom were Christians, the whole of Arabia now followed the Islâmic Faith.   Officers were sent to the provinces and to the various tribes for the purpose of teaching the people the duties of Islâm, administering justice, and collecting the tithes or *zakât*.   Mu'âz ibn-Jabal was sent to Yemen, and Mohammed's parting injunction to him was to rely on his own judgment in the administration of affairs in the event of not finding any authority in the Koran.   To Ali, whom he deputed to Yemâma, he said, " When two parties come before you for justice, do not decide before hearing both."

11 A. H. 29th March 632 to 18th March 633 A.C.

Preparations were also commenced for sending an expedition under Osâma, the son of Zaid, who was killed at Mûta, against the Byzantines to exact the long-delayed reparation for the murder of the envoy in Syria.   In fact, the troops were already encamped outside the city ready for the start.   But the poison which had been given to the Prophet by the Jewess at Khaibar, and which had slowly penetrated into his system, began now to show its effects, and it became evident that he had not long to live.   The news of his approaching end led to the stoppage of the expedition under Osâma.   It had also the effect of producing disorder in some of the outlying provinces.   Three pretenders started up claiming divine commission for their reign of licentiousness and plunder.   They gave themselves out as prophets, and tried by all kinds of imposture to win over their tribes.   One of these, the most dangerous of all, was Ayhala ibn-Ka'b, better known as al-Aswad (the black).   He

---

[1] Abdullâh the son of Ubayy, the head of the *Munâfikîn*, died in the month of Zu'l Ka'da (February, 631 A.C.).   In his last moments he solicited the Prophet to say the funeral prayers over him.   Mohammed, who never rejected the wishes of a dying man, against the remonstrances of Omar, who reminded him of the persistent opposition and calumny of Abdullâh, offered the prayers and with his own hands lowered the body into the grave.

was a chief of Yemen, a man of great wealth and equal sagacity, and a clever conjuror. Among his simple tribesmen, the conjuring tricks he performed invested him with a divine character. He soon succeeded in gaining them over, and, with their help, reduced to subjection many of the neighbouring towns. He killed Shahr, who had been appointed by Mohammed to the governorship of Sanâ' in the place of Bâzân, his father, who had just died. Bâzân had been the viceroy of Yemen under the Chosroes of Persia, and after his adoption of Islâm was continued in his viceroyalty by the Prophet. He had during his lifetime exercised great influence, not only over his Persian compatriots settled in Yemen, who were called by the name of *Abnâ*, but also over the Arabs of the province. His example had led to the conversion of all the Persian settlers of Yemen. Al-Aswad, the impostor, had massacred Shahr, and forcibly married his wife Marzbâna. He was killed by the *Abnâ*, assisted by Marzbâna, when he was lying drunk, after one of his orgies. The other two pretenders, Tulaiha, son of Khuwailid, and Abû Thumama Hârân, son of Habîb, commonly called Mosailima, were not suppressed until the accession of Abû Bakr to the Caliphate. Mosailima had the audacity to address the Prophet in the following terms : " From Mosailima, prophet of God, to Mohammed, prophet of God, salutations ! I am your partner : the power must be divided between us : half the earth for me, the other half for your Koreishites. But the Koreishites are a grasping people, not given to justice." Mohammed's reply reveals his sterling nature. " In the name of God the merciful and compassionate, from Mohammed, the Prophet of God, to Mosailima the Liar.[1] Peace is on those who follow the right path. The earth belongs to God ; He bestows it on such of His servants as He pleaseth. The future is to the pious [*i.e.* only those prosper who fear the Lord] ! "

The last days of the Prophet were remarkable for the calmness and serenity of his mind, which enabled him, though weak and feeble, to preside at the public prayers until within three days of his death. One night, at midnight, he went to the place where his old companions were lying in the slumber of death, and prayed and wept by their tombs, invoking God's

---

[1] *Kazzâb*, superlative of *Kâzib*.

blessings for his " companions resting in peace." He chose
'Âyesha's house, close to the mosque, for his stay during his
illness, and, as long as his strength lasted, took part in the
public prayers. The last time he appeared in the mosque he
was supported by his two cousins, Ali and Fazl, the son of
Abbâs. A smile of inexpressible sweetness played over his
countenance, and was remarked by all who surrounded him.
After the usual praises and hymns to God, he addressed the
multitude thus : " Moslems, if I have wronged any one of you,
here I am to answer for it ; if I owe aught to any one, all I may
happen to possess belongs to you." Upon hearing this, a man
in the crowd rose and claimed three dirhems which he had
given to a poor man at the Prophet's request. They were
immediately paid back, with the words, " Better to blush in
this world than in the next." The Prophet then prayed and
implored heaven's mercy for those present, and for those who
had fallen in the persecutions of their enemies ; and recommended to all his people the observance of religious duties
and the practice of a life of peace and good-will, and concluded
with the following words of the Koran : " The dwelling of the
other life we will give unto them who do not seek to exalt
themselves on earth or to do wrong ; for the happy issue shall
attend the pious." [1]

After this, Mohammed never again appeared at public
prayers. His strength rapidly failed. At noon on Monday
(12th of Rabi I., 11 A.H.—8th June 632 A.C.), whilst praying
earnestly in whisper, the spirit of the great Prophet took flight
to the " blessed companionship on high." [2]

So ended a life consecrated, from first to last, to the service
of God and humanity. Is there another to be compared to
his, with all its trials and temptations ? Is there another which
has stood the fire of the world, and come out so unscathed ?
The humble preacher had risen to be the ruler of Arabia, the
equal of Chosroes and of Cæsar, the arbiter of the destinies of
a nation. But the same humility of spirit, the same nobility

[1] Koran, sura xxviii. ver. 83 ; Ibn ul-Athîr, vol. ii. p. 241 ; Tabari, vol. iii.
p. 207 et seq.

[2] Ibn-Hishâm, p. 1009 ; Ibn ul-Athîr, vol. ii. pp. 244, 245 ; Abulfedâ, p. 91.
Comp. Caussin de Perceval, vol. iii. p. 322 and note ; al-Halabi, in loco.

of soul and purity of heart, austerity of conduct, refinement
and delicacy of feeling, and stern devotion to duty which had
won him the title of al-Amîn, combined with a severe sense of
self-examination, are ever the distinguishing traits of his
character.   Once in his life, whilst engaged in a religious conversation with an influential citizen of Mecca, he had turned
away from a humble blind seeker of the truth.   He is always
recurring to this incident with remorse, and proclaiming God's
disapprobation.[1]   A nature so pure, so tender, and yet so
heroic, inspires not only reverence, but love.   And naturally
the Arabian writers dwell with the proudest satisfaction on the
graces and intellectual gifts of the son of Abdullâh.   His
courteousness to the great, his affability to the humble, and
his dignified bearing to the presumptuous, procured him
universal respect and admiration.   His countenance reflected
the benevolence of his heart.   Profoundly read in the volume
of nature, though ignorant of letters, with an expansive mind,
elevated by deep communion with the Soul of the Universe, he
was gifted with the power of influencing equally the learned
and the unlearned.   Withal, there was a majesty in his face,
an air of genius, which inspired all who came in contact with
him with a feeling of veneration and love.[2]

His singular elevation of mind, his extreme delicacy and
refinement of feeling, his purity and truth, form the constant
theme of the traditions.   He was most indulgent to his inferiors,

[1] The Sura in connection with this incident is known by the title of " He
frowned," and runs thus :—

"The Prophet frowned, and turned aside,
Because the blind man came to him.
And how knowest thou whether he might not have been cleansed from
his sins.
Or whether he might have been admonished, and profited thereby ?
As for the man that is rich,
Him thou receivest graciously ;
And thou carest not that he is not cleansed.
But as for him that cometh unto thee earnestly seeking his salvation,
And trembling anxiously, him dost thou neglect.
By no means shouldst thou act thus."

After this, whenever the Prophet saw the poor blind man, he used to go
out of his way to do him honour, saying, " The man is thrice welcome on
whose account my Lord hath reprimanded me " ; and he made him twice
governor of Medîna.   See the remark of Bosworth Smith on Muir about this
incident.

[2] *Mishkât*, Bk. xxiv. chap. 3, pt. 2.

and would never allow his awkward little page to be scolded
whatever he did. " Ten years," said Anas, his servant, " was
I about the Prophet, and he never said so much as ' Uff ' to
me." [1] He was very affectionate towards his family. One of
his boys died on his breast in the smoky house of the nurse, a
blacksmith's wife. He was very fond of children. He would
stop them in the streets, and pat their little cheeks. He never
struck any one in his life. The worst expression he ever made
use of in conversation was, " What has come to him ? May
his forehead be darkened with mud ! " [2] When asked to curse
some one, he replied, " I have not been sent to curse, but to
be a mercy to mankind."

He visited the sick, followed every bier he met, accepted the
invitation of a slave to dinner, mended his own clothes, milked
his goats, and waited upon himself, relates summarily another
tradition.[3] He never first withdrew his hand from another's
palm, and turned not before the other had turned. His hand
was the most generous, his breast the most courageous, his
tongue the most truthful ; he was the most faithful protector
of those he protected ; the sweetest and most agreeable in

---

[1] *Ibid.* Bk. xxiv. chap. 4, pt. 1.

[2] *Ibid.* Bk. xxiv. chap. 4, pt. 1.

Mr. Poole's estimate of Mohammed is so beautiful and yet so truthful that
I cannot resist the temptation to quote it here : " There is something so
tender and womanly, and withal so heroic, about the man, that one is in peril
of finding the judgment unconsciously blinded by the feeling of reverence and
well-nigh love that such a nature inspires. He who, standing alone braved
for years the hatred of his people, is the same who was never the first to withdraw his hand from another's clasp ; the beloved of children, who never passed
a group of little ones without a smile from his wonderful eyes and a kind word
for them, sounding all the kinder in that sweet-toned voice. The frank friendship, the noble generosity, the dauntless courage and hope of the man, all
tend to melt criticism into admiration."

" He was an enthusiast in that noblest sense when enthusiasm becomes the
salt of the earth, the one thing that keeps men from rotting whilst they live.
Enthusiasm is often used despitefully, because it is joined to an unworthy
cause, or falls upon barren ground and bears no fruit. So was it not with
Mohammed. He was an enthusiast when enthusiasm was the one thing
needed to set the world aflame, and his enthusiasm was noble for a noble cause.
He was one of those happy few who have attained the supreme joy of making
one great truth their very life-spring. He was the messenger of the one God ;
and never to his life's end did he forget who he was, or the message which was
the marrow of his being. He brought his tidings to his people with a grand
dignity sprung from the consciousness of his high office, together with a most
sweet humility, whose roots lay in the knowledge of his own weakness."

[3] *Mishkât*, Bk. xxiv. chap. 4, pt. 2.

conversation ; those who saw him were suddenly filled with
reverence ; those who came near him loved him ; they who
described him would say, " I have never seen his like, either
before or after." He was of great taciturnity ; and when he
spoke, he spoke with emphasis and deliberation, and no one
could ever forget what he said. " Modesty and kindness,
patience, self-denial, and generosity pervaded his conduct, and
riveted the affections of all around him. With the bereaved
and afflicted he sympathised tenderly . . . He shared his food
even in times of scarcity with others, and was sedulously
solicitous for the personal comfort of every one about him."
He would stop in the streets listening to the sorrows of the
humblest. He would go to the houses of the lowliest to
console the afflicted and to comfort the heart-broken. The
meanest slaves would take hold of his hand and drag him to
their masters to obtain redress for ill-treatment or release from
bondage.[1] He never sat down to a meal without first invoking
a blessing, and never rose without uttering a thanks-giving.
His time was regularly apportioned. During the day, when
not engaged in prayers, he received visitors and transacted
public affairs. At night he slept little, spending most of the
hours in devotion. He loved the poor and respected them,
and many who had no home or shelter of their own slept at
night in the mosque contiguous to his house. Each evening it
was his custom to invite some of them to partake of his humble
fare. The others became the guests of his principal disciples.[2]
His conduct towards the bitterest of his enemies was marked
by a noble clemency and forbearance. Stern, almost to
severity, to the enemies of the State, mockings, affronts,
outrages, and persecutions towards himself were, in the hour
of triumph—synonymous with the hour of trial to the human
heart—all buried in oblivion, and forgiveness was extended to
the worst criminal.

Mohammed was extremely simple in his habits. His mode
of life, his dress and his belongings, retained to the very last a
character of patriarchal simplicity. Many a time, Abû Huraira
reports, had the Prophet to go without a meal. Dates and

---

[1] *Hayat-ul-Kulûb* (Shiah) and the *Rouzat-ul-Ahbab* (Sunni).
[2] Abulfedâ, p. 99 ; al-Halabi, *Insân ul-'Uyûn*, vol. iii. p. 362.

water frequently formed his only nourishment. Often, for months together, no fire could be lighted in his house from scantiness of means. God, say the Moslem historians, had indeed put before him the key to the treasures of this world, but he refused it !

The mind of this remarkable Teacher was, in its intellectualism and progressive ideals, essentially modern. Eternal " striving " was in his teachings a necessity of human existence : " Man cannot exist without constant effort " ; [1] " The effort is from me, its fulfilment comes from God." [2] The world, he taught, was a well-ordered Creation, regulated and guided by a Supreme Intelligence overshadowing the Universe—" Everything is pledged to its own time," [3] he declared. And yet human will was free to work for its own salvation. His sympathy was universal ; it was he who invoked the mercy of the Creator on all living beings.[4] It was he who pronounced the saving of one human life as tantamount to the saving of humanity.

His social conception was constructive not disintegrating. In his most exalted mood he never overlooked the sanctity of family life. To him the service of humanity was the highest act of devotion. His call to his faithful was not to forsake those to whom they owed a duty ; but in the performance of that duty to earn " merit " and reward. Children were a trust from God, to be brought up in tenderness and affection ; parents were to be respected and loved. The circle of duty embraced in its fold kindred, neighbour, and the humble being " whose mouth was in the dust."

Fourteen centuries have passed since he delivered his message, but time has made no difference in the devotion he inspired, and to-day as then the Faithful have in their hearts and on their lips those memorable words :—

مـروبحی فـداك يـارسـول اللّٰه

" May my life be thy sacrifice, O Prophet of God."

[1] لَيْسَ لِلْاِنْسَانِ اِلَّا مَا سَعٰى   [2] اَلسَّعْىُ مِنِّى وَ الْاِتْمَامُ مِنَ اللّٰه

[3] كُلُّ اُمَّةٍ صَدْحُونَ بِأَذْقَانِهِ   [4] رَحْمَةً لِلْعَالَمِين

CHAPTER X

THE APOSTOLICAL SUCCESSION

وَٱعْتَصِمُوا بِحَبْلِ ٱللَّهِ جَمِيعًا وَ لَا تَفَرَّقُوا

THE spiritual life the Prophet had infused into his people did not end with his life. From the first it was an article of faith that he was present in spirit with the worshippers at their prayers, and that his successors in the ministry were his representatives. The immanence of the Master's spirit during the devotions establishes the harmony between the soul of man and the Divine Essence. Amongst all the dynastic rivalries and schismatic strife this mystical conception of his spiritual presence at the prayers has imparted a force to the Faith which cannot be over-estimated.

The two great sects into which Islâm became divided at an early stage are agreed that the religious efficacy of the rites and duties prescribed by the Law (*the Shari'at*) depends on the existence of the vice-gerent and representative of the Prophet, who, as such, is the religious Head (*Imâm*) of the Faith and the Faithful.

The adherents of the Apostolical Imâms have a development and philosophy of their own quite distinct from " the followers of the traditions." According to them the spiritual heritage bequeathed by the Prophet devolved on Ali and his descendants by Fâtima, the Prophet's daughter. They hold that the Imâmate descends by Divine appointment in the apostolic line. They do not regard the Pontificate of Abû Bakr, Omar and Osman as rightful ; they consider that Ali, who was indicated by the Prophet as his successor, was the first rightful

Caliph and Imâm of the Faithful, and that after his assassination the spiritual headship descended in succession to his and Fâtima's posterity in " the direct male line " until it came to Imâm Hasan al-'Askari, eleventh in descent from Ali, who died in the year 874 A.C. or 260 of the Hegira in the reign of the Abbaside Caliph Mu'tamid. Upon his death the Imâmate devolved upon his son Mohammed, surnamed *al-Mahdi* (the " Guide "), the last Imâm. The story of these Imâms of the House of Mohammed is intensely pathetic. The father of Hasan was deported from Medîna to Sâmarra by the tyrant Mutawakkil, and detained there until his death. Similarly, Hasan was kept a prisoner by the jealousy of Mutawakkil's successors. His infant son, barely five years of age, pining for his father, entered in search of him a cavern not far from their house. From that cavern the child never returned. The pathos of this calamity culminated in the hope, the expectation, which fills the hearts of all Shiahs, that the child may return to relieve a sorrowing and sinful world of its burden of sin and oppression. So late as the fourteenth century of the Christian era, when Ibni Khaldûn [1] was writing his great work, the Shiahs were wont to assemble at eventide at the entrance of the cavern and supplicate the missing child to return to them. After a long and wistful waiting, they dispersed to their homes, disappointed and sorrowful. This, says Ibn Khaldûn, was a daily occurrence. " When they were told it was hardly possible the child could be alive," they answered that, " as the Prophet Khizr [2] was alive why should not their Imâm be alive also ? " This Imâm bears among the Shiahs the titles, the *Muntazar*, the Expected—the *Hujja* or the Proof (of the Truth), and the *Kâim*, the Living.

The philosophical student of religions will not fail to observe the strange similarity of the Shiah and the Sunni beliefs to older ideas. Among the Zoroastrians the persecution of the Seleucidæ engendered the belief that a divinely appointed Saviour, whose name was Sosiosch, would issue from Khorasân to release them from the hated bondage of the foreigner. The same causes gave birth to that burning anticipation

[1] See *post*, p. 126.   [2] See Appendix III.

among the Jews in the, advent of the Messiah. The Jew
believes that the Messiah is yet to come ; the Sunni, like him,
believes that the Saviour of Islâm is still unborn. The
Christian believes that the Messiah has come and gone, and
will come again ; the Asna-'asharia,[1] like the Christian, awaits
the reappearance of the *Mahdi*, the Guide, who is to save the
world from evil and oppression. The origin of these conceptions
and the reasons of their diversity are traceable to like causes.
The phenomena of the age in which the idea of the *Mahdi*
took shape in its two distinct forms were similar to those
visible in the history of the older faiths. Every eventide
the prayer goes up to heaven in Islâm, as in Judaism and
Christianity, for the advent of the divinely-appointed Guide,
to redeem the world from sorrow and sin.

The Shiah believes that the Imâm though *ghâib* (absent),
is always present in spirit at the devotions of his fold. The
expounders of the law and the ministers of religion are his
representatives on earth ; and even the secular chiefs represent
him in the temporal affairs of the world. Another point of
difference between them and the Sunnis consists in the qualities
required for the Imâmate. According to the Shiahs. the
Imâm must be sinless or immaculate (*m'asûm*), a quality which
their Imâms alone possess, and that he must be the most excellent (*afzal*) of mankind.

The Sunni doctrines which govern the lives, thoughts, and
conduct of the bulk of the Moslem world are diametrically
opposed to the Shiah conception. The Sunni religious law
insists that the Imâm must be actually present in person to
impart religious efficacy to the devotions of the Faithful ;
and that, where it is not possible for him to lead the prayers,
he should be represented by persons possessing the necessary
qualifications.

These doctrines are enunciated in detail in most works on
jurisprudence and scholastic theology. The *Khilâfat*, it is
explained, is the Vice-gerency of the Prophet ; it is ordained
by Divine Law for the perpetuation of Islâm and the continued
observance of its laws and rules. For the existence of Islâm,
therefore, there must always be a Caliph, an actual and direct

representative of the Master. The Imâmate is the spiritual leadership ; but the two dignities are inseparable ; the Vice-gerent of the Prophet is the only person entitled to lead the prayers when he can himself be present. No one else can assume his functions unless directly or indirectly " deputed " by him. Between the Imâm and the *mâmûm* [1] or congregation, there is a spiritual tie which binds the one to the other in the fealty to the Faith. There is no inconsistency between this dogma and the rule that there is no priesthood in Islâm. Each man pleads for himself before his Lord, and each soul holds communion with God without the intermediation of any other human being. The Imâm is the link between the individual worshipper and the evangel of Islâm. This mystical element in the religion of Islâm forms the foundation of its remarkable solidarity.

The above remarks serve to emphasise the statement in the *Durr-ul-Mukhtâr* that Imâmate is of two kinds, the *Imâmat-al-Kubrâ* and the *Imâmat-as-Sughrâ*, the supreme spiritual Headship and the minor derivative right to officiate at the devotions of the Faithful. The *Imâm al-Kabîr*, the supreme Pontiff, is the Caliph of the Sunni world. He combines in his person the spiritual and temporal authority which devolves on him as the vicegerent of the Master. Secular affairs are conducted by him in consultation with councillors as under the first four Caliphs, or, as in later times, by delegates, collect-ively or individually. Similarly with religious and spiritual matters. But in the matter of public prayers, unless physically prostrate, he is bound to conduct the congregational service in person.

Among the Shiahs, even Friday prayers and prayers offered at the well-known festivals, may validly be performed indi-vidually and in private. According to the Sunni doctrines congregational prayers, where mosques or other places of public worship are accessible, are obligatory ; abstention from attendance without valid reason is a sin, and the defaulters incur even temporal penalties. In Najd, under the rule of the Wahâbis, who have been called the Covenanters of Islâm,

---

[1] This is the term used in the *Fatâwai-Alamgiri.* The individual follower is usually called the *Muktadi.*

laggards were whipped into the mosque. And to-day under
Ibni S'aûd, his followers who designate themselves *Ikhwân*, or
" Brothers in faith," pursue the same method for enforcing
the observance of religious rites. Prayers *bi'l jamâ'at* being
obligatory (*farz'ain*) naturally made the presence of the Imâm
absolutely obligatory.[1]

The Sunnis affirm that when stricken by his last illness the
Prophet deputed Abû Bakr to lead the prayers. On his
death, but before he was consigned to his grave, the Master's
nomination was accepted by the " congregation " and Abû
Bakr was installed as his vicegerent by the unanimous suffrage
of the Moslems. And this has ever since been the universal
practice in all regular lines.

Amongst the qualifications necessary for occupying the
pontifical seat, the first and most essential is that he must
be a Moslem belonging to the Sunni communion, capable of
exercising supreme temporal authority, free of all outside
control. The Sunnis do not require that the Imâm should
be *ma'sûm*, or that he should be " the most excellent
of mankind," nor do they insist on his descent from the
Prophet. According to them he should be an independent
ruler, without any personal defects, a man of good character,
possessed of the capacity to conduct the affairs of State, and to
lead at prayers. The early doctors, on the authority of a saying
of the Prophet, have included a condition which comes at the
end of the passage relating to the qualities necessary for the
Imâmate—viz., that the Caliph-Imâm should be a Koreish by
birth. The avowed object of inserting this condition, as is stated
both in the *Durr-ul-Mukhtâr* and the *Radd-ul-Muhtâr*, was to
nullify the Shiah contention that the Imâmate was restricted
to the House of Mohammed, the descendants of Ali and Fâtima,
and to bring in the first three Caliphs, and the Ommeyyade
and the Abbaside Caliphs, into the circle of legitimate Imâms.
The great jurist and historian, Ibn Khaldûn,[2] a contemporary
of Tamerlane, who died in the year 1406 A.C., long before the

[1] There is absolute consensus on these points among the different Sunni
schools. The Jurist Khalil ibn Ishâk, the author of the monumental work
on Mâliki Law, enunciates the rules in the same terms as the Hanafis and
the Shâfeïs.

[2] For many years Mâlikite Chief Kâzi of Cairo.

House of Othman attained the Caliphate, has dealt at great
length with this condition in his *Mukaddamât* (Prolegomena).
He does not dispute the genuineness of the saying on which
it is based, but explains that it was a mere recommendation
which was due to the circumstances of the times.   He points
out that when the Islâmic Dispensation was given to the world
the tribe of Koreish were the most advanced and most powerful
in Arabia ; and in recommending or desiring that the temporal
and spiritual guardianship of the Moslems should be confined
to a member of his own tribe, the Prophet was thinking of the
immediate future rather than of laying down a hard and fast
rule of succession.   At that time a qualified and capable ruler
of Islâm could only be found among the Koreish ; hence the
recommendation that the Caliph and Imâm should be chosen
from among them.   This view eloquently expressed by one of
the most learned of Sunni Jurisconsults is universally accepted
by the modern doctors (the *Mutâkherîn*), that subject to the
fulfilment of all other conditions the law imposes no tribal or
racial restriction in the choice of an Imâm.   Abû Bakr before
his death had nominated Omar his successor in the Vice-
gerency, and the appointment was accepted by the " universality " of the people, including the House of Mohammed.
Omar died from the effects of a mortal wound inflicted on
him by a Christian or Magian fanatic who considered himself
aggrieved by the acts of this great Caliph.   To avoid all
imputation of favouritism Omar had, before his death,
appointed an electoral committee consisting of six eminent
members of the Moslem congregation to choose his successor.
Their choice fell on Osmân, a descendant of Ommeyya, who
was installed as Caliph with the suffrage of the people.   On
Osmân's unhappy death, Ali, the son-in-law of the Prophet,
who, according to the Shiahs, was entitled by right to the
Imâmate in direct succession to the Prophet, was proclaimed
Caliph and Imâm.   The husband of Fâtima united in his
person the hereditary right with that of election.   But his
endeavour to remedy the evils which had crept into the
administration under his aged predecessor raised against him
a host of enemies.   Mu'âwiyah, an Ommeyyade by descent,
who held the governorship of Syria under Osmân, raised the

standard of revolt. Ali proceeded to crush the rebellion but, after an indecisive battle, was struck down by the hand of an assassin whilst at his devotions in the public Mosque of Kûfa in 'Irak. With 'Ali ended what is called by the early Sunni doctors of law and theologians, the *Khilâfat-al-Kâmila*, " the Perfect Caliphate," for in each case their title to the rulership of Islâm was perfected by the universal suffrage of the Moslem nation.

On Ali's death Mu'âwiyah obtained an assignment of the Caliphate from Hasan, the eldest son of Ali, who had been elected to the office by the unanimous voice of the people of Kûfa and its dependencies ; and received the suffrage of the people of Syria to his assumption of the high office. This happened in 661 A.C.

It should be noted here that the Ommeyyades and Hâshimides were two offshoots from one common stock, that of Koreish. Bitter rivalry existed between these families which it was the great aim of the Prophet throughout his ministry to remove or reconcile. The Hâshimides owe their designation to Hâshim, the great grandfather of the Prophet. His son Abdul Muttalib had several sons ; one of them, Abbâs, was the progenitor of the Abbâside Caliphs. Abû Talib, another son, was the father of Ali the Caliph, whilst the youngest, Abdullah, was the Prophet's father.

Mu'âwiyah was the first Caliph of the House of Ommeyya. On the death of Mu'âwiyah's grandson, another member of the same family belonging to the Hakamite branch, named Merwân, assumed the Caliphate. Under his son 'Abdul Malik and grandson Walîd, the Sunni Caliphate attained its widest expansion ; it extended from the Atlantic to the Indian Ocean and from the Tagus to the sands of the Sahara and the confines of Abyssinia. In 749 A.C. Abu'l Abbâs, surnamed Saffâh, a descendant of Abbâs, the uncle of the Prophet, overthrew the Ommeyyade dynasty and was installed as Caliph, in place of Merwân II., the last Pontiff of that House, in the Cathedral Mosque of Kûfa, where he received the *Bai'at* [1] of the people. He then ascended the pulpit, recited the public sermon which the Imâm or his representative delivers at the public prayers.

---

[1] The sacramental oath of fealty.

This notable address, religiously preserved by his successors, is to be found in the pages of the Arab historian Ibn-ul-Athîr. It is in effect a long vindication of the rights of the children of Abbâs to the Caliphate. Abu'l Abbâs was henceforth the legitimate ruler of the Sunni world and the rightful spiritual Head of the Sunni Church. His first six successors were men of remarkable ability ; those who followed were of varying capacity, but a few possessed uncommon talent and learning. Mansûr, the brother of Saffâh, who succeeded him in the Caliphate, founded Bagdad, which became their capital and seat of Government, and was usually called the *Dâr-ul-Khilâfat* and the *Dâr-us-salâm*, " The Abode of the Caliphate " and " The Abode of Peace." Here the house of Abbâs exercised undisputed spiritual and temporal authority for centuries. Their great rivals of Cairo became extinct in Saladin's time ; the brilliant Ommeyyade dynasty of Cordova disappeared in the first decade of the eleventh century. The Almohades, the Almoravides, and the many Berber and Arab dynasties which, on the decline of the Almoravides, followed each other in succession in Morocco, had no valid title to the headship of the Sunni Church. The right of the Abbâsides to the Sunni Imâmate stood unchallenged from the Atlantic to the Ganges, from the Black Sea and the Jaxartes to the Indian Ocean. In 493 of the Hegira (1099 A.C.) Yusuf bin Tâshfin, the Almohade conqueror after the epoch-making battle of az-Zallâka, where the Christian hordes were decisively beaten, obtained from the Abbâside Caliph al-Muktadi, a formal investiture with the title of *Ameer-al-Muslimin* ; and this was confirmed to him by the Caliph al-Mustazhir. It should be borne in mind that neither the " Caliphs " of Cordova nor any of the Moslem sovereigns in after ages assumed the dignity of the representative of the Prophet (*Khalîfat-ar-Rasûl*) or arrogated the title of *Ameer-ul-Mominin*.

For full five centuries Bagdad was the centre of all intellectual activity in Islâm ; and here the rules and regulations appertaining to the Caliphate, as also to other matters, secular and religious, were systematised. And the conception that the Caliph-Imâm was the divinely-appointed Vice-gerent of the Prophet became, as it is to-day, welded into the religious life of the people. It will thus be seen that according to the Sunni doctrines the Caliph is not merely a secular sovereign ; he is the religious head of a Church and a commonwealth, the actual representative of Divine government.[1]

The Abbâside Caliphate lasted for five centuries from its first establishment until the destruction of Bagdad by the Mongols in 1258 of the Christian era. At that time Musta'sim b'Illah was the Caliph, and he, together with his sons and the principal members of his family, perished in the general massacre ; only those scions of the House of Abbâs escaped the slaughter who were absent from the capital, or succeeded in avoiding detection.

For two years after the murder of Musta'sim b'Illah the Sunni world felt acutely the need of an Imâm and Caliph ; both the poignancy of the grief at the absence of a spiritual Head of the Faith, and the keenness of the necessity for a representative of the Prophet to bring solace and religious merit to the Faithful, are pathetically voiced by the Arab historian of the Caliphs.[2] The devotions of the living were devoid of that religious efficacy which is imparted to them by the presence in the world of an acknowledged Imâm ; the prayers for the dead were equally without merit. Sultan Baibars felt with the whole Sunni world the need of a Caliph and Imâm. The right to the Caliphate had become vested by five centuries of undisputed acknowledgment in the House of Abbâs ; and a member of this family, Abu'l Kâsim Ahmed, who had succeeded in making his escape from the massacre by the Mongols, was invited to Cairo for installation in the pontifical seat. On his arrival in the environs of Cairo, the Sultan, accompanied by the judges and great officers of State, went forth to greet him. The ceremony of installation is described as imposing and sacred. His descent had to be proved first before the Chief Kazi or Judge. After this was done, he was installed in the chair and acknowledged as Caliph, under the title of al-Mustansir b'Illah, " Seeking the help of the Lord." The first to take the oath of *Bai'at* was the Sultan Baibars himself ; next came the Chief Kâzi Taj-ud-din, the principal sheikhs and the ministers of State, and lastly the

[1] Suyûti.   [2] *Ibid.*

nobles, according to their rank. This occurred on May 12th, 1261, and the new Caliph's name was impressed on the coinage and recited in the Khutba. On the following Friday he rode to the mosque in procession, wearing the black mantle of the Abbâsides,[1] and delivered the pontifical sermon. As his installation as the Caliph of the Faithful was now complete, he proceeded to invest the Sultan with the robe and diploma so essential in the eyes of the orthodox for legitimate authority.

The Abbâside Caliphate thus established in Cairo lasted for over two centuries and a-half. During this period Egypt was ruled by sovereigns who are designated in history as the Mameluke Sultans. Each Sultan on his accession to power received his investiture from the Caliph and " Imâm of his time " (*Imâm-ul-Wakt*) and he professed to exercise his authority as the lieutenant and delegate of the Pontiff. The appointment of ministers of religion and administrators of justice was subject to the formal sanction of the Caliph. Though shorn of all its temporal powers, the religious prestige of the Caliphate was so great, and the conviction of its necessity as a factor in the life of the people so deep-rooted in the religious sentiments of the Sunni world, that twice after the fall of Bagdad the Musulman sovereigns of India received their investiture from the Abbâside Caliphs. The account of the reception in 1343 A.C. of the Caliph's envoy by Sultan Mohammed Juna Khan Tughlak, the founder of the gigantic unfinished city of Tughlakabad, gives us an idea of the veneration in which the Pontiffs were held even in Hindustan, in those days said to be full six months' journey from Egypt. On the approach of the envoy the King, accompanied by the Syeds and the nobles, went out of the capital to greet him ; and when the Pontiff's missive was handed to the Sultan he received it with the greatest reverence. The formal diploma of investiture legitimised the authority of the King. The whole of this incident is celebrated in a poem still extant in India by the poet laureate, the famous Badr-ud-din Châch.

---

[1] Black was the colour of the Abbâsides, white of the Ommeyyades and green of the Fatimides, the descendants of Mohammed.

About the end of the fifteenth century the star of Selim I., also surnamed Saffâh, of the House of Othman, rose in the horizon. His victories over the enemies of Islâm had won for him the title of " Champion of the Faith " ; and no other Moslem sovereign—not even his great rival Shah Isma'îl, the founder of the Sûfi dynasty in Persia and the creator of the first orthodox Shiah State,—equalled the Osmanli monarch in greatness and power.

The closing decades of that century had witnessed a vast change in the condition of Egypt, and the anarchy that had set in under the later Mameluke Sultans reached its climax some years later. Invited by a section of the Egyptian people to restore order and peace in the distracted country, Selim easily overthrew the incompetent Mamelukes, and incorporated Egypt with his already vast dominions. At this period the Caliph who held the Vice-gerency of the Prophet bore the pontifical name of Al-Mutawakkil 'alâ-Allâh (" Contented in the grace of the Lord "). According to the Sunni records, he perceived that the only Moslem sovereign who could combine in his own person the double functions of Caliph and Imâm, and restore the Caliphate of Islâm in theory and in fact, and discharge effectively the duties attached to that office, was Selim. He accordingly, in 1517, by a formal deed of assignment, transferred the Caliphate to the Ottoman conqueror, and, with his officials and dignitaries, " made the Bai'at on the hand of the Sultan." In the same year Selim received the homage of the Sharîf of Mecca, Mohammed Abu'l Barakât, a descendant of Ali, who presented by his son Abu Noumy on a silver salver the keys of the Kaaba and took the oath by the same proxy. The combination in Selim of the Abbâside right by assignment and by Bai'at, and the adhesion of the representative of the Prophet's House who held at the time the guardianship of the Holy Cities, perfected the Ottoman Sultan's title to the Caliphate, " just as the adhesion of (the Caliph) Ali had completed the title of the first three Caliphs." The solemn prayers with the usual Khutbas offered in Mecca and Medina for the Sultan gave the necessary finality to the right of Selim. Henceforth Constantinople, his seat of government, became the Dâr-ul-Khilâfat, and began to be called

" Islâmbol," " The City of Islâm."   Before long envoys arrived
in Selim's Court and that of his son, Solyman the Magnificent,
from the rulers of the Sunni States to offer their homage ;
and thus, according to the Sunnis, the Caliphate became the
heritage of the House of Othman, which they have enjoyed
for four centuries without challenge or dispute.

PART II.

THE SPIRIT OF ISLÂM

CHAPTER I

THE IDEAL OF ISLÂM

هَلُمَّ إِلَيَّ لَا تَقْصِدْ سِوَائِي

أَنَا الْمُعْطَانُ فَاطْلُبْنِي تَجِدْنِي

أَتَذْكُرُ لَيْلَةً نَادَيْتَ سِرًّا

فَلَمْ أَسْمَعْكَ فَاطْلُبْنِي تَجِدْنِي

إِذَا الْمُضْطَرُّ قَالَ أَلَا تَرَانِي

نَظَرْتُ إِلَيْهِ فَاطْلُبْنِي تَجِدْنِي

إِذَا عَبْدِي عَصَانِي لَمْ تَجِدْنِي

سَرِيعَ الْأَخْذِ فَاطْلُبْنِي تَجِدْنِي [1]

THE religion of Jesus bears the name of Christianity, derived from his designation of Christ; that of Moses and of Buddha are known by the respective names of their teachers. The religion of Mohammed alone has a distinctive appellation. It is Islâm.

In order to form a just appreciation of the religion of Mohammed it is necessary to understand aright the true significance of the word Islâm. *Salam* (*salama*), in its primary sense, means, to be tranquil, at rest, to have done one's duty, to have paid up, *to be at perfect peace*; in its secondary sense,

[1] For translation, see Appendix.

to surrender oneself to Him with whom peace is made. The
noun derived from it means peace, greeting, safety, salvation.
The word does not imply, as is commonly supposed, absolute
submission to God's will, but means, on the contrary, *striving
after righteousness*.

The essence of the ethical principles involved and embodied
in Islâm is thus summarised in the second chapter of the
Koran : " There is no doubt in this book—a guidance to the
pious, who believe in the Unseen, who observe the prayers,
and distribute (charity) out of what We have bestowed on
them ; and who believe in that which We have commissioned
thee with, and in that We commissioned others with before thee,
and who have assurance in the life to come ;—these have
received the direction of their Lord." [1]

The principal bases on which the Islâmic system is founded
are (1) a belief in the unity, immateriality, power, mercy, and
supreme love of the Creator ; (2) charity and brotherhood
among mankind ; (3) subjugation of the passions ; (4) the
outpouring of a grateful heart to the Giver of all good ; and
(5) accountability for human actions in another existence.
The grand and noble conceptions expressed in the Koran of
the power and love of the Deity surpass everything of their
kind in any other language. The unity of God, His immateriality, His majesty, His mercy, form the constant and never-
ending theme of the most eloquent and soul-stirring passages.
The flow of life, light, and spirituality never ceases. But
throughout there is no trace of dogmatism. Appeal is made to
the inner consciousness of man, to his intuitive reason alone.

Let us now take a brief retrospect of the religious conceptions
of the peoples of the world when the Prophet of Islâm commenced his preachings. Among the heathen Arabs the idea
of Godhead varied according to the culture of the individual
or of the clan. With some it rose, comparatively speaking,
to the " divinisation " or deification of nature ; among others
it fell to simple fetishism, the adoration of a piece of dough,
a stick, or a stone. Some believed in a future life ; others
had no idea of it whatever. The pre-Islâmite Arabs had their
groves, their oracle-trees, their priestesses, like the Syro-

[1] Koran, sura ii. 1-6.

Phœnicians. Phallic worship was not unknown to them; and the generative powers received adoration, like the hosts of heaven, under monuments of stone and wood. The wild denizens of the desert, then as now, could not be impervious to the idea of some unseen hand driving the blasts which swept over whole tracts, or forming the beautiful visions which rose before the traveller to lure him to destruction. And thus there floated in the Arab world an intangible, unrealised conception of a superior deity, the Lord of all.[1]

The Jews, those great conservators of the monotheistic idea, as they have been generally regarded in history, probably might have assisted in the formation of this conception. But they themselves showed what strange metamorphoses can take place in the thoughts of a nation when not aided by a historical and rationalistic element in their religious code.

The Jews had entered Arabia at various times, and under the pressure of various circumstances. Naturally, the conceptions of the different bodies of emigrants, refugees, or colonists would vary much. The ideas of the men driven out by the Assyrians or Babylonians would be more anthropomorphic, more anthropopathic, than of those who fled before Vespasian, Trajan, or Hadrian. The characteristics which had led the Israelites repeatedly to lapse into idolatry in their original homes, when seers were in their midst to denounce their backslidings, would hardly preserve them from the heathenism of their Arab brothers. With an idea of " the God of Abraham " they would naturally combine a materialistic conception of the deity, and hence we find them rearing " a statue representing Abraham, with the ram beside him ready for sacrifice," in the interior of the Kaaba.

Amongst the later comers the Shammaites and the Zealots formed by far the largest proportion. Among them the worship of the law verged upon idolatry, and the Scribes and Rabbins claimed a respect almost approaching adoration. They believed themselves to be the guardians of the people, the preservers of law and tradition, " living exemplars and mirrors, in which the true mode of life, according to the law,

[1] Shahristâni; Tiele calls the religion of the pre-Islâmite Arabs "animistic polydæmonism."

was preserved." [1] They looked upon themselves as the
" flower of the nation," and they were considered, through
their intercourse with God, to possess the gift of prophecy.
In fact, by their people as well as by themselves they were
regarded as the prime favourites of God.[2] The veneration of
the Jews for Moses went so far, says Josephus, that they
reverenced his name next to that of God ; and this veneration
they transferred to Ezra, the restorer of national life and law
under the Kyânian dynasty.[3]

Besides, the mass of the Jews had never, probably, thoroughly
abandoned the worship of the Teraphim, a sort of household
gods made in the shape of human beings, and consulted on all
occasions as domestic oracles, or regarded perhaps more as
guardian penates.[4] This worship must have been strengthened
by contact with the heathen Arabs.

When Jesus made his appearance in Judæa, the doctrine of
divine unity and of a supreme Personal Will, overshadowing the
universe with its might and grace, received acceptance only
among one race—the worshippers of Jehovah. And even
among them, despite all efforts to the contrary, the conception
of the divinity had either deteriorated by contact with heathen
nations, or become modified by the influence of pagan philosophies. On the one hand, Chaldæo-Magian philosophy
had left its finger-mark indelibly impressed on the Jewish
traditions ; on the other, their best minds, whilst introducing
among the Greek and Roman philosophers the conception of a
great Primal Cause, had imbibed, in the schools of Alexandria,
notions hardly reconcilable with their monotheistic creed.

The Hindus, with their multitudinous hordes of gods and
goddesses ; the Mago-Zoroastrians, with their two divinities
struggling for mastery ; the Greeks, Romans, and Egyptians,
with their pantheons full of deities whose morality was below
that of the worshippers,—such was the condition of the civilised
world when Jesus. commenced his preachings. With all his
dreams and aspirations, his mind was absolutely exempt from

[1] Döllinger, *The Gentile and the Jew*, vol. ii. p. 308.
[2] Josephus, *Antiquities*, xvii. 24. They were, so to speak, the Brahmans of Judaism.
[3] Ezra vii. 10 *et seq.*   [4] Judges xviii. 14.

those pretensions which have been fixed on him by his over-zealous followers. He never claimed to be a " complement of God," or to be a " hypostasis of the Divinity."

Even modern idealistic Christianity has not been able yet to shake itself free from the old legacy bequeathed by the anthropomorphism of bygone ages. Age after age everything human has been eliminated from the history of the great Teacher, until his personality is lost in a mass of legends. The New Testament itself, with " its incubation of a century," leaves the revered figure clothed in a mist. And each day the old idea of " an Æon born in the bosom of eternity," gathers force until the Council of Nice gives it a shape and consistency, and formulates it into a dogma.

Many minds, bewildered by the far-offness of the universal Father, seek a resting-place midway in a human personality which they call divine. It is this need of a nearer object of adoration which leads modern Christianity to give a name to an ideal, clothe it with flesh and blood, and worship it as a man-God.

The gifted author of the *Defects of Modern Christianity* considers the frequency with which the Nazarene Prophet asserted that he was " the Son of God," and demanded the same worship as God Himself, a proof of his Divinity. That Jesus ever maintained he was the Son of God, in the sense in which it has been construed by Christian divines and apologists, we totally deny. Matthew Arnold has shown conclusively that the New Testament records are in many respects wholly unreliable. So far as the divinity of Christ is concerned, one can almost see the legend growing. But assuming that he made use of the expressions attributed to him, do they prove that he claimed to be " the only-begotten of the Father " ? Has the apologist not heard of the Eastern dervish, famous now as al-Hallâj, who claimed to be God Himself ? " *An-al-Hakk*," " I am God—I am the Truth," said he ; and the Musulman divines, like the Jewish Sanhedrim, pronounced him guilty of blasphemy, and condemned him to death ? A poor simple heart, kindling with an exalted mysticism, was thus removed from earth. The Bâbî still believes that his master, " the Gate " to eternal life, was not killed, but miraculously removed to heaven. Can it be said that when Abû Mughis al-Hallâj [1] and the Bâb called themselves " Truth " and the " Gate to heaven," they meant to imply that they were part of the Divinity, or, if they did, that their " claim " is tantamount to proof ? But, as we said before, we deny that Jesus, whose conceptions, when divested of the *Aberglaube* of his followers, were singularly free from exaggeration as to his own character or personality, ever used any expression to justify the demand attempted to be fixed upon him. His conception of the " Fatherhood " of God embraced all humanity. All mankind were the children of God, and he was their Teacher sent by the Eternal Father.[2] The Christian had thus a nobler exemplar before him. The teachings of the Prophet of Nazareth should have elevated him to a purer conception of the Deity. But six centuries had surrounded the figure of Jesus with those myths which, in opposition to his own words, resolved him into a manifestation of the Godhead. The " Servant " took the place of the Master in the adoration of the world. The vulgar masses, unable to comprehend or realise this wonderful mixture of Neo-Pythagoreanism, Platonism, Judæo-Hellenistic philosophy, and the teachings of Jesus, adored him as God incarnate, or reverted to the primitive worship of relics and of a tinselled goddess who represented the pure mother of Jesus.[3] The Collyridians, who were by no means an unimportant sect, went so far as to introduce in the Christian pantheon the Virgin Mary for God, and worship her as such, offering her a sort of twisted cake called *collyris*, whence the sect had its name. At the Council of Nice which definitely settled the nature of Jesus, there were men who held that besides " God the Father," there were two other gods—

[1] Abû Mughis ibn Mansûr, *al-Hallâj*, died in the prime of life. He was a man of pure morals, great simplicity, a friend of the poor, but a dreamer and an enthusiast. For an account of the Bâb and Bâbism, see Gobineau, *Les Religions et les Philosophies dans l'Asie Centrale* and the *History of the Bâb* by Professor E. G. Browne.

[2] The use of the word " Father " in relation to God was cut out from Islâm owing to the perversion of the idea among the then Christians.

[3] The Isaurian sovereigns, indirectly inspired by Islâm, for over a century battled against the growing degradation of Christianity, strived with all their might to make it run back in the channel pointed out by the great Teacher, but to no purpose.

Christ and the Virgin Mary.[1] And the Romanists even now, it is said, call the mother of Jesus the *complement* of the Trinity.

In the long night of superstition the Christians had wandered far away from the simplicity of the Nazarene teachings. The worship of images, saints, and relics had become inseparably blended with the religion of Jesus. The practices which he had denounced, the evils which he had reprehended, were, one by one, incorporated with his faith. The holy ground where the revered Teacher had lived and walked was involved in a cloud of miracles and visions, and " the nerves of the mind were benumbed by the habits of obedience and belief." [2]

Against all the absurdities we have described above, the life-aim of Mohammed was directed. Addressing, with the voice of truth, inspired by deep communion with the God of the Universe, the fetish-worshippers of the Arabian tribes on one side and the followers of degraded Christianity and Judaism on the other, Mohammed, that " master of speech," as he has been truly called, never travelled out of the province of reason, and made them all blush at the monstrousness of their beliefs. Mohammed, the grand apostle of the unity of God, thus stands forth in history in noble conflict with the retrogressive tendency of man to associate other beings with the Creator of the universe. Ever and anon in the Koran occur passages, fervid and burning, like the following : " Your God is one God ; there is no God but He, the Most Merciful. In the creation of the heaven and earth, and the alternation of night and day, and in the ship which saileth on the sea, laden with what is profitable to mankind ; and in the rain-water which God sendeth from heaven, quickening again the dead earth, and the animals of all sorts which cover its surface ; and in the change of winds, and the clouds balanced between heaven and earth,—

[1] Mosheim, vol. i. p. 432.

[2] Mosheim's *Ecclesiastical Hist.* vol. i. p. 432 ; comp. also Hallam, *Const. Hist. of England*, chap. ii. p. 75. From the text it will be seen how much truth there is in the assertion that Islâm derived " everything good it contains " from Judaism or Christianity. " It has been the fashion," says Deutsch, " to ascribe whatever is good in Mohammedanism to Christianity. We fear this theory is not compatible with the results of honest investigation. For of Arabian Christianity at the time of Mohammed, the less said, perhaps, the better . . . By the side of it . . . even modern Amharic Christianity, of which we possess such astounding accounts, appears pure and exalted."—*Quarterly Review*, No. 954, p. 315.

are signs to people of understanding ; yet some men take idols
beside God, and love them as with the love due to God." [1]
What a depth of sympathy towards those benighted people
do these words convey ! Again : " It is He who causeth the
lightning to appear unto you (to strike) fear and (to raise)
hope ; and formeth the pregnant clouds. The thunder
celebrateth His praise, and the angels also. . . . He launcheth
His thunderbolts, and striketh therewith whom He pleaseth
while they dispute concerning Him. . . . It is He who of right
ought to be invoked, and those (the idols) whom they invoke
besides Him shall not respond to them at all ; otherwise than
as he who stretched forth his hands to the water that it may
ascend to his mouth when it cannot ascend (thither). [2] He
hath created the heavens and the earth to (manifest His)
justice ; far be that from Him which they associate with Him.
He hath created man . . . and behold he is a professed disputer.
He hath likewise created the cattle for you, and they are a
credit unto you when they come trooping home at evening-
time, or are led forth to pasture in the morn. . . . And He
hath subjected the night and day to your service ; and the sun
and the moon and the stars are all bound by His laws. . . . It
is He who hath subjected the sea unto you, and thou seest the
ships ploughing the deep . . . and that ye might render thanks.
. . . Shall He therefore who createth be as he who createth
not ? Do ye not therefore take heed ? If ye were to reckon
up the blessings of God, ye shall not be able to compute their
number ; God is surely gracious and merciful. He knoweth
that which ye conceal and that which ye publish. But those
[the idols] whom ye invoke, besides the Lord, create nothing,
but are themselves created. They are dead and not
living." [3]

   " God ! there is no God but He—the Living, the Eternal.
No slumber seizeth Him.. Whatsoever is in heaven or in earth
is His. Who can intercede with Him but by His own permission ? He knows what has been before, and what shall be
after them ; yet nought of His knowledge shall they grasp
but He willeth. His Throne reacheth over the heavens and

---

[1] Sura ii. 158-160.   [2] Sura xiii. 13-15.
[3] Sura xvi. 3-21.

the earth, and the upholding of them both burdeneth Him not, . . .[1] He throweth the veil of night over the day, pursuing it quickly. He created the sun, moon, and stars subjected to laws by His behest. Is not all creation and all empire His ? Blessed be the Lord of the worlds.[2] Say, He alone is God : God the Eternal. He begetteth not, and He is not begotten ; there is none like unto Him. Praise be to God, the Lord of the worlds, the Compassionate, the Merciful, King on the day of reckoning ; Thee only do we worship, and to Thee do we cry for help. Guide us on the straight path,—the path of those to whom Thou art gracious, with whom Thou art not angry ; such as go not astray.[3] . . . Against the evil in His creation I betake me to the Lord of the daybreak." " Thou needest not raise thy voice, for He knoweth the secret whisper, and what is yet more hidden. Say, Whose is what is in the heavens and the earth ? Say, God's who has imposed mercy on Himself.[4] . . . With Him are the keys of the unseen. None knows them save He ; He knows what is in the land and in the sea ; no leaf falleth but He knoweth it ; nor is there a grain in the darkness under the earth, nor a thing, green or sere, but it is recorded by itself. He taketh your souls in the night, and knoweth what the work of your day deserveth ; then He awaketh you, that the set life-term may be fulfilled ; then unto Him shall ye return, and then shall He declare unto you what you have wrought.[5] Verily, God it is who cleaves out the grain and the date-stone ; He brings forth the living from the dead, and it is He who brings the dead from the living. There is God ! How then can ye be beguiled ? "

" It is He who cleaves out the morning, and makes night a repose, and the sun and the moon two reckonings ; that is the decree of the Mighty, the Wise.[6]

.   .   .   .

" There is God for you, your Lord ! There is no God but He, the Creator of everything ; then worship Him, for He over everything keeps guard ! "

[1] Sura ii. 255.   [2] Sura vii. 54.
[3] This is the Surat-ul-Fâtiha, the opening chapter of the Koran.
[4] Sura vi. 12.   [5] Sura vi. 59, 60.
[6] Sura vi. 97.

" Sight perceives Him not, but he perceives men's sights ; for He is the knower of secrets the Aware." [1]

.　　.　　.　　.　　.　　.

" Say, Verily my prayers and my devotion, and my life and my death, belong to God, the Lord of the worlds." [2]

" Dost thou not perceive that all *creatures* both in heaven and earth praise God ; and the birds also ?

" Every one knoweth His prayer and His praise.

" Unto God belongeth the kingdom of heaven and earth ; and unto God shall be the return.

" Whose is the kingdom of the heavens and of the earth ? There is no God but He !　He maketh alive and killeth.[3] . . . He is the Living One.　No God is there but He.　Call then upon Him, and offer Him a pure worship.　Praise be to God, the Lord of the worlds ! . . .　My prayers and my worship and my life and my death are unto God, Lord of the worlds. He hath no associate.[4]　It is He who hath brought you forth, and gifted you with hearing and sight and heart ; yet how few are grateful ! . . .　It is He who hath sown you in the earth, and to Him shall ye be gathered.[5] . . .　O my Lord, place me not among the ungodly people.[6] . . .　He it is who ordaineth the night as a garment and sleep for rest, and ordaineth the day for waking up to life." [7]

" Is not He the more worthy who answereth the oppressed when they cry to Him, and taketh off their ills, and maketh you to succeed your sires on the earth ? [8]　God the Almighty, the All-knowing, Forgiver of Sin, and Receiver of Penitence." [9]

" Shall I seek any other Lord than God, when He is Lord of all things ?　No soul shall labour but for itself, and no burdened one shall bear another's burden." [10]

" At last ye shall return to your Lord, and He will declare that to you about which you differ.[10]　Knower of the hidden and the manifest ! the Great, the Most High ! . . .　Alike to Him is that person among you who concealeth his words, and

---

[1] Sura vi. 104.　　　　　[2] Sura vi. 163.
[3] Sura vii. 153.　　　　　[4] Sura vii. v. 158.
[5] Sura lxvii. 23, 24.　　　[6] Sura xxiii. 94.
[7] Sura xxv. 47.　　　　　[8] Sura xxvii. 62.
[9] Sura xl. 1-2.　　　　　[10] Sura ii. 286.

he that telleth them abroad ; he who hideth him in the night, and he who cometh forth in the day." [1]

" God is the light of the heavens and the earth ; His light is as a niche in which is a lamp, and the lamp is in a glass ; the glass is as though it were a glittering star ; it is lit from a blessed tree, an olive neither of the east nor of the west, the oil of which would well-nigh give light though no fire touched it—light upon light ! God guides to His light whom He pleases ; and God strikes out parables for men, and God all things doth know."

" In the houses God has permitted to be reared and His name to be mentioned therein, His praises are celebrated therein mornings and evenings."

" Men whom neither merchandise nor selling divert from the remembrance of God, and steadfastness in prayer and giving alms, who fear a day when hearts and eyes shall be upset, that God may recompense them for the best they have done, and give them increase of His grace ; for God provides whom He pleases without count."

" But those who misbelieve, their works are like the mirage in a plain,—the thirsty counts it water till when he comes to it he finds nothing, but he finds that God is with him, and He will pay him his account, for God is quick to take account."

" Or like darkness on a deep sea ; there covers it a wave, above which is a wave, above which is a cloud,—darknesses one above the other,—when one puts out his hand he can scarcely see it, for he to whom God has given no light he has no light."

" Hast thou seen that God ? All who are in the heavens and the earth celebrate His praises, and the birds, too, spreading out their wings ; each one knows its prayer and its praise, and God knows what they do."

" Hast thou not seen that God drives the clouds, and then reunites them, and then accumulates them, and thou mayest see the rain coming forth from their midst ; and He sends down from the sky mountains with hail therein, and He makes it fall on whom He pleases, and He turns it from whom He pleases ; the flashing of His lightning well-nigh goes off with their sight."

[1] Sura xiii. 9, 10, 11.

" God interchanges the night and the day ; verily in that is a lesson to those endowed with sight."

The chapter entitled " The Merciful," which has been well called the *Benedicite* of Islâm, furnishes one of the finest examples of the Prophet's appeal to the testimony of nature.

" The sun and the moon in their appointed time,
The herbs and the trees adore,
And the heavens He raised them, and set the Balance that
    ye should not be outrageous in the balance ;
But weigh ye aright and stint not the measure.
And the earth, He has set it for living creatures ;
Therein are fruits, and palms with sheaths, and grain with
    chaff and frequent shoots.

.   .   .   .

He created man of crackling clay like the potter's, and He
    created the firmament from the smokeless fire.

.   .   .   .

The Lord of the two easts and the Lord of the two wests,
He has let loose the two seas that meet together ; between
    them is a barrier they cannot pass.
He brings forth from each pearls both great and small !

.   .   .   .

His are the ships which rear aloft in the sea like mountains.
Every one upon it is transient, but the face of thy Lord
    endowed with majesty and honour shall endure.

.   .   .   .

Of Him whosoever is in the heaven and in the earth does
    beg ; every day is He in [some fresh] work.
Blessed be the name of thy Lord, possessed of majesty and
    glory."

" Every man's actions have we hung round his neck, and on the last day shall be laid before him a wide-opened Book." [1] . . . " By a soul, and Him who balanced it, and intimated to it its wickedness and its piety, blest now is he who hath kept it pure, and undone is he who hath corrupted it." [2] . . . " No defect canst thou see in the creation of the God of mercy ;

[1] Sura xvii. 13.   [2] Sura xci. 7-9.

repeat the gaze, seest thou a single flaw, then twice more repeat the gaze, thy gaze shall return to thee dulled and weary." [1] . . . " He quickeneth the earth when it is dead ; so too shall you be brought to life."

" The heavens and the earth stand firm at His bidding ; hereafter when at once He shall summon you from the earth, forth shall ye come." [2] . . . " When the sun shall be folded up, and the stars shall fall, and when the mountains shall be set in motion ; when the she-camels shall be left, and the wild beasts shall be gathered together ; when the seas shall boil, and souls be re-paired [with their bodies] ; when the female child that was buried alive shall be asked for what crime she was put to death ; when the leaves of the Book shall be unrolled, and the heavens shall be stripped away, and the fire of hell blaze forth, and paradise draw nigh, then shall every soul know what it hath done." [3] . . . " What knowledge hast thou [Mohammed] of the hour ?   Only God knoweth its period. It is for thee only to warn those who fear it." . . . " What shall teach thee the inevitable ?   Thamûd and Âd treated the Day of Decision as a lie. They were destroyed with thunderbolts and roaring blasts."

And yet with all His might, His tender care and pity are all-embracing :

" By the noonday brightness, and by the night when it darkeneth, thy Lord hath not forsaken thee, neither hath He been displeased. Surely the future shall be better for thee than the past ; and in the end He shall be bounteous to thee, and thou shalt be satisfied. Did He not find thee an orphan, and give thee a home ; erring, and guided thee ; needy, and enriched thee ? As to the orphan, then, wrong him not ; and chide not away him that asketh of thee, and tell abroad the favours of thy Lord." [4]   " Did ye think We had made you for sport, and that ye should not be brought back again to us ? " " O our God, punish us not if we forget and fall into sin ; blot out our sins and forgive us." " Have mercy, O Lord, for of the merciful, Thou art the best." [5]   " The heavy laden

[1] Sura lxvii. 4.   [2] Sura xxx. 25.
[3] Sura lxxxi.   [4] Sura xciii.
[5] Sura xxiii. 118.

shall not bear another's load. We never punished till we had sent an apostle." " This clear Book, behold, on a blessed night have we sent it down for a warning to mankind." " Not to sadden thee have we sent it thee."

And so on goes this wonderful book, appealing to the nobler feelings of man,—his inner consciousness and his moral sense, proving and manifesting the enormity of idolatrous beliefs. Scarcely a chapter but contains some fervid passages on the power, mercy, and unity of God. The Islâmic conception of the Almighty has been misunderstood by Christian writers. The God of Islâm is commonly represented as " a pitiless tyrant, who plays with humanity as on a chess-board, and works out His game without regard to the sacrifice of the pieces." Let us see if this estimate is correct. The God of Islâm is the All-mighty, the All-knowing, the All-just, the Lord of the worlds, the Author of the heavens and the earth, the Creator of life and death, in whose hand is dominion and irresistible power ; the great, all-powerful Lord of the glorious Throne. God is the Mighty, the Strong, the Most High, the Producer, the Maker, the Fashioner, the Wise, the Just, the True, the Swift in reckoning, who knoweth every ant's weight of good and of ill that each man hath done, and who suffereth not the reward of the faithful to perish. But the Almighty, the All-wise, is also the King, the Holy, the Peaceful, the Faithful, the Guardian over His servants, the Shelterer of the orphan, the Guide of the erring, the Deliverer from every affliction, the Friend of the bereaved, the Consoler of the afflicted ; in His hand is good, and He is the generous Lord, the Gracious, the Hearer, the Near-at-Hand, the Compassionate, the Merciful, the Very-forgiving, whose love for man is more tender than that of the mother-bird for her young.

The mercy of the Almighty is one of the grandest themes of the Koran. The very name [Ar-Rahmân] with which each chapter opens, and with which He is invoked, expresses a deep, all-penetrating conviction of that love, that divine mercy which enfolds creation.[1]

The moral debasement of the followers of the two previous Dispensations wrings the Teacher's heart, and then burst forth

[1] Sura iii. 124, xxv. 50, xxviii. 74, xlii. 3, etc. etc.

denunciations on the Christians and the Jews for the superstitious rites they practised in defiance of the warnings of their
prophets. The fire of religious zeal, that had burned in the
bosoms of Isaiah and Jeremiah, was rekindled in the breast
of another and far greater man. He denounces; but above
the wail, the cry of agony at the degradation of humanity, is
heard the voice of hope.

The Korân severely censures the Jews for their "worship
of false gods and idols," the *teraphim* before referred to, and
for their exaggerated reverence for the memory of Ezra;
the Christians, for their adoration of Jesus and his mother.
" Hast thou not seen those to whom a portion of the Scriptures
have been given ? They believe in false gods and idols. They
say to the unbelievers they are better directed in the right
way than those that believe [the Moslems]." [1] " The Jews
say, Ezra is the son of God ; the Christians say, al-Masîh
(Jesus) is the son of God. How infatuated they are ! They
take their priests and their monks for their lords besides
God. . . . They seek to extinguish the light of God with
their mouths." [2] . . . " The Jews and the Christians say,
We are the children of God, and His beloved." [3] " Many
of those unto whom the Scriptures have been given [4] desire
to render you again unbelievers, after ye have believed. . . .
Be constant in prayer, and give alms ; and what good ye have
sent before you for your souls, ye shall find it with God." . . .
" They say, Verily, none shall enter paradise except those who
are Jews or Christians. . . . Say, Produce your proof if ye
speak the truth. Nay, but he who directeth towards God,
and doth that which is right, he shall have his reward with
his Lord." [5]

" O ye who have received the Scriptures, exceed not the just
bounds in your religion, neither say of God otherwise than the
truth. Verily, al-Masîh, the son of Mary, is the apostle of
God and His word. Believe therefore in God and His apostles,
and say not, There are three Gods; forbear this . . . al-Masîh
doth not proudly disdain to be a servant unto God." [6] " It

[1] Sura iv. 45.   [2] Sura ix. 30-32.   [3] Sura v. 18.
[4] The Jews, the Christians, and the Zoroastrians.   [5] Sura v. 105, 106.
[6] Sura iv. 171,

beseemeth not a man, that God should give him the Scriptures, and the wisdom, and the gift of prophecy, and that then he should say to his followers, 'Be ye worshippers of me, as well as of God,' but rather, 'Be ye perfect in things pertaining to God, since ye know the Scriptures, and have studied deep.'"

The following passage shows the feeling with which such religious conceptions were regarded: "They say the God of mercy hath gotten to himself a son.[1] Now have ye uttered a grievous thing ; and it wanted but little that the heaven should be torn open, and that the earth cleave asunder, and the mountains fall down, for that they attribute children unto the Merciful ; whereas it is not meet for God to have children. Verily there is none in heaven or on earth but shall approach the Merciful as His servant. He encompasseth them."[2] . . .

But the inspired Preacher whose mission it is to proclaim the Truth does not confound the good with the bad : "Yet they are not all alike ; there are of those who have received the Scriptures, upright people ; they meditate on the signs of God in the night season, and worship ; they believe in God and the last day ; and command that which is just ; and forbid that which is unjust, and zealously strive to excel in good works ; these are of the righteous."[3]

The mutual and burning hatred of Jew and Christian, the savage wars of Nestorian and Monophysite, the meaningless wrangle of the sects, the heartless and heart-rending logomachy of the Byzantine clergy, ever and anon bring down denunciations like the following :

"To Jesus and other apostles we gave manifest signs ; and if God had pleased, their followers would not have fallen into these disputes. But God doeth what He will!" "Mankind was but one people, and God sent them prophets of warning and glad tidings, and the Book of Truth to settle all disputes. Yet none disputed like those to whom the Book had been sent ; for they were filled with jealousy of each other." "O people of the Book, why wrangle about Abraham? Why contend about that whereof ye know nothing?"

The primary aim of the new Dispensation was to infuse or

[1] Sura iii. 78.   [2] Sura xix. 91-94.   [3] Sura iii. 112. 113.

revive in the heart of humanity a living perception of truth
in the common relations of life. " The moral ideal of the new
gospel," to use the phraseology of an eminent writer, " was
set in the common sense of duty and the familiar instances of
love."

"Verily, those people [1] have now passed away; they have
the reward of their deeds; and ye shall have the meed of
yours; of their doings ye shall not be questioned." [2] " Every
soul shall bear the good and the evil for which it has laboured;
and God will burden none beyond its power." " Blessed is
he who giveth away his substance that he may become pure,
and who offereth not favours to any one for the sake of recompense . . . but only as seeking the approval of his Lord the
Most High." [3]

"They are the blest who, though longing for it themselves,
bestowed their food on the poor and the orphan and the
captive [saying], ' We feed you for the sake of God: we seek
from you neither recompense nor thanks.' " [4]

"Worship God alone; be kind to kindred and servants,
orphans and the poor; speak righteously to men, pray, and
pay alms." " Defer humbly to your parents; with humility
and tenderness say, O Lord, be merciful to them, even as they
brought me up when I was helpless." " Abandon the old
barbarities, blood-vengeance, and child-murder, and be united
as one flesh." " Do thy alms openly or in secret, for both
are well." Give of that which hath been given you before
the day cometh when there shall be no trafficking, nor friendship, nor intercession." " Wouldst thou be taught the steep
[path]? It is to ransom the captive, to feed the hungry, the
kindred, the orphan, and him whose mouth is in the dust."
"Be of those who enjoin steadfastness and compassion on
others." [5] "Woe to them that make show of piety, and
refuse help to the needy." " Make not your alms void by
reproaches or injury." " Forgiveness and kind speech are
better than favours with annoyance." " Abandon usury."
" He who spendeth his substance to be seen of men, is like a

---

[1] *I.e.* Abraham, Ishmael, and Isaac, and the tribes.
[2] Sura ii. 128.   [3] Sura xcii. 18, 20.
[4] Sura lxxvi. 8, 9.   [5] Sura xc. 12-17.

rock with thin soil over it, whereon the rain falleth and leaveth it hard. But they who expend their substance to please God and establish their souls, are like a garden on a hill, on which the rain falleth and it yieldeth its fruits twofold ; and even if the rain doth not fall, yet is there a dew."

" Judge between men with truth, and follow not thy passions, lest they cause thee to err from the way of God." [1] " Covet not another's gifts from God." " There is no piety in turning the face east or west, but in believing in God only and doing good." " Make the best of all things ; enjoin justice and avoid the foolish ; and if Satan stir thee to evil, take refuge in God." " Touch not the goods of the orphan.[2] Perform your covenant, and walk not proudly on the earth." " The birth of a daughter brings dark shadows on a man's face." . . . " Kill not your children for fear of want : for them and for you will We provide. Verily the killing them is a great wickedness." [3] " God hath given you wives that ye may put love and tenderness between you."

" Reverence the wombs that bear you." " Commit not adultery ; for it is a foul thing and an evil way." [4] " Let the believer restrain his eyes from lust ; let women make no display of ornaments, save to their own kindred."

" Know ye that this world's life is a cheat, the multiplying of riches and children is like the plants that spring up after rain, rejoicing the husbandman, then turn yellow and wither away. In the next life is severe chastisement, or else pardon from God and His peace." " Abandon the semblance of wickedness and wickedness itself. They, verily, whose only acquirement is iniquity, shall be rewarded for what they shall have gained." [5] " Those who abstain from vanities and the indulgence of their passions, give alms, offer prayers, and tend well their trusts and their covenants, these shall be the heirs of eternal happiness." [6] " Show kindness to your parents, whether one or both of them attain to old age with thee : and say not to them ' Fie ! ' neither reproach them ; but speak to them both with respectful speech and tender affection." [7]

---

[1] Sura xxxviii. 25.   [2] Sura xvii. 37.   [3] Sura xvii. 33.
[4] Sura xvii. 32.   [5] Sura vi. 121.   [6] Sura xxiii. 8.
[7] Sura xvii. 23.

" And to him who is of kin render his due, and also to the poor and to the wayfarer ; yet waste not wastefully." [1]

" And let not thy hand be tied up to thy neck ; nor yet open it with all openness, lest thou sit thee down in rebuke in beggary." [2] " Enjoin my servants to speak in kindly sort." [3] " Turn aside evil with that which is better." [4] " Just balances will We set up for the day of the Resurrection, neither shall any soul be wronged in aught ; though were a work but the weight of a grain of mustard seed, We would bring it forth *to be weighed* : and Our reckoning will suffice." [5] " Seek pardon of your Lord and be turned unto Him : verily, my Lord is merciful, loving." [6] " And your Lord saith, ' Call upon me, I will hearken unto you." [7] " Say : O my servants who have transgressed to your own injury, despair not of God's mercy, for all sins doth God forgive. Gracious, merciful is He ! " [8] " The good word riseth up to Him, and the righteous deed will He exalt." [9]

" Truly my Lord hath forbidden filthy actions, whether open or secret, and iniquity, and unjust violence." [10]

" Call upon your Lord with lowliness and in secret, for He loveth not transgressors. And commit not disorders on the well-ordered earth after it hath been well ordered ; and call on Him with fear and longing desire : Verily the mercy of God is nigh unto the righteous." [11] " Moreover, We have enjoined on man to show kindness to his parents. With pain his mother beareth him ; with pain she bringeth him forth ; and he saith, ' O my Lord ! stir me up to be grateful for Thy favours wherewith Thou hast favoured me and my parents, and to good works which shall please Thee ; and prosper me in my offspring : for to Thee am I turned, and am resigned to Thy will.' " [12] " For them is a dwelling of peace with their Lord ; and in recompense for their works shall He be their protector." [13] " Lost are they who, in their ignorance, have foolishly slain their children, and have forbidden that which

---

[1] Sura xvii. 26.
[2] Sura xvii. 29.
[3] Sura xvii. 53.
[4] Sura xxiii. 96.
[5] Sura xxi. 47.
[6] Sura xi. 90.
[7] Sura xi. 60.
[8] Sura xxxix. 53.
[9] Sura xxxv. 10.
[10] Sura vii. 33.
[11] Sura vii. 55-58.
[12] Sura xlvi. 15.
[13] Sura vi. 28.

God hath given them for food, devising an untruth against God! Now have they erred; and they were not rightly guided." [1]

"The likeness of those who expend their wealth for the cause of God, is that of a grain of corn which produceth seven ears, and in each ear a hundred grains; they who expend their wealth for the cause of God, and never follow what they have laid out with reproaches or harm, shall have their reward with their Lord; no fear shall come upon them, neither shall they be put to grief. A kind speech and forgiveness is better than alms followed by injury." [2]

"God will not burden any soul beyond its power. It shall enjoy the good which it hath acquired, and shall bear the evil for the acquirement of which it laboured." ... "O Lord! punish us not if we forget, or fall into sin, O our Lord! and lay not on us a load like that which Thou hast laid on those who have been before us, O our Lord! And lay not on us that for which we have not strength: but blot out our sins and forgive us and have pity on us." [3] "The patient and the truthful, the lowly and the charitable, they who seek pardon at each daybreak": [4] ... "Who give alms, alike in prosperity and in success, and who master their anger, and forgive others! God loveth the doers of good"; [5] [theirs a goodly home with their Lord.] "O our Lord! forgive us then our sin, and hide away from us our evil deeds, and cause us to die with the righteous": [6] ... "And their Lord answereth them, 'I will not suffer the work of him among you that worketh, whether of male or female, to be lost, the one of you is the issue of the other.'" [7] "And fear ye God, in whose name ye ask favours of each other—and respect women." [8]

"And marry not women whom your fathers have married: for this is a shame, and hateful, and an evil way." [9]

"Covet not the gifts by which God hath raised some of you above others." [10]

"Be good to parents, and to kindred, and to orphans, and

[1] Sura vi. 141.   [2] Sura ii. 261-263.
[3] Sura ii. 286.   [4] Sura iii. 16.   [5] Sura iii. 128.
[6] Sura iii. 192.   [7] Sura iii. 194.   [8] Sura iv. 1.
[9] Sura iv. 22.   [10] Sura iv. 32.

to the poor, and to a neighbour, whether kinsman or new-comer, and to a fellow-traveller, and to the wayfarer, and to the slaves whom your right hands hold ; verily, God loveth not the proud, the vain boaster." [1] " He who shall mediate between men for a good purpose shall be the gainer by it. But he who shall mediate with an evil mediation shall reap the fruit of it. And God keepeth watch over everything." [2] " O ye Moslems ! stand fast to justice, when ye bear witness before God, though it be against yourselves, or your parents or your kindred, whether the party be rich or poor. God is nearer than you to both. Therefore follow not passion, lest ye swerve from truth." [3]

Do the preachings of this desert-born Prophet, addressing a larger world and a more advanced humanity, in the nobility of their love, in their strivings and yearnings for the true, the pure, and the holy, fall short of the warnings of Isaiah or " the tender appeals of Jesus ? "

The poor and the orphan, the humble dweller of the earth " with his mouth in the dust," the unfortunate being bereft in early life of parental care, are ever the objects of his tenderest solicitude. Ever and again he announces that the path which leads to God is the helping of the orphan, the relieving of the poor, and the ransoming of the captive. His pity and love were not confined to his fellow-beings, the brute creation shared with them his sympathy and tenderness.

" A man once came to him with a bundle, and said : ' O Prophet, I passed through a wood and heard the voice of the young of birds, and I took them and put them in my carpet, and their mother came fluttering round my head.' And the Prophet said : ' Put them down ' ; and when he had put them down the mother joined the young. And the Prophet said : ' Do you wonder at the affection of the mother towards her young ? I swear by Him who has sent me, Verily, God is more loving to His servants than the mother to these young birds. Return them to the place from which ye took them, and let their mother be with them.' " " Fear God with regard to animals," said Mohammed ; " ride them when they are fit to be ridden, and get off when they are tired. Verily, there are

[1] Sura iv. 36.   [2] Sura iv. 85.   [3] Sura iv. 135.

rewards for our doing good to dumb animals, and giving them water to drink."

In the Koran, animal life stands on the same footing as human life in the sight of the Creator. "There is no beast on earth," says the Koran, "nor bird which flieth with its wings, but the same is a people like unto you—unto the Lord shall they return." It took centuries for Christendom to awaken to a sense of duty towards the animal creation. Long before the Christian nations ever dreamt of extending towards animals tenderness and humanity, Mohammed proclaimed in impressive words the duty of mankind towards their dumb and humble servitors. These precepts of tenderness so lovingly embalmed in the creed are faithfully rendered into a common duty of everyday life in the world of Islâm.

CHAPTER II

THE RELIGIOUS SPIRIT OF ISLÂM

قُلْ لِمَنْ مَّا فِي السَّمَـٰوَٰتِ وَٱلْأَرْضِ

قُلْ لِلَّهِ ۚ كَتَبَ عَلَىٰ نَفْسِهِ الرَّحْمَةَ

قُلْ تَعَالَوْا أَتْلُ مَا حَرَّمَ رَبُّكُمْ عَلَيْكُمْ أَلَّا تُشْرِكُوا بِهِ شَيْئًا وَبِالْوَالِدَيْنِ
إِحْسَانًا ۖ وَلَا تَقْتُلُوا أَوْلَادَكُمْ مِنْ إِمْلَاقٍ ۖ نَحْنُ نَرْزُقُكُمْ وَإِيَّاهُمْ ۖ
وَلَا تَقْرَبُوا الْفَوَاحِشَ مَا ظَهَرَ مِنْهَا وَمَا بَطَنَ ۖ وَلَا تَقْتُلُوا النَّفْسَ
الَّتِي حَرَّمَ اللَّهُ إِلَّا بِالْحَقِّ ۚ ذَٰلِكُمْ وَصَّاكُمْ بِهِ لَعَلَّكُمْ تَعْقِلُونَ ۖ
وَلَا تَقْرَبُوا مَالَ الْيَتِيمِ إِلَّا بِالَّتِي هِيَ أَحْسَنُ حَتَّىٰ يَبْلُغَ أَشُدَّهُ ۖ
وَأَوْفُوا الْكَيْلَ وَالْمِيزَانَ بِالْقِسْطِ ۖ لَا نُكَلِّفُ نَفْسًا إِلَّا وُسْعَهَا ۖ
وَإِذَا قُلْتُمْ فَاعْدِلُوا وَلَوْ كَانَ ذَا قُرْبَىٰ ۖ وَبِعَهْدِ اللَّهِ أَوْفُوا ۚ ذَٰلِكُمْ
وَصَّاكُمْ بِهِ لَعَلَّكُمْ تَذَكَّرُونَ ۖ

FOR the conservation of a true religious spirit, Mohammed attached to his precepts certain practical duties, of which the following are the principal: (1) prayer, (2) fasting, (3) alms-giving, and (4) pilgrimage.

Man's consciousness of a supreme, all-pervading Power; his helplessness in the eternal conflict of nature; his sense of

benefaction,—all lead him to pour out the overflowing sentiments of his heart in words of gratitude and love, or repentance
and solicitation, to One who is every-wakeful and merciful.
Prayers are only the utterance of the sentiments which fill
the human heart. All these emotions, however, are the result
of a superior development. The savage, if supplications do
not answer his purpose, resorts to the castigation of his fetish.
But every religious system possessing any organic element
has recognised, in some shape, the efficacy of prayer. In
most, however, the theurgic character predominates over the
moral ; in some, the moral idea is entirely wanting.

The early Hindu worship consisted of two sets of acts—
oblations and sacrifice accompanied with invocations. In
the infancy of religious thought the gods are supposed to
possess the same appetites and passions as human beings ;
and thus whilst man needs material benefits, the gods require
offerings and propitiation. This idea often finds expression
in the old hymns of the *Rig Veda*. With the development of
religious conceptions, it is probable that, among at least the
more advanced or thoughtful minds, the significance attached
to oblations and sacrifice underwent considerable modification.
But as the hold of the priestly caste, which claimed the possession of a " secret virtue " transmissible only through the blood,
strengthened on the minds of the masses, Brahmanism crystallised into a literally sacrificial cult. The sacrifice could be
performed only by the priest according to rigid and unalterable
formulæ ; whilst he recited the *mantras* and went through the
rites in a mechanical spirit, without religious feeling or
enthusiasm, the worshipper stood by, a passive spectator of
the worship which was performed on his behalf. The smallest
mistake undid the efficacy of the observances. The devotional
spirit, however, could not have been entirely wanting, or the
Bhagavad Gita could not have been composed. But for the
people as a whole, their worship had become a vast system of
sacrifice, the value of which depended not so much upon the
moral conduct of the individual worshipper as upon the
qualification of the officiating priest. The former had only
to believe in the efficacy of the rite and be in a state of legal
purity at the time.

The Mago-Zoroastrian and the Sabæan lived in an atmosphere of prayer. The Zoroastrian prayed when he sneezed, when he cut his nails or hair, while preparing meals, day and night, at the lighting of lamps, etc. Ormuzd was first invoked, and then not only heaven, earth, the elements and stars, but trees, especially the moon-plant,[1] and beasts. The formulæ were often to be repeated as many as twelve hundred times.[2] The moral idea, however pure with the few, would be perfectly eliminated from the minds of the common people. But even the sort of spiritual life enjoyed by exceptional minds was monopolised by the ministers of religion. The barriers of special holiness which divided the priesthood from the laity, shut out the latter from all spiritual enjoyments of a nobler type. The Magians, like the Ophici, had two forms of worship, or rather, two modes of understanding the objects of worship : one esoteric, especially reserved for the priestly classes ; the other exoteric, in which alone the vulgar could participate.[3]

The Mosaic law contained no ordinances respecting prayers ; only on the payment of tithes to the priests, and the domestic solemnity of the presentation of the firstlings, was there a prescribed formula of a prayer and acknowledgment, when the father of the house, on the strength of his having obediently performed the behests of the law, supplicated blessings from Jehovah on Israel, " even as He had sworn unto their fathers." [4] But, with the rise of a more spiritual idea of the Deity among the people and the teachers, and the decline of an uncompromising anthropomorphism, the real nature of prayer, as the medium of intercommunication between God and man, began to be understood. Tradition and custom, in default of any express regulation by the law, made the Jews at last, as Döllinger says, a people of prayer.[5] Three hours daily were consecrated to devotional exercises, viz. nine, twelve, and three o'clock. The necessity, however, for the service of priests, combined

---

[1] Called *Soma* by the Sanscritic, and *Homa* or *Haoma* by the Zend races.

[2] Döllinger, *The Gentile and the Jew*, vol. i. p. 398. The Zend Avesta itself is a grand repertory of prayers, hymns, invocations, etc., to a multitude of deities, among whom Ormuzd ranks first. In fact, it is a book of liturgies. Comp. Clarke, *Ten Great Religions*, pp. 187, 202.

[3] Reland, *Dissertationes Miscellanæ*, part i. p. 191 ; Shahristâni.

[4] Deut. xxvi. 12-15.   [5] Döllinger, vol. ii. p. 372.

with the absence of any positive precedent coming down from the Lawgiver himself, tended to make prayer, in the majority of cases, merely mechanical. Phylacteries were in use in the time of Jesus, and the Koran reproaches the Jews in bitter terms for " selling the signs of God." [1]

The teachings of Jesus, representing a later development of the religious faculty in man, recognised the true character of prayer. He consecrated the practice by his own example.[2] The early disciples, in the spirit of their Master, laid great stress on the habit of devotion and thanksgiving to God.[3] But the want of some definite rule for the guidance of the masses, in process of time, left them completely adrift in all that regarded the practice of devotion, and under subjection to the priests, who monopolised the office of regulating the number, length, and the terminology of prayers. Hence missals, liturgies, councils, and convocations to settle articles of faith and matters of conscience ; hence also, the mechanical worship of droning monks, and the hebdomadal flocking into churches and chapels on one day in the week to make up for the deficiency of spiritual food during the other six ; hence also the " presbyter," who, merely a " servant " at first,[4] came to regard himself as " the Lord of the spiritual heritage " bequeathed by Jesus.

All these evils had culminated to a point in the seventh century, when the Prophet of Arabia began to preach a re-formed religion. In instituting prayers, Mohammed recognised the yearning of the human soul to pour out its love and gratitude to God, and by making the practice of devotion periodic, he impressed that disciplinary character on the observance of prayer which keeps the thoughts from wandering into the regions of the material.[5] The formulæ, consecrated by his example and practice, whilst sparing the Islâmic world the evils of contests regarding liturgies, leave to the individual worshipper the amplest scope for the most heartfelt outpouring of devotion and humility before the Almighty Presence.

---

[1] Sura ii. 42.   [2] Luke ix. 1-4.
[3] *E.g.* Eph. vi. 18 ; Col. i. 12 *et seq.*
[4] Mosheim, vol. i. 99 *et seq.*
[5] Comp. Oelsner, *Des Effets de la Religion de Mohammed*, p. 6.

The value of prayer as the means of moral elevation and the purification of the heart, has been clearly set forth in the Koran :

" Rehearse that which hath been revealed unto thee of the Book, and be constant at prayer, for prayer preserveth from crimes and from that which is blameable ; and the remembering of God is surely a most sacred duty." [1]

The forms of the supplicatory hymns, consecrated by the example of the Prophet, evince the beauty of the moral element in the teachings of Islâm :

" O Lord ! I supplicate Thee for firmness in faith and direction towards rectitude, and to assist me in being grateful to Thee, and in adoring Thee in every good way : and I supplicate Thee for an innocent heart, which shall not incline to wickedness ; and I supplicate Thee for a true tongue, and for that virtue which Thou knowest ; and I pray Thee to defend me from that vice which Thou knowest, and for forgiveness of those faults which Thou knowest. O my Defender ! assist me in remembering Thee and being grateful to Thee, and in worshipping Thee with the excess of my strength. O Lord ! I have injured my own soul, and no one can pardon the faults of Thy servants but Thou ; forgive me out of Thy loving-kindness, and have mercy on me ; for verily Thou art the forgiver of offences and the bestower of blessings on Thy servants." [2]

Another traditional prayer, called the prayer of David, runs thus ; " O Lord, grant to me the love of Thee ; grant that I may love those that love Thee ; grant that I may do the deeds that may win Thy love ; make Thy love to be dearer to me than self, family or than wealth." [3]

The two following prayers of Ali (the Caliph) evince the highest devotional spirit.

" Thanks be to my Lord ; He the Adorable, and only to be adored. My Lord, the Eternal, the Ever-existing, the Cherisher, the True Sovereign whose mercy and might overshadow the universe ; the Regulator of the world, and Light of the creation. His is our worship ; to Him belongs all worship ; He existed before all things, and will exist after all that is living has

---

[1] Koran xxix. 45.   [2] *Mishkât*, bk. iv. chap. 18, parts 2, 3.
[3] *Tasfsîr-Jalâli*, p. 288.

ceased. Thou art the adored, my Lord ; Thou art the Master, the Loving and Forgiving ; Thou bestowest power and might on whom Thou pleasest ; him whom Thou hast exalted none can lower ; and him whom Thou hast lowered none can exalt. Thou, my Lord, art the Eternal, the Creator of all, All-wise Sovereign Mighty ; Thy knowledge knows everything ; Thy beneficence is all-pervading ; Thy forgiveness and mercy are all-embracing. O my Lord, Thou art the Helper of the afflicted, the Reliever of all distress, the Consoler of the broken-hearted ; Thou art present everywhere to help Thy servants. Thou knowest all secrets, all thoughts, art present in every assembly, Fulfiller of all our needs, Bestower of all blessings. Thou art the Friend of the poor and bereaved ; my Lord, Thou art my Fortress ; a Castle for all who seek Thy help. Thou art the Refuge of the weak ; the Helper of the pure and true. O my Lord, Thou art my Supporter, my Helper, the Helper of all who seek Thy help. . . . O my Lord, Thou art the Creator, I am only created ; Thou art my Sovereign, I am only Thy servant ; Thou art the Helper, I am the beseecher ; Thou, my Lord art my Refuge ; Thou art the Forgiver, I am the sinner ; Thou, my Lord, art the Merciful, All-knowing, All-loving ; I am groping in the dark ; I seek Thy knowledge and love. Bestow, my Lord, all Thy knowledge and love and mercy ; forgive my sins, O my Lord, and let me approach Thee, my Lord."

" O my Lord, Thou the Ever-praised, the Eternal, Thou art the Ever-present, Ever-existing, the Ever-near, the All-knowing. Thou livest in every heart, in every soul, all-pervading ; Thy knowledge is ingrained in every mind." " He bears no similitude, has no equal, One, the Eternal ; thanks be to the Lord whose mercy extends to every sinner, who provides for even those who deny Him. To Him belong the beginning and the end, all knowledge and the most hidden secret of the heart. He never slumbers, the Ever-just, the Ever-wakeful. He forgiveth in His mercy our greatest sins,—loveth all creation. I testify to the goodness of my Lord, to the truth of His Messenger's message, blessings on him and his descendants and his companions." [1]

<hr>

[1] *Sahîfat-Kâmila.*

" It is one of the glories of Islâm," says an English writer,
" that its temples are not made with hands, and that its
ceremonies can be performed anywhere upon God's earth or
under His heaven." [1] Every place in which the Almighty
is faithfully worshipped is equally pure.   The Moslem, whether
he be at home or abroad, when the hour of prayer arrives, pours
forth his soul in a brief but earnest supplicatory address ;
his attention is not wearied by the length of his prayers, the
theme of which is always self-humiliation, the glorification of
the Giver of all good, and reliance on His mercy. [2] The intensity
of the devotional spirit embalmed in the church of Mohammed
has hardly been realised by Christendom.   Tradition, that
faithful chronicler of the past, with its hundred corroborative
witnesses, records how the Prophet wept during his prayers
with the fervour of his emotions ; how his noble cousin and
son-in-law became so absorbed in his devotions that his body
grew benumbed.

The Islâm of Mohammed recognises no caste of priesthood,
allows no monopoly of spiritual knowledge or special holiness
to intervene between man and his God.   Each soul rises to its
Creator without the intervention of priest or hierophant.   No
sacrifice, [3] no ceremonial, invented by vested interests, is
needed to bring the anxious heart nearer to its Comforter.
Each human being is his own priest ; in the Islâm of Mohammed
no one man is higher than the other.

European rationalists have complained of the complex
character of the Moslem prayers, but the ritual of the Koran
is astonishing in its simplicity and soberness.   It includes
the necessary acts of faith, the recital of the creed, prayer,
almsgiving, fasting, and pilgrimage, but lays down scarcely
any rules as to how they are to be performed.   " Observe the
prayers and the mid-day prayer, and stand ye attent before
God ; seek aid from patience and prayer.   Verily, God is
with the patient ; " but nothing is said regarding the manner
in which the prayers should be offered.   " When ye journey

---

[1] Hunter, *Our Indian Musalmans*, p. 179.

[2] Sura ii. 127, 239, etc., vii. 204, 205, xvii. 79, xx. 130, xxx. 16, 17, etc. etc.
See the *Kitâb ul-Mustatraf*.

[3] The annual sacrifice at the Hajj and the Bairam is a mere memorial
observance.

about the earth," says the Koran, " it is no crime to you that ye come short in prayer if ye fear that those that disbelieve will set upon you.   God pardons everything except associating aught with Him."

The practice of the Prophet has, however, attached certain rites and ceremonies to the due observance of prayers.   At the same time it is pointed out in unmistakeable terms that it is to the devotional state of the mind the Searcher of the spirit looks : " It is not the flesh or the blood of that which ye sacrifice which is acceptable to God : it is your piety which is acceptable to the Lord." [1]   " It is not righteousness," continues the Koran, " that ye turn your faces in prayer towards the east or the west ; but righteousness is of him who believeth in God ; . . . who giveth money for God's sake unto his kindred, and unto orphans, and the needy, and the stranger, and those who ask, and for the redemption of captives ; who is constant at prayers and giveth alms ; and of those who perform their covenant, when they have covenanted ; and who behave themselves patiently in hardship and adversity, and in times of violence : these are they who are true." [2] . . .

It was declared that prayer without " the presence of the heart " was of no avail, and that God's words which were addressed to all mankind and not to one people, should be studied with the heart and lips in absolute accord.   And the Caliph Ali held that devotion offered without understanding was useless and brought no blessing.[3]   The celebrated Imâm al-Ghazzâli [4] has pronounced that in reading the sacred book [5] heart and intelligence must work together ; the lips only utter the words ; intelligence helps in the due apprehension of their meaning ; the heart, in paying obedience to the dictates of duty.[6]   " It is not a sixth nor a tenth of a man's devotion," said the Prophet, " which is acceptable to God, but only such portion thereof as he offers with understanding and true devotional spirit." [7]

The practice of baptism in the Christian Church, even the

---

[1] Sura xxii. 37.   [2] Sura ii. 177.
[3] *Ghurrar wa'd Durrar*.   [4] See *post*, chap. xx.
[5] The Koran.   [6] The *Kitâb ul-Mustatraf*, chap. i.
[7] From Muâz ibn Jabal, reported by Abû Dâûd and Nisâî.

lustrations, which the Egyptians, the Jews, or the hierophants
of the heathen religions in the East and the West, required as
preliminary to the performance of devotional or religious
exercises, show the peculiar sanctity which was attached to
external purifications. Mohammed, by his example, consecrated this ancient and beneficent custom. He required
cleanliness as a necessary preliminary to the worship and
adoration of God.[1] At the same time, he especially inculcated
that mere external, or rather physical, purity does not imply
true devotion. He distinctly laid down that the Almighty
can only be approached in purity and humility of spirit.[2]
Imâm al-Ghazzâli expressly says, as against those who are only
solicitous about external purifications, and have their hearts
full of pride and hypocrisy, that the Prophet of God declared
the most important purification to be the cleansing of the
heart from all blameable inclinations and frailties, and the
mind from all vicious ideas, and from all thoughts which
distract attention from God.[3]

In order to keep alive in the Moslem world the memory of
the birthplace of Islâm, Mohammed directed that during
prayers the Moslem should turn his face towards Mecca, as the
glorious centre which saw the first glimmerings of the light of
regenerated truth.[4] With the true instinct of a prophet he
perceived the consolidating effect of fixing a central spot round
which, through all time, should gather the religious feelings of
his followers ; and he accordingly ordained that everywhere
throughout the world the Moslem should pray looking towards
the Kaaba. " Mecca is to the Moslem what Jerusalem is to
the Jew. It bears with it all the influence of centuries of
associations. It carries the Moslem back to the cradle of his
faith, the childhood of his Prophet, it reminds him of the
struggle between the old faith and the new, of the overthrow
of the idols, and the establishment of the worship of the one

[1] Sura v. 6.
The Koran, in its universality, speaks of ablutions, but where water is not
available it allows any cleansing substitute for lavation, but nowhere lays
down the details of the *Wuzú*. As usual, the manner of performing the
lavations or ablutions, derived from the practice of the Prophet, has given
rise to considerable discussions and difference among the theologians.

[2] Sura vii. 206.   [3] Compare the *Kitâb ul-Mustatraf*, chap. i. sec. 1.
[4] Sura ii. 139, 144, etc.

God ; and, most of all, it bids him remember that all his
brother Moslems are worshipping towards the same sacred
spot ; that he is one of a great company of believers, united
by one faith, filled with the same hopes, reverencing the same
things, worshipping the same God. Mohammed showed his
knowledge of the religious emotions in man when he preserved
the sanctity of the temple of Islâm." [1]   But that this rule is
not an essential requisite for devotion, is evident from the
passage of the Koran quoted above.[2]

The institution of fasting has existed more or less among all
nations.   But it may be said that throughout the ancient world
the idea attached to it was, without exception, more of penitence than of abstinence.   Even in Judaism the notion of
fasting as an exercise of self-castigation or self-abnegation was
of later growth.   The Essenians (from their connection with
the Pythagoreans, and, through them, with the asceticism
of the further East) were the first among the Jews to grasp
this moral element in the principle of fasting ; and Jesus
probably derived this idea, like other conceptions, from them.

The example of Jesus consecrated the custom in the Church.
But the predominating idea in Christianity, with respect to
fasts generally, is one of penitence or expiation ; [3] and partially,
of precedent.[4]   Voluntary corporal mortifications have been
as frequent in the Christian Church as in other Churches ;
but the tendency of such mortifications has invariably been
the destruction of mental and bodily energies, and the fostering
of a morbid asceticism.   The institution of fasting in Islâm,
on the contrary, has the legitimate object of restraining the
passions, by diurnal abstinence for a limited and definite

---

[1] Stanley Lane-Poole, Introd. to the *Selections from the Koran*, p. lxxxv.
[2] See *ante*, p. 166.

[3] Mosheim, vol. i. p. 131. Mosheim distinctly says that fasting came early
to be regarded " as the most effectual means of repelling the force, and dis-
concerting the stratagems of evil spirits, and of appeasing the anger of an
offended deity."   Vol. i. p. 398.

[4] " The weekly and yearly festivals of the Christians," says Neander,
" originated in the same fundamental idea, . . . the idea of imitating Christ,
the crucified and risen Saviour."   And, again, " by the Christians—who were
fond of comparing their calling to a warfare, a militia Christi—such fasts,
united with prayers, were named *stationes*, as if they constituted the watches
of the soldiers of Christ (the *milites Christi*) " ; Neander, *Church Hist.* vol. i.
pp. 408, 409.

period, from all the gratifications of the senses, and directing
the overflow of the animal spirits into a healthy channel.
Useless and unnecessary mortification of the flesh is discountenanced, nay, condemned.   Fasting is prescribed to the able-
bodied and the strong, as a means of chastening the spirit by
imposing a restraint on the body.   For the weak, the sickly,
the traveller, the student (who is engaged in the pursuit of
knowledge—the *Jihâd-ul-Akbar*), the soldier doing God's
battle against the assailants of the faith, and women in their
ailments, it is disallowed.   Those who bear in mind the
gluttony of the Greeks, the Romans, the Persians, and the
pre-Islâmite Arabs, their excesses in their pleasures as well
as their vices, will appreciate the value of the regulation, and
comprehend how wonderfully adapted it is for keeping in
check the animal propensities of man, especially among semi-
civilised races.

Mark the wisdom of the rule as given in the Koran : " O
ye that have believed, a fast is ordained to you . . . that ye
may practise piety, a fast of a computed number of days.
But he among you who shall be ailing, or on a journey, (shall
fast) an equal number of other days ; and they that are able
to keep it (and do not), shall make atonement by maintaining
a poor man. . . .   But if ye fast, it will be better for you if
ye comprehend ; . . . God willeth that which is easy for you." [1]

This rule of abstinence is restricted to the day ; in the night,
in the intervals of prayer and devotion, the Moslem is allowed,
perhaps indeed, is bound, to refresh the system by partaking
in moderation of food and drink, and otherwise enjoying himself
lawfully.   In the true spirit of the Teacher, the legists invariably laid down the rule that, during the fast, abstinence of
mind from all base thoughts is as incumbent as the abstinence
of the body. [2]

No religion of the world prior to Islâm had consecrated
charity, the support of the widow, the orphan, and the helpless
poor, by enrolling its principles among the positive enactments
of the system.

The *agapæ*, or feasts of charity among the early Christians,
depended on the will of individuals ; their influence, therefore,

---

[1] Sura ii. 183-4.   [2] The *Kitâb ul-Mustatraf*, chap. i. sec. 4.

could only be irregular and spasmodic. It is a matter of history that this very irregularity led to the suppression of the " feasts of charity or love-feasts " only a short time after their introduction.[1]

By the laws of Islâm every individual is bound to contribute a certain part of his substance towards the help and assistance of his poorer neighbours. This portion is usually one part of forty, or $2\frac{1}{2}$ per cent. on the value of all goods, chattels, emblements, on profits of trade, mercantile business, etc. But alms are due only when the property amounts to a certain value,[2] and has been in the possession of a person for one whole year ; nor are any due from cattle employed in agriculture or in the carrying of burdens. Besides, at the end of the month of Ramazân (the month of fasting), and on the day of the *Id-ul-Fitr*, the festival which celebrates the close of the Moslem Lent, each head of a family has to give away in alms, for himself and for every member of his household, and for each guest who breaks his fast and sleeps in his house during the month, a measure of wheat, barley, dates, raisins, rice, or any other grain, or the value of the same.

The rightful recipients of the alms, as pointed out by the practice of Mohammed and his disciples, are (1) the poor and the indigent ; (2) those who help in the collection and distribution of the obligatory alms ; (3) slaves, who wish to buy their freedom and have not the means for so doing ; (4) debtors, who cannot pay their debts ; (5) travellers and strangers.[3] General charity is inculcated by the Koran in the most forcible terms,[4] But the glory of Islâm consists in having embodied the beautiful sentiment of Jesus [5] into definite laws.

---

[1] Neander, vol. i. p. 450 *et seq.* ; Mosheim, vol. ii. p. 56. I do not mean to say that this was the only form in which Christian charity expressed itself. The support of the widow, the poor, and orphan was as much insisted upon in Christianity as in Islâm. But even this divine charity taught by Jesus received an impress of exclusiveness from the disciples, in whose hands he left his work. The widow, in order to claim the benefits of charity, was required to be " threescore years of age, to have been the wife of one man, to have brought up children," etc. Compare throughout Blunt's *History of the Christian Church*, p. 27 *et seq.*

[2] For example, no alms are due from a man unless he own twenty camels.

[3] *Jâmaa ut-Tirmizi*, chapter on " Alms-giving " ; *Jâmaa-Abbâsi* ; Querry, *Droit Musulman.* Comp. also the *Mabsût.*

[4] Sura ii. 267, 270, 271, etc., ix. 60, etc.   [5] Matt. xxv. 35, 36.

The wisdom which incorporated into Islâm the time-honoured custom of annual pilgrimage to Mecca and to the shrine of the Kaaba, has breathed into Mohammed's religion a freemasonry and brotherhood of faith in spite of sectarian divisions.   The eyes of the whole Moslem world fixed on that central spot, keep alive in the bosom of each some spark of the celestial fire which lighted up the earth in that century of darkness. Here, again, the wisdom of the inspired Lawgiver shines forth in the negative part of the enactment, in the conditions necessary to make the injunction obligatory :—(1) ripeness of intelligence and discernment ; (2) perfect freedom and liberty ; (3) possession of the means of transport and subsistence during the journey ; (4) possession of means sufficient to support the pilgrim's family during his absence ; (5) the possibility and practicability of the voyage.[1]

Owing to the minute regulations, almost Brahminical in their strictness, in force among the heathen Arabs regarding the lawful or unlawful character of various kinds of food, the Teacher of Islâm had frequently to admonish his followers that, with certain exceptions, all food was lawful. " And eat of what God hath given you for food that which is lawful and wholesome : and fear God, in whom ye believe." [2]   " Say," says the Koran, " I find not in what hath been revealed to me aught forbidden to the eater to eat, except it be that which dieth of itself, or blood poured forth, or swine's flesh, for that is an abomination, and meat which has been slain in the name of other than God [idols]." This is amplified in the fifth sura, which is also directed against various savage and idolatrous practices of the pagan Arabs. " That which dieth of itself, and blood, and swine's flesh, and all that hath been sacrificed under the invocation of any other name than that of God,[3] and the strangled, and the killed by a blow or by a fall, or by goring,[4] and that which hath been eaten by beasts of prey,

---

[1] *Radd-ul-muhtâr*, chapter on *Hajj* ; Querry, *Droit Musulman*, vol. i. ; the *Mabsût*.

[2] Sura v. 98.

[3] The heathen Arabs, when killing any animal for food, used to consecrate it by invoking the names of their gods and goddesses.

[4] The idolatrous Arabs had different savage methods of killing animals. This prohibition has reference to the brutal processes employed by them.

unless ye give the death-stroke yourselves, and that which
hath been sacrificed on the blocks of stone,[1] is forbidden to
you : and to make division of the slain by consulting the
arrows, is impiety in you." [2]   " Eat ye of the good things
wherewith we have provided you and give thanks to God." [3]

Intoxication and gambling, the curse of Christian communities, and the bane of all uncultured and inferior natures,
and excesses of all kinds, were rigorously prohibited.

Nothing can be simpler or more in accord with the advance
of the human intellect than the teachings of the Arabian
Prophet. The few rules for religious ceremonial which he
prescribed were chiefly with the object of maintaining discipline
and uniformity, so necessary in certain stages of society ;
but they were by no means of an inflexible character. He
allowed them to be broken in cases of illness or other causes.
" God wishes to make things easy for you, for," says the
Koran, " man was created weak." The legal principles which
he enunciated were either delivered as answers to questions
put to him as the Chief Magistrate of Medîna, or to remove or
correct patent evils. The Prophet's Islâm recognised no

---

[1] Sacrificial stones placed round the Kaaba or at the entrance of houses
over which the offerings were made to the idols.

[2] Sura v. 3.

[3] Things by nature abhorrent to man, such as the flesh of carnivorous
animals, birds of prey, snakes, etc., required no specific prohibition. The
idea prevalent in India, borrowed from the Hindus, that Moslems should not
partake of food with Christians, is entirely fallacious, and opposed to the
precept contained in the following passage of the Koran (sura v. 5) : " This
day things healthful are legalised to you, and the meats of those who have
received the Scriptures are allowed to you, as your meats are to them." With
regard to the sumptuary regulations, precepts, and prohibitions of Mohammed,
it must be remembered that they were called forth by the temporary circumstances of the times and people. With the disappearance of such
circumstances, the need for these laws has also disappeared. To suppose,
therefore, that every Islâmic precept is necessarily immutable, is to do an
injustice to history and the development of the human intellect. Ibn
Khaldûn's words are, in this connection, deserving of our serious consideration :
" It is only by an attentive examination and well-sustained application that
we can discover the truth, and guard ourselves against errors and mistakes.
In fact, if we were merely to satisfy ourselves by reproducing the records
transmitted by tradition without consulting the rules furnished by experience,
the fundamental principles of the art of government, the nature, even, of the
particular civilisation, or the circumstances which characterise the human
society ; if we are not to judge of the wants which occurred in distant times
by those which are occurring under our eyes, if we are not to compare the past
with the present we can hardly escape from falling into errors and losing the
way of truth." *Prolègomenes d'Ibn Khaldoun*, traduits par M. de Slane,
Première Partie, p. 13.

ritual likely to distract the mind from the thought of the one God ; no law to keep enchained the conscience of advancing humanity.

The ethical code of Islâm is thus summarised in the fourth Sura : " Come, I will rehearse what your Lord hath enjoined on you—that ye assign not to Him a partner ; that ye be good to your parents ; and that ye slay not your children because of poverty : for them and for you will We provide ; and that ye come not near to pollutions, outward or inward ; and that ye slay not a soul whom God hath forbidden, unless by right ... and draw not nigh to the wealth of the orphan, save so as to better it ... and when ye pronounce judgment then be just, though it be the affair of a kinsman. And God's compact fulfil ye ; that is, what He hath ordained to you. Verily, this is my right way ; follow it, then." [1] And again, " Blessed are they who believe and humbly offer their thanks-giving to their Lord ... who are constant in their charity, and who guard their chastity, and who observe their trust and covenants ... Verily, God bids you do justice and good, and give to kindred their due ; and He forbids you to sin and to do wrong and oppress."

" Faith and charity," to use the words of the Christian historian, " are not incompatible with external rites and positive institutions, which, indeed, are necessary in this imperfect state to keep alive a sense of religion in the common mass." [2] And, accordingly, Mohammed had attached a few rites to his teachings in order to give a more tangible conception to the generality of mankind. Jesus himself had instituted two rites, baptism and the " Holy Supper." [3] Probably, had he lived longer, he would have added more. But one thing is certain, that had a longer career been vouchsafed to him, he would have placed his teachings on a more systematic basis. This fundamental defect in Christianity has been, in fact, the real cause of the assembling of councils and convocations for the establishment of articles and dogmas, which snap asunder at every slight tension of reason and free thought. The work of Jesus was left unfinished. It was reserved for another Teacher to systematise the laws of morality.

[1] Sura iv. 155 et seq.   [2] Mosheim, vol. i. p. 124.   [3] Ibid.

Our relations with our Creator are matters of conscience ; our relations with our fellow-beings must be matters of positive rules ; and what higher sanction—to use a legal expression— can be attached to the enforcement of the relative duties of man to man than the sanction of religion. Religion is not to be regarded merely as a subject for unctuous declamations by " select preachers," or as some strange theory for the peculiar gratification of dreamy minds. Religion ought to mean the rule of life ; its chief object ought to be the elevation of human- ity towards that perfection which is the end of our existence. The religion, therefore, which places on a systematic basis the fundamental principles of morality, regulating social obligations and human duties, which brings us nearer and nearer, by its compatibility with the highest development of intellect, to the All-Perfect—that religion, we say, has the greatest claim to our consideration and respect. It is the distinctive character- istic of Islâm, as taught by Mohammed, that it combines within itself the grandest and the most prominent features in all ethnic and catholic [1] religions compatible with the reason and moral intuition of man. It is not merely a system of positive moral rules, based on a true conception of human progress, but it is also " the establishment of certain principles, the enforcement of certain dispositions, the cultivation of a certain temper of mind, which the conscience is to apply to the ever- varying exigencies of time and place." The Teacher of Islâm preached, in a thousand varied ways, universal love and brotherhood as the emblem of the love borne towards God. " How do you think God will know you when you are in His presence—by your love of your children, of your kin, of your neighbours, of your fellow-creatures ? " [2] " Do you love your Creator ? love your fellow-beings first." [3] " Do you wish to approach the Lord ? love His creatures, love for them what you love yourself, reject for them what you reject for yourself, do unto them what you wish to be done unto you." He condemned in scathing language the foulness of impurity, the meanness of hypocrisy, and the ungodliness of self-deceit.

---

[1] For the use of these words see Clarke, *Ten Great Religions*, chap. i.

[2] *Mishkât*, bks. xxii., xxiii. chaps. xv. and xvi.

[3] Comp. Kastalâni's *Commentary on the Sahîh of Bukhâri*, pt. i. p. 70.

He proclaimed, in unmistakable terms, the preciousness of truth, charity, and brotherly love.

The wonderful adaptability of Islâmic precepts to all ages and nations ; their entire concordance with the light of reason ; the absence of all mysterious doctrines to cast a shade of sentimental ignorance round the primal truths implanted in the human breast,—all prove that Islâm represents the latest development of the religious faculties of our being. Those who have ignored the historic significance of some of its precepts have deemed that their seeming harshness, or unadaptability to present modes of thought ought to exclude it from any claim to universality. But a little inquiry into the historic value of laws and precepts, a little more fairness in the examination of facts, would evince the temporary character of such rules as may appear scarcely consonant with the requirements or prejudices of modern times. The catholicity of Islâm, its expansiveness, and its charity towards all moral creeds, has been utterly mistaken, perverted, or wilfully concealed by the bigotry of rival religions.

" Verily," says the Koran, " those who believe (the Moslems), and those who are Jews, Christians, or Sabæans, whoever hath faith in God and the last day (future existence), and worketh that which is right and good,—for them shall be the reward with their Lord ; there will come no fear on them ; neither shall they be grieved." [1]

The same sentiment is repeated in similar words in the fifth Sura ; and a hundred other passages prove that Islâm does not confine " salvation " to the followers of Mohammed alone :—
" To every one have we given a law and a way. . . . And if God had pleased, He would have made you all (all mankind) one people (people of one religion). But He hath done otherwise, that He might try you in that which He hath severally given unto you : wherefore press forward in good works. Unto God shall ye return, and He will tell you that concerning which ye disagree." [2]

Of all the religions of the world that have ruled the conscience

[1] Sura v. 69. Compare the spirit of these teachings with that of the Athanasian Creed.
[2] Sura v. 48. Compare also xxix. 46, xxxii. 23, 24, xxxix. 41, xl. 13, etc.

of mankind, the Islâm of Mohammed alone combines both the conceptions which have in different ages furnished the main-spring of human conduct,—the consciousness of human dignity, so valued in the ancient philosophies, and the sense of human sinfulness, so dear to the Christian apologist. The belief that man will be judged by his work solely, throws the Moslem on the practice of self-denial and universal charity; the belief in Divine Providence, in the mercy, love, and omnipotence of God, leads him to self-humiliation before the Almighty, and to the practice of those heroic virtues which have given rise to the charge that the virtues of Islâm are stoical," [1] patience, resignation, and firmness in the trials of life. It leads him to interrogate his conscience with nervous anxiety, to study with scrupulous care the motives that actuate him, [2] to distrust his own strength, and to rely upon the assistance of an Almighty and All-Loving Power in the conflict between good and evil.

In some religions the precepts which inculcated duties have been so utterly devoid of practicability, so completely wanting in a knowledge of human nature, and partaking so much of the dreamy vagueness of enthusiasts, as to become in the real battles of life simply useless. [3] The practical character of a religion, its abiding influence on the common relations of mankind, in the affairs of everyday life, its power on the masses, are the true criteria for judging of its universality. We do not look to exceptional minds to recognise the nature of a religion. We search among the masses to understand its true character. Does it exercise deep power over them? does it elevate them? does it regulate their conception of rights and duties? does it, if carried to the South Sea islander, or preached to the Caffrarians, improve or degrade them?— are the questions we naturally ask. In Islâm is joined a lofty idealism with the most rationalistic practicality. It did not ignore human nature; it never entangled itself in the tortuous pathways which lie outside the domains of the actual

[1] Clarke, *Ten Great Religions*, p. 484.
[2] Compare the first Apologue in the *Akhlâk* (Ethics) of Husain Wâiz on *Ikhlâs*.
[3] Compare M. Ernest Havet's remarks in his valuable and learned work, *Le Christianisme et ses Origines*, Pref. p. xxxix.

and the real.   Its object, like that of other systems, was the
elevation of humanity towards the absolute ideal of perfection ;
but it attained, or tries to attain, this object by grasping the
truth that the nature of man is, in this existence, imperfect.
If it did not say, " If thy brother smite thee on one cheek,
turn thou the other also to him " ; if it allowed the punishment
of the wanton wrong-doer to the extent of the injury he had
done,[1] it also taught, in fervid words and varied strains, the
practice of forgiveness and benevolence, and the return of good
for evil :—" Who speaketh better," says the Koran, " than
he who inviteth unto God, and worketh good ? . . .   Good and
evil shall not be held equal.   Turn away evil with that which
is better." [2]   And again, speaking of paradise, it says, " It
is prepared for the godly, who give alms in prosperity and
adversity, who bridle their anger, and forgive men ; for God
loveth the beneficent." [3]

The practice of these noble precepts does not lie enshrined
in the limbo of false sentimentalism.   With the true follower
of the Prophet they form the active principles of life.   History
has preserved, for the admiration of wondering posterity,
many examples of patience under suffering exhibited by the
followers of other creeds.   But the practice of the virtue of
patient forgiveness is easier in adversity, when we have no
power to punish the evil-doer, than in prosperity.   It is related
of Husain, the noble martyr of Kerbela, that a slave having
once thrown the contents of a scalding dish over him as he sat
at dinner, fell on his knees and repeated the verse of the Koran,
" Paradise is for those who bridle their anger."   " I am not
angry," answered Husain.   The slave proceeded, " and for
those who forgive men."   " I forgive you."   The slave, however, finished the verse, adding, " for God loveth the beneficent."
" I give you your liberty and four hundred pieces of silver,"
replied Husain.[4]

---

[1] Koran, sura xxii. 39, 40.   Thonissen's remark, that Mohammed allowed
the punishment of the wilful wrong-doer for the purpose of preventing
enormous evils, must always be borne in mind.—*L'Hist. du Droit Criminel
des Peuples Anciens*, vol. ii. p. 67.

[2] Koran, sura xli. 33, 34.   [3] Koran, sura xlii. 37.

[4] This anecdote has been told by Sale in a note to the third chapter of his
translation of the Koran, and also by Gibbon ; but both have, by mistake,

The author of the *Kashshâf* thus sums up the essence of the Islâmic teachings : " Seek again him who drives you away ; give to him who takes away from you ; pardon him who injures you : [1] for God loveth that you should cast into the depth of your soul the roots of His perfections." [2]

In the purity of its aspiration, can anything be more beautiful than the following : " The servants of the Merciful are they that walk upon the earth softly ; and when the ignorant speak unto them, they reply, Peace ! they that spend the night worshipping their Lord, prostrate, and standing, and resting : those that, when they spend, are neither profuse nor niggardly, but take a middle course : . . . those that invoke not with God any other God, and slay not a soul that God hath forbidden otherwise than by right ; and commit not fornication : . . . they who bear not witness to that which is false ; and when they pass by vain sport, they pass it by with dignity : who say, ' Oh, our Lord, grant us of our wives and children such as shall be a comfort unto us, and make us examples unto the pious,'—these shall be the rewarded, for that they persevered ; and they shall be accosted in paradise with welcome and salutation :—For ever therein,—a fair abode and resting-place ! " [3]

This is the Islâm of Mohammed. It is not " a mere creed ; it is a life to be lived in the present "—a religion of right-doing, right-thinking, and right-speaking, founded on divine love, universal charity, and the equality of man in the sight of the Lord. However much the modern professors of Islâm may have dimmed the glory of their Prophet (and a volume might also be written on the defects of modern Mohammedanism), the religion which enshrines righteousness and " justification by work " [4] deserves the recognition of the lovers of humanity.

---

applied the episode to Hasan, the brother of Husain.   See the *Tafsîr-Husaini*, Mirat Ed. p. 199.

[1] Compare this with the precept of Mohammed reported by Abû Dardâ, *Mishkât*, bk. iv. chap. i. part ii., and the whole chapter on " Forgiveness " (chap. xxxvi.) in the *Mustatraf*.

[2] Zamakhshari (the *Kashshâf*), Egypt. Ed. part i. p. 280.

[3] Koran, sura xxv. 63-76.

[4] Mr. Cotter Morrison, in his *Service of Man*, calls the other doctrine the most disastrous to human morality.

مي تواني از ره آسمان شدن بر آسمان

راست باش و راست رو کانجا نباشد کاستني

" Wishest thou to approach God ?
Live purely, and act righteously."

Jalâl ud-din Rûmi says,—

از بهایم بهره داری وز ملایک نیز هم

بگذر از بهایم تا از ملایک هم بگذری

" Thou partakest of the nature of the beast as well as the angel ;
Leave the nature of the beast, that thou mayest surpass the angel."

The present life was the seed-ground of the future. To work in all humility of spirit for the human good, to strive with all energy to approach the perfection of the All-Perfect, is the essential principle of Islâm. The true Moslem is a true Christian, in that he accepts the ministry of Jesus, and tries to work out the moral preached by him. Why should not the true Christian do honour to the Preacher who put the finishing stroke to the work of the earlier Masters ? Did not he call back the wandering forces of the world into the channel of progress ?

Excepting for the conception of the sonship of Jesus, there is no fundamental difference between Christianity and Islâm. In their essence they are one and the same ; both are the outcome of the same spiritual forces working in humanity. One was a protest against the heartless materialism of the Jews and the Romans ; the other a revolt against the degrading idolatry of the Arabs, their ferocious customs and usages. Christianity, preached among a more settled and civilised people subject to an organised government, had to contend with comparatively milder evils. Islâm, preached among warring tribes and clans, had to fight against all the instincts of self-interest and ancient superstition. Christianity, arrested in its progress towards the East by a man of cultured but bizarre character, who, though a Jew by birth, was by education an Alexandrian Greek, was carried to Greece and Rome, and there gathering up the pagan civilisation of centuries, gave

birth to new ideas and doctrines. Christianity ceased to be
Christian the moment it was transplanted from the home of
its birth. It became the religion of Paul, and ceased to be that
of Jesus. The pantheons of ancient paganism were tottering
to their fall. Greek and Alexandrian philosophy had prepared
the Roman world for the recognition of an incarnate God—a
demiurgus, an Æon born in the bosom of eternity, and this
conception imbedded itself in Pauline Christianity. Modern
idealistic Christianity, which is more a philosophy than a
positive religion, is the product of centuries of pre-Christian
and post-Christian civilisation. Islâm was preached among
a people, among conditions social and moral, wholly divergent.
Had it broken down the barrier which was raised against it by
a degraded Christianity, and made its way among the higher
races of the earth, its progress and its character would have
presented a totally different aspect from what it now offers
to the observer among the less cultured Moslem communities.
Like rivers flowing through varied tracts, both these creeds
have produced results in accordance with the nature of the
soil through which they have found their course. The Mexican
who castigates himself with cactus leaves, the idol-worshipping
South American, the lower strata of Christian nations, are
hardly in any sense Christians. There exists a wide gulf
between them and the leaders of modern Christian thought.
Islâm, wherever it has found its way among culturable and
progressive nations, has shown itself in complete accord with
progressive tendencies, it has assisted civilisation, it has
idealised religion.[1]

A religion has to be eminently positive in its " commandments and prohibitions " to exercise an abiding salutary
influence on the ignorant and uncultured. The higher and
more spiritualised minds are often able to forge on the anvils
of their own hearts, lines of duty in relation to their fellow
creatures without reference to outside directions. They are

---

[1] The faith which could give birth to the heroic devotion of Ali, the gentleness of Ja'far (the Sâdik), the piety and patience of Mûsa, the divine purity
of Fâtima, the saintliness of Râbi'a ; the religion which could produce men
like Ibn-Sîna, Al-Beiruni, Ibn-Khaldûn, Sanâi, Jalâl ud-din Rûmi, Farîd
ud-din (the Attâr), Ibrâhim Adham, and a host of others, surely contains
every element of hopefulness.

in commune with God and are guided by the consciousness of right and wrong, of truth and purity which had grown up with their being.   Plato and Aristotle, who had never received the light of the Semitic revelations, spoke to the world of the highest principles of morality in as distinct terms as the great prophets.   They too had heard the voice of God, and were lifted up to Him by their own thoughts.

To the mass of mankind, however, sunk either in ignorance or barbarism, for the uncultured and the sodden, moral enunciations convey no meaning unless they are addressed in a positive form and formulated with the precision of enactments surrounded with definite sanctions.   The ethical side of a religion does not appeal to their feelings or sentiments ; and philosophical conceptions exercise no influence on their minds, their daily conduct or their lives.

They are swayed far more by authority and precedent than by sermons on abstract principles.   They require definite prescriptions to regulate not only their relations towards their fellow-beings but also towards their Creator whom, in the absence of such rules, they are apt to forget.

The success of Islâm in the seventh century of the Christian era, and its rapid and marvellous diffusion over the surface of the globe, were due to the fact that it recognised this essential need of human nature.   To a world of wrangling sects and creeds, to whom words were of far greater importance than practice, it spoke in terms of positive command from an Absolute Source.   Amidst the moral and social wreck in which it found its birth, it aimed at the integration of the worship of a Personal Will, and thereby to recall humanity to the observance of duty which alone pointed to the path of spiritual development.   And by its success in lifting up the lower races to a higher level of social morality it proved to the world the need of a positive system.   It taught them sobriety, temperance, charity, justice and equality as the commandments of God.   Its affirmation of the principle of equality of man and man and its almost socialistic tendency represented the same phase of thought that had found expression on the shores of Galilee.   But even in his most exalted mood the great Teacher of Islâm did not forget the limitations imposed on individual capacity which occasion economic inequalities.

Alas for the latter-day professors of Islâm ! The blight of patristicism has ruined the blossom of true religion and a true devotional spirit.

A Christian preacher has pointed out with great force the distinction between religion and theology, and the evils which have followed in his Church from the confusion of the two.[1] What has happened in Christianity has happened in Islâm. Practice has given way to the mockery of profession, ceremonialism has taken the place of earnest and faithful work,— doing good to mankind for the sake of doing good, and for the love of God. Enthusiasm has died out, and devotion to God and His Prophet are meaningless words. The earnestness without which human existence is no better than that of the brute creation, earnestness in right-doing and right-thinking, is absent. The Moslems of the present day have ignored the spirit in a hopeless love for the letter. Instead of living up to the ideal preached by the Master, instead of " striving to excel in good works," " of being righteous " ; instead of loving God, and for the sake of His love loving His creatures,—they have made themselves the slaves of opportunism and outward observance. It was natural that in their reverence and admiration for the Teacher his early disciples should stereotype his ordinary mode of life, crystallise the passing incidents of a chequered career, imprint on the heart orders, rules, and regulations enunciated for the common exigencies of the day in an infant society. But to suppose that the greatest Reformer the world has ever produced, the greatest upholder of the sovereignty of Reason, the man who proclaimed that the universe was governed and guided by law and order, and that the law of nature meant progressive development, ever contemplated that even those injunctions which were called forth by the passing necessities of a semi-civilised people should become immutable to the end of the world, is doing an injustice to the Prophet of Islâm.

No one had a keener perception than he of the necessities of this world of progress with its ever-changing social and moral

[1] Professor Momerie in his *Defects of Modern Christianity*.

phenomena, nor of the likelihood that the revelations vouch-safed to him might not meet all possible contingencies.   When Muâz was appointed as governor of Yemen, he was asked by the Prophet by what rule he would be guided in his administra-tion of that province.   " By the law of the Koran," said Muâz. " But if you find no direction therein ? "   " Then I will act according to the example of the Prophet."   " But if that fails ? "   " Then I will exercise my own judgment."   The Prophet approved highly of the answer of his disciple, and commended it to the other delegates.

The great Teacher, who was fully conscious of the exigencies of his own times, and the requirements of the people with whom he had to deal,—people sunk in a slough of social and moral despond,—with his keen insight and breadth of views, perceived, and one may say foretold, that a time would come when the accidental and temporary regulations would have to be differ-entiated from the permanent and general.   " Ye are in an age," he declared, " in which, if ye abandon one-tenth of what is ordered, ye will be ruined.   After this, a time will come when he who shall observe one-tenth of what is now ordered will be redeemed." [1]

وَعَنْ اَبِي هُرَيْرَةَ قَالَ قَالَ رَسُولُ اللَّهِ صَلَّى اللَّهُ عَلَيْهِ وَسَلَّمَ اِنَّكُمْ فِي زَمَانٍ مَنْ تَرَكَ مِنْكُمْ عُشْرَ مَا اُمِرَ بِهِ هَلَكَ ثُمَّ يَاتِي زَمَانٌ مَنْ عَمِلَ مِنْهُمْ عُشْرَ مَا اُمِرَ بِهِ نَجَا رَوَاهُ التِّرْمِذِيُّ - مِشْكُوةُ الْمَصَابِيحِ - بَابُ الْاِعْتِصَامِ بِالْكِتَابِ وَالسُّنَّةِ

As we have already observed, the blight which has fallen on Musulman nations is not due to the teachings of the Master. No religion contained greater promise of development, no faith was purer, or more in conformity with the progressive demands of humanity.

The present stagnation of the Musulman communities is principally due to the notion which has fixed itself on the minds of the generality of Moslems, that the right to the exercise of private judgment ceased with .the early legists,

[1] This authentic tradition is given in the *Jâma‘ ut-Tirmizi* and is to be found also in the *Mishkât.*

that its exercise in modern times is sinful, and that a Moslem in order to be regarded as an orthodox follower of Mohammed should belong to one or the other of the schools established by the schoolmen of Islâm, and abandon his judgment absolutely to the interpretations of men who lived in the ninth century, and could have no conception of the necessities of the twentieth.

Among the Sunnis, it is the common belief that since the four Imâms,[1] no doctor has arisen qualified to interpret the laws of the Prophet. No account is taken of the altered circumstances in which Moslems are now placed; the con- clusions at which these learned legists arrived several centuries ago are held-to be equally applicable to the present day. Among the Shiahs, the Akhbâri will not allow his judgment to travel beyond the dictates of " the expounders of the law." The Prophet had consecrated reason as the highest and noblest function of the human intellect. Our schoolmen and their servile followers have made its exercise a sin and a crime.

As among Christians, so among Moslems. The lives and conduct of a large number of Moslems at the present day are governed less by the precepts and teachings of the Master, and more by the theories and opinions of the *mujtahids* and *imâms* who have tried, each according to his light, to construe the revelations vouchsafed to the Teacher. Like men in a crowd listening to a preacher who from a lofty position addresses a large multitude and from his vantage ground overlooks a vast area, they observed only their immediate surroundings, and, without comprehending the wider meaning of his words or the nature of the audience whom he addressed, adapted his utterances to their own limited notions of human needs and human progress. Oblivious of the universality of the Master's teachings, unassisted by his spirit, devoid of his inspiration, they forgot that the Prophet, from the pinnacle of his genius, had spoken to all humanity. They mixed up the temporary with the permanent, the universal with the particular. Like many of the ecclesiastics of Christendom, not a few were the servants of sovereigns and despots whose demands were not consistent with the precepts of the Master. Canons were invented, theories started, traditions discovered, and glosses

[1] Abû Hanîfa, Shâfe'i, Mâlik, and Ibn Hanbal.

put upon his words utterly at variance with their spirit. And hence it is that most of the rules and regulations which govern now the conscience of so many professors of the faith are hardly derived from any express and positive declarations of the Koran, but for the most part from the lego-religious books with which the Islâmic world was flooded in the later centuries. " Just as the Hebrews deposed their Pentateuch in favour of the Talmud," justly observes an English writer, " so the Moslems have abolished the Koran in favour of the traditions and decisions of the learned." " We do not mean to say," he adds most pertinently, " that any Mohammedan if asked what was the text-book of his religion, would answer anything but the ' Koran ' ; but we do mean that practically it is not the Koran that guides his belief or practice. In the Middle Ages of Christendom it was not the New Testament, but the *Summa Theologica* of Thomas Aquinas, that decided questions of orthodoxy ; and in the present day, does the orthodox churchman usually derive his creed from a personal investigation of the teaching of Christ in the Gospels ? Probably, if he refers to a document at all, the Church Catechism contents him ; or if he be of a peculiarly inquiring disposition, a perusal of the Thirty-nine Articles will resolve all doubts. Yet he too would say his religion was drawn from the Gospels, and would not confess to the medium through which it was filtered. In precisely the same way modern Mohammedanism is constructed, and a large part of what Moslems now believe and practise is not to be found in the Koran at all."

And yet each system, each school contains germs of improvement, and if development is now stopped, it is not even the fault of the lawyers. It is due to a want of apprehension of the spirit of the Master's enunciations, and even of those of the fathers of the Church.[1]

In the Western world, the Reformation was ushered in by the Renaissance and the progress of Europe commenced when

---

[1] The *Radd ul-Muhtâr* of Mohammed Amîn the Syrian, and the *Majma' ul-Anhâr* of the Shaikh Zâdeh are as much in advance of the *Multeka* and the *Hedâya* as the views of an Eldon or Mansfield upon those of a Coke or Blackstone. The opinions of Shaikh Murtaza, in their liberal and liberalising tendencies, are far above those of the narrow-minded self-opinionated Mohakkik. But the servile Akhbâri follows the latter in preference to the former.

it threw off the shackles of Ecclesiasticism. In Islâm also, enlightenment must precede reform ; and, before there can be a renovation of religious life, the mind must first escape from the bondage which centuries of literal interpretation and the doctrine of "conformity" have imposed upon it. The formalism that does not appeal to the heart of the worshipper must be abandoned ; externals must be subordinated to the inner feelings ; and the lessons of ethics must be impressed on the plastic mind ; then alone can we hope for that enthusiasm in the principles of duty taught by the Prophet of Islâm. The reformation of Islâm will begin when once it is recognised that divine words rendered into any language retain their divine character and that devotions offered in any tongue are acceptable to God. The Prophet himself had allowed his foreign disciples to say their prayers in their own tongue.[1] He had expressly permitted others to recite the Koran in their respective dialects ; and had declared that it was revealed in seven languages.

In the earliest ages of Islâm there was a consensus of opinion that devotion without understanding was useless. Imâm Abû Hanifa considered the recitation of the *namâz* and also of the *Khutba* or sermon, lawful and valid in any language.[2] The disciples of Abû Hanîfa, Abû Yusuf and Mohammed, have accepted the doctrine of their master with a certain variation. They hold that when a person does not know Arabic, he may validly offer his devotions in any other language.[3]

There is, however, one great and cogent reason why the practice of reciting prayers in Arabic should be maintained wherever it is possible and practicable. Not because it was the language of the Prophet, but because it has become the language of Islâm and maintains the unity of sentiment

[1] Salmân the Persian, whom Ali had saved from a lion, was the first to whom this permission was granted.

[2] *Jawâhir ul-Akhlâti : Durr ul-Mukhtâr, Bâb us-Salât* (Chapter on Prayer). This view is also given in the *Tajnîs*. Tahtâwi states that the Imâm's opinion is authoritative and should be followed. The commentator of the *Durr ul-Mukhtâr* also recognises the validity of reciting prayers in Persian.

[3] This is construed by the *Ulemas* of the present day to mean, when the worshipper is unable to pronounce Arabic words ! The absurdity of the explanation is obvious.

throughout the Islâmic world.   And wherein lies more strength than in unity ?

NOTE I.

The sumptuary prohibitions of Mohammed may be divided into two classes, *qualitative* and *quantitative*.   The prohibition against excess in eating and drinking and others of the like import belong to the latter class.   They were called forth in part by the peculiar semi-barbarous epicureanism which was coming into fashion among the Arabs from their intercourse with the demoralised Syrians and Persians, and in part by circumstances of which only glimpses are afforded us in the Koran.   The absolute prohibition of swine's flesh, which may be classed under the head of qualitative prohibitions, arose, as is evident, from hygienic reasons and this prohibition must remain unchanged as long as the nature of the animal and the diseases engendered by the eating of the flesh remain as at present.   The prohibition against dancing was directed against the orgiastic dances with which the heathen Arabs used to celebrate the Syro-Phœnician worship of their Ashtoreth, Moloch and Baal.

CHAPTER III

THE IDEA OF FUTURE LIFE IN ISLÂM

يَا أَيَّتُهَا النَّفْسُ الْمُطْمَئِنَّـــةُ • ارْجِعِي إِلَى رَبِّكِ رَاضِيَةً مَرْضِيَّةً •

فَادْخُلِي فِي عِبَادِي • وَادْخُلِي جَنَّتِي • [1]

THE idea of a future existence—of an existence after the separation of the living principle of our nature from the mortal part—is so generally shared by races of men, otherwise utterly distinct from each other, that it has led to the belief that it must be one of the first elementary constituents of our being. A more careful examination of facts, however, connected with the infancy of races and tribes, leads us to the conclusion that the conception of a future existence is also the result of the natural development of the human mind.

The wild savage has scarcely any idea of a life separate and distinct from that which he enjoys on earth. He looks upon death as the end of existence. Then comes a later stage when man has passed out of his savage state, his hopes and aspirations are bounded no more by an earthly death ; he now anticipates another course of existence after the course here has been fulfilled. But even in this stage the conception of immortality does not rise out of the groove of daily life. Life after death is a mere continuation of life on earth. This idea of a continued life beyond the grave must have been developed from the yet unconscious longing of the human soul for a more extended

[1] See translation at end of this chapter.

sphere, where the separation of dear friends, so painful to both savage and civilised man, should end in reunion.

The next stage is soon reached ; man comes to believe that present happiness and misery are not, cannot be, the be-all and end-all of his existence ; that there *will be* another life, or that there *is* another life after death, where he will be happy or miserable in proportion to his deserts.

Now we have reached a principle and a law.

The mind of man goes no further towards developing the idea of future existence. The nihilistic philosopher makes no discovery, asserts no new position. He is only treading in the footsteps of our savage ancestor, whose field of vision was restricted to this life alone.

It is a well-authenticated fact, however, that all those ideas which represent the various stages, from a subjective point of view, exist simultaneously not only among different nations but even in the same nation, in different combinations, according to the individual development.

The Egyptians are said to have been the first to recognise the doctrine of a future life, or, at least, to base the principles of human conduct on such a doctrine.[1] With an idea of metempsychosis they joined an idea of future recompense and punishment. Man descended into the tomb only to rise again. After his resurrection he entered on a new life, in company with the sun, the principle of generation, the self-existent cause of all. The soul of man was considered immortal like the sun, and as accomplishing the same pilgrimages. All bodies descended into the lower world, but they were not all assured of resurrection. The deceased were judged by Osiris and his forty-two assessors. Annihilation was often believed to be the lot of those adjudged guilty. The righteous, purified from venial faults, entered into perfect happiness, and as the companions of Osiris, were fed by him with delicious food.[2]

We might naturally expect that the long stay of the Israelites in Egypt would introduce among them some conception of a

[1] Rawlinson's *History of Ancient Egypt*, vol. ii. p. 423.

[2] Comp. Lenormant, *Ancient History of the East*, vol. i. pp. 319-322 ; and Alger, *History of the Doctrine of a Future Life*, p. 102 *et seq.*

future life with its concomitant idea of rewards and punishments.   But pure Mosaism (or the teachings which pass under
that name) does not recognise a state of existence differing
from the present.   The pivot on which the entire system of
Mosaic legislation turns consists of tangible *earthly* rewards and
punishments.[1]   The vitality of the laws is confined within a
very small compass.   The doctrine of a resurrection, with the
ideas arising from it, which appears in later Judaism,—especially
in the writings of Daniel and Ezekiel,—is evidently a fruit of
foreign growth derived from Zoroastrian sources.   Even the
descriptions of Sheol, the common sojourn of departed beings,
equally of the just and unjust, which appear in comparatively
early writings, do not seem of true Hebraic origin.   In Sheol
man can no longer praise God or remember His loving-kindness.[2]
It is a shadow-realm, a Jewish counterpart of the heathen
Hades, in which the souls lead a sad, lethargic, comfortless
existence ; knowing nothing of those who were dear to them
on earth, mourning only over their own condition.[3]

But later Judaism is full of the strongest faith in a future
life.   Tradition revels in the descriptions of the abodes of bliss,
or of the horrors of the damned.[4]   Zoroastrianism thus acted
on the Hebraic race in a double way.   It not only developed
in them a purer and more spiritual conception of a future
existence, but later Mago-Zoroastrianism, itself a product of
Chaldæism, strongly coloured the Rabbinical beliefs with
materialistic ideas of punishments and rewards hereafter.[5]   It
was, however, among the Aryan nations of the East that the
doctrine of a future life after visible death was distinctly and
vividly recognised.   In one branch of the Aryan family, it took
the shape either of an eternal metempsychosis, a ceaseless whirl
of births and deaths, or of utter absorption after a prolonged
probation in absolute infinity, or endless unfathomable space,

[1] Comp. Alger, *History of the Doctrine of a Future Life*, p. 157 ; also Milman's
Christianity, vol. i. pp. 21, 25, 75, etc.

[2] Ps. vi. 5.

[3] Job xiv. 22.   Comp. Döllinger, vol. ii. p. 389 ; and Alger, *History of the
Doctrine of a Future Life*, pp. 151, 152 *et seq.*

[4] See Milman, *History of Christianity*, vol. i. p. 242, notes.

[5] See the chapter of Alger, tracing the influence of the Persian system on
later Judaism, p. 165 *et seq.*

or nothing.[1] In the other branch, this doctrine was clothed in the shape of a graduated scale of rewards and punishments, in the sense in which human accountability is understood by the modern Christian or Moslem. Whether the Mago-Zoroastrians from the beginning believed in a corporeal resurrection is a question on which scholars are divided. Döllinger, with Burnouf and others, believes that this notion was not really Zoroastric, and that it is of later growth, if not derived from Hebrews.[2]

However this be, about the time of the Prophet of Arabia, the Persians had a strong and developed conception of future life. The remains of the Zend-Avesta which have come down to us expressly recognise a belief in future rewards and punishments. The Zoroastrianism of the Vendidad and the Bunde-hesh, enlarging upon the beliefs of the Avesta, holds that after a man's death the demons take possession of his body, yet on the third day consciousness returns. Souls that in their lifetime have yielded to the seductions of evil cannot pass the terrible bridge Chinevad, to which they are conducted on the day following the third night after their death. The good successfully pass it, conducted by the Yazatas (in modern Persian, *Izad*), and, entering the realms of bliss, join Ormuzd and the Amshaspands in their abode, where seated on thrones of gold, they enjoy the society of beautiful fairies (*Hoorân-i-Behisht*) and all manner of delights. The wicked fall over the bridge or are dragged down into the gulf of *Duzakh* where they are tormented by the *Dævas*. The duration of this punishment is fixed by Ormuzd, and some are redeemed by the prayers and intercessions of their friends. Towards the end of the world a prophet is to arise, who is to rid the earth of injustice

---

[1] And yet the Brahmanical priests painted the horrors of hell and the pleasures of heaven with the vividness of a thoroughly morbid imagination. The Arabic scholar is referred to the appreciative account of the Buddhistic doctrines (not so much regarding future life as generally) in Shahristâni, p. 446.

[2] Alger has furnished us with strong reasons for supposing that the early Zoroastrians believed in a bodily resurrection. The extreme repugnance with which the Mago-Zoroastrians regarded corpses is no reason for discarding this conclusion, as most probably this repugnance arose under Manichæan influences ; see Alger, p. 138 *et seq.* *Apropos* of the repugnance with which the Persians in Mohammed's time looked upon corpses, consult Döllinger, vol. ii. p. 409.

and wickedness, and usher in a reign of happiness—the Zoroastrian millennium, Ormuzd's kingdom of heaven.[1] After this, a universal resurrection will take place, and friends and relatives will meet again. After the joys of recognition there will follow a separation of the good from the bad. The torments of the unrighteous will be fearful. Ahriman will run up and down Chinevad overwhelmed with anguish. A blazing comet, falling on the earth, will ignite the world. Mountains will melt and flow together like liquid metal. All mankind, good and bad alike, will pass through this glowing flood, and come out purified. Even Ahriman will be changed and *Duzakh* purified. Evil thenceforth will be annihilated, and all mankind will live in the enjoyment of ineffable delights.

Such is the summary of a religion which has influenced the Semitic faiths in an unmistakable manner, and especially the eclectic faith of Mohammed.

About the time when Jesus of Nazareth made his appearance, the Phœnicians and Assyrians had passed away. The hellenised Roman ruled the world, checked in the East, however, by triumphant and revived Mago-Zoroastrianism.

The Jew had lost his independence for ever. A miserable sycophant occupied the throne of David. A mightier power than that of the Seleucidæ kept in subjection his spirit of unruliness. Like every nation animated by a fierce love of their country, creed, and individuality, the Jews, as their fate grew darker and darker, became more and more inspired with the hope that some heaven-commissioned ministrant, like Gideon or Maccabeus, would restore their original glory, and enable them to plant their foot on the necks of their many oppressors.[2] The appearance of a Messiah portrayed in vivid colours by all their patriotic seers, the Jewish bards, was founded on one grand aspiration—the restoration of the

---

[1] Shahristânî calls this prophet Ushîzerbekâ (Cureton's ed. p. 188) ; but according to Western authors his name is said to be Sosiosch; who is to be preceded by two other prophets, called Oscheder Bami and Oschédermah (Döllinger v. ii. p. 401). De Sacy calls him Pashoutan (*Sur Div. Ant. de la Perse*, p. 95).

[2] It is not necessary, as Alger supposes, that because the Jews looked forward to the reappearance of Elijah or some other prophet among them for these national purposes, we must conclude that they believed in transmigration.

kingdom of Israel. Under the influences of the Mago-Zoroastrians and Chaldæans in the East, and the Grecian schools of
philosophy in the West, among some classes of society
(especially among those whom the hellenising tendencies of
Herod had withdrawn from the bosom of Israel), the belief in
a personal Messiah was either faint and indistinct, or a mere
echo from the vulgar masses. But, as Milman beautifully
observes, the Palestinian Jews had about this time moulded
out of various elements a splendid though confused vision of
the appearance of the Messiah, the simultaneous regeneration
of all things, the resurrection of the dead, and the reign of
Messiah upon earth. All these events were to take place at
once, or to follow close upon each other.[1] The Messiah was to
descend from the line of David ; he was to assemble all the
scattered descendants of the tribes, and to expel and destroy
their hateful alien enemies. Under the Messiah a resurrection
would take place, but would be confined to the righteous of
their race.[2]

Amidst all this enthusiasm and these vague aspirations, the
hopes of eternal life and future bliss were strangely mingled.
The extremes of despair and enthusiastic expectation of
external relief always tend to the development of such a state
of mind among the people. One section appears to look
forward to an unearthly kingdom, a reign of peace and law
under divine agency, as an escape from the galling yoke of
brute force ; the other looks forward to the same or cognate
means for securing the kingdom of heaven by the blood of
aliens and heathens.[3]

The traditions which record the sayings of Jesus have gone

[1] Milman, *History of Christianity*, vol. i. p. 76.

[2] The similarity between the Zoroastrian idea of a deliverer and restorer
of religion and order on earth, and the Messianic conception among the Jews,
is, to say the least, wonderful. The Jews, it is certain, derived this conception from the Zoroastrians ; and in their misfortunes developed it in more
vivid terms. But I am strongly disposed to think that the idea of a Sosiosch,
whatever its prophetic significance, arose among the Persians also when
labouring under a foreign yoke—whether of the Semitic Assyrians or the Greek
Macedonians it is difficult to say. The very country in which the scene of
his appearance is laid—Kanguédez in Khorasân, according to De Sacy,
Cansoya, according to Döllinger's authorities—shows that the Persians, in their
misfortunes, looked to the East, especially to the " Land of the Sun," for
assistance and deliverance.

[3] Like the modern, though obscure, sect of Christadelphians.

through such a process of elimination and selection, that it is hardly possible at the present moment to say which are really his own words and which are not.[1]   But taking them as they stand, and on the same footing as we regard other religious documents (without ignoring their real spirit, yet without trying to find mysterious meanings like the faithful believer), we see that throughout these traditional records the notion of an immediate advent of a new order of things, " of a kingdom of heaven," is so predominant in the mind of Jesus as to overshadow all other ideas.   The Son of Man has appeared, the kingdom of God is at hand ; such is the burden of every hopeful word.[2]   This kingdom was to replace the society and government which the Prophet of Nazareth found so imperfect and evil.   At times his words led the disciples to conclude that the new Teacher was born to lead only the poor and the famished to glory and happiness ; that under the hoped-for theocratic *régime* these alone would be " the blessed," and would constitute the predominating element, for " woe " is denounced in awful terms against the rich and the well-fed.[3]   At other times, the realm of God is understood to mean the literal fulfilment of the apocalyptic visions or dreams connected with the appearance of the Messiah.   Sometimes, however, the kingdom of God is a realm of souls, and the approaching deliverance is merely a spiritual deliverance from the bondage

[1] Milman himself admits that the traditions regarding the acts and sayings of Jesus, which were floating about among the Christian communities, were not cast into their present shape till almost the close of the first half of the second century (*History of Christianity*, vol. i. p. 126).   Necessarily, therefore, the ancient collectors and modellers of the Christian Gospels, or as Milman regards them, rude and simple historians, must have exercised a discretionary latitude in the reception of the traditions.   They must have decided everything on dogmatic grounds.   " If a narrative or scripture was, in its tone and substance, agreeable to their (preconceived) views, they looked upon defective external evidence as complete ; if it was not agreeable, the most sufficient was explained away as a misunderstanding."   Hence a great many additions were made, though unconsciously, to the sayings and doings of Jesus.   On this point the testimony of Celsus, with every allowance for exaggeration, must be regarded as conclusive when he says the Christians were in the habit of coining and remodelling their traditional accounts (*Origen c. Celsus*, ii. 27). And this on the principle laid down by Sir W. Muir in Canon III. p. lxxxi. vol. i. (*Life of Mahomet*).

[2] Matt. iv. 17, x. 7, etc.

[3] Luke vii. 20 *et seq*.   In Matthew " the poor in spirit " are mentioned. But the simpler statement of Luke, from a comparison of all the circumstances, seems more authentic.

of this mundane existence. All these conceptions appear at one period to have existed in the mind of Jesus simultaneously.[1] But the fierceness and bigotry of the dominant party and the power of the Roman eagle made any immediate social change impossible. As every hope of present amelioration died away, hopes and aspirations of a brighter future took possession of the heart. Jesus felt the present state could not last long ; that the time of the regeneration of mankind was at hand,[2] when he himself would appear in the clouds of heaven, clothed in divine garments, seated on a throne, surrounded by angels and his chosen disciples.[3] The dead would rise from their graves,[4] and the Messiah would sit in judgment. The angels would be the executors of his sentence. He would send the elect to a delightful abode prepared from the beginning of the world, and the unrighteous into " everlasting fire prepared for the devil and his angels," [5] where there would be weeping and gnashing of teeth. The chosen, not numerically large,[6] would be taken into an illuminated mansion, where they would partake of banquets presided over by the father of the race of Israel, the patriarchs, and the prophets,[7] and in which Jesus himself will share.[8]

[1] Renan, *Vie de Jesus*, p. 282.

[2] Matt. xix. 18.
There can be no doubt that Jesus himself believed in a corporeal resurrection, and in tangible rewards and punishments in a future life. He often spoke of " the blessed " in his kingdom eating and drinking at his table. But whilst in the early traditions passing under the name of the four apostles, the accounts, owing to careful pruning, are meagre enough, later traditionists enlarge upon the descriptions of paradise and hell, and revel in the most gorgeous fantasies, which go under the name of revelations (*vide* Rev. xxi. 8-21, xxii. 1, 2). In puerility even the Christian traditionists do not fall short of the followers of other creeds. The tradition handed down by Irenæus on the authority of John declares Jesus to have said, " Days shall come in which there shall be vines, which shall have each ten thousand branches, and every one of these branches shall have ten thousand lesser branches, and every one of these branches shall have ten thousand twigs, and every one of these twigs shall have ten thousand clusters of grapes, and in every one of these clusters there shall be ten thousand grapes, and every one of these grapes being pressed shall yield two hundred and seventy-five gallons of wine ; and when a man shall take hold of one of these sacred bunches, another bunch shall cry out, I am a better bunch, take me, and bless the Lord by me," etc.

[3] Matt. xvi. 27, xxiv. 30, 31, xxv. 31 *et seq.* etc.

[4] Rev. xx. 12, 13. Compare these notions with the Zoroastrian belief.

[5] Matt. xxv. 41.   [6] Luke xiii. 23.

[7] Matt. viii. 11 ; Luke xiii. 28, xxii. 30.   [8] Matt. xxvi. 29.

That the inauguration of the new *régime* with the second advent of Jesus and the resurrection of the human race was considered not to be distant, is apparent from the words of the Master himself, when he impressed upon his hearers the approach of the kingdom of God, and the utter futility of every provision for the occupations and exigencies of the present life.[1]

The words of the Teacher, acting in unison with the state of mind engendered by the circumstances of the age,[2] had sunk deep into the hearts of his disciples, and all looked forward, with a vividness of expectation hardly surpassed in the annals of human beliefs, to the literal fulfilment of the prophecies concerning the millennium.

" If the first generation of the Christians had a profound and constant belief, it was that the world was approaching its end, and that the great ' revelation ' of Christ was to happen soon." [3] It is only when the Christian Church becomes a regular organisation that the followers of Jesus expand their views beyond the restricted horizon of the Judaic world, and, forgetting their millenarian dream, they pass into the Greek and Roman system, and extend the empire of their creed over untold legions of barbarians fresh from their forests, who looked upon Jesus and his mother as the counterparts of their own Odin and Freya worshipped in their primeval homes.

But ever and anon the Christian world has been agitated in moments of convulsions and disasters by the millenary excitement and fierce expectation of the apocalyptic appearance of the great Prophet of Nazareth. The idea, however, of the realm of God has, with the lapse of ages and the progress of thought, taken either a spiritual shape or utterly faded away from the mind, or, where it has been retained, derives its character from the surroundings of the individual believers. The Jew, the Mago-Zoroastrian, and the Christian all believed in a bodily resurrection. The crude notions of primitive Mosaism had made way for more definite ideas derived chiefly

---

[1] Matt. x. 23 ; Mark xiii. 30 ; Luke xiii. 35 ; Matt. vi. 25-34, viii. 22.

[2] Mark the bitter term which Jesus applies to his generation.

[3] Renan, *Vie de Jesus*, p. 287.   Comp. also Milman's *History of Christianity*, vol. i. p. 378.

from the Chaldæo-Zoroastrian doctrines.   We know how among the Persians the old worship of the mountains, the simple teachings of the early teachers, had grown, under the magic wands of the Babylonian wizards, into a complex system of graduated rewards and punishments,—how Chaldæan philosophy had permeated Mago-Zoroastrianism to its innermost core. Primitive Christianity, with its vivid belief in the immediate advent of the material kingdom of Christ, had imbibed notions from Chaldæan, Mago-Zoroastrian, and Alexandrian sources which had considerably altered the old conceptions. Jew, Christian, and Zoroastrian all looked, more or less, to material rewards and punishments in a future existence.

The popular Christian notion, fostered by ecclesiasticism, that Mohammed denied souls to women, is by this time, we believe, exploded. It was a calumny concocted to create an aversion against Islâm. But the idea that the Arabian Prophet promised his followers a sensual paradise with *hooris*, and a graduated scale of delights, still lingers. It is a sign alike of ignorance and ancient bigotry. There is no doubt that in the Suras of the intermediate period, before the mind of the Teacher had attained the full development of religious consciousness, and when it was necessary to formulate in language intelligible to the common folk of the desert, the realistic descriptions of heaven and hell, borrowed from the floating fancies of Zoroastrian, Sabæan, and the Talmudical Jew, attract the attention as a side picture, and then comes the real essence—the adoration of God in humility and love. The *hooris* are creatures of Zoroastrian origin, so is paradise,[1] whilst hell in the severity of its punishment is Talmudic. The descriptions are realistic, in some places almost sensuous ; but to say that they are sensual, or that Mohammed, or any of his followers, even the ultra-literalists accepted them as such, is a calumny. The wine " that does not inebriate " and the attendants " that come not nigh," can hardly be said to represent sensual pleasures !

The chief and predominating idea in Islâm respecting a future life is founded upon the belief that, in a state of existence hereafter, every human being will have to render an account of his

[1] In Persian, *firdous*.

or her actions on earth, and that the happiness or misery of individuals will depend upon the manner in which they have performed the behests of their Creator. His mercy and grace are nevertheless unbounded, and will be bestowed alike upon His creatures. This is the pivot on which the whole doctrine of future life in Islâm turns, and this is the only doctrinal point one is required to believe and accept. All the other elements, caught up and syncretised from the floating traditions of the races and peoples of the time, are mere accessories. Setting aside from our consideration the question of subjectivity involved in all ideas of future rewards and punishments, we may say, in all ideas of a life-after death, we must bear in mind that these ideas have furnished to the moral teachers of the world the most powerful instrument for influencing the conduct of individuals and nations. But though every religion, more or less, contains the germ of this principle of future account-ability in another state, all have failed thoroughly to realise its nature as a continuous agency for the elevation of the masses. Virtue, for its own sake, can only be grasped by minds of superior development ; for the average intellect, and for the uneducated, sanctions, more or less comprehensible, will always be necessary.

To turn now to the nature of these sanctions, it must be remembered that it is scarcely ever possible to convey an idea of spiritual pleasure or spiritual pain to the apprehensions of the generality of mankind without clothing the expressions in the garb of tangible personalities, or introducing sensible objects into the description of such pleasure or pain. Philosophy has wrangled over abstract expressions, not dressed in tangible phraseology. Such expressions and conceptions have seen their day, have flourished, and have died without making them-selves felt beyond a restricted circle of dreamers, who lived in the indefinable vagueness of their own thoughts.

Mohammed was addressing himself not only to the advanced minds of a few idealistic thinkers who happened to be then living, but to the wide world around him engrossed in materialism of every type. He had to adapt himself to the comprehensions of all. To the wild famished Arab, what more grateful, or what more consonant to his ideas of paradise than rivers of unsullied incorruptible water, or of milk and honey ; or anything more acceptable than unlimited fruit, luxuriant vegetation, inexhaustible fertility ? He could conceive of no bliss unaccompanied with these sensuous pleasures. This is the contention of that portion of the Moslem world which, like Sanâî and Ghazzâlî, holds that behind the descriptions of material happiness portrayed in objects like trees, rivers, and beautiful mansions with fairy attendants, lies a deeper meaning ; and that the joy of joys is to consist in the beatific visions of the soul in the presence of the Almighty, when the veil which divides man from his Creator will be rent, and heavenly glory revealed to the mind untrammelled by its corporeal, earthly habiliments. In this they are upheld by the words of the Koran as well as the authentic sayings of the Prophet. " The most favoured of God," said Mohammed, " will be he who shall see his Lord's face (glory) night and morning, a felicity which will surpass all the pleasures of the body, as the ocean surpasses a drop of sweat." One day, talking to his friend, Abû Huraira, the Prophet said, " God has prepared for His good people what no eye hath seen, nor ear heard, nor hath it entered into the heart of anyone," and then recited the following verse of the Koran : " No soul knoweth the joy which is secretly prepared for it as a reward for that it may have wrought." [1] Another tradition [2] reports that Mohammed declared the good will enjoy the beatific vision of God, to which reference, he said, is made in the following verse of the Koran : " And God inviteth unto the dwelling of peace . . . For those who do good there is excellent reward and superabundant addition." [3]

As to the parabolical nature of the Koranic expressions, this school of thinkers bases its convictions on the following passage of the inspired Book : " It is He who hath sent down unto thee ' the Book.' Some of the signs (verses) are firm (i.e. perspicuous or clear to understand)—these are the basis (or fundamental part) of the book—and others are figurative." [4]

[1] Koran xxxii. 17 ; Mishkât, bk. xxiii. chap. xiii. pt. i.   [2] From Suhaib.
[3] Koran x. 26. Consult here Zamakhsharî (the *Kashshâf*), Egyp. Ed., pt. i. p. 244 ; he gives the fullest references to the opinions of the different theologians and schools, and especially mentions the doctrines of the *Mushhabbahâs* and the *Jabarias*.
[4] Koran iii. 5.

Another section looks upon the joys and pains of the Here-after as entirely subjective. It holds that as extreme mental pain is far more agonising than physical pain, so is mental pleasure of the higher type far more rapturous than any sensuous pleasure ; that as, after physical death, the indi-vidual soul " returns," to use the Koranic expression, to the Universal Soul, all the joys and pains, portrayed in vivid colours by the inspired Teacher to enable the masses to grasp the truth, will be mental and subjective. This section includes within its bosom some of the greatest philosophers and mystics of the Moslem world.

Another, and by far perhaps the larger class, however, believe in the literal fulfilment of all the word-paintings of the Koran.

Without venturing to pass any opinion on these different notions, we may take this occasion to state our own belief with regard to the Koranic conception of future rewards and punishments.

A careful study of the Koran makes it evident that the mind of Mohammed went through the same process of development which marked the religious consciousness of Jesus. Moham-med and Jesus are the only two historic Teachers of the world, and for this reason we take them together. How great this development was in Jesus is apparent, not only from the idealised conception towards the end of his earthly career regarding the Kingdom of Heaven, but also from the change of tone towards the non-Israelites. Thoroughly exclusive at first,[1] with a more developed religious consciousness wider sympathies awaken in the heart.[2]

As with Jesus so with Mohammed.

The various chapters of the Koran which contain the ornate descriptions of paradise, whether figurative or literal, were delivered wholly or in part at Mecca. Probably in the infancy of his religious consciousness, Mohammed himself believed in some or other of the traditions which floated around him. But with a wider awakening of the soul, a deeper communion with the Creator of the Universe, thoughts, which bore a material

[1] Matt. x. 5, xv. 22-26.
[2] Matt. xxviii. 19, etc. ; comp. throughout Strauss, *New Life of Jesus* (1865), vol. i. p. 296 *et seq.*

aspect at first, became spiritualised. The mind of the Teacher
progressed not only with the march of time and the development of his religious consciousness, but also with the progress
of his disciples in apprehending spiritual conceptions. Hence,
in the later *suras* we observe a merging of the material in the
spiritual, of the body in the soul. The gardens " watered by
rivers," perpetual shade,[1] plenty and harmony, so agreeable to
the famished denizen of the parched, shadeless, and waterless
desert, at perpetual discord with himself and all around him,
—these still form the groundwork of beautiful imageries ; but
the happiness of the blessed is shown to consist in eternal peace
and goodwill in the presence of their Creator. " But those,"
says the Koran, " who are pious shall dwell in gardens, amidst
fountains ; they shall say unto them, ' Enter ye therein in
peace and security ' ; and all rancour will we remove from their
bosoms ; they shall sit as brethren, face to face,[2] on couches ;
weariness shall not affect them therein, neither shall they be
repelled thence for ever." [3]

What can be nobler or grander in its conception or imagery,
or give a better idea of the belief in the Prophet's mind
when conveying his final message concerning the nature
of the present and future life, than the following passage :
" It is He who enableth you to travel by land and by sea ; so
that ye go on board of ships, which sail on with them, with
favourable breeze, and they rejoice therein. But if a tempestuous wind overtake, and the waves come on them from
every side, and they think they are encompassed therewith,
they call on God, professing unto Him sincere religion ; (saying)
wouldst Thou but rescue us from this, then we will ever be
indeed of the thankful. But when We have rescued them,
Behold ! they commit unrighteous excesses on the earth. O
men ! verily the excesses ye commit to the injury of your own
souls are only for the enjoyment of this earthly life ; soon shall
ye return to Us, and We will declare unto you that which ye
have done. Verily, the likeness of this present life is not
otherwise than the water which We send down from heaven ;
and the productions of the earth, of which men and cattle eat,

---

[1] Koran xiii. 34, xlvii. 16, 17. Comp. also chaps. ix., x., and xiv.
[2] *I.e.* with peace and good-will in their hearts.   [3] Koran xv. 48.

are mixed therewith, till the earth has received its beautiful raiment, and is decked out, and they who inhabit it imagine they have power over it ! (But) Our behest cometh unto it by night or by day, and We make it as if it had been mown, as though it had not teemed (with fertility) only yesterday. Thus do we make our signs clear unto those who consider. And God inviteth unto the abodes of peace, and guideth whom He pleaseth into the right way.[1] For those who do good is excellent reward and superabundant addition of it ; neither blackness nor shame shall cover their faces. These are the inhabitants of paradise ; therein do they abide for ever. But those who have wrought evil shall receive the reward of evil equal thereunto ; [2] and shame shall cover them (for there will be none to protect them against God) as though their faces were covered with a piece of the night of profound darkness." [3]

Then again, what can be purer in its aspirations than the following :

" Who fulfil the covenant of God and break not their compact ; and who join together what God hath bidden to be joined ; and who fear their Lord and dread an ill-reckoning ; and who, from a sincere desire to please their Lord,[4] are constant amid trials, and observe prayers and give alms, in secret and openly, out of what We have bestowed on them ; and turn aside evil with good : for them there is the recompense of that abode, gardens of eternal habitation, into which they shall enter, together with such as shall have acted rightly from among their fathers, their wives, and their posterity ; and the angels shall go in unto them by every portal, (saying) ' Peace be with you ! because ye have endured with patience.' Excellent is the reward in that abode ! " [5]

Enough has been said to show the utter falsehood of the theory that Mohammed's pictures of future life were all

[1] Baizâwi explains the expression " whom He pleaseth," as " those who repent " (p. 67, n. 1, chap. iv). Compare Zamakhsharî (the *Kashshâf*).

[2] Observe the reward of virtue will not be confined to an exact measure of man's works ; it will far exceed his deserts ; but the recompense of evil will be strictly proportioned to what one has done.

[3] Koran x. 23-27.

[4] This may also be translated as " from a desire to see the face (glory) of their Lord."

[5] Koran xiii. 20-24. Compare throughout Zamakhsharî (the *Kashshâf*).

sensuous.   We will conclude this chapter with the following passage from the Koran to show the depth of spirituality in Islâm, and the purity of the hopes and aspirations on which it bases its rule of life : " O thou soul which art at rest, return unto thy Lord, pleased and pleasing Him, enter thou among my servants, and enter thou my garden of felicity." [1]

[1] Koran lxxxix. 27-30.

CHAPTER IV

THE CHURCH MILITANT OF ISLÂM

لا إكْراهَ فِي الدِّينِ ۱

إنَّ الَّذِينَ آمَنُوا وَالَّذِينَ هَادُوا وَالصَّابِئِينَ وَالنَّصَارَى مَنْ آمَنَ
بِاللَّهِ وَالْيَوْمِ الْآخِرِ وَعَمِلَ صَالِحًا فَلَا خَوْفٌ عَلَيْهِمْ وَلَا هُمْ يَحْزَنُونَ ۲

THE extraordinary rapidity with which the religion of the Arabian Prophet spread over the surface of the globe is one of the most wonderful phenomena in the history of religions. For centuries Christianity had hidden itself in byways and corners ; not until it had largely absorbed and assimilated paganism, not until a half-pagan monarch had come to its assistance with edicts and orders, was it able to rear its head among the creeds of the world. Islâm, within thirty years of the death of its Teacher, found its way into the hearts of millions of people. And before a century was well over the voice of the Recluse of Hira had rolled across three continents. The legions of the Cæsars and the Chosroes, who endeavoured to stop the onrush of the new democracy preached in Arabia, were shattered to pieces by the children of the desert. Its remarkable success and marvellous effect upon the minds of men have given rise to the charge that, as a religion of the sword, Islâm was propagated

---

[1] Sura ii. 261, " Let there be no compulsion in religion."
[2] Sura v. 69 ; see p. 175. Compare this with the thunders of the Athanasian Creed.

by the sword and upheld by the sword. We propose, therefore, carefully to examine the circumstances and facts connected with the rise of Islâm, to see whether there is any truth in the statement.

At the time of the Prophet's advent into Medîna, the two tribes of Aus and Khazraj, who had been engaged in deadly conflict for years, had just ended their strife by a hollow peace. There was every prospect of the war breaking out again with fiercer animosity. The Jews, who after the onslaught of Jabala had accepted the clientage of the Medinite Arabs, were fast recovering their strength and were openly threatening their pagan compatriots with the vengeance of the Messiah, whose appearance was hourly expected. The surrounding tribes, among whom the influence of the Koreish was supreme, were arrayed in all their desert ferocity against Medîna. The moment Mohammed appeared among the Medinites the elements of danger which threatened the new religion became apparent. The Meccan disciples who had braved death, and now faced destitution and exile for their Master and the light which he had brought to their hearts, were few and weak. His Medinite followers were not many ; they were divided amongst themselves, actuated by tribal jealousies. An important faction, headed by an influential chieftain, an aspirant to the throne of Medîna, worked in the city on the side of the heathens.[1] The Jews, compact and united, jealously and relentlessly, with poison and with treachery, opposed him in every direction. But the heart, which did not fail when the Koreish threatened him with death, was not daunted when the existence of others depended on him. He at once set himself to the task of organising into a social entity the varied elements which had gathered round him as the minister of God. He substituted referees for the old tribal vendetta ; he abolished the distinction of Aus and Khazraj ; he comprehended the Jews and Christians in his little commonwealth, and planted germs of cordial relations among all believers ; he proclaimed that a Jew, Sabæan, or Christian, whoever believed in God and future life and acted righteously, " on him shall come no fear." To a people wedded to the worst type of heathenism, to a race with

[1] See *ante*, p. 57.

whom the shedding of blood was a second nature, he taught purity and truth, self-restraint, charity, and love of one's kind. "It shall be an expiation with God," he said to them, "when one shall drop his right of retaliation." "He who shall mediate between men for a good purpose shall be the gainer thereby, but the mediator for evil shall reap the fruit of his doing." [1]

Whilst engaged in this divine work of humanising his people, raising them from the abyss of degradation, purifying them from abominations, he is attacked by his enemies, ruthless and untiring in their vengeance. They had sworn his death and the extirpation of his creed. The apostates from the faith of their fathers, as the Koreish regarded Mohammed and his followers to be, had betaken themselves to the rival city, to plant the germs of revolutionary doctrines. United Arabia must annihilate these crazy enthusiasts who had forsaken home and wealth for the sake of an unseen God, so exacting in His worship, so insistent on the common duties of love, charity, and benevolence, on purity of thought and deed. From the moment of his entry into Medîna, Mohammed's destiny had become intertwined with that of his people, and of those who had invited and welcomed him into their midst. His destruction meant the destruction of the entire body of people who had gathered round the minister of God. Surrounded by enemies and traitors, the whole of Arabia responding to the call of the Koreish, the ancient servitors of the national gods marching to their slaughter, his followers would have inevitably perished but for the swords in their hands. And it was not until their enemies were upon them that it was declared, "The infidels regard not in a believer either ties of blood or covenant ; when they break their oaths of alliance, and attack you, defend yourself " ; and again, "Defend yourself against your enemies ; but attack them not first : God hateth the aggressor." [2] To the Moslems self-defence had become a question of self-preservation. They must either submit to be massacred or fight when they were attacked. They chose the latter alternative, and succeeded, after a long struggle, in subduing their enemies.

The bitter animosity of the Jews, their repeated violations of

[1] Sura iv. 85.　　　[2] Sura ii. 190.

the most solemn engagements, their constant seditiousness, and
their frequent endeavours to betray the Moslems to the idolaters,
led naturally to severe chastisement.   It was essentially necessary for the safety of the weak and small community, more as
a deterrent warning than as a vindictive punishment.

We have no right to assume that because some of the great
teachers who have from time to time appeared on earth have
succumbed under the force of opposing circumstances and
become martyrs, that because others have created in their
brains an unrealised Utopia, that because dreamers have
existed, and enthusiasts have suffered, Mohammed was bound
to follow their example, and leave the world before he had
fulfilled his mission.   Nor was he obliged to sacrifice himself
and the entire community over which he was called to preside,
for the sake of carrying out what, in the present time, would
be called an ' Idea.'

Let us compare the struggles of the Moslems in self-defence,
and for self-preservation, with the frightful wars of the Jews
and the Christians, and even of the gentle Parsis, for the
propagation of their respective faiths.   In the case of the Jews,
aggression and extirpation were sanctified by religion.   They
were cursed for sparing.

In the case of the early Christians, the doctrine of humility
and meekness, preached by the Prophet of Nazareth, was soon
forgotten in the pride of power.   From the moment Christianity
became a recognised force,—the dominant faith of a community,
—it became aggressive and persecuting.   Parallels have been
drawn between Jesus and Mohammed by different writers.
Those fully penetrated with the conviction of the godhead of
Jesus have recognised in the " earthly " means employed by
the Arabian Prophet for the regeneration of his people the
result of " Satanic suggestions," while the non-employment of
such means (perhaps from want of opportunity to use them)
has been looked upon as establishing the divinity of the Prophet
of Nazareth.   We shall furnish reasons to show that such com-
parisons are unfair, based as they are on what is not only false
to history, but false to human nature.

The circumstances attending the lives of Jesus and
Mohammed were wholly different.   During his short ministry

the influence of Jesus remained confined to a small body of
followers, taken chiefly from the lower and uneducated ranks.
He fell a victim [1] to the passions he had evoked by his scathing
denunciations of the lifeless sacerdotalism of the priestly classes
—to the undying hatred of a relentless race—before his followers
had become either numerous or influential enough to require
practical rules for their guidance, or before they could form an
organisation, either for purposes of spiritual teaching, or as a
safeguard against the persecutions of the dominant creed.
Drawn from among a people with settled laws, the observance
of which was guaranteed by the suzerain power, the followers
of Jesus had no occasion to constitute themselves into an
organised body, nor had the Teacher any need to frame rules
of practical positive morality.   The want was felt when the
community became more extensive, and the genius of a scholar,
well-versed in the Neo-Platonic lore, destroyed the individuality
and simplicity of the teachings of the Master.

Mohammed, like Jesus, was followed from the commencement of his career as a preacher and reformer by the hostility
and opposition of his people.   His followers also, in the
beginning, were few and insignificant.   He also was preceded
by men who had shaken off the bondage of idolatry, and had
listened to the springs of the life within.   He, too, preached
gentleness, charity, and love.

But Mohammed appeared among a nation steeped in barbarous usages, who looked upon war as the object of life,—a nation
far removed from the materialising, degrading influences of the
Greeks and the Romans, yet likewise far from their humanising
influences.   At first his enunciations evoked scorn, and then
vengeful passions.   His followers, however, increased in number
and strength until at last the invitation of the Medinites
crowned his glorious work with success.   From the moment he
accepted the asylum so nobly proffered, from the moment he
was called upon to become their chief magistrate as well as

---

[1] I write according to the generally received opinion among Western
scholars ; that Mohammed, in accordance with the traditions current in his
time, believed that Jesus miraculously disappeared, there is no doubt.   In
spite of this so-called apocryphal Gnostic tradition being opposed to the
general body of Christian traditions, there is as much historic probability on
one side as the other.

their spiritual teacher, his fate became involved in theirs ; from that time the hostilities of the idolaters and their allies required an unsleeping vigilance on the part of the Moslems. A single city had to make head against the combined attacks of the multitudinous tribes of Arabia. Under these circumstances, energetic measures were often necessary to sustain the existence of the Moslem commonwealth. When persuasion failed, pressure was required.

The same instinct of self-preservation which spoke so warmly within the bosom of the great Prophet of Nazareth,[1] when he advised his disciples to look to the instruments of defence, caused the persecuted Moslems to take up arms when attacked by their relentless enemies.

Gradually, by gentle kindness and energy, all the disjointed fragments of the Arabian tribes were brought together to the worship of the true God, and then peace settled upon the land. Born among a people the most fiery of the earth, then as now vehement and impulsive by nature, and possessed of passions as burning as the sun of their desert, Mohammed impressed on them habits of self-control and self-denial such as have never before been revealed in the pages of history.

At the time of Mohammed's advent international obligations were unknown. When nations or tribes made war upon each other, the result usually was the massacre of the able-bodied, the slavery of the innocent, and plunder of the household penates.

The Romans, who took thirteen centuries to evolve a system of laws which was as comprehensive as it was elevated in conception,[2] could never realise the duties of international morality or of humanity. They waged war for the sole purpose of subjugating the surrounding nations. Where they succeeded, they imposed their will on the people absolutely. The sacredness of treaties was unknown ; pacts were made and broken, just as convenience dictated. The liberty of other nations was never of the slightest importance in their estimation.[3] The

---

[1] Luke xxii. 256.

[2] In justice to the Semitic races, I must say that almost all the great jurists of Rome were Semites,—Phœnicians, Syrians, or Carthaginians.

[3] Compare Döllinger, *The Gentile and the Jew*, throughout on this subject.

introduction of Christianity made little or no change in the views entertained by its professors concerning international obligations. War was as inhuman and as exterminating as before ; people were led into slavery without compunction on the part of the captors ; treaties were entered into and broken just as suited the purpose of some designing chieftain. Christianity did not profess to deal with international morality, and so left its followers groping in the dark.

Modern thinkers, instead of admitting this to be a real deficiency in the Christian system, natural to the unfinished state in which it was left, have tried to justify it. A strange perversion of the human intellect ! Hence, what is right in the individual comes to be considered wrong in the nation, and *vice versâ*. Religion and morality, two convertible terms, are kept apart from the domain of law. Religion, which claims to regulate the ties of individual men, ignores the reciprocal relations of the various aggregates of humanity. Religion is thus reduced into mere sentimentalism, an object of gushing effusion, or mutual laudation at debating societies, albeit sometimes rising to the dignity of philosophical morality.

The basis of international obligations consists in the recognition of nations as individuals, and of the fact that there is not one standard for individuals and another for nations ; for as individuals compose a nation, so nations compose humanity ; and the rights of nations and their obligations to each other in nowise differ from those existing between individuals.[1]

True it is, that the rise of the Latin Church in the West, and the necessary augmentation of the power of the bishops of Rome, introduced in the Latin Christian world a certain degree of international responsibility. But this was absolutely confined to the adherents of the Church of Rome, or was occasionally extended as a favour to Greek Christianity. The rest of the world was unconditionally excluded from the benefits of such responsibility. " The name of religion served as the plea and justification of aggression upon weaker nations ; it led to their spoliation and enslavement." Every act of violation was sanctified by the Church, and, in case of extreme iniquity,

[1] Comp. David Urquhart's essay on the " Effects of the Contempt of International Law," reprinted from *The East and West*, Feb. 1867.

absolution paved the criminal's way to heaven. From the first slaughters of Charlemagne, with the full sanction of the Church, to the massacre and enslavement of the unoffending races of America, there is an unbroken series of the infringement of international duties and the claims of humanity. This utter disregard of the first principles of charity led also to the persecution of those followers of Jesus who ventured to think differently from the Church.[1]

The rise of Protestantism made no difference. The wars and mutual persecutions of the several religious factions form a history in themselves. " Persecution," says Hallam, " is the deadly original sin of the Reformed Church, that which cools every honest man's zeal for their cause, in proportion as his reading becomes more expansive." [2]

But, however much the various new-born Churches disagreed among themselves, or from the Church of Rome, regarding doctrinal and theological points, they were in perfect accord with each other in denying all community of interests and rights to nations outside the pale of Christendom.[3]

The spirit of Islâm, on the contrary, is opposed to isolation and exclusiveness. In a comparatively rude age, when the world was immersed in darkness, moral and social, Mohammed preached those principles of equality which are only half-realised in other creeds, and promulgated laws which, for their expansiveness and nobility of conception, would bear comparison with the records of any faith. " Islâm," says an able writer, " offered its religion, but never enforced it ; and the acceptance of that religion conferred co-equal rights with the conquering body, and emancipated the vanquished States from the conditions which every conqueror, since the world existed up to the period of Mohammed, had invariably imposed."

[1] Compare Milman, *Latin Christianity*, vol. i. p. 352, and Lecky, *History of Rationalism in Europe*, chap. on " Persecution."

[2] Hallam's *Const. Hist. of England*, vol. i. chap. ii. p. 62. When Calvin burnt Servetus for his opinions regarding the Trinity, his act was applauded, says Lecky, by all sections of Protestants. Melanchthon, Bullinger, and Farel wrote to express their warm approbation of the crime. Beza defended it in an elaborate treatise ; Lecky, *Hist. of Rationalism*, vol. ii. p. 49. A study of the penal laws of England against the Catholics, Dissenters, and non-Conformists is enough to shock any candid mind.

[3] Grotius, the founder, perhaps, of international law in Europe, formally excepted the Moslems from all community of rights with the European nations.

By the laws of Islâm, liberty of conscience and freedom of worship were allowed and guaranteed to the followers of every other creed under Moslem dominion. The passage in the Koran, " Let there be no compulsion in religion," [1] testifies to the principle of toleration and charity inculcated by Islâm. " If thy Lord had pleased, verily all who are in the world would have believed together." " Wilt thou then force men to believe when belief can come only from God ? "—" Adhere to those who forsake you ; speak truth to your own heart ; do good to every one that does ill to you " : these are the precepts of a Teacher who has been accused of fanaticism and intolerance. Let it be remembered that these are the utterances, not of a powerless enthusiast or philosophical dreamer paralysed by the weight of opposing forces. These are the utterances of a man in the plenitude of his power, of the head of a sufficiently strong and well-organised State, able to enforce his doctrines with the edge of his reputed sword.

In religion, as in politics, individuals and sects have preached toleration, and insisted upon its practice only so long as they have been powerless and feeble. The moment they have acquired strength enough to battle with the forces which they wish to supersede, tolerance gives way to persecution. With the accession of Constantine to the throne of the Cæsars, Christianity was safe from molestation. But from that period commenced a system of religious persecution in its atrocity paralleled only by that of the Jews. " From the very moment," says Lecky, " the Church obtained civil power under Constantine, the general principle of coercion was admitted and acted on, both against the Jews, the heretics, and pagans." [2] They were tortured with every refinement of cruelty ; they were burnt at a slow-consuming fire to enable them to think of the charity and humanity of the church of Christ. Father after father wrote about the holiness of persecution. One of the greatest saints of the Church, " a saint of the most tender and exquisite piety "—supplied arguments for the most atrocious persecution. Except during the titanic struggles in Europe at the beginning of the nineteenth century, the Christian

---

[1] Sura ii. 257 (a Medîna sura).
[2] Comp. Hallam, *Const. Hist. of England*, vol. i. chap. iii. p. 98.

church, purporting to derive its authority from the Apostles, has never hesitated to encourage war,[1]—or to give its sanction, in the name of religion and " the glory of Christ," to exterminating enterprises against heretics and heathens. These had no claims on Christian humanity or the law of nations ; nor have the poor black races now ! In the fifteenth century, the Pope granted a special charter by which the non-Christian world was allotted to the Portuguese and Spaniards in equal shares with absolute power to convert the inhabitants in any way they chose ! History records how liberally they construed the permission. And all the atrocious doctrines relating to persecution and the treatment of non-Christians are unjustly based upon the words of Jesus himself ! Did not the Master say, " Compel them to come in " ?

In the hour of his greatest triumph, when the Arabian Prophet entered the old shrine of Mecca and broke down the idols, it was not in wrath or religious rage, but in pity, that he said—" Truth is come, darkness departeth,"—announcing amnesty almost universal, commanding protection to the weak and poor, and freeing fugitive slaves.

Mohammed did not merely preach toleration ; he embodied it into a law. To all conquered nations he offered liberty of worship. A nominal tribute was the only compensation they were required to pay for the observance and enjoyment of their faith. Once the tax or tribute was agreed upon, every interference with their religion or the liberty of conscience was regarded as a direct contravention of the laws of Islâm.[2] Could so much be said of other creeds ? Proselytism by the sword was wholly contrary to the instincts of Mohammed, and wrangling over creeds his abhorrence. Repeatedly he exclaims, " Why wrangle over that which you know not ; try to excel in good works ; when you shall return to God, He will tell you about that in which you have differed."

We must now return to our examination of the wars of the Prophet. We have seen that the various conflicts of the

---

[1] In the colossal and devastating struggle of the twentieth century, in which all the great nations of Christendom were engaged, the ministers of religion on both sides took vehement part in fostering the warlike spirit.

[2] See chapter on *The Political Spirit of Islâm*.

Moslems under Mohammed with the surrounding tribes were occasioned by the aggressive and unrelenting hostility of the idolaters, and were necessary for self-defence.

The battle of Mûta and the campaign of Tabûk, the earliest demonstrations against a foreign State, arose out of the assassination of an envoy by the Greeks. Probably we should not have heard of the promulgation of Islâm by the sword had the Moslems not punished the eastern Christians for this murder. The battle of Mûta was indecisive, and the campaign of Tabûk, which was entirely defensive in its nature (being undertaken to repulse the gathering of the forces of Heraclius), left this international crime unpunished during the lifetime of the Prophet ; but his successors did not forget it, and a heavy penalty was exacted.

The extent of the Greek empire brought the Moslems into a state of belligerency with the greatest portion of Christendom. Besides, the anomalous position occupied by the governors of the provinces under the waning suzerainty of the Byzantine emperors rendered it impossible for the Moslem Chiefs to put an end to this condition of affairs by means of treaty-stipulations with any one of them. Before one could be subdued and brought to terms another committed some act of hostility, and compelled the Moslems to punish him. Hence the career once entered upon, they were placed in just warfare with nearly the whole of Christendom.[1]

Religion has often furnished to designing chieftains, among Moslems as among Christians, a pretext for the gratification of ambition. The Moslem casuists, like the Christian jurists and divines, have divided the world into two regions—the *Dâr*

[1] See Urquhart's *Islâm as a Political System*. I do not mean to assert that the Moslems were never actuated by the spirit of aggression or by cupidity. It would be showing extreme ignorance of human nature to make such an assertion. It was hardly possible, that after the unprecedented progress they had made against their enemies and assailants, and after becoming aware of the weakness of the surrounding nations, they should still retain their moderation, and keep within the bounds of the law. Nor do I shut my eyes to the fact that there have been wars among the followers of Mohammed perhaps as cruelly waged as among the Christians. But these wars have been invariably dynastic. The persecutions to which certain sects have been subjected have arisen also, for the most part, from the same cause. The persecution of the descendants of Mohammed, the children of Ali and Fâtima, by the Ommeyyades, found its origin in the old hatred of the Koreish to Mohammed and the Hâshimis, as I shall show hereafter.

ul-Harb and the *Dâr ul-Islâm*, the counterparts of Heathendom and Christendom.   An examination, however, of the principles upon which the relations of Moslem states with non-Moslem countries were based, shows a far greater degree of liberality than has been evinced by Christian writers on international law.   It is only in recent times, and under stress of circumstances that non-Christian states have been admitted into the " comity of nations."   The Moslem jurists, on the other hand, differentiate between the condition of belligerency and that of peace.   The expression, *Dâr ul-Harb*,[1] thus includes countries with which the Moslems are at war ; whilst the States with which they are at peace are the *Dâr ul-Amân*.[2]   The *harbi*, the inhabitants of the *Dâr ul-Harb*, is an alien, pure and simple. He has no right to enter Islâmic States without express permission.   But once he receives the *amân* or guarantee of safety from even the poorest Moslem, he is perfectly secure from molestation for the space of one year.   On the expiration of that period, he is bound to depart.   The inhabitant of the *Dâr ul-Amân* is a *mustâmin*.   The *amân* may be for ever or for a limited duration ; but so long as it lasts, the *mustâmin's* treatment is regulated in strict accordance with the terms of the treaty with his country.[3]   The *mustâmins* were governed by their own laws, were exempt from taxation and enjoyed other privileges.

The spirit of aggression never breathed itself into that code which formally incorporated the Law of Nations with the religion ; and the followers of Mohammed, in the plenitude of their power, were always ready to say to their enemies, " Cease all hostility to us, and be our allies, and we shall be faithful to you ; or pay tribute, and we will secure and protect you in all your rights ; or adopt our religion, and you shall enjoy every privilege we ourselves possess."

The principal directions of Mohammed, on which the Moslem laws of war are founded, show the wisdom and humanity which animated the Islâmic system : " And fight for the religion of God against those who fight against you ; but

---

[1] Lit. *The country of war*.   [2] *The country of peace*.
[3] These *Amâns* formed the origin of the Capitulations which have proved the ruin of Turkish resources.

transgress not (by attacking them first), for God loveth not
the transgressors ; . . . if they attack you, slay them ; . . . but
if they desist, let there be no hostility, except against the
ungodly." [1]

In turning their arms against Persia the Moslems were led
on by circumstances. The Munzirs, a dynasty of semi-Arab
kings who reigned under the shadow of the Persian monarchy,
though politically hostile, were allied to the Byzantines by ties
of faith and community of interests. The first conflicts of the
Moslems with the Greeks naturally re-acted on the Hirites, the
subjects of the Munzirs. The Hirite territories comprehended
a large tract of country, from the banks of the Euphrates westward, overlapping the desert of Irâk, and almost reaching the
pasturage of the Ghassânide Arabs, who owned allegiance to
the Byzantines.

The position of Hîra under the Persians was similar to that
of Judæa under Augustus or Tiberias. About the time of the
Moslem conquest a Persian nominee ruled this principality ;
but the jealousy of the Chosroes associated a *marzbân*, or
satrap, with the successor of the Munzirs, whose subjects, as
impatient of control then as their descendants now, engaged
in predatory raids on the neighbouring tribes, and became
involved in hostilities with the Moslems. A strong government
under the guidance of a single ruler, whose power had become
doubly consolidated after the suppression of the revolts of the
nomads on the death of the Prophet, was little inclined to
brook quietly the insults of the petty dependency of a tottering
empire. A Moslem army marched upon Hîra ; the *marzbân*
fled to Madâin (Ctesiphon), the capital of the Persian empire,
and the Arab chief submitted, almost without a struggle, to
the Moslems under Khâlid bin-Walîd.

The conquest of Hîra brought the Moslems to the threshold
of the dominions of the Chosroes. Persia had, after a long
period of internecine conflict, signalised by revolting murders
and atrocities, succeeded in obtaining an energetic ruler, in the
person of Yezdjard. Under the directions of this sovereign,
the Persian general brought an imposing force to bear on the
Moslems. The great Omar who now ruled at Medîna, before

[1] Sura ii. 186, compare ver. 257.

taking up the challenge, offered to Yezdjard, through his
deputies, the usual terms by which war might be avoided.
These terms were, the profession of Islâm, which meant the
reform of the political abuses that had brought the Sasanian
empire so low ; the reduction of all those heavy taxes and
perquisites,[1] which sucked out the life-blood of the nation ;
and the administration of justice by the code of Mohammed,
which held all men, without distinction of rank or office, equal
in the eye of the law. The alternative offer was the payment
of tribute in return for protection. These terms were disdain-
fully refused by the Persian monarch and the days of Kâdesia
followed. After the conquest of Madâin (Ctesiphon), the
Caliph promulgated peremptory orders that under no circumstance should the Moslems cross the Tigris towards the East,
and that that river should for ever form the boundary between
the Persian and the Saracenic empires. Upon this basis a
peace was concluded. But Irân chafed under the loss of
Mesopotamia ; and the successive breaches of faith by the
Persians led to Nehâvend. The Kesrâ's power was irretrievably
shattered ; many of his nobles and the chiefs of the priesthood,
whose interest it was to keep up the reign of disorder and
oppression, were cut off, and he himself became a fugitive like
another Darius. The nation at large hailed the Moslems as
their deliverers.[2] The advance of the Saracens from the Tigris
to the Elburz and from the Elburz to Transoxiana was not
different from that of the British in India and due to similar
causes.

The general conversion of the Persians to the religion of
Mohammed is often taken as a proof of the intolerant character
of Islâm. But, in the blindness of bigotry, even scholars forget
the circumstances under which the Moslems entered the
country. Every trace of religious life was extinct among the
people ; the masses were ground down by the worst of all
evils, a degenerate priesthood and a licentious oligarchy. The
Mazdakian and Manichæan heresies had loosened every rivet

[1] Save the tenth on landed property, and 2½ per cent. of every man's means
for the poor, the distribution of which would have been left to himself and
his officers.

[2] Yezdjard, like Darius, was assassinated by his own people. See *The
Short History of the Saracens* (Macmillan, 1921), p. 32.

in the social fabric. Kesrâ Anûshirvân had only postponed for a time the general disruption of society.

The consequence was, that as soon as the Moslems entered the country as the precursors of law and order, a general conversion took place, and Persia became for ever attached to Islam.[1]

An impartial analyst of facts will now be able to judge for himself how much truth there is in the following remark of Muir : " It was essential to the permanence of Islâm that its aggressive course should be continuously pursued, and that its claim to an universal acceptance, or, at the least, to an universal supremacy, should be enforced at the point of the sword." [2] Every religion, in some stage of its career, has, from the tendencies of its professors, been aggressive. Such also has been the case with Islâm ; but that it ever aims at proselytism by force, or that it has been more aggressive than other religions, must be entirely denied.[3]

Islâm seized the sword in self-defence, and held it in self-defence, as it will ever do. But Islâm never interfered with the dogmas of any moral faith, never persecuted, never established an Inquisition. It never invented the rack or the stake for stifling difference of opinion, or strangling the human conscience, or exterminating heresy. No one who has a competent knowledge of history can deny that the Church of Christ, when it pretended to be most infallible, " shed more innocent blood than any other institution that has ever existed among mankind " ; whilst the fate of the man or woman who forsook the Church, or even expressed a preference for any other creed, was no less cruel.[4] In 1521, death and confiscation of property was decreed by Charles V. against all heretics. Burnings and hangings, and tearing out and twisting of tongues

[1] As a testimony to the spirit which animated the Moslems, we quote the following from Gibbon : " The administration of Persia was regulated by an actual survey of the people, the cattle, and the fruits of the earth ; and this monument, which attests the vigilance of the Caliphs, might have instructed the philosophers of every age."—*Decline and Fall of the Roman Empire*, vol. v. p. 97. See also Suyûtî, *Târîkh ul-Khulafâ* (*History of the Caliphs*).

[2] Muir, *Life of Mahomet*, vol. iii. p. 251.

[3] Compare Niebuhr's remarks in his *Description de l'Arabie*.

[4] In the seventeenth century a young man was hanged for having said, it is stated, that he did not think Mohammed was a bad man.

were the usual penalties of refusal to adopt the orthodox communion. In England, after it became Protestant, the Presbyterians, through a long succession of reigns, were imprisoned, branded, mutilated, scourged, and exposed in the pillory. In Scotland, they were hunted like criminals over the mountains ; their ears were torn from the roots ; they were branded with hot irons ; their fingers were wrenched asunder by thumbkins ; the bones of their legs were shattered in the boots. Women were scourged publicly through the streets. The Catholics were tortured and hanged. Anabaptists and Arians were burnt alive. But as regards non-Christians, Catholics and Protestants, orthodox and un-orthodox, were in perfect accord. Musulmans and Jews were beyond the pale of Christendom. In England, the Jews were tortured and hanged. In Spain, the Moslems were burnt. Marriages between Christians and Jews, and Christians and " infidels," were null and void, in fact prohibited under terrible and revolting penalties. Even now, Christian America burns alive a Christian negro marrying a Christian white woman ! Such has been the effect produced by Christianity.

To this day, wherever scientific thought has not infused a new soul, wherever true culture has not gained a foothold, the old spirit of exclusiveness and intolerance, the old ecclesiastical hatred of Islâm, displays itself in writings, in newspaper attacks, in private conversations, in public speeches. The spirit of persecution is not dead in Christianity ; it is lying dormant, ready to burst into flame at the touch of the first bigot.

Let us turn from this picture to the world of Islâm. Whilst orthodox Christianity persecuted with equal ferocity the Jews and Nestorians,—the descendants of the men who were supposed to have crucified its Incarnate God, and the men who refused to adore his mother,—Islâm afforded them both shelter and protection. Whilst Christian Europe was burning witches and heretics, and massacring Jews and " infidels," the Moslem sovereigns were treating their non-Moslem subjects with consideration and tolerance. They were the trusted subjects of the State, councillors of the empire. Every secular office was open to them along with the Moslems. The Teacher himself had declared it lawful for a Moslem to intermarry with a Christian, Hebrew, or Zoroastrian. The converse was not allowed, for obvious political reasons. Moslem Turkey and Persia entrust their foreign interests to the charge of their Christian subjects. In Christendom, difference of faith has been a crime ; in Islâm it is an accident. " To Christians," says Urquhart, " a difference of religion was indeed a ground for war, and that not merely in dark times and amongst fanatics." From the massacres, in the name of religion, of the Saxons, the Frisians and other Germanic tribes by Charlemagne ; from the burning to death of the thousands of innocent men and women ; from the frightful slaughters of the Arians, the Paulicians, the Albigenses and the Huguenots, from the horrors of the sacks of Magdeburg and Rome, from the sanguinary scenes of the Thirty Years' War, down to the cruel persecutions of Calvinistic Scotland and Lutheran England, there is an uninterrupted chain of intolerance, bigotry, and fanaticism. Can anything be more heart-rending than the wholesale extermination of the unoffending races of America in the name of Christ ?

It has been said that a warlike spirit was infused into mediæval Christianity by aggressive Islâm ! The massacres of Justinian and the fearful wars of Christian Clovis in the name of religion, occurred long before the time of Mohammed.

Compare, again, the conduct of the Christian Crusaders with that of the Moslems. " When the Khalif Omar took Jerusalem, A.D. 637, he rode into the city by the side of the Patriarch Sophronius, conversing with him on its antiquities. At the hour of prayer, he declined to perform his devotions in the Church of the Resurrection, in which he chanced to be, but prayed on the steps of the Church of Constantine ; for, said he to the Patriarch, ' had I done so, the Musulmans in a future age might have infringed the treaty, under colour of imitating my example.' But in the capture by the Crusaders, the brains of young children were dashed out against the walls ; infants were pitched over the battlements ; men were roasted at fires ; some were ripped up, to see if they had swallowed gold ; the Jews were driven into their synagogue, and there burnt ; a massacre of nearly 70,000 persons took place ; and the pope's legate was seen partaking in the triumph ! " [1] When Saladin recaptured the city, he released all Christians, gave them money and food, and allowed them to depart with a safe-conduct.[2]

Islâm " grasped the sword " in self-defence ; Christianity grasped it in order to stifle freedom of thought and liberty of belief. With the conversion of Constantine, Christianity had become the dominant religion of the Western world. It had thenceforth nothing to fear from its enemies ; but from the moment it obtained the mastery, it developed its true character of isolation and exclusiveness. Wherever Christianity prevailed, no other religion could be followed without molestation. The Moslems, on the other hand, required from others a simple guarantee of peace and amity, tribute in return for protection, or perfect equality,—the possession of equal rights and privileges,—on condition of the acceptance of Islâm.

[1] Draper, *History of the Intellectual Development of Europe*, vol. ii. p. 22.
[2] For a full account, see *The Short History of the Saracens*, p. 356.

CHAPTER V

THE STATUS OF WOMEN IN ISLÂM

الجنة نحت اقدام الامّهات [1]

IN certain stages of social development, polygamy, or more
properly speaking, polygyny,—the union of one man with
several women,—is an unavoidable circumstance. The
frequent tribal wars and the consequent decimation of the male
population, the numerical superiority of women, combined
with the absolute power possessed by the chiefs, originated
the custom which, in our advanced times, is justly regarded as
an unendurable evil.

Among all Eastern nations of antiquity, polygamy was a
recognised institution. Its practice by royalty, which everywhere bore the insignia of divinity, sanctified its observance
to the people. Among the Hindus, polygamy, in both its
aspects, prevailed from the earliest times. There was,
apparently, as among the ancient Medes, Babylonians,
Assyrians, and Persians, no restriction as to the number of
wives a man might have. A high caste Brahman, even in
modern times, is privileged to marry as many wives as he
chooses. Polygamy existed among the Israelites before the
time of Moses, who continued the institution without imposing
any limit on the number of marriages which a Hebrew husband
might contract. In later times, the Talmud of Jerusalem
restricted the number by the ability of the husband to maintain the wives properly ; and though the Rabbins counselled
that a man should not take more than four wives, the Karaites

[1] " Paradise is at the foot of the mother ; " the Prophet.

differed from them, and did not recognise the validity of any
limitation.

To the Persians, religion offered a premium on the plurality
of wives.[1]

Among the Syro-Phœnician races, whom the Israelites displaced, conquered, or destroyed, polygamy was degraded into
bestiality.[2]

Among the Thracians, Lydians, and the Pelasgian races
settled in various parts of Europe and Western Asia, the
custom of plurality of marriages prevailed to an inordinate
extent, and dwarfs all comparison with the practice prevailing
elsewhere.[3]

Among the Athenians, the most civilised and most cultured
of all the nations of antiquity, the wife was a mere chattel
marketable and transferable to others, and a subject of testa-
mentary disposition.   She was regarded in the light of an evil,
indispensable for the ordering of a household and procreation
of children.   An Athenian was allowed to have any number of
wives ; and Demosthenes gloried in the possession by his
people of three classes of women, two of which furnished the
legal and semi-legal wives.[4]

Among the Spartans, though the men were not allowed,
unless under especial circumstances, to have more than one
wife, the women could have, and almost always had, more
than one husband.[5]

The peculiar circumstances under which the Roman State
was originally constituted probably prevented the introduction
of legal polygamy at the commencement of its existence.
Whatever the historical truth of the Rape of the Sabines, the
very existence of the tradition testifies to the causes which
helped to form the primitive laws of the Romans on the subject
of matrimony.   In the surrounding states generally, and
especially among the Etruscans, plurality of marriage was a
privileged custom.   The contact, for centuries, with the other

---

[1] Döllinger, *The Gentile and the Jew*, pp. 405, 406.   [2] Lev. xviii. 24.
[3] *Encyclopedie Universelle*, art. " Mariage " ; Döllinger, *The Gentile and the
Jew*, vol. ii. p. 233.
[4] Döllinger, *The Gentile and the Jew*, vol. ii. pp. 233-238.
[5] Grote, *History of Greece*, vol. vi. p. 136.

nations of Italy, the wars and conquests of ages, combined with the luxurious habits which success engendered, at last resulted in making the sanctity of marriage a mere by-word amongst the Romans. Polygamy was not indeed legalised, but " after the Punic triumphs the matrons of Rome aspired to the common benefits of a free and opulent republic, and their wishes were gratified by the indulgence of fathers and lovers." [1] Marriage soon became a simple practice of promiscuous concubinage. Concubinage recognised by the laws of the State acquired the force of a privileged institution. The freedom of women, the looseness of the tie which bound them to men, the frequency with which wives were changed or transferred, betoken in fact the prevalence of polygamy, only under a different name.

In the meantime, the doctrines of primitive Christianity preached on the shores of Galilee began to irradiate the whole Roman world. The influence of the Essenes, which is reflected visibly in the teachings of Jesus, combined with an earnest anticipation of the Kingdom of Heaven, had led the Prophet of Nazareth to depreciate matrimony in general, although he never interdicted or expressly forbade its practice in any shape.

Polygamy flourished in a more or less pronounced form until forbidden by the laws of Justinian. But the prohibition contained in the civil law effected no change in the moral ideas of the people, and polygamy continued to be practised until condemned by the opinion of modern society. The wives, with the exception of the one first married, laboured under severe disabilities. Without rights, without any of the safe-guards which the law threw around the favoured first one, they were the slaves of every caprice and whim of their husbands. Their children were stigmatised as bastards, precluded from all share in the inheritance of their father, and treated as outcasts from society.

Morganatic and left-handed marriages were not confined to the aristocracy. Even the clergy, frequently forgetting their vows of celibacy, contracted more than one legal or illegal union. History proves conclusively that, until very recent

[1] Gibbon, *Decline and Fall of the Roman Empire*, vol. ii. p. 206.

times, polygamy was not considered so reprehensible as it is now.   St. Augustine [1] himself seems to have observed in it no intrinsic immorality or sinfulness, and declared that polygamy was not a crime where it was the legal institution of a country. The German reformers, as Hallam points out, even so late as the sixteenth century, admitted the validity of a second or a third marriage contemporaneously with the first, in default of issue and other similar causes.

Some scholars, whilst admitting that there is no intrinsic immorality in a plurality of wives, and that Jesus did not absolutely or expressly forbid the custom, hold that the present monogamous practice, in one sense general throughout Europe, arose from the engrafting of either Germanic or Hellenic-Roman notions on Christianity.[2]   The latter view is distinctly opposed to fact and history and deserves no credit.   As regards the Germans, the proof of their monogamous habits and customs rests upon the uncorroborated testimony of one or two Romans, of all men the most untrustworthy witnesses to facts when it was to their interest to suppress them.   Besides, we must remember the object with which Tacitus wrote his *Manners of the Germans*.   It was a distinct attack upon the licentiousness of his own people, and, by contrasting the laxity of the Romans with the imaginary virtues of barbarians, was intended to introduce better ideas into Rome.   Again, supposing that Tacitus is right, to what cause should we ascribe the polygamous habits of the higher classes of the Germans, even up to the nineteenth century ? [3]

Whatever may have been the custom of the Romans in early times, it is evident that in the latter days of the republic and the commencement of the empire, polygamy must have been accepted as an institution, or, at least, not regarded as illegal.   Its existence is assumed, and its practice recognised, by the edict which interfered with its universality.   How far the Prætorian Edict succeeded in remedying the evil, or diverting the current of public opinion, appears from the rescript of

[1] St. Augustine, lib. ii. *cont. Faust*, ch. xlvii.

[2] M. Barthelemy St. Hilaire appears to hold the opinion that monogamy was engrafted upon Christianity from Hellenic and Roman sources.

[3] Comp. *Encyclopédie Universelle*, art. *Mariage*.

the Emperors Honorius and Arcadius towards the end of the fourth century, and the practice of Constantine and his son, both of whom had several wives. The Emperor Valentinian II., by an edict, allowed all the subjects of the empire, if they pleased, to marry several wives ; nor does it appear from the ecclesiastical history of those times that the bishops and the heads of the Christian Churches made any objection to this law.[1] Far from it, all the succeeding emperors practised polygamy, and the people generally were not remiss in following their example.

This state of the laws continued until the time of Justinian, when the concentrated wisdom and experience of thirteen centuries of progress and development in the arts of life resulted in the proclamation of the laws which have shed a factitious lustre on his infamous reign. But this laws owed little to Christianity, at least directly. The greatest adviser of Justinian was an atheist and a pagan. Even the prohibition of polygamy by Justinian failed to check the tendency of the age. The law represented the advancement of thought ; its influence was confined to a few thinkers, but to the mass it was a perfectly dead letter.

In the western parts of Europe, the tremendous upheaval of the barbarians, the intermingling of their moral ideas with those of the people among whom they settled, tended to degrade the relations between man and wife. Some of the barbaric codes attempted to deal with polygamy,[2] but example was stronger than precept, and the monarchs, setting the fashion of plurality of wives, were quickly imitated by the people.[3] Even the clergy, in spite of the recommendation to perpetual celibacy held out to them by the Church, availed themselves of the custom of keeping several left-handed wives by a simple licence obtained from the bishop or the head of their diocese.[4]

[1] Comp. *Encyclopédie Universelle*, art. *Mariage* and Davenport, *Apology for Mahomet*.

[2] Like the laws of Theodoric. But they were based on advanced Byzantine notions.

[3] For polygamy among the Merovingian and Carlovingian sovereigns, see *The Short History of the Saracens*, p. 626.

[4] Comp. Hallam's *Constitutional History of England*, vol. i. p. 87, and note ; *Middle Ages*, p. 353 (1 vol. ed.).

The greatest and most reprehensible mistake committed by Christian writers is to suppose that Mohammed either adopted or legalised polygamy.   The old idea of his having introduced it, a sign only of the ignorance of those who entertained that notion, is by this time exploded ; but the opinion that he adopted and legalised the custom is still maintained by the common masses, as well as by many of the learned in Christendom.   No belief can be more false.

Mohammed found polygamy practised, not only among his own people, but amongst the people of the neighbouring countries, where it assumed some of its most degrading aspects. The laws of the Christian empire had indeed tried to correct the evil, but without avail.   Polygamy continued to flourish unchecked, and the wretched women, with the exception of the first wife, selected according to priority of time, laboured under severe disabilities.

The corruptness of morals in Persia about the time of the Prophet was deplorable.   There was no recognised law of marriage, or, if any existed, it was completely ignored.   In the absence of any fixed rule in the Zend-Avesta as to the number of wives a man might possess, the Persians indulged in a multitude of regular matrimonial connections, besides having a number of concubines.[1]

Among the ancient Arabs and the Jews there existed, besides the system of plurality of wives, the custom of entering into conditional, as well as temporary contracts of marriage. These loose notions of morality exercised a disastrous influence on the constitution of society within the peninsula.

The reforms instituted by Mohammed effected a vast and marked improvement in the position of women.   Both among the Jews and the non-nomadic Arabs the condition of women was degraded in the extreme.   The Hebrew maiden, even in her father's house, stood in the position of a servant ; her father could sell her if a minor.   In case of his death, the sons could dispose of her at their will and pleasure.   The daughter inherited nothing, except when there were no male heirs.[2] Among the settled pagan Arabs, who were mostly influenced

[1] Döllinger, *The Gentile and the Jew*, vol. i. p. 406.
[2] Num. xxx. 17.

by the corrupt and effete civilisation of the neighbouring
empires, a woman was considered a mere chattel ; she formed
an integral part of the estate of her husband or her father ;
and the widows of a man descended to his son or sons by right
of inheritance, as any other portion of his patrimony.   Hence
the frequent unions between step-sons and step-mothers which,
when subsequently forbidden by Islâm, were branded under
the name of *Nikâh ul-Mékt* (" shameful or odious marriages ").
Even polyandry was practised by the half-Jewish, half-Sabæan
tribes of Yemen.[1]

The pre-Islâmite Arabs carried their aversion to women so
far as to destroy, by burying alive, many of their female
children.   This fearful custom, which was most prevalent
among the tribes of Koreish and Kindah, was denounced in
burning terms by Mohammed and was prohibited under severe
penalties, along with the inhuman practice, which they, in
common with other nations of antiquity, observed, of sacri-
ficing children to their gods.

In both the empires, the Persian and the Byzantine, women
occupied a very low position in the social scale.   Fanatical
enthusiasts, whom Christendom in later times canonised as
saints, preached against them and denounced their enormities,
forgetting that the evils they perceived in women were the
reflections of their own jaundiced minds.   It was at this time,
when the social fabric was falling to pieces on all sides, when all
that had hitherto kept it together was giving way, when the
cry had gone forth that all the older systems had been weighed
in the scale of experience and found wanting, that Mohammed
introduced his reforms.

The Prophet of Islâm enforced as one of the essential teachings of his creed, " respect for women."   And his followers, in
their love and reverence for his celebrated daughter, proclaimed
her " the Lady of Paradise," as the representative of her sex.
" Our Lady of Light "[2] is the embodiment of all that is divine
in womanhood,—of all that is pure and true and holy in her
sex,—the noblest ideal of human conception.   And she has
been followed by a long succession of women, who have

---

[1] Lenormant, *Ancient History of the East*, vol. ii. p. 318.
[2] *Khâtûn-i-jinnat, Fâtima'l-az-zahrâ*:

consecrated their sex by their virtues. Who has not heard of the saintly Râbi'a and a thousand others her equals ?

In the laws which the Arabian Prophet promulgated he strictly prohibited the custom of conditional marriages, and though at first temporary marriages were tacitly allowed, in the third year of the Hegira even these were forbidden.[1] Mohammed secured to women, in his system, rights which they had not before possessed ; he allowed them privileges the value of which will be more fully appreciated as time advances. He placed them on a footing of perfect equality with men in the exercise of all legal powers and functions. He restrained polygamy by limiting the maximum number of contemporaneous marriages, and by making absolute equity towards all obligatory on the man. It is worthy of note that the clause in the Koran which contains the permission to contract four contemporaneous marriages, is immediately followed by a sentence which cuts down the significance of the preceding passage to its normal and legitimate dimensions. The passage runs thus, " You may marry two, three, or four wives, but not more." The subsequent lines declare, " but if you cannot deal equitably and justly with all, you *shall* marry only one." The extreme importance of this proviso, bearing especially in mind the meaning which is attached to the word " equity ." ('*adl*) in the Koranic teachings, has not been lost sight of by the great thinkers of the Moslem world. '*Adl* signifies not merely equality of treatment in the matter of lodgment, clothing and other domestic requisites, but also complete equity in love, affection and esteem. As absolute justice in matters of feeling is impossible, the Koranic prescription amounted in reality to a prohibition. This view was propounded as early as the third century of the Hegira.[2] In the reign of al-Mâmûn, the first Mu'tazilite doctors taught that the developed Koranic laws

---

[1] A section of the Shiahs still regard temporary marriages as lawful. But with all deference to the Mujtahids, who have expounded that view, I cannot help considering that it was put forward to suit the tastes of the times, or of the sovereigns under whom these lawyers flourished. In many of their doctrines one cannot fail to perceive the influence of personal inclinations.

[2] *The Radd ul-Muhtâr* distinctly says " some doctors [the Mu'tazila] hold that '*adl* includes equality in love and affection, but *our* masters differ from this view and confine it to equal treatment in the matter of *nafkah*, which in the language of law, signifies food, clothing and lodgment."

inculcated monogamy. And though the cruel persecution of the mad bigot, Mutawakkil, prevented the general diffusion of their teachings, the conviction is gradually forcing itself on all sides, in all advanced Moslem communities, that polygamy is as much opposed to the teachings of Mohammed as it is to the general progress of civilised society and true culture.[1]

The fact must be borne in mind, that the existence of polygamy depends on circumstances. Certain times, certain conditions of society, make its practice absolutely needful, for the preservation of women from starvation or utter destitution. If reports and statistics speak true, the greatest proportion of the mass of immorality prevalent in the centres of civilisation in the West arises from absolute destitution. Abbé Huc and Lady Duff Gordon have both remarked that in the generality of cases sheer force of circumstances drives people to polygamy in the East.

With the progress of thought, with the ever-changing conditions of this world, the necessity for polygamy disappears, and its practice is tacitly abandoned or expressly forbidden. And hence it is, that in those Moslem countries where the circumstances which made its existence at first necessary are disappearing, plurality of wives has come to be regarded as an evil, and as an institution opposed to the teachings of the Prophet ; while in those countries where the conditions of society are different, where the means which, in advanced communities, enable women to help themselves are absent or wanting, polygamy must necessarily continue to exist. Perhaps the objection may be raised, that as the freedom of construction leaves room for casuistical distinctions, the total extinction of polygamy will be a task of considerable difficulty. We admit the force of this objection, which deserves the serious consideration of all Moslems desirous of freeing the Islâmic teachings from the blame which has hitherto been attached to them, and of moving with advancing civilisation. But it must be remembered that the elasticity of laws is the greatest test of their beneficence and usefulness. And this is the merit of the Koranic provision. It is adapted alike for the acceptance

[1] Compare the remarks on this subject of Moulvi Chirâgh Ali in his able work called *Are Reforms possible in Mohammedan States ?*

of the most cultured society and the requirements of the least civilised. It ignores not the needs of progressive humanity, nor forgets that there are races and communities on the earth among whom monogamy may prove a dire evil. The task of abolishing polygamy, however, is not so difficult as is imagined. The blight that has fallen on the Moslem nations is due to the patristic doctrine which has prohibited the exercise of individual judgment (*Ijtihâd*). The day is not far distant when an appeal to the Teacher's own words will settle the question whether the Moslems will follow Mohammed or the Fathers of the Church, who have misused the Master's name to satisfy their own whimsicalities, or the capricious dictates of Caliphs and Sultans, whose obsequious servants they were. Europe has gone through the same process herself, and instead of hurling anathemas at the Church of Mohammed, ought to watch, with patience and sympathy, the efforts of regenerated Islâm to free itself from patristic bondage. When once the freedom from the enthralment of old ideas is achieved, it will be easy for the jurists of each particular Moslem State to abolish, by an authoritative dictum, polygamy within that State. But such a consummation can only result from a general progress in the conception of facts, and a proper understanding of the Prophet's teachings. Polygamy is disappearing, or will soon disappear, under the new light in which his words are being studied.

As remarked already, the compatibility of Mohammed's system with every stage of progress shows their Founder's wisdom. Among unadvanced communities, polygamy, hedged by all the safeguards imposed by the Prophet, is by no means an evil to be deplored. At least it is preferable to those polyandrous customs and habits and modes of life which betoken an utter abandonment of all moral self-restraint. As culture advances, the mischiefs resulting from polygamy are better appreciated, and the meaning of the prohibition better comprehended. We are by no means prepared to say that the Musulmans of India have benefited greatly by their intermixture with the Brahmanical races, among whom prostitution was a legalised custom. Their moral ideas have become lax ; the conception of human dignity and spiritual purity has become degraded ; the class of *hetairai* has become as popular among them as among their non-Moslem neighbours. And yet there are signs visible which bid us hope that God's light, which lit up Arabia in the seventh century, will fall on their hearts and bring them out of the darkness in which they are now plunged. The Mu'tazila is, by conviction, a strict monogamist ; according to him the law forbids a second union during the subsistence of a prior contract. In other words, a Mu'tazila marriage fulfils in every respect the requirements of an essentially monogamous marriage as a " voluntary union for life of one man and one woman to the exclusion of all others."

Even among the archaic sects, a large and influential body hold polygamy to be unlawful, the circumstances which rendered it permissible in primitive times having either passed away or not existing in the present day.

As a matter of fact, the feeling against polygamy is becoming a strong social, if not a moral, conviction, and many extraneous circumstances in combination with this growing feeling, are tending to root out the custom from among the Indian Musulmans. It has been customary among all classes of the community to insert in the marriage-deed a clause, by which the intending husband formally renounces his supposed right to contract a second union during the continuance of the first marriage. Among the Indian Musulmans ninety-five men out of every hundred are at the present moment, either by conviction or necessity, monogamists. Among the educated classes, versed in the history of their ancestors, and able to compare it with the records of other nations, the custom is regarded with disapprobation. In Persia, only a small fraction of the population enjoy the questionable luxury of plurality of wives.[1] It is earnestly to be hoped that, before long, a general synod of Moslem doctors will authoritatively declare that polygamy, like slavery, is abhorrent to the laws of Islâm.

We now turn to the subject of Mohammed's marriages, which to many minds not cognisant of the facts, or not honest enough to appreciate them, seem to offer a fair ground of reproach against the Prophet of Islâm. His Christian

[1] Only two per cent, according to Col. Macgregor.

assailants maintain that in his own person by frequent marriages he assumed a privilege not granted by the laws, and that he displayed in this manner a weakness of character little compatible with the office of Prophet. Truer knowledge of history, and a more correct appreciation of facts, instead of proving him to be a self-indulgent libertine, would conclusively establish that the man, poor and without resource himself, when he undertook the burden of supporting the women whom he married in strict accordance with the old patriarchal institution, was undergoing a self-sacrifice of no light a character. And we believe that a thorough analysis of motives from the standpoint of humanity will demonstrate the falsehood and uncharitableness of the charges levelled at " the Great Arabian." When Mohammed was only twenty-five years of age, in the prime of life, he married Khadîja, much his senior in years. For twenty-five years his life with her was an uninterrupted sunshine of faithfulness and happiness. Through every contumely and outrage heaped on him by the idolaters, through every persecution, Khadîja was his sole companion and helper. At the time of Khadîja's death Mohammed was in the fifty-first year of his age. His enemies cannot deny, but are forced to admit, that during the whole of this long period they find not a single flaw in his moral character. During the lifetime of Khadîja, the Prophet married no other wife, notwithstanding that public opinion among his people would have allowed him to do so had he chosen.

Several months after Khadîja's death and on his return, helpless and persecuted, from Tâyef, he married Sauda, the widow of one Sakrân, who had embraced Islâm, and had been forced to fly into Abyssinia to escape the persecution of the idolaters. Sakrân had died in exile, and left his wife utterly destitute. According to the customs of the country, marriage was the only means by which the Teacher could protect and help the widow of his faithful disciple. Every principle of generosity and humanity would impel Mohammed to offer her his hand. Her husband had given his life in the cause of the new religion ; he had left home and country for the sake of his faith ; his wife had shared his exile, and now had returned to Mecca destitute. As the only means of assisting the poor

234

woman, Mohammed, though straitened for the very means of daily subsistence, married Sauda.

Abdullah, the son of Osmân Abû Kuhâfa, known afterwards in history as Abû Bakr, was one of the most devoted followers of Mohammed. He was one of the earliest converts to the faith of the Prophet; and in his sincere, earnest and unvarying attachment to Mohammed he might almost be compared with Ali.

Abû Bakr, as by anticipation we may well call him, had a little daughter named Âyesha, and it was the desire of his life to cement the attachment which existed between himself and the Prophet, who had led him out from the darkness of scepticism, by giving Mohammed his daughter in marriage. The child was only seven years of age, but the manners of the country recognised such alliances. At the earnest solicitation of the disciple, the little maiden became the wife of the Prophet.

Some time after the arrival of the fugitives at Medîna there occurred an incident which throws considerable light on the conditions of life among the Arabs of the time. Those who know the peculiarities of the Arab character—" pride, pugnacity, a peculiar point of honour, and a vindictiveness of wonderful force and patience "—will be able to appreciate the full bearing of the story. Even now " words often pass lightly between individuals," says Burton, " which suffice to cause a blood-feud amongst Bedouins." Omar Ibn ul-Khattâb, who afterwards became the second Caliph of Islâm, had a daughter of the name of Hafsa. This good lady had lost her husband at the battle of Badr, and being blessed with a temper as fiery as that of her father, had remained ever since without a husband. The disciples bent upon matrimony fought shy of her. It was almost a reflection on the father; and Omar, in order to get rid of the scandal, offered his daughter's hand to Abû Bakr, and, upon his declining the honour, to Osmân. He also met the offer with a refusal. This was little less than a direct insult, and Omar proceeded in a towering rage to Mohammed to lay his complaint before the Prophet. The point of honour must, anyhow, be settled in his favour. But neither Abû Bakr nor Osmân would undertake the burden of Hafsa's temper :—a dispute, ludicrous in its origin from our point of view, but sufficiently serious then to throw into commotion the small body of the Faithful.   In this extremity the chief of the Moslems appeased the enraged father by marrying the daughter.   And public opinion not only approved, but was jubilant over it.[1]

Hind Umm Salmâ, Umm Habîba, and Zainab Umm ul-Masâkîn,[2] three other wives of the Prophet, had also been widows, whom the animosity of the idolaters had bereft of their natural protectors, and whom their relations were either unable or unwilling to support.

Mohammed had married his devoted friend and freedman, Zaid, to a high-born lady of the name of Zainab, descended from two of the noblest families of Arabia.   Proud of her birth, and perhaps also of her beauty, her marriage with a freedman rankled in her breast.   Mutual aversion at last culminated in disgust.   Probably this disgust on the husband's part was enhanced by the frequent repetition, in a manner which women only know how to adopt, of a few words which had fallen from the lips of Mohammed on once seeing Zainab. He had occasion to visit the house of Zaid, and upon seeing Zainab's unveiled face, had exclaimed, as a Moslem would say at the present day when admiring a beautiful picture or statue, " Praise be to God, the ruler of hearts ! "

The words, uttered in natural admiration, were often

---

[1] The story told by Muir, Sprenger, and Osborn, with some amount of gloating, of the domestic squabble between Hafsa and Mohammed, concerning Mary, the Coptic girl presented to the Prophet's household by the Negus, is absolutely false and malicious.   A tradition, which is repudiated by all the respectable commentators of the Koran, and which must have been invented in the time of some Ommeyyade or Abbasside sensualist, founded on the weakest authority, has been seized with avidity by these critics for the vilification of the Prophet.   The verse in the Koran which has been supposed to refer to this story, refers, in truth, to a wholly different circumstance.   Mohammed, in his boyhood, when he tended the flocks of his uncle, had acquired a fondness for honey, which was often supplied by Zainab. Hafsa and Âyesha set to work to make him give up honey, and they succeeded in inducing him to vow he would never touch it.   But after he had made the vow to her came the thought that he was making something unlawful in which there was nothing unlawful, simply to please his wives.   His conscience smote him as to his weakness, and then came the verse, " O Prophet, why holdest thou that to be prohibited which God has made lawful, seeking to please thy wives ? "—(Zamakhsharî.)

[2] " Mother of the poor," so called from her charity and benevolence.

repeated by Zainab to her husband to show how even the Prophet praised her beauty, and naturally added to his displeasure. At last he came to the decision not to live any longer with her, and with this determination he went to the Prophet and expressed his intention of being divorced. " Why," demanded Mohammed, " hast thou found any fault in her ? " " No," replied Zaid, " but I can no longer live with her." The Prophet then peremptorily said, " Go and guard thy wife ; treat her well and fear God, for God has said ' Take care of your wives, and fear the Lord ! ' " But Zaid was not moved from his purpose, and in spite of the command of the Prophet he divorced Zainab. Mohammed was grieved at the conduct of Zaid, more especially as it was he who had arranged the marriage of these two uncongenial spirits.

After Zainab had succeeded in obtaining a divorce from Zaid, she commenced importuning Mohammed to marry her, and was not satisfied until she had won for herself the honour of being one of the wives of the Prophet.[1]

Another wife of Mohammed was called Juwairiya. She was the daughter of Hârith, the chief of the Banî Mustalik, and was taken prisoner by a Moslem in an expedition undertaken to repress their revolt. She had made an agreement with her captor to purchase her freedom for a stipulated sum. She petitioned Mohammed for the amount, which he immediately gave her. In recognition of this kindness, and in gratitude for her liberty, she offered her hand to Mohammed, and they were married. As soon as the Moslems heard of this alliance, they said amongst themselves the Banû Mustalik are now connections of the Prophet, and we must treat them as such. Each victor thereupon hastened to release the captives he had made in the expedition, and a hundred families, thus

---

[1] Tabari (Zotenberg's translation), vol. iii. p. 58. This marriage created a sensation amongst the idolaters, who, whilst marrying their step-mothers and mothers-in-law, looked upon the marriage of the divorced wife of an adopted son (as Zaid at one time was regarded by Mohammed) by the adoptive father as culpable. To disabuse the people of the notion that adoption creates any such tie as real consanguinity, some verses of chap. xxxiii. were delivered, which destroyed the pagan custom of forbidding or making sacred the person of a wife or husband, or intended wife or husband, by merely calling her mother, sister, father, or brother—much less by her or him being first allied to an adopted son or daughter. One of the greatest tests of the Prophet's purity is that Zaid never swerved from his devotion to his master.

regaining their liberty, blessed the marriage of Juwairiya with Mohammed.[1]

Safiya, a Jewess, had also been taken prisoner by a Moslem in the expedition against Khaibar. Her, too, Mohammed generously liberated, and elevated to the position of his wife at her request.

Maimûna, whom Mohammed married in Mecca, was his kinswoman, and was already above fifty. Her marriage with Mohammed, besides providing for a poor relation the means of support, gained over to the cause of Islâm two famous men, Ibn-Abbâs and Khâlid bin-Walîd, the leader of the Koreish cavalry in the disastrous battle of Ohod, and in later times the conqueror of the Greeks.

Such was the nature of the marriages of Mohammed. Some of them may possibly have arisen from a desire for male offspring, for he was not a god, and may have felt the natural wish to leave sons behind him. He may have wished also to escape from the nickname which the bitterness of his enemies attached to him.[2] But taking the facts as they stand, we see that even these marriages tended in their results to unite the warring tribes, and bring them into some degree of harmony.

The practice of *Thâr* (vendetta) prevailed among the heathen Arabs; blood-feuds decimated tribes. There was not a family without its blood-feud, in which the men were frequently murdered, and the women and children reduced to slavery. Moses had found the practice of *Thâr* existing among his people (as it exists among all people in a certain stage of development); but failing to abolish it, had legalised it by the institution of sanctuaries. Mohammed, with a deeper conception of the remedies to be applied, connected various rival families and

---

[1] Ibn-Hishâm, p. 729.

[2] With savage bitterness the enemies of the Prophet applied to him the nickname of *al-abtar* on the death of his last son. This word literally means " one whose tail has been cut off." Among the ancient Arabs, as among the Hindoos, a male issue was regarded as the continuation of the blessings of the gods; and the man who left no male issue behind was looked upon as peculiarly unfortunate. Hence the bitter word applied to the Prophet; Koran, chap. cviii. (see the *Kashshâf*). Hence, also, the idolatrous Arabs used to bury alive their female offspring, which Mohammed denounced and reprehended in burning terms; comp. Koran xvii. 34, etc.

powerful tribes to each other and to himself by marriage ties. Towards the close of his mission, standing on the Mount of Arafat, he proclaimed that from that time all blood-feuds should cease.

The malevolence of unfair and uncandid enemies has distorted the motives which, under the sanction of the great patriarchs of ancient times, led Mohammed to have a plurality of wives, and so provide helpless or widowed women with subsistence in the lack of all other means. By taking them into his family, Mohammed provided for them in the only way which the circumstances of the age and the people rendered possible.

People in the West are apt to regard polygamy as intrinsically evil, and its practice not only illegal, but the result of licentiousness and immorality. They forget that all such institutions are the offspring of the circumstances and necessities of the times. They forget that the great patriarchs of the Hebraic race, who are regarded by the followers of all Semitic creeds as exemplars of moral grandeur, practised polygamy to an extent which, to our modern ideas, seems the culmination of legalised immorality. We cannot perhaps allow their practice or conduct to pass unquestioned, in spite of the sanctity which time-honoured legend has cast around them. But in the case of the Prophet of Arabia, it is essential we should bear in mind the historic value and significance of the acts.

Probably it will be said that *no* necessity should have induced the Prophet either to practise or to allow such an evil custom as polygamy, and that he ought to have forbidden it absolutely, Jesus having overlooked it. But this custom, like many others, is not absolutely evil. Evil is a relative term. An act or usage may be primarily quite in accordance with the moral conceptions of societies and individuals ; but progress of ideas and changes in the condition of a people may make it evil in its tendency, and, in process of time, it may be made by the State, illegal. That ideas are progressive is a truism ; but that usages and customs depend on the progress of ideas, and are good or evil according to circumstances, or as they are or are not in accordance with conscience,—" the spirit of the time " —is a fact much ignored by superficial thinkers.

One of the most remarkable features in the history of early

Christianity is its depreciation of marriage. Matrimony was regarded as a condition of inferiority, and the birth of children an evil. Monasticism had withdrawn from the world the most vigorous minds ; the lay-clergy were either not allowed to marry, or to marry but once. This morbid feature was partly due to the example of the Master, and partly the resultant of a variety of circumstances which pressed upon the early Christian organisation.

The Nazarene Prophet's intimate connection with the Essene ascetics, his vivid anticipation of the immediate advent of a kingdom of God, where all social relations would be at an end, and the early cessation of his ministry, all explain his depreciation of matrimony, and we may add, perhaps, his never entering the married state. His association with the Baptist, himself an Essene, throws light upon the history of a short but most pathetic life. The strong and inexplicable antipathy of Paul towards the female sex, joined to the words of the Master, strengthened in the Church the Essenic conception that the union of man and woman in the holiest of ties was an act of sinfulness, an evil to be avoided as far as possible. Marriage was regarded as having for its sole object the procreation of children and the gratification of " man's carnal lusts," and the marriage services of most of the Christian Churches bear to this day the impress of this primitive notion. It was under these influences, the idea engrafted itself upon Christianity, which still retains its hold where not displaced by humanitarian science, that a person who has never married is a far superior being to one who has contaminated himself by marriage. The ash-covered Yogis of India, the matted-locked ascetics of the East generally, the priests of Buddha, were celibates. According to them, " knowledge was unattainable without sundering all the loving ties of home and family, and infinity impossible of realisation without leading a life of singleness." Celibacy passed into Christianity through many hands from Eastern Gnosticism and Asceticism. The " sinlessness " of Jesus has been regarded by some as a proof of his divinity, by others as an indication of his immeasurable superiority over the rest of the teachers of the world. To our mind, the comparison or contrast which is so falsely instituted between Jesus and

Mohammed appears wholly misconceived, and founded upon a wrong estimate of moral ideals. If never marrying constitutes a man an ideal being, then all the ascetics, the hermits, the dervishes are perfect. A perfect life would then imply a total abandonment of all domestic relations. Surely this view would be a perversion of nature, and end in disastrous consequences to humanity. But if it be not so, then why this disparagement of the Prophet, who fulfilled the work of Jesus? Is it because he married more wives than one? We have shown what these marriages meant; we have at least endeavoured to show that in those very deeds which have been used to calumniate him, he was undergoing a sacrifice.

But let us look for a moment at his marriages from an abstract point of view. Why did Moses marry more than one wife? Was he a moral, or a sensual man for doing so? Why did David, " the man after God's heart," indulge in unlimited polygamy? The answer is plain—each age has its own standard. What is suited for one time is not suited for the other, and we must not judge of the past by the standard of the present. Our ideals do not lose their greatness or their sublimity by having acted truthfully and honestly up to the standard of their age. Would we be justified in calling Jesus a vain, ambitious, unpractical dreamer, or Moses and David sanguinary sensualists, because the mind of one was filled with vague imaginings of expected sovereignty, and the lives of the others were so objectionable from the twentieth century point of view? In both cases we would be entirely wrong; the aspirations of the one, the achievements of the others, were all historical facts, in accord with their times. It is the truest mark of the Prophet that, in his most exalted mood, he does not lose sight of the living in his anticipation of the yet unborn. In his person he represents the growth and development of humanity. Neither Jesus nor Mohammed could at once efface existing society, or obliterate all national and political institutions. Like Jesus, Mohammed contented himself, except where ordinances were necessary, to meet the requirements of the moment, " with planting principles in the hearts of his followers which would, when the time was ripe for it, work out their abolition."

As regards the statement that Mohammed assumed to himself a privilege which he denied to his followers, only thus much need be said, that it is founded on a misconception resulting from ignorance. The limitation on polygamy was enunciated at Medîna some years after the exile ; and the provision regarding himself, instead of being a privilege assumed by a libertine, was a burden consciously imposed on a self-conscious, self-examining soul. All his marriages were contracted before the revelation came restricting polygamy ; and with that came the *other* which took away from him all privileges. Whilst his followers were free (subject to the conditions imposed by the law), to marry to the limit of four, and by the use of the power of divorce, which, in spite of the Prophet's denunciations, they still exercised, could enter into fresh alliances, he could neither put away any of his wives, whose support he had undertaken, nor could he marry any other. Was this the assumption of a " privilege " ; or was it not a humane provision for those already allied to him—and to himself, a revelation of perfect self-abnegation in his prophetic task ?

The subject of divorce has proved a fruitful source of misconception and controversy ; but there can be no question that the Koranic laws concerning the treatment of women in divorce are of " better humanity and regard for justice than those of any other scripture."

Among all the nations of antiquity, the power of divorce has been regarded as a necessary corollary to the law of marriage ; but this right, with a few exceptions, was exclusively reserved for the benefit of the stronger sex ; the wife was under no circumstance entitled to claim a divorce.

The progress of civilisation and the advancement of ideas led to a partial amelioration in the condition of women. They, too, acquired a qualified right of divorce, which they were never backward in exercising freely, until the facility with which marriages were contracted and dissolved under the Roman emperors passed into a bye-word.

Under the ancient Hebraic Law, a husband could divorce his wife for any cause which made her disagreeable to him, and there were few or no checks to an arbitrary and capricious use of his power. Women were not allowed to demand a divorce from their husbands for any reason whatsoever.[1]

In later times, the Shammaites, to some extent, modified the custom of divorce by imposing certain restrictions on its exercise, but the school of Hillel upheld the law in its primitive strictness.

At the time of the Prophet's appearance, the Hillelite doctrines were chiefly in force among the Jewish tribes of Arabia, and repudiations by the husbands were as common among them as among the pagan Arabs.

Among the Athenians the husband's right to repudiate the wife was as unrestricted as among the ancient Israelites.

Among the Romans, the legality of the practice of divorce was recognised from the earliest times. The laws of the Twelve Tables admitted divorce. And if the Romans, as is stated by their admirers, did not take advantage of this law until five hundred years after the foundation of their city, it was not because they were more exemplary than other nations, but because the husband possessed the power of summarily putting his wife to death for acts like poisoning, drinking, and the substitution of a spurious child. But the wife had no right to sue for a divorce ;[2] and if she solicited separation, her temerity made her liable to punishment. But in the later Republic, the frequency of divorce was at once the sign, the cause, and the consequence of the rapid depravation of morals.

We have selected the two most prominent nations of antiquity whose modes of thought have acted powerfully on modern ways of thinking and modern life and manners. The laws of the Romans regarding divorce were marked by a progressive spirit, tending to the melioration of the condition of women, and to their elevation to an equality with men. This was the result of the advancement of human ideas, as much as of any extraneous cause.

" The ambiguous word which contains the precept of Jesus is flexible to any interpretation that the wisdom of the legislator

---

[1] Ex. xxi. 2 ; Deut. xxi. 14, xxiv. 1. Compare also Döllinger, *The Gentile and the Jew*, vol. ii. pp. 339, 340 ; and Selden's *Uxor Hebraica, in loco*.

[2] Döllinger, *The Gentile and the Jew*, vol. ii. p. 255.

can demand." [1]   We may well suppose that at the time Jesus uttered the words, " What God has joined, let not man put asunder," he had no other idea than that of stemming the torrent of moral depravity, and he did not stop to consider the ultimate tendency of his words.   The subsequent rule, which makes fornication [2] (using the translated word) the only ground of valid divorce, shows abundantly that Jesus was alive to the emergency.[3]   But the " wisdom " of subsequent legislators has not confined itself to a blind adherence to a rule laid down probably to suit the requirement of an embryonic community, and delivered verbally.   The rule may be regarded as inculcating a noble sentiment ; but that it should be considered as the typical law of divorce is sufficiently controverted by the multitudinous provisions of successive ages in Christian countries.

Among the Arabs, the power of divorce possessed by the husband was unlimited.   They recognised no rule of humanity or justice in the treatment of their wives.   Mohammed looked upon the custom of divorce with extreme disapproval, and regarded its practice as calculated to undermine the foundations of society.[4]   He repeatedly declared that nothing pleased God more than the emancipation of slaves, and nothing more displeased Him than divorce.   It was impossible, however, under the existing conditions of society to abolish the custom entirely.   He was to mould the mind of an uncultured and semi-barbarous community to a higher development so that in the fulness of time his spiritual lessons might blossom in the hearts of mankind.   The custom was not an unmixed evil ;

[1] Gibbon, *Decline and Fall of the Roman Empire*, vol. iv. (2nd Ed.) p. 209.

[2] Matt. xxix. 9.

[3] Two of the Christian Gospels make no mention of the reason for which Jesus allowed his followers " to put away " their wives (Mark x. 11 and Luke xvi. 18).   If the traditions recorded by these two Gospels be considered of higher authority than those passing under the name of Matthew, then our contention is that Jesus, whilst preaching noble sentiments, and inculcating high principles of morality, did not intend his words should be considered as an immutable and positive law, nor had he any other idea than that of stemming the rising tide of immorality and irreligion.   Selden thinks that by an evasive answer, Jesus wanted to avoid giving offence either to the school of Shammai or that of Hillel, *Uxor Hebraica*, I. iii. c. 18-22, 28, 31.   Compare Gibbon's valuable note on the interpretation of the Greek word πορνεία, rendered " fornication " in the English version, vol. iv. (2nd Ed.) p. 209.

[4] Koran, sura ii. 226.

and accordingly he allowed the exercise of the power of divorce
to husbands under certain conditions. He permitted to
divorced parties three distinct and separate periods within
which they might endeavour to become reconciled and resume
their conjugal relationship ; but should all attempts at reconciliation prove unsuccessful, then the third period in which
the final separation was declared to have arrived, supervened.
In case of conjugal disputes, he advised settlement by means
of arbiters chosen by the two disputants.

M. Sédillot, than whom no Western writer has analysed the
laws of Mohammed better, has the following passage on the
subject :

" Divorce was permitted, but subject to formalities which
allowed (and, we will add, recommended), a revocation of a
hurried or not well-considered resolution. Three successive
declarations, at a month's interval, were necessary in order to
make it irrevocable." [1]

The reforms of Mohammed marked a new departure in the
history of Eastern legislation. He restrained the power of
divorce possessed by the husbands ; he gave to the women the
right of obtaining a separation on reasonable grounds ; and
towards the end of his life he went so far as practically to
forbid its exercise by the men without the intervention of
arbiters or a judge. He pronounced " talâk to be the most
detestable before God of all permitted things," for it prevented
conjugal happiness and interfered with the proper bringing up
of children. The permission, therefore, in the Koran though
it gave a certain countenance to the old customs, has to be read
with the light of the Lawgiver's own enunciations. When it
is borne in mind how intimately law and religion are connected
in the Islâmic system, it will be easy to understand the bearing
of his words on the institution of divorce.

Naturally, great divergence exists among the various schools
regarding the exercise of the power of divorce by the husband
of his own motion and without the intervention of the judge.
A large and influential body of jurists regard talâk emanating
from the husband as really prohibited, except for necessity,
such as the adultery of the wife. Another section, consisting

[1] Sédillot, *Histoire des Arabes*, vol. i. p. 85.

chiefly of the Mu'tazilas,[1] consider *talâk* as not permissible or lawful without the sanction of the *Hâkim ush-shara'*. They hold that any such case as may justify separation and remove *talâk* from the category of being *forbidden*, should be tested by an unbiased judge ; and, in support of their doctrine, they refer to the words of the Prophet already cited, and to his direction that in case of disputes between the married parties, arbiters should be appointed for the settlement of their differences.

The Hanafîs, the Mâlikîs, the Shâfe'îs and the bulk of the Shiahs hold *talâk* to be *permitted*, though they regard the exercise of the power without any cause to be unlawful.

The *Radd ul-Muhtâr*, after stating the arguments against the proposition that *talâk* is unlawful, proceeds to say, " no doubt, it is forbidden, but it becomes *mubâh* (permitted) for certain outside reasons, and this is the meaning of those jurists who hold that it is really forbidden."

Although " the Fathers of the Church " have taken up the temporary permission as the positive rule, and ignored many of the principles of equity inculcated by the Master, the rules laid down by the legists are far more humane and just towards women than those of the most perfect Roman law developed in the bosom of the Church.[2] According to the legists, the wife also is entitled to demand a separation on the ground of ill-usage, want of proper maintenance, and various other causes ; but unless she showed very good and solid grounds for demanding the separation, she lost her " settlement " or dowry. In every case, when the divorce originated with the husband (except in cases of open infidelity), he had to give up to her everything he settled upon her at her marriage.[3]

---

[1] See *post*.   [2] Milman's *Latin Christianity*, vol. i. pp. 368, 369.

[3] M. Sédillot also speaks of the condition which (according to the Sunnite doctrines) requires that in such cases of complete separation, prior to the husband and wife coming together again, the latter should marry another and be divorced anew,—as a very wise measure which rendered separation more rare. Muir censures Mohammed for making such a condition necessary (vol. iii. p. 306). He ignores that, among a proud, jealous, and sensitive race like the Arabs, such a condition was one of the strongest antidotes for the evil. The very proverb he quotes ought to have shown the disgrace which was attached to the man who would make his wife go through such " a disgusting ordeal." I am afraid, in his dislike towards Mohammed, Sir W. Muir forgot that this condition was intended as a check on that other

The frequent admonitions in the Koran against separations, the repeated recommendation to heal quarrels by private reconciliation, show the extreme sacredness of the marriage tie in the eyes of the Arab Legislator :

" If a woman fear ill-usage or aversion from her husband, it shall not be blameable in them [1] if they agree with mutual agreement, for reconciliation (or agreement) is best. (Men's) souls are prone to avarice ; but if ye act kindly and deal piously, verily God is well acquainted with what ye do. And ye will not have it at all in your power *to treat your wives alike with equity*, even though you fain wanted to do so ; [2] yet yield not to your inclinations ever so much as to leave her in suspense ; and if ye agree and act piously, then, verily, God is forgiving and merciful." [3]

And, again, in a preceding verse, it is declared :

" And if ye fear a breach between them (man and wife), then send a judge chosen from his family and a judge chosen from her family ; if they desire a reconciliation, God will cause them to agree ; verily, God is knowing and apprised of all." [4]

The sanctity attached to the institution of marriage in the Islâmic system has either not been apprehended or sufficiently appreciated by outsiders. " Marriage," says the *Ashbâh w'an-Nazâir*, " is an institution ordained for the protection of

" revolting " practice rife both among the Jews and the heathen Arabs, and by example also among the Christians, of repudiating a wife on every slight occasion, at every outburst of senseless passion or caprice. This check was intended to control one of the most sensitive nations of the earth, by acting on the strongest feeling of their nature, the sense of honour (compare Sale, *Preliminary Discourse*, p. 134). Sir W. Muir also forgot that many of the Shiite doctors do not recognise the obligation or validity of the wife's being married to a third person, prior to her being taken back (compare Malcolm, *History of Persia*, vol. ii. p. 241, and the *Mabsût, in loco*).

For my part, I believe in the correctness of the construction, namely, that the verse which says, " When ye divorce women, and the time for sending them away is come, send them away with generosity ; but retain them not by constraint so as to be unjust towards them " abrogates the preceding verse, which requires the intervention of a third person.

[1] The Arabic expression implies " it will be commendable," etc.

[2] This furnishes another argument against those Mohammedans who hold that the developed laws of Islâm allow plurality of wives. It being declared that " equity " is beyond human power to observe, we must naturally infer that the Legislator had in view the merging of the lower in the higher principle, and the abolition of a custom which though necessary in some state of society, is opposed to the later development of thought and morals.

[3] Koran, sura iv. 128, 129.   [4] Koran, sura iv. 35.

society, and in order that human beings may guard themselves from foulness and unchastity." "Marriage is a sacrament, insomuch that in this world it is an act of 'ibâdat or worship, for it preserves mankind free from pollution." ... "It is instituted by divine command among members of the human species." "Marriage when treated as a contract is a permanent relationship based on mutual consent on the part of a man and a woman between whom there is no bar to a lawful union."

It has been frequently said that Mohammed allowed his followers, besides the four legitimate wives, to take to themselves any number of female slaves. A simple statement of the regulation on this point will show at once how opposed this notion is to the true precepts of Islâm. " Whoso among you hath not the means to marry a free believing woman, then let him marry such of your maid-servants whom your right hands possess and who are believers. This is allowed unto him among you who is afraid of committing sin ; but if ye abstain from allying yourself with slaves, it will be better for you."

On this slender basis, and perhaps on some temporary and accidental circumstances connected with the early rise of the Moslem commonwealth, have our legists based the usage of holding (jârias) female slaves. And this, though opposed to the spirit of the Master's precepts, has given rise to some of the strongest animadversions of rival religionists.

Concubinage, the union of people standing to each other in the relation of master and slave, without the sanction of matrimony, existed among the Arabs, the Jews, the Christians, and all the neighbouring nations. The Prophet did not in the beginning denounce the custom, but towards the end of his career he expressly forbade it.

" And you are permitted to marry virtuous women who are believers, and virtuous women of those who have been given the Scriptures before you, when you have provided them their portions, living chastely with them without fornication, and not taking concubines." [1]

Compare the spirit of the first part of this commandment with the exclusiveness of Christian ecclesiasticism, which

[1] Sura v. 5.

refused to recognise as valid or lawful the union of a Christian
with a non-Christian. The stake frequently was the lot of the
" infidel " who indulged in the temerity of marrying a
Christian. Mohammed's rule was a distinct advance in
humanity.

The prohibition directed against Moslem women entering
into marriage with non-Moslems, which has furnished a handle
for attacks, was founded upon reasons of policy and the necessities of the early commonwealth.

It cannot be denied that several institutions which the
Musulmans borrowed from the pre-Islâmic period, " the Days
of Ignorance," and which exist simply as so many survivals of
an older growth, have had the tendency to retard the advancement of Mohammedan nations. Among them the system of
the seclusion of women is one. It had been in practice among
most of the nations of antiquity from the earliest times. The
gynaikonitis was a familiar institution among the Athenians ;
and the inmates of an Athenian *harem* were as jealously guarded
from the public gaze as the members of a Persian household
then, or of an Indian household now. The *gynaikonomoi*, like
their Oriental counterpart, were the faithful warders of female
privacy, and rigorously watched over the ladies of Athens.
The seclusion of women naturally gave birth to the caste of
Hetairai, various members of whom played such an important
part in Athenian history. Were it not for the extraordinary
and almost inexplicable spectacle presented by the Byzantine
empire and modern Europe and America, we should have said
that in every society, at all advanced in the arts of civilised
life, the growth of the unhappy class of beings whose existence
is alike a reproach to humanity and a disgrace to civilisation,
was due to the withdrawal of women from the legitimate
exercise of their ennobling, purifying, and humanising influence
over the minds of men. The human mind, when it does not
perceive the pure, hankers after the impure. The Babylonians, the Etruscans, the Athenians and the pre-Islâmite
Meccans furnish the best exemplification of this view in ancient
times. The enormity of the social canker eating into the heart
and poisoning the life-blood of nations in modern times is
due, however, to the spread of a godless materialism covered

with a thin veneer of religion, be it Christianity, be it Mohammedanism, or any other form of creed. Mohammed had, in
early life, observed with pain and sorrow the depravity
prevailing among the Meccans, and he took the most effective
step suited to the age and the people to stamp out the evil.
" By his severe laws at first," to use the expressive language
of Mr. Bosworth Smith, " and by the strong moral sentiment
aroused by these laws afterwards, he has succeeded, down to
this very day, and to a greater extent than has ever been
the case elsewhere, in freeing all Mohammedan countries "—
where they are not overgrown by foreign excrescences—" from
those professional outcasts who live by their own misery,
and, by their existence as a recognised class, are a standing
reproach to every member of the society of which they form
a part."

The system of female seclusion undoubtedly possesses many
advantages in the social well-being of unsettled and uncultured
communities ; and even in countries, where the diversity of
culture and moral conceptions is great, a modified form of
seclusion is not absolutely to be deprecated. It prevails at
the present moment, in forms more or less strict, among
nations far removed from Moslem influences, to which is
ascribed the existence of the custom in India and other Oriental
countries. In Corea, female seclusion is carried to the height
of absurdity. In China and among the Spanish colonies of
South America, which are not within the immediate ambit of
the European social code,. the *Purdah* is still observed. The
Prophet of Islâm found it existing among the Persians and
other Oriental communities ; he perceived its advantages, and
it is possible that, in view of the widespread laxity of morals
among all classes of people, he recommended to the women-folk
the observance of privacy. But to suppose that he ever
intended his recommendation should assume its present
inelastic form, or that he ever allowed or enjoined the *seclusion*
of women, is wholly opposed to the spirit of his reforms. The
Koran itself affords no warrant for holding that the seclusion
of women is a part of the new gospel.

" O Prophet ! speak to thy wives and to thy daughters, and
to the wives of the Faithful, that they let their wrappers fall

low. Thus will they more easily be known, and they will not be affronted. God is indulgent, merciful." [1]

" And speak to the believing women, that they refrain their looks and observe continence ; and that they display not their ornaments except those which are external, and that they draw their kerchiefs over their bosoms." [2]

Directions easy to understand [3] in the midst of the social and moral chaos from which he was endeavouring, under God's Guidance, to evolve order,—wise and beneficent injunctions having for their object the promotion of decency among women, the improvement of their dress and demeanour, and their protection from insult.[4] It is a mistake, therefore, to suppose there is anything in the law which tends to the perpetuation of the custom. Considerable light is thrown on the Lawgiver's recommendation for female privacy, by the remarkable immunity from restraint or seclusion which the members of his family always enjoyed. 'Âyesha, the daughter of Abû Bakr, who was married to Mohammed on Khadîja's death, personally conducted the insurrectionary movement against Ali. She commanded her own troops at the famous " Battle of the Camel." Fâtima, the daughter of the Prophet, often took part in the discussions regarding the succession to the Caliphate. The grand-daughter of Mohammed, Zainab the sister of Husain, shielded her youthful nephew from the Ommeyyades after the butchery of Kerbela. Her indomitable spirit awed equally the ferocious Obaidullah ibn Ziyâd and the pitiless Yezîd.

The depravity of morals, which had sapped the foundations

[1] Sura xxxiii. 59.   [2] Sura xxiv. 31.

[3] Those who have travelled in Europeanised Egypt and in the Levant will understand how necessary these directions must have been in those times.

[4] Hamilton, the translator of the *Hedâya*, in his preliminary discourse dealing with the *Book of Abominations*, has the following : " A subject which involves a vast variety of frivolous matter, and must be considered chiefly in the light of a treatise upon *propriety* and *decorum*. In it is particularly exhibited the scrupulous attention paid to female modesty, and the avoidance of every act which may tend to violate it, even in thought. It is remarkable, however, that this does not amount to that *absolute seclusion* of women supposed by some writers. In fact, this seclusion is a result of *jealousy* or *pride*, and not of any *legal injunction*, as appears in this and several other parts of the *Hedâya*. Neither is it a custom universally prevalent in Mohammedan countries." Marsden, in his *Travels*, says : " The Arab settlers in Java never observed the custom, and the Javanese Mussulman women enjoy the same amount of freedom as their Dutch sisters."

of society among the pre-Islâmic Arabs, as well as among the
Jews and the Christians, urgently needed some correction.
The Prophet's counsel regarding the privacy of women served
undoubtedly to stem the tide of immorality, and to prevent
the diffusion among his followers of the custom of disguised
polyandry, which had evidently, until then, existed among
the pagan Arabs.

According to von Hammer, " the *harem* is a sanctuary : it
is prohibited to strangers, not because women are considered
unworthy of confidence, but on account of the sacredness with
which custom and manners invest them. The degree of
reverence which is accorded to women throughout higher
Asia and Europe (among Mohammedan communities) is a
matter capable of the clearest demonstration."

The idealisation of womanhood is a natural characteristic of
all the highest natures. But national pride and religious
bigotry have given rise to two divergent theories regarding
the social exaltation of women among the cultured classes in
modern Christendom. The one attributes it to Mariolatry, the
other to Mediæval chivalry, alleged to be the offspring of
Teutonic institutions. Of Christianity, in its relation to
womankind, the less said the better. In the early ages, when
the religion of the people, high and low, the ignorant and
educated, consisted only of the adoration of the mother of
Jesus, the Church of Christ had placed the sex under a ban.
Father after father had written upon the enormities of women,
their evil tendencies, their inconceivable malignity. Tertullian
represented the general feeling in a book in which he described
women as " the devil's gateway, the unsealer of the forbidden
tree, the deserter of the divine law, the destroyer of God's
image—man." Another authority declared with a revolting
cynicism, " among women he sought for chastity but found
none." Chrysostom, who is recognised as a saint of high
merit, " interpreted the general opinion of the Fathers," says
Lecky, " when he pronounced women to be a necessary evil,
a natural temptation, a desirable calamity, a domestic peril,
a deadly fascination, a painted ill." The orthodox Church
excluded women from the exercise of all religious functions
excepting the lowliest. They were excluded absolutely from

society ; they were prohibited from appearing in public, from going to feasts or banquets. They were directed to *remain in seclusion*, to observe silence, to obey their husbands, and to apply themselves to weaving and spinning and cooking. If they ever went out they were to be clothed from head to foot. Such was the position of women in Christianity when Mariolatry was recognised and practised by all classes. In later times, and in the gloomy interval which elapsed between the overthrow of the Western empire and the rise of modern society in Europe, a period which has been described as one of " rapine, falsehood, tyranny, lust, and violence," Christianity, by introducing convents and nunneries, served, in some respects, to improve the lot of women. This questionable amelioration, however, was only suited for an age when the abduction of women was an everyday occurrence, and the dissoluteness of morals was such as to defy description. But the convents were not always the haunts of virtue, nor the inculcation of celibacy the surest safeguard of chastity. The *Registrum Visitationem,* or the diary of the pastoral visits of Archbishop Rigaud, throws a peculiar light upon the state of morality and the position of the sex during the most glorious epoch of the Age of Faith. The rise of Protestantism made no difference in the social conditions or in the conception of lawyers regarding the status of women. Jesus had treated woman with humanity ; his followers excluded her from justice.

The other theory to which we have adverted is in vogue among the *romanceurs* of Europe. They have represented each historical figure in the Middle Ages to be a Bayard or a Crichton. The age of chivalry is generally supposed to extend from the beginning of the eighth to the close of the fourteenth century —a period, be it noted, almost synchronous with the Saracenic domination in Spain. But, during this period, in spite of the halo which poetry and romance have cast around the conditions of society, women were the frequent subjects of violence. Force and fraud were the distinguishing characteristics of the golden age of Christian chivalry. Roland and Arthur were myths until the West came in contact with the civilisation and culture of the East. Chivalry was not the product of the wilds of Scandinavia or of the gloomy forests of Germany ;—

prophecy and chivalry alike were the children of the desert.
From the desert issued Moses, Jesus, and Mohammed ; from
the desert issued 'Antar, Hamza, and Ali.

The condition of women among the Arabs settled in the cities
and villages, who had adopted the loose notions of morality
prevalent among the Syrians, Persians, and Romans, was, as
we have already stated, degraded in the extreme. Among
some of the nomads, however, they enjoyed great freedom,
and exercised much influence over the fortunes of their tribes.
" They were not, as among the Greeks," says Perron, " the
creatures of misery." They accompanied the warriors to
battle, and inspired them to heroism ; the cavaliers rushed into
the fights singing the praises of sister, wife, or lady-love. The
guerdon of their loves was the highest prize of their prowess.
Valour and generosity were the greatest virtues of the men,
and chastity that of the women.   An insult offered to a woman
of a tribe would set in flame the desert tribes from end to end of
the peninsula. The " Sacrilegious Wars," which lasted for forty
years, and were put an end to by the Prophet, had their origin
in an insult offered to a young girl at one of the fairs of Okâz.

Mohammed rendered a fitful custom into a permanent creed,
and embodied respect for women in his revelations. With
many directions, which reflect the rude and patriarchal
simplicity of the age, his regulations breathe a more chivalrous
spirit towards the sex than is to be found in the teachings of
the older masters. Islâm, like Christianity, is different with
different individuals and in different ages, but on the whole,
true chivalry is more intimately associated with true Islâm
than with any other form of positive faith or social institution.

The hero of Islâm, the true disciple of the founder of the
Hilf-ul-Fuzûl, was as ready with lance and sword to do battle
with God's enemies as to redress the wrongs of the weak and
oppressed. Whether on the plains of Irâk or nearer home,
the cry of distress never failed to bring the mailed knight to
the succour of the helpless and suffering. His deeds translated
into legends, and carried from the tent to the palace, have
served to influence the prowess of succeeding ages. The caliph
in his banqueting-hall puts down the half-tasted bowl on being
told that an Arab maiden, carried into captivity by the Romans,

had cried out, " Why does not Abd ul-Malik come to my help ? "
—he vows that no wine or water shall wet his lips until he has
released the maiden from bondage.   Forthwith he marches his
troops upon the Roman caitiffs, and only when the maiden has
attained her liberty is he freed from his vow.   A Mogul emperor,[1] sore pressed by relentless foes, is marching towards the
frontiers when he receives the bracelet of an alien queen—the
token of brotherhood and call for succour.   He abandons his
own necessities, retraces his steps, defeats her foes, and then
resumes his march.

Oelsner calls 'Antar " the father of chivalry." Ali was its
beau-ideal—an impersonation of gallantry, of bravery, of
generosity ; pure, gentle, and learned, " without fear and without reproach," he set the world the noblest example of chivalrous grandeur of character.   His spirit, a pure reflection of
that of the Master, overshadowed the Islâmic world, and formed
the animating genius of succeeding ages.   The wars of the
Crusades brought barbarian Europe into contact with the
civilisation of the Islâmic East, and opened its eyes to the
magnificence and refinement of the Moslems ; but it was
especially the influences of Mohammedan Andalusia on the
neighbouring Christian provinces which led to the introduction
of chivalry into Europe.   The troubadours, the trouveurs of
Southern France, and the minnesingers of Germany, who sang
of love and honour in war, were the immediate disciples of the
romanceurs of Cordova, Granada, and Malaga.   Petrarch and
Boccaccio, even Tasso and Chaucer, derived their inspiration
from the Islâmic fountain-head.   But the coarse habits and
thoughts of the barbarian hordes of Europe communicated a
character of grossness to pure chivalry.

In the early centuries of Islâm, almost until the extinction
of the Saracenic empire in the East, women continued to occupy
as exalted a position as in modern society.   Zubaida, the wife
of Hârûn, plays a conspicuous part in the history of the age, and
by her virtues, as well as by her accomplishments, leaves an
honoured name to posterity.   Humaida, the wife of Fârûk, a

[1] The Emperor Humâyûn, pursued by the Afghans, received, on his march
to Cabul, the bracelet from the Jodhpur queen, and at once came to her help.
I have mentioned two instances of Moslem chivalry, which might be multiplied
by hundreds.

Medinite citizen, left for many years the sole guardian of her
minor son, educates him to become one of the most distinguished
jurisconsults of the day.[1]   Sukaina, or Sakîna, the daughter of
Husain,[2] and the grand-daughter of Ali, was the most brilliant,
most accomplished, and most virtuous woman of her time,—
"la dame des dames de son temps, la plus belle, la plus gracieuse,
la plus brillante de qualités," as Perron calls her.   Herself no
mean scholar, she prized the converse of learned and pious
people.   The ladies of the Prophet's family were noted for
their learning, their virtues, and their strength of character.
Bûrân, the wife of the Caliph Mâmûn, Umm-ul-Fazl, Mâmûn's
sister, married to the eighth Imam of the house of Ali, Umm
ul-Habîb, Mâmûn's daughter, were all famous for their scholarship.   In the fifth century of the Hegira, the Sheikha Shuhda,
designated *Fakhr un-nisa* (" the glory of women "), lectured
publicly, at the Cathedral Mosque of Bagdad, to large
audiences on literature, rhetoric, and poetry.   She occupies in
the annals of Islâm a position of equality with the most distinguished *'ulama*.   What would have befallen this lady had
she flourished among the fellow-religionists of St. Cyril can be
judged by the fate of Hypatia.   Possibly she would not have
been torn to pieces by enthusiastic Christians, but she would,
to a certainty, have been burnt as a witch.   Zât ul-Hemma,
corrupted into Zemma, " the lion-heart," the heroine of many
battles, fought side by side with the bravest knights.[3]

The improvement effected in the position of women by the
Prophet of Arabia has been acknowledged by all unprejudiced
writers, though it is still the fashion with bigoted controversialists to say the Islâmic system lowered the status of
women.   No falser calumny has been levelled at the great
Prophet.   Nineteen centuries of progressive development
working with the legacy of a prior civilization, under the most
favourable racial and climatic conditions, have tended to place

---

[1] Fârûk was away for twenty-seven years engaged in wars in Khorâsân.
His son's name is Râbya-ar-Ray.

[2] Husain was married to one of the daughters of Yezdjard, the last
Sasanian king of Persia.

[3] For a full account of the distinguished women who have flourished in
Islâm, see the article in the May number of the *Nineteenth Century* for 1899
and *The Short History of the Saracens* (Macmillan).

women, in most countries of Christendom, on a higher social level than the men,—have given birth to a code of etiquette which, at least ostensibly, recognises the right of women to higher social respect. But what is their legal position even in the most advanced communities of Christendom ? Until very recently, even in England, a married woman possessed no rights independently of her husband. If the Moslem woman does not attain in another hundred years, the social position of her European sister, there will be time enough to declaim against Islâm as a system and a dispensation. But the Teacher who in an age when no country, no system, no community gave any right to woman, maiden or married, mother or wife, who, in a country where the birth of a daughter was considered a calamity, secured to the sex rights which are only unwillingly and under pressure being conceded to them by the civilised nations in the twentieth century, deserves the gratitude of humanity. If Mohammed had done nothing more, his claim to be a bene-factor of mankind would have been indisputable. Even under the laws as they stand at present in the pages of the legists, the legal position of Moslem females may be said to compare favourably with that of European women. We have dealt in another place at length with this subject. We shall do no more here than glance at the provisions of the Moslem codes relating to women. As long as she is unmarried she remains under the parental roof, and until she attains her majority she is, to some extent, under the control of the father or his repre-sentative. As soon, however, as she is of age, the law vests in her all the rights which belong to her as an independent human being. She is entitled to share in the inheritance of her parents along with her brothers, and though the proportion is different, the distinction is founded on the relative position of brother and sister. A woman who is *sui juris* can under no circumstances be married without her own express consent, " not even by the sultan." [1] On her marriage she does not lose her individuality. She does not cease to be a separate member of society.

---

[1] Centuries after the principle was laid down by the Moslem jurists, the sovereigns and chiefs of Christendom were in the habit of forcibly marrying women to their subjects.

An ante-nuptial settlement by the husband in favour of the wife is a necessary condition, and on his failure to make a settlement the law presumes one in accordance with the social position of the wife.   A Moslem marriage is a civil act, needing no priest, requiring no ceremonial.   The contract of marriage gives the man no power over the woman's person, beyond what the law defines, and none whatever upon her goods and property.   Her rights as a mother do not depend for their recognition upon the idiosyncrasies of individual judges.   Her earnings acquired by her own exertions cannot be wasted by a prodigal husband, nor can she be ill-treated with impunity by one who is brutal.   She acts, if *sui juris*, in all matters which relate to herself and her property in her own individual right, without the intervention of husband or father.   She can sue her debtors in the open courts, without the necessity of joining a next friend, or under cover of her husband's name. She continues to exercise, after she has passed from her father's house into her husband's home, all the rights which the law gives to men.   All the privileges which belong to her as a woman and a wife are secured to her, not by the courtesies which " come and go," but by the actual text in the book of law.   Taken as a whole, her status is not more unfavourable than that of many European women, whilst in many respects she occupies a decidedly better position.   Her comparatively backward condition is the result of a want of culture among the community generally, rather than of any special feature in the laws of the fathers.

CHAPTER VI

BONDAGE (SLAVERY)

*" And as to your slaves, see that ye feed them as ye feed yourselves
and clothe them as ye clothe yourselves."*—THE PROPHET.

SLAVERY in some of its features has been aptly compared
with polygamy. Like polygamy, it has existed among
all nations, and has died away with the progress of
human thought and the growth of a sense of justice among
mankind. Like polygamy it was the natural product of
passion and pride so strongly marked in certain phases of
the communal and individual development. But unlike
polygamy, it bears from its outset the curse of inherent
injustice.

In the early stages, when humanity has not risen to the full
appreciation of the reciprocal rights and duties of man ; when
laws are the mandates of one, or of the few, for the many ;
when the will of the strong is the rule of life and the guide of
conduct—then the necessary inequality, social, physical, or
mental, engendered by nature among the human race, invariably takes the form of slavery, and a system springs into
existence which allows absolute power to the superior over the
inferior.[1] This complete subserviency of the weak to the
strong has helped the latter to escape from the legendary curse
laid on man—" In the sweat of thy face shalt thou eat bread
till thou return to the ground," and allowed them to employ
the leisure thus acquired in congenial pursuits. " The simple
wish," says the author of *Ancient Law*, " to use the bodily
powers of another person as the means of ministering to one's

[1] Comp. throughout *L'Influence des Croisades sur l'État des Peuples de
l'Europe*, by Maxime de Choiseul D'Aillecourt,. Paris, 1809.

own ease or pleasure, is doubtless the foundation of slavery, and as old as human nature." [1]

The practice of slavery is co-eval with human existence. Historically, its traces are visible in every age and in every nation. Its germs were developed in a savage state of society, and it continued to flourish even when the progress of material civilisation had done away with its necessity.

The Jews, the Greeks, the Romans, and the ancient Germans, [2] —people whose legal and social institutions have most affected modern manners and customs,—recognised and practised both kinds of slavery, prædial servitude as well as household slavery.

Among the Hebrews, from the commencement of their existence as a nation, two forms of slavery were practised. The Israelite slave, given into bondage as a punishment for crime or for the payment of a debt, occupied a higher position than a slave of alien birth. The law allowed the former his liberty after six years of servitude, unless he refused to avail himself of his right. But the foreign slaves, whether belonging to the people whom the Israelites had reduced into absolute helotage by a merciless system of warfare, or whether acquired in treacherous forays or by purchase, were entirely excluded from the benefits of this arrangement, an arrangement made in a spirit of national partiality and characteristic isolation. [3] The lot of these bondsmen and bondswomen was one of unmitigated hardship. Helots of the soil or slaves of the house, hated and despised at the same time, they lived a life of perpetual drudgery in the service of pitiless masters.

Christianity, as a system and a creed, raised no protest against slavery, enforced no rule, inculcated no principle for the mitigation of the evil. Excepting a few remarks on the disobedience of slaves, [4] and a general advice to masters to give servants their due, the teachings of Jesus, as portrayed in the Christian traditions, contained nothing expressive of disapproval of bondage. On the contrary, Christianity enjoined

---

[1] Maine, *Ancient Law*, p. 104.

[2] Cæsar (*De Bell. Gall.* lib. vi.), Tacitus (*De Moribus German.* cap. 24, 25), and Pothier (*De Stat. Servor. apud Germ.* lib. i.) all testify to the extreme severity of German servitude.

[3] Lev. xxv. 44, 45.　　　　　　[4] 1 Tim. iv. 1, 2.

on the slave absolute submission to the will of his or her pro-
prietor. It found slavery a recognised institution of the
empire ; it adopted the system without any endeavour to
mitigate its baneful character, or to promote its gradual
abolition, or to improve the status of slaves. Under the civil
law, slaves were mere chattels. They remained so under the
Christian domination. Slavery had flourished among the
Romans from the earliest times. The slaves, whether of native
or of foreign birth, whether acquired by war or purchase, were
regarded simply as chattels. Their masters possessed the
power of life and death over them. But that gradual improvement which had raised the archaic laws of the Twelve Tables
to the comprehensive code of Hadrian, did not fail to introduce
some amelioration in the condition of the slaves. In spite,
however, of the changes which the humanity or the wisdom of
the emperors had effected in the old laws, the person of the
slave was absolutely subject to the will of the master. Each
magnate of the empire possessed thousands of slaves, who were
tortured and subjected to lashings for the most trivial of faults.

The introduction of the religion of Jesus into Europe affected
human chattelhood only in its relation to the priesthood. A
slave could become free by adopting monachism, if not claimed
within three years.[1] But in other respects, slavery flourished
as much and in as varied shapes as under the pagan domination.
The Digest, compiled under a Christian emperor, pronounced
slavery a constitution of the law of nature ; and the Code fixed
the maximum price of slaves according to the professions for
which they were intended. Marriages between slaves were
not legal, and between the slave and the free were prohibited
under severe penalties.[2] The natural result was unrestrained
concubinage, which even the clergy recognised and practised.[3]

Such was slavery under the most advanced system of laws
known to the ancient world. These laws reflected the wisdom
of thirteen centuries, and towards the close of their develop-

[1] Comp. Milman, *Latin Christianity*, vol. i. p. 358.
[2] One of the punishments was, if a free woman married a slave, she was
to be put to death and the slave burnt alive. Comp. the splendid though
apologetic chapter of Milman on the subject, *Latin Christianity*, vol. ii.
[3] Comp. Milman, *Latin Christianity*, vol. ii. p. 369 ; and also Du Cange,
Concubina.

ment had engrafted upon themselves some faint offshoots of the teachings of one of the greatest moral preceptors of the world.

With the establishment of the Western and Northern barbarians on the ruins of the Roman empire, besides personal slavery, territorial servitude scarcely known to the Romans, became general in all the newly settled countries. The various rights possessed by the lords over their vassals and serfs exhibited a revolting picture of moral depravity and degradation.[1] The barbaric codes, like the Roman, regarded slavery as an ordinary condition of mankind ; and if any protection was afforded to the slave, it was chiefly as the property of his master, who alone, besides the State, had the power of life and death over him.

Christianity had failed utterly in abolishing slavery or alleviating its evils. The Church itself held slaves, and recognised in explicit terms the lawfulness of this baneful institution. Under its influence the greatest civilians of Europe had upheld slavery, and have insisted upon its usefulness as preventing the increase of pauperism and theft.[2] And it was under the same influences that the highly cultured Christians of the Southern States of North America practised the cruellest inhumanities upon the unfortunate beings whom they held as slaves,—many of their own kith,—and shed torrents of blood for the maintenance of the curse of slavery in their midst. The least trace of the blood of an inferior race, however imperceptible, subjected the unfortunate being to all the penalties of slavery. The white Christian could never legitimatise the issue of his illicit connection with his negro slave-women. With her he could never contract a legal union. The mother of his illegitimate children and her descendants, however remote,

[1] Comp. De Choiseul, and also consult on this subject the comprehensive chapter of Stephen's *Commentaries on the Laws of England*, bk. ii. pt. i. chap. ii. One of the miserable and disgusting privileges possessed by the lord was designated in Britain the custom of *culiage*, which was afterwards commuted into a fine. This custom, as has been correctly supposed, gave rise to the law of inheritance, prevalent in some English counties, and known by the name of Borough English.

[2] Pufendorff, *Law of Nature and Nations*, bk. vi. c. 3, s. 10 ; Ulricus Huberus, *Praelect Jur. Civ.* l. i. tit. 4, s. 6 ; Pothier, *De Statu Servorum* ; and Grotius, *De Jure Bell.*, l. ii. c. 5, s. 27.

could be sold by his legitimate white issue at any time. Christianity failed to grasp the spirit of its Master's teachings in regard to the equality of man in the sight of God.

Islâm recognises no distinction of race or colour; black or white, citizens or soldiers, rulers or subjects, they are perfectly equal, not in theory only, but in practice. In the field or in the guest-chamber, in the tent or in the palace, in the mosque or in the market, they mix without reserve and without contempt. The first Muezzin of Islâm, a devoted adherent and an esteemed disciple, was a negro slave. To the white Christian, his black fellow-religionist may be his equal in the kingdom of heaven, but certainly not in the kingdom of this world; in the reign of Christ, perhaps, but not in the reign of Christianity. The law may compel him, a larger humanity with torrents of blood may force him to give his black brother civic rights, but the pride of race and colour acknowledges no equality, and even in the house of God a strict separation is observed.

The Islâmic teachings dealt a blow at the institution of slavery which, had it not been for the deep root it had taken among the surrounding nations and the natural obliquity of the human mind, would have been completely extinguished as soon as the generation which then practised it had passed away

It has been justly contended that, as the promulgation of the laws, precepts, and teachings of Islâm extended over twenty years, it is naturally to be expected many of the pre-Islâmic institutions, which were eventually abolished, were, at first, either tacitly permitted or expressly recognised.[1] In one of these categories stood the usage of slavery. The evil was intertwined with the inmost relations of the people among whom Mohammed flourished. Its extinction was only to be achieved by the continued agency of wise and humane laws, and not by the sudden and entire emancipation of the existing slaves, which was morally and economically impossible. Numberless provisions, negative as well as positive, were accordingly introduced in order to promote and accomplish a gradual enfranchisement. A contrary policy would have produced an utter collapse of the infant commonwealth.

The Prophet exhorted his followers repeatedly in the name

[1] *Tahzib ul-Akhlâk* (15th Rajab, 1288), p. 118.

of God to enfranchise slaves, " than which there was not an act more acceptable to God." He ruled that for certain sins of omission the penalty should be the manumission of slaves. He ordered that slaves should be allowed to purchase their liberty by the wages of their service ; and that in case the unfortunate beings had no present means of gain, and wanted to earn in some other employment enough for that purpose, they should be allowed to leave their masters on an agreement to that effect.[1] He also provided that sums should be advanced to the slaves from the public treasury to purchase their liberty. In certain contingencies, it was provided that the slave should become enfranchised without the interference and even against the will of his master. The contract or agreement in which the least doubt was discovered, was construed most favourably in the interests of the slave, and the slightest promise on the part of the master was made obligatory for the purposes of enfranchisement. He placed the duty of kindness towards the slave on the same footing with the claims of " kindred and neighbours, and fellow-travellers, and wayfarers " ; encouraged manumission to the freest extent, and therewith the gift of " a portion of that wealth which God hath given you " ; and prohibited sensual uses of a master's power over the slave, with the promise of divine mercy to the wronged. To free a slave is the expiation for ignorantly slaying a believer, and for certain forms of untruth. The whole tenor of Mohammed's teaching made " permanent chattelhood " or caste impossible ; and it is simply " an abuse of words ". to apply the word slavery, in the English sense, to any status known to the legislation of Islâm.

The Lawgiver ordained, that a fugitive fleeing to the territories of Islâm should at once become enfranchised ; that the child of a slave woman should follow the condition of the father, while the mother should become free at his death ; that the slave should be able to contract with his master for his emancipation ; and that a part of the poor-tax should be devoted to the ransom of those held in bondage. The masters were forbidden to exact more work than was just and proper. They were ordered never to address their male or female slaves by that degrading appellation, but by the more affectionate

[1] Koran xxiv. 33, etc.

name of " my young man," or " my young maid " ; it was
enjoined that all slaves should be dressed, clothed, and fed
exactly as their masters and mistresses. Above all, it was
ordered that in no case should the mother be separated from
her child, nor brother from brother, nor father from son, nor
husband from wife, nor one relative from another.[1]

In the moral rules laid down for the treatment of those then
in bondage, the Arabian Teacher did not prescribe the reciprocal
duties of master and slave in the one-sided manner so often
visible in other creeds.[2] With a deeper and truer knowledge
of human nature, he saw that it was not so needful to lay down
the duties the weak owe to the strong, as those the strong owe
to the weak. In Islâm no discredit is attached to the status
of slavery. It is an accident, and not, as in the civil law and
patristic Christianity, " a constitution of nature." Zaid, the
freedman of the Prophet, was often entrusted with the command
of troops, and the noblest captains served under him without
demur ; and his son 'Osâma was honoured with the leadership
of the expedition sent by Abû Bakr against the Greeks. Kutb
ud-dîn, the first king of Delhi, and the true founder, therefore,
of the Musulman empire in India, was a slave. The slavery
which was allowed in Islâm had, in fact, nothing in common
with that which was in vogue in Christendom until recent
times, or with American slavery until the holy war of 1865 put
an end to that curse.

In Islâm the slave of to-day is the grand vizier of to-morrow.
He may marry, without discredit, his master's daughter, and
become the head of the family. Slaves have ruled kingdoms
and founded dynasties. The father of Mahmûd of Ghazni
was a slave. Can Christianity point to such records as these ?
Can Christianity show, in the pages of history, as clear, as
humane an account of her treatment of slaves as this ?

From all that we have said it is abundantly clear that the
Legislator himself looked upon the custom as temporary in its

---

[1] I see no need of quoting authorities on these points, as they are admitted
facts. But I may refer the curious reader to the traditions collected in the
Mishkât, the *Sahîh* of Bukhâri, and the *Bihâr ul-Anwâr*. The latter contains
the noblest monument of generosity and charity practised by the Prophet's
immediate descendants.

[2] See Col. iii. 22 ; 1 Tim. vi. 1.

nature, and held that its extinction was sure to be achieved by
the progress of ideas and change of circumstances.   The Koran
always speaks of slaves as " those whom your righ: hands have
acquired," indicating thus the only means of acquisition of
bondsmen or bondswomen.   It recognised, in fact, only one
kind of slavery—the servitude of men made captives in *bonâ
fide* lawful warfare, *Jihâd-i-Shara'i*.   Among all barbarous
nations the captives are spared from a motive of selfishness
alone,[1] in order to add to the wealth of the individual captor,
or of the collective nation, by their sale-money or by their
labour.[2]   Like other nations of antiquity, the Arab of the
pre-Islâmic period spared the lives of his captives for the sake
of profiting by them.   Mohammed found this custom existing
among his people.   Instead of theorising, or dealing in vague
platitudes, he laid down strict rules for their guidance, enjoining that those only may be held in bond who were taken in
bonâ fide legal war until they were ransomed, or the captive
bought his or her own liberty by the wages of service.   But
even when these means failed, an appeal to the pious feelings
of the Moslem, combined with the onerous responsibilities
attached to the possession of a slave, was often enough to
secure the eventual enfranchisement of the latter.   Slave-
lifting and slave-dealing, patronised by dominant Christianity,[3]
and sanctified by Judaism, were utterly reprobated and condemned.   The man who dealt in slaves was declared the
outcast of humanity.   Enfranchisement [4] of slaves was pronounced to be a noble act of virtue.   It was forbidden in
absolute terms to reduce Moslems to slavery.   To the lasting
disgrace of a large number of professed Moslems it must

[1] Comp. Milman, *Latin Christ.* vol. ii. p. 387.   The ancient jurists based the
right of enslaving the captive on the prior right of killing him.   In this they
are followed by Albericus Gentilis (*De Jur. Gent. cap. de Servitude*), Grotius,
and Pufendorff.   Montesquieu, indeed, was the first to deny this mythical
right of killing a captive, unless in case of absolute necessity, or for self-
preservation.   And this the author of the *Spirit of Laws* denied, because of
his freedom from the thraldom of the Church.

[2] Comp. Milman, *Hist. of the Jews*, vol. iii. p. 48.

[3] After the massacre of Drogheda by Cromwell, and the suppression of the
insurrection in Ireland, the English Protestants sold the Irish, men and
women, wholesale to the colonists in Virginia, Pennsylvania, and other places.
The same was done after Monmouth's rebellion.

[4] According to an authentic and well-known tradition from Imâm Ja'far
as-Sâdik (*Bihâr ul-Anwâr*).

be said, however, that, whilst observing, or trying to observe the letter, they have utterly ignored the spirit of the Teacher's precepts, and allowed slavery to flourish (in direct contravention of the injunctions of the Prophet) by purchase and other means. The possession of a slave, by the Koranic laws, was conditional on a *bonâ fide* struggle, in self-defence, against unbelieving and idolatrous aggressors, and its permission was a guarantee for the safety and preservation of the captives. The cessation of the state of war in which the Moslem community was at first involved, from the animosity of the surrounding tribes and nations, would have brought about the extinction of slavery by a natural process—the stoppage of future acquisition and the enfranchisement of those in bondage. However, whether from contact with the demoralised nations of the East and the West, and the wild races of the North, or from the fact that the baneful institution was deeply rooted among all classes of society, many Moslems, like the Christians and the Jews, recognised slavery, and to some extent do so even now. But the wild Turkoman, or the African Arab, who glories in slave-lifting, is no more a representative of Islâm than is the barbarous Guacho, who revels on the savage prairies of South America, of Christianity.[1] Like polygamy, the institution of slavery, prevalent universally among mankind at some stage or other of their growth, has, at least among the nations which claim to be civilised, outlived the necessities which induced its practice, and must sooner or later become extinct. It will be seen, therefore, that Islâm, did not " consecrate " slavery, as has been maliciously affirmed, but provided in every

[1] In order not to break the letter of his Prophet's Commandments, the Turkoman (himself a violent Sunni) forced his captive (whether a Sunni or a Shiah) to acknowledge himself a heretic. And the African Arab calls his murderous *razzias*, on the pagan negroes, *Jihâds*. Mr. Joseph Thompson, the well-known African traveller, in a letter to the London *Times* of the 14th of November, 1887, thus writes on the subject of slavery in East Africa : " I unhesitatingly affirm, and I speak from a wider experience of Eastern Central Africa than any of your correspondents possess, that if the slave trade thrives it is because Islâm has not been introduced in these regions, and for the strongest of all reasons, that the spread of Mahommedanism would have meant the concomitant suppression of the slave trade." His account of " the peaceful and unassuming agencies " by which Islâm has been spread in Western Africa and Central Soudan deserves the attention of every reader. " Here," he says, " we have Islâm as a living, active force, full of the fire and energy of its early days, proselytizing too with much of the marvellous success which characterized its early days."

way for its abolition and extinction by circumscribing the means of possession within the narrowest limits. Islâm did not deal capriciously with this important question. Whilst proclaiming in the most emphatic terms the natural equality of human beings, it did not, regardless of consequences, enfranchise the men and women already in bondage, which would have only been productive of evil in a world not then ripe for that consummation of human liberty, moral and intellectual.

The mutilation of the human body was also explicitly forbidden by Mohammed, and the institution which flourished both in the Persian and the Byzantine empires was denounced in severe terms. Slavery by purchase was unknown during the reigns of the first four Caliphs. There is at least no authentic record of any slave having been acquired by purchase during their tenure of the office. But with the accession of the usurping house of Ommeyya a change came over the spirit of Islâm. Muâwiyah was the first Musulman sovereign who introduced into the Moslem world the practice of acquiring slaves by purchase. He was also the first to adopt the Byzantine custom of guarding his women by eunuchs. During the reigns of the early Abbassides, the Shiah Imâm Ja'far as-Sâdik preached against slavery.

The time is now arrived when humanity at large should raise its voice against the practice of servitude, in whatever shape or under whatever denomination it may be disguised. The Moslems especially, for the honour of their great Prophet, should try to efface that dark page from their history—a page which would never have been written but for their contravention of the spirit of his laws, however bright it may appear by the side of the ghastly scrolls on which the deeds of the professors of the rival creeds are recorded. The day is come when the voice which proclaimed liberty, equality, and universal brotherhood among all mankind should be heard with the fresh vigour acquired from the spiritual existence and spiritual pervasion of fourteen centuries. It remains for the Moslems to show the falseness of the aspersions cast on the memory of the great and noble Prophet, by proclaiming in explicit terms that slavery is reprobated by their faith and discountenanced by their code.

CHAPTER VII

THE POLITICAL SPIRIT OF ISLÂM

" The blood of the *Zimmi* is like the blood of the Moslem "—ALI.

HITHERTO, we have considered the teachings of the Arabian Prophet solely from one point of view—as furnishing the rule of human conduct, and supplying the guide of man's duty to his Creator and to his fellow-creatures. We now propose to examine the influence of Islâm on collective humanity—on nations, and not merely on the individual, in short, on the destiny of mankind in the aggregate.

Seven centuries had passed since the Master of Nazareth had come with his message of the Kingdom of Heaven to the poor and the lowly. A beautiful life was ended before the ministry had barely commenced. And now unutterable desolation brooded over the empires and kingdoms of the earth, and God's children, sunk in misery, were anxiously waiting for the promised deliverance which was so long in coming.

In the West, as in the East, the condition of the masses was so miserable as to defy description. They possessed no civil rights or political privileges. These were the monopoly of the rich and the powerful, or of the sacerdotal classes. The law was not the same for the weak and the strong, the rich and the poor, the great and the lowly. In Sasanide Persia, the priests and the landed proprietors, the *Dehkâns*, enjoyed all power and influence, and the wealth of the country was centred in their hands. The peasantry and the poorer classes generally were ground to the earth under a lawless despotism. In the Byzantine Empire, the clergy and the great magnates, courtezans, and other nameless ministrants to the vices of Cæsar and proconsul, were the happy possessors of wealth, influence and power. The people grovelled in the most abject misery. In the barbaric kingdoms—in fact, wherever feudalism had established itself—by far the largest proportion of the population were either serfs or slaves.

Villeinage or serfdom was the ordinary status of the peasantry. At first there was little distinction between prædial and domestic slavery. Both classes of slaves, with their families, and their goods and chattels, belonged to the lord of the soil, who could deal with them at his own free will and pleasure.[1]   In later times the serfs or villeins were either annexed to the manor, and were bought and sold with the land to which they belonged, or were annexed to the person of the lord, and were transferable from one owner to another. They could not leave their lord without his permission ; and if they ran away, or were purloined from him, might be claimed and recovered by action, like beasts or other chattels. They held, indeed, small portions of land by way of sustaining themselves and their families, but it was at the mere will of the lord, who might dispossess them whenever he pleased. A villein could acquire no property, either in land or goods ; but if he purchased either, the lord might enter upon them, oust the villein, and seize them to his own use.

An iron collar round the neck was the badge of both prædial servitude and domestic slavery. The slaves were driven from place to place in gangs, fed like swine, and housed worse than swine, with fettered feet and manacled hands, linked together in a single chain which led from collar to collar. The trader in human flesh rode with a heavy knotted lash in his hands, with which he ' encouraged ' the weary and flagging. This whip when it struck, and that was frequently, cut the flesh out of the body. Men, women, and children were thus dragged about the country with rags on their body, their ankles ulcerated, their naked feet torn. If any of the wretches flagged and fell, they were laid on the ground and lashed until the skin was flayed and they were nearly dead. The horrors of the Middle Passage,

[1] The Church retained its slaves longest. Sir Thomas Smith in his *Commonwealth* speaks bitterly of the hypocrisy of the clergy.

the sufferings of the poor negroes in the Southern States of North America before the War of Emancipation, the cruelties practised by the Soudanese slave-lifters, give us some conception of the terrible sufferings of the slaves under Christian domination at the time when Islâm was first promulgated, and until the close of the fifteenth century.[1] And even after the lapse of almost two thousand years of Christ's reign, we still find Christians lashing to death helpless women, imprisoned for real or imaginary political offences by one of the most powerful empires of the civilised world.[2]

The condition of the so-called freemen was nowise better than that of the ordinary serfs. If they wanted to part with their lands, they must pay a fine to the lord of the manor. If they wanted to buy any, they must likewise pay a fine. They could not take by succession any property until they had paid a heavy duty. They could not grind their corn or make their bread without paying a share to the lord. They could not harvest their crops before the Church had first appropriated its tenth, the king his twentieth, the courtiers their smaller shares. They could not leave their homes without the leave of the lord, and they were bound, at all times, to render him gratuitous services. If the lord's son or daughter married, they must cheerfully pay their contributions. But when the freeman's daughter married, she must first submit to an infamous outrage —and not even the bishop, the servant of Christ, when he happened to be the lord of the manor, would waive the atrocious privilege of barbarism. Death even had no solace for these poor victims of barbarism. Living, they were subject to the inhumanities of man ; dead, they were doomed to eternal perdition ; for a *felo-de-se* was the unholiest of criminals, there was no room for his poor body in consecrated ground ; he could only be smuggled away in the dead of night and buried in some unhallowed spot with a stake through his body as a warning to others.

---

[1] In the Parliamentary War both sides sold their opponents as slaves to the colonists. After the suppression of the Duke of Monmouth's rebellion all his followers were sold into slavery. The treatment of the slaves in the colonies at the hands of " the Pilgrim Fathers " and their descendants will not bear description.

[2] This was written before the fall of the Romanoffs.

Such was the terrible misery which hung over the people ! But the baron in his hall, the bishop in his palace, the priest in his cloister, little recked they of the sufferings of the masses. The clouds of night had gathered over the fairest portion of Europe and Africa.   Everywhere the will of the strongest was the measure of law and right.   The Church afforded no help to the downtrodden and oppressed.   Its teachings were opposed to the enfranchisement of the human race from the rule of brute force.   "The early Fathers" had condemned resistance to the constituted authorities as a deadly sin.   No tyranny, no oppression, no outrages upon humanity were held to justify subjects in forcibly protecting themselves against the injustice of their rulers.   The servants of Jesus had made common cause with those whom he had denounced,—the rich and powerful tyrant.   They had associated themselves with feudalism, and enjoyed all its privileges as lords of the soil, barons and princes.

The non-Christians—Jews, heretics, or pagans—enjoyed, under Christian domination, a fitful existence.   It was a matter of chance whether they would be massacred or reduced to slavery.   Rights they had none ; enough if they were suffered to exist.   If a Christian contracted an illicit union with a non-Christian,—a lawful union was out of the question,—he was burnt to death.   The Jews might not eat or drink or sit at the same table with the Christians, nor dress like them.   Their children were liable to be torn from their arms, their goods plundered, at the will of the baron or bishop, or a frenzied populace.   And this state of things lasted until the close of the seventeenth century.

Not until the Recluse of Hira sounded the note of freedom, —not until he proclaimed the practical equality of mankind, not until he abolished every privilege of caste, and emancipated labour,—did the chains which had held in bond the nations of the earth fall to pieces.   He came with the same message which had been brought by his precursors and *he* fulfilled it.

The essence of the political character of Islâm is to be found in the charter, which was granted to the Jews by the Prophet after his arrival in Medîna, and the notable message sent to the Christians of Najrân and the neighbouring territories after

Islâm had fully established itself in the Peninsula. This latter document has, for the most part, furnished the guiding principle to all Moslem rulers in their mode of dealing with their non-Moslem subjects, and if they have departed from it in any instance the cause is to be found in the character of the particular sovereign. If we separate the political necessity which has often spoken and acted in the name of religion, no faith is more tolerant than Islâm to the followers of other creeds.[1] " Reasons of State " have led a sovereign here and there to display a certain degree of intolerance, or to insist upon a certain uniformity of faith ; but the system itself has ever maintained the most complete tolerance. Christians and Jews, as a rule, have never been molested in the exercise of their religion, or constrained to change their faith. If they are required to pay a special tax, it is in lieu of military service, and it is but right that those who enjoy the protection of the State should contribute in some shape to the public burdens. Towards the idolaters there was greater strictness in theory, but in practice the law was equally liberal. If at any time they were treated with harshness, the cause is to be found in the passions of the ruler or the population. The religious element was used only as a pretext.

In support of the time-worn thesis that the non-Moslem subjects [2] of Islâmic States labour under severe disabilities, reference is made not only to the narrow views of the later canonists and lawyers of Islâm, but also to certain verses of the Koran, in order to show that the Prophet did not view non-Moslems with favour, and did not encourage friendly relations between them and his followers.[3] In dealing with this subject, we must not forget the stress and strain of the life-and-death struggle in which Islâm was involved when those verses were promulgated, and the treacherous means that were often employed by the heathens, as well as the Jews and the Christians, to corrupt and seduce the Moslems from the new Faith. At such a time, it was incumbent upon the Teacher

---

[1] Comp. Gobineau, *Les Religions et les Philosophies dans l'Asie Centrale.*

[2] In the Islâmic system the non-Moslem subjects of Moslem States are called *Ahl-us-zimmah* or *Zimmis, i.e* " people living under guarantees."

[3] See Sell's Essays on Islâm.

to warn his followers against the wiles and insidious designs of hostile creeds. And no student of comparative history can blame him for trying to safeguard his little commonwealth against the treachery of enemies and aliens. But when we come to look at his general treatment of non-Moslem subjects, we find it marked by a large-hearted tolerance and sympathy.

Has any conquering race or Faith given to its subject nationalities a better guarantee than is to be found in the following words of the Prophet? " To [the Christians of] Najrân and the neighbouring territories, the security of God and the pledge of His Prophet are extended for their lives, their religion, and their property—to the present as well as the absent and others besides ; there shall be no interference with [the practice of] their faith or their observances ; nor any change in their rights or privileges ; no bishop shall be removed from his bishopric ; nor any monk from his monastery, nor any priest from his priesthood, and they shall continue to enjoy every thing great and small as heretofore ; no image or cross shall be destroyed ; they shall not oppress or be oppressed ; they shall not practise the rights of blood-vengeance as in the Days of Ignorance ; no tithes shall be levied from them nor shall they be required to furnish provisions for the troops." [1]

After the subjugation of Hîra, and as soon as the people had taken the oath of allegiance, Khâlid bin-Walîd issued a proclamation by which he guaranteed the lives, liberty and property of the Christians, and declared that " they shall not be prevented from beating their *nâkûs* [2] and taking out their crosses on occasions of festivals." " And this declaration," says Imâm Abû-Yusuf,[3] " was approved of and sanctioned by the Caliph [4] and his council." [5]

---

[1] *I.e.* nor shall troops be quartered on them ; *Futûh ul-Buldân* (Balâzuri), p. 65 ; *Kitâb-ul-Kharâj* of Imâm Abû Yusuf. Muir gives this guarantee of the Prophet in an abridged form, vol. ii. p. 299 ; see Appendix.

[2] A piece of wood used in Eastern Christian churches in place of a bell.

[3] The Chief Kâzi of Hârûn ar-Rashîd.

[4] Abû Bakr.

[5] Consisting of Omar, Osmân and Ali and the other leading Companions of the Prophet ; see the *Kitâb ul-Kharâj*, p. 84.

The non-Moslem subjects were not precluded from building new churches or temples. Only in places exclusively inhabited by Moslems a rule of this kind existed in theory. " No new Church or temple," said Abdullah bin Abbâs,[1] " can be erected in a town solely inhabited by Moslems ; but in other places where there are already *Zimmis* inhabiting from before, we must abide by our contract with them." [2] In practice, however, the prohibition was totally disregarded. In the reign of Mâmûn, we hear of eleven thousand Christian churches, besides hundreds of synagogues and fire-temples within the empire. This enlightened monarch, who has been represented as " a bitter enemy " of the Christians, included in his Council the representatives of all the communities under his sway,— Moslems, Jews, Christians, Sabæans and Zoroastrians ; whilst the rights and privileges of the Christian hierarchy were carefully regulated and guaranteed.

It is a notable fact, with few parallels even in modern history, that after the conquest of Egypt the Caliph Omar scrupulously preserved intact the property dedicated to the Christian churches and continued the allowances made by the former government for the support of the priests.[3]

The best testimony to the toleration of the early Moslem government is furnished by the Christians themselves. In the reign of Osmân (the third Caliph), the Christian Patriarch of Merv addressed the Bishop of Fars, named Simeon, in the following terms : " The Arabs who have been given by God the kingdom (of the earth) do not attack the Christian faith ; on the contrary they help us in our religion ; they respect our God and our Saints, and bestow gifts on our churches and monasteries."

In order to avoid the least semblance of high-handedness, no Moslem was allowed to acquire the land of a *zimmi* even by purchase. " Neither the Imâm nor the Sultan could dispossess a *zimmi* of his property."

The Moslems and the *zimmis* were absolutely equal in the eye of the law. " Their blood," said Ali the Caliph, " was like our blood." Many modern governments, not excepting

---

[1] A cousin of the Prophet and a jurist of recognised authority.
[2] *Kitâb ul-Kharâj*, p. 88.　　　[3] Makrîzi, pp. 492, 499.

some of the most civilised, may take the Moslem administration for their model. In the punishment of crimes there was no difference between the rulers and the ruled. Islâm's law is that if a *zimmi* is killed by a Moslem, the latter is liable to the same penalty as in the reverse case.[1]

In their anxiety for the welfare of the non-Moslem subjects, the Caliphs of Bagdad, like their rivals of Cordova, created a special department charged with the protection of the *zimmis* and the safeguarding of their interests. The head of this department was called, in Bagdad, *Kâtib-ul-Jihbâzeh* ; in Spain, *Kâtib-uz-Zimâm*.[2]

Mutawakkil, who rased to the ground the mausoleum of the martyr Husain and forbade pilgrimages to the consecrated spot, excluded non-Moslems, as he excluded the Moslem Rationalists, from the employment of the State and subjected them to many disabilities. In the later works of law, written whilst the great struggle was proceeding between Islâm and Christendom, on one side for life, on the other for brute mastery, there occur no doubt passages which give colour to the allegation that in Islâm *zimmis* are subject to humiliation. But no warrant for this statement will be found in the rules inculcated by the Teacher, or his immediate disciples or successors. It must be added, however, that the bigoted views of the later canonists were never carried into practice ; and the toleration and generosity with which the non-Moslems were treated are evidenced by the fact that *zimmis* could be nominated as executors to the wills of Moslems ; that they often filled the office of rectors of Moslem universities and educational institutions, and of curators of Moslem endowments so long as they did not perform any religious functions. And when a non-Moslem of worth and merit died, the Moslems attended his funeral in a body.

In the beginning military commands, for obvious reasons,

[1] Zail'i in his *Takhrîj-ul-Hedâya* mentions a case which occurred in the Caliphate of Omar. A Moslem of the name of Bakr bin Wâil killed a Christian named Hairût. The Caliph ordered that " the killer should be surrendered to the heirs of the killed." The culprit was made over to Honain, Hairût's heir, who put him to death, p. 338, Delhi edition. A similar case is reported in the reign of Omar bin Abdul Aziz.

[2] With a *Zâl* ; see *The Short History of the Saracens*, p. 573.

were not entrusted to non-Moslems, but all other posts of emolument and trust were open to them equally with Moslems. This equality was not merely theoretical, for from the first century of the Hegira we find important offices of state held by Christians, Jews and Magians. The Abbasides, with rare exceptions, recognised no distinction among their subjects on the score of religion. And the dynasties that succeeded them in power scrupulously followed their example.

If the treatment of non-Moslems in Islâmic countries is compared with that of non-Christians under European Governments, it would be found that the balance of humanity and generosity, generally speaking, inclines in favour of Islâm. Under the Mogul Emperors of Delhi, Hindus commanded armies, administered provinces and sat in the councils of the sovereign. Even at the present time can it be said that in no European empire, ruling over mixed nationalities and faiths, is any distinction made of creed, colour or race?

That which Islâm had almost exclusively in view was to inculcate among mankind the principle of divine unity and human equality preached by the Prophet. So long as the central doctrine of the unity of God and the message of the Prophet is recognised and accepted, Islâm allows the widest latitude to the human conscience. Consequently, wherever the Moslem missionary-soldier made his appearance, he was hailed by the down-trodden masses and the persecuted heretics as the harbinger of freedom and emancipation from a galling bondage. Islâm brought to them practical equality in the eye of the law, and fixity of taxation.

The battle of Kâdesia, which threw Persia into the hands of the Moslems, was the signal of deliverance to the bulk of the Persians, as the battles of Yermuk and Ajnâdin were to the Syrians, the Greeks, and the Egyptians. The Jews, whom the Zoroastrians had massacred from time to time, the Christians, whom they hunted from place to place, breathed freely under the authority of the Prophet, the watchword of whose faith was the brotherhood of man. The people everywhere received the Moslems as their liberators. Wherever any resistance was offered, it was by the priesthood and the aristocracy. The masses and the working classes in general, who were under the ban of Zoroastrianism, ranged themselves with the conquerors. A simple confession of an everlasting truth placed them on the same footing as their Moslem emancipators.

The feudal chiefs of the tribes and villages retained all their privileges, honours, and local influence,—" more than we believe," says Gobineau, " for the oppressions and persecutions of the Musulmans have been greatly exaggerated."

The conquest of Africa and Spain was attended with the same result. The Arians, the Pelagians, and other heretics hitherto the victims of orthodox fury and hatred,—the people at large, who had been terribly oppressed by a lawless soldiery and a still more lawless priesthood,—found peace and security under Islâm. By an irony of fate, which almost induces a belief in the Nemesis of the ancients, the Jews, whose animosity towards the Prophet very nearly wrought the destruction of the Islâmic commonwealth, found in the Moslems their best protectors. " Insulted, plundered, hated and despised by all Christian nations," they found that refuge in Islâm, that protection from inhumanity, which was ruthlessly denied to them in Christendom.

Islâm gave to the people a code which, however archaic in its simplicity, was capable of the greatest development in accordance with the progress of material civilisation. .It conferred on the State a flexible constitution, based on a just appreciation of human rights and human duty. It limited taxation, it made men equal in the eye of the law, it consecrated the principles of self-government. It established a control over the sovereign power by rendering the executive authority subordinate to the law,—a law based upon religious sanction and moral obligations. " The excellence and effectiveness of each of these principles," says Urquhart " (each capable of immortalising its founder), gave value to the rest ; and all combined, endowed the system which they formed with a force and energy exceeding those of any other political system. Within the lifetime of a man, though in the hands of a popula-tion, wild, ignorant, and insignificant, it spread over a greater extent than the dominions of Rome. While it retained its primitive character, it was irresistible." [1]

[1] Urquhart, *Spirit of the East*, vol. i. Introd. p. xxviii.

The short government of Abû Bakr was too fully occupied with the labour of pacifying the desert tribes to afford time for any systematic regulation of the provinces. But with the reign of Omar—a truly great man—commenced that sleepless care for the welfare of the subject nations which characterised the early Moslem governments.

An examination of the political condition of the Moslems under the early Caliphs brings into view a popular government administered by an elective chief with' limited powers. The prerogatives of the head of the State were confined to administrative and executive matters, such as the regulation of the police, control of the army, transaction of foreign affairs, disbursement of the finances, etc. But he could never act in contravention of the recognised law.

The tribunals were not dependent on the government. Their decisions were supreme ; and the early Caliphs could not assume the power of pardoning those whom the regular tribunals had condemned. The law was the same for the poor as for the rich, for the man in power as for the labourer in the field.

As time advances the stringency of the system is relaxed but the form is always maintained. Even the usurpers, who, without right, by treachery and murder seized the reins of government, and who in their persons represented the pagan oligarchy which had been displaced by the teachings of Islâm, observed more or less the outward semblance of law-abiding executive heads of a representative government. And the rulers of the later dynasties, when they overstepped the bounds, often unlimited, of arbitrary power, were restrained by the sentence of the general body of jurisconsults, which in all Musulman States serves as a constitutional check on the sovereign. In the early times, however, the " Companions " of the Master formed as it were an effective Council of State. The consideration attached to the title of " Companion of the Prophet " was as great in the camp as in the city. The powerful influence which they possessed increased with the conquests of the Moslems. The quality of *ashâb* carried with it a character of sanctity and nobleness. When a person bearing this title was in an action, the crowd flocked to his side and followed his lead. In the first degree were those who had accompanied the Prophet from Mecca—the Exiles, and the Ansâr who had received him with devotion, and who had battled in defence of the Faith at Badr and Ohod ; those who were charged with any work by him and those who had talked with him, seen him, or heard him. In the last rank came those who had served under any of the *sahâba*, and thus came indirectly within the magic influence of the Master.

An incident which occurred during the Caliphate of Omar shows the absolute equality of all men in Islâm. Jabala, king of the Ghassanides, having embraced the Faith, had proceeded to Medîna to pay his homage to the Commander of the Faithful. He had entered the city with great pomp and ceremony, and been received with much consideration. Whilst performing the *tawâf*, or circumambulation of the Kaaba, a humble pilgrim engaged in the same sacred duties accidentally dropped a piece of his pilgrim's dress over the royal shoulders. Jabala turned round furiously and struck him a blow which knocked out the poor man's teeth. The rest of this episode must be told in the memorable words of Omar himself to Abû Obaidah, commanding the Moslem troops in Syria. " The poor man came to me," writes the Caliph, " and prayed for redress ; I sent for Jabala, and when he came before me I asked him why he had so ill-treated a brother-Moslem. He answered that the man had insulted him, and that were it not for the sanctity of the place he would have killed him on the spot. I answered that his words added to the gravity of his offence, and that unless he obtained the pardon of the injured man he would have to submit to the usual penalty of the law. Jabala replied, ' I am a king, and the other is only a common man.' " King or no king, both of you are Musulmans and both of you are equal in the eye of the law.' He asked that the penalty might be delayed until the next day ; and, on the consent of the injured, I accorded the delay. In the night Jabala escaped, and has now joined the Christian dog.[1] But God will grant thee victory over him and the like of them . . ."

This letter was read by Abû Obaidah at the head of his

---

[1] Such was the designation usually given to the Byzantine emperors by the early Moslems.

troops.   These communications appear to have been frequent under the early Caliphate.   No person in the camp or in the city was a stranger to public affairs.   Every Friday after divine service, the Commander of the Faithful mentioned to the assembly the important nominations and events of the day. The prefects in their provinces followed the example.   No one was excluded from these general assemblies of the public.   It was the reign of democracy in its best form.   The Pontiff of Islâm, the Commander of the Faithful, was not hedged round by any divinity.   He was responsible for the administration of the State to his subjects.   The stern devotion of the early Caliphs to the well-being of the people, and the austere simplicity of their lives, were in strict accordance with the example of the Master.   They preached and prayed in the mosque like the Prophet ;   received in their homes the poor and oppressed, and failed not to give a hearing to the meanest. Without cortege, without pomp or ceremony, they ruled the hearts of men by the force of their character.   Omar travelled to Syria to receive the capitulation of Jerusalem, accompanied by a single slave.   Abû Bakr on his death-bed left only a suit of clothes, a camel, and a slave to his heir.   Every Friday, Ali distributed his own allowance from the public treasury among the distressed and suffering ;   and set an example to the people by his respect for the ordinary tribunals.   Whilst the Republic lasted none of the Caliphs could alter, or act contrary to, the judgment of the constituted courts of justice.[1]

Naturally, it is difficult for a new government, introduced by force of arms, to conciliate the affection of the people at once. But the early Saracens offered to the conquered nations motives for the greatest confidence and attachment.   Headed by chiefs of the moderation and gentleness of Abû Obaidah, who tempered and held in check the ferocity of soldiers like Khâlid, they maintained intact the civil rights of their subjects.   They accorded to all the conquered nations the completest religious toleration.   Their conduct might furnish to many of the civilised governments of modern times the noblest example of

---

[1] The first sentence of a court of justice which was not carried into execution was under Mu'âwiyah, who pardoned a man found guilty by the judge upon the criminal reciting a poem in praise of the usurper.

civil and religious liberty.   They did not lash women to death. They did not condemn innocent females to Siberian mines and the outrages of their guards.   They had the sagacity not to interfere with any beneficent civil institution, existing in the conquered countries, which did not militate with their religion.

The measures taken by Omar to secure the agricultural prosperity of the people evince an ever-present solicitude to promote their well-being and interests.   Taxation on land was fixed upon an equable and moderate basis ;   aqueducts and canals were ordered to be made in every part of the empire. The feudal burdens, which had afflicted the cultivators of the soil, were absolutely withdrawn, and the peasantry were emancipated from the bondage of centuries.   The death of this remarkable man at the hands of an assassin was an un-doubted loss to the government.   His character, stern and yet just, his practical commonsense and knowledge of men, had eminently fitted him to repress and hold in check the ambitious designs of the children of Ommeyya.   On his death-bed Omar entrusted to six electors the task of nominating a successor to the office.   The Caliphate was offered to the son of Abû Tâlib, but Ommeyyade intrigue had annexed to the proposal a condition which they knew Ali would not accept.   He was required to govern, not only in accordance with the laws and precedents of the Prophet, but also with those established by his two predecessors.   With characteristic independence Ali refused to allow his judgment to be so fettered.   The Caliphate was then offered, as it was expected by the Ommeyyades, to their kinsman Osmân.   The accession of this venerable chief to the vicegerency of the Prophet proved in the sequel an unqualified disaster to the commonwealth of Islâm.   He was a member of that family which had always borne a deep-rooted animosity towards the children of Hâshim.   They had per-secuted the Teacher with rancorous hatred, and had driven him from his home.   They had struggled hard to crush the Faith in its infancy, and had battled against it to the last. Strongly united among themselves, and exercising great influence among all the tribes of Mozar,[1] of which they were

[1] With a *Zâd.*

the prominent members, the Ommeyyades had watched with ill-concealed jealousy the old power and prestige slip away from their hands. After the fall of Mecca they had accepted the inevitable, but never forgave the house of Hâshim or Islâm for the ruin which the son of Abdullah had wrought to them. Whilst the Prophet lived, his commanding personality overawed all these traitors. Many of them had made a nominal profession of the Faith from self-interest [1] and a greed to secure a part of the worldly goods which the success of the Moslems brought to the Islâmic commonwealth. But they never ceased to hate the democracy proclaimed by Mohammed. Libertines and profligates, unscrupulous and cruel, pagans at heart, they chafed at a religion of equal rights, a religion which exacted strict observance of moral duties and personal chastity. They set themselves, from the commencement, to undermine the government to which they had sworn allegiance, and to destroy the men upon whom the Republic depended. The first two successors of the Prophet had kept their ambition within bounds, and repressed their intrigues and treacherous designs. With the election of Osmân, they flocked to Medîna like vultures scenting the prey. His accession was the signal for that outburst of hatred, that pent-up profligacy on the part of the Ommeyyades, which convulsed the Islâmic world to its innermost core, and destroyed its noblest and most precious lives.

Under Osmân there was a complete reversal of the policy and administration of his two predecessors, whose decisions he had engaged to follow. All the old governors and commanders taken from among the immediate disciples of the Prophet and his Companions were displaced. Merit and faithful service were wholly disregarded. All offices of trust and emolument were seized by the Ommeyyades. The governorships of the provinces were bestowed on men who had proved themselves most inimical to Islâm, and the treasury was emptied in their favour. We shall have to describe the subsequent events in some detail when dealing with the divisions in the Church of Mohammed ; suffice it for us to say, that the corruptness of the administration, the total disregard of all precedent, the gross

---

[1] They were, therefore, called the *Muallafat ul-kulûb*.

favouritism displayed by the old Caliph towards his kinsmen,
and his refusal to listen to any complaint, gave rise to serious
disaffection among the old companions of the Prophet and the
general body of the Moslems, ending in revolt in which Osmân
lost his life. On Osmân's tragical death, Ali was elected to
the vacant Caliphate by the consensus of the people. The
rebellions which followed are matters of history. " Had Ali
been allowed to reign in peace," says Oelsner, " his virtues,
his firmness, and his ascendancy of character would have
perpetuated the old republic and its simple manners." [1] The
dagger of an assassin destroyed the hope of Islâm. " With
him," says Major Osborn, " perished the truest-hearted and
best Moslem of whom Mohammedan history has preserved the
remembrance." Seven centuries before, this wonderful man
would have been apotheosised ; thirteen centuries later his
genius and talents, his virtues and his valour, would have
extorted the admiration of the civilised world. As a ruler, he
came before his time. He was almost unfitted by his uncompromising love of truth, his gentleness, and his merciful nature,
to cope with the Ommeyyades' treachery and falsehood.

With the establishment of an autocracy under Mu'âwiyah
the political spirit of Islâm underwent a great change. The
sovereigns were no more the heads of a commonwealth, elected
by the suffrage of the people, and governing solely for the
welfare of their subjects and the glory of the Faith. From the
time of Mu'âwiyah the reigning Caliph nominated his successor ;
and the oath of fealty taken by the people in his presence, or
in that of his proxy, confirmed his nomination. This system
combined the vices of democracy and despotism without the
advantages of either. Under the Republic not only were
the Caliphs assisted by a council of the Companions of the
Prophet, but the provincial governors had similar advisory
bodies. During the Ommeyyade rule the government was a
pure autocracy tempered by the freedom of speech possessed
by the desert Arabs and the learned or holy, which enabled
them, often by a phrase or verse from the Koran or from the
poets, to change the mood of the sovereign. Under the first
five Caliphs of the Abbaside dynasty also the government

[1] Oelsner, *Des Effets de la religion de Mohammed.*

continued to be more or less autocratic, although the departmental ministers and prominent members of the family formed a body of unauthorised councillors. A regular Council composed of the leading representatives of communities owning allegiance to the Caliph was for the first time established in the reign of Mâmûn the Great. The Buyides, the Sâmânides, the Seljukides, and the Ayyûbides all had their councils in which the people were more or less represented.

But absolutism in the hands of the early Abbasides helped in the intellectual development and material prosperity of the Islâmic nations. In the vigour of their rule and the firmness with which they held the reins of government they may be compared with the Tudors of England. The political and administrative machinery of the Abbaside Caliphate, which was afterwards adopted by the succeeding dynasties, owes its origin to the genius of Mansûr, the founder of Bagdad. In its effective distribution of work and its control of details it ranks with the most perfectly organised systems of modern times.

At the very commencement of their rule, which lasted for several centuries, they established a Chamber of Finance and a Chancellery of State, the first being charged with the duty of receiving the taxes and disbursing the expenses of the empire, the second with the duty of impressing a character of authenticity on the mandates of the sovereigns. Later, for the better subdivision of work, other departments of state (called *diwâns*) were created, of which the following are the principal :—the *Diwân-ul-Kharâj* (Central Office of Taxes) or Department of Finance ; the *Diwân-ud-Diä* (Office of the Crown Property) ; the *Diwân-uz-zimâm* (Audit or Accounts Office) ; the *Diwân-ul-Jund* (War Office) ; the *Diwân-ul-Mawâli wa'l Ghilmân* (Office for the Protection of Clients and Slaves), where a register was kept of the freedmen and slaves of the Caliph, and arrangements made for their maintenance ; the *Diwân-ul-Barîd* (the Post Office) ; *Diwân-uz-Zimâm an-Nafakât* (Household Expense Office) ; the *Diwân-ur-Rasâil* (Board of Correspondence or Chancery Office) ; the *Diwân-ut-Toukia* (Board of Requests) ; the *Diwân un nazr fi'l Mazâlim* (Board for the Inspection of Grievances) ; the *Diwân-ul-Ahdâs w'ash-Shurta*

(Militia and Police Office) ; and the *Diwân-ul-'Atâ* (Donation Office), analogous to the paymaster-general's department, charged with the payment of the regular troops. The protection of the interests of non-Moslems was entrusted to a special office, the head of which was called the *Kâtib-ul-jihbâzèh.*

Each Government office was presided over by a director who was designated the *Raîs,* or *Sadr,* and the practical work of control and supervision was carried on by inspectors, called *Mushrifs,* or *Nâzirs.*[1]

To this organisation the Abbaside Caliphs added the appointment of an officer with the designation of *Hâjib,* who introduced the foreign ambassadors, and also formed a Court of Appeal from the decrees of the Kâzis. They instituted the office of *Vizier,* or Prime Minister, whose duty it was to submit for the consideration of the sovereign the various matters requiring his decision. They gave regularity to the provincial administration, and fixed definitely the contributions due from the provinces. They constructed caravanserais, built cisterns and aqueducts along the road from Bagdad to Mecca, planted trees along the route, and everywhere founded wayside resting-places for the travellers and pilgrims. They made a route between Mecca and Medîna, and laid relays of horses and camels between Hijâz and Yemen to facilitate communication between these two provinces. They established couriers in every city for the despatch of the post. They formed a central office in the metropolis for the custody and preservation of the archives of the empire, and created an efficient police in every part of their dominions. They formed a syndicate of merchants, charged with the supervision of commercial transactions, the decision of disputes between mercantile men, and the duty of suppressing fraud. Not only did each centre of commerce possess its corporation of merchants but most cities of importance had their town councils. They created the office of *Muhtesib,* or intendant of the market, who went round daily to examine the weights and measures of the tradespeople. They fostered self-government and protected and encouraged municipal institutions. Agriculture was promoted by advances

---

[1] For a full account of the political and administrative machinery of the Abbasides, see *The Short History of the Saracens,* pp. 402-443.

to the peasantry, and periodical reports were required from the provincial officers respecting the prosperity of the people and the state of the country. Many of them, in the midst of their pomp and circumstance, tried to maintain a semblance of republican virtue. Books written by them, baskets woven by them, used to be sold in the market, and the proceeds were supposed to supply the personal expenses of the Caliphs. Their zeal to promote the well-being of their subjects may perhaps be taken into the great Account against their cruelties towards the Alides. Under Mâmûn and his two immediate successors the Abbaside empire attained the zenith of prosperity.

Spain furnishes one of the most instructive examples of the political character of Islâm and its adaptability to all forms and conditions of society. This country had suffered frightfully under the barbarian hordes which had swept over the land, destroying and levelling every institution they found existing. The kingdoms they had formed over the ruins of the Roman administration had effaced the germs of political development. Their subjects were weighted down with feudal burdens, and all the terrible consequences flowing therefrom. Vast areas were completely denuded of population. The introduction of the Islâmic Code enfranchised the people as well as the land from feudal bondage. The desert became fruitful, thriving cities sprang into existence on all sides, and order took the place of anarchy. Immediately on their arrival on the soil of Spain, the Saracens published an edict assuring to the subject races, without any difference of race or creed, the most ample liberty, Suevi, Goth, Vandal, Roman, and Jew were all placed on an equal footing with the Moslem. They guaranteed to both Christian and Jew the full exercise of their religions, the free use of their places of worship, and perfect security of person and property. They even allowed them to be governed, within prescribed limits, by their own laws, to fill all civil offices and serve in the army. Their women were invited to intermarry with the conquerors. Does not the conduct of the Arabs in Spain offer an astonishing contrast to that of many European nations, even in modern times, in their treatment of conquered nationalities? Whilst to compare the Arab rule with that of the Normans in England, or of the Christians in Syria during the Crusades, would be an insult to common-sense and humanity.   The fidelity of the Arabs in maintaining their promises, the equal-handed justice which they administered to all classes, without distinction of any kind, secured them the confidence of the people.   And not only in these particulars, but also in generosity of mind and in amenity of manner, and in the hospitality of their customs, the Arabians were distinguished above all other people of those times.[1]   The Jews had, owing to the influence of the Christian priesthood, suffered bitterly under the barbarians, and they profited most by the change of government.   Spanish ladies of the highest rank, among them the sister of Pelagius and the daughter of Roderick, contracted marriages with " the Infidels,"-as the orthodox Jean Mariana calls the Moslems.   They enjoyed all the rights and privileges which their rank gave them with full liberty of conscience.   The Moslems invited all the landed proprietors, whom the violence of Roderick had driven into the mountains, to abandon their retreats.   Unhappily the depopulation was so great that this measure had no effect in supplying inhabitants to the soil.   They, accordingly, held forth the most generous advantages to foreign cultivators who wished to establish themselves in the Peninsula.   These offers brought large and industrious colonies from Africa and Asia.   Fifty thousand Jews at one time, accompanied by their women and children, settled in Andalusia.

For seven centuries the Moslems held Spain, and the beneficence of their rule, in spite of intestine quarrels and dynastic disputes, is testified to and acknowledged even by their enemies.   The high culture attained by the Spanish Arabs has been sometimes considered as due principally to frequent marriages between Moslems and Christians.   This circumstance undoubtedly exercised a great influence on the development of the Spanish Moslems and the growth of that wonderful civilisation to which modern Europe owes so much of its advance in the arts of peace.[2]   What happened in Spain happened also in other places.   Wherever the Moslems entered a change came

[1] Condé's *History of the Spanish Moors.*
[2] Renan, *Averroes et Averroisme.*

over the countries; order took the place of lawlessness, and peace and plenty smiled on the land. As war was not the privileged profession of one caste, so labour was not the mark of degradation to another. The pursuit of agriculture was as popular with all classes as the pursuit of arms.[1]

The importance which Islâm attaches to the duties of sovereigns towards their subjects, and the manner in which it promotes the freedom and equality of the people and protects them against the oppression of their rulers, is shown in a remarkable work [2] on the reciprocal rights of sovereigns and subjects, by *Safi-ud-dîn* Mohammed bin Ali bin Taba Taba, commonly known as Ibn ut-Tiktaka.[3] The book was composed in 701 A.H. (1301-2), and is dedicated to *Fakhr ud-dîn* ʻIsa bin Ibrâhim, Ameer of Mosul.

The first part deals with the duties of sovereigns to their subjects, and the rules for the administration of public affairs and political economy. The author describes the qualities essential for a sovereign,—wisdom, justice, knowledge of the wants and wishes of his people, and the fear of God; and adds emphatically that this latter quality is the root of all good, and the key to all blessings, " for when the king is conscious of the presence of God, His servants will enjoy the blessings of peace and security." The

و هذه الخصلة هي أصلُ كل خيرٍ و مِفتاحُ كلِّ بركةٍ إنّ الملكَ

متى خاف الله آمنهُ عبادُ الله

sovereign must also possess the quality of mercy, العفو عن الذنوب and " this is the greatest of all good qualities." He must have an ever-present desire to benefit his subjects, and consult with them on their wants; for the Prophet consulted always with his Companions, and God hath said,[4] " Consult with them [5] on every affair." In the administration of public affairs, it is the

[1] Oelsner.

[2] This work is generally known as the *Kitâb-i-Târikh-ud-Duwal* Hist. of Dynasties; but its proper title is *Kitâb-ul-fakhri fi'l âdâb-ul-Sultaniyat wa'd duwal ul-Islâmia*, " the book of Fakhri, concerning the conduct of sovereigns and the Islamic dynasties"; Derenbourg's Edition; see Appendix.

[3] With a hard *kâf*.   [4] In the Koran.   [5] *I.e.* The people.

sovereign's duty to superintend the public income, guard the lives and property of his subjects, maintain peace, check the evil-doer, prevent injuries.   He must always keep his word, and then, adds the author significantly, " the duty of the subject is obedience, but no subject is bound to obey a tyrant." Ibn Rushd (the great Averroes) says, " the tyrant is he who governs for himself, and not for his people."

The laws of the Moslems, based on equitable principles, and remarkable for their simplicity and precision, did not demand an obedience either difficult to render or incompatible with the intelligence of mankind.   The countries where the Moslems established themselves remained exempt from the disastrous consequences of the feudal system and the feudal code.[1] " Admitting no privilege, no caste, their legislation produced two grand results,—that of freeing the soil from factitious burdens imposed by barbarian laws, and of assuring to individuals perfect equality of rights." [2]

---

[1] In Corsica, Sardinia, Sicily, and Lower Italy, the feudal system was introduced after the expulsion of the Arabs.

[2] Oelsner.

CHAPTER VIII

THE POLITICAL DIVISIONS AND SCHISMS OF ISLÂM

جنگ هفتاد و در ملت همه را عذر بنه

چون ندیدند حقیقت ره افسانه زدند

HÂFIZ.

TO every philosophical student of the history of religion the heading of this chapter must cause surprise, if not pain ; to every Islâmist devoted to the Founder of his Faith it must cause sorrow and shame. Alas ! that the religion of humanity and universal brotherhood should not have escaped the curse of internecine strife and discord ; that the Faith which was to bring peace and rest to the distracted world should itself be torn to pieces by angry passions and the lust of power. The evils, which we deplored in Christianity arose from the incompleteness of the system, and its incompatibility with human needs ; in Islâm, the evils that we shall have to describe arose from the greed of earthly advancement, and the revolutionary instincts of individuals and classes impatient of moral law and order.

Nothing evinces so clearly the extraordinary genius of the Arabian Teacher, his wonderful personality, and the impressiveness of his call to religious unity and universal citizenship, as the world-movement of which he was the cause, and which, in spite of internal dynastic wars, carried his people on a tidal wave of conquest from one end of the globe to the other. Arabia, hitherto the home of warring tribes and clans, each with its blood-feud of centuries, was suddenly animated with a common purpose. Until now the wars of the Arabs and their alliances, their virtues and their vices, their love of independence and

their clannish feeling, had alike prevented community of action.
Suddenly a nation of shepherds is turned into a nation of kings,
a race of semi-nomades transformed into masters of " a world-
faith and law." With unexampled energy and self-mastering
devotion the congeries of wandering clans planted between
three continents take up the banner of the Faith and bear it
aloft to every quarter of the earth. " You have been elected
to carry to all mankind the message of mercy, the announcement
of divine unity," is the call addressed to them, and they respond
to it with a determination which acknowledges no obstacle.
The intensity of conviction, which alone could carry them
through the barriers of hostile creeds and races, explains the
mystery of the revolution !

Truth is eternal : Mohammed's message was not new. It
had been delivered before, but had not reached the heart of
man. *His* voice quickened the dead into life, revived the
dying, and made the pulse of humanity beat with the accumulated force of ages. The exodus of the Saracens under this
mighty impulse, its magnitude and its far-reaching effects,
form the most marvellous phenomenon of modern times. They
issued from their desert-fastnesses as the preceptors of
humanity. Within thirty years—the term prophesied for the
true Caliphate—they were knocking at the gate of every nation,
from the Hindu Kush to the shores of the Atlantic, to deliver
their message. In the short space of time which elapsed from
the death of the Prophet to the subversion of the Republic,
they built up an empire, which, in its vastness, exceeded that
achieved by the Romans after thirteen centuries of continuous
expansion. Turn over the pages of Ibn ul-Athîr, Tabari, or
Abulfedâ, you will find a continuous record of the wave rolling
onward, fertilising every soil over which it passes, assimilating
in its way all that is good.

The same causes, however, which, until the advent of the
Prophet, had prevented the growth of the Arabs into a nation,
—the same tribal jealousies, the same division of clan and clan,
the marks of which are still visible throughout the Moslem
world,—led eventually, not only to the ruin of the Republic,
but also to the downfall of the Saracenic empire. " Had the
followers of Mohammed marched on the lines of the Master

and adopted the character of the early Caliphs," says d'Ohsson, " their empire would have been still more vast and more durable than that of the Romans." But the greed of the Ommeyyade, the unruliness of the Arab, and his spirit of individualism, which showed itself even when arrayed against a common foe, caused the overthrow of the stupendous fabric which the heroism and devotion of the early Moslems had raised. Owing to this, they lost Tours, even whilst victory was within their grasp ; they were driven out of Spain because they could not forget the old jealousies of the desert, and make common cause against the enemy.

But though the Republic fell, and the imperial sceptre passed from the hands of the Saracens, the Faith lived. It was the outcome of ages of evolution. It represented the latest phase in the religious development of man ; it did not depend for its existence or its growth on the life of empires or men. And as it spread and fructified, each race and each age profited by its teachings according to their own spiritual necessities and intellectual comprehension !

The Church of Mohammed, like the Church of Christ, has been rent by intestine divisions and strifes. Difference of opinion on abstract subjects, about which there cannot be any certitude in a finite existence, has always given rise to greater bitterness and a fiercer hostility than ordinary differences on matters within the range of human cognition. The disputes respecting the nature of Christ deluged the earth with the blood of millions ; the question of Free-will in man caused, if not the same amount of bloodshed, equal trouble in Islâm. The claim to infallibility on the part of the Pontiffs of Rome convulsed Christendom to its core ; the infallibility of the people and of the Fathers became in Islâm the instrument for the destruction of precious lives.

Most of the divisions in the Church of Mohammed owe their origin primarily to political and dynastic causes,—to the old tribal quarrels, and the strong feeling of jealousy which animated the other Koreishites against the family of Hâshim. It is generally supposed that the Prophet had not expressly designated any one as his successor in the spiritual and temporal Government of Islâm ; but this notion is founded on a

mistaken apprehension of facts, for there is abundant evidence
that many a time the Prophet had indicated Ali for the vice-
gerency.   Notably on the occasion of the return journey from
the performance of " the Farewell Pilgrimage," during a halt
at a place called Khumm, he had convoked an assembly of the
people accompanying him, and used words which could leave
little doubt as to his intention regarding a successor.   " Ali,"
said he, " is to me what Aaron was to Moses.   Almighty God !
be a friend to his friends and a foe to his foes ; help those who
help him, and frustrate the hopes of those who betray him ! " [1]
On the other hand, the nomination of Abû Bakr to lead prayers
during the Prophet's illness might point to a different choice.
The question came up for discussion and settlement on his
decease, when it became necessary to elect a leader for Islâm.
The Hâshimites maintained that the office had devolved by
appointment as well as by succession upon Ali.   The other
Koreishites insisted upon proceeding by election.   Whilst the
kinsmen of Mohammed were engaged in his obsequies, Abû
Bakr was elected to the Caliphate by the votes of the Koreish
and some of the Medinite Ansâr.   The urgency of an immediate
selection for the headship of the State might explain the haste.
With his usual magnanimity and devotion to the Faith,
scrupulously anxious to avoid the least discord among the
disciples of the Master, Ali at once gave in his adhesion to
Abû Bakr.   Three times was he set aside, and on every occasion
he accepted the choice of the electors without demur.   He
himself had never stood forth as a candidate for the suffrages
of the electors, and whatever might have been the feeling of
his partisans, he had never refrained from giving to the first
two Caliphs his help and advice in the governance of the
Commonwealth : and they on their side had always deferred
to his counsel and his exposition of the Master's teachings.
We have already referred to the circumstances connected with
the elevation of Osmân to the Caliphate.   We will here trace

[1] Ibn Khallikân, vol. i. p. 383. " According to Al-Hâzimi," says Ibn-
Khallikân, " Khumm is the name of a valley lying between Mecca and Medina,
and in the neighbourhood of at-Tuhfa. It contains a pond (Ghadîr) near
which the Prophet pronounced his invocation." This took place on the 18th
of Zu'l-Hijja, for Ibn-Khallikân says the 18th of that month " is the
anniversary of the Feast of Ghadîr (Id-ul-Ghadîr), which is the same as that
of Ghadîr-i-Khumm."

the events which followed upon his accession to elucidate the history of the deplorable schism which has for so long divided the Moslem world into two sects. Osmân possessed neither the shrewdness of Abû Bakr nor the intellectual vigour or the moral fibre of Omar. His amiability and easy good nature made him a pliable tool in the hands of his kinsfolk. The venerable Caliph surrounded by his hungry kinsmen, the provinces crying for redress, and the general body of Moslems sullenly watching the proceedings of the head of the State, form an instructive though sad picture of the times. The character of the deluded Pontiff has been graphically portrayed by Dozy. " The personality of Osmân did not justify his election to the Caliphate. It is true he was rich and generous, had assisted Mohammed and the religion by pecuniary sacrifices, and that he prayed and fasted often, and was a man of amiable and soft manners. He was, however, not a man of spirit, and was greatly enfeebled by old age. His timidity was such that when placed on the pulpit he knew not how to commence his sermon. Unhappily for this old man, he possessed an inordinate fondness for his kinsmen, who formed the Meccan aristocracy, and who, for twenty years, had insulted, persecuted, and fought against Mohammed. Soon they dominated over him completely. His uncle, Hishâm, and especially Hishâm's son, Merwân, in reality governed the country, only allowing the title of Caliph to Osmân, and the responsibility of the most compromising measures, of which he was often wholly ignorant. The orthodoxy of these two men, especially of the father, was strongly suspected. Hishâm had been converted only when Mecca was taken. Having betrayed state-secrets, he had been disgraced and exiled. Abû Bakr and Omar had maintained the order passed (by the Prophet). Osmân, on the contrary, not only recalled him from his exile, but gave him on his arrival a hundred thousand pieces of silver from the public treasury, and a piece of land belonging to the State. He made Merwân his secretary and vizier, and married him to one of his daughters, and enriched him with the spoils of Africa." [1] . . . He confirmed Mu'âwiyah, the son of Abû Sufiân and Hind, who had fought against Mohammed with such ferocity at Ohod, in the

[1] Dozy, *Hist. des Mussulmans dans l'Espagne*, vol. i. p. 44.

governorship of Syria ; and his foster-brother, Abdullah ibn Sa'd ibn Surrah, to the satrapy of Egypt.   This Abdullah was at one time a secretary to the Prophet, and when the Master dictated his revelations, he used to change the words and " denaturalise " their meaning.   His sacrilege being discovered, he had fled, and had relapsed into idolatry.   Walîd, an uterine brother of the old Caliph, was made governor of Kûfa.   His father had often ill-treated Mohammed, and once nearly strangled him.   An abandoned debauchee, a profligate drunkard, his life was a scandal to the Moslems.   He appeared in the mosque at the time of morning-prayers helpless from intoxication, falling prostrate on the ground as he attempted to perform the duties of an Imâm, or leader of prayer ; and when the by-standers hurried up to assist him to his feet, shocked them by demanding more wine, in a husky and stammering voice.   These were the men whom the Caliph favoured ! They fastened upon the provinces like famished leeches, heaping up wealth by means of pitiless extortion.   Complaints poured into Medîna from all parts of the empire.   But the complaints were invariably dismissed with abuses and hard words.[1]   A deputation, consisting of twelve thousand men, headed by Mohammed, the son of the Caliph Abû Bakr, came to the capital to lay before Osmân the grievances of the people, and to seek redress.   Sore pressed at their demands for justice, he had recourse to the intervention of the son-in-law of the Prophet whose advice he had hitherto persistently refused to heed.   Ali persuaded the deputation to depart to their homes, by giving them a pledge that their complaints should be redressed.   On their way back, and hardly at a day's journey from Medîna, they intercepted a letter written by Osmân's secretary, which bore the Caliph's own seal, containing a mandate to the unscrupulous Mu'âwiyah to massacre them in a body.   Enraged at this treachery, they returned to Medîna, entered the old Caliph's house, and killed him.   His death furnished to the Ommeyyades what they were long thirsting for, a plea for a revolt against Islâm,—against its democracy, its equal rights, and its stern rules of morality.   It furnished to the Meccans and their allies an excuse for organising a conspiracy against

[1] Ibn ul-Athîr, vol. iii. p. 125.

Medinite dominance, which they hated so bitterly. Ali had tried hard to save Osmân, at first by wise counsels not to abandon himself absolutely into the hands of his unprincipled kinsmen, and at the last crisis by placing himself before the infuriated soldiery, and asking for consideration for the venerable though misguided pontiff. He had nearly sacrificed his own sons in his endeavours to protect Osmân. On Osmân's death he was raised to the Caliphate by the unanimous voice of the people. Since the death of the Prophet, Ali, though he had never failed to attend the councils of State, had always maintained a dignified reserve and a noble independence of character. In his retirement he had chiefly devoted himself to study and the peaceable occupations of domestic life. Called to the helm of the State, he received the oath of fealty with his usual simplicity, declaring his readiness to resign the office to any one more worthy.

" Had," says Sédillot, " the principle of hereditary succession (in favour of Ali) been recognised at the outset, it would have prevented the rise of those disastrous pretensions which engulfed Islâm in the blood of Moslems. . . . The husband of Fâtima united in his person the right of succession as the lawful heir of the Prophet, as well as the right by election. It might have been thought that all would submit themselves before his glory ; so pure and so grand. But it was not to be." Zubair and Talha, who had hoped that the choice of the people might fall on either of them for the Caliphate, baulked in their ambitious designs, and smarting under the refusal of the new Caliph to bestow on them the governorships of Basra and Kûfa, were the first to raise the standard of revolt. They were assisted by 'Âyesha, the daughter of Abû Bakr, who had taken a decisive part in the former elections. This lady had always borne an inveterate dislike towards the son-in-law of Khadîja, and now this feeling had grown into positive hatred. She was the life and soul of the insurrection, and herself accompanied the insurgent troops to the field, riding a camel. The Caliph, with his characteristic aversion to bloodshed, sent his cousin Abdullah bin Abbâs to adjure the insurgents by every obligation of the Faith to abandon the arbitrament of war. But to no avail. Zubair and Talha gave battle at a place called

Khoraiba, and were defeated and killed.[1] 'Âyesha was taken
prisoner. She was treated with courtesy and consideration,
and escorted with every mark of respect to Medîna. Hardly
had this rebellion been suppressed, when Ali learnt of the
insurrection of Mu'âwiyah in Syria. The son of Abû Sufiân,
like most of his kinsmen whom Osmân had appointed to the
governorships of the provinces, had, with the gold lavished
upon him by the late Pontiff and the wealth of Syria, collected
round him a large band of mercenaries. Ali had been advised
by several of his councillors to defer the dismissal of the corrupt
governors appointed by the late Caliph until he himself was
secure against all enemies. " The Bayard of Islâm, the hero,
without fear and without reproach," [2] refused to be guilty of
any duplicity or compromise with injustice. The fiat went
forth removing from their offices all the men whom Osmân had
placed in power, and who had so grossly betrayed the public
trust. Mu'âwiyah at once raised the standard of revolt.
Defeated in several consecutive battles on the plains of Siffîn,
on the last day when his troops were flying like chaff before
the irresistible charge of Mâlek al-Ashtar, he bethought himself
of a ruse to save his men from impending destruction. He
made some of his soldiers tie copies of the Koran to their
spears, and advance towards the Moslems shouting, " Let the
blood of the Faithful cease to flow ; if the Syrian army be
destroyed, who will defend the frontier against the Greeks ?
If the army of Irâk be destroyed, who will defend the frontier
against the Turks and Persians ? Let the Book of God decide
between us." The Caliph, who knew well the character of the
arch-rebel and his fellow-conspirator, Amr(u) the son of al-'Âs,
saw through the artifice, and tried to open the eyes of his
people to the treachery ; but a large body of his troops refused
to fight further, and demanded that the dispute should be
referred to arbitration. In answer to the Caliph's assurances
that the son of Abû Sufiân was only using the Koran as a device
for delivering himself from the jaws of death, these refractory

[1] The battle is called the " Battle of the Camel," from 'Âyesha's presence in
a litter on a camel. The place where the fight actually took place and where
these men were killed, is called *Wâdi us-Saba'*, " Valley of the Lion."

[2] These are the designations given to Ali by Major Osborn.

spirits threatened open defection.[1] Mâlek al-Ashtar was recalled, the battle was stopped, and the fruits of a victory already won were irretrievably lost.[2] An arbitration was arranged. The bigots, who had compelled Ali to sheathe the sword at the moment of victory, forced upon him, against his own judgment and wishes, Abû Mûsa al-Asha'ri as the representative of the House of Mohammed. This man, who was also secretly hostile to Ali, was altogether unfitted by his vanity and religious conceit and a somewhat simple nature to cope with the astute and unscrupulous Amr the son of al-'Âs, who acted as the representative of Mu'âwiyah, and he soon fell into the trap laid for him by the latter. Amr led Abû Mûsa to believe that the removal of both Ali and Mu'âwiyah (of the one from the Caliphate and of the other from the governorship of Syria), and the nomination of another person to the Headship of Islâm, was necessary to the well-being of the Moslems. The trick succeeded ; Abû Mûsa ascended the pulpit and solemnly announced the deposition of Ali. After making this announcement he descended aglow with the sensation of having performed a virtuous deed. And then Amr smilingly ascended the pulpit vacated by Abû Mûsa the representative of Ali, and pronounced that he accepted the deposition of Ali, and appointed Mu'âwiyah in his place. Poor Abû Mûsa was thunder-struck ; but the treachery was too patent, and the Fâtimides refused to accept the decision as valid.[3] This happened at Dûmat ul-Jandal. The treachery of the Ommeyyades exasperated the Fâtimides, and both parties separated vowing undying hatred towards each other. Ali was shortly after assassinated whilst engaged in prayer in a mosque at Kûfa.[4] His assassination enabled the son of Abû Sufiân to consolidate his power both in Syria and Hijâz. On the death of Ali, Hasan, his

---

[1] Shahristânî, pt. i. p. 85.   [2] Ibid.

[3] Those very men who had forced upon the Caliph the arbitration afterwards repudiated it, and rose in rebellion against him for consenting to their demand for arbitration. They were the original Khawârij (insurgents), who became afterwards an enormous source of evil to Islâm ; see post.

[4] With the chivalrous generosity which distinguished him, the Caliph Ali, even in his war against his treacherous foe, always ordered his troops to await the enemy's attack, to spare the fugitive, and respect the captive, and never to insult the women. With his dying breath he commanded his sons to see that the murderer was killed with one stroke of the sword, and that no unnecessary pain might be inflicted on him.

eldest son, was raised to the Caliphate. Fond of ease and quiet, he hastened to make peace with the enemy of his House, and retired into private life. But the Ommeyyade's animosity pursued him even there, and before many months were over he was poisoned to death. The star of Hind's son was now in the ascendant, and Abû Sufiân's ambition to become the king of Mecca was fulfilled on a grander scale by Mu'âwiyah. Thus was the son of the two most implacable foes of the Prophet, by the strangest freak of fortune recorded in history, seated on the throne of the Caliphs. Lest it be considered our estimate of Mu'âwiyah's character is actuated by prejudice, we give the words of a historian who cannot be accused of bias in favour of either side. " Astute, unscrupulous, and pitiless," says Osborn, " the first Khalif of the Ommayas shrank from no crime necessary to secure his position. Murder was his accustomed mode of removing a formidable opponent. The grandson of the Prophet he caused to be poisoned ; Mâlek-al-Ashtar, the heroic lieutenant of Ali, was destroyed in a like way. To secure the succession of his son Yezid, Mu'âwiyah hesitated not to break the word he had pledged to Husain, the surviving son of Ali. And yet this cool, calculating, thoroughly atheistic Arab ruled over the regions of Islâm, and the sceptre remained among his descendants for the space of nearly one hundred and twenty years. The explanation of this anomaly is to be found in two circumstances, to which I have more than once adverted. The one is, that the truly devout and earnest Muhammadan conceived that he manifested his religion most effectually by withdrawing himself from the affairs of the world. The other is the tribal spirit of the Arabs. Conquerors of Asia, of Northern Africa, of Spain, the Arabs never rose to the level of their position. Greatness had been thrust upon them, but in the midst of their grandeur they retained, in all their previous force and intensity, the passions, the rivalries, the petty jealousies of the desert. They merely fought again on a wider field ' the battles of the Arabs before Islâm.' "

With the rise of Mu'âwiyah the oligarchical rule of the heathen times displaced the democratic rule of Islâm. Paganism, with all its attendant depravity, revived, and vice and immorality followed everywhere in the wake of

Ommeyyade governors and the Syrian soldiery. Hijâz and Irâk groaned under the usurper's rule ; but his hold on the throat of Islâm was too strong to be shaken off with impunity. The wealth which he pitilessly extracted from his subjects, he lavished on his mercenaries, who in return helped him to repress all murmurings. Before his death, he convened the chief officers of his army and made them take the oath of fealty to his son Yezîd, whom he had designated as his successor to the throne. This was Yezîd's title to the Caliphate ! On Mu'âwiyah's death, the Domitian of the house of Ommeyya ascended the throne founded by his father on fraud and treachery. As cruel and treacherous as Muâwiyah, he did not, like his father, possess the capacity to clothe his cruelties in the guise of policy. His depraved nature knew no pity or justice. He killed and tortured for the pleasure he derived from human suffering. Addicted to the grossest of vices, his boon companions were the most abandoned of both sexes. Such was the Caliph—the Commander of the Faithful ! Husain, the second son of Ali, had inherited his father's chivalric nature and virtues. He had served with honour against the Christians in the siege of Constantinople. He united in his person the right of descent from Ali, with the holy character of grandson of the Apostle. In the terms of peace signed between Mu'âwiyah and Hasan, his right to the Caliphate had been expressly reserved. Husain had never deigned to acknowledge the title of the tyrant of Damascus, whose vices he despised, and whose character he regarded with abhorrence ; and when the Moslems of Kûfa besought his help to release them from the curse of the Ommeyyade's rule, he felt it his duty to respond to the Irâkians' appeal for deliverance. The assurances he received, that all Irâk was ready to spring to its feet to hurl the despot from his throne the moment he appeared on the scene, decided him to start for Kûfa with his family. He traversed the desert of Arabia unmolested, accompanied by his brother Abbâs, a few devoted followers, and a timorous retinue of women and children ; but as he approached the confines of Irâk he was alarmed by the solitary and hostile face of the country, and suspecting treachery, the Ommeyyade's weapon, he encamped his small band at a place called

Kerbela near the western bank of the Euphrates. No event in history surpasses in pathos the scenes enacted on this spot. Husain's apprehensions of betrayal proved to be only too true. He was overtaken by an Ommeyyade army under the brutal and ferocious Obaidullah ibn-Ziyâd. For days their tents were surrounded ; and as the cowardly hounds dared not come within the reach of the sword of Ali's son they cut the victims off from the waters of the Tigris. The sufferings of the poor band of martyrs were terrible. In a conference with the chief of the enemy, Husain proposed the option of three honourable conditions : that he should be allowed to return to Medîna, or be stationed in a frontier garrison against the Turks, or safely conducted to the presence of Yezîd.[1] But the commands of the Ommeyyade tyrant were stern and inexorable— that no mercy should be shown to Husain or his party, and that they must be brought as criminals before the " Caliph " to be dealt with according to the Ommeyyade sense of justice. As a last resource, Husain besought these monsters not to war upon the helpless women and children, but to kill him and be done with it. But they knew no pity. He pressed his friends to consult their safety by a timely flight ; they unanimously refused to desert or survive their beloved master. One of the enemy's chiefs, struck with horror at the sacrilege of warring against the grandson of the Prophet, deserted with thirty followers " to claim the partnership of inevitable death." In every single combat and close fight the valour of the Fâtimides was invincible. But the enemy's archers picked them off from a safe distance. One by one the defenders fell, until at last there remained but the grandson of the Prophet. Wounded and dying he dragged himself to the river-side for a last drink ; they turned him off with arrows from there. And as he re-entered his tent he took his infant child in his arms ; him they transfixed with a dart. The stricken father bowed his head to heaven. Able no more to stand up against his pitiless foes,

---

[1] The author of the *Rouzat-us-Safâ*, after stating the above, adds that an attendant of Husain, who by chance escaped the butchery of Kerbela, denied that his master, so far as he was aware, ever made any such proposal to the Ommeyyade leader. It is possible, however, that such denial was made in order to show that Husain did not lower himself by proposing terms to the enemy. To my mind, however, it detracts in no way from the grandeur of Husain's character that he proposed terms to the Ommeyyades.

alone and weary, he seated himself at the door of his tent.
One of the women handed him a cup of water to assuage his
burning thirst ; as he raised it to his lips he was pierced in the
mouth with a dart ; and his son and nephew were killed in his
arms.   He lifted his hands to heaven,—they were full of blood,
—and he uttered a funeral prayer for the living and the dead.
Raising himself for one desperate charge, he threw himself
among the Ommeyyades, who fell back on every side.   But
faint with loss of blood he soon sank to the ground, and then
the murderous crew rushed upon the dying hero.   They cut
off his head, trampled on his body, and subjected it to every
ignominy in the old spirit of Hind.   They carried the martyr's
head to the castle of Kûfa, and the inhuman Obaidullah struck
it on the mouth with a cane : " Alas ! " exclaimed an aged
Musulman, " on these lips have I seen the lips of the Apostle
of God."   " In a distant age and climate," says Gibbon, " the
tragic scene of the death of Husain will awaken the sympathy
of the coldest reader."   It will now be easy to understand, if
not to sympathise with, the frenzy of sorrow and indignation
to which the adherents of Ali and his children give vent on the
recurrence of the anniversary of Husain's martyrdom.

Thus fell one of the noblest spirits of the age, and with him
perished all the male members of his family,—old and young,—
with the solitary exception of a sickly child, whom Husain's
sister, Zainab (Zenobia), saved from the general massacre.   He,
too, bore the name of Ali, and in after-life received the noble
designation of Zain ul-'Âbidîn, " the Ornament of the Pious."
He was the son of Husain by the daughter of Yezdjard, the
last Sasanide king of Persia, and in him was perpetuated the
house of Mohammed.   He represented also, in his mother's
right, the claims of the Sasanians to the throne of Irân.

The tragical fate of Husain and his children sent a thrill of
horror through Islâm ; and the revulsion of feeling which it
caused proved eventually the salvation of the Faith.   It
arrested the current of depravity which flowed from the
Ommeyyade court of Damascus.   It made the bulk of Moslems
think of what the Master had done, and of the injuries which
the children of his enemies were inflicting on Islâm.   For a
hundred years, however, the Ommeyyades ruled with the free

help of the sword and poison.   They sacked Medîna, and drove
the children of the Helpers into exile in far-away lands.   The
city which had sheltered the Prophet from the persecution of
the idolaters, and which he loved so dearly, the hallowed
ground he had trod in life, and every inch of which was sanctified by his holy work and ministry, was foully desecrated ;
and the people who had stood by him in the hour of his need,
and helped him to build up the arch of the Faith, were subjected to the most terrible and revolting atrocities, which find
a parallel only in those committed by the soldiers of the Con-
stable of France and the equally ferocious Lutherans of George
Frundsberg at the sack of Rome.   The men were massacred,
the women outraged, the children reduced into slavery.   The
public mosque was turned into a stable, the shrines demolished
for the sake of their ornaments.   During the whole period of
Ommeyyade domination the holy city remained a haunt of
wild beasts.[1]   The paganism of Mecca was once more triumphant.   And " its reaction," says Dozy, " against Islâm was
cruel, terrible, and revolting."   The Meccans and the Ommeyyades thus repaid the clemency and forbearance shown to them
in the hour of Islâm's triumph !   The Ommeyyades produced
many notable men eminent for piety and virtue, chief amongst
them Omar bin-'Abdul Azîz, the Marcus Aurelius of the Arabs,
a virtuous sovereign, a good ruler, and a God-fearing Moslem,
who modelled his life after his great namesake the second
Caliph.   For the rest they were unabashed pagans and revelled
in the disregard of the rules and discipline of the religion they
professed.

But for the Ommeyyades, the difference between the followers
of the *Ahl-ul-Bait*,[2] the upholders of Ali's right to the apostolical
succession, and those who maintained the right of the people
to elect their own *spiritual* as well as temporal chiefs, would
never have grown into a schism ; it would have ended in a
compromise or coalition after the accession of Ali to the Caliphate.   The violence and treachery of the children of Ommeyya
rendered this impossible.   They had waded to the throne

---

[1] Abdul Malik ibn-Merwân went so far as to issue an edict forbidding pilgrims
to visit the sepulchre of the Prophet at Medîna.

[2] For the meaning of this word see note 2, page 313.

through manifold crimes and oceans of blood ; it was necessary
for them to impart a semblance of validity to their tenure of
the office of Caliph.   They claimed to have the title of *Ameer-
ul-Mominîn* by right of election—election by their own mercenaries and pagan partisans.   After the sack of Medîna and
the destruction and dispersion of the family of Mohammed and
the Muhâjirîn and Ansâr, it was easy to draw precedents from
the early Caliphate, and when that failed, to manufacture
traditions.   Nor was it difficult to appropriate a title which
might have been assumed, but was not, by those who supported
the right of the universality of the people to elect their chiefs.
The giants who had built up the Republic were dead or destroyed ; their children were fugitives or slaves ; who was to
question the validity of the title so adroitly usurped ?   The
Ommeyyade policy was pursued by the dynasty which took
its place.   The same fierce jealousy with which the Bani-
Ommeyya had pursued or persecuted the Banî-Fâtima, characterised the conduct of the Banî-Abbâs towards the descendants of Mohammed.   They had no claim to the Caliphate
themselves ; they made the affection of the people for the
children of Fâtima the means for their own elevation, and when
they had attained the desired end they rewarded the Fâtimides
with bitter persecution.   Their title also was founded on quasi-
election, and naturally they hunted, like the Ommeyyades, all
who questioned the legality of their claim, or who upheld in
explicit terms the doctrine of the devolution of the Imâmate
by succession in the line of Mohammed.   Every difference of
opinion was strictly repressed ; even the jurists of the time
were punished if they ventured to express opinions which did
not find favour with the sovereigns.[1]   If we did not keep in
view the circumstances which led to the sudden and unexpected
rise of the Abbasides, we would be apt to regard it as pheno-
menal.   The terrible cruelties inflicted by the Ommeyyades on
the children of Fâtima, and the sublime patience with which
they had borne their sufferings and their wrongs, had given
rise to a universal feeling of horror against the tyrants, and
had invested the objects of persecution, in the eyes of their

[1] Imâm Mâlik ibn Anas, the third pillar of the Sunni Church, was publicly
punished for an offence of this nature.

followers and disciples, with a superhuman halo. Persecution,
however fierce, has always failed to achieve its end ; instead
of stamping out the faith or devotion of a sect or community,
it has diverted it into new channels and imparted to it greater
vitality. In Islâm, as in Christianity, the dangers of the battlefield and the pains of persecution have " clothed with more
than earthly splendour the objects for whom they were endured."
And the children of Fâtima, saints who had submitted to the
injustice of man and devoted themselves to intellectual pursuits
and the practice of religion,—without arms, without treasure,
and without subjects,—ruled more firmly over the hearts of
their followers, and enjoyed the veneration of the people to a
greater degree, than the caliph in his palace, the master of
legions. The cup of Ommeyyade iniquity was full to overflowing, and men were crying aloud in the anguish of their
hearts, O Lord, how long ! On every side there was an eager
and passionate longing engendered by the vices and misrule of
the pseudo-caliphs that the House of Mohammed might be
restored to its rights. They looked wistfully to the Imâms to
give the sign, but these saints had retired from the world ;
their domain was no more of this earth. Successive avengers [1]
of their wrongs had risen in arms, and gone down before the
serried ranks of their Syrian enemies. The people waited for
authority from the divinely-appointed leaders of the Faithful,
but they condemned the use of force. What was to be done ?
Several scions of the House who had risen against the Banî-
Ommeyya, contrary to the counsel and without the sanction
of the heads of the family, had sacrificed themselves to their
ambition or their religious zeal. It was at this juncture, at
this moment of unrest, when the Moslems were longing for a
sign from the House of Mohammed, that the Banî-Abbâs
appeared on the scene. The Banî-Abbâs were the descendants
of Abbâs, an uncle of the Prophet. Abbâs had always taken
a deep interest in the progress of Islâm ; he was Mohammed's
companion when the famous " Pledge of the Women " was
taken from the Medînites. But from some weakness of character or from policy, he did not embrace Islâm definitely until
about the time Mecca fell. He was, however, always treated

[1] Sulaimân ibn Surrâd, al-Mukhtâr, and Yezîd ibn Muhallib.

with the greatest affection and consideration by Mohammed. The Prophet's example was imitated by Abû Bakr, Omar, and Osmân. They dismounted if they met him walking ; and not unfrequently would accompany him to his residence.[1] He died in A.H. 32,—according to some, two years later,—leaving four sons, Abdullah (*Abu'l Abbâs* Abdullah *ibn Abbâs*), Fazl, Obaidullah, and Kaithân. Abdullah, better known in history and tradition as Ibn Abbâs, was born at Mecca in A.C. 619, three years before the Hegira. He was instructed in the Koran and jurisprudence by Ali himself. His reputation as a scholar and expounder of the Koran and of the decisions of the Caliphs stood so high that crowds flocked from all parts to hear his lectures. He gave public lessons one day in the week on the interpretation of the Koran ; another day, on law ; the third, on grammar ; the fourth, on the history of the Arabs, and the fifth on poetry. He gave an impulse to the study and preservation of pre-Islâmic Arab literature and history by frequently quoting verses from the ancient poets to explain and illustrate the difficult and obscure passages of the Koran. He was wont to say, " When you meet with a difficulty in the Koran, look for its solution in the poems of the Arabs, for these are the registers of the Arab nation."[2] The steady and unvarying devotion of Ibn Abbâs and his brothers to Ali was proverbial. All four brothers were present at " the Battle of the Camel," and at Siffîn, Ibn Abbâs, who was no less an accomplished soldier than a scholar, commanded the cavalry of Ali. He acted frequently as the envoy of the Caliph, and it was he whom Ali desired to nominate as the representative of the House of Mohammed when forced by the refractory troops to refer the dispute between himself and Mu'âwiyah to arbitration.[3] Ibn Abbâs died at Tâyef of a broken heart, after the murder of Husain, in A.H. 67, in the seventieth year of his age. His son, who was named Ali after the great Caliph, walked in the footsteps of his father in his zealous attachment to the children of Fâtima. He died in A.H. 117,

[1] Abbâs may be called the John of Gaunt of Moslem history.

[2] Once he was asked how he had acquired his extensive knowledge : his reply was, " By means of an inquiring tongue and an intelligent heart."

[3] Shahristânî, pt. i. p. 86.

and was succeeded in the headship of his family by his son Mohammed.

At this time, Persia, Irâk, and Hijaz, which had suffered most from the atrocities of the Banî-Ommeyya, were honey-combed by secret organisations for the overthrow of the hated family. The Banî-Abbâs were the most active in the move-ment to subvert the Ommeyyade rule, at first, perhaps, from a sincere desire to restore to the Fâtimides their just rights, but afterwards in their own interests. Mohammed, the son of Ali ibn Abdullah, was the first to conceive the project of seizing the Caliphate for himself. He was a man of great ability and unbounded ambition. Whilst working ostensibly for the Fâti-mides, he contrived gradually to establish the pretensions of his own family. He started a new doctrine to justify the claims of his house to the Imâmate : that on the murder of Husain at Kerbela, the spiritual headship of Islâm was not transmitted to his surviving son Ali (Zain ul-'Âbidîn), but to Mohammed ibn al-Hanafiya, a son of the Caliph Ali by a different mother, whom he had married after the death of Fâtima, belonging to the tribe of Hanifa ; that upon his death the office descended upon his son Hâshim, who had assigned it formally to the Abbaside Mohammed. This story received credence in some quarters ; but for the bulk of the people, who clung to the descendants of the Prophet, the *dâ'is* [1] of the Abbasides affirmed that they were working for the *Ahl-ul-bait*. Hitherto, the Abbasides had professed great devotion to the House of Fâtima, and had ascribed to all their movements and plans the object of securing justice for the descendants of Mohammed. The representatives and adherents of the *Ahl-ul-bait*, little suspecting the treachery which lay behind their professions, extended to Mohammed bin Ali and to his party the favour and protection which was needed to impress upon his action the sanction of a recognised authority. The attach-ment of the Persians to the Fâtimide cause was due to historical and national associations. The Fâtimides represented in their persons, through the daughter of Yezdjard, the right to the throne of Irân. From the first commencement of the Islâmic preachings, Ali had extended the utmost consideration and

---

[1] Missionaries or political agents.

friendship to the Persian converts.   Salmàn the Persian, one
of the most notable disciples of the Prophet, was long the
associate and friend of the Caliph.   After the battle of Kâdesia,
Ali used to devote his share of the prize-money to the redemption of the captives, and repeatedly by his counsel induced
Omar to lighten the burden of the subjects.   The devotion of
the Persians to his descendants was intelligible.   Mohammed
bin Ali beguiled the Persians by preaching to them their
approaching deliverance from the hated rule of their Arab
oppressors.   To the Yemenites settled in Khorâsân, Fars, and
other provinces of Irân, who were equally attached to the
Ahl-ul-bait, and whose animosity against their old enemies, the
descendants of Mozar, was inflamed by many recent injuries,
he proclaimed he was acting solely on behalf of the Imâms of
the House of Mohammed.   He succeeded in winning over to
his side Abû Muslim, the ablest general of his time, and hitherto
a devoted partisan of the children of Ali.   Before his death,
which took place in 125 A.H., he named his sons Ibrâhim,
Abdullah Abu'l Abbâs (surnamed *Saffâh*), Abdullah Abû Ja'far
(surnamed *al-Mansûr*) as his successors, one after the other.

The furious struggle which broke out about the middle of the
eighth century between the Yemenites and Mozarites in
Khorâsân served as a signal to apply the torch to the well-laid
mine.   Abû Muslim sent word to his partisans in every city
and village of the Province to raise at once the standard of
revolt.   The cause proclaimed was " the rights of the *Ahl-ul-
bait* " against the usurping Banî-Ommeyya.   A short time
previously, Yahya, a grandson of the Imâm Ali Zain-ul-'Âbidîn,
had revolted and been killed, and his body was exposed, by the
order of Merwân, upon a gibbet.   Abû Muslim ordered the
remains of the young chief to be taken down and buried with
every mark of respect ; and his followers clothed themselves
in black in token of their sorrow, and their determination to
avenge the death of Yahya.   From that day black became the
distinguishing symbol of the Abbaside cause.   And when
the order went forth summoning the people to arms against the
usurpers, the crowd, clothed in black, which flocked to the
trysting-places showed the widespread character and strength
of the revolt.   The gathering was to take place on the night

of the 25th of Ramazân A.H. 127, and the people were to be
summoned by large bonfires lighted on the tops of the hills.
Vast multitudes poured from every quarter into Merv, where
Abû Muslim was dwelling at the time. Ibrâhim, who had
succeeded Mohammed bin Ali as the head of the Abbasides,
was seized by Merwan and killed ; but before his death he
contrived to pass to his second brother, Abu'l Abbâs, a document assigning him the authority in accordance with the
testament of their father. Abû Muslim soon made himself
master of the whole of Khorâsân, and marched his victorious
troops towards Irâk. Nothing as yet was divulged as to the
ultimate purpose of the movement. The *Ahl-ul-bait* was the
watchword which rallied all classes of people round the black
standard. Kûfa surrendered at once. Hasan ibn Kahtaba,
the lieutenant of Abû Muslim, entered the city at the head of
his troops, and was joined at once by Abû Salma Ja'ar ibn
Sulaimân al-Khallâl, " who," says the author of the *Rouzat-us-
Safâ,* " was designated the vizier of the descendants of Mohammed." Apparently this man acted as the agent of the head of
the family. He was received with the greatest consideration
by the Abbaside general, " who kissed his hand, and seated
him in the place of honour," [1] and told him that it was Abû
Muslim's orders that he should be obeyed in all things. Abû
Salma's vanity was flattered, but as yet he was wholly unaware
of the Abbaside design. A proclamation was issued in the
joint names of Abû Salma and Hasan ibn Kahtaba, inviting
the inhabitants of Kûfa to assemble the next day at the *Masjid-
al-Jâmi'* (the public mosque). The people flocked to the
mosque expecting some announcement ; but the plot had not
yet thickened, and Hasan and the other Abbaside partisans
considered the moment inopportune for the proclamation of
their design. In the meantime, Abu'l Abbâs, with his brother
Abû Ja'far, had successfully evaded the Ommeyyade guards,
and had arrived at Kûfa, where they kept themselves concealed, waiting for the next event of the drama. Abû Salma,
who was still faithful to the masters he purported to serve,
sent a message secretly to the Imâm (Ja'far as-Sâdik) to come
and take up his right. The Imâm, knowing well the nature of

---

[1] *Rouzat-us-Safâ* ; Ibn ul-Athîr, vol. v. p. 312 *et seq.*

Irâkian communications, burnt the missive unopened. But before any answer could reach Abû Salma, he had already accepted Abu'l Abbâs as the Caliph. He then issued a proclamation, still acting ostensibly in the name of the *Ahl-ul-bait*, inviting the inhabitants, one and all, to assemble on the following day, which was a Friday, to elect a Caliph. On that day Kûfa presented a strange aspect. Large crowds of people, clothed in the sable garments of the Bani-Abbâs, were hastening from every quarter to the *Masjid-al-jâmi'* to hear the long-deferred announcement. In due time Abû Salma appeared on the scene, and, strangely, dressed. in the same sombre black. Few, excepting the partisans of Abu'l Abbâs, knew how he had come to sell himself to the Abbaside cause. He preferred his head to the interests of his masters. After leading the prayers he explained to the assemblage the object of the meeting. Abû Muslim, he said, the defender of the Faith and the upholder of the right of the House, had hurled the Ommeyyades from the height of their iniquity ; it was now necessary to elect an Imâm and Caliph ; there was none so eminent for piety, ability, and all the virtues requisite for the office as Abu'l Abbâs ; and him he offered to the Faithful for election. Up to this Abû Salma and the Abbasides were dubious of the impression on the people. They were afraid that even the Kûfians might not view their treachery to the house of Ali with approbation. But the proverbial fickleness of the Irâkians was now proved. They had again and again risen in arms in support of the Fâtimide cause, and as often betrayed those whom they had pledged themselves to help or whose help they had invoked. Swayed by the passing whim of the moment, they had as often shown themselves to be traitors, as the defenders of truth. After the massacre of Kerbela they had been so struck with remorse that twenty thousand of them, after spending a night over the tomb of Husain praying for forgiveness, had hurled themselves against the serried legions of Yezîd. But the remorse did not last long ; fickle and turbulent, faithless and unreliable, Hajjâj ibn-Yusuf, the veritable " Scourge of God," had alone kept them in order. And now, no sooner had the words passed from the lips of Abû Salma, proposing Abu'l Abbâs as the Caliph, than they burst forth with loud acclamations of the *takbir* [1] signifying their approval. A messenger was sent in haste to fetch Abu'l Abbâs from his concealment, and when he arrived at the mosque there was a frantic rush on the part of the multitude to take his hand and swear fealty. The election was complete. He ascended the pulpit, recited the *khutba*, and was henceforth the Imâm and Caliph of the Moslems.[2] Thus rose the Abbasides to power on the popularity of the children of Fâtima, whom they repaid afterwards in a different coin. The greed of earthly power is the worst form of ambition. It has caused greater disasters to humanity than any other manifestation of human passion. It never hesitates as to the choice of means to attain its object ; it uses indiscriminately both crime and virtue, the one to disguise its design, the other to achieve its ends. It has even pressed religion into its service. Ambition disguised in the cloak of religion has been productive of fearful calamities to mankind. The popes of Rome, in their incessant endeavour to maintain unimpaired their temporal power, deluged the civilised world with human blood. The pontiffs of Islâm, Abbaside, Egyptian Fâtimide, and Ommeyyade, seized with avidity upon the claim prepared by willing minions to supreme spiritual and temporal rule, and in their desire to maintain the undivided allegiance of their subjects, caused equal bloodshed and strife in the bosom of Islâm.

The early Abbaside Caliphs were men of great ability, and possessed of vast foresight and statesmanship. From the moment they were raised to the Caliphate by the acclamation of the people of Kûfa, they directed their whole energy towards consolidating the spiritual and temporal power in their hands, and to give shape and consistency to the doctrine of divine sanction to popular election. Henceforth it became a point of vital importance to disavow the principle of apostolical succession by descent, and to make the election by the people almost sacramental.

During Saffâh's [3] reign, Abû Muslim enjoyed some considera-

[1] *I.e. Allâho-Akbar*, God is great.
[2] For a full account, see *The Short History of the Saracens* (Macmillan).
[3] Abu'l Abbâs Abdullah received the title of Saffâh, " blood-spiller," or " sanguinary," on account of his unsparing use of the sword against his

tion, but the king-maker was hated and suspected for his ill-concealed Fâtimide proclivities. Under Saffâh's successor he was accused of heresy—stigmatised with the opprobrious epithet of *Zendîk* [1]—and killed. The pure and unsullied lives of the leading representatives of the House of Mohammed, the extreme veneration in which they were held by the people, frequently evoked the jealousy of the Abbasides, and exposed the children of Fâtima to periodic outbursts of persecution. Hârûn destroyed the Barmekides, who were the bulwarks of his empire and had made for him the fame which he so largely appropriated, solely on suspicion of conspiracy with the Fâtimides. This state of affairs lasted until the reign of Abdullah al-Mâmûn, the noblest Caliph of the house of Abbâs, who, on his accession to the Caliphate, resolved to restore to the children of Fâtima their just rights. He accordingly named Ali ibn Mûsa, surnamed Rizâ (" the acceptable or agreeable "), the eighth Imâm of the Fâtimides, as his successor, and gave his sister Umm ul-Fazl in marriage to this prince. He also abandoned the black, the Abbaside colour, in favour of the green, which was the recognised standard of the Fâtimides.[2] Ali ibn Mûsa ar-Rizâ was poisoned by the infuriated Abbasides, and Mâmûn was forced to resume the black as the colour of his house. The tolerance shown by him to the Fâtimides was continued by his two immediate successors (Mu'tasim and Wâsik).[3] The accession of Mutawakkil was the signal for a new and fierce persecution, which lasted during the whole fifteen years of a reign signalised by gross cruelty and debauchery. He was succeeded by his son Muntasir, whose first care was to restore the tombs of Ali and Husain, destroyed by Mutawakkil, and to re-establish the sacredness of their memory so wantonly outraged by his father. The sagacity of this Caliph was imitated by his successors, and some degree of toleration was thenceforward extended to the Shiahs. In the year 334 A.H. (A.C. 945) Muizz ud-dowla (the Deilemite), of the House of Buwaih, became the

enemies ; one of his successors (Mu'tazid b'illâh) received the title of Saffâh as-Sâni (Saffah II.), and the Ottoman, Selim I., bore the same designation.

[1] *I.e.* a Magian, Guebre, from *Zend.*

[2] The Fâtimides had adopted green, the colour of the Prophet, as the symbol of their cause ; the Banî-Ommeyya, the white ; and the Banî-Abbâs, black.

[3] Mu'tasim-b'illâh (Mohammed) and Wâsik b'illâh (Hârûn).

Mayor of the Palace at Bagdad. An enthusiastic partisan of
the Fâtimides, he entertained at one time the design of deposing
the Abbaside Caliph Muti'ullah, and placing in his stead some
scion of the house of Ali, but was restrained by motives of
policy from carrying this project into effect. Muizz ud-dowla
also instituted the *Yaum-i-'âshûra*, the day of mourning, in
commemoration of the martyrdom of Hussain and his family
on the plains of Kerbela. In the year A.H. 645 (A.C. 1247),
under Musta'sim b'illâh, another fierce persecution of the
Shiahs broke out, the consequences of which proved in the end
disastrous to Saracenic civilisation, engulfing in one common
ruin the Western Asians. Impelled by the perfidious counsels
of the fanatics who surrounded him, this imbecile pontiff of
the Sunni Church doomed the entire male population of the
Shiahs to massacre. By a terrible edict, which reminds us of
the fate of the Albigenses and the Huguenots, he permitted the
orthodox to plunder the goods, demolish the houses, ravage
the fields, and reduce to slavery the women and children of
the Shiahs. This atrocious conduct brought upon the ill-fated
city of Bagdad the arms of the avenging Hulâkû, the grandson
of Chengîz. For three days the Tartar chief gave up the town
to rapine and slaughter. On the third day the thirty-seventh
Caliph of the house of Abbâs was put to death with every
circumstance of ignominy; and so ended the Abbaside
dynasty ! [1]

Until the time of Mu'âwiyah the adherents of the *Ahl-ul-bait* [2]
had not assumed or adopted any distinctive appellation. They

---

[1] A scion of the house of Abbâs escaped into Egypt, and the titular Caliphate
flourished there until the Ottoman Selim obtained a renunciation in his favour
from the last of the Abbasides ; see *ante*, p. 130.

[2] The *Ahl-ul-bait*, " People of the House " (of Mohammed), is the designation usually given to Fâtima and Ali and their children and descendants.
This is the name by which Ibn-Khaldûn invariably designates them, and
their followers and disciples,—the Shiahs or *adherents* of the " People of the
House." Sanâi represents the general feeling with which the descendants
of Mohammed were regarded in the following verse :—

جز کتاب الله و عترت ز احمد مرسل نماند

یادگاری کو توان تا روز محشر داشتن

" Excepting the Book of God and his family (descendants) nothing has
been left by Ahmed the Prophet, memorials such as these can never be obtained
till the Day of Judgment."

were known simply as the Banî-Hâshim. There was no difference between the Banî-Fâtima and the Banî-Abbâs ; they were all connected with each other by the closest ties of blood. After Mu'âwiyah's seizure of the sovereign power the followers of the House of Mohammed began to call themselves *Shiahs* (adherents) and their enemies either *Nawâsib* (rebels) or *Khawârij* (insurgents or deserters).[1] The Ommeyyades called themselves *Amawis* (children of Ommeyya). As yet the name of *Ahl-us-Sunnat wa'l Jamâ'at* was wholly unknown. Under Mansûr and Hârûn this designation first came into existence. In the tenth century, a member of the house of Ali wrested Egypt from the Abbasides, and established a dynasty which ruled over that country and Syria until the rise of Saladin. The anathemas which the Caliphs of Bagdad and Cairo hurled at each other, the multitudinous traditions which were unearthed to demolish the claims of the one and the other, and the *fatwas* emanating from the doctors of the two Caliphates, accentuated the strife and bitterness of partisans. Saladin overthrew the Fâtimide dynasty in Egypt, and restored the predominance of the Sunni Church in Eastern Africa. Various other branches of the Banî-Fâtima, however, succeeded in establishing the supremacy of their family in different parts of the two continents.[2] The *Isnâ-'asharias*[3] alone, the followers of the saintly Imâms, who reprehended the use of force, and who claimed and exercised only a spiritual dominion, maintained an attitude of complete withdrawal from temporal interests, until Shah Ismail the great Safawi monarch made *Isnâ-'ashariaism* the State religion of Persia. Himself a philosopher and a Sûfi, he perceived in the sympathy and devotion of the people to the House of Mohammed, whose descendant he was, a means of national awakening and consolidation. Since then *Isnâ-'ashariaism* is the national church of Persia.

[1] The name of Khâwarij was especially given to the troops who deserted Ali at Dûmat ul-Jandal and formed a confederacy hostile to Islâm, and was afterwards applied to those who adopted their pernicious doctrines ; see *post*.

[2] Besides the Banî-Fâtima of Egypt, other branches of Fâtimides have ruled under the different denominations of Ameer, Imâm, Sharif, and Caliph in different parts of the Musulman world, such as the Banî-Ukhaydur, the Banî-Mûsa, the Banî-Kitâdah at Mecca, the Banî-Taba-Taba in Northern Yemen, the Banî-Ziyâd in Southern Yemen, and the Banî-Idris in Morocco.

[3] *Isnâ* with a ث ; see *post*.

The Bahmani and 'Âdil Shâhi dynasties of Southern India which Aurungzeb overthrew, thus paving the way for the rise of the Mahratta marauders whom the Bahmani sovereigns had kept in check with an iron hand, were attached to the doctrines of the Imâms.   Such has been the political fate of the Fâtimides, which has left its impress on their doctrines.

The title of the Banî-Abbâs to the spiritual and temporal headship of Islâm was founded on *bai'at* or nominal election. Since Saffâh's accession, the Abbaside Caliphs had taken the precaution of obtaining during their lifetime the fealty of the chiefs for their intended successors.   And it became necessary to impress on the doctrine of election a sanctity derived from precedent and ancient practice.   The rise of the Fâtimides in Egypt, their persistent endeavour to wrest the dominion of the East from the Caliphs of Bagdad, made it doubly necessary to controvert the pretensions of the children of Fâtima, and to give form and consistency to the orthodox doctrines recognising the Abbaside Pontiffs as the spiritual chiefs of Islâm.[1]

Every corner of Irâk and Hijâz was ransacked for traditions in support of the right of the house of Abbâs.   The doctors of law were required to formulate the principles of orthodoxy in explicit terms : and gradually the grand superstructure of the Sunni church was raised on the narrow foundations of Abbaside self-interest.   Much of the success of the doctors and legists who assisted in the growth and development of Sunnism was due to the Manichæism of the Egyptian Fâtimides.   The nature of their doctrines, which were at variance with the teachings

---

[1] Arslân al-Basâsiri, a general in the service of the Abbasides, but an adherent of the Egyptian Fâtimides, drove al-Kâim-ba-amr illâh, the then Caliph of Bagdad, from the city, and compelled him to take refuge with the phylarch of the Arabs (the Ameer-ul-Arab, a title analogous to the Il-Khâni of Persia), until restored by Tughril, the father of Alp Arslân and the founder of the Seljukide dynasty.   During the whole of this period the *Khutba* was read in Bagdad itself in the name of the Fâtimide Caliph.   The *Khutba* is the name given to the sermon pronounced on Fridays from the pulpits of the great mosques in all Moslem countries ; it begins by a declaration of God's attributes and unity, and an invocation of His blessings upon the Prophet, his family, and successors; then follows a prayer for the reigning Caliph and for the prince who exercises civil power in the State. The right of being named in the *Khutba* and that of coining money are two of the principal privileges possessed by the temporal sovereign, and the special marks of his legitimacy.

of both the Shiah Imâms and the Sunni doctors ; the assassinations of the best men committed at the instance of Hasan Sabbâh (" the Old Man of the Mountain ") ; the disintegrating character of the heresies, which under the influence of the ancient Chaldæo-Magism had sprung up in various quarters, and which were subversive of all order and morality,—added greatly to the strength of a system which formed, in the opinion of the masses, a bulwark against the enemies of Islâm.   The Shiah Imâms strongly condemned the impious or communistic doctrines of the antitypes of Mâni and Mazdak, but they lacked the power, even if willing to use it, to suppress heresy or enforce uniformity.   Sunnism, associated with the temporal power of the Abbaside Caliphs, possessed the means and used it, and thereby won the sympathy and acceptance of all who cared little about the disputes on the abstract question of apostolical descent.

Until the rise of the House of Abbâs there was little or no difference between the assertors of the right of the *Ahl-ul-bait* to the pontificate and the upholders of the right of the people to elect their own spiritual and temporal chiefs.   The people of Hijâz and the Medinite Ansâr especially, who were so ruthlessly destroyed by the Ommeyyades, whilst they insisted on the principle of election, abhorred the injustice done to the children of Fâtima.   After the murder of Husain, a cry of horror had gone forth from the heart of Islâm, and the people of the holy cities had risen in arms against the tyrant, and suffered bitterly for it.   The adherents of the *Ahl-ul-bait* and the followers of the first three Caliphs together underwent fearful cruelties in the cause of the common Faith.   But when it became necessary for dynastic reasons to create a gulf between the two parties the elements of divergence came ready to hand on both sides.   Their doctrinal and legal differences began from this time to assume the type and proportions they retain at the present moment

During the enlightened rule of Mâmûn and of his two immediate successors, when humanitarian science and philosophy influenced the conceptions of all classes of society, there was a break in the development of the Sunni Church.   With the exception of this period the entire duration of the Abbaside

Caliphate [1] was occupied in the consolidation of its dogmas. The Church and State were linked together ; the Caliph was the Imâm—temporal chief as well as spiritual head. The doctors of law and religion were his servants. He presided at the convocations, and guided their decisions. Hence the solidarity of the Sunni church. Many of the sects [2] into which it was originally split up have gradually disappeared, but it is still divided into four principal denominations, differing from each other on many questions of dogma and ritual. Their differences may perhaps be likened to those existing between the Roman Catholic and the Greek, Armenian, and Syrian orthodox churches.

Shiahism, on the other hand, shows how the Church and the State have become dissociated from each other, and how the "Expounders of the Law" have assumed, at least among a section, the authority and position of the clergy in Christendom. The freedom of judgment, which in Protestantism has given birth to one hundred and eighty sects, has produced an almost parallel result in Shiahism, and the immense diversity of opinion within the church itself is due to the absence of a controlling temporal power, compelling uniformity at the point of the sword.

The question of the Imâmate,[3] or the spiritual headship of

---

[1] From 750 A.C. to 1252 A.C.

[2] According to Imâm Ja'far Tûsi (quoted in the *Dabistân*), the Sunnis were originally divided into sixty-five sects.

[3] A very good definition of the word "Imâm" is given by Dr. Percy Badger : "The word 'Imâm' comes from an Arabic root signifying to aim at, to follow after,—most of the derivatives of which partake, more or less, of that idea. Thus *Imâm* means, primarily, an exemplar, or one whose example ought to be imitated. It is applied in that sense, κατ' ἐξοχήν, to Mohammed, as being the leader and head of the Muslims in civil and religious matters, and also to the Khalîfahs, or legitimate *Successors*, as his representatives in both capacities. It is also given—in its religious import only—to the heads of the four orthodox sects, namely, the el-Hanafy, esh-Shâfa'iy, el-Mâliky, and el-Hanbaly ; and, in a more restricted sense still, to the ordinary functionary of a mosque who leads in the daily prayers of the congregation,—an office usually conferred on individuals of reputed piety, who are removable by the *Nâzirs* or wardens, and who, with their employment and salary, lose the title also."

"The term is used in the Koran to indicate the Book, or Scriptures, or record of a people ; also, to designate a teacher of religion. Hence, most probably, its adoption by the Muslims in the latter sense. 'When the Lord tried Abraham with certain words, which he fulfilled, He said, I have made thee an Imâm to the people.' Again, referring to Abraham, Isaac and Jacob, 'We have made them Imâms, that they may direct others at our

the Musulman commonwealth, is henceforth the chief battleground of the two sects.[1] The Shiahs hold that the spiritual
heritage bequeathed by Mohammed devolved on Ali and his
descendants. They naturally repudiate the authority of the
Jamâ'at (the people) to elect a spiritual head who should supersede the rightful claims of the Prophet's family. According to
the Shiahs, therefore, the Imâmate descends by divine appointment in the apostolical line. The Imâm, besides being a
descendant of the Prophet, must possess certain qualities,—he
must be *Ma'sûm* or sinless, bear the purest and most unsullied
character, and must be distinguished above all other men for
truth and purity. It is not proper, nor could it be the intention
of the Almighty, they argue, that a man whose character is not
unimpeachable should have the direction of the human conscience. Human choice is fallible, as is proved by the history
of mankind ; and the people have often accepted the worst
men for their leaders. God could never have left the religious
needs of man to his unaided faculty. If an Imâm be needed,
he must be one whom the conscience must accept. Accordingly
they declare that if the choice of an Imâm be left to the
community, it would be subversive of all morality ; and

command.' And again, ' We delivered to Moses the Book, therefore be not
in doubt of his reception thereof, and we ordained it to be a guide unto the
children of Israel. And we appointed some of them to be Imâms, to direct
the people according to our command.' "—Badger's *Imâms and Seyyids of
Oman*, App. A.

[1] " The question of the Imâmate forms a subject of controversy," says Mas'ûdi,
" between the followers of different sects, particularly between those who
adhere to the doctrine of appointment, القائلون با النص and the followers
of the doctrine of election, اصحاب الاختيار. The defenders of the doctrine of
appointment are the Imâmias, اهل الإمامة who form a section of the
Adherents, Shiahs الشيعة of Ali ibn Abi Tâlib and his holy children (by
Fâtima) الطاهرون من ولد ه. They believe that God does not leave mankind at any time without a man who maintains the religion of God (and acts
as their Imâm). Such men are either prophets or their legates. The doctrine
of election is defended by a section of the Khawârij الخوارج, the Murjias
المرجية, by many of those *who admit the traditions and the generally received
opinions (Ahl-us-Sunnat)*, by some of the Mu'tazalas, and by a section of the
Zaidias, الزيديون. They believe that it is the will of God and his Prophet
that the nation should choose a man amongst themselves, and make him their
Imâm, for there are times when God does not send a legate. The Shiahs
consider such Imâms as usurpers of the dignity."—*Murûj-uz-zahab*.

consequently the spiritual guidance of mankind has been entrusted to divinely-appointed persons.[1]

According to the Sunnis, the Imâmate is not restricted to the family of Mohammed. The Imâm need not be just, virtuous, or irreproachable (Ma'sûm) in his life, nor need he be the most excellent or eminent being of his time افضل الباهى ; so long as he is free, adult, sane, and possessed of the capacity to attend to the ordinary affairs of State, he is qualified for election. Another doctrine in which they agree with the Church of Rome was full of momentous consequences to Islâm. They hold that neither the vices nor the tyranny of the Imâm would justify his deposition ; [2] nor can the perversity or evil conduct of the Imâm or those who preside at the public divine service invalidate the prayers of the Faithful.[3] They also hold that the Imâmate is indivisible, and that it is not lawful to have two Imâms at one and the same time. As Christianity could yield obedience to but one Pope, so the Moslem world could yield obedience to but one lawful Caliph. But as three Popes have often pretended to the triple crown, so have three

---

[1] " It is neither the beauty of the sovereign," says Ibn-Khaldûn, " nor his great learning, perspicacity, or any other personal accomplishment which is useful to his subject. . . . The sovereign exists for the good of his people." " The necessity of a ruler," continues this remarkable writer, whose keenness of observation was equalled by his versatility, " arises from the fact that human beings have to live together, and unless there is some one to maintain order, society would break to pieces. A temporal sovereign only enforces such orders as are promulgated by man, but the laws framed by a divinely-inspired legislator have two objects in view—the moral as well as social well-being of mankind. The Caliph is the Vicar and Lieutenant of the Prophet. He is more than a temporal ruler, he is a spiritual chief as well. The Caliph is thus designated the Imâm, his position being similar to that of the leader of the congregation at the public prayers." " This establishment of an Imâm," continues Ibn-Khaldûn, " is a matter of obligation. The law which declares its necessity is founded on the general accord of the Companions of the Prophet. The Imâm is the spiritual head, whilst the Caliph or Sultan represents the temporal power."

[2] In spite of this doctrine, promulgated at the order of tyrants anxious to avoid the penalty of their oppression, the people have never approved of it entirely. Under the Ommeyyade Walîd, surnamed for his vices the Fâsik (the Wicked), they rose in revolt and deposed him. Similarly, when the iniquities of Mutawakkil (the Abbaside) became intolerable, he was deposed by his own son, Muntasir the Good. The history of the Ottoman Turks contains many examples of the people rising in revolt against a vicious or incapable sovereign, the last being under the unhappy Abdul Azîz.

[3] Against this doctrine there is now a widespread revolt in the Sunni Church ; the Ghair-Mukallidîn, whom we shall describe later, holding that if the Imâm is not chaste in his life, the prayers of the congregation are invalid.

Ameer ul-Muslimin laid claim to supreme rule. After the downfall of the Ommeyyades in Asia a member of that house succeeded in setting up an independent state in Spain, whilst the family of Abbâs exercised power on the banks of the Tigris, and that of Fâtima on the Nile. The fact that at various times two or three sovereigns have assumed simultaneously the Headship of Islâm has given rise to an opinion that the rule of indivisibility applies only to one and the same country, or to two countries contiguous to each other ; but when the countries are so far apart that the power of one Imâm cannot extend to the other, it is lawful to elect a second Imâm. The Imâm is the patron and syndic of all Musulmans, and the guardian of their interests during their lives as well as after their death. He is vested with the power to nominate his successors, subject to the approval of the Moslems. As the office is for the temporal and spiritual benefit of the community, the nomination is dependent on the choice of the people.[1]

It might have been expected that persecution would keep the Shiahs united among themselves ; but although all were agreed on the question that the supreme pontificate of Islâm is confined to the line of the Prophet, many of them fell away from the recognised heads of the family, and attached themselves from design or predilection to other members of the House. Whilst the acknowledged Imâms and their disciples lived in holy retirement, the others found leisure amidst their foreign hostilities for domestic quarrels. They preached, they disputed, they suffered.

Shahristâni divides the Shiahs into five sects, viz. the *Zaidia*, the *Isma'ilia*, the *Isnâ-'asharia* or *Imâmia*, the *Kaisânia*, and the *Ghâllia* or *Ghullât*. As a matter of fact, however, as we shall show hereafter, some of these sects, and especially the branches into which they bifurcated, had, excepting in a more or less exaggerated attachment to Ali, nothing in common with Shiahism proper. On the contrary, they derived their origin from sources other than Islâmic.

The *Zaidias*, says Shahristâni, are the followers of Zaid, son of Ali II. (Zain-ul-'Âbidîn), son of Husain. They affirm that the Imâmate descended from Ali to Hasan, then to Husain ;

[1] Ibn-Khaldûn ; see *ante*, part i. chapter x.

from Husain it devolved upon Ali II. (Zain-ul-'Âbidîn) ; and
from him it passed to Zaid, and not, as is held by the *Isnâ-
'Asharias*, and, in fact, by most Moslems, to Mohammed
al-Bâkir. In their doctrines they closely approach the *Ahl
us-Sunnat*. They hold that the people have the right of
choosing their spiritual head from among the descendants
of the Prophet, combining thus the principle of election with
the principle which restricts the Imâmate to the family of
Mohammed. They also affirm that it is lawful to elect the
mafzûl (*the less eminent*) whilst the *afzal* (*the most eminent*) is
present. As a consequence of this principle, they accept the
Imâmate of the first three Caliphs, whose pontificate is generally
disclaimed by the other Shiahs. They hold that though Ali
was the most eminent of all the Companions of the Prophet,
and by right of descent as well as by his *qualities* entitled to
the Imâmate, yet for reasons of policy, and to allay the disorders which had broken out upon the death of the Prophet,
to settle the minds of the people and to compose the differences
among the tribes, a man of a maturer age was required to fill
the office. Besides, owing to the struggle in which Ali had
been engaged in defence of the Faith, the feeling of retaliation
was strong in the bosom of those who had fought against Islâm,
and who had been only recently reduced to subjection ; and
these people would not willingly have bowed before the grandeur
of Ali. They hold that the same reason applies to the election
of Omar.[1] Their acceptance of the Imâmate of the first two
Caliphs brought upon the Zaidias the name of *Rawâfiz*, or Dissenters, by the other Shiahs. Another doctrine held by them
is too important to escape notice. They maintain that in
addition to piety, truth, knowledge, and innocence or sinlessness, qualities required by the Shiahs proper for the pontifical
office, the Imâm should possess bravery, and the capacity to
assert by *force of arms* his right to the Imâmate. The Imâm
Mohammed al-Bâkir, who had succeeded his father Ali II.,
maintained that the use of force was reprehensible. Zaid
differed from his brother in this opinion. He rose in arms
against the tyrants in the reign of Hishâm ibn Abdul Malik
(the Ommeyyade), and was killed in the neighbourhood of

[1] Shahristânî, pt. i. p. 115.

Kûfa. He was succeeded by Yahya, his son, who followed the example of his father, and, against the advice of Imâm Ja'far as-Sâdik, proceeded to assert his right by force of arms. He collected a large following in Khorâsân, but was defeated and killed by one of the generals of Hishâm.

On the death of Yahya, the Imâmate, say the *Zaidias*, passed to another member of the family, Mohammed ibn Abdullah, surnamed *an-Nafs-uz-Zakiya* (" the Pure Soul "). Mohammed assumed the title of Mahdi, and rose in arms in Hijâz against the Abbaside Mansûr. He was defeated and killed at Medîna by 'Isâ, Mansûr's nephew. He was succeeded by his brother Ibrâhîm, who lost his life similarly in a vain struggle against the Abbasides. Isâ, another brother, who also endeavoured to assert his claims by force, was seized by Mansûr, and imprisoned for life. After mentioning these facts, Shahristâni adds that " whatever befell them was prognosticated by Ja'far as-Sâdik, who said that temporal dominion was not for their family, but that the Imâmate was to be a toy in the hands of the Abbasides."

According to a branch of the *Zaidias*, the Imâmate passed from Ibrâhîm to Idrîs, the founder of the Idriside dynasty in Mauritania (مغرب الاقصى), and of the city of Fez. After the fall of the Idrisides, the *Zaidias* became disorganised, but members of this sect are still to be found in different parts of Asia and Africa. A branch of the *Zaidias* ruled in Tabaristan for a long time, and there is a Zaidia Imâm still in Northern Yemen. The *Zaidias*, according to Shahristâni, were divided into four subsections, *viz.* the *Jârudias*, *Sulaimânias*, *Tabarias*, and *Sâlehias*. They differ from each other about the devolution of the Imâmate from Zaid's grandson. The *Jârudias*, who upheld the claims of Mohammed *Nafs-uz-Zakiya* in supersession of Isâ, suffered bitterly under Mansûr. The *Sulaimânias* were named after their founder, Sulaimân ibn Jarîs, who declared that the Imâmate depended upon the consensus of the people ; . . . " that the Imâmate is not intended for regulating religion or for the acquisition of a knowledge of the Deity, or His unity or the laws which He has made for the government of the world, for these are acquired through Reason. The Imâmate is intended for the government of the earth, inflicting punishments

on wrong-doers, dealing out justice, and defending the State.
It is not necessary for the Imâm to be *afzal*. . . ." "A section
of the *Ahl-us-Sunnat* hold similar opinions, for they say that
it is not required for the Imâm to be learned or a *Mujtahid*,
so long as he is wise and has some one with him capable of
expounding the law." [1] The *Sulaimânias* and the *Sâlehias*
agree in accepting the Imâmate of the first two Caliphs ; the
latter hold that Ali, having himself abandoned his preferential
claim in favour of Abû Bakr and Omar, the people have no
right to question *their* Imâmate : but as regards Osmân they
are in doubt, for they say " when we see how he travailed for
the support of the Banî Ommeyya, we find his character
different from the other *Sahâba*."

The *Ismailias*, also sometimes called *Sabi'yûn* (*Seveners*),[2]
derive their names from Isma'îl, a son of Imâm Ja'far as-Sâdik,
who predeceased his father.   They hold that upon the death
of Imâm Ja'far as-Sâdik, the Imâmate devolved on Isma'îl's
son, Mohammed (surnamed *al-Maktûm*,[3] the *hidden or unrevealed*), and not on Ja'far's son, Mûsa al-Kâzim, as believed
by the *Isnâ-'Asharias* and generally by the other Moslems.
Mohammed *al-Maktûm* was succeeded, according to the *Isma'îlias*, by Ja'far *al-Musaddak*, whose son Mohammed *al-Habîb*
was the last of the *unrevealed Imâms*.

His son, Abû Mohammed Abdullah, was the founder of the
Fâtimide dynasty which ruled Northern Africa for three centuries. He had been thrown into prison by the Abbaside
Caliph, Mu'tazid-b'illâh Saffâh II., but, escaping from his
dungeon at Segelmessa, he appeared in Barbary, where he
assumed the title of *Obaidullah* and *Mahdi* (*the promised Guide*).
Followers gathered round him from all sides, and, assisted by

---

[1] Shahristânî, pt. i. pp. 119, 120.

[2] Because they acknowledge only seven Imâms—(1) Ali, (2) Hasan, (3)
Husain, (4) Ali II., (5) Mohammed al-Bâkir, (6) Ja'far as-Sâdik (the True),
and (7) Isma'îl.

[3] So called, says Makrîzi, because his followers kept him " concealed," to
escape the persecution of the Abbasides. Isma'îl was the eldest son of Imâm
Ja'far as-Sâdik, and a man of sweet disposition and engaging manners, and
according to Makrîzi, had a considerable following in Yemen, in Ketama,
and the African provinces. During the lifetime of Isma'îl's mother, says
Shahristânî, the Imâm Ja'far never had any other wife, " like the Prophet
with Khadîja, and Ali with Fâtima."

a Sûfi, he soon overthrew the Aghlabites, who were ruling the African provinces in the name of the Caliphs of Bagdad, and founded an empire which extended from Mauritania to the confines of Egypt. One of his successors (Ma'dd Abû Temim), *al-Muizz-li-dîn-illâh* (*Exalter of the Faith of God*), wrested Egypt and a portion of Syria from the Abbasides. Muizz, to mark his victory over the enemies of his House, founded Cairo (*Kâhira, the Victorious City*), and removed his capital from Mahdièh, near Kairwân, established by Obaidullah al-Mahdi, to the new city. At this time his dominions included, besides the whole of Northern Africa, the islands of Sardinia and Sicily. He founded in Cairo the mosque of *al-Azhar* (*Jâmi'-al-azhar, the Brilliant Mosque*), a vast public library, and several colleges, and endowed them richly. At these colleges, students received instruction in grammar, literature, the interpretation of the Koran, jurisprudence, medicine, mathematics, and history. "The distinctive character of his reign," says the historian, "was justice and moderation." [1]

Almost all the accounts we possess of the Egyptian Fâtimides have come down to us from hostile sources. Since Jouhar, the general of Muizz, conquered Egypt and Syria from the Caliphs of Bagdad, there was an incessant struggle between the two Caliphates as to the legitimacy of their respective titles. The hold which the claim of the Fâtimides to be descended from Mohammed enabled them to acquire over the people, gave rise to an unceasing desire on the part of the Abbasides to annihilate the genuineness of their rivals' genealogy, and to impress on the world the anti-Islâmic character of the doctrines adopted by them. In the reign of Kâdir-b'illâh, a secret assemblage of the doctors of the law was held at Bagdad at the instance of

---

[1] Marcel. The orthodox Jamâl ud-din bin Taghri-bardi (in his *Maured ul-Latâfat*, الطافة مورد ال‏) says, "though Muizz was a schismatic, he was wise, learned, generous, and just to his subjects,"

و كان المعزرافضيا الا انه كان فاضلا عاقلا اديبا حازما جوادا
ممدحا فيه عدل الرعية

For a full account of the Fâtimide dynasty, see *Short History of the Saracens* (Macmillan).

the frightened Caliph, to fulminate against the Fâtimides an anathema declaring that they were not the genuine descendants of Fâtima. The Fâtimides, on their side, replied by a counter-anathema, signed by the leading doctors of Cairo, among them many belonging to the Mâliki and Shâfe'i persuasions. In spite, however, of the doubts thrown on their legitimacy by the Abbaside doctors, great historians like Makrîzi, Ibn Khaldûn, and Abulfedâ have accepted the genuineness of the claims of the Fâtimides.

Makrîzi is extremely outspoken on the subject, and plainly charges the partisans of the Banî-Abbâs with misrepresentation and forgery. Dealing with the Abbaside statement that Obaidullah al-Mahdi was not a descendant of Mohammed, he goes on to say, " a little examination of facts will show that this is a fabrication. The descendants of Ali, the son of Abû Talib, at that time were numerous, and the Shiahs regarded them with great veneration. What was it then that could have induced their partisans to forsake them, the descendants of Mohammed, and to recognise in their stead as Imâm an offspring of the Magi, a man of Jewish origin ? No man, unless absolutely devoid of commonsense, would act thus. The report that Obaidullah al-Mahdi was by descent a Jew or a Magian owes its origin to the artifices of the feeble Abbaside princes, who did not know how to rid themselves of the Fâtimides, for their power lasted without interruption for 270 years, and they despoiled the Abbasides of the countries of Africa, Egypt, Syria, the Diâr-bakr, the two sacred cities (Mecca and Medîna), and of Yemen. The *Khutba* was even read in their names at Bagdad during forty weeks. The Abbaside armies could not make head against them ; and, therefore, to inspire the people with aversion against the Fâtimides, they spread calumnies about their origin. The Abbaside officers and Ameers who could not contend successfully with the Fâtimides gladly adopted these slanders as a means of revenge. The Kâzis, who attested the act of convocation under Kâdir b'illâh, acted under the orders of the Caliph, and only upon hearsay ; and since then historians have heedlessly and without reflection given currency to a calumny which was invented by the Abbasides." Nothing can be more explicit than this statement by a critical historian and a distinguished jurisconsult whose reputation stands high among all Orientals.[1]

Probably the doctrines professed by the Egyptian Fâtimides were subjected to the same process of misrepresentation. Still there can be little doubt that they adopted largely the esoteric doctrines of Abdullah ibn Maimûn, surnamed the *Kaddâh* (the *Oculist*), and made use of his degrees of initiation for the purposes of a political propaganda.

The protracted struggle between pope and emperor for the suzerainty of Christendom ; the Thirty Years' War, with its concomitant miseries ; the persecution of the Huguenots, in which dynastic ambitions played as important a part as religious bigotry,—give us some conception of the evils that have flowed from the greed of earthly power. In Islâm it has been the same. The Abbasides battling with the Ommeyyades, and then with the Egyptian Fâtimides, produced the same disastrous results.

The eastern provinces of the ancient Persian empire were at this time the home of a variety of congenial spirits. Here had gathered not only the Mago-Zoroastrians, fleeing before the Islâmic wave, but also the representatives of various Indian sects, with their ideas of metempsychosis, the incarnation of Vishnu, the descent of Krishna from heaven, and his free and easy intercourse with the *gopis*. The revolutionary opinions and heresies which under the later Sasanides had shaken the temple and palace alike, and which Kesrâ Anûshirvân had endeavoured to exterminate with fire and sword, had survived all persecutions. At least they retained sufficient vitality to reappear in Islâm in various shapes and forms.

---

[1] Makrîzi died in 845 A.C. Jamâl ud-din Abu'l Mahâsin Yusuf bin Taghribardi, in his نجوم الزاهرة في ملوك مصروالقاهرة, speaks of Makrîzi thus :—

توفى الشيخ الامام العالم المحدّث المقتن عمــــدة المورّخيـــن وراس المحدّثين تقيّ الدين احمد بن على بن عبد القادر بن محمد بن ابراهيم بن محمد بن نعيم بن عبد الصمد البعلبكى الاصل المصرى المولد

" In this year died the learned sheikh and Imâm, jurisconsult, and that eminent historian and traditionist, Taki ud-din Ahmed, son of Ali," etc. etc.

The *Râwendis*, an Indo-Magian sect who maintained the doctrine of the transmigration of souls, and the *Safidjâmagân*,[1] founded by Hâkim bin Hâshim, the infamous Mokanna,[2] revolted in Khorâsân, and were suppressed by the Caliph Al-Mahdi. Mokanna taught that God had assumed the human form, since He had commanded the angels to adore the first man ; and that, since that period, the divine nature had passed from prophet to prophet until it had descended to himself.[3]

About the same time Mazdakism, which two centuries and a half before had involved the empire of the Chosroes in a general conflagration, and was ruthlessly trampled under foot by the great Anûshirvân, raised its head again under the Caliphs. The snake had only been half killed. Bâbek, surnamed Khurrami (from Khurram, his place of birth), preached, like his prototype Mazdak, the same nihilistic doctrines,—the community of women and goods, and the indifference of all human actions. For a space of twenty years he filled the whole circuit of the Caliphate with carnage and ruin, until at length, in the reign of Mu'tasim b'illâh, he was overthrown, taken prisoner, and put to death in the Caliph's presence. It was a repetition of the old story. Islâm had to pass through the same throes as Christianity. From the beginning of the second to the end of the ninth century there was an unceasing struggle in Christianity with the ancient cults, which were appearing in diversified characters throughout the wide area in which the religion of Jesus was professed. After this struggle was over, a deadly pall settled over Christendom ; orthodoxy had succeeded in crushing not only the revolutionary Montanists, the Manichæan Paulicians, but also the rationalistic Arians. Ecclesiasticism and orthodoxy, convertible terms, held in bondage the mind of man until the Reformation. Islâm had

[1] So called because they dressed themselves in white, like the Taborides of Europe.

[2] This is the impostor whom Moore has made famous as " the Veiled Prophet of Khorasan." He was called *Mokanna* because, either to conceal his ugliness, or to impress his followers with a sense of inaccessibility, he always wore a veil. He was also called the *Sâzendeh-i-Mah* (Moon-maker), because on one occasion he had, by a piece of jugglery, caused an illumination, like that of the moon, at Nakhsheb.

[3] Ibn Khaldûn's *General History, Kitâb ul-'Ibar. &c.* (Egypt. ed.), vol. iii. p. 206.

to pass through the same ordeal, but *its* Reformation is only just commencing.

Islâm required from its votaries a simple confession of an eternal truth, and the practice of a few moral duties. In other respects it allowed them the widest latitude of judgment. In the name of divine unity it held forth to all creeds and sects the promise of a democratic equality. Naturally the persecuted heretics of every faith rallied round the standard of the Prophet who had emancipated human judgment from the bondage of priesthood ; and "Avestan scripturalists" and Zoroastrian free-thinkers, Manichæans, Christians, Jews, and Magi all hailed the advent of a new dispensation which realised the dream of religious unity. The swarms of gnostic sects which had distracted the Church of Jesus from the second to the sixth century had either merged in the Church of Mohammed, or lived in peace, unmolested by the orthodox Greeks or Catholics, under the large tolerance of the Caliphs. The former, whilst they adopted the faith of Mohammed, retained their primitive conceptions, and gave birth to the docetic sects of Islâm, which we shall describe later on.

The national characteristics of a people, the climatic conditions under which they exist, the natural features of the country in which they dwell, the influence of older cults, all give a colour and a complexion to their faiths and doctrines. It is the same in Christendom and in Islâm. Irân gave birth to agnosticism ; from there emanated the docetic conceptions which permeated the Roman world and impressed upon the primitive belief of the judaical Christians the conception of a divinity who discoursed familiarly with mankind on earth. Manichæism, that wonderful mixture of fancy and philosophy, to which Christianity owes so much and acknowledges so little, was, in spite of the persecution of Zoroastrian and Christian, alive, not dead. Will it ever die, that child of a bizarre genius, the outcome of a nation's character ? Theologians may try, but will never kill it. The morbidism of the Fathers of the Sunni Church gave place in Irân to imaginative philosophy. Ali's personality fired the imagination of Manichæism. It took the place of the docetic Christ among the people. The process of deification was not confined to Ali. His successors were deified with him.

Shiaism, like Sunnīsm, presents therefore two aspects. One is the pure, simple *Shiaism* of Mohammed's immediate descendants, which we shall describe shortly. The other is docetic Shiaism, fantastic and transmogrified according to the primitive beliefs of the people among whom it spread. Ultra-Shiaism is again as different from docetic Shiaism as ultra-Sunnīsm or *Nawâsibism* is from docetic Sunnīsm. Narrow-minded exclusiveness is not the peculiar characteristic of any one faith or creed ; nor are the thunders of the Athanasian Creed confined to Christianity. In Islâm also (be it said with certain exceptions) each sect condemns the others to perdition, not eternal (as the orthodox Christian charitably hopes it will be), but sufficiently prolonged to make them feel the evils of a different 'doxy from its own. Still, notwithstanding the anathemas of hell-fire and brimstone which have been hurled by contending parties and sects against each other, the philosophical student will not fail to observe the universality of Islâm.

About the middle of the seventh century Constantine Sylvanus founded the Manichæan sect of Paulicians, who derived their name from St. Paul, whose disciples they professed themselves to be. The Paulicians disclaimed the designation of Manichæan ; but their doctrines bear the closest analogy to those taught by Mâni, and all the Christian writers, with the exception of Milner, ascribe their origin to Manichæism. The Paulicians were the real progenitors of the Reformed Churches of Europe. Their abhorrence of images and relics was probably a reflex of Islâmic influences. In their aversion towards Mariolatry and saint-worship, and in the repudiation of all visible objects of adoration, they closely approached the Moslems. They believed, however, with Mâni, that Christ was a pure spirit which bore on earth only the semblance of a body, and that the crucifixion was a mere delusion. They maintained the eternity of matter ; the origin of a second principle, of an active being, who has created this visible world, and exercises his temporal reign till the final consummation of sin and death. In the interpretation of the Christian Gospels they indulge in allegories and figures, and claimed, like Mâni, an esoteric insight into the meaning of words. An outward and expedient profession of another faith, a doctrine which in modern Persia has become famous as *ketmân* or *takiyyè*,[1] was held to be commendable.

The Paulicians were persecuted by the Greek Church and the Byzantine Court with terrible fury, and for nearly two hundred years they waged a not unequal contest in North Armenia and Cappadocia with the fanatics and despots of Byzantium, in which both sides perpetrated the most fearful atrocities.[2] At last they succumbed to superior force ; but though their fortresses were razed and their cities ruined, the sect lived. It passed its doctrines to the Bulgarians, who have always been regarded with disfavour by the Orthodox Churches. The Paulicians after their destruction in Asia appeared in South Provence and Savoy in the thirteenth century. Their fate in those countries is known to every reader of European history. They were annihilated with fire and sword,—not even women and children were spared ; such of the latter as escaped were reduced to slavery. But Paulicianism did not die ; it showed itself in England, where its followers, under the name of Lollards, suffered like their predecessors in Asia, in Savoy, and in Provence ; it reappeared in Bohemia under Huss ; and finally it triumphed under Luther and Calvin over its orthodox persecutors. We have traced so far the fate of this peculiar sect, as in its original home it exercised no inconsiderable influence over the religio-political movements which were proceeding about the same time in Islâm.

During the tempestuous epoch, when Chyroseir the Paulician was devastating the eastern portion of the Byzantine dominions, and had filled the cities of Asia Minor with carnage and ruin, there lived at Ahwâz, in Fars, a man who equalled Mâni in the versatility of his genius, the variety of his information, and the profundity of his knowledge, and who was destined to play an almost equal part in the history of religion. Abdullah ibn Maimûn al-Kaddâh has been represented by his enemies as a Magian by birth : whilst his disciples have declared him

---

[1] See *post*, p. 335.

[2] A hundred thousand Paulicians are said to have been destroyed under the orders of the second Theodora, the mother of Manuel, by the sword, the gibbet, or the flames.

to be a descendant of Ali.[1] However that may be, it is clear that he was a devoted adherent of the House of Mohammed. Considering the disastrous consequences which directly or indirectly have flowed from his teachings, it was impossible for even historians like Ibn Khaldûn [2] to avoid viewing the man and his doctrines with an unfavourable bias. They think Abdullah ibn Maimûn was animated by a desire to subvert the dominion of Islâm by the same insidious means which were adopted by his great prototype against Christianity. Aware of the risk attendant upon an open war against constituted authority so long as the conscience of the people and temporal power were at its back, he determined (they say) to work in secret like Mâni. He accordingly enveloped his system in a veil of mystery, and, in order to annihilate all positive religion and authority, he resolved to divide his followers into seven degrees, like the Pythagoreans. The last degree inculcated the vanity of all religion,—the indifference of actions, which, according to him, are neither visited with recompense nor chastisement, either now or hereafter. He appointed emissaries whom he despatched to enlist disciples, and to initiate them according to their capacity in some or all of the degrees. The pretensions of the son of Isma'îl served them as a political mask ; whilst working ostensibly for him, they were secretly, but in reality, the apostles of impiety.[3]

Shahristâni's account,[4] however, of the tenets of the sect is in a more philosophical spirit ; whilst Mohsin Fâni's description in the *Dabistân*, derived from members of the fraternity, is coloured with a slightly roseate hue. But, studied carefully, they render it more than probable that Abdullah ibn Maimûn was a materialistic theist ; that like Mâni, he was fired with the ambition of creating an eclectic naturalism, which would reconcile philosophy with positive religion ; and that his degrees of initiation were analogous to the mystical degrees of the Sûfis. It is evident from what Mirkhond states that the

[1] Abdullah ibn Maimûn is stated to have been at one time in the service of Imâm Ja'far as Sâdik.

[2] Pronounced in Arabic Ibn (u) Khaldûn ; in Persian, Ibn (i) Khaldûn.

[3] Nuwairi, *Journal Asiatique*, vol. iv. p. 298.

[4] Shahristâni, part i. p. 147.

Egyptian Fâtimides adopted most of their mystical doctrines from Abdullah ibn Maimûn.[1]

Abdullah proceeded from Ahwâz to Basra, and thence to Syria, where he settled at Salemiyè. In the course of his travels he came in contact with the Paulicians, and imbibed many of their doctrines. The long-continued struggle of the Paulicians with the Byzantines, and the success of their pro-selytising endeavours, undoubtedly influenced him in his project of religion. He moulded his doctrines partly upon those actually taught by Mâni and partly upon those of the Moslem mystics. Manichæism itself was essentially pan-theistic, founded upon a substratum of Pythagorean philo-sophy, Zervanism, and Christianity. Abdullah's followers have received the designation of *Bâtinis* or *Esotericians*, on account of their claim to an esoteric insight into the precepts of positive religion—a claim similar to that advanced by the Manichæans and Paulicians.

Abdullah ibn Maimûn seems to have affirmed the eternity of matter. He declared further " that God is not separate from His manifestations ; that it cannot be predicated of him inde-pendently that He is existent or non-existent, omniscient or non-omniscient, for to affirm regarding Him any of these things is to assume that there is some resemblance between Him and His creatures ; that the First Cause evolved by a simple command (*amr-i-wâhid*), or a mere act of volition, a Principle which was embosomed in Eternity, and is called *Akl* or Reason, and *this* Principle evolved a subordinate Principle called the *Nafs* or soul, whose relation to the other is that of a child to the parent ; that the essential attribute of this Principle is *Life*, as that of Reason is *Knowledge* ; that this second Principle gave shape to pre-existent Matter, the essential attribute of which is passivity, and afterwards created Time and Space, the elements, the planets, and the astral bodies, and all other objects in creation ; that in consequence of an incessant desire on the part of the Second Principle (*the Demiurgus*) to raise

[1] The Egyptian Fâtimides differed from the general body of the *Isma'ilias* in one essential feature. Whilst the latter held that Isma'il, their last Imâm, had only disappeared, and would reappear in the fulness of time when " the kingdom of heaven " would be revealed, the Egyptians taught that he had reappeared in the person of Obaidullah al-Mahdi and his successors.

itself to the level of the First Created Principle, it manifested
itself in matter in the shape of human beings ; that the aim of
all human souls is to struggle upwards to the Creative Principle
or Wisdom ; that the Prophets are embodiments or manifestations of that Principle to help the human soul to struggle with
matter ; the Prophets are therefore called *Nâtik*, ناطق, ' speaking apostles ' ; that they are seven in number like the planets ;
that the progress of the world is in cycles, and at the last stage
will occur the Resurrection (قیامت کبری), when the sanctions
of positive religion and law will be withdrawn, for the motion
of the heavens and the adoption of the precepts of religion are
for the purpose that the Soul may attain Perfection, and its
perfection consists in attaining to the degrees of Reason and
its junction or assimilation with it in fact ; and this is the great
Resurrection (قیامت کبری), when all things, the heavens, the
elements, and organic substances, will be dissolved ; and the
earth will be changed, and the heavens will be closed like a
written book, and the good will be differentiated from the bad,
and the obedient from the disobedient, and the good will be
merged in the Universal Soul, and the bad will join with the
Principle of Evil ; thus from the commencement of motion to
its cessation (according to Abdullah ibn Maimûn) is the initial
stage (مبدأ), and from the cessation of motion or activity to
amalgamation with infinity is the stage of perfection ; [1] that

كما نحركت الافلاك بنحريك النفس و العقل و الطبائع [1]
كذلك نحركت النفوس و الاشخاص بالشرائع بنحريك النبي
والوصي في كل زمان دائرا على سبعة سبعة حدى ينتهى
انى الدور الاخير و يدخل زمان القيامة و نرتفع التكاليف
و تضمحل السنن و الشرائع و انما هذه الحركات الفلكية و السنن
الشرعية لتبلغ النفس الى حال كمالها و كمالها بلوغها الى
درجة العقل و اتحادها به و وصولها الى مرتبة فعلا و ذلك هو
القيامة الكبرى فتنحل تراكيب الافلاك و العناصر والمركبات
و ينشق السماء و تتنافر الكوكب و تبدل الارض غير الارض

all the precepts of religion and law have their measures " . . .
" and that each letter and word have two meanings, for every
revelation (*tanzîl*) has an interpretation (*tâvîl*), and everything
visible has its counterpart in the invisible world ; that knowledge of truth cannot be acquired by reason but by instruction."
Abdullah ibn Maimûn's disciples developed his doctrines still
further by declaring that Resurrection means the Advent or
Revelation of the Imâm and of a Heavenly Kingdom in which
all the burdens of positive religion and traditions would be
removed ; that deception in religion is allowable ; that all the
precepts of the Koran have an esoteric sense ; that religion does
not consist in external observances, but in an inner sense and
feeling ; that every thing or act which is not injurious is lawful ;
that fasting is nothing but keeping the secret of the Imâm ;
that the prohibition against fornication implies that the
disciple must not disclose the mysteries of the faith ; and that
zakât means the giving of the tithes to the Imâm *ma'sûm*—a
peculiar and fantastical medley of many cults and philosophies,
and in its tendency subversive of law and morality.

Abdullah ibn Maimûn settled in Syria, the home of Christian
Gnosticism, where he still further developed his doctrines.
Here he converted Hamadân, also called Karmath, whose name
has become infamous in the annals of Islâm.

The method of proselytising adopted by the followers of
Abdullah ibn Maimûn was the old Manichæan one of throwing
the acolyte into a sea of doubt with insidious questions and
equivocal replies, " not," says Mohsin Fâni's informant, " with
any evil object, but simply to bring the seeker after truth and
wisdom to the goal of perfection." [1] The process varied with
the religious standpoint of the person whom they desired to

و تطوى السماوات كطى السجل لكتاب المرقوم فيه و يحاسب
الخلق و يذميز الخير عن الشر والمطيع عن العاصى و ينصـــل
جزئيات الحــــق بالنفس الكل و جزئيات البـــاطل بالشيطان
المبطل etc.

—Shahristâni, pt. i. pp. 148, 149.

[1] *Dabistân*, p. 356.

convert. The *Dâ'i* [1] (the missionary) would at first give a tacit
recognition of the faith of the intended proselyte, and then by
an insinuation of doubt and difficulties, gradually unsettle his
mind, and end by suggesting as the only possible solution the
peculiar tenets of the *Bâtini* system. For example, if the *Dâ'i*
had to proselytise a Shiah, he would represent himself as a
devoted partisan of the House of Mohammed. He would
expatiate on the cruelty and injustice with which they were
treated—on the martyrdom of Husain and the butchery of
Kerbela; having thus prepared the way, he would instil into
the now receptive mind the esoteric doctrines of the *Bâtinis*.
If he had a Jew to deal with, he spoke disparagingly of the
Christians and the Musulmans, and while agreeing with his
intended convert in still looking forward to a promised Messiah,
by degrees persuaded the neophyte that this promised Messiah
can be none other than the *Isma'ilite* Imâm. If it was a Christian
whom he hoped to win over, he enlarged on the obstinacy of the
Jews and the ignorance of the Musulmans, he conformed to all
the chief articles of the Christian creed, at the same time hinting
that they were all symbolic, and pointed to a deeper meaning
which the *Bâtini* system alone could solve. And after the
mind of the neophyte had been so far moulded he would suggest
that the Christians had misinterpreted the doctrine of the
Paraclete, and that the *Isma'ilia* Imâm was the real Paraclete. [2]
Abdullah ibn Maimûn also formulated in precise terms the
doctrine of *takeyyè*—outward conformity with an alien
religious belief or practice. It had been in vogue among all
the Manichæan sects—not excepting the Paulicians. It was
re-introduced by Abdullah ibn Maimûn, partly to escape persecution, partly to facilitate the work of proselytism. *Takeyyè*
is the natural defence of the weak and suffering against the
strong. All people have not the fibre of a martyr; and the
majority of them have to submit where they cannot oppose.
The primitive Christians had to practise *takeyyè*. The *Isma'ilias*
had special reasons for concealing their religious views in all
countries within the sway of the Abbaside Caliphs; and this
long-enforced habit became at last a second nature with them.
From them the Shiahs proper borrowed the practice of *takeyyè*.

[1] راعی, one who invites.   [2] Mâni, in fact, claimed to be the Paraclete.

Before Persia and Turkey had entered upon terms of amity, a Shiah was unable to perform the Hajj unless he conformed to the Sunni rites, and *takeyyè* in such cases was almost a necessity with the devout Shiah wishing to visit the holy shrines. But *takeyyè*, " the natural offspring of persecution and fear," has become so habitual with the Persians that they conform to it even in circumstances when there is no necessity. They practise it to avoid giving offence or wounding susceptibilities, just as the modern Protestant shows a certain deference to Romish rites in Catholic countries.

Hamadân, otherwise called Karmath, had broken away from his master and formed a sect of his own. Abdullah ibn Maimûn had disavowed the use of force in his proselytism ; Karmath advocated it as the corner-stone of his sect. Possibly, like Chyroseir, he was driven to it by the persecution of the ortho-dox. He raised an insurrection in al-Ahsa and al-Bahrain. The weakness of the Caliph's troops gave him the victory. Collecting a large following he issued from al-Bahrain, and, like the Paulician Chyroseir, marked his progress by slaughter and ruin. The Karmathites, from their fastnesses in al-Bahrain and al-Ahsa, waged for nearly a hundred years a sanguinary contest with the Pontiffs of Bagdad. They pillaged even Mecca, and carried away the sacred stone, the symbol of Abrahamitic antiquity, like the Wahâbis 900 years later. In this sacrilege they imitated the example of their *congeners*, the Paulicians, who had pillaged Ephesus, destroyed the sepulchre of St. John, and turned his cathedral into a stable for mules and horses. They were destroyed ultimately by the Caliph Mu'tazid b'illâh.

After the destruction of the Karmathites, *Isma'ilism* was proscribed ; its votaries were placed under the ban, and hunted like vermin. *Isma'ilism* had to hide itself on all sides until Obaidullah al-Mahdi wrested Africa from the Abbasides.

The Fâtimides of Egypt were grand supporters of learning and science. Yet in their desire to promote the diffusion of knowledge among their subjects, they did not ignore the political advantages of the propaganda established by Abdullah ibn Maimûn, whose esoteric and Manichæan doctrines they partially adopted for their own purposes. They established colleges, public libraries, and scientific institutes (*Dâr ul-hikmat*), richly furnished with books, mathematical instruments, to which were attached numerous professors and attendants. Access to, and the use of, these literary treasures were free to all, and writing materials were afforded gratis.[1] The Caliphs frequently held learned disputations, at which the professors at these academies appeared, divided according to the different faculties,—logicians, mathematicians, jurists, and physicians, dressed in their *Khala'*, or doctoral mantles. The gowns of the English universities still retain the original form of the Arabic *Khala'* or *Kaftan*.

Two hundred and fifty-seven thousand ducats, raised by a carefully regulated taxation, was the amount of the annual revenue of the institutes, for the salaries of the professors and officials, for the provision of the requisites for teaching, and other objects of public scientific instruction. In these institutes they taught every branch of human knowledge. To the central *Dâr ul-hikmat* was attached a grand Lodge, where the candidates for initiation into the esoteric doctrines of *Isma'ilism* were instructed in the articles of the faith. Twice a week, every Monday and Wednesday, the *Dâ'i ud-du'ât*, the Grand Prior of the Lodge, convened meetings, which were frequented by both men and women, dressed in white, occupying separate seats. These assemblages were named *Majâlis ul-hikmat*, or Conferences of Wisdom. Before the initiation the *Dâ'i ud-du'ât* waited on the Caliph, who was the Grand Master, and read to him the discourse he proposed to deliver to the neophytes, and received his sign-manual on the cover of the manuscript.[2] After the lecture the pupils kissed the hands of the Grand Prior, and touched the signature of the Master reverently with their foreheads. Makrîzi's account of the different degrees of initiation adopted in this Lodge forms an invaluable record of freemasonry. In fact, the Lodge at Cairo became the model of all the Lodges created afterwards in Christendom. Abdullah ibn Maimûn had established seven degrees of initiation. Seven was the sacred number : there were seven planets, seven days in the week, and seven Imâms. At Cairo, where Egyptian hierophantism with the old mystic

[1] Makrîzi ; Chrestomathie Arabe (De Sacy), vol. i. p. 158.　　[2] Makkari.

ceremonies became superimposed on the Manichæan foundation, the number was increased to nine.[1]   The first degree was the most difficult of all, and required the longest time to mould the mind of the neophyte, and incline him to take that most solemn oath by which he bound himself to the secret doctrine with blind faith and unconditional obedience.   After this the process was simple enough : the acolyte was led gradually to recognise all the doctrines, and to become the instrument of insatiable ambition.

The Grand Lodges of Mahdièh and afterwards of Cairo became thus the centres of a vast and far-reaching political propaganda.   But the knowledge of the doctrines upon which they worked was confined to a few.   Like the mysteries of

---

[1] A very good description of the different stages of initiation is given by De Sacy in the *Journal Asiatique*, vol. iv. p. 298.   In order to induce the neophyte to take the oath of the first degree, his mind was perplexed by the Dâ'î with doubts.   The contradictions of positive religion and reason were dwelt upon, but it was pointed out that behind the apparent literal signification there lay a deeper meaning, which was the kernel, as the words were mere husks.   The curiosity of the novice was, however, not satisfied until he had taken an unrestricted oath ; on this he was admitted to the second degree. This inculcated the recognition of divinely-appointed Imâms, who were the source of all knowledge.   As soon as the faith in them was well established, the third degree taught their number, which could not exceed the holy seven ; for, as God had created seven heavens, seven earths, seven seas, seven planets, seven colours, seven musical sounds, and seven metals, so had He appointed seven of the most excellent of His creatures as revealed Imâms :   these were Ali, Hasan, Husain, Ali II. (Zain ul-'Âbidîn), Mohammed al-Bâkir, Ja'far as-Sâdik, and Isma'il his son, as the last and seventh.   In the fourth degree they taught that since the beginning of the world there have been seven speaking apostles (ناطق), embodiments of the Logos, each of whom had always, by the command of Heaven, altered the doctrine of his predecessor ; each of these had seven coadjutors, who succeeded each other in the epoch from one Nâtik to another, but who, as they did not manifest themselves, were called *Sâmit* (صامت) or *Silent*.   The seven *Nâtiks* were Adam, Noah, Abraham, Moses, Jesus, Mohammed, and Isma'il (the son of Ja'far as-Sâdik) or *Imâm-i-zamân* (Lord or Imâm of all times).   Their seven colleagues were Seth, Shem, Ishmâel son of Abraham, Aaron, Simeon, Ali, and Mohammed son of Isma'il.   The object of having a *Sâmit* attached to a *Nâtik* was to allow a free hand to the teachers and emissaries to put forward any one they liked as the *Sâmit* apostle of the time.   The fifth degree inculcated that each of the seven *Sâmits* had twelve *Nakîbs* or delegates for the extension of the true faith, for the number twelve is the most excellent after seven ; hence the twelve signs of the Zodiac, the twelve months, the twelve tribes of Israel, etc. In the sixth degree, the principles of Manichæan philosophy were instilled into the heart of the neophyte, and only when he was fully impressed with the wisdom of those doctrines was he admitted to the seventh, where he passed from philosophy to mysticism.   He then became one of the *knowers* ('árifîn). In the eighth he shook off the trammels of positive religion : The " veil " was lifted, and henceforth " everything was pure to the pure."   The tendency of these doctrines can be better imagined than described.

Eleusis, or the secret principles of the Templars, the Illuminati, and the Revolutionists of France, they were imparted only to the adepts—in whole or in part ; wholly to those alone who were intended to be used for the purpose of undermining the power of their enemies. For the masses and the uninitiated, the State-religion was Islâm, and its moral precepts and religious observances were enforced in all its austerity. Most of the Caliphs, especially al-Muizz, were in their lives and practice strict religionists and observers of the duties enjoined by the moral law.[1] The doctors of law and the officers of State were pious Moslems. Nevertheless the fact of the existence of a secret body working on mysterious lines loosened the bonds of society. The organisation of secret emissaries weakened the control of the Abbasides without permanently strengthening the hold of the Fâtimides or extending their temporal power.

The Fâtimides of Egypt have been called the Western Isma'ilias, in contradistinction to the followers of Hasan ibn Mohammed Sabbâh Himyari, commonly known as Hasan Sabbâh, infamous in the history of the West as the founder of the order of the Assassins,[2] but known to his followers as "Syedna," "our lord." His disciples are sometimes designated

[1] Mohsin Fâni says :—

ایمهٔ اسمعیلیهٔ مغرب همه مقید بامور ظاهر شرعی بودند

Hâkim bi-amr-illâh, the sixth Fâtimide Caliph of Cairo, who is regarded even at the present day by the Druses (a branch of the Isma'ilias) as an incarnation of the Divinity, has been represented as "a monster of iniquity." His was a strangely contradictory character ; and, as Makrîzi rightly thinks, his mind was probably affected. He was at times atrociously cruel ; at other times, a wise and humane sovereign. He abolished all distinction of race and creed in his dominions ; he introduced the system of lighting up the streets of Cairo for the protection of wayfarers ; he organised a system of police ; he repressed violence. For an account of Hâkim bi-amr-illâh, see *Short History of the Saracens*, p. 602. It may be noticed, as a remarkable coincidence, that Ivan the Terrible, who has been termed just such another monster, was regarded by the average Russian of his day as a monarch of singular force of character and ability. The fact is that the cruelties practised by Galeazzo Maria Sforza, by the Norman chief of Sicily who was in the habit of disembowelling his victims, by the Popes Paul and Alexander VI., by the Kings of England, Richard and John, and others, show only too clearly how little difference creed or country is apt to make in the misdeeds of irresponsible power joined to an innately cruel nature.

[2] Sylvestre de Sacy derives the name from the word *hashish* (the Indian *bhang*) with which Hasan Sabbâh's followers drugged themselves, and this derivation is now generally accepted. See Professor Browne's *Literary Hist. of Persia* vol. ii. pp. 204-5. Mohsin Fâni describes this man's life and

as the *Eastern Isma'ilias* or *Alamûtias*, or the *Malâhida* of
Kuhistân (" the impious atheists " of Kuhistân).

Hasan was the son of a learned Shiah doctor, an Arab by
descent, as his name betokens, residing in the city of Khoi in
Persia. He had been carefully trained in all the learning of his
time. It is said that at one time he was a fellow-student
of Nizâm ul-Mulk (afterwards the renowned minister of Alp
Arslân and of Malik Shah, the two great Seljukian sovereigns of the East) and of the famous mystical poet Omar
Khayyâm. But the story appears now to be discredited.[1]
Baulked in his ambition at the court of Malik Shah, he
proceeded to the pontifical court at Cairo, and was there
initiated into the mysteries of the Cairene Lodge. Persia at
that time was in the most rigid bonds of Sunni orthodoxy,
the Seljukian Sultans having always been among the most
devoted upholders of the straitest traditions of Asha'rism.
Hasan returned from Egypt to Asia, and partly by force and
partly by fraud possessed himself of an almost impregnable
fortress called in the archaic Persian or Pahlavi *Alamût*, or
the Eagles' Nest,[2] seated on one of the most inaccessible
mountain-fastnesses of Upper Persia ;[3] and during the thirty-
five years that he held the dominion of that place, he organised
from there a system of terror throughout Asia and Africa[4] and
Eastern Europe, fighting the sword with the dagger, and avenging persecution with assassination. He himself was a strict
observer of all the precepts of religion, and would not allow
drunkenness or dancing or music within the circuit of his rule.
His esotericism appears to have been different from that of the

doctrines according to the Isma'ilias themselves, " as hitherto his life had been
written with the pen of prejudice."

چون احوال او در تواریخ باقلام تعصب نگارش یافته لاجرم
بر تحریر آن چنانچه نزد اسمعیلیه است مبادرت می نماید

[1] Professor E. G. Browne's *Lit. Hist. of Persia*, vol. ii. pp. 190-193.
[2] Wassâf, قلعۀ الموت یعنی آن آشیانۀ عقابست
[3] Near Kazwin.
[4] Wassâf says :—

و از قتل و هتک و هنک و هتک ملاحده اهن و امان از میان
مسلمانان مرفوع شد

Western Isma'ilias, and is explained in detail by Shahristâni and Moshin Fâni, both of whom speak of him with some awe, which induces the conviction that they were not quite unapprehensive of the dagger of his *fidâis*.[1] Leaving the mystical portion of his doctrines aside, it may be said that he admitted only four degrees of initiation. Those who had obtained the first three degrees were named respectively *Fidâi*, *Rafîk*, and *Dâ'i*,—fellows, companions, and knights,—to use the terms of a system to which Hasan's institution bears the closest resemblance, viz. that of the Templars. Hasan was the first Grand Master of this institution, though he always paid a formal homage to the Egyptian Caliphs. The fourth Grand Master, Hasan bin Mohammed, of the Alamûtia Lodge, who, in order to further his ends, did not hesitate to claim descent from the Caliph Mustansir billâh of Cairo through his son Nizâr, abolished all the ordinances of religion. The Resurrection had arrived ; the revelation of the Imâm had taken place in his person ; and the Kingdom of Heaven was ushered in with freedom and licence from the ordinary trammels of the moral law.[2] This

[1] That their apprehensions were not unjustified will be apparent from the following anecdote concerning Imâm Fakhr ud-din Râzi. This learned Imâm used to lecture on jurisprudence in his native city of Rai (Rhages). Once he had occasion to denounce the Isma'ilias from his professorial chair. The news of this audacious conduct was carried to the Eagles' Nest, and a Fidâi was promptly deputed to bring the careless professor to reason. The Fidâi on his arrival at Rai entered himself as a student in the Imâm's college. For seven months he waited for an opportunity to carry his design into effect. At last one day he found the Imâm alone in his chamber ; he locked the door, and throwing the Imâm on the ground pointed the dagger at his throat. " Why kill me ? " asked the frightened professor. " Because you have cursed the Isma'ilias," answered the Fidâi. The Imâm offered to bind himself solemnly never again to disparage the brotherhood. The Fidâi refused to accept the Imâm's word unless he agreed to receive a pension from the Grand Master, thus binding himself by the debt of " bread and salt."

[2] Hasan died in 508 A.H. Wassâf, following Juwaini, the vizier of Hûlâku and the author of the *Jahân-Kushâ*, gives an extremely bitter but not unjust account of these Isma'ilias.

چون امام غشوم بمنبر برآمد و چون مرغ شوم بر درخت

زَقّوم نشست و از تحمیدی فرا خور معتقد مذموم فارغ شده مژده

داد که ابواب رحمت بمفتاح هدایت کشاده است و قیامت

موعود منقود شده : قبیح بن مُذمّم اعنی حسن ابن محمد

mad revolutionist is known in the history of the Alamûtias as
'ala-Zikrihi-as-Salâm, "may his name be blessed"—corrupted
into Zikr-us-Salâm. From this time, until the destruction of
Alamût, the disciples of the two Hasans maintained a remorse-
less fight with civil society, in which no quarter was shown on
either side. They were, in fact, the Nihilists of Islâm. Under
their stilettoes fell both Christians and Moslems. They were
attacked by Hulâku, and after the destruction of their fortresses
in the mountains, they were hunted and killed like vermin.[1]

From the Isma'ilias the Crusaders borrowed the conception
which led to the formation of all the secret societies, religious
and secular, of Europe. The institutions of Templars and
Hospitallers ; the Society of Jesus, founded by Ignatius
Loyola, composed of a body of men whose spirit of self-sacrifice
and devotion to their cause can hardly be surpassed in our
times ; the ferocious Dominicans, the milder Franciscans,—
may all be traced either to Cairo or to Alamût. The Knights
Templars especially, with their system of grand masters, grand
priors and religious devotees, and their degrees of initiation,
bear the strongest analogy to the Eastern Isma'ilias. Small
sections of the Western Isma'ilias are still to be found in Yemen,
in Egypt, and Barbary, where they cannot be distinguished
from the general body of Moslems. On the western coast of
India there exists, however, a large community called Khojahs,
who are the direct representatives of the original Eastern

امام بحتى و.. خليفه مطلق است و مولانا فاها بفهم ايشانرا
بخدای رسانید و انواع تكليف برداشت و چون. از منبر نزول
كرد سماط عيد گسترد وانرا عيد قيام خواند و بشرب خمور
و نشر لهو و سرير اشتغال نمود و ابن حسن را باصطلاح بي استصلاح
علی ذكره السلام گفتندی.—Wassâf.

---

[1] For a full account of the Alamûtias and their crimes against humanity,
see Von Hammer's *History of the Assassins*, translated into English by Wood.
Even the Christian sovereigns frequently availed themselves of the services of
the Alamûtia assassins to get rid of their enemies. Richard of England had
Conrad of Montferrat assassinated by a *Fidâi* of Alamût ; and one of the
Popes employed another, though unsuccessfully, to remove Frederick Barba-
rossa. After the destruction of Alamût, Rudbâr, and the other castles of the
Assassins, the Alamûtias were massacred without compunction by the Tartars.

Isma'ilias. Hindus by origin, they were converted to Isma'ilism, in the eleventh or twelfth century of the Christian era, by
one Pîr Sadr ud-dîn, an Isma'ilian *Dâ'î*. His teachings fitted
in with their own religious conceptions, for part of the old cult
was incorporated with the Isma'ilia doctrines.[1]

The *Kaisânias* and *Hâshimias*, both of them exclusively
political in their character, but tinted by Magianism, are now
completely extinct, and hardly require any mention.

The *Ghâllias* or the *Ghulât* (Extravagantists), supposed by
Ibn Khaldûn and Shahristâni to be a sect of the Shiahs, are, in
reality, the descendants of the old Gnostics, whose Islâm consisted merely in the substitution of Mohammed or Ali, chiefly
the latter, for Christ. They are, in fact, the Docetes of Islâm.
The *Nusairis*, who believe in the divinity of Ali, the *Ishâkias*,
the *Numânias*, the *Khitâbias*, and others, anthropomorphists,
believers in incarnations and metempsychosis,—represent the
notions which were prevalent among the Marcionites, the
Valentinians, and the other docetic Christians. Some of these
have replaced the Christian triad by a pentad. These believe
that Mohammed, Ali, Fâtima, Hasan, and Husain jointly
represent the Divinity. A form of Docetism is in vogue also
in Sunnîsm. In the mountains of Kurdistân a Sunni Saint[2]
occupies almost a similar place in the popular faith to Jesus
among the Gnostics.

The *Roushenias*, as their name implies, were the exact
counterparts of the Illuminati of Christendom. This sect had
its origin in Afghânistân in that dark, turbulent, and sanguinary period which preceded the accession of Akbar to the
throne of India. Their founder, Bâyezîd,[3] by birth an Afghan,
but of Arab extraction, appears to have been a man of great
natural abilities and extreme subtlety of genius. In his early
youth he acquired a taint of Manichæism from the Isma'ilias

[1] Numbers of Isma'ilias are also to be found in the mountains of Gilgat and
Hunza.
[2] Sheikh Abdul Kâdir Ghilâni. There are Sunnis who pay an extravagant
veneration, verging on adoration, to this Saint. He has received the title
among them of *Ghaus-i-'âzam, Mahbûb-i-Subhâni, Kutb-i-Rabbâni*—" The
great Saint, the beloved of God, the Pole-star of holiness " (see the *Guldastai-
Kerâmat*). Sheikh Abdul Kâdir was a mystic, and a Fâtimide by descent.
He takes a high position in the hierarchy of the mystics and the dervishes ;
see chapter xi.
[3] Afterwards called Miân *Roushan* Bâyezîd.

who still flourished in considerable numbers in some of the mountainous districts of Khorâsân. The doctrines which he first propagated seem not to have differed essentially from those of the *Sûfis*; but as he proceeded he diverged wider and wider from the pale of dogmatic Islâm. As his sect increased in numbers and power, it assumed a political as well as a religious aspect; and soon made such formidable progress that, at last, it embraced nearly the whole of Afghânistân.

The doctrines taught by Bâyezîd, when examined critically, show a superstructure of mysticism and pantheism upon a basis of Isma'ilism. The observant reader, however, will not fail to perceive a strange and fantastic analogy between his teachings and the practices and theories of the brotherhood of Fakîrs. He taught that God is all-pervading, and that all existing objects are only forms of the Deity; that the *Pîrs* or religious teachers were the great manifestations of the Divinity; that the sole test of right and wrong was to follow the path pointed out by the *Pîr*, who is the representative of the Divinity; that the ordinances of the law have therefore a mystical meaning, and are ordained only as the means of acquiring religious perfection; and that the mystic sense of the law is only attainable by religious exercises and through the instructions of a *Pîr*; it is the source of religious perfection, and this perfection being attained, the exterior ordinances of the law cease to be binding, and are virtually annulled.

The *Bâtinis*, the *Isma'ilias*, and all the cognate sects differ from the general body of Moslems in making *faith* the keystone of their doctrines. In this they closely approach most of the Reformed Churches of Christendom. They " believe," like Luther, in " justification by faith." Luther has strenuously inculcated that " faith in Christ " would save all sinners. The Bâtinis and the Isma'ilias with their offshoots made " faith " or " *îmân*," which included a firm reliance on the divine Imâm, an essential factor in their creed. So long as an individual was blessed with *îmân*, his outward acts were immaterial.

We now come to the Shiahs proper, the followers of the Imâms of the house of Mohammed, generally known as the *Isnâ-'Asharias* (the *Duo decemians*), so named because they accept the leadership of twelve Imâms. The *Isnâ-'Asharias* hold that the Imâmate descended by express appointment in the following order :—

1. Ali, the Caliph, usually styled *Murtaza Asad-ullah al-Ghâlib, the Chosen, the Lion of God, the Victorious* (d. A.H. 40, A.C. 661).

2. Hasan, styled *Mujtaba, the Approved* (A.H. 44, A.C. 664).

3. Husain, *Shahîd-i-Kerbela, the Martyr of Kerbela* (A.H. 60, A.C. 679).

4. Ali II., surnamed for his piety *Zain ul-'Âbidîn*, the *Ornament of the Pious* (died A.H. 94, A.C. 713).

5. Mohammed *al-Bâkir, the Explainer of Mysteries*, or *the Profound*, a man of great learning and ascetic austerity (born A.H. 57, A.C. 676 ; died A.H. 113, A.C. 731).

6. Ja'far *as-Sâdik, the True*, was the eldest son of Mohammed *al-Bâkir*. Ja'far was born in Medîna, in the year of the Hegira A.H. 80 (A.C. 699). As a scholar, a littérateur, and a jurisconsult, his reputation stands high among all sects of Moslems. His learning and his virtues, the transcendental purity and truth of his character, won him the veneration even of the enemies of his family. He died at an advanced age in his native town, in the reign of Abû Ja'far al-Mansûr, the second Abbaside Caliph, in the year of the Hegira 148 (A.C. 765).

7. *Abu'l Hasan* Mûsa *al-Kâzim*, the son of Ja'far as-Sâdik, was also surnamed *al-Abd us-Sâleh, the Holy Servant*, on account of his piety and " his efforts to please God." He was born at Medîna in the year 129 A.H. (A.C. 746-747). He died at Bagdad on the 25th of Rajab 183 (1st September, 799 A.C.) in a prison where he was confined for a number of years by Hârûn, who was extremely jealous of the veneration in which the Imâm was held in Hijâz. De Sacy says Mûsa was put to death secretly in his confinement by order of Hârûn. His sufferings and his pure and exalted character endeared him greatly to all classes of people, and gained for him the title of *Kâzim, " the Patient."*

8. Ali III., *Abu'l Hasan* Ali, surnamed *ar-Riza*, the *Acceptable*, for the purity of his character. He was a scholar, a poet, and a philosopher of the first rank. He was born in Medîna in the year 153 A.H. (A.C. 770), and died at Tûs in Khorâsân in A.H. 202 (A.C. 817). He married a sister of Mâmûn, named Umm ul-Fazl.

9. *Abû Ja'far* Mohammed, surnamed *al-Jawwâd* for his munificence and generosity, and *Takî* for his piety. He was a nephew of Mâmûn, and was also married to his daughter, named Umm ul-Habîb. He was held in the highest estimation by that Caliph and his successor Mu'tasim (born A.H. 195, A.C. 811 ; and died in A.H. 220, A.C. 835).

10. Ali IV., surnamed *Nakî, the Pure*, died A.H. 260, A.C. 868.

11. Abû Mohammed al-Hasan ibn Ali *al-'Askari*, surnamed *al-Hâdi, the Director*, and called 'Askari from his long residence under the surveillance of Mutawakkil at Surra man-Raâ [1] which also went by the name of al-'Askar, " the Encampment." He was a man of eminent piety and great nobility of character, a distinguished poet and littérateur. He was born at Medîna A.H. 231 (A.C. 845-6), and died at al-'Askar in A.H. 260 (A.C. 874). He is said to have been poisoned by Mutawakkil.

12. Mohammed *al-Mahdi* (A.H. 265, A.C. 878-9). This last Imâm disappeared, according to the Shiah belief, in a grotto at Surra-man-Raâ in the fifth year of his age.[2] He is believed to be still alive, and they look forward with earnest anticipation to his reappearance to re-establish the universal Caliphate, and to restore the purity of the human race. He is styled the Imâm *Ghâib* (the absent Imâm), the *Muntazar*, " the Expected," and the *Kâim*, " the Living." [3]

The Isnâ-'Asharias, now called Shiahs or Imâmias *par excellence*, are divided into two sub-sects—*Usûlis* and *Akhbâris* (*i.e. the followers of principles* and *the followers of traditions*). There is no difference between them on the question of the Imâmate or its descent to the last Imâm. But they differ on the amount of authority to be attached to the exposition of the *Mujtahids*, who call themselves the representatives of the Imâm. The Usûli repudiates entirely the authority of the expounders of the law to fetter his judgment. He contends that the law is clear, and that it is his duty to construe it for himself with the light of reason and progress of human thought, and not to be

[1] A place several days' journey to the north-west of Bagdad.

[2] For an account of this pathetic incident, see ante, p. 123, and *Short History of the Saracens* (Macmillan), p. 295.

[3] Compare especially the belief of the Christadelphians, according to whom Christ will reappear to bring about an earthly kingdom.

guided in his judgment by the dictates of men as fallible as himself, and interested in maintaining the world in ignorance   He holds that God's revelations had not the object of hiding the Divine meaning in words difficult to apprehend.   They were addressed through his Prophet to humanity to apprehend and to obey.   Thus God's teachings delivered through His Messenger do not require the interpretation of priest or lawyer.   The Akhbâri, on the other hand, obeys slavishly the expositions of the Mujtahids.

According to the Usûli doctrines, the oral precepts of the Prophet are in their nature supplementary to the Koranic ordinances, and their binding effect depends on the degree of harmony existing between them and the teachings of the Koran. Thus, those traditions which seem to be in conflict with the spirit of the Koranic precepts are considered apocryphal.   The process of elimination is conducted upon recognised principles, founded upon logical rules and definite data.   These rules have acquired a distinctive type among the Mu'tazilas, who have eliminated from the *Hadîs Kudsî* (*the holy traditions*) such alleged sayings of the Prophet as appeared incompatible and out of harmony with his developed teachings as explained and illustrated by the philosophers and jurists of his family.

The Usûlis divide the traditions under four heads, viz. :— (*a*) *Sahîh*, " authentic " ;   (*b*) *Hasan*, " good " ;   (*c*) *Mûsak*, " strong " ;   and (*d*) *Za'îf*, " weak." A *hadîs sahîh*, or an authentic tradition, is one the authority of which can be conclusively traced to the *Aimma-i-Ma'sûm* (the *sinless Imâms*), according to the narration of an *Imâm 'âdil*, " *a just or trustworthy Imâm*," about whose integrity there is a consensus among the " masters of traditions " (*arbâb-i-hadîs*).   The narration must be through a succession of such '*âdils.* A *hadîs-hasan*, or a good tradition, is one the authority of which goes back, like that of the *hadîs sahîh*, to the *Ma'sûm* ; but, according to the narrative of a venerable Imâm, in this way, that although, in regard to the narrator of it, the words *sikah 'âdil*, " *trustworthy and just*," have not been used by the historians, yet they have praised him in other words. A *hadîs-mûsak*, or a *strong tradition*, is one handed down by people who are acknow- ledged to be *sikah* and '*âdil*, " *virtuous and just*," by the historians, though some or all of the narrators might not be *Imâmias*, "followers of Ali." A *hadîs-za'îf*, or a *weak tradition*, is one which complies with neither of these conditions. It is only the first three kinds of *hadîs* that are accepted or relied upon by the *Usûlis*.

Again, a tradition before it can be accepted must have been handed down in *regular succession.* A tradition is in regular succession when a large number of people in the regular course of time make the same narration until it is traced to the *Ma'sûm*, subject to the condition that the number of narrators, in each particular age, is so great as to exclude the idea of their having combined in telling a falsehood. A tradition is without a regular succession, when the number of narrators does not, in all or several stages, reach to such a body of witnesses ; and this kind of tradition is called, " in the peculiar idiom of the masters of traditions, *the information of one.*"

The *Usûli* exercises his own judgment in the construction of the law, and the reception, application, and interpretation of the traditions. He does not consider himself bound to follow the exposition of a Mujtahid, if his judgment and conscience tell him that that exposition is against the revealed or natural law, or justice, or reason. They protest against the immoderate number of traditions accepted by the *Akhbâris* without any criticism, or any application of the rules of exegesis. The *Usûlis* represent the Broad Church, if not of Islâm, at least of Shiahism.

According to the *Dabistân*, the *Akhbâris* derive their title from the fact that they rely entirely upon *akhbâr*, or traditions, and repudiate *ijtihâd* (the exercise of private judgment), as they consider it contrary to the practice of the Imâms. They accept as authentic whatever tradition happens to be current, if only it is labelled with the name of an Imâm or of the Prophet. It is enough that it is called a *hadîs* ; it becomes *ipso facto* authentic in their eyes,[1] and further inquiry is not required to test the source from which it emanates. It need not be said that under colour of this easy principle a vast number of traditions and maxims have become incorporated with the Islâmic

---

[1] *Adilla-i-Kati'*, conclusive evidence, which admits of no questioning, and requires no exercise of judgment.

teachings which have little in common with them. The ancient faith had never completely died out of the hearts of the masses, and it was impossible that with the growth of a national Church many of the old thoughts should not find expression in new and more approved garbs. Gobineau has, somewhat harshly, but not quite without reason, charged ultra-Akhbârîsm with having converted the great hero of Islâm into an Ormuzd, and his descendants into Amshaspands.

Akhbârîsm is the favourite creed of the uneducated, who require a leading string for their guidance, or of the half-educated Mullas. Usûlîsm finds acceptance among the most intellectual classes of the people and the most learned of the clergy. One of the most notable advocates of the Usûli doctrines within recent times was Mulla Sadra [1] (Mohammed bin Ibrâhim), a native of Shirâz, and probably the ablest scholar and dialectician of his time. He was the reviver of philosophy and humanitarian science among the Persians. From the fall of the Buwaihs to the rise of the Safawis, Irân had remained under a cloud. Patristic orthodoxy had proscribed philosophy and science ; the very name of Avicenna had become hateful, and his works were publicly burnt. During these centuries many Mazdeistic traditions dressed in Islâmic garb naturally had found acceptance among the uneducated classes. The true Fâtimide scholars had retired into seclusion, and a body of ecclesiastics strongly imbued with national predilections and prejudices had sprung up to maintain the people in ignorance. Mulla Sadra had thus to contend against a clergy as tenacious of their rights as those of Christendom, and as ready to take offence at the slightest approach to an attack on their preserve of orthodoxy. But Mulla Sadra was gifted with great perseverance and tact, and succeeded after considerable difficulty in reviving the study of philosophy and science. Usûlîsm came to the front once more. Its philosophical counterpart, Mu'tazilaism, is unquestionably the most rationalistic and liberal phase of Islâm. In its liberalism, in its sympathy with all phases of human thought, its grand hopefulness and expansiveness, it represents the ideas of the philosophers of the House of Mohammed who reflected the thoughts of the Master.

[1] Mulla Sadra flourished in the reign of Shah Abbâs II.

The political factions which have hitherto kept the Shiahs divided among themselves are disappearing, and the rest of the sects are fast merging into the Isnâ-'Asharias. The Shiahs of Persia, Arabia, West Africa, and India belong for the most part to this sect. *Isnâ-'Ashariaism* has thus become synonymous with Shiahism.

Like the Akhbâris, the Sunnis base their doctrines on the entirety of the traditions. But they differ from them in accepting such only of the traditions as can stand the test of certain rules of criticism peculiar to their school. In this they approach the Usûlis. They regard the concordant decisions of the successive Caliphs and of the general assemblies (*Ijmâ'-ul-Ummat*) as supplementing the Koranic rules and regulations, and as almost equal in authority to them.

The Sunnis are divided into several sub-sects, each differing from the other on various points of dogma and doctrine. These minor sectarian differences have often given rise to great bitterness and persecutions. In the main, however, they are agreed on the fundamental bases of their doctrines and laws, deriving them from four unvarying sources, viz. :—(1) The *Koran* ; (2) The *Hadîs* or *Sunnat* (traditions handed down from the Prophet) ; (3) The *Ijmâ'-ul-Ummat* (concordance among the followers) ; and (4) The *Kiyâs* (private judgment). The *Hadîs* (*pl. Ahâdis*) embraces (*a*) all the words, counsels, and oral precepts of the Prophet (*Kawl*) ; (*b*) his actions, his works, and daily practice (*Fi'l*) ; (*c*) and his silence (*Takrîr*), implying a tacit approbation on his part of any individual act committed by his disciples. The rules deduced from these subsidiary sources vary considerably in respect of the degree of authority which is attached to them. If the rules, or traditional precepts, are of public and universal notoriety (*Ahâdîs-i-Mutawâtireh*), they are regarded as absolutely authentic and decisive. If the traditions, though known publicly by a great majority of people, do not possess the character of universal notoriety, they are designated *Ahâdîs-i-Mashhúra*, and stand next in rank to the *Ahâdîs-i-Mutawâtireh* ; whilst the *Akhbâr-i-wâhid*, which depend for their authenticity upon the authority of isolated individuals, have little or no value attached to them. Thus every tradition purporting to be handed down by the contemporaries and companions of the Prophet, regardless of their actual relationship to him, is considered to be authentic and genuine, provided certain arbitrary conditions framed with the view of testing the value of personal testimony are complied with. The expression *Ijmâ'-ul-Ummat* implies general concordance. Under this collective name are included all the apostolic laws, the explanations, glosses, and decisions of the leading disciples of the Prophet, especially of the first four Caliphs (the *Khulafâi Râshidîn*), on theological, civil, and criminal matters.

Since the eighth century of the Christian era, however, all these sources of law and doctrine have been relegated to the domain of oblivion. And each sect has followed blindly its own doctors in the interpretation of the law and the exposition of doctrines. This is called *Taklîd*. No man is considered " orthodox " unless he conforms to the doctrines of one or the other of the principal doctors.

The four most important persuasions or sects [1] among the Sunnis are designated Hanafi, Shâfe'î, Mâliki, and Hanbali, after their respective founders.

Abû Hanîfa,[2] who gave his name to the first school, was born in the year 80 of the Hegira, during the reign of Abdul Malik ibn Merwân. He was educated in the Shiah school of law, and received his first instructions in jurisprudence from Imâm Ja'far as-Sâdik, and heard traditions from Abû Abdullah ibn al-Mubarak and Hâmid ibn Sulaimân. Abû Hanîfa often quotes the great Shiah Imâm as his authority. On his return to his native city of Kûfa, though he continued to remain a zealous and consistent partisan of the house of Ali, he seceded from the Shiah school of law and founded a system of his own, diverging completely in many important points from the doctrines of the Shiahs ; and yet, so close is the resemblance between his exposition of the law and their views, that there is no reason for doubt as to the source from which he derived his original inspiration. The latitude which he allows to private judgment in the interpretation of the law seems to be unquestionably a reflex of the opinions of the Fâtimide doctors. He

[1] Called the *Mazâhib-arba'a*.
[2] Abû Hanîfa an-No'man ibn Thâbit (A.C. 699-769).

is called by his followers the *Imâm-ul-Na'zam* (the great Imâm).[1] He died in the year A.H. 150. The doctrines taught by him are in force among the major portion of the Indian Musulmans, among the Afghans, Turkomans, almost all Central Asian Moslems, the Turks, and the Egyptians. His school owns by far the largest number of followers.

The founder of the second school was (Abû Abdullah) Mâlik ibn Anas, who died in the year A.H. 179, in the Caliphate of Hârûn ar-Rashîd.

Shâfe'î was the originator of the third school. He was born at Ghazza in Syria, in the same year in which Abû Hanîfa died. He died in Egypt in the year A.H. 204 (A.C. 819), during the Caliphate of Mâmûn. He was a contemporary of the Fâtimide Imâm Ali ibn Mûsa ar-Rizâ. Shâfe'î's doctrines are generally followed in Northern Africa, partially in Egypt, in Southern Arabia, and the Malayan Peninsula, and among the Musulmans of Ceylon. His followers are also to be found among the Borahs [1] of the Bombay Presidency.

The fourth school was originated by Ibn-Hanbal. He flourished during the reigns of Mâmûn and his successor Mu'tasim b'illâh. These two Caliphs were Mu'tazilas. Ibn-Hanbal's extreme fanaticism, and the persistency with which he tried to inflame the bigotry of the masses against the sovereigns, brought him into trouble with the rulers. He died in the odour of great sanctity in the year A.H. 241. Ibn-Hanbal and his patristicism are responsible for the ill-success of Mâmûn in introducing the Mu'tazila doctrines throughout the empire, and for the frequent outbursts of persecution which deluged the Mohammedan world with the blood of Moslems.

I have in another place [2] described the legal differences of the various Sunni schools ; their doctrinal divergences run into the minutiæ of the ceremonials of worship, unnecessary to detail in a work intended for the general student. It may be said, however, that the Hanbalites were the most pronounced anthropomorphists. To them God was a being in the similitude of man enthroned in heaven. Among the other sects the conceptions varied considerably according

---

[1] These Borahs are partly Shâfe'îs and partly Isma'ilias of the Egyptian type.
[2] "Mohammedan Law."

to the age and the people. Anthropomorphism was, however, the predominating element. There is no doubt that
Hanafīsm was originally the most liberal of these sects,
whilst Shâfe'īsm and Mâlikīsm were both exclusive and
harsh in their sympathies and ideas. With the advance
of time, and as despotism fixed itself upon the habits and
customs of the people, and the Caliph or sovereign became the
arbiter of their fate without check or hindrance from jurisconsult or legist, patristicism took hold of the mind of all classes
of society. The enunciations of the Fathers of the Church
became law. The Hanafis, who styled themselves, and were
styled by their brethren of the rival schools, *ahl-ur-rai w'al
kiyâs*, " people of judgment and analogy," in contradistinction
to the others, who were called *ahl-ul-hadîs*, traditionists *par
excellence*, have long ceased to exercise their judgment in
the domains of law or doctrine. What has been laid down
by the Fathers is unchangeable, and beyond the range of
discussion. The Faith may be carried to the land of the
Esquimaux, but it must go with rules framed for the guidance
of Irâkians !

Patristicism has thus destroyed all hope of development
in the Sunni fold. But its endeavours to ensure uniformity
of faith and practice have led within the last hundred years to
two notable revolts within the bosom of the Sunni Church.
Wahâbīsm, which made its appearance at the beginning of
the nineteenth century, derived its breath from the Desert.
Ghair-mukallidism springs from the innermost recesses of
the human heart, seeking an escape from the strait-laced
pharisaism of the established Church. The *Ghair-mukallid* is
a non-conformist, though he has been wrongly and unjustly
confounded with the Wahâbis. He is undoubtedly more
philosophical and rationalistic than the followers of the other
denominations of Sunnīsm. Narrow, no doubt, admittedly
limited and unsympathetic in its scope, *Ghair-Mukallidism* is
nevertheless the one movement in the Sunni Church which
contains great promise for the future.

The dispute which ushered in the Reformation in Europe has
already commenced among the Hanafis, and is sure before long
to make itself felt among all sects and schools of Moslems.

Does the translation of the Koran stand on the same footing as the Arabic Koran ; are prayers offered in the vulgar tongue, in the tongue of the worshipper ignorant of Arabic, as meritorious as those offered in the language of Hijâz—such are the questions which are now agitating the Moslem world in India. The controversy has already caused much bitterness and given rise to a few anathemas on the side of the orthodox, and the reformers may well be congratulated that the movement which they have set on foot is conducted under a neutral Government. To the old plea, which vested interests have always urged against every innovation, the leaders of the reform answer by asking, Is Arabic the sole language which God understands ? If not, what is the purpose of the prayer instituted by the Prophet ? If it is to bring the worshipper nearer to God, and to purify and ennoble his heart, then how can he feel the elevating effect of prayer if he only mumbles what he cannot understand ? From reason they appeal to the example of the Prophet, who allowed his Persian converts to offer their prayers in their own tongue.[1] This movement, still unknown to Europeans, contains the germ of great development. It is the beginning of the Reformation. Hitherto the theologians of Islâm, like the Christian clergy in the Middle Ages, have exercised, through the knowledge of a language not known to the masses or the sovereigns, a dominating influence. Once the principle for which the reformers are working is accepted, the prescriptions framed in the ninth and tenth centuries of the Christian era, for people utterly apart from the culture and civilisation of the present day, will have to be understood and explained with the light of a thousand years.

Khawârijism has been often regarded as a branch of Sunnism, though in reality it came into existence long before the foundations of the Sunni Church were laid. The refractory troops, who had forced the Caliph Ali to abandon the fruits of the well-earned victory at Siffin, and who afterwards rose in arms against him at Nahrwân, were the first to receive the name of *Khawârij* (deserters or rebels). Shahristâni has given a very lucid account of this insurrection. These were the men who were most eager in referring to arbitration the dispute of the

[1] See *ante*, p. 186.

arch-rebel Mu'âwiyah with the Caliph. They had forced upon their chief, against his own judgment, Abû Mûsa as the representative of the House of Mohammed ; but no sooner had the terms been settled than these soldier-theologians, these Covenanters of Islâm, fell into a hot controversy amongst themselves about the sinfulness of submitting any cause to human judgment. In order to prevent the spectacle of Moslems slaughtering each other in the presence of the enemy, Ali retired to Kûfa with the greater part of his army, leaving a small detachment at Dûmat ul-Jandal to await the result of the arbitration. The rebels to the number of twelve thousand deserted the Caliph at Kûfa, and, retiring to Nahrwân, took up a formidable position from which they threatened the Caliphate. With the repugnance to shed blood which was ever the distinguishing trait in Ali's character, he besought them repeatedly to return to their allegiance. In reply they threatened him with death. Human patience could not bear this contumacy longer. They were attacked and defeated in two successive battles. A few of the rebels escaped, says Shahristâni, and betaking themselves to al-Bahrain, that harbour of refuge for all the free lances of Islâm, spread their noxious doctrines among the wild inhabitants of that tract. They reappeared in the time of Abdul Malik, who drove them back into their fastnesses in al-Ahsa and al-Bahrain. They issued again under Merwan II., and spread themselves in Yemen, Hijâz, and the Irâk. They were attacked and defeated, and forced to take refuge in Oman, where they have remained settled ever since. Under the Abbasides they spread their doctrines among the Berbers of Africa, whom they raised repeatedly against the Pontiffs of Bagdad. The Khawârij are the Calvinists of Islâm. Their doctrines are gloomy and morose, hard and fanatical. They are strict predestinarians. They do not accept the Imâmate of any of the Caliphs after Omar, their own chiefs being, according to them, the lawful Imâms. They differ from the other Sunnis, in maintaining that it is not requisite for a person to be either a Koreishite or a free man for election as Imâm of the Moslems. Slaves and non-Koreishites were eligible for the Imâmate equally with Koreishites and free men. According to Shahristâni, the Khawârij are divided into six groups, the most important of whom are the *Azârika* (the followers of Abû Râshid Nafè ibn Azrak) ; the *Ibâdhia* (the followers of Abdullah ibn Ibâdh, who appeared in the reign of Merwân II., the last of the Ommeyyades) ; the *Nejdat Azâria* (the followers of Nejdat ibn 'Âmir) ; the *Ajârida* (of Abdul Karîm bin 'Ajrad) ; and the *Sufâruz Ziadia.* .

Of these, the *Azârika* are the most fanatical, exclusive, and narrow. According to them, every sect besides their own is doomed to perdition, and ought to be forcibly converted or ruthlessly destroyed. No mercy ought to be shown to any infidel or *Mushrik* (an expansive term, including Moslems, Christians, and Jews). To them every sin is of the same degree : murder, fornication, intoxication, smoking, all are damning offences against religion. Whilst the other Moslems, Shiah as well as Sunni, hold that every child is born into the world in the faith of Islâm,[1] and remains so until perverted by education, the Azraki declares that the child of an infidel is an infidel. The orthodox Christian maintains that every child who is not *baptized* is doomed to perdition ; the Khâriji, like the Christian, declares that every child who has not pronounced the formula of the Faith is beyond the pale of salvation. The *Azârika* were destroyed by Hajjâj ibn Yusuf ; but their sanguinary, fierce, and merciless doctrines found expression nine centuries later in Wahâbïsm.

The *Ibâdhia* were decidedly less fanatical. They were, for the most part, settled in Oman, and are still to be found in the principality of Muscat. The *Azârika*, and afterwards the Wahâbis, were at deadly feud with the *Ibâdhias*.

According to them, the general body of Moslems are unbelievers, but not *Mushrik* (polytheists), and that consequently they can intermarry with them. They differ from the *Azârika* in this and in other respects. They accept the evidence of Moslems against their people ; hold that the taking of the goods of the Moslems except in time of war, is unlawful, and " pronounce no opinion," says Shahristâni, " on the infidelity of the children of infidels " ; but they agree with their brethren, the

كل مولود يولد على فطرة الاسلام !

Azârika, in denouncing and anathematising the chief companions of the Prophet (the *Ashâb-i-Kabâr*).

The *Ibâdhias* have held Oman until now. Sore pressed by the Wahâbis, they have succeeded in maintaining their power on the coast of Eastern Arabia, but they seem to be fast merging into the general body of Sunnis.

The Wahâbis have been depicted in rather favourable colours by Mr. Palgrave, in his *Travels in Central Arabia*, but, in fact, they are the direct descendants of the *Azârika*, who, after their defeat by Hajjâj ibn Yusuf, had taken refuge in the recesses of Central Arabia. Abdul Wahâb's doctrines bear the closest resemblance to those held so fiercely by the followers of Nâfe ibn al-Azrak. Like them, the Wahâbis designate all other Moslems as unbelievers, and permit their despoilment and enslavement. However commendable their revolt against the anthropolatrous usages in vogue among the modern Moslems, their views of religion and divine government, like those of the *Ikhwân* of the present day in Nejd, are intensely morose and Calvinistic, and in absolute conflict with progress and development.

Bâbism, which made its appearance in Persia in the early part of the nineteenth century, has been represented in widely divergent colours. According to the Moslem authorities, it is nothing but a new form of Mazdakism, an Eastern socialistic communism. Its mixed gatherings of men and women are regarded in the same light as the ancient *Agapæ* of the primitive Christians were considered by the followers of the older faiths. On the other hand, a European scholar [1] of great research and learning, who has studied the religious literature of the Bâbis, and mixed familiarly with them, represents Bâbism as the latest expression of an eclectic evolution growing out of the innate pantheism of the Iranian mind.

During the reign of Mohammed Shah,[2] the hypocrisy and vices of the national clergy, says this writer, had reached such a pitch that a change was inevitable. The political and social condition of the people was deplorable. In this

---

[1] Gobineau.

[2] The third Kajar King of Persia, who ascended the throne on the death of his grandfather, Fathi Ali Shah.

P

state of affairs a young Mullah of Shirâz, Mirza Ali Mohammed, supposed to be a Fâtimide by descent, who had studied much, had travelled a great deal and made the pilgrimage to the holy cities, and had for many years resided in Arabia and Syria, began to preach a social and moral reform. He denounced the hypocrisy of the ordinary mullahs, and their reception of the most doubtful traditions to justify practices condemned by Islâm. His words struck a sympathetic chord in minds already prepared for the reception of his views, and evoked extraordinary enthusiasm. He obtained numerous disciples, among them a young lady of Kazwîn, whose learning and eloquence supplied a powerful support to his cause. She is venerated now as *Kurrat-ul-'Ayn*, "Light of the Eyes." Mirza Ali Mohammed, either carried away by the enthusiasm of his followers, or unhinged by his own exaltation, in a fit of pantheistical insanity, assumed the title of *Bâb Hazrat-i-â'ala*, and styled himself a part of the Divinity. His followers rose in arms against the constituted authorities and failed. The fanaticism of the clergy and political expediency gave rise to a persecution, for which even Gobineau thinks the Bâbis were primarily responsible. The Bâb was killed with most of his prominent disciples. But his teachings have survived. His social precepts are said by Gobineau to be much in advance of the received doctrines. He attached great importance to the marriage-relations, and during the continuance of the first marriage he allowed the taking of a second wife only under certain conditions. He absolutely interdicted concubinage, forbade divorce, and allowed the appearance of women in public. The custom of seclusion, as Gobineau justly observes, creates infinite disorders, and exercises a pernicious influence on the early education of children. The usage itself does not depend on any religious prescription, it is simply a convenience. The ancient kings of Persia observed it as a sign of grandeur, and the Moslem sovereigns and chiefs imitated their example, and adopted the custom. Among the Arabs the women of the tribes are perfectly free to move about as they wish. The ladies of the Prophet's family conversed with the disciples, received their visits, and often shared in the repasts of the men. Mirza Ali Mohammed therefore, says

Gobineau, made no innovation in endeavouring to free women from the bondage of a mischievous custom. His religious doctrines are essentially pantheistic, and his code of morals, far from being lax, is strict and rigid.[1]

Some Moslem writers have divided the religious sects into two comprehensive groups, viz. the *Ahl-ul-bâtin*, the *Intuitionalists*, and the *Ahl-uz-zâhir*, *those who look into the meaning of precepts*, and *those who look only to the literal sense*. The *Ahl-ul-bâtin*, however, must not be confounded with the *Bâtinis*. The *Ahl-ul-bâtin* include the mystical Sûfis, the philosophical *mutakallimín*, and the Idealists in general, " all those," to use the words of Zamakhsharí's comment, " who strive to implant in their hearts the roots of divine perfection," who strive and struggle to attain the highest standard of human excellence, and who, whilst conforming to the prescriptions of the law, perceive in them the divine intent to promote concord and harmony among the races of the earth, peace and goodwill among mankind.[2]

---

[1] The most recent account of this remarkable religious movement, from the Bâbi point of view, is to be found in Professor E. G. Browne's *New History of the Bâb*, which purports to be a translation of a Bâbi work called *Târíkh-i-Jadíd*. Professor Browne's Introduction is extremely interesting. From the *Târíkh* one can picture the fascinating personality of *Kurrat-ul-'Ayn* ; see Appendix III. This great scholar has given to the world in his new work, called *Materials for the Study of the Bâbi Religion*, considerable additional information regarding its development and diffusion. Bahâism, its latest phase, which flourishes chiefly in the United States of America, appears to have largely assimilated the doctrines of Christian Science.

[2] See *post*, chap. xi.

CHAPTER IX

THE LITERARY AND SCIENTIFIC SPIRIT OF ISLÂM

تعلموا العلم فان تعلمه لله حسنة ، ودراسته تسبيح والبحث عنه
جهاد ، وطلبه عبادة ، وتعليمه صدقة ، وبذله لاهله قربة[1]

WE have already referred to the Arabian Prophet's devotion to knowledge and science as distinguishing him from all other Teachers, and bringing him into the closest affinity with the modern world of thought. Medîna, the seat of the theocratic commonwealth of Islâm, had, after the fall of Mecca, become the centre of attraction, not to the hosts of Arabia only, but also to inquirers from abroad. Here flocked the Persian, the Greek, the Syrian, the Irâkian, and African of diverse hues and nationalities from the north and the west. Some, no doubt, came from curiosity, but most came to seek knowledge and to listen to the words of the Prophet of Islâm. He preached of the value of knowledge : " Acquire knowledge, because he who acquires it in the way of the Lord performs an act of piety ; who speaks of it, praises the Lord ; who seeks it, adores God ; who dispenses instruction in it, bestows alms ; and who imparts it to its fitting objects, performs an act of devotion to God. Knowledge enables its possessor to distinguish what is forbidden from what is not ; it lights the way to Heaven ; it is our friend in the desert, our society in solitude, our companion when bereft of friends ; it guides us to happiness ; it sustains us in misery ; it is our ornament in the company of friends ; it serves as an armour

---

[1] The translation of this *Hadís* is given in the text : " Acquire knowledge, etc."

against our enemies. With knowledge, the servant of God rises to the heights of goodness and to a noble position, associates with sovereigns in this world, and attains to the perfection of happiness in the next." [1]

He would often say, " the ink of the scholar is more holy than the blood of the martyr " ; and repeatedly impress on his disciples the necessity of seeking for knowledge " even unto China." [2]   " He who leaves his home in search of knowledge, walks in the path of God."   " He who travels in search of knowledge, to him God shows the way to paradise." [3]

The Koran itself bears testimony to the supreme value of learning and science.   Commenting on the Súrat-ul-'alak,[4] Zamakhsharî thus explains the meaning of the Koranic words : " God taught human beings that which they did not know, and this testifieth to the greatness of His beneficence, for He has given to His servants knowledge of that which they did not know.   And He has brought them out of the darkness of ignorance to the light of knowledge, and made them aware of the inestimable blessings of *the knowledge of writing*, for great benefits accrue therefrom which God alone compasseth ; and without the knowledge of writing no other knowledge ('ulûm) could be comprehended, nor the sciences placed within bounds, nor the history of the ancients be acquired and their sayings be recorded, nor the revealed books be written ; and if that knowledge did not exist, the affairs of religion and the world, امور الدين و الدنيا. could not be regulated."

Up to the time of the Islâmic Dispensation, the Arab world, properly so called, restricted within the Peninsula of Arabia and some outlying tracts to the north-west and the north-east, had shown no signs of intellectual growth.   Poetry, oratory, and judicial astrology formed the favourite objects of pursuit among the pre-Islâmic Arabs.   Science and literature possessed no votaries.   But the words of the Prophet gave a new impulse to the awakened energies of the race.   Even within

---

[1] Tradition from the *Bihâr-ul-Anwâr* of Mulla Bâkir ibn Mohammed Taki *al-majlisi*, vol. i. chap. on Knowledge, handed down by the Imâm Ja'far as-Sâdik, also quoted from Mu'âz ibn-Jabal in the *Mustatraf*, chap. iv. ; also in the *Kashf uz-Zunûn* of Hâji Khalîfa, Fluegel's ed. p. 44.

[2] *Misbâh ush-Sharîat.*   [3] *Jâmi' ul-Akhbâr.*

[4] Koran, sura xcvi. ; see also other suras.

his lifetime was formed the nucleus of an educational institution, which in after years grew into universities at Bagdad and Salerno, at Cairo and Cordova. Here preached the Master himself on the cultivation of a holy spirit : " One hour's meditation on the work of the Creator [in a devout spirit] is better than seventy years of prayer." [1] " To listen to the instructions of science and learning for one hour is more meritorious than attending the funerals of a thousand martyrs,— more meritorious than standing up in prayer for a thousand nights ; " " To the student who goes forth in quest of knowledge, God will allot a high place in the mansions of bliss ; every step he takes is blessed, and every lesson he receives has its reward ; " " The seeker of knowledge will be greeted in Heaven with a welcome from the angels ; " " to listen to the words of the learned, and to instil into the heart the lessons of science, is better than religious exercises, . . . better than emancipating a hundred slaves ; " " Him who favours learning and the learned, God will favour in the next world ; " " He who honours the learned honours me." Ali lectured on branches of learning most suited to the wants of the infant commonwealth. Among his recorded sayings are the following : " Eminence in science is the highest of honours ; " " He dies not who gives life to learning ; " " The greatest ornament of a man is erudition."

Naturally such sentiments on the part of the Master and the chief of the Disciples gave rise to a liberal policy, and animated all classes with a desire for learning. The art of Kûfic writing, which had just been acquired by a disciple at Hîra, furthered the primitive development of the Moslems. It was, however, pre-eminently an age of earnestness and faith, marked by the uprise of the soul against the domination of aimless, lifeless philosophy. The practice of religion, the conservation of a devotional spirit, and the special cultivation of those branches of learning which were of practical value in the battle of every-day life, were the primary objects of the Moslem's attention.

The age of speculation was soon to commence ; its germs were contained in the positive precepts of the Master ; and even whilst he was working, the scholarly Disciple was thinking. The Master had himself declared that whosoever desired to

[1] *Jâmi' ul-Akhbâr.*

realise the spirit of his teachings must listen to the words of the Scholar.[1] Who more able to grasp the meaning of the Master's words than Ali, the beloved friend, the trusted Disciple, the devoted cousin and son ? The gentle, calm teachings instilled in early life into the young mind bore their fruit.

In spite of the upheaval of the Arab race under the early Caliphs, literature and arts were by no means neglected in the metropolis of primitive Islâm. Ali and Ibn Abbâs, his cousin, gave public lectures on poetry, grammar, history, and mathematics ; others taught the art of recitation or elocution ; whilst some gave lessons in caligraphy,—in ancient times an invaluable branch of knowledge.

On Osmân's tragical death the Scholar was called by the voice of the people to the helm of the State. During his retirement Ali had devoted himself to the study of the Master's precepts by the light of reason. " But for his assassination," to quote the language of a French historian, " the Moslem world might have witnessed the realisation of the Prophet's teachings, in the actual amalgamation of Reason with Law, and in the impersonation of the first principles of true philosophy in positive action." The same passionate devotion to knowledge and learning which distinguished Mohammed, breathed in every word of his Disciple. With a liberality of mind—far beyond that of the age in which he lived—was joined a sincere devoutness of spirit and earnestness of faith. His sermons, faithfully preserved by one of his descendants, and his litanies or psalms, portray a devout uplooking toward the Source of All Good, and an unbounded faith in humanity. The accession of the Ommeyyades to the rulership of Islâm was a blow to the progress of knowledge and liberalism in the Moslem world. Their stormy reigns left the nation little leisure to devote to the gentler pursuits of science ; and to this, among the sovereigns, was joined a characteristic idolatry of the past. Their thoughts were engrossed by war and politics. During the comparatively long rule of a century, the House of

انا مدينة العلم علي بابها [1]

" I am the city of learning, Ali is its gate."

Ommeyya produced only one man devoted to the cultivation of letters ; and this man was Abû Hâshim Khâlid ibn Yezîd, " the philosopher of the Merwânian family," [1] as he has been called, who was set aside from the succession on account of his learning.

The jealous suspicion and the untiring animosity of the children of Abû Sufîan and Hind had obliged the descendants of the Prophet to live a life of humble retirement. " In the night of misery and unhappiness " they followed truly and faithfully the precepts of their ancestor, and found consolation in intellectual pursuits. Their ardent love of knowledge, their passionate devotion to the cause of humanity,—their spirit looking upwards far above the literalness of common interpretations of the law,—show the spirituality and expansiveness of Islâm. [2] The definition by the Imâm Ja'far as-Sâdik of sciences or knowledge gives some idea of their faith in the progress of man : " The enlightenment of the heart is its essence ; Truth its principal object ; Inspiration, its guide ; Reason, its accepter ; God, its inspirer ; and the words of man its utterer." [3]

Surrounded by men whom love, devotion, and sympathy with their patience had gathered around them, the early descendants of the Prophet were naturally more or less influenced by the varied ideas of their followers. Yet their philosophy never sinks to that war of words without life and without earnestness which characterised the schools of Athens or Alexandria under the Ptolemies.

But though literature and philosophy were at a discount among the rulers, the example of the Imâms naturally exercised no small influence on the intellectual activity of the Arabs and the subject races. Whilst the Ommeyyades discouraged the peaceful pursuits of the mind, the children of Fâtima, with remarkable liberalism, favoured learning. They were not

---

[1] *Mâkhaz-i-'ulûm* of Moulvi Syed Kerâmat Ali. This learned scholar was nearly forty years curator of the Imambara at Houghly.

[2] See the *Hadîs-i-Ihlilaj*, from the Imâm Ali bin-Mûsa ar-Raza, reported by Mufazal bin-Omar Joufi, *Bihâr ul-Anwâr*.

[3] *Târikh ul-Hukamâ*, by Jamâl ud-dîn al-Kifti, founded upon another work bearing the same name, by Shihâb ud-dîn Suhrwardi ; Shihâb ud-dîn was a Platonist—an Ishrâki—an idealist, and was condemned and put to death by the orthodox synod in the reign of Saladin's son. Compare the first *Khutba* of the *Nahj-ul-Balâghat*, and the traditions on knowledge in the *Bihâr ul-Anwâr*.

devoted to the past,—the *salaf* was not their guide.   With
the Master's precepts to light their path, they kept in view the
development of humanity, and devoted themselves to the
cultivation of science and learning in all its branches.   Like
the Master and the early Caliphs, the " Philosophers of the
House of Mohammed " [1] received with distinction the learned
men whom the fanatical persecution of Justinian's successors
drove for refuge into foreign lands.   The academies of philosophy and medicine, founded by the Nestorians at Edessa and
Nisibis, had been broken up ; its professors and students were
refugees in Persia and Arabia.   Many betook themselves—as
their predecessors had done before, in the time of the Prophet
and the Caliph Abû Bakr—to Medîna, which, after its sack by
the Ommeyyades, had again gathered round Ja'far as-Sâdik
a galaxy of talented scholars.   The concourse of many and
varied minds in the City of the Prophet gave an impetus to the
cultivation of science and literature among the Moslems.   From
Medîna a stream of unusual intellectual activity flowed towards
Damascus.   Situated on the northern confines of the Arabian
Desert, along the trade-route from Mecca and Medîna to Syria,
Damascus had been associated from ancient times with the
Ommeyyades ; and the Syrian Arabs were closely allied by
interest and kinship to the family whom they had assisted to
elevate to the rulership of Islâm.   The Ommeyyades had
naturally fixed upon this city as the seat of their empire ; and
though shunned with horror by the devout Moslems, it formed
the gathering place for the representatives of the many races
who had come under the sway of Islâm.   The controversies of
Greek and Saracen furnished a strong incentive to the study of
dialectics and Greek philosophy ; and the invention of the
diacritical and vowel points furthered the cultivation of
grammar and philology.   At this time flourished two Christian
writers of note, who, fleeing before their orthodox persecutors,
had taken shelter in Damascus.   These were Johannes Damas-
cenus and Theodorus Abucara.   Their polemical writings
against the Moslems, their rationalistic and philosophical
disputes with their own orthodox brethren, joined to the
influence of the Medinite school, which flourished under

[1] *Mâkhaz-i-'Ulûm.*

Mohammed al-Bâkir and Ja'far as-Sâdik, soon led to the growth of philosophical tendencies among the Saracens. For centuries Greek philosophy had been known to the Persians and the Arabs ; the Nestorians had spread themselves in the dominions of the Chosroes since the beginning of Justinian's reign, but it was not until all the varied elements had been fused into an organic whole by Islâm that Greek science and culture exercised any real effect on the intellectual development of Western Asia. It was towards the close of the Ommeyyade rule that several Moslem thinkers came into prominence, whose lectures on subjects then uppermost in the minds of the people attracted great attention. And their ideas and conceptions materially moulded the thoughts of succeeding generations.

It was in the second century, however, that the literary and scientific activity of the Moslems commenced in earnest, and the chief impulse to this was given by the settlement of the Arabs in towns. Hitherto they had lived in camps isolated from the races they had subjugated. Osmân had laid a prohibition on their acquiring lands in the conquered countries, or contracting marriages with the subject nations. The object of this policy was apparent ; it has its parallel in the history of all nations, ancient and modern. In British India and in French Algeria it is still in force. During the whole period of the Ommeyyade rule the Arabs had constituted the dominant element,—the aristocratic military caste amongst their subjects. The majority of them were occupied in warlike pursuits. The gentler avocations of learning and science were left to the suspected Hâshimis and the children of the Ansâr,—to the descendants of Ali, Abû Bakr, and Omar. The Arabs had carried with them into distant regions the system of clientage which had existed in Arabia, as it had existed among the Romans, from ancient times. Clientage afforded to the subjects protection and consideration ; to the conquerors, the additional strength gained by numbers. Thus, both in the East and in the West, the leading families allied themselves with members of the prominent desert clans, and became the *maulas* or *clients*, not *freedmen*, as has been incorrectly supposed, of their conquerors. To these *clients*, besides the Hâshimites and the children of the Ansâr and Muhâjirîn, such as had survived the sack of Medîna, was left scholarship and the cultivation of arts and sciences during the Ommeyyade rule. With the rise of the Abbasides commenced a new era. They rose to power with the assistance of the Persians ; and they relied for the maintenance of their rule more upon the attachment of the general body of their subjects, than the fickle affection of the military colonists of Arabia. Abu'l Abbâs Saffâh held the reins of government for but two years. His brother and successor, al-Mansûr, though cruel in his treatment of the Fâtimides, was a statesman of the first rank. He organised the State, established a standing army and a corps of police, and gave firmness and consistency to the system of administration. The Arabs had hitherto devoted themselves almost exclusively to the profession of arms ; the method of government adopted by al-Mansûr gave a new bent to their genius. They settled in cities, acquired landed properties, and devoted themselves to the cultivation of letters with the same ardour which they had displayed in the pursuit of war.

The rich and fertile valley of the Euphrates, watered by the two great rivers of Western Asia, has, from the most ancient times, been the seat of empire and the centre of civilisation. It was in this region that Babylon, Ctesiphon, and Seleucia had risen successively. Here existed at this epoch Basra and Kûfa, with their unruly and volatile inhabitants. Basra and Kûfa had, from the first conquest of the Moslems, formed important centres of commercial activity. The latter city was at one time the seat of government. To Basra and Kûfa had come all the active spirits of the East, who either could not or would not go to the depraved capital of the Ommeyyades. For the Abbasides, Damascus had not only no attraction, but was a place of peril ; and the uncertain and fickle temperament of the people of Basra and Kûfa made those cities undesirable as the seat of government. Al-Mansûr cast about for a site for his capital, and at last fixed upon the locality where Bagdad now stands—a six days' journey by river from Basra.

Bagdad is said to have been a summer retreat of Kesrâ Anûshirvân, the famous monarch of Persia, and derived from his reputation as a just ruler the name it bears,—the " Garden of Justice." With the disappearance of the Persian monarchy had disappeared the famous Garden where the Lord of Asia dispensed justice to his multitudinous subjects ; tradition, however, had preserved the name. The beautiful site, central and salubrious, attracted the eyes of Mansûr, and the glorious city of the Caliphs arose, like the sea-goddess issuing from the waves, under the magic wand of the foremost architects of the day.

The Bagdad of Mansûr was founded in the year 145 of the Hegira on the western bank of the Tigris. Soon, however, another city—a new Bagdad—sprang up on the eastern bank under the auspices of the heir-apparent, the Prince Imperial of the Caliphate, who afterwards assumed the title of al-Mahdi. This new city vied in the splendour of its structures with the beauty and magnificence of the Mansuriêh. In the days of its glory, before the destroying hordes of Chengîz sweeping over Western Asia had engulfed in ruin every vestige of Saracenic civilisation, Bagdad presented a beautiful and imposing appearance—a fit capital for the Pontiffs of Islâm.[1]

The beauty and splendour of the city, before its sack by the Mongols, have been immortalised in glowing lines by Anwarî— most brilliant of panegyrists :— [2]

" Blessed be the site of Bagdad, seat of learning and art—
    None can point in the world to a city equal to her,
    Her suburbs vie in beauty with the blue vault of heaven,
    Her climate in quality equals the life-giving breezes of
        heaven,
    Her stones in their brightness rival gems and rubies,

[1] For a description of Bagdad under the Abbasides, see *Short History of the Saracens* (Macmillan), p. 444.

[2] This English rendering gives an inadequate idea of the beauty of the original :—

خوشا نواحى بغداد جاى فضل : هنر

که کس نشان ندهد در جهان چنان کشور

سواد او بمنزل چون سپهر مینا رنگ

هواى او بصفت چون نسیم جان پرور

بخاصیت همه سنگش عقیق لولو بار

> Her soil in beneficence has the fragrance of the amber,
> The morning breeze has imparted to the earth the freshness
>   of *Tûba* (the tree of Paradise),
> And the winds have concealed in her water the sweetness
>   of *Kausar* (the spring of Eden),
> The banks of the Tigris with their beautiful damsels surpass
>   (the city of) *Khullakh*,[1]
> The gardens filled with lovely nymphs equal Cashmere,
> And thousands of gondolas on the water,
> Dance and sparkle like sunbeams in the sky."

Its designation of the *City of Peace, Dâr us-Salâm*, was derived from a prophecy made by the astronomer-royal Noubakht, that none of the Caliphs would die within the walls of the city, and the strange fulfilment of this prognostication in the case of thirty-seven Pontiffs. The great number of holy men who have found their last resting-place within or about its walls, and whose tombs are objects of veneration to all Moslems, gave to Bagdad the title of *Bulwark of the Holy*. Here are the mausoleums of the greatest Imâms and the most pious Sheikhs. Here reposes the Imâm Mûsa al-Kâzim, and here lie buried Abû Hanîfa, the Sheikhs Junaid, Shibli, and Abdul Kâdir Ghilâni, the chiefs of the Sûfis.

In the midst of the monuments of the Imâms and Sheikhs stood those of the Caliphs and their consorts. Of the numerous academies, colleges, and schools which filled the city, two nstitutions surpassed all others in importance by their wealth

منفعت همه خاكش عبير غاليه بر

صبا سرشته بخاكش طراوت طوبى

هوا نهفتـه در آبش حـلاوت كوثر

كنار دجلـه ز تركان سيمتـن خلخ

ميان رجبـه ز خوبان ماهـرخ كشمر

هزار زورق خورشيد شكل بر سر آب

بدان صفت كه برافكنده به سپهر شرر

---

[1] A city in Cathay famous for the beauty of its women.

and the number of their students. These were the Nizamièh and Mustansarièh ; the first established in the first half of the fifth century of the Hegira by Nizâm ul-Mulk, the great Vizier of Malik Shah, Sultan of the Seljuks ; and the second, built two centuries later, by the Caliph Al-Mustansir b'illâh.

" It is a remarkable fact," says the historian of Culture under the Caliphs, " that the sovereign who makes us forget some of the darker sides of his nature by his moral and mental qualities, also gave the impetus to the great intellectual movement which now commenced in the Islâmic world." [1] It was by Mansûr's command that literary and scientific works in foreign languages were first translated into Arabic. Himself no mean scholar and mathematician he had the famous collections of Indian fables (the Hitopadesa), the Indian treatise on astronomy called the *Siddhanta*, several works of Aristotle, the *Almagest* of Claudius Ptolemy, the books of Euclid, as well as other ancient Greek, Byzantine, Persian, and Syrian productions, translated into the language of the Arabs. Mas'ûdi mentions that no sooner were these translations published than they were studied with much avidity. Mansûr's successors were not only warm patrons of the learned, who flocked to the metropolis from all quarters, but were themselves assiduous cultivators of every branch of knowledge. Under them the intellectual development of the Saracens, in other words of the conglomerate races of the vast empire which constituted the Caliphate, proceeded with wonderful rapidity.

Each great nation of the world has had its golden age. Athens had her Periclean era ; Rome, her Augustan age ; so, too, had the Islâmic world its epoch of glory ; and we may with justice look upon the period which elapsed from the accession of Mansûr to the death of Mu'tazid-b'illâh, with only a brief intermission during the reign of Mutawakkil, as an epoch of equal, if not of superior greatness and magnificence. Under the first six Abbaside Caliphs, but especially under Mâmûn, the Moslems formed the vanguard of civilisation. The Saracenic race by its elastic genius as well as by its central position,—with the priceless treasures of dying Greece and Rome on one side, and of Persia on the other, and India and

[1] Kremer, *Culturgeschichte des Orients unter den Chalifen*, vol. ii. p. 412.

China far away sleeping the sleep of ages,—was pre-eminently fitted to become the teacher of mankind. Under the inspiring influences of the great Prophet, who gave them a code and a nationality, and assisted by their sovereigns, the Saracens caught up the lessons of wisdom from the East and the West, combined them with the teachings of the Master, and " started from soldiers into scholars." " The Arabs," says Humboldt, " were admirably situated to act the part of mediators, and to influence the nations from the Euphrates to the Guadalquivir and Mid-Africa. Their unexampled intellectual activity marks a distinct epoch in the history of the world."

Under the Ommeyyades we see the Moslems passing through a period of probation, preparing themselves for the great task they were called upon to undertake. Under the Abbasides we find them the repositories of the knowledge of the world. Every part of the globe is ransacked by the agents of the Caliphs for the hoarded wealth of antiquity ; these are brought to the capital, and laid before an admiring and appreciating public. Schools and academies spring up in every direction ; public libraries are established in every city free to every comer ; the great philosophers of the ancient world are studied side by side with the Koran. Galen, Dioscorides, Themistius, Aristotle, Plato, Euclid, Ptolemy, and Apollonius receive their due meed of appreciation. The sovereigns themselves assist at literary meetings and philosophical disquisitions. For the first time in the history of humanity a religious and autocratic government is observed to ally itself with philosophy, preparing and participating in its triumphs.

Every city in the empire sought to outrival the other in the cultivation of the arts and sciences. And governors and provincial chiefs tried to emulate the sovereign. Travelling in search of knowledge was, according to the precept of the Master, a pious duty. From every part of the globe students and scholars flocked to Cordova, to Bagdad, and to Cairo to listen to the words of the Saracenic sages. Even Christians from remote corners of Europe attended Moslem colleges. Men who became in after-life the heads of the Christian Church,[1] acquired their scholarship from Islâmic teachers. The rise of Cairo

[1] Such as Gerbert, afterwards Pope Sylvester II., who studied in Cordova.

372 THE SPIRIT OF ISLÂM II.

under al-Muizz li-dîn-illâh added a spirit of rivalry to the
patronage of learning on the part of the Caliphs of the Houses
of Abbâs and Fâtima. Al-Muizz was the Mâmûn of the West
—the Mæcenas of Moslem Africa, which then embraced the
whole of the continent from the eastern confines of Egypt to
the shores of the Atlantic and the borders of the Sahara. During
the reign of al-Muizz and his first three successors, the arts and
sciences flourished under the especial and loving protection of
the sovereigns. The free university of Cairo, the *Dâr-ul-Hikmat*
—Scientific Institute—established by al-Muizz, " anticipated
Bacon's ideal with a fact." The Idrîsides at Fez, and the
Moorish sovereigns in Spain, outvied each other in the cultivation of arts and letters. From the shores of the Atlantic
eastward to the Indian Ocean, far away even to the Pacific,
resounded the voice of philosophy and learning, under Moslem
guidance and Moslem inspiration. And when the House of
Abbâs lost its grasp on the empire of the East, the chiefs who
held the reins of government in the tracts which at one time
were under the undivided temporal sway of the Caliphs,
extended the same protection to science and literature as the
Pontiffs from whom they still derived their title to sovereignty.
This glorious period lasted, in spite of the triumph of patristicism and its unconcealed jealousy towards scientific and
philosophical pursuits, until the fall of Bagdad before the
Tartar hordes. But the wild savages who overturned the
Caliphate and destroyed civilisation, as soon as they adopted
Islâm, became ardent protectors of learning !

What was the condition of learning and science in Christendom at this epoch ? Under Constantine and his orthodox
successors the Æsclepions were closed for ever ; the public
libraries established by the liberality of the pagan emperors
were dispersed or destroyed ; learning was " branded as magic
or punished as treason " ; and philosophy and science were
exterminated. The ecclesiastical hatred against human learning had found expression in the patristic maxim, " Ignorance
is the mother of devotion " ; and Pope Gregory the Great,
the founder of ecclesiastical supremacy, gave effect to this
obscurantist dogma by expelling from Rome all scientific
studies, and burning the Palatine Library founded by Augustus

Cæsar. He forbade the study of the ancient writers of Greece
and Rome. He introduced and sanctified the mythologic
Christianity which continued for centuries the predominating
creed of Europe, with its worship of relics and the remains of
saints. Science and literature were placed under the ban by
orthodox Christianity, and they succeeded in emancipating
themselves only when Free Thought had broken down the
barriers raised by orthodoxy against the progress of the human
mind.

Abdullah al-Mâmûn has been deservedly styled the Augustus
of the Arabs. " He was not ignorant that they are the elect
of God, his best and most useful servants, whose lives are
devoted to the improvement of their rational faculties . . . that
the teachers of wisdom are the true luminaries and legislators
of the world." [1]

Mâmûn was followed by a brilliant succession of princes who
continued his work. Under him and his successors, the principal distinguishing feature of the school of Bagdad was a true
and strongly marked scientific spirit, which dominated over all
its achievements. The deductive method, hitherto proudly
regarded as the invention and sole monopoly of modern Europe,
was perfectly understood by the Moslems. " Marching from
the known to the unknown, the school of Bagdad rendered to
itself an exact account of the phenomena for the purpose of
rising from the effect to the cause, accepting only what had
been demonstrated by experience ; such were the principles
taught by the (Moslem) masters." " The Arabs of the ninth
century," continues the author we are quoting, " were in the
possession of that fecund method which was to become long
afterwards, in the hands of the moderns, the instrument of
their most beautiful discoveries."

Volumes would be required to enumerate the host of scientific
and learned men who flourished about this epoch, all of whom
have, in some way or other, left their mark on the history of
progress. Mâshallâh and Ahmed ibn Mohammed al-Nehâvendi, the most ancient of the Arab astronomers, lived in the
reign of Mansûr. The former, who has been called the Phœnix
of his time by Abu'l Faraj, wrote several valuable treatises on

[1] Abu'l Faraj.

the astrolabe and the armillary sphere, and the nature and movements of celestial bodies—works which still evoke the admiration of scientists. Ahmed al-Nehâvendi wrote from his own observations an astronomical table, *al-Mustamal*, which formed a decided advance upon the notions of both the Greeks and the Hindus. Under Mâmûn, the *Almagest* of Ptolemy was re-translated, and the *Verified Tables* prepared by famous astronomers like Send ibn Ali, Yahya ibn Abi-Mansûr, and Khâlid ibn Abdul Malik. Their observations connected with the equinoxes, the eclipses, the apparitions of the comets, and other celestial phenomena, were valuable in the extreme, and added greatly to human knowledge.

Mohammed ibn Mûsa al-Khwârizmi made a new translation, under the orders of Mâmûn, of the *Siddhanta*, or the Indian Tables, with notes and observations. Al-Kindi wrote two hundred works on various subjects—arithmetic, geometry, philosophy, meteorology, optics and medicine. Thoroughly versed in the language of the Greeks, he derived from the schools of Athens and Alexandria part of the information which he embodied in his invaluable treatises. " His works," says Sédillot, " are full of curious and interesting facts." Abû-Ma'shar (corrupted by the Europe of the Middle Ages into Albumazar) made the celestial phenomena his special study ; and the *Zîj-abî-Ma'shar*, or the Table of Abû-Ma'shar, has always remained one of the chief sources of astronomical knowledge. The discoveries of the sons of Mûsa ibn Shâkir,[1] who flourished under Mâmûn and his two immediate successors, especially with respect to the evaluations of the mean movement of the sun and other astral bodies, are almost as exact as the latest discoveries of Europe. They ascertained with wonderful precision, considering the appliances they possessed, the obliquity of the ecliptic, and marked for the first time the variations in the lunar altitudes. They also observed and determined with remarkable accuracy the precession of the equinoxes, and the movements of the solar apogee (which were utterly unknown to the Greeks). They calculated the size of the earth from the measurement of a degree on the shore of the Red Sea—this at a time when Christian Europe was

[1] Mohammed, Ahmed, and Hasan.

asserting the flatness of the globe. Abu'l Hasan invented the telescope, of which he speaks as " a tube to the extremities of which were attached diopters." These " tubes " were improved and used afterwards in the observatories of Marâgha and Cairo with great success. Al-Nairèzi and Mohammed ibn Isa Abû Abdullah continued the great work of Mûsa ibn Shâkir's sons.[1] By the time al-Batâni appeared, the Moslems had evolved from the crude astronomy of the ancients a regular and harmonious science. Al-Batâni,[2] though surpassed by his successors, occupies a high position among astronomers, and a competent judge pronounces his *rôle* to be the same among the Saracens as that of Ptolemy among the Greeks. His Astronomical Tables, translated into Latin, furnished the groundwork of astronomy in Europe for many centuries. He is, however, best known in the history of mathematics as the introducer of the sine and co-sine instead of the chord in astronomical and trigonometrical calculations.

Among the numerous astronomers who lived and worked in Bagdad at the close of the tenth century, the names of two men, Ali ibn Amajûr and Abu'l Hasan Ali ibn Amajûr, generally known as Banû-Amajûr, stand prominently forward. They are noted for their calculation of the lunar movements.

Owing to the weakness of the central power, and an increasing inability to maintain the sway of the Caliphate in outlying and distant parts, there arose on the confines of the empire, towards the end of the tenth century, several quasi-independent chiefs. Spain had been lost to the Abbasides at the commencement of their rule ; about this period the Banî-Idrîs established themselves at Fez, the Banî-Rustam at Tahârt, and the Banî-Aghlab at Kairowân in Africa. Soon, however, the whole of the northern part of that continent was brought under the domination of the Banî-Fâtima, and then another era of glory for arts and literature commenced. Fez, Miknâsa, Segelmessa, Tahârt, Tlemcen, Kairowân, but above all, Cairo, became centres of culture and learning. In Khorâsân the Tâherides,

[1] For their names, see *ante*, p. 374. Mohammed ibn Musa ibn Shâkir died in A.H. 259 (A.C. 873).

[2] Abû Abdullah Mohammed ibn Jâbir ibn Sinân al-Batâni was a native of Harran, died A.H. 317 (A.C. 929-30).

in Transoxiana the Sâmânides, the Buyides in Tabaristan and afterwards in Persia and Bagdad, as mayors of the palace, extended a lavish patronage to scientists and scholars. Abdur Rahman Sûfi, one of the most brilliant physicists of the age, was an intimate friend of the Buyide Ameer 'Azud ud-Dowla, deservedly called the second Augustus of the Arabs. Abdur Rahman improved the photometry of the stars. 'Azud ud-Dowla,[1] himself a scholar and a mathematician, welcomed to his palace as honoured guests the learned men who flocked to Bagdad from every part of the globe, and took part in their scientific controversies. Ja'far, the son of the Caliph Muktafi b'illâh, made important observations regarding the erratic movements of comets, and wrote a treatise on them ; and other princes cultivated the sciences side by side with their subjects.

Under the Buyides flourished a host of astronomers, physicists, and mathematicians, of whom only two need be mentioned here, Al-Kohî and Abu'l-Wafâ. Al-Kohî studied and wrote on the movements of the planets His discoveries concerning the summer solstice and the autumnal equinox added materially to the store of human knowledge. Abu'l-Wafâ was born in 939 A.C. at Buzjân in Khorâsân ; he established himself in Irâk in 959, where he applied himself chiefly to mathematics and astronomy. His *Zij-ush-Shâmil (the Consolidated or General Table)* is a monument of industry and keen and accurate observation. He introduced the use of the secant and the tangent in trigonometry and astronomical observations. " But this was not all," says M. Sédillot ; " struck by the imperfection of the lunar theory of Ptolemy, he verified the ancient observations, and discovered, independently of *the equation of the centre and the eviction*, a third inequality, which is no other than the variation determined six centuries later by Tycho Brahe." [2]

Under the Fâtimides of Egypt, Cairo had become a new intellectual and scientific centre. Here flourished, in the reigns

[1] To 'Azud ud-Dowla (Malik Fanâkhusrû) Bagdad owed several hospitals for the sick and refuges for orphans. He built magnificent mausoleums over the tombs of Ali and Husain at Najaf and Kerbela. He rendered navigable the river which flows by Shirâz by erecting the famous dvke called *Bend-emir*.

[2] Abu' Walâ died in A.H. 387 (A.C. 997).

of Azîz b'illâh [1] and Hâkim bi-amr-illâh, one of the master-
spirits of the age, Ibn Yunus,[2] the inventor of the pendulum
and the measurement of time by its oscillations. He is, however, famous for his great work named after his patron and
sovereign, *Zîj-ul-Akbar-al-Hâkimi*, which soon displaced the
work of Claudius Ptolemy. It was reproduced among the
Persians by the astronomer-poet Omar Khayyâm (1079) ;
among the Greeks, in the Syntax of Chrysococca ; among the
Mongols by Nasîr ud-dîn Tûsi, in the *Zîj-îl-Khâni* ; and
among the Chinese, in the astronomy of Co-Cheou-king in 1280 ;
and thus what is attributed to the ancient civilisation of China
is only a borrowed light from the Moslems.[3]

Ibn Yunus died in 1009, and his discoveries were continued
by Ibn un-Nabdi, who lived in Cairo in 1040, and Hasan ibn
Haitham, commonly called in Europe Alhazen, and famous for
the discovery of atmospheric refraction. He flourished about
the end of the eleventh century, and was a distinguished
astronomer and optician. He was born in Spain, but resided
chiefly in Egypt. He is best known in Europe by his works
on optics, one of which has been translated into Latin by
Risner. He corrected the Greek misconception as to the
nature of vision, and demonstrated for the first time that the
rays of light come from external objects to the eye, and do not
issue forth from the eye, and impinge on external things. He
determined the retina as the seat of vision, and proved that the
impressions made upon it were conveyed along the optic nerves
to the brain. He explained the phenomena of a single vision
by the formation of visual images on symmetrical portions of
the two retinas. He discovered that the refraction of light
varies with the density of the atmosphere, and that atmospheric
density again varies with the height. He explained accurately
and clearly how in consequence of this refraction, astral bodies
are seen before they have actually risen and after they have
set, and demonstrated that the beautiful phenomenon of

---

[1] 'Azîz b'illâh was one of the greatest sovereigns Egypt ever had. " He
loved his people as they loved him." He was married to a Christian lady,
whose brothers, Jeremiah and Arvenius, held the posts of patriarchs, one of
Jerusalem and the other of Alexandria. Both of them belonged to the
orthodox or *melkite* sect.

[2] See Appendix III.   [3] Sédillot.

twilight was due to the effect of atmospheric refraction combined with the reflecting action of the air upon the course of the rays of light. In his book called the *Balance of Wisdom* he discusses dynamical principles, generally supposed to be the monopoly of modern science. He describes minutely the connection between the weight of the atmosphere and its density, and how material objects vary in weight in a rare and in a dense atmosphere. He discusses the submergence of floating bodies, and the force with which they rise to the surface when immersed in light or heavy media ; he fully understands the principle of gravitation, and recognises gravity as a force. He knows correctly the relation between the velocities, spaces, and times of falling bodies, and has very distinct ideas of capillary attraction.[1]

In Spain the same activity of mind was at work from the Pyrenees to the Straits : Seville, Cordova, Granada, Murcia, Toledo, and other places possessed their public libraries and colleges, where they gave free instruction in science and letters. Of Cordova, an English writer speaks thus : " Beautiful as were the palaces and gardens of Cordova, her claims to admiration in higher matters were no less strong. The mind was as lovely as the body. Her professors and teachers made her the centre of European culture ; students would come from all parts of Europe to study under her famous doctors, and even the nun Hroswitha far away in her Saxon convent of Gaudersheim, when she told of the martyrdom of Eulogius, could not refrain from singing the praises of Cordova, ' the brightest splendour of the world.' Every branch of science was seriously studied there, and medicine received more and greater additions by the discoveries of the doctors and surgeons of Andalusia than it had gained during all the centuries that had elapsed since the days of Galen. . . . Astronomy, geography, chemistry, natural history, all were studied with ardour at Cordova ; and as for the graces of literature there never was a time in Europe when poetry became so much the speech of everybody—when people

[1] The annalist 'Ayni says that at this period the public library of Cairo contained over two million books, of which six thousand treated exclusively of mathematics and astronomy. I have only mentioned a few of the names among the thousands of mathematicians and physicists who flourished during this epoch, when the scientific spirit of Islâm was at its zenith.

of all ranks composed those Arabic verses which perhaps suggested models for the ballads and canzonettes of the Spanish minstrels and the troubadours of Provence and Italy. No speech or address was complete without some scrap of verse, improvised on the spur of the moment, by the speaker or quoted by memory from some famous poet." [1] To these we may add the words of Renan : " The taste for science and literature had, by the tenth century, established, in this privileged corner of the world, a toleration of which modern times hardly offer us an example. Christians, Jews, and Musulmans spoke the same tongue, sang the same songs, participated in the same literary and scientific studies. All the barriers which separated the various peoples were effaced ; all worked with one accord in the work of a common civilisation. The mosques of Cordova, where the students could be counted by thousands, became the active centres of philosophical and scientific studies." [2]

The first observatory in Europe was built by the Arabs. The Giralda, or tower of Seville, was erected under the superintendence of the great mathematician Jâbir ibn Afiâh in 1190 A.C. for the observation of the heavens. Its fate was not a little characteristic. After the expulsion of the Moors, it was turned into a belfry, the Spaniards not knowing what else to do with it !

Omar ibn Khaldûn, Ya'kûb ibn Târik, Muslimah al-Maghr'ibi, and the famous Averroes (Abu'l Walîd Mohammed ibn Rushd) are some of the physicists whom we may mention here. Nor was Western Africa inactive during this period : Ceuta and Tangier, Fez, and Morocco, rivalled Cordova, Seville, and Granada ; their colleges sent out able professors, and numerous learned works testified to the indefatigable ardour of the Moslem mind in all departments of learning.

The beginning of the eleventh century saw a great change in the political condition of Central Asia. The rise of

[1] Stanley Lane-Poole, *The Moors in Spain*, p. 144. For a full account of Cordova, see *Short History of the Saracens* (Macmillan), p. 515.

[2] Renan, *Averroes et Averroism*, p. 4. The golden age of literature and science in Spain was under Hakam *al-Mustansir b'illâh* who died in 976 A.C. The catalogue of his library consists of forty-four quartos. He employed agents in every quarter of the globe to procure for him, at any price, scientific works, ancient and modern. He paid to Abu'l Faraj al-Isphahâni 1000 dinars of gold for the first copy of his celebrated Anthology (*Kitâb ul-Aghâni*).

Mahmûd,[1] the great Ghaznavide conqueror, *Yemîn ud-Dowla* and *Amîn ul-Millat*, " right hand of the empire " and " custodian of the Faith," brought Transoxiana, Afghânistân, and Persia under the sovereignty of Ghazni. He collected round him a body of scholars and litterateurs who shed a glorious lustre on his brilliant reign. Attached to the renovated " orthodoxy " of al-Asha'ri, and consequently piously inimical to the rationalistic school of thinkers, chary in his munificence to the poets who made his name famous in the annals of the world, he yet had the genius to perceive the merits of men like *Abû Raihân Mohammed ibn Ahmed* al-Beirûnî, philosopher, mathematician, and geographer. Firdousi, the prince of poets, Dakîki, and Unsuri. Al-Beirûnî's mind was encyclopædic. His work on astronomy, entitled after his patron Sultan Masû'd,[2] *al-Kânûn-al-Mas'ûdi, Canon Masudicus*, is a monument of learning and research. He travelled into India, and studied the language of the Hindus, their sciences, their philosophy and literature, and embodied his observations in a work which has recently been furnished to us in an English garb. The philosophical and scientific, not to say sympathetic, spirit which animates al-Beirûnî in the treatment of his subject is in marked contrast to the mode still in vogue among Western nations, and serves as an index to the intellectual character of Islâm. The Ἰνδικα[3] of al-Beirûnî shows the extent to which the Moslems had utilised the treasures of Greek learning, and turned them to fruitful purposes. Besides these two great works, he wrote on mathematics, chronology, mathematical geography, physics, and chemistry.

Al-Beirûnî communicated to the Hindus the knowledge of the Bagdadian school in return for their notions and traditions. He found among them the remains of Greek science, which had been transported to India in the early centuries of the Christian era, or perhaps earlier, during the existence of the Græco-Bactrian dynasties. The Hindus do not seem to have possessed any advanced astronomical science of their own ; for, had it

---

[1] A.C. 996-1030.   [2] The son and successor of the Conqueror.

[3] *Fi't Tahkîk mâ li'l Hind* ; see *Short History of the Saracens* (Macmillan), p. 463. Another remarkable work of his is the *Âsâr ul-Bâkièh* or the Vestiges of the Past, translated into English by Dr. Sachau.

been otherwise, we doubtless would have heard about it, as Sédillot rightly observes, from the Greek writers of the times of Alexander and the Seleucidæ. They, like the Chinese, borrowed most of their scientific ideas from foreign sources, and modified them according to their national characteristics.

Under the successors of Mahmûd learning and arts flourished abundantly. The rise of the Seljukides and their grand munificence towards scholarship and science rivalled that of the golden days of the Abbaside rule. Tughril, Alp Arslân, Malik Shah, and Sanjar were not only remarkable for the greatness of their power, the clear comprehension of what constituted the welfare of their subjects, but were equally distinguished for their intellectual gifts and ardent enthusiasm in the cause of learning. *Jalâl ud-dîn* Malik Shah [1] and his vizier, Khwâja Hasan *Nizâm ul-Mulk*,[2] collected round them a galaxy of astronomers, poets, scholars, and historians. The astronomical observations conducted in his reign by a body of savants, with Omar Khayyâm and Abdur Rahman al-Hâzini at their head, led to the reform of the Calendar which preceded the Gregorian by six hundred years and is said by a competent authority to be even more exact.[3] The era which was introduced upon these observations was named after Malik Shah, the *Jalâlian*.

The destructive inroads of the Christian marauders who called themselves Crusaders was disastrous to the cause of learning and science in Western Asia and Northern Africa. Barbarous savages, hounded to rapine and slaughter by crazy priests, they knew neither mercy for the weakness of sex or age, nor the value of letters or arts. They destroyed the splendid library of Tripoli without compunction ; they reduced to ashes many of the glorious centres of Saracenic culture and arts. Christian Europe has held up to obloquy the apocryphal destruction of the Alexandrian library, which had already been burned in the time of Julius Cæsar, but it has no word of blame for the crimes of her Crusaders five centuries later. The calamities inflicted by the Crusaders were lasting in their effect ; and in spite of the endeavours of Saladin and his sons to restore the intellectual life of Syria, it has remained dead from that day to this.

[1] 1073-1092 A.C.   [2] *i.e.* the Administrator of the Empire.   [3] Sédillot.

In the interval which elapsed between the rise of Mahmûd and the fall of Bagdad, there flourished a number of philosophers and scientists, among whom shine the great Avicenna (*Abû Ali* Husain Ibn-Sîna),[1] Fath ibn Nâbeghah Khâkâni,[2] Mubashshar ibn Ahmed,[3] and his son Mohammed.[4]

The eruption of the Mongols upon the Saracenic world was not like the invasion of the Roman empire by the northern barbarians. These had proceeded slowly ; and in their comparatively gradual progress towards the heart of the empire they had become partially softened, and had to some extent cast off their pristine ferocity. The case was otherwise with the hordes of the devastator Chengîz. They swept like overwhelming torrents over Western Asia. Wherever they went they left misery and desolation.[5] Their barbarous campaigns and their savage slaughters put an end for a time to the intellectual development of Asia. But the moment the wild savages adopted the religion of the Prophet of Arabia a change came over them. From the destroyers of the seats of learning and arts they became the founders of academies and the protectors of the learned. Sultan Khoda-Bendah (Uljaitû-Khan), sixth in descent from Chengîz, was distinguished for his attainments and his patronage of the sciences. But the fearful massacres which the barbarians had committed among the settled and cultured population of the towns destroyed most of the gifted classes, with the result that, though the great cities like Bokhâra and Samarcand rose again into splendour, they became, nevertheless, the seats of a narrower culture, more casuistical and theological than before. And yet the Mongols protected philosophers like Nasîr ud-dîn Tûsi, Muwayyad ud-dîn al-Orezi of Damascus, Fakhr ud-dîn al-Marâghi, Mohi ud-dîn al-Maghribi, Ali Shah al-Bokhâri, and many others. The successors of Hulâku tried thus to restore to Islâm what their ancestor had destroyed. Whilst the Mongols in Persia were employed in making some amends to civilisation, Kublai Khan transported to China the learning of the Arabs. Co-

---

[1] Died in 1037 A.C.   [2] Died in 1082 A.C.
[3] Died in 1135 A.C.   [4] Died in 1193 A.C.
[5] For a full account of the havoc and ruin caused by the Tartars, see *Short History of the Saracens*, pp. 391-400.

Cheou-king received in 1280 from Jamâl ud-dîn the tables of Ibn-Yunus, and appropriated them for Chinese purposes.

Ibn-Shâthir, who lived in the reign of Mohammed ibn Kalâun, the Mameluke sovereign of Egypt, developed still further the mathematical and astronomical sciences.   And now arose on the eastern horizon the comet-like personality of Timûr. " From his throne in Samarcand this Titan of the fourteenth century called into being the greatest empire ever seen in Asia, and seemed to extinguish in his one resistless will the immemorial antagonism of Irân and Tûran."   He was a patron of science and poetry, himself fond of the society of the scholars and artists of his day, an author, as well as a legislator of no mean order.[1] Magnificent colleges, splendid mosques, vast libraries, testified to the taste for letters of this remarkable man. His vast system of colonisation filled the great cities of Eastern Asia, especially Samarcand, with the splendour of all the arts and sciences known to the West.   Timûr established " the most brilliant empire known to the history of Islâm, except that of the Ommeyyads in Spain, and that of the first Abbasides in Arabistan."   Jâmi, master of sciences ; Suhailî, translator of Pilpay ; Ali Shèr Ameer, were some of the men who shed lustre on the reigns of his successors.   The college founded by his consort, Bibi Khânam, and known by her name, still strikes the observer as one of the most imposing and most beautiful products of Saracenic architecture.   Timûr's son, Shah Rukh Mirza, imitated his father in the cultivation and patronage of arts and letters.   His peaceful reign of nearly half a century was remarkable for high intellectual culture and scientific study.   When he transported his government from Samarcand to Herat, the former city lost none of its splendour.   Ulugh Beg, his son, charged with the government of Transoxiana, maintained the literary and scientific glories of Samarcand. Himself an astronomer of a high rank, he presided at the observations which have immortalised his name.   The tables in which those observations were embodied complete the cycle of Arabian thought.   Ulugh Beg is separated by only a century and a half from Kepler, the founder of modern astronomy.

---

[1] The *Malfûzât-i-Timûri* (" The Institutes of Timûr ") are couched in the style of the old Assyrian and Kyânian monarchs.

It was, however, not astronomy only which the Moslems cultivated and improved. Every branch of higher mathematics bears traces of their genius. The Greeks are said to have invented algebra, but among them, as Oelsner has justly remarked, it was confined to furnishing amusement " for the plays of the goblet." The Moslems applied it to higher purposes, and thus gave it a value hitherto unknown. Under Mâmûn they had discovered the equations of the second degree, and very soon after they developed the theory of quadratic equations and the binomial theorem. Not only algebra, geometry, and arithmetic, but optics and mechanics made remarkable progress in the hands of the Moslems. They invented spherical trigonometry ; they were the first to apply algebra to geometry, to introduce the tangent, and to substitute the sine for the arc in trigonometrical calculations. Their progress in mathematical geography was no less remarkable. The works of Ibn-Haukal, of Makrîzî, al-Istakhri, Mas'ûdi, al-Beirûnî, al-Kumi and al-Idrîsî, Kazwînî, Ibn ul-Wardi, and Abu'l Fedâ, show what the Saracens attained in this department of science, called by them the *rasm-ul-arz.* At a time when Europe firmly believed in the flatness of the earth, and was ready to burn any foolhardy person who thought otherwise, the Arabs taught geography by globes.

The physical sciences were as diligently cultivated. The method of *experimentation* was substituted for theorising ; and the crude ideas of the ancients were developed into positive sciences.[1] Chemistry, botany, geology, natural history, among others occupied the attention and exercised the energies of the ablest men.

Chemistry, as a science, is unquestionably the invention of the Moslems. Abû Mûsa Jâbir (the Geber of Christian writers)[2] is the true father of modern chemistry. " His name is memorable in chemistry, since it marks an epoch in that science of equal importance to that of Priestley and

---

[1] Humboldt calls the Arabs the real founders of the physical sciences.

[2] Abû Mûsa Jâbir ibn Hayyân was a native of Tarsus. Ibn Khallikân says " Jâbir compiled a work of two thousand pages in which he inserted the problems of his master (the Imâm) Ja'far as-Sâdik which formed five hundred treatises " ; see also the *Târîkh-ul-Hukama.*

IX.   THE LITERARY AND SCIENTIFIC SPIRIT   385

Lavoisier." He was followed by others, whose originality and industry, profoundness of knowledge, and keenness of observation, evoke the astonishment of students, and make them look with regret upon the inertness of the latter-day Moslem.

The science of medicine and the art of surgery, the best index to a nation's genius and a severe test to the intellectual spirit of a faith, were developed to the highest degree. Medicine had undoubtedly attained a high degree of excellence among the Greeks, but the Arabs carried it far beyond the stage in which their predecessors in the work of civilisation had left it, and brought it close to the modern standard. We can give here but a small conception of the work done by the Saracens for several centuries in this department of human study, and in the development of the natural sciences.

The study of medical substances, the idea of which struck Dioscorides in the Alexandrian school, is, in its scientific form, a creation of the Arabs. They invented chemical pharmacy, and were the first founders of those institutions which are now called ·dispensaries.[1] They established in every city public hospitals, called Dâr ush-Shifa, "the house of cure," or Mâristân (an abbreviation of bimâristan, "the patient's house") and maintained them at the expense of the State.

The names of the Arab physicians in the biographical dictionary of Abû Usaibi'a fill a volume. Abû Bakr Mohammed ibn Zakaria ar-Râzi (known to mediæval Europe as Rhazes), who flourished in the beginning of the tenth century,[2] Ali ibn-Abbâs,[3] Avicenna (Abû Ali Husain ibn-Sîna), Albucasis (Abû'l

---

[1] The persons in charge of the dispensaries were under the control of Government. The price and quality of medicine were strictly regulated. Many dispensaries were maintained by the State. There were regular examinations for physicians and pharmacists, at which licences were given to passed candidates. The licence-holders were alone entitled to practise. Compare Kremer and Sédillot.

[2] This great physician, surnamed Râzi, from the place of his birth, Rai (ancient Rhages), filled successively the office of principal of the public hospitals at Rai, Jund-Shapur, and Bagdad. He wrote the Hâwî, which Sédillot calls " un corpus medical fort estimé." His treatises on smallpox and measles have been consulted by the physicians of all nations. He introduced the use of minoratives, invented the seton, and discovered the nerve of the larynx. He wrote two hundred medical works, some of which were published in Venice in 1510. Ar-Râzi died in A.H. 311 (A.C. 923-4).

[3] Ali ibn-Abbâs flourished fifty years later than Rhazes. He published a medical work, consisting of twenty volumes, on the theory and practice of

Kâsim Khalaf ibn Abbâs), Aven-Zoar [1] (Abû Merwân ibn Abdul Malik *ibn Zuhr*), Averroes (Abu'l Walîd Mohammed *ibn Rushd*),[2] and Aben-Bethar (Abdullah ibn Ahmed ibn Ali *al-Beithâr*, the *veterinary*),[3] are some of the most brilliant and most distinguished physicians who have left an enduring impression on the world of thought. Albucasis was not only a physician but a surgeon of the first rank. He performed the most difficult surgical operations in his own and the obstetrical department. In operations on women, we are informed by him, in which considerations of delicacy intervened, the services of properly instructed women were secured. The ample description he has left of the surgical instruments employed in his time gives an idea of the development of surgery among the Arabs.[4] Avicenna was unquestionably the most gifted man of his age ; a universalist in genius, and encyclopædic in his writings. A philosopher, mathematician, astronomer, poet, and physician, he has left his influence impressed on two continents, and well deserves the title of Aristotle of the East. In spite of patristic jealousy, his philosophic ideas exercised an undisputed sway for several centuries in the schools of the East as well as of Europe. Avicenna is commonly known in Asia as *the Sheikh par excellence*.

medicine, which he dedicated to the Buyide Ameer 'Azud ud-dowla. This work was translated into Latin in 1227, and printed at Lyons in 1523 by Michel Capella. Ali ibn-Abbâs corrected many of the errors of Hippocrates and Galen.

[1] Ibn Zuhr or Aven-Zoar was one of the most distinguished physicians of his age. Born at Penaflor, he entered, after finishing his medical and scientific studies, the service of Yusuf bin Tâshfin, the great Almoravide monarch of Africa, who covered the rising physician with honours and riches. Ibn Zuhr joined, like Albucasis, the practice of medicine with surgery. He was the first to conceive the idea of bronchotomy, with exact indications of the luxations and fractures, and discovered several important maladies with their treatment. His son followed in his father's steps and was the chief surgeon and physician of Yusuf bin Tâshfin's army.

[2] Averroes was the Avicenna of the West. His life and writings have been given to the world by Renan. He was a contemporary of Ibn Zuhr, Ibn Bâja, and Ibn Tufail. Of Averroes and his contemporaries we shall have to speak in the next chapter.

Besides these may be mentioned Abu'l Hasan ibn Tilmîz, author of *Almalihi* ; Abû Ja'far Ahmed ibn Mohammed at-Tâlib, who wrote on pleurisy, etc. ; and Hibatulla.

[3] Al-Beithâr travelled all over the East to find medicinal herbs, on which he wrote an exhaustive treatise. The Arab physicians introduced the use of the rhubarb, cassia, senna, camphor, the pulp of the tamarind (*tamr—* تمر *-hindi*—Indian date), etc.

[4] In lithotomy he was equal to the foremost surgeons of modern times.

He was born in the year 980 A.C. at a village called Afshanah, in Transoxiana, of which place his father was the governor. He finished his medical studies in Bokhâra at the age of eighteen, when commenced an extraordinary political and philosophical career. His tenacity in refusing the liberal offers of Mahmûd the Conqueror to join his service led to his expulsion from the Ghaznavide dominions. He soon became the vizier of Shams ud-dowla, Ameer of Hamadân, and afterwards of 'Ala ud-dowla, Ameer of Isphahân, where he pursued his scientific and philosophical studies, and wrote his great works, the *Kânûn* and the *Arjûza*, afterwards the foundation of all medical knowledge.

The Greeks possessed crude notions of anatomy, and their knowledge of pharmacy was restricted within a very narrow compass. The Moslems developed both anatomy and pharmacy into positive sciences. The wide extent of the empire enabled researches and investigations in every quarter of the globe, with the result that they enriched the existing pharmacopœia by innumerable and invaluable additions. Botany they advanced far beyond the state in which it had been left by Dioscorides, and augmented the herbalogy of the Greeks by the addition of two thousand plants. Regular gardens existed both in Cordova and Bagdad, at Cairo and Fez for the education of pupils, where discourses were delivered by the most learned in the sciences.

Ad-Damîrî (Aldemri) is famous in the Moslem world for his history of animals—a work which forestalled Buffon by seven hundred years.

Geology was cultivated under the name of '*Ilm-i-Tashrîh-ul-Arz*, " the science of the anatomy of the earth."

The superiority of the Moslems in architecture requires no comment, for the glorious remains of Saracenic art in the East and in the West still evoke the admiration of the modern world. Their religion has been charged with their backwardness in painting and sculpture, but it must be borne in mind that the prohibition contained in the Koran is similar to the Levitical commandment. It was but a continuation of the Mosaic Law, which had so effectually suppressed the making of " graven images " among the Jews, and its signification rests upon the inveterate idolatry of the pre-Islâmite Arabs. To the early Moslems, therefore, painting and statuary were odious and unlawful, as emblematic of heathenism, and this deeply implanted iconoclasm undoubtedly saved them from relapsing, as other nations had done, into idolatry. But with the gradual development of the primitive commonwealth into a civilised and cultured empire, and with the ascendency of learning and science, the Moslems grasped the spirit of the prohibition, and cast off the fetters of a narrow literalism. No doubt the spirit of rationalism, which so deeply influenced the early Abbaside and Spanish Caliphs, was the actual cause of the impetus given by them to art. Hence throughout the Moslem world a taste for painting and sculpture arose simultaneously with the progress of literature and science. The palaces of the Caliphs, the mansions of the sovereigns who followed in their footsteps, and the houses of the grandees were decorated with pictures and sculptures.

To the Prophet's prohibition of graven images or painting in mosques the world is indebted for the art of arabesque— which possesses such peculiar charm in the decoration of Oriental buildings, and which has been widely adopted by Western art. With the gradual enlightenment of the Moslems by contact with the arts of other nations, animals and flowers, birds and fruits were introduced into arabesque ; but the figures of animated beings were throughout absolutely inter- dicted in the decoration of places of worship. In purity of form and simplicity of outline, in the gracefulness of design and perfection of symmetry, in the harmony of every detail, in the exquisiteness of finish and sublimity of conception, Moslem architecture is equal to any in the world, and the chaste and graceful ornamentation with which so many of the grandest monuments are adorned, indicates a refinement of taste and culture surpassing any of the great monumental relics of ancient Greece or modern Europe. Another branch of Moslem decorative art is that of ornamental writing, which is so often utilised with remarkable effect in the adornment of mosques, mausolea, and palaces, where whole chapters of the Koran are carved or inlaid round domes and minarets, doors and arches, testifying to the same religious earnestness, yet in a purely monotheistic spirit, as the pictures of saints and martyrs which decorate Christian churches.

Before the promulgation of Islâm the profession of music among the Arabs was confined to the slaves of both sexes imported from Syria and Persia, or to the class of hetairai called *Kyân*. The Prophet had discountenanced, for obvious moral reasons, the songs and dances of these degraded women. But under the Abbasides and the Spanish Arab kings, when music was elevated to the rank of a science, and its cultivation was recognised as an art, a love for music spread among all classes of society.   A large literature grew up on the subject ; songs were collected and classified according to their melodies and keys, and the musical instruments of the ancients were improved and new ones invented.   The sharp conflict between Rationalism and Patristicism, between Idealism and Literalism, which marked the middle of the twelfth century, drove this sweetest of arts back into the arms of the servile classes or forced it to seek a refuge in the chapels of the dervishes.

A large general literature existed on the subject of commerce, agriculture, handicraft and manufacture, the latter including every conceivable subject, from porcelain to weapons of war.

In historical research the Moslems have not been behind any other nation, ancient or modern.   At first attention was devoted chiefly to the history of the Prophet, but soon the primitive idea widened into a broad conception.   Archæology, geography, and ethnology were included in history, and the greatest minds applied themselves to the pursuit of this captivating branch of study.   Between the simple work of Ibn-Ishâk and the universal history of Ibn-Khaldûn there is a great difference, but the intervening space is occupied by a host of writers, the product of whose labours supplies some index to the intellectual activity of the Saracenic nations under the inspiration of Islâm.

Balâzuri, who died in 279 A.H. (A.C. 892), was born at Bagdad, where he lived and worked.   His " Conquest of the Countries " (*Futûh ul-Buldân*) is written in admirable style, and marks a distinct advance of the historical spirit.

Hamadâni, who flourished towards the end of the third and the beginning of the fourth century of the Hegira, gave to the world a comprehensive history of Southern Arabia, with an account of its tribes, its numerous remains of interest, with explanations of their inscriptions, as well as the ethnography and geography of Yemen. It is, however, in the monumental works of Mas'ûdi, of al-Beirûni, of Ibn ul-Athîr, of Tabarî, of Ibn-Khaldûn, called by Mohl the Montesquieu of Islâm, of Makrîzî, Makkari, Abu'lfedâ, Nuwairi, and Mirkhond that the mental vigour of the Moslem races in this department of knowledge is found in full play. These men were not specialists only; they were encyclopædists—philosophers, mathematicians, geographers, as well as historians. Mas'ûdi was a native of Bagdad, but by descent a Northern Arab, who in his early youth travelled and saw the greater part of the Mohammedan world. He first went to India, visited Multan and Mansûra, then travelled over Persia and Kerman, again went to India, remained for some time at Cambay (Kambâja) and the Deccan, went to Ceylon, sailed from there to Kambalu (Madagascar), and went from there to Oman, and perhaps even reached the Indo-Chinese Peninsula and China. He had travelled far in Central Asia, and reached the Caspian Sea. After finishing his travels, he lived for some time in Tiberias and Antioch, and afterwards took up his abode in Basrah, where he first published his great work, called the *Murûj-uz-Zahab* (مروج الذهب). Afterwards he removed to Fostat (old Cairo), where he published the *Kitâb ut-Tanbîh*, and later the *Mirât-uz-Zamân*, or the *Mirror of the Times*, a voluminous work, which is only partially preserved.[1] In the *Murûj-uz-Zahab* (the " Golden Meadows ") " he tells the rich experiences of his life in the amiable and cheerful manner of a man who had seen various lands, experienced life in all its phases, and who takes pleasure, not only in instructing, but in amusing his reader. Without burdening us with the names of the authorities, without losing himself in long explanations, he delights in giving prominence to that which strikes him as wonderful, rare, and interesting, and to portray people and manners with conciseness and anecdotic skill."

---

[1] I am told that the Library in Vienna contains a historical work by the same author consisting of some thirty volumes which bears the name of the *Akhbâr-uz-Zamân*. Perhaps this is the same work as *Mirât-us-Zamân*.

Tabari (Abû Ja'far Mohammed ibn Jarîr), surnamed the Livy of the Arabs, who died in Bagdad in 922 A.C., brought his work down to the year 302 of the Hegira (914 A.C.). It was continued to the end of the twelfth century by al-Makîn or Elmacin.

Ibn ul-Athîr (ابن الاثير), surnamed *Izz ud-din,* "glory of religion," was a native of Jazîreh-banî-Omar, in Irâk, but resided chiefly at Mosul, where his house was the resort of the most distinguished scholars and savants of the time. His universal history, known as the *al-Kâmil,* which ends with the year 1231 A.C., may be compared with the best works of modern Europe.

Makrîzî [1] (Taki ud-din Ahmed) was a contemporary of Ibn-Khaldûn. His works on Egypt furnish a vivid picture of the political, religious, social, commercial, archæological, and administrative condition of the country.

Abu'lfedâ, whom we have already mentioned as a geographer, was the Prince of Hamah at the commencement of the fourteenth century. Distinguished alike in the pursuit of arms as in letters, gifted with eminent qualities, he occupies a prominent place among the scholars and scientists of the East. The portion of his great work which deals with the political and literary history of Islâm, and its relations to the Byzantines from the eighth to the twelfth century, is extremely valuable.

Ibn Khaldûn flourished in the fourteenth century of the Christian era. Born in Tunis in 1332, he was in the midst of all the revolutions of which Africa was the theatre in the fourteenth century. His magnificent history is preceded by a Prolegomena, in itself a store-house of information and philosophical dissertation. In the Prolegomena he traces the origin of society, the development of civilisation, the causes which led to the rise and fall of kingdoms and dynasties; and discusses, among other questions, the influence of climate on the formation of a nation's character. He died in the year 1406 A.C.

The Arabs invented the mariner's compass, and voyaged to all parts of the world in quest of knowledge or in the pursuit of commerce. They established colonies in Africa, far to the south in the Indian Archipelago, on the coasts of India, and on the Malayan Peninsula. Even China opened her barred gates

[1] Died in 1442 A.C.

to Moslem colonists and mercenaries. They discovered the Azores, and, it is even surmised, penetrated as far as America. Within the confines of the ancient continents they gave an unprecedented and almost unparalleled impulse in every direction to human industry. The Prophet had inculcated labour as a duty ; he had given the impress of piety to industrial pursuits ; he had recommended commerce and agriculture as meritorious in the sight of the Lord. These precepts had their natural result ; the merchants, the traders, the industrial classes in general, were treated with respect ; and governors, generals, and savants disdained not to call themselves by the title of their professions. The peace and security with which caravans travelled the empire ; the perfect safety of the roads ; the cisterns, and tanks, and reservoirs, and rest-houses which existed everywhere along the routes—all aided in the rapid development of commerce and trade, and arts and manufactures.

The Arabs covered the countries where they settled with networks of canals. To Spain they gave the system of irrigation by flood-gates, wheels, and pumps. Whole tracts of land that now lie waste and barren were covered with olive groves, and the environs of Seville alone, under Moslem rule, contained several thousand oil-factories. They introduced the staple products, rice, sugar, cotton, and nearly all the fine garden and orchard fruits, together with many less important plants, such as ginger, saffron, myrrh, etc. They opened up the mines of copper, sulphur, mercury, and iron. They established the culture of silk, the manufacture of paper and other textile fabrics ; of porcelain, earthenware, iron, steel, and leather. The tapestries of Cordova, the woollen stuffs of Murcia, the silks of Granada, Almeria, and Seville, the steel and gold work of Toledo, the paper of Salibah were sought all over the world. The ports of Malaga, Carthagena, Barcelona, and Cadiz were vast commercial emporiums for export and import. In the days of their prosperity the Spanish Arabs maintained a merchant navy of more than a thousand ships. They had factories and representatives on the Danube. With Constantinople they possessed a great trade, which ramified from the Black Sea and the eastern shores of the Mediterranean into the interior of Asia, and reached the ports of India and China

and extended along the African coast as far as Madagascar.
" In the midst of the tenth century, when Europe was about
in the same condition that Caffraria is now, enlightened Moors,
like Abul Cassem, were writing treatises on the principles of
trade and commerce." In order to supply an incentive to
commercial enterprise, and to further the impulse to travel,
geographical registers, gazetteers, and itineraries were published under the authority of Government, containing minute
descriptions of the places to which they related, with particulars of the routes and other necessary matters. Travellers
like Ibn-i-Batûta visited foreign lands in quest of information,
and wrote voluminous works on the people of those countries,
on their fauna and flora, their mineral products, their climatic
and physical features, with astonishing perspicacity and keenness of observation.

The love of learning and arts was by no means confined to
one sex. The culture and education of the women proceeded
on parallel lines with that of the men, and women were as keen
in the pursuit of literature and as devoted to science as men.
They had their own colleges ; [1] they studied medicine and
jurisprudence, lectured on rhetoric, ethics, and *belles-lettres*,
and participated with the stronger sex in the glories of a
splendid civilisation. The wives and daughters of magnates
and sovereigns spent their substance in founding colleges and
endowing universities, in establishing hospitals for the sick,
refuges for the homeless, the orphan, and the widow.[2]

The division and jealousy of the Arab tribes, which had
prevented the assimilation and fusion of their several dialects,
had nevertheless conduced to the enrichment of the national
language as spoken in Hijâz, and the annual conflux of people

---

[1] One well-known institution of this kind was established in Cairo in 684 A.H.
by the daughter of the Mameluke Sultan Malik Tâher.

[2] Zubaida, the wife of Hârûn, founded several such refuges ; and the hospital
built by the wife of 'Azud ud-dowla rivalled her husband's. The daughter of
Malik Ashraf, known as the Khâtûn, erected a splendid college at Damascus.
Another college was founded by Zamurud Khâtûn, wife of Nâsir ud-dowla of
Hems.
Many Moslem ladies were distinguished in poetry. Fâtima, the Prophet's
daughter, holds a high rank among poets. So does the daughter of Aurangzeb,
Zêb un-nisâ, surnamed *Makhfî*. When Urquhart travelled in Turkey, three
of the most celebrated living poets were ladies, and one of them, Perishek
Khânam, acted as private secretary to Sultan Mustafa.

at Okâz, with the periodical contest of the poets, had imparted to it a regularity and polish. But it was the Koran—" a book by the aid of which the Arabs conquered a world greater than that of Alexander the Great, greater than that of Rome, and in as many tens of years as the latter had wanted hundreds to accomplish her conquests ; by the aid of which they alone of all the Shemites came to Europe as kings, whither the Phœnicians had come as tradesmen, and the Jews as fugitives or captives ; came to Europe to hold up, together with these fugitives, the light to humanity ;—they alone, while darkness lay around, to raise up the wisdom and knowledge of Hellas from the dead, to teach philosophy, medicine, astronomy, and the golden art of song to the West as to the East, to stand at the cradle of modern science, and to cause us late epigoni for ever to weep over the day when Granada fell," [1]—it was this book which fixed and preserved for ever the Arabic tongue in all its purity. The simple grandeur of its diction, the chaste elegance of its style, the variety of its imageries, the rapid transitions, like flashes of lightning, which show the moralist teaching, the philosopher theosophising, the injured patriot denouncing in fervent expressions the immorality and degradation of his people, and withal the heavenly Father calling back through His servant His erring children,—all mark its unique character among religious records. And the awe and veneration with which the greatest poets of the day listened to its teachings, show how deeply it must have moved the people. Delivered at different times,—in moments of persecution and anguish, or of energetic action, or enunciated for purposes of practical guidance,—there is yet a vitality, an earnestness and energy in every word, which differentiates it from all other Scriptures. Lest it be thought we are biassed in our opinion, we give the words of the great orientalist whom we have already quoted : " Those grand accents of joy and sorrow, of love, and valour, and passion, of which but faint echoes strike on our ears now, were full-toned at the time of Mohammed ; and he had not merely to rival the illustrious of the illustrious, but excel them ; to appeal to the superiority of what he said and sang as a very sign and proof of his mission . . . The poets

[1] Deutsch.

before him had sung of love . . .   Antara, himself the hero of
the most famous novel, sings of the ruin, around which ever
hover lovers' thoughts, of the dwelling of Abla, who is gone,
and her dwelling-place knows her not.   Mohammed sang none
of these.   No love-minstrelsy his, not the joys of this world,
nor sword nor camel, not jealousy or human vengeance, not
the glories of tribe or ancestors, nor the unmeaning, swiftly
and forever-extinguished existence of man, were his themes.
He preached *Islâm*.   And he preached it by rending the skies
above and tearing open the ground below, by adjuring heaven
and hell, the living and the dead."

Another great writer speaks of the Koran in the following
terms :   " If it is not poetry,—and it is hard to say whether it
be or not,—it is more than poetry.   It is not history, nor
biography.   It is not anthology, like the Sermon on the
Mount ;   nor metaphysical dialectics, like the Buddhist Sûtras ;
nor sublime homiletics like Plato's conferences of the wise
and foolish teachers.   It is a prophet's cry, Semitic to the core ;
yet of a meaning so universal and so timely that all the voices
of the age take it up, willing or unwilling, and it echoes over
palaces and deserts, over cities and empires, first kindling its
chosen hearts to world-conquest, then gathering itself up into
a reconstructive force that all the creative light of Greece and
Asia might penetrate the heavy gloom of Christian Europe,
when Christianity was but the Queen of Night." [1]

In general literature, embracing every phase of the human
intellect, ethics, metaphysics, logic, rhetoric, the Moslem
writers may be counted by hundreds.   In poetry, the fertility
of the Moslem mind has not been yet surpassed.   From Mutanabbi the Arab (not to go back to the poets who flourished in
the time of the Prophet) to Hâlî the Indian, there is an endless
succession of poets.   Mutanabbi flourished in the ninth century,
and enjoyed the patronage of Ameer Saif ud-dowla (Abu'l
Hasan Ali bin Hamdân).   He was followed by Ibn-Duraid,[2]
Abû-Ula,[3] Ibn Fâridh,[4] Tantarâni,[5] and others.   The Spanish
Arabs were nature's poets ;   they invented the different kinds
of poetry, which afterwards were adopted as models by the

---

[1] Johnson.   [2] Died in A.C. 933.   [3] Died in A.C. 1057.
[4] Died in A.C. 1255.   [5] Died in A.C. 1092.

Christian nations of southern Europe. Among the great poets
who flourished in Spain the name of Ahmed ibn Mohammed
(Abû-Omar)[1] is the most famous. We have already mentioned
the poets who lived under Mahmûd ; Firdousi, who brought
back to life the dead heroes of Irân, rivals the fame of the
sovereign whom first he praised and afterwards satirised.
Under the later Ghaznavides and the Seljukides flourished the
lyric poets Suzeni,[2] the creator of the Persian metrical system,
and Watwât ; the panegyrists Anwarî,[3] Khâkânî,[4] and Zahîr
Fâryâbi ; [5] the great mystics, Sanâî,[6] whose *Hadîka* is valued
wherever the Persian language is known and appreciated, and
Farîd ud-dîn 'Attâr ; [7] and the romancist Nizâmi, the immortal
bard of Khusrû and Shîrîn and of Alexander. Under the
Atâbegs, who rose to power on the decline of the Seljukides,
flourished the moralist Sa'di and the mystic Jalâl ud-din
Rûmi. Under Timûr lived the sweet singer Hâfiz (Shams
ud-dîn), called the Anacreon of Persia. These are but a very
few of the names famous in the realm of poetry. The pages
of Ibn-Khallikân, and of Lutf Ali Âzar [8] speak more eloquently
of the poetical genius of the Moslems.

Such were the glorious achievements of the Moslems in the
field of intellect ; and all was due to the teachings of one man.
Called by his voice from the abyss of barbarism and ignorance
in which they had hitherto dwelt, with little hope of the present,
with none of the future, the Arab went into the world, to
elevate and civilise. Afflicted humanity awoke into new life.
Whilst the barbarians of Europe, who had overturned an effete
empire, were groping in the darkness of ignorance and brutality,
the Moslems were building up a great civilisation. During
centuries of moral and intellectual desolation in Europe, Islâm
led the vanguard of progress. Christianity had established

[1] A.C. 1175, A.H. 569. [2] A.C. 1177, A.H. 573.

[3] Anwarî's panegyric on Sultan Sanjar is one of the finest poems in the
Persian language. The Hindustâni poet Sauda in the *Kasîda* in honour of
Âsaf ud-Dowla of Oudh has imitated Anwarî with great success.

[4] A.C. 1186, A.H. 582. [5] A.C 1201, A.H. 598.

[6] A.C. 1180, A.H. 576. [7] A.C. 1190, A.H. 586.

[8] The *Âtesh-Kadèh* (" Fire Temple ") of Lutf Ali Âzar is the lives of the
Persian poets from the earliest times, with specimens of their poetry.

itself on the throne of the Cæsars, but it had failed to regenerate the nations of the earth.   From the fourth century of the Christian era to the twelfth, the gloom that overshadowed Europe grew deeper and deeper.   During these ages of ferocious bigotry Ecclesiasticism barred every access through which the light of knowledge, humanity, or civilisation could enter.   But though jealously shut out from this land of fanaticism, the benignant influences of Islâmic culture in time made themselves felt in every part of Christendom.   From the schools of Salerno, of Bagdad, of Damascus, of Cordova, of Granada, of Malaga, the Moslems taught the world the gentle lessons of philosophy and the practical teachings of stern science.[1]

The first manifestation of Rationalism in the West occurred in the province most amenable to the power of Moslem civilisation. Ecclesiasticism crushed this fair flower with fire and with sword, and threw back the progress of the world for centuries. But the principles of Free Thought, so strongly impressed on Islâm, had communicated their vitality to Christian Europe. Abelard had felt the power of Averroes' genius, which was shedding its light over the whole of the Western world.   Abelard struck a blow for Free Thought which led to the eventual emancipation of Christendom from the bondage of Ecclesiasticism.   Avenpace and Averroes were the precursors of Descartes, Hobbes, and Locke.

The influence of Abelard and of his school soon penetrated into England.   Wycliffe's originality of thought and freedom of spirit took their rise from the bold conceptions of the former thinkers.   The later German reformers, deriving their notions on one side from the iconoclasts of Constantinople, and on the other from the movements of the Albigenses and the Wycliffites, completed the work which had been commenced by others under foreign rationalistic influence.

While Christian Europe had placed learning under the ban of persecution ; while the Vicar of Christ set the example of stifling the infant lispings of Free Thought ; while the priests

[1] The impetus which Islâm gave to the intellectual development of mankind is evidenced by the fact that the Arabs were joined in the race for progress by members of nationalities which had hitherto lain absolutely dormant.   Islâm quickened the pulse of humanity and awakened new life in communities which were either dead or dying ; see Appendix III.

led the way in consigning to the flames thousands of inoffensive beings for mere aberration of reason ; while Christian Europe was exorcising demons and worshipping rags and bones— learning flourished under the Moslem sovereigns, and was held in honour and veneration as never before. The Vicegerents of Mohammed allied themselves to the cause of civilisation, and assisted in the growth of Free Thought and Free Inquiry, originated and consecrated by the Prophet himself. Persecution for the sake of the faith was unknown ; and whatever the political conduct of the sovereigns, the world has never had superior examples in their impartiality and absolute toleration of all creeds and religions. The cultivation of the physical sciences—that great index to the intellectual liberty of a nation —formed a popular pursuit among the Moslems.

The two failures of the Arabs, the one before Constantinople and the other in France, retarded the progress of the world for ages, and put back the hour-hand of time for centuries. Had the Arabs been less keen for the safety of their spoils, less divided among themselves, had they succeeded in driving before them the barbarian hosts of Charles Martel, the history of the darkest period in the annals of the world would never have been written. The Renaissance, civilisation, the growth of intel- lectual liberty, would have been accelerated by seven hundred years. We should not have had to shudder over the massacre of the Albigenses or of the Huguenots, or the ghastly slaughters of the Irish Catholics by the English Protestants under the Tudors and the Protectorate. We should not have had to mourn over the fate of a Bruno or a Servetus, murdered by the hands of those who had revolted from their mother-church. The history of the *auto-da-fe*, of the murders of the Inquisition, of the massacres of the Aztecs and the Incas ; the tale of the Thirty Years' War, with its manifold miseries,—all this would have remained untold. Above all, Spain, at one time the favoured haunt of learning and the arts, would not have become the intellectual desert it now is, bereft of the glories of centuries. Who has not mourned over the fate of that noble race, exiled by the mad bigotry of a Christian sovereign from the country of its adoption, which it had made famous among nations ? Justly has it been said, " In an ill-omened hour the Cross

supplanted the Crescent on the towers of Granada." The shades
of the glorious dead, of Averroes and Avenpace, of Wâlâdèh
and Âyesha, sit weeping by the ruined haunts of their people
—haunts silent now to the voice of minstrelsy, of chivalry, of
learning, and of art,—only echoing at times the mad outcries
of religious combatants, at times the fierce sounds of political
animosities. Christianity drove the descendants of these
Moslem Andalusians into the desert, sucked out every element
of vitality from beautiful Spain, and made the land a synonym
for intellectual and moral desolation.[1]

If Maslamah had succeeded in capturing Constantinople,—
the capital of Irene, the warm advocate of orthodoxy and cruel
murderess of her own son,—the dark deeds which sully the
annals of the Isaurians, the Comneni, the Palæologi, the terrible
results which attended the seizure of Byzantium by the Latins,
above all, the frightful outburst of the unholy wars, in which
Christian Europe tried to strangle the nations of Asia, would
probably never have come to pass.   One thing at all events is
certain, that if Constantinople had fallen into the hands of the
Moslems, the iconoclastic movement would not have proved
altogether abortive, and the reformation of the Christian
Church would have been accomplished centuries earlier.
Providence willed otherwise. The wave of Free Thought,
which had reached the Isaurian emperors from the Islâmic
regions, broke upon the rocks of ignorance, superstition, and
bigotry ; its power was not felt until the combined action of
the schools of Salerno and Cordova—the influence of Averroes,
and perhaps of some Greeks who had imbibed learning at the
Saracenic fountain—had battered down the rampart of
Ecclesiasticism.

Islâm inaugurated the reign of intellectual liberty. It has
been truly remarked, that so long as Islâm retained its pristine
character, it proved itself the warm protector and promoter of
knowledge and civilisation,—the zealous ally of intellectual
freedom. The moment extraneous elements attached themselves to it, it lagged behind in the race of progress.

But, to explain the stagnation of the Moslems in the present

[1] For the economic condition of Spain and the state of arts and learning
under the Arabs, see *Short History of the Saracens*, pp. 474-580.

day, it is necessary to glance back for a moment at the events that transpired in Spain, in Africa, and in Asia between the twelfth and the seventeenth centuries. In the former country, Christianity destroyed the intellectual life of the people. The Moslems had turned Spain into a garden ; the Christians converted it into a desert. The Moslems had covered the land with colleges and schools ; the Christians transformed them into churches for the worship of saints and images. The literary and scientific treasures amassed by the Moslem sovereigns were consigned to the flames. The Moslem men, women, and children were ruthlessly butchered or burnt at the stake ; the few who were spared were reduced to slavery. Those who fled were thrown on the shores of Africa helpless beggars. It would take the combined charity of Jesus and Mohammed to make Islâm forget or forgive the terrible wrongs inflicted by the Christians of Spain upon the Andalusian Moslems. But the punishment was not long in coming. Before the world was a century old, Spain's fire had sunk into a heap of ashes !

In Western Africa, the triumph of Patristicism under the third Almohade sovereign,[1] and the uprise of Berber fanaticism turned back the tide of progress, arrested the civilisation of centuries, and converted the seats of learning and arts into centres of bigotry and ignorance. The settlement of the Corsairs on the Barbary coast and the anarchy which prevailed in Egypt under the later Mamelukes, discouraged the cultivation of peaceful knowledge. In Asia the decadence of the Timûride dynasty, the eruption of the wild and fanatical Uzbegs, and the establishment of their power in the capital of Timûr, destroyed the intellectual vitality of the people. In Persia, under the Safawis, literature and science had begun

---

[1] On the decadence of the Fâtimide power in Western Africa there arose a dynasty descended from a *Marabout* or saint of the country, hence called Almoravide or *al-Murâbatia* (المرابطيه). To this family belonged Yusuf ibn Tâshfin, the patron of Ibn-Zuhr. His son and successor was defeated and killed by Abdu'l Momin, the founder of the dynasty of Almohades (*al-Muwahidin*, الموحدين, the *Unitarians*), who sacked and destroyed Morocco and Fez. They were akin to the Wahâbis and the *Ikhwân* of Central Arabia, and probably not very different from the Mahdists of Lybia. The first two sovereigns of this dynasty, Abdu'l Momin and Yusuf, encouraged learning and arts ; in the reign of Ya'kûb al-Mansûr, the third Almohade king, fanaticism became rampant.

to breathe once more ; but this renaissance was only temporary, and with the irruption of the barbarous Ghihzais the renovated life of Irân came to an end.   A deathlike gloom settled upon Central Asia, which still hangs heavy over these unhappy countries, and is slowly lifting in Afghanistan.

Under Selim I., Solyman and the Murads, learning received support in the Ottoman dominions ; but the Osmanlis were on the whole a military race.   At first from ambition, afterwards from sheer necessity and for self-preservation, they had been at war with a relentless foe, whose designs knew no slackening, whose purpose was inscrutable.   That enemy has disappeared, but the nation has still to fight for its existence.   Letters and arts, under such conditions, can make but little progress. Dealing with the charge of obscurantism, often levelled against Islâm, M. Gobineau makes the following pregnant observation : " Imagine in any European country the absolute predominance of military and administrative despotism during a period of two hundred and fifty years, as is the case in Turkey ; conceive, something approaching the warlike anarchy of Egypt under the domination of foreign slaves—Circassians, Georgians, Turks, and Albanians ; picture to yourself an Afghan invasion, as in Persia after 1730, the tyranny of Nâdir Shah, the cruelties and ravages that have marked the accession of the dynasty of the Kajars,—unite all these circumstances with their naturally concomitant causes, you will then understand what would have become of any European country although European, and it will not be necessary to look further for any explanation of the ruin of Oriental countries, nor to charge Islâm with any unjust responsibility."

From the time of its birth in the seventh century up to the end of the seventeenth, not to descend later, Islâm was animated by a scientific and literary spirit equal in force and energy to that which animates Europe of our own day.   It carried the Moslems forward on a wave of progress, and enabled them to achieve a high degree of material and mental develop- ment.   Since the eruption of the Goths and the Vandals, the progress of Europe has been on a continuous scale.   No such calamity as has afflicted Asia, in the persons of the Tartars or the Uzbegs, has befallen Christendom since Attila's retreat from France. Her wars, cruel and bitter, fierce and inhuman, have been waged on equal terms of humanity or inhumanity. Catholics and Protestants have burnt each other ; but Europe has never witnessed, since the wholesale butcheries of the poor Spanish Moors, the terrible massacres committed by the Tartars in all the centres of civilisation and culture, in which fell the gifted classes who formed the backbone of the nation.[1]

And now,

پرده داری می کند در قصر قیصر عنکبوت

بوم نوبت می زند بر گنبد افراسیاب

The spider holds watch in the palace of Cæsar,
The owlet beats the drum on the tower of Afrâsiâb.

[1] The sack of Bagdad by the Mongols exemplifies what happened in other cities, but in order to give a true conception of the fearful atrocities perpetrated by the savages, it requires to be painted by another Gibbon. For three days the streets ran with blood, and the water of the Tigris was dyed red for miles along its course. The horrors of rapine, slaughter, and outraged humanity lasted for six weeks. The palaces, mosques, and mausoleums were destroyed by fire or levelled to the earth for their golden domes. The patients in the hospitals and the students and professors in the colleges were put to the sword. In the mausoleums the mortal remains of the sheikhs and pious imâms, and in the academies the immortal works of great and learned men, were consumed to ashes ; books were thrown into the fire, or, where that was distant and the Tigris near, were buried in the waters of the latter. The accumulated treasures of five centuries were thus lost for ever to humanity. The flower of the nation was completely destroyed. It was the custom of Hulâku, from policy and as a precaution, to carry along with his horde the princes and chiefs of the countries through which they swept. One of these princes was Sa'di bin Zangi, the Atabek of Fars. The poet Sa'di had, it appears, accompanied his friend and patron. He was thus an eye-witness to the terrible state of Bagdad and its doomed inhabitants. In two pathetic couplets he has given expression to its magnitude and horrors, see Appendix II.

CHAPTER X

THE RATIONALISTIC AND PHILOSOPHICAL
SPIRIT OF ISLÂM

اِنَّ اللّٰهَ لَا يُغَيِّرُ مَا بِقَوْمٍ حَتَّى يُغَيِّرُوا مَا بِاَنْفُسِهِمْ [1]

LIKE all other nations of antiquity, the pre-Islâmite Arabs were stern fatalists. The remains of their ancient poetry, sole record of old Arab thought and manners, show that before the promulgation of Islâm the people of the Peninsula had absolutely abandoned themselves to the idea of an irresistible and blind fatality. Man was but a sport in the hands of Fate. This idea bred a reckless contempt of death, and an utter disregard for human life. The teachings of Islâm created a revolution in the Arab mind ; with the recognition of a supreme Intelligence governing the universe, they received the conception of self-dependence and of moral responsibility founded on the liberty of human volition. One of the remarkable characteristics of the Koran is the curious, and, at first sight, inconsistent, manner in which it combines the existence of a Divine Will, which not only orders all things, but which acts directly upon men and addresses itself to the springs of thought in them, with the assertion of a free agency in man and of the liberty of intellect. Not that this feature is peculiar to the Moslem scripture ; the same characteristic is to be found in the Biblical records. But in the Koran the conception of human responsibility is so strongly developed that the question naturally occurs to the mind, How can these two ideas be

[1] " God changes not as to what concerns any people until they change in respect to what depends upon themselves."

reconciled with each other ? It seems inconsistent at first
sight that man should be judged by his works, a doctrine which
forms the foundation of Islâmic morality, if all his actions are
ruled by an all-powerful Will.   The earnest faith of Mohammed
in an active ever-living Principle, joined to his trust in the
progress of man, supplies a key to this mystery.   I propose to
illustrate my meaning by a reference to a few of the passages
which give expression to the absolutism of the Divine Will and
those which assert the liberty of human volition : " And
God's ordering is in accordance with a determined decree ;
. . . and the sun proceeding to its place of rest—that is an
ordinance (تقدير) of the Almighty, the All-wise ; [1] . . . and
among His signs is the creation of the heavens and the earth
and of the animals which He hath distributed therein, which
He has sovereign power to gather when He will ; [2] . . . and do
they not see that God who created the heavens and the earth,
and faltered not in creating these, has power to vivify the dead
—nay, He has sovereign control over all things ; [3] and other
things which are not at your command, but which are truly
within His grasp, inasmuch as God is sovereign disposer of all
things (على كل شئ قديرا) ; [4] nor is there anything not provided beforehand by Us, or which We send down otherwise
than according to a fore-known decree ; [5] . . . the secrets of
the heavens and the earth are God's ; . . . God has all things
at command ; [6] . . . and propound to them a similitude of this
present life, which is like water sent down by Us from heaven,
so that the plants of the earth are fattened by it, and on the
morrow become stubble, scattered by the winds,—God disposes
of all things ; [7] . . . and it pertains to God's sovereignty to
defend them ; [8] . . . God creates what He will ; [9] . . . and who
created all things, and determined respecting the same with
absolute determination ; [10] . . . and thy Lord is a supreme
sovereign ; [11] . . . behold thou the imprints of the mercy of
God : how He vivifies the earth, after it has died—in very
deed, a restorer of life to the dead is there, and all things are
at His bidding ; [12] . . . to God belongs whatsoever is in the

[1] xxxvi. 38.   [2] xlii. 28.   [3] xlvi. 29.   [4] xlviii. 21.   [5] xv. 21.
[6] xvi. 77.   [7] xviii. 45.   [8] xxii. 40.   [9] xxiv. 45.   [10] xxv. 2.
[11] xxv. 54.   [12] وهو على كل شئ قدير ., xxx. 50.

heavens and whatsoever is on the earth ; and whether ye disclose that which is within you or conceal it, God will reckon
with you for it ; and He pardons whom He will, and punishes
whom He will—inasmuch as God is a Supreme Sovereign ; [1]
. . . say thou : O God, Sovereign Disposer of dominion, Thou
givest rule to whom Thou wilt, and takest away power from
whom Thou wilt, Thou exaltest whom Thou wilt, and humblest
whom Thou wilt : all good is at Thy disposal—verily, Thou art
a Supreme Sovereign ; [2] . . God punishes whom He will, and
pardons whom He will ; [3] . . . to God belongs the dominion of
the heavens and the earth, and whatsoever they contain is
His, and He is Sovereign over all things. [4] . . . Verily, God
accomplishes what He ordains—He hath established for everything a fixed decree ; [5] . . . but God has the measuring out
(يقدّر) of the night and the day ; [6] . . . extol the name of Thy
Lord, the Most High, who made the world, and fashioned it to
completeness, who fore-ordained, and guides accordingly ; [7]
. . . as for the unbelievers it matters nothing to them whether
thou warnest them or dost not warn them ; they will not
believe ; God hath sealed up their hearts and their ears ; [8] . .
and the darkness of night is over their eyes ; [9] . . and God
guides into the right path whomsoever He will ; [10] . . . God is
pleased to make your burthens light, inasmuch as man is by
nature infirm. . . . God changes not as to what concerns any
people until they change in respect to what depends upon
themselves ; [11] . . . say thou : Verily, Gods leads astray whomsoever He will, and directs to Himself those who are penitent." [12]
    It will be noticed that, in many of these passages by " the
decree of God " is clearly meant the law of nature. The stars
and planets have each their appointed course ; so has every
other object in creation. The movements of the heavenly
bodies, the phenomena of nature, life and death, are all
governed by law. Other passages unquestionably indicate the
idea of Divine agency upon human will ; but they are again
explained by others, in which that agency is " conditioned "
upon human will. It is to the seeker for Divine help that God

[1] ii. 284.   [2] iii. 25.   [3] v. 18.   [4] v. 120.   [5] lxv. 3.
[6] lxxiii. 20.   [7] lxxxvii. 1-3.   [8] ii. 5-6.   [9] ii. 7.   [10] xiii. 31.
[11] انّ الله لا يغيّر ما بقوم حتّى يغيّروا ما بانفسهم: , xiii. 11.   [12] xiii. 27.

renders His help ; it is on the searcher of his own heart, who purifies his soul from impure longings, that God bestows grace. To the Arabian Teacher, as to his predecessors, the existence of an Almighty Power, the Fashioner of the Universe, the Ruler of His creatures, was an intense and vivid reality. The feeling of " an assured trust " in an all-pervading, ever-conscious Personality has been the motive power in the world of every age. To the weary mariner, " sailing on life's solemn main," there is nothing more assuring, nothing that more satisfies the intense longing for a better and purer world, than the consciousness of a Power above humanity to redress wrongs, to fulfil hopes, to help the forlorn. Our belief in God springs from the very essence of Divine ordinances. They are as much laws, in the strictest sense of the word, as the laws which regulate the movements of the celestial bodies. But the will of God is not an arbitrary will : it is an educating will, to be obeyed by the scholar in his walks of learning as by the devotee in his cell.

The passages, however, in which human responsibility and the freedom of human will are laid down in emphatic terms define and limit the conception of absolutism. " And whosoever gets to himself a sin, gets it solely on his own responsibility ; [1] ... and let alone those who make a sport and a mockery of their religion, and whom this present world has deluded, and thereby bring to remembrance that any soul perishes for what it has got to itself ; [2] and when they commit a deed of shame they say : We have found that our fathers did so, and God obliges us to do it ; say thou : Surely, God requireth not shameful doing : [3] ... they did injustice to themselves ; [4] yonder will every soul experience that which it hath bargained for ; [5] ... so then, whosoever goes astray, he himself bears the whole responsibility of wandering." [6]

---

[1] iv. 111 ومن يكسب اثما فانّما يكسبه على نفسه
[2] vi. 70, ان تبسل نفسى بما كسبت
[3] vii. 29, انّ اللہ لا يأمر بالفحشاء
[4] ix. 70. و لكن كانوا انفسهم يظلمون
[5] x. 30, هنالك تبلوا كلّ نفس ما اسلفت
[6] x. 108. فمن اهتدى فا نما يهتدى لنفسه ومن ضلّ فانما يضلّ عليها

Man, within the limited sphere of his existence, is absolute master of his conduct. He is responsible for his actions, and for the use or misuse of the powers with which he has been endowed. He may fall or rise, according to his own " inclination." There was supreme assistance for him who sought Divine help and guidance. Is not the soul purer and better in calling to its Lord for that help which He has promised ? Are not the weak strengthened, the stricken comforted—by their own appeal to the Heavenly Father for solace and strength ? Such were the ideas of the Teacher of Islâm with regard to Divine sovereignty and the liberty of human volition. His recorded sayings handed down from sources which may be regarded as unquestionably authentic, help in explaining the conception he entertained about freewill and predestination (جبر و اختیار or قضا و قدر). Not only his own words, but those of his son-in-law, " the legitimate heir to his inspiration," and his immediate descendants, who derived their ideas from him, may well furnish us with a key to the true Islâmic notion on the question of the free agency of man—a subject which has for ages, both in Islâm and in Christianity, been the battleground of sectarian disputes. In discussing this subject, we must not, however, lose sight of the fact that most of the traditions which have supplied to Patristicism its armoury of weapons against the sovereignty of reason, bear evident traces of being ' made to order.' They tell their own story of how, and the circumstances under which, they came into existence. Some of the traditions which purport to be handed down by men who came casually in contact with the Teacher, show palpable signs of changes and transformations in the minds and in the memories of the mediaries. The authentic sayings, however, are many, and I shall refer only to a few to explain what I have already indicated, that in Mohammed's mind an earnest belief in the liberty of human will was joined to a vivid trust in the personality of the heavenly Father. Hereditary depravity and natural sinfulness were emphatically denied. Every child of man was born pure and true ; every departure in after-life from the path of truth and rectitude is due to education. " Every man is born religiously constituted ; it is his parents who make him afterwards a Jew, Christian, or a

Sabæan, like as ye take up the beast at its birth—do ye find upon it any mutilation, until ye yourselves mutilate it?"[1] Infants have no positive moral character: for about those who die in early life, "God best knows what would have been their conduct" [had they lived to maturity]. "Every human being has two inclinations,—one prompting him to good and impelling him thereto, and the other prompting him to evil and thereto impelling him;[2] but the godly assistance is nigh, and he who asks the help of God in contending with the evil promptings of his own heart obtains it." "It is your own conduct which will lead you to paradise or hell, as if you had been destined therefor." No man's conduct is the outcome of fatality, nor is he borne along by an irresistible decree to heaven or hell; on the contrary, the ultimate result is the creation of his own actions, for each individual is primarily answerable for his future destiny. "Every moral agent is furthered to his own conduct," or, as it is put in another tradition: "Every one is divinely furthered in accordance with his character."[3] Human conduct is by no means fortuitous; one act is the result of another; and life, destiny and character mean the connected series of incidents and actions which are related to each other, as cause and effect, by an ordained law, "the assignment" of God. In the sermons of the Disciple we find the doctrine more fully developed. "Weigh your own soul before the time for the weighing of your actions arrives; take count with yourself before you are called upon to account for your conduct in this existence; apply yourself to good and pure actions, adhere to the path of truth and rectitude before the soul is pressed to leave its earthly abode: verily, if you will not guide and warn yourself, none other can direct you."[4] "I adjure you to

---

[1] قال رسول الله صلى الله عليه و سلم ما من مولود الا يولد على الفطرة فأبواه يهوّدانه و ينصّرانه و يمجّسانه كما قنتج البهيمة بهيمة جمعاء هل تـمّـون فيها من جدعاء

[2] Bukhâri's *Collections*, chapter on the Hadîs, "He is secured whom God helps"; reported by Abû Sa'îd al-Khuzri.

[3] اعملوا فكل ميسر لما خلق له

[4] *Nahj ul-Balâghat*, p. 43 (a collection of the *Khutbas* of the Caliph Ali by one of his descendants, named Sharîf Riza, mentioned by Ibn-Khallikân), printed at Tabriz in 1299 A.H.

worship the Lord in purity and holiness. He has pointed out
to you the path of salvation and the temptations of this world.
Abstain from foulness, though it may be fair-seeming to your
sight ; avoid evil, however pleasant. . . . For ye knoweth how
far it takes you away from Him. . . . Listen, and take warning
by the words of the Merciful Guardian." [1] . . . And again, " O
ye servants of my Lord, fulfil the duties that are imposed on
you, for in their neglect is abasement : your good works alone
will render easy the road to death. Remember, each sin
increases the debt, and makes the chain [which binds you]
heavier. The message of mercy has come ; the path of truth
is clear ; obey the command that has been laid on you ; live
in purity, and work in piety, and ask God to help you in
your endeavours, and to forgive your past transgressions." [2]
" Cultivate humility and forbearance : comport yourself with
piety and truth. Take count of your actions with your own
conscience (نفسى), for he who takes such count reaps a great
reward, and he who neglects incurs great loss. He who acts
with piety gives rest to his soul ; he who takes warning understands the truth ; he who understands it attains the perfect
knowledge." These utterances convey no impression of predestinarianism ; on the contrary, they portray a soul animated
with a living faith in God, and yet full of trust in human
development founded upon individual exertion springing from
human volition. Mohammed's definition of reason and knowledge, of the cognition of the finite and infinite, reminds us of
Aristotelian phraseology and thought, and Ali's address to his
son may be read with advantage by the admirer of Aristotelian
ethics.

The *Ihtijâj ut-Tabrasi* [8] supplies further materials to form a
correct opinion on the question of predestinarianism in Islâm.
The Caliph Ali was one day asked the meaning of *Kazâ* (قضا)
and *Kadar* (قدر) ; he replied, " The first means obedience
to the commandments of God and avoidance of sin ; the latter,
the ability to live a holy life, and to do that which brings one
nearer to God and to shun that which throws him away from

---

[1] *Ibid.* p. 136.   [8] *Nahj ul-Balâghat*, p. 170.
[8] *Evidences of Tabrasi*, a collection of traditions by the Shaikh ut-Tabrasi.

His perfection. . . . Say not that man is *compelled*, for that is attribution of tyranny to God ; nor say that man has absolute discretion,[1]—rather that we are furthered by His help and grace in our endeavours to act righteously, and we transgress because of our neglect (of His commands)." One of his interlocutors, 'Utba ibn Rabi'a Asadi, asked him once as to the meaning of the words " there is no power nor help but from God," لا حول و لا قوة الا بالله. " It means," said the Caliph, " that I am not afraid of God's anger, but I am afraid of his purity ; nor have I the power to observe His commandment, but my strength is in His assistance." [2] . . . God has placed us on earth to try each according to his endowments. Referring to the following and other passages of the Koran, the Caliph went on to say, " God says, ' We will try you to see who are the *strivers* (مجاهدين) [after truth and purity], and who are the forbearing and patient, and We will test your actions.' . . . and ' We will help you by degrees to attain what ye know not.' [3] . . . These verses prove the liberty of human volition." [4] Explaining the verse of the Koran, " God directs him whom He chooses, and leads astray him whom He chooses," the Caliph said that this does not mean that He compels men to evil or good, that He either gives direction or refuses it according to His caprice, for this would do away with all responsibility for human action ; it means, on the contrary, that God points out the road to truth, and lets men choose as they will.[5]

Arabian philosophy, nurtured afterwards in other cradles, drew its first breath in the school of Medîna. The freedom of human will, based on the doctrine that man would be judged by the use he had made of his reason, was inculcated in the teachings of the Master, along with an earnest belief in a Supreme Power ruling the universe. The idea assumed a more definite shape in the words of the Disciple, and grew into a philosophy. From Medîna it was carried to Damascus, Kûfa, Basra, and

---

[1] *I.e.* to decide what is right and what is wrong.

[2] *Ihtijâj ut-Tabrasi*, p. 236.

[3] ر لنبلونكم حتى نعلم المجاهدين منكم والصابرين و نبلو اخباركم و فى نوله

ونستدرجهم من حيث لا يعلمون

[4] *Ibid*, p. 237.   [5] *Ibid*.

Bagdad, where it gave birth to the eclectic schools, which shed such lustre on the reigns of the early Abbasides.

The butchery of Kerbela and the sack of Medîna had led to the closing of the lecture-room of the Imâms. With the appearance of Jaafar as-Sâdik as the head of Mohammed's descendants, it acquired a new life. Extremely liberal and rationalistic in his views,—a scholar, a poet, and a philosopher, apparently well read in some of the foreign languages,—in constant contact with cultured Christians, Jews, and Zoro-astrians, with whom metaphysical disputations were frequent, —he impressed a distinct philosophical character on the Medînite school. Some of his views respecting predestination deserve to be mentioned. Speaking of the doctrine of *Jabr* (*compulsion* or predestinarianism), which had about this period made its appearance in Damascus, he expressed the following opinion : " Those who uphold *Jabr* make out God to be a participator in every sin they commit, and a tyrant for punish-ing those sins which they are impelled to commit by the compulsion of their being : this is infidelity." Then (giving the analogy of a servant sent by his master to the market to purchase something which he, the master, knows well that he cannot bring, not possessing the wherewithal to buy it, and, nevertheless, the master punishes him) the Imâm adds, " the doctrine of *Jabr* converts God into an unjust Master." [1] As regards the opposite doctrine of *absolute liberty* (*Tafwîz, delega-tion of authority*)—meaning not the freedom of human will, but unqualified discretion in the choice of wrong and right, he declared that to affirm such a principle would destroy all the foundations of morality, and give to all human beings absolute licence in the indulgence of their animal propensities ; for if each individual is vested with a discretion to choose what is right or wrong, no sanction, no law can have any force. [2] *Ikhtiâr* (اختيار) is therefore different from *Tafwîz* (تفويض), " God has endowed each human being with the capacity to under-stand His commands and to obey them. They who exert themselves to live purely and truly, them He helps : they are those who please Him ; whilst they who disobey Him are sinners." These views are repeated with greater emphasis by

[1] *Ihtijâj ut-Tabrasi*, p. 236.　　[2] *Ibid.* p. 235.

the eighth Imâm, Ali ar-Rizâ, who denounced *Jabr* (predestinarianism) and *Tashbîh* (anthropomorphism) as absolute infidelity,[1] and declared the upholders of those doctrines to be "the enemies of the Faith." He openly charged the advocates of *Jabr* and *Tashbîh* with the fabrication of traditions. At the same time he warned his followers against the doctrine of *discretion* or *Tafwîz*. He laid down in broad terms, "God has pointed out to you the two paths, one of which leads you to Him, the other takes you far away from His perfection; you are at liberty to take the one or the other; pain or joy, reward or punishment, depend upon your own conduct. But man has not the capacity of turning evil into good, or sin into virtue."

The Ommeyyades, many of whom remained pagans at heart even after the profession of Islâm, were, like their forefathers, fatalists. Under them arose a school which purported to derive its doctrines from the "ancients," the *Salaf*, a body of primitive Moslems. All of them were dead; it was consequently easy to fabricate any tradition and pass it as handed down by one or other of them. Jahm bin Safwân was the founder of this school, which was called *Jabria*. The *Jabrias*[2] rivalled Calvin in the absolute denial of free-will to man. They maintained "that man is not responsible for any of his actions which proceed entirely from God;[3] that he has no determining power to do any act, nor does he possess the capacity of free volition; that he is the subject of absolute Divine sovereignty in his actions, without ability on his part, or will or power of choice; and that God absolutely creates actions within him just as He produces activity in all inanimate things; ... and that reward and punishment are subject to absolute Divine sovereignty in human actions." The *Jabrias* maintained certain views regarding Divine attributes which have no

---

[1] He who believes in *Jabr* is a *Kâfir*; *Ihtijâj ut-Tabrasi*, p. 214.

[2] Shahristâni divides the *Jabrias* into two branches, one being *Jabrias* pure and simple, and the other more moderate. The first maintained that neither action nor the ability to act belongs in any sense to man (نثبت للعبد فعلا ولا قدرة على الفعل اصلا); the latter held that man has an ability which is not at all efficacious (نثبت للعبد قدرة غير موثرة اصله).

[3] الجبر هو نفى , الفعل حقيقة عن العبد و اضافته الى الرب تعالى

particular significance.[1]   According to Shahristâni, the *Jabrias*
were divided into three sects, viz. : the *Jahmia*, the *Najjâria*,
and the *Zirâria*, differing from each other on minor points ;
but, so far as the doctrine of predestination was concerned, all
of them were agreed in denying free agency.   The *Najjârias*,
who, after undergoing several transformations, developed two
centuries later into the Asha'rias, maintained that God creates
the conduct of His creatures, good and bad, virtuous and
vicious, while man appropriates the same.   The *Jabria*
doctrines found favour with the Ommeyyade rulers, and soon
spread among the people.

The uncompromising fatalism of the *Jabrias* occasioned
among the thinking classes a revolt, which was headed by
Ma'bad al-Juhani, Yûnus al-Aswâri, and Ghailân Dimishki (*i.e.*
of Damascus), who had evidently derived many of their ideas
from the Fâtimides.   They boldly asserted in the capital of the
Ommeyyades, in the very stronghold of predestinarianism, the
free agency of man.[2]   But in the assertion of human liberty
they sometimes verged on the doctrine of *Tafwîz*.   From
Damascus the dispute was carried to Basra, and there the
differences of the two parties waxed high.   The *Jabrias*
merged into a new sect, called the *Sifâtias*,[3] who, with predestinarianism, combined the affirmation of certain attributes
in the Deity as distinct from His Essence, which the *Jabrias*
denied.   The *Sifâtias* claimed to be the direct representatives
of the *Salaf*.   According to Shahristâni, these followers of the
Salaf " maintained that certain eternal attributes pertain to
God, namely, knowledge, power, life, will, hearing, · sight,
speech, majesty, maġnanimity, bounty, beneficence, glory, and
greatness,—making no distinction between attributes of essence
and attributes of action. . . .   They also assert certain descriptive attributes (صفات خبرية) as, for example, hands and
face, without any other explanation than to say that these
attributes enter into the *revealed* representation of the Deity,
and that, accordingly, they had given them the name of
descriptive attributes."   Like the *Jabrias*, they adhered to
the doctrine of predestination in all its gloominess and intensity.

---

[1] Shahristâni, part i. p. 59.   [2] Shahristâni, part i. pp. 59-63.
[3] *Lit.* Attributists.

From the *Sifâtias* sprang the *Mushabbihas*, " who likened the Divine attributes to the attributes of created things," [1] and turned God into a similitude of their own selves. [2] At this period one of the most noted professors belonging to the anti-predestinarian party was Imâm Hasan, surnamed al-Basri (from his place of residence). He was a Medînite by birth, and had actually sat at the feet of " the Philosophers of the family of Mohammed." He had imbibed their liberal and rationalistic ideas, and, on settling at Basra, had started a lecture-room, which was soon thronged by the students of Irâk. Here he discoursed on the metaphysical questions of the day in the spirit of his masters.

One of his most prominent pupils was Abû Huzaifa Wâsil bin 'Atâ al-Ghazzâl, [3] a man of great mental powers, thoroughly versed in the sciences and traditions, who had also studied in the lecture-room of Medîna. He differed from the Imâm on a question of religious dogma, and was made to withdraw from the lecture-room. He thereupon founded a school of his own. His followers have, from this fact, been called *Mu'tazilas*, or *Ahl-ul-I'tizâl*, Dissenters. [4] He soon rivalled the fame of his master, whose school before long practically merged in that of the pupil. In his antagonism against intellectual tyranny he often overstepped the bounds of moderation, and gave utterance to views, especially on the controversy raised by Mu'âwiyah, which were in conflict with those entertained at Medîna. Yet the general rationalism of his school rallied the strongest and most liberal minds round his standard. Proceeding upon the lines of the Fatimide philosophers, and appropriating

---

[1] التشبيه بصفات المحدثات

[2] Shahristâni draws a distinction between the *Sifâtia* anthropomorphists and those who came into existence later. " At a later period certain persons went beyond what had been professed by any who held to the primitive faith, and said that undoubtedly those expressions (denoting the attributes) are used in the literal sense, and are to be interpreted just as they stand, without resort to figurative interpretation, and at the same time, without insisting upon the literal sense alone, whereby they fell into pure anthropomorphism (التشبيه الصرف) in violation of the primitive Moslem faith."

[3] ابو حذيفة واصل بن عطا الغزال. He lived in the days of Abd ul-Malik, Walîd and Hishâm. He was born in 83 A.H. (699-700 A.C.) and died in 131 A.H. (748-9 A.C.).

[4] Shahristâni, p. 31; *Gouhar-i-Murâd* (*vide post*). *Mu'tazala* spelt with a *fatha* (*a*) in the third syllable in the *Ghyâs-ul-lughat* and the *Farhang* (Lucknow, 1889). See Appendix III.

the principles which they had laid down and the ideas to which they had often given forcible expression, he formulated into theses the doctrines which constitute the basis of his difference from the predestinarian schools and from Patristicism generally. For several centuries his school dominated over the intellects of men, and with the support of the enlightened rulers who during this period held the reins of government, it gave an impetus to the development of national and intellectual life among the Saracens such as had never been witnessed before. Distinguished scholars, prominent physicists, mathematicians, historians—all the world of intellect in fact, including the Caliphs, belonged to the Mu'tazilite school.[1]

Men like Abu'l Huzail Hamdân,[2] Ibrâhîm ibn Sayyâr an-Nazzâm,[3] Ahmed ibn Hâit, Fazl al-Hadasi, and Abû Ali Mohammed al-Jubbâî,[4] well read in Greek philosophy and logic, amalgamated many ideas borrowed from those sources with the Medînite conceptions, and impressed a new feature on the philosophical notions of the Moslems. The study of Aristotle, Porphyry, and other Greek and Alexandrian writers gave birth to a new science among the Mu'tazilas, which was called *Ilm-ul-Kalâm*, "the science of reason" (*Kalâm*, *logos*),[5] with which they fought both against the external as well as the internal enemies of the Faith,—the non-Moslems who assailed the teachings of Islâm from outside, and the patristic Moslems who aimed at its degradation from within. The extreme views of Wâsil on the political questions which had agitated the Caliphate of Ali were before long abandoned, with the result that moderate Mu'tazilaism became substantially amalgamated with the rationalism of the Fâtimide school, whence it had sprung. It is a well-known fact that the chief doctors of the Mu'tazilite school were educated under the Fâtimides, and there can hardly be any doubt that moderate Mu'tazilaism

[1] We may mention here two or three prominent Mutazilas whose names are still famous, *e.g.* Imâm Zamakhshari, the author of the *Kashshâf*, admittedly the best and most erudite commentary on the Koran; Mas'ûdi, "Imâm, historian, and philosopher"; the famous Al-Hazen, Abu'l Wafâ, and Mirkhond.

[2] Died A.H. 235 (A.C. 849-850), in the beginning of al-Mutawakkil's Caliphate.

[3] A nephew of Abu'l Huzail.　　　　[4] Born in 861; died in 933.

[5] Shahristâni, p. 18; Ibn-Khaldûn *in loco*.

represented the views of the Caliph Ali and the most liberal of
his early descendants, and probably of Mohammed himself.
A careful comparison of the Mu'tazilite doctrines will show
that they were either word for word the same as were taught
by the early Fâtimides, or were modifications of those doctrines
induced by the requirements of a progressive society, and
partly, perhaps, by the study of Greek and Alexandrian
philosophy.

The Caliph Ali had condemned in emphatic language all
anthropomorphic and anthropopathic conceptions of the Deity.
" God was not like any object that the human mind can conceive ; no attribute can be ascribed to Him which bore the least
resemblance to any quality of which human beings have
perception from their knowledge of material objects. The
perfection of piety consists in *knowing* God ; the perfection of
knowledge is the affirmation of His verity ; and the perfection
of verity is to acknowledge His unity in all sincerity ; and the
perfection of sincerity is to deny all attributes to the Deity . . .
كمال الاخلاص له نفي الصفات عنه , He who refers an attribute to
God believes the attribute to be God, and he who so believes an
attribute to be God, regards God as two or part of one. . . .
He who asks where God is, assimilates Him with some object.
God is the Creator, not because He Himself is created ; God is
existent, not because He was non-existent. He is with every
object, not from resemblance or nearness ; He is outside of everything not from separation. He is the Primary Cause (فاعل),
not in the meaning of motion or action ; He is the Seer, but no
sight can see Him. He has no relation to place, time, or
measure.[1] . . . God is Omniscient, because knowledge is His
Essence ; Mighty, because Power is His Essence ; Loving,
because Love is His Essence . . . not because these are attributes
apart from His Essence. . . . The conditions of time or space
were wholly inapplicable to Him." . . . [2] *Takdîr* (تقدير),
construed by the followers of the *Salaf* to mean predestination,
meant " weighing," " probation," " trial."

Let us see now what Mu'tazilaism is. On many minor and
subsidiary points the prominent Mu'tazilite doctors differed

[1] *Nahj-ul-Balâghat* ; see the comment of Ibn-i-Abi'l Hadîd, the Mu'tazilite.
[2] From the Imâm Ja'far as-Sâdik, *ibid.*

among themselves ; but I shall give here a sketch of the doctrines on which they were in accord. According to Shahri-stâni, the Mu'tazilas [1] declare that " eternity is the distinguish-ing attribute of the Divine Being ; that God is Eternal, for Eternity is the peculiar property of His Essence ; they unanimously deny the existence of eternal (Divine) qualities (الصفات القديمة) [as distinct from His being], and maintain that He is Omniscient as to His being ; Living as to His being ; Almighty as to His being ; but not through any knowledge, power, or life existing in Him as eternal attributes ; for know-ledge, power, and life are part of His Essence. Otherwise, if they are to be looked upon as eternal attributes of the Deity (separate from His Essence), it would tend to the affirmation of a multiplicity of eternal entities. . . . They also maintain that the WORD of God is created, and when created, is expressed in letters and sounds. . . . In like manner they unanimously denied that willing, hearing, and seeing are ideas subsistent in the Divine Being, though differing as to the modes of their existence and their metaphysical grounds." [2] " They deny unanimously that God can be beheld in the *Dâr-ul-Karâr* (in the Abode of Rest) with the corporeal sight. They forbid the describing of God by any quality belonging to material objects, either by way of direction, or location, or appearance, or body, or change, or cessation of action, or dissolution ; and they have explained the passages of the Koran in which expres-sions implying these qualities have been used, by asserting that the expressions are used figuratively and not literally. And this doctrine they call *Tauhîd*, ' assertion of Divine unity.' . . .

---

[1] " The Mu'tazilas called themselves," says Shahristâni, " *Ashâb-ul-'adl wa't-tauhid*, ' people of justice and unity,' and sometimes *Kadarias*." As a matter of fact, however, the designation of *Kadaria* was never applied by the Mu'tazilas to themselves ; it was applied by their enemies to the extreme Mu'tazilas who maintained the doctrine of *Tafwîz*, and which was condemned by the Fâtimide Imâms. They always repudiated that designation, and applied it to the predestinarians, who asserted that God is the Creator of every human action. Shahristâni admits this, and says :—

و قالوا لفظ القدرية يطلق على من يقول بالقدر خيره و شره من الله تعالي

But he tries to refute the applicability of the word *Kadaria* to the pre-destinarians. " How can it apply to those who *trust* in God " ; Shahristâni, p. 30.

[2] Shahristâni, p. 30.

They also agree in believing that man is the creative efficient of his actions, good and bad لا نعاله خيرها و شرهاان العبد قادر خالق and gets reward and punishment in the future world by merit for what he does ; and that no moral evil, or iniquity of action, or unbelief, or disobedience, can be referred to God, because, if He had caused unrighteousness to be, He would be Himself unrighteous (لانه لو خلق الظلم كان ظالما) . . . They also unanimously maintain that the All-wise does only that which is beneficial and good (لا يفعل الا الصلاح و الخير), and that a regard in the light of wisdom (من حيث الحكمة) for the good of humanity (مصالح العباد) is incumbent upon Him, though they differed as to His being obligated to secure the highest good, and to bestow grace (و اما الاصلح و اللطف وفي وجوبه خلاف عندهم). And this doctrine they call the doctrine of 'adl, or justice."

They further hold that there is no eternal law as regards human actions ; that the Divine ordinances which regulate the conduct of men are the result of growth and development ; that God has commanded and forbidden by a law which grew gradually. At the same time, they say that he who works righteousness merits rewards, and he who works evil deserves punishment ; and this, they say, is consonant with reason. The Mu'tazilas also say that all knowledge is attained through reason, and must necessarily be so obtained. They hold that the cognition of good and evil is also within the province of reason ; that nothing is known to be wrong or right until reason has enlightened us as to the distinction ; and that thankfulness for the blessings of the Benefactor is made obligatory by reason, even before the promulgation of any law on the subject. They maintain that the knowledge of God is within the province of reason ; and, with the exception of Himself, everything else is liable to change or to suffer extinction. " They also maintain that the Almighty has sent His Prophets to explain to mankind His commandments. . . . They differ among themselves as to the question of the Imâmate ; some maintaining that it descended by appointment, others holding to the right of the people to elect." The Mu'tazilas are, therefore, the direct antitheses of the Sifâtias, for " these and all *other Ahl-us-Sunnat* hold that God does whatever He pleases, for He is the

Sovereign Lord of His dominions, and whatever He wishes He orders ... and this is *'adl* (justice) according to them. According to the *Ahl-ul-I'tizâl*, what accords with Reason and Wisdom only is justice (*'adl*), and the doing of acts for (or according to) the good and well-being [of mankind], على وجه الصواب و المصلحة . The *Ahl-ul-'adl* say that God has commanded and forbidden by created words. According to the *Ahl-us-Sunnat* (the Sifâtias), all that is obligatory is known from hearsay (سمع) ; (secular) knowledge only is attained by reason ; Reason cannot tell us what is good, or what is bad, or what is obligatory. The *Ahl-ul-'adl* say (on the contrary) that *all* knowledge comes through reason.[1] They referred that term of tradition ' pre-destination ' to trial and deliverance, adversity and prosperity, sickness and health, death and life, and other doings of God, exclusive of moral good and evil, virtue and vice, regarding men as responsible for the latter,

(دون الخير و الشر و الحسن و القبيح الصادرين من اكساب العباد)

and it is in the same sense that the whole community of the Mu'tazila employ that term.''

Thus far we have given the views of the school as a body ; but there were certain opinions held by the prominent doctors individually, which, though not accepted beyond the immediate circle of their particular disciples, are yet deserving of notice. For example Abû-Huzail Hamdân maintained that the Creator is knowing by virtue of knowledge, but that His knowledge is His Essence ; powerful by virtue of power, but that His power is His Essence ; living by virtue of life, but that His life is His Essence. '' A view,'' says Shahristâni, '' adopted from the Philosophers,'' but really taken from the Medînite school. He also affirmed that free will (السلامة) is an accident (عرض), additional to perfection of development and soundness (الصحة). Ibrâhîm ibn Sayyâr an-Nazzâm, '' a diligent student of the books of the Philosophers,'' maintained '' that without a revelation, man is capable, by reflection, of recognising the Creator, and of distinguishing between virtue and vice ... and that the Doer of Righteousness possessed not the capacity to do wrong.'' Mu'ammar ibn Abbâd as-Sulami advanced

[1] Shahristâni, p. 31.

the Platonic theory of "archetypes." He maintained that accidents are permanent in the several species of things to which they belong (لاتناهى في كل نوع). and that every accident subsists in a subject, though its subsistence therein is only by virtue of some idea (in the human mind). Mu'ammar and his followers were in consequence of this doctrine called Idealists (.اصحاب المعاني). Abû Ali Mohammed ibn Abdul Wahhâb, known as Abû Ali al-Jubbâi, maintained that action pertains to man in the way of origination and first production ; and ascribed to man moral good and evil, obedience and disobedience, in the way of sovereignty and prerogative ; and that free-will (الاستطاعة) is a pre-requisite to action, and a power additional to bodily completeness and soundness of the members. Abu'l Ma'âli al-Juwaini,' [1] *Imâm-ul-Haramain* (*i.e.* of the two sacred cities), who, however, did not call himself a Mu'tazila, and is generally claimed by the upholders of the opposite doctrine as belonging to their body, held that the denial of ability and free-will is something which reason and consciousness disavow ; that to affirm an ability without any sort of efficacy is equivalent to denying ability altogether, and that to affirm some unintelligible influence (of ability), which constitutes *a motive cause*, amounts to the denial of any special influence, and that, inasmuch as *conditions and states*, on the principle of those who maintain them, are not to be characterised as existing or non-existing (but must be explained by reference to their origin), action on the part of man (regarded as an existing state) is to be attributed really to his own ability, —though not in the way of origination and creation, for by creation is meant the causing of something to come into being by supreme power which was not previously in existence ; and that action depends for its existence upon ability (in man), which itself depends for its existence upon some other cause, its relation to that cause being the same as the relation of (human) action to (man's) ability, and so one cause depends upon another until the *causa causans* (مسبب الاسباب), the Creator of causes and of their operations, the Absolute Self-

---

[1] Died 1085.

sufficing, is reached. " This view," adds Shahristâni, " was borrowed by Abu'l Ma'âli from the Philosophers of the theistic school, but he presented it in the garb of the *Kalâm* (scholastic theology)." [1]

This is the general outline of the philosophical notions of the Mu'tazilas respecting some of the most burning questions which have agitated the mind of man in every age and country, and have so frequently led to sanguinary strifes and fratricidal wars both in the East and in the West.

As the assertors of divine Unity, shorn of all anthropomorphic conceptions, and the advocates of moral responsibility, they naturally called themselves *ashâb-ul-'adl wa't-tauhîd*, " upholders of the unity and justice of God," and designated their opponents *Mushabbihas* (" assimilators " or anthropomorphists). They reasoned thus : If sin emanated from, or was created by God, and man was pre-ordained to commit it, the imposition of any penalty for its commission would make the Creator an Unrighteous God,—which is infidelity : thus reason and revelation both tell us that piety and sin, virtue and vice, evil and good, are the product of human volition ; man has absolute control over his actions, though he has been told what is right and what is wrong. Evil and good depend upon what is just ; for God's creation is ruled by justice. Reason and justice are the guiding principles of human actions ; and general usefulness and the promotion of the happiness of mankind at large, the chief criterion of right and wrong. Has not God Himself declared that " the two Paths were shown to mankind for their own good ? Has He not Himself called upon them to exercise their understanding ? " Rationalists and Utilitarians, they based the foundations of the moral law on the concordance of Reason with positive revelation. They walked in the footsteps of the Master and his immediate descendants. They upheld the doctrine of Evolution in regarding every law that regulates the mutual relations of man to man as the result and outcome of a process of continuous development. In their ideas of the long

---

[1] Comp. Juwaini's views with those of Ibn-Rushd (Averroes). Shahristâni evidently had not made himself acquainted with the views of the Fâtimide Imâms ; Shahristâni, part i. pp. 70, 71. The views of Abu'l Ma'âli do not commend themselves to the " orthodox " Shahristâni.

R

422 THE SPIRIT OF ISLÂM II.

antiquity of man on earth,[1] they occupy a vantage ground in relation to the natural philosophers of the modern world.

Mu'tazilaism spread rapidly among all the thinking and cultured classes in every part of the Empire, and finding its way into Spain took possession of the Andalusian colleges and academies. Mansûr and his immediate successors encouraged Rationalism, but made no open profession of the Mu'tazilite doctrines. Mâmûn, who deserves more justly than any other Asiatic sovereign the title of " Great," acknowledged his adhesion to the Mu'tazilite school ; and he and his brother Mu'tasim and nephew Wâsik, endeavoured to infuse the rationalistic spirit into the whole Moslem world. Under them Rationalism acquired a predominance such as it has not gained perhaps even in modern times in European countries. The Rationalists preached in the mosques and lectured in the colleges ; they had the moulding of the character of the nation's youth in their hands ; they were the chief counsellors of the Caliphs, and it cannot be gainsaid that they used their influence wisely. As professors, preachers, scientists, physicians, viziers, or provincial governors, they helped in the growth and development of the Saracenic nation. The rise of the Banî-Idrîs in Western Africa, and the establishment of the Fâtimide power imparted a new life to Mu'tazilaism after its glory had come to an end in Asia.

The question now naturally occurs to the mind, how is it that predestinarianism and the subjection of Reason to blind authority, though discountenanced by the Prophet and the Philosophers of his family, became finally predominant in the speculations and practice of the Moslem world ? Before we furnish an answer to this inquiry, let us trace the development of another phase of the Moslem intellect. Mu'tazilaism has been, with considerable plausibility, compared to the scholastic philosophy of the Middle Ages in Europe. Scholasticism is said to have been the " movement of the intellect to justify by reason several of the dogmas of the Faith." Mu'tazilaism also directed its endeavours to establish a concordance between

[1] They derived this notion from a *Hadîs* reported from Ali, *Bihâr-ul-Anwâr*, chapter on Creation.

Reason and positive revelation. But there the parallel ends. In the Christian Church, the dogmas requiring explanation and justification were many. The doctrine of the trinity in unity, of the three " Natures " in one, of original sin, of transubstantiation, all gave rise to a certain intellectual tension. The dogmas of the Church accordingly required some such " solvent " as scholasticism before science and free thought could find their way into Christendom. In Islâm the case was otherwise ; with the exception of the unity of God—the doctrine of *Tauhîd*, which was the foundation of Mohammed's Church—there was no *dogma* upon which insistence was placed in any such form as to compel Reason to hold back its acceptance. The doctrine of " origin and return "—*mabdâ* (مبدا) and *maâd* (معاد), " coming (from God) and returning (to Him) "—and of the moral responsibility of man, was founded on the conception of a Primal Cause—the Originator of all things. That the *Ego* will not be entirely lost after it has been set apart from its earthly habiliments, that it will exist as a self-conscious entity after the dissolution of the body, is a notion which has been shared alike by the wise and the ignorant. Some few have denied a future existence, but the generality have believed in it, though all have differed as to the nature of that existence. So also as regards moral responsibility, there is great divergence of opinion on the mode in which man shall discharge the obligation ; but there is little difference on the question that he is responsible for the use or misuse of his powers. On both these questions the words of the Teacher allow the greatest latitude of judgment ; so long as the original conceptions were retained and accepted, Mohammed's Church permitted the broadest and most rationalistic view. Hence it was that Islâm passed at once from the Age of Receptivity into the Age of Activity, from the Age of Faith into the Age of Reason, without any such intermediate stage as was required in Christianity.

In the Prophet's time, as well as under the *Râshidîn* Caliphs, no doubt, free independent inquiry was naturally, and perhaps rightly, discouraged. But no questioning was avoided, no doubt was silenced by the terror of authority, and if the teacher was unable to answer the question, the inability was avowed in all humility.[1] Mu'tazilaism holds therefore a distinctive place in the development of the human intellect. It bears an analogy to European scholasticism, but in reality it is akin in genius to modern rationalism. Scholasticism worked under the shadow of the Church. Mu'tazilaism worked in conjunction with the heads of the Church. The real scholasticism of Islâm came later.

The cultivation of the physical sciences gave a new direction to Saracenic genius. A body of thinkers sprang up, who received the generic name of *Hukamâ* (pl. of *hakîm*, a scientist or philosopher), whose method of reasoning was analogous to that of modern science. They were mostly Mu'tazilas, but the conceptions of a few were tinged by the philosophical notions of Aristotle and the Neo-Platonic school of Alexandria. Though bigotry and ignorance stigmatised them with the opprobrious epithets of infidel and heretic, historical verity must admit that they did not exclude themselves from Islâm, nor advance any theory for which they were unable to find a warrant in the sayings of the Founder of the Faith or his immediate descendants.

The doctrine of evolution and progressive development to which these philosophers adhered most strongly has been propounded in clear terms by one of their prominent representatives, the famous Al-Hazen. The philosophical notions on this subject may be summarised thus : " In the region of existing matter, the mineral kingdom comes lowest, then comes the vegetable kingdom, then the animal, and finally the human being. By his body he belongs to the material world, but by his soul he appertains to the spiritual or immaterial. Above him are only the purely spiritual beings,—the angels,[2]— above whom only is God ; thus the lowest is combined by a chain of progress to the highest. But the human soul perpetually strives to cast off the bonds of matter, and, becoming free, it soars upwards again to God, from whom it emanated." And these notions found expression later in the *Masnavi* of

[1] The answer was, " God knows best."

[2] The author of the *Gouhar-i-Murâd*, to which I shall refer later in some detail, explains that what are called in " the language of theology " " angels," are the forces of nature in the language of *Hikmat*.

Moulâna Jalâl ud-dîn, whose "orthodoxy" can hardly be questioned,—

از جمادی مردم و نامی شدم
وز نما مردم بحیــــوان ســـرزدم
مردم از حیوانی و آدم شدم
پس چه ترسم کی ز مردن کم شوم
حملـهٔ دیگر بمیـــــرم از بشر
تا بر آرم از ملائک بال و پر
بار دیگـــر از ملــک پران شوم
آنچـــه اندروهم ناید آن شوم
پس عدم گردم عدم چون ارغنون
گویــد کانا الیـــه راجعـــون

"Dying from the inorganic we developed into the vegetable kingdom. Dying from the vegetable we rose to the animal. And leaving the animal we became men. Then what fear that death will lower us ? The next transition will make us angels. From angels we shall rise and become what no mind can conceive ; we shall merge in Infinity as in the beginning. Have we not been told, ' All of us will return unto Him ' ? "

The greatest of the philosophers were al-Kindi, al-Fârâbi, Ibn-Sîna, Ibn-Bâja, Ibn-Tufail, and Ibn-Rushd.[1]

Al-Kindi [2] (Abû Yusuf Ya'kûb ibn Ishâk), surnamed the Philosopher *par excellence*, was a descendant of the illustrious family of Kinda, and counted among his ancestors several of the princes of Arabia. His father, Ishâk bin as-Sabbâh, was the governor of Kûfa under al-Mahdi, al-Hâdi, and Hârûn. Al-Kindi, who prosecuted his studies at Basra and Bagdad, rendered himself famous under the Caliphs Mâmûn and Mu'tasim by the versatility of his genius and the profoundness of his knowledge. He wrote on philosophy, mathematics,

---

[1] Shahristâni mentions several others, such as—Yahya al-Nahwy, Abu'l Faraj al-Mufassir, Abû Sulaimân al-Sajzy, Abû Bakr Sâbit bin Kurrah, Abû Sulaimân Mohammed al-Mukaddasi, Abû Tamâm Yûsuf bin Mohammed Nishâpûri, Abû Zaid Ahmed bin Saha al-Balkhî, Abû Muhârib al-Hasan bin-Sahl bin Muhârib al-Kúmy, Ahmed bin Tayyeb al-Sarrakhsy, Talhâ bin Mohammed al-Nafsy, Abû Hâmid Ahmed bin Mohammed al-Safzâri, 'Isa bin Ali al-Wazîr, Abû Ali Ahmed bin Muskuya, Abû Zakaria Yahya bin 'Adi al-Zumairi, Abu'l Hasan al-'Âmri. He does not mention a single Spanish philosopher.

[2] 813 to 842 A.C. ; see Appendix II.

astronomy, medicine, politics, music, etc. Versed in the languages of the Greeks, the Persians, and the Indians, thoroughly acquainted with their sciences and philosophy, he was selected by Mâmûn for the work of translating Aristotle and other Greek writers into Arabic. "Cardan," says Munk, "places him among the twelve geniuses of the first order who had appeared in the world up to the sixteenth century."

Abû Nasr *Fârâbi* (Abû Nasr Mohammed bin Mohammed Turkhân *al-Fârâbi*), so called from his native city of Fârâb in Transoxiana, was a distinguished physician, mathematician, and philosopher. He is regarded as the most learned and subtle of the commentators of Aristotle. He enjoyed the patronage of Saif ud-dowla Ali bin Hamdân, Prince of Aleppo, and died at Damascus in the month of Rajab 339 A.H. December (950 A.C.). Among his various works some may be mentioned here to show the tendency of the Arab mind in that prolific age. In the *Encyclopædia of Science* (*Ihsâ ul-ulûm*) he gives a general review of all the sciences. A Latin epitome of this work gives an idea of the range over which it extends, being divided into five parts dealing with the different branches of science, viz. language, logic, mathematics, natural sciences, and political and social economy. Another celebrated work of Fârâbi, largely utilised by Roger Bacon and Albertus Magnus, was his commentary on Aristotle's *Organon*. His *Tendency of the Philosophies of Plato and Aristotle*, his treatise on ethics, entitled *as-Sîrat ul-Fazilâ*, and another on politics, called *as-Siyâsat ul-Medîneyya*, which forms part of a larger and more comprehensive work bearing the name of *Mabâdi-ul-Moujûdât*, show the versatile character of his intellect. Besides philosophy and medicine, Fârâbi cultivated music, which he elevated into a science. He wrote several treatises both on the theory and the art of music, as well as the manufacture of musical instruments. In one he compared the systems of music among the ancients with that in vogue in his own time. Abu'l Kâsim Kinderski, no mean judge, places Fârâbi on a level with his great successor, Ibn-Sîna.[1]

---

[1] See also the *'Uyûn-ul-Masâil* (Dieterici's ed. p. 52), where he establishes by deductive reasoning that Creation is the work of a Supreme Intelligence, and that nothing in the universe is fortuitous or accidental.

Of Ibn-Sîna I have already spoken as a physician. As a philosopher he occupies a position hardly inferior to that of the great Stagyrite. He was unquestionably the master-spirit of his age, and in spite of the opposition raised against him by fanaticism and self-interest, he left his impress in undying characters on the thoughts of succeeding ages. His voluminous works testify to the extraordinary activity of his mind.[1] He systematised Aristotelian philosophy, and filled " the void between God and man " in Aristotle's fragmentary psychology by the doctrine of the intelligence of the spheres conceived after a scientific method. The great object of the Arabian philosophers was to furnish the world with a complete theory of the unity of the Cosmos which would satisfy, not the mind only, but also the religious sense. And accordingly they endeavoured to reconcile the ethical and spiritual with the philosophical side of science. Hence the development of the theory of the two intellects—the passive Reason, or Abstract Soul, in contact with material forms, and subject through them to change and death ; and the Active Reason (Akl-i-fa'âl), conversant with the immutable, and so remaining unchanged in itself. By patient discipline of the heart and soul man can elevate himself to conjunction with this Higher Reason. But the discipline needed was as much moral and spiritual as intellectual. Ibn-Sîna represented these ideas in the highest degree. He was the truest and most faithful exponent of the philosophical aspirations of his time. " For ethical earnestness it would be hard to find anything more impressive than the teaching of Avicenna." A severely logical treatment of his subjects is the distinctive character of his writings. His main endeavour was directed towards the demonstration of the theory that there existed an intimate connexion between the human Soul and the Primary Absolute Cause—a conception which is traced in every line of Jalâl ud-dîn Rûmi.

Shahristâni gives a brief but exhaustive sketch of Ibn-Sîna's views, culled, as he says, from his various books. After describing Ibn-Sîna's treatment of the sciences, logic, and other

[1] His two greatest works on philosophy and science, the *Shifâ* and the *Najât*, still exist intact.

cognate subjects, Shahristâni states that the Philosopher discussed metaphysics under ten theses ; under the first five, he deals with the origin of knowledge, experimentation, induction, and deduction ; matter and force ; the relation of cause and effect ; the primary and accidental, universals and particulars. Under the sixth and seventh he demonstrates that the Primal Cause—the being whose existence is necessary by virtue of his Essence—is one and Absolute. Under the eighth and ninth he deals with the unity of the Cosmos, the relation of human souls to the Primal Cause and the Active Intellect, the first created. And lastly, he discusses the conception of future existence, the doctrine of " Return " (معاد). He proclaims the individual permanence of the human soul, and argues that it will retain its individuality after its separation from the corporeal body ; but that the pleasure and pain of the future existence will be purely spiritual, depending on the use or misuse by man of his mental, moral and physical powers to attain the Perfection. He argues under the last head the necessity for mankind of prophetism. The Prophet expounds to men the Divine laws, explains to them the ethical demands of God and Humanity in parables comprehensible to common folk, which appeal to and settle their hearts. The Prophet dissuades from jealousy, rancour, and misdeeds ; lays the foundations of social and moral development, and is God's veritable messenger on earth.

Abû Bakr Mohammed ibn Yahya, surnamed *Ibn-ul-Sâyeh*, popularly called Ibn-Bâja, corrupted by the European scholiasts into Avenpace, is one of the most celebrated philosophers among the Arabs of Spain. He was not only a distinguished physician, mathematician, and astronomer, but also a musician of the first rank. He was born at Saragossa towards the end of the eleventh century of the Christian era, and in 1118 A.C. we find him mentioned as residing in Seville. He afterwards proceeded to Africa, where he occupied a high position under the Almoravides. He died at Fez in 1138 A.C. Several of his works have come down to us in their entirety and show the free range of the Moslem intellect in those days.

Ibn-Tufail (Abû Bakr Mohammed ibn Abdul Malik ibn-

Tufail al-Kàisi) was born in the beginning of the twelfth century at Gaudix (Wâdi-ash), a small city of Andalusia, in the province of Granada. He was celebrated as a physician, mathematician, philosopher, and poet, and was held in great esteem at the court of the first two sovereigns of the Almohade dynasty. From 1163 to 1184 he filled the office of vizier and physician to Abû Ya'kûb Yusuf, the second Almohade king. Ibn-Tufail died in Morocco in 1185 A.C. He belonged to the contemplative school of Arab philosophy which was designated *Ishrâki*, an offshoot of ancient Neo-Platonism, and akin in its aspirations to modern mysticism. His contemplative philosophy is not founded on mystical exaltation, but on a method in which intuition is combined with reasoning. His famous work, called *Hayy ibn Yakzân*, represents the gradual and successive development of intelligence and the power of perception in a person wholly unassisted by outside instruction.[1]

Ibn-Rushd or Averroes (Abu'l Walîd Mohammed ibn Ahmed) was born in 520 A.H. (1126 A.C.) at Cordova, where his family had for a long time occupied a prominent position. His grandfather was the *Kâzi ul-Kuzât* of all Andalusia under the Almoravides. Ibn-Rushd was a jurisconsult of the first rank, but he applied himself mainly to medicine, mathematics, and philosophy. Introduced to Abû Ya'kûb Yusuf by Ibn-Tufail, he was received with great favour by that sovereign. In 1169-1170 we find him holding the office of Kâzi of Seville, and in 1182 of Cordova. For a few years after the accession of Ya'kûb al-Mansûr to the throne of the Almohades, Ibn-Rushd enjoyed the consideration and esteem of that monarch, but when the pent-up Berber fanaticism burst forth he was the first to fall a victim to the fury of the lawyers and Mullahs whom he had offended by his philosophical writings, and who were jealous of his genius and his learning. Ibn-Rushd was without question one of the greatest scholars and philosophers the Arab world has produced, and " one of the profoundest commentators," says Munk, " of Aristotle's works." Ibn-Rushd held that the highest effort of man ought to be directed towards the attainment of perfection, that is, a complete

[1] See Appendix III.

identification with the Active Universal Intellect ; that this perfection can only be attained by study and speculation, and abandoning all the desires which belong to the inferior faculties of the soul, and especially to the senses,—but not by mere sterile meditation. He also held that prophetic revelations were necessary for spreading among mankind the eternal verities proclaimed equally by religion and philosophy ; that religion itself directs their search by means of science ; that it teaches truths in a popular manner comprehensible to all people : that philosophy alone is capable of seizing the true religious doctrines by means of interpretation ; but the ignorant apprehend only the literal meaning. On the question of pre-destination he held that man was neither the absolute master of his actions nor bound by fixed immutable decrees. But the truth, says Ibn-Rushd, lies in the middle, الامر بين الامرين words used by the Fâtimide Imâms, and explained by them somewhat similarly. Our actions depend partly on our own free will and partly on causes outside us. We are free to wish and to act in a particular manner ; but our will is always restrained and determined by exterior causes. These causes spring from the general laws of nature ; God alone knows their sequence. It is this which, in the language of theology, is called *Kazâ* and *Kadar*. Ibn-Rushd's political theories were directed against human tyranny in every shape. He regarded the Arab republic under the Râshidîn Caliphs as the model government in which was realised the dream of Plato. Mu'âwiyah, he says, in establishing the Ommeyyade autocracy, overthrew this ideal, and opened the door to all disasters. Ibn-Rushd considered women to be equal in every respect to men, and claimed for them equal capacity—in war, in philosophy, in science. He cites the example of the female warriors of Arabia, Africa, and Greece ; and refers to their superiority in music in support of his contention, that, if women were placed in the same position as men, and received the same education, they would become the equals of their husbands and brothers in all the sciences and arts ; and he ascribes their inferiority to the narrow lives they lead.

In Ibn-Rushd Arabian philosophy reached its apogee. Six centuries divide him from the Prophet. Within these centuries the Arab intellect had broadened in every direction. Men like Ibn-Sîna and Ibn-Rushd thought with the accumulated wealth of ages on all the most important questions which occupy human attention in modern times, and formulated their ideas, little different from those held by the most advanced scientists of the present day, with logical precision. All these thinkers claimed to be Moslems, and were recognised as such by the best minds of their times. Ibn-Sîna repudiated with indignation and contempt the charge of infidelity levelled against him by fanatics or enemies jealous of his fame ; and one of the greatest mystical poets of Islâm, Sanâî, whose orthodoxy, though doubted by his personal foes, is no longer questioned, has embodied his veneration for " Bû Ali Sîna " in an immortal poem.[1]

Ibn-Rushd wrote on the concord of religion with philosophy ; and one of his intimate friends, Abd ul-Kabîr, a highly religious person, described him as one anxious to establish a harmony between religion and philosophy.[2] Al-Ansâri and Abd ul-Walîd speak of Ibn-Rushd as sincerely attached to Islâm ; and his latest biographer says : " There is nothing to prevent our supposing that Ibn-Rushd was a sincere believer in Islâmism, especially when we consider how little irrational the supernatural element in the essential dogmas of this religion is, and how closely this religion approaches the purest Deism." [3]

The close of the tenth century was full of the darkest omens for rationalism and science. The star of the son of Sîna had not yet risen on the horizon ; but masters like Kindi and Fârâbi had appeared and departed after shedding an abiding lustre on the Saracenic race. Patristicism was triumphant in every quarter which owned the temporal or spiritual sway of the Abbasides : the college of jurists had placed under the ban of heresy the rationalists and philosophers who had made the name of Moslems glorious in the annals of the world ; a heartless, illiberal, and persecuting formalism dominated the

---

[1] See Appendix III.

[2] In the *Fasl-ul-Makâl* (Muller's ed. published in Munich, 1859), which is said to have been written in A.H. 575 for the Almohade sovereign Yusuf ibn Tâshfîn, he establishes this concordance.

[3] Renan, *Averroes et Averroism*, p. 163.

spirit of the theologians ; a pharisaical epicureanism had taken possession of the rich, and an ignorant fanaticism of the poor ; the gloom of night was fast thickening, and Islâm was drifting into the condition into which ecclesiasticism had led Christianity. It was at this epoch of travail and sorrow for all lovers of truth that a small body of thinkers formed themselves into a Brotherhood to keep alive the lamp of knowledge among the Moslems, to introduce a more healthy tone among the people, to arrest the downward course of the Moslems towards ignorance and fanaticism, in fact, to save the social fabric from utter ruin. They called themselves the " Brothers of Purity," *Ikhwân-us-Safâ*. The society of the " Pure Brethren " was established in Basra, which still held rank in the fast-dwindling Caliphate as the second city of the empire, the home of rationalism and intellectual activity. To this " Brotherhood " none but men of unsullied character and the purest morals were admitted ; the passport for admission into the select circle was devotion to the cause of knowledge and humanity. There was nothing exclusive or esoteric in their spirit ; though, from the necessities of their situation, and working under a rigid theological and political despotism, their movements were enshrouded in some degree of mystery. They met together quietly and unobtrusively in the residence of the head of the society, who bore the name of Zaid the son of Rifâ'a, and discussed philosophical and ethical subjects with a catholicity of spirit and breadth of views difficult to rival even in modern times. They formed branches in every city of the Caliphate, wherever, in fact, they could find a body of thoughtful men, willing and qualified to work according to their scientific method. This philanthropic and scientific movement was led by five men, who, with Zaid, were the life and soul of the " Brotherhood." Their system was eclectic in the highest and truest sense of the word. They contemned no field of thought ; they " culled flowers from every meadow." In spite of the mysticism which slightly tinged their philosophical conceptions, their views on social and political problems were highly practical and intensely humane. As the result of their labours, they gave to the world a general *résumé* of the knowledge of the time in separate treatises, which were collectively known as the *Rasâil* [1]-*i-Ikhwân-us-Safâ wa-Khullân-ul-Wafâ*, " Tracts of the Brothers of Purity and Friends of Sincerity " ; or, shortly, *Rasâil-i-Ikhwân-us-Safâ*.[2] These *risâlas* range over every subject of human study—mathematics, including astronomy, physical geography, music, and mechanics ; physics, including chemistry, meteorology, and geology ; biology, physiology, zoology, botany, logic, grammar, metaphysics, ethics, the doctrine of a future life. They form, in fact, a popular encyclopædia of all the sciences and philosophy then extant. The theory of these evolutionists of the tenth century as to the development of animal organism may be compared with advantage with that entertained in present times. But I am not concerned so much with the scientific and intellectual side of their writings as with the ethical and moral. The ethics of the " Pure Brethren " are founded on self-study and the purification or abstraction of human thought from all impurity. Moral endowments are prized above intellectual gifts ; and the strength of soul founded upon patient self-discipline and self-control is regarded as the highest of virtues.[3] " Faith without work, knowing without doing, were vain." Patience and forbearance, mildness and loving gentleness, justice, mercy, and truth, the sublimity of virtue, the sacrifice of self for others, are taught in every line : cant, hypocrisy, and deceit, envy and pride, tyranny and falsehood, are reprobated in every page ; and the whole is pervaded by a purity of sentiment, a fervent love of humanity, an earnest faith in the progress of man, a universal charity, embracing even the brute creation in its fold.[4] What can be more beautiful, more truly humane, than the disputation between the " animals and mankind " ? Their ethics form the foundation of all later works.[5] Their religious idea was identical with that of Fârâbi and Ibn Sîna,—the universe was an emanation from God, but not directly ; the Primal Absolute Cause created Reason, or the Active Intel-

---

[1] Plural of *Risâla*, a tract, a chapter, a monograph.

[2] Published in 4 vols., at Bombay, in 1305 A.H., by Haji Nûr ud-dîn.

[3] See the third *Risâla*, vol. iv.

[4] See the fourth *Risâla*, vol. iv.

[5] Such as the *Akhlâk-i-Nâsiri* of Nasîr ud-din Tûsi, the *Akhlâk-i-Jâlâli*, and the *Akhlâk-i-Muhsini* of Husain Wâiz Kâshifi.

ligence : and from this proceeded the *Nafs-i-nufús*, the Abstract Soul, from which sprang primary matter, the protoplasm of all material entities ; the Active Intelligence moulded this primary matter, and made it capable of taking shapes and forms, and set it in motion, whence were formed the spheres and the planets. Their morality is founded on this very conception of the Primal Absolute Cause being connected by an unbroken chain with the lowest of His creation ; for the Abstract Soul individualised in humanity is always struggling to attain by purity of life, self-discipline, intellectual study, the goal of Perfection,—to get back to the source from which it emanated. This is *Ma'âd* ; this is the " Return " which the Prophet taught; this is the rest and peace inculcated in the Scripture. It was thus that the " Pure Brethren " taught. Whatever we may think of their psychology there is no denying that their morality was of the purest, their ethics of the highest that can be conceived, standing on a different plane from those of the theologians who induced the bigot Mustanjid to burn their encyclopædia in Bagdad, before Bagdad itself was burnt by the Mongols.

Aristotelian philosophy, which was founded on " observation and experience," was, however, more akin to the Saracenic genius and the positive bent of the Arab mind. Aristotelian logic and metaphysics naturally exercised a great influence on the conceptions of Arab scientists and scholars. Neo-Platonism based on intuition and a certain vague and mystical contemplation, did not take root among the Arabs until it was made popular by the writings of the unfortunate Shihâb ud-dîn Suhrwardi. The Aristotelian conception of the First Cause pervades accordingly many of the philosophical and metaphysical writings of this period. And it was in consequence of the influence exercised by the Stagyrite that a section of Arab thinkers tended towards a belief in the eternity of matter. These men received the name of *Dahrîs* (from *dahr*, or *nature*). " The fundamental idea of these philosophers," says Kremer, " was the same as has gained ground, in modern times, owing to the extension of natural science." But they were not, as their enemies called them, *atheists*. Atheism is the negation of a power or Cause beyond and outside the visible and material world. These philosophers affirmed no such thing ; they only held that it was impossible to predicate of the *Causa Causans* any attribute whatsoever, or to explain the mode in which He works on the universe. They were, in fact, the exponents of the doctrine of *ta'lil* or agnosticism.

It appears clear, therefore, that the Islâm of Mohammed contains nothing which in itself bars progress or the intellectual development of humanity. How is it, then, that, since the twelfth century of the Christian era, philosophy has almost died out among the followers of Islâm and an anti-rationalistic patristicism has taken possession of the bulk of the people ? How is it that predestinarianism, though only one phase of the Koranic teachings, has become the predominant creed of a large number of Moslems ? As regards the supposed *extinction* among them of philosophy, I should like to call attention to the revival of *Avicennism* under the Safawi sovereigns of Persia to show that rationalism and free-thought are not yet dead in Islâm. But the questions which I have formulated apply to the general body of Moslems, and I propose to explain the causes which have led to this result.

Before the Abbaside Mutawakkil's accession to the throne, Islâm presented a spectacle similar to that of Christendom in the seventeenth and eighteenth centuries. It was divided into two camps, one of Authority, the other of Reason ; the one advocated the guidance of humanity in matters, natural as well as supernatural, by precedent, pure and simple ; the other, by human judgment tempered so far as practicable by precedent. Between these two parties the difference was irreconcilable. The first was composed chiefly of the lawyers—a class of people who have been regarded in every age and country, and not always without reason, as narrow-minded, self-opinionated, and extremely jealous of their interests as a body. To them were joined the ignorant populace. " The creed of the bishop is the creed of the grocer. But the philosophy of that grocer is in no sense the philosophy of a professor. Therefore it is that the bishop will be revered where the professor will be stoned. Intellect is that which man claims as specially his own ; it is the one limiting distinction ; and thus the multitude, so tolerant of the claims of an aristocracy of birth or of wealth, is uneasy under the claims of an aristocracy of intelligence." [1]

As I have had occasion to mention in a previous chapter, most of the legal decisions pronounced by the Prophet were called forth by the passing necessities of a primitive and archaic society. After him the Caliph Ali was the expositor of the new Faith. In the Koran these legal doctrines were extremely few, and adaptable to any circumstance or time, and, during the reigns of the Râshidîn Caliphs, were expounded chiefly by Ali and his disciple Ibn Abbâs.

Upon their death, the men who had attended their lectures or listened to their judgments opened classes of jurisprudence on their own account. *Fakîhs* or lawyers multiplied ; they discussed religio-legal questions, gave opinions on points of casuistry, the rites of religion, as well as on the ordinary relations of life. Gradually they became the keepers of the conscience of the people. Naturally there was a keen desire to discover how the Prophet had acted in any particular case ; traditions multiplied. The supply was in proportion to the demand. But, excepting in the school of Medîna, there was no uniformity of system or method. The immediate descendants of Mohammed followed one definite rule ; if they found any precedent of the time of the Prophet or of the Caliph Ali, authenticated by their own ancestors, *which was applicable to the circumstances of the case*, they based their decision upon it ; if not, they relied on their own judgment. Law was with them inductive and experimental ; and they decided according to the exigencies and requirements of each particular case. Under the early Ommeyyades there was no fixed rule ; the governors ruled sharply by the sword, according to their own judgment, leaving matters of conscience to the *Fakîhs*. Under the later Ommeyyades, however, the lawyers assumed great preponderance, chiefly on account of their influence with the fickle populace. When the Abbasides rose to power the lecture-room of Imâm Ja'far as Sâdik was attended by two men who afterwards became the bulwarks of the Sunni Church, —one was Abû Hanîfa,[2] and the other Mâlik son of Anas.[3]

[1] Lewes's *History of Philosophy*, vol. ii.p. 59.
[2] See *ante*, p. 351.   [3] See *ante*, p. 352.

Abû Hanîfa was a native of Irâk ; Mâlik, of Medîna. Both were men of severe morals and great kindliness of nature, and anxious to broaden the foundations of the Church. They were devoted to the family of the Prophet, and suffered in consequence of their attachment. Abû Hanîfa on his return to Kûfa opened a class which became the nucleus of the now famous Hanafî school. He rejected most of the traditions [1] as untrue, and relied solely on the Koran ; and by " analogical deductions " endeavoured to make the simple Koranic utterances applicable to every variety of circumstance. Abû Hanîfa knew nothing of human kind ; nor had he ever been to any city except Medîna and Bagdad. He was a speculative legist, and his two disciples, Abû Yusuf, who became Chief Kâzi of Bagdad under Hârûn, and Mohammed ash-Shaibâni, fixed Abû Hanîfa's conceptions on a regular basis. Mâlik proceeded on different lines. He excluded from his system all inferences and " deductions." He applied himself to discover in Medîna, so full of the Prophet's memories, every real or supposititious incident in the Master's life and based his doctrines thereupon. His was " the Beaten Path," [2] and to the simple Arabs and the cognate races of Africa Mâlik's enunciations were more acceptable, being suited to their archaic forms of society, than the rationalised views of the Fâtimide Imâms, or the speculative theories of Abû Hanîfa. Soon after came Shâfeˈi, a man of strong and vigorous mind, better acquainted with the world than Abû Hanîfa and Mâlik, and less casuistical than Abû Yusuf and Mohammed ash-Shaibâni. He formed, from the materials furnished by Jaˈfar as-Sâdik, Mâlik, and Abû Hanîfa, an eclectic school, which found acceptance chiefly among the middle classes. Less adaptable than original Hanafîsm to the varying necessities of a growing and mixed population, it contained sufficient germs of improvement which, had they not been killed by the rigid formalism of later times, would have been productive of substantial good. [3] Four different systems of law and doctrine, more or less distinct from

[1] Ibn Khallikân.

[2] The *Muwatta*, *i.e.* " The Beaten Path," is the name of his work on jurisprudence.

[3] Shâfeˈism is spreading rapidly among the educated Hanafis of India.

each other, thus established themselves in the Islâmic world. The Fâtimide system was chiefly in force among the Shiahs, who were dispersed all over the empire ; Mâlikism among a large part of the Arabs in the Peninsula, among the Berbers, and most of the Spanish Moslems ; Shâfe'ism among the fairly well-to-do classes ; and Hanafism among the more respectable sections of society in Mesopotamia, Syria, and Egypt. The position of Hanafism in the Caliphate was similar to that of Pharisaism among the Jews. It received the countenance of the Court as the only school with sufficient expansiveness to meet the requirements of a mixed population. To have acknowledged the Fâtimide system would have been to give too great a preponderance to the descendants of the Prophet ; to have adopted Mâlikism and Shâfe'ism for the administration of a liberal State would have jeopardised the interests of the empire. Hence, whilst rationalism ruled in the colleges and *Madrasas*,[1] Hanafism held possession of the pulpits and *Mahkamas*.[2] In its theological views, Hanafism inclined towards *Sifâtism* ; but it varied its opinions according to those of the rulers. At this period Hanafism was remarkable for its flexibility. Ahmed ibn Hanbal, commonly known as Imâm Hanbal, made his appearance at this juncture,—a red hot puritan, breathing eternal perdition to all who differed from him, he was shocked with the pharisaical liberalism of Hanafism, and disgusted both with the narrowness of Mâlikism and the common-place character of Shâfe'ism, he applied himself to frame a new system, based on traditions, for the whole empire. Abû Hanîfa had rejected the majority of the current traditions ; Ibn Hanbal's system included a mass of incongruous, irrational, and bewildering stories, the bulk of which were wholly incon- sistent with each other, and bearing upon their face the marks of fabrication. And now commenced a serious struggle between the parties of progress and retrogression. Ibn Hanbal adopted the extreme *Sifâtia* views ; he inculcated that the Deity was visible to the human sight ; that His attributes were separate from His essence ; that the statements about His being seated on the throne were to be accepted in their literal sense ; that

---

[1] *Madrasa* is a place where lectures are given, hence a college, school, etc.

[2] Courts of justice.

man was in no sense a free agent ; that every human action was the direct act of the Deity, and so forth. He denounced learning and science, and proclaimed a holy war against Rationalism. The populace, carried away by his eloquence or his vehemence, took up the cry ; the Hanafî jurists, whose power materially depended on their influence over the ignorant masses, and who were jealous of the prominence of the scientists and philosophers in the Court of Hârûn and Mâmûn, made common cause with the new reformer. The pulpits began to fulminate brimstone and fire against the upholders of reason and the advocates of philosophy and science. The streets of Bagdad became the scenes of frequent rioting and bloodshed. Mu'tasim and Wâsik repressed the fanatical violence of the fiery puritans with some severity. The prime mover of the disturbances was put in prison, where he died in the odour of great sanctity ; his bier was followed to the grave by a crowd consisting of a hundred and forty thousand men and women.[1] His system never took root among any large body of people : but, mixing with Hanafîsm, it gave a new character to the doctrines of Abû Hanîfa. Henceforth Hanafîsm represents a mixture of the teachings of Abû Hanîfa and of Ibn Hanbal.

When Mutawakkil was raised to the throne the position of the various parties stood thus :—the Rationalists were the directing power of the State ; they held the chief offices of trust ; they were professors in colleges, superintendents of hospitals, directors of observatories ; they were merchants ; in fact, they represented the wisdom and the wealth of the empire ; Rationalism was the dominating creed among the educated, the intellectual, and influential classes of the community. *Sifâtism* was in force among the lower strata of society, and most of the Kâzis, the preachers, the lawyers of various degree were attached to it. A cruel drunken sot, almost crazy at times, Mutawakkil had the wit to perceive the advantage of an alliance with the latter party. It would make him at once the idol of the populace, and the model Caliph of the bigots. The fiat accordingly went forth for the expulsion of the party of progress from their offices under government.

[1] See Appendix II.

The colleges and universities were closed; literature, science, and philosophy were interdicted; and the Rationalists were hunted from Bagdad. Mutawakkil at the same time demolished the mausoleum of the Caliph Ali and his sons. The fanatical lawyers, who were now the priests and rabbis of Islâm, became the ruling power of the State. Mutawakkil's death and Mustansir's accession gave the victory once more to the Progressists. But their success was short-lived. Under the pitiless and sanguinary Mu'tazid b'illâh the triumph of Patristicism was complete. He mercilessly persecuted the Rationalists. They inculcated that " justice " was the animating principle of human actions; that God Himself governed the universe by " justice," which was His Essence; that the test of right and wrong was not any individual will, but the good of humanity. These doctrines were terribly revolutionary; they were aimed at the divine right of the Caliph to do wrong. Tom Paine could scarcely preach worse. On the other hand, the clerical party taught very properly " God is the Sovereign; as the sovereign does no wrong, so God can do no wrong." There could be no question which of these two doctrines was true. The days of Rationalism were now over under the Abbasides. Expelled from Bagdad, it took refuge in Cairo, which was worse, for if there was one place which the Abbaside Caliphs hated with the hatred of death, that was Cairo. The very name of Rationalism became one of dire import to the Pontiffs of Bagdad. A College of Jurists was established to ferret out " heresy " in the writings of the philosophers and scientists, whose misfortune was still to live within the reach of the patristic influences. The works in which the smallest taint was observed were committed to the flames; their authors were subjected to tortures and to death. Islâm now presented the spectacle of orthodox Christendom. There was a time when, in spite of the fact that the temporal power was arrayed against it, Rationalism would have regained its hold on the masses. In their constant disputations the clerical party always found themselves worsted; and though, on these occasions, they not infrequently invoked the more forcible reasoning of the sword and bricks and stones, their defeats in argument perceptibly told on the ranks of their followers.

It was at this period that the retrogressive party received the assistance of an unexpected ally. Hitherto they had fought against Reason with their usual repertory of traditions. Abu'l Hasan al-Asha'ri,[1] a descendant of the famous Abû Mûsa al-Asha'ri, who had been tricked by 'Amr ibn al-'Âs into abandoning the rights of the Caliph Ali, was educated among the Mu'tazilas. He had learnt their logic, their philosophy, their science of reasoning. Actuated by vanity, and partly perhaps by ambition, he one day in the *Jâmi'* mosque of Basra, in the presence of a large congregation, made a public disavowal of the Mu'tazilite doctrines, and declared his adherence to *Sifâtism*. His theatrical manner and his eloquent words impressed the people, and the waverers at once went over to him. Asha'ri was now the greatest man in the Caliphate ; he was petted by the legists, idolised by the populace, respected by the Caliph. He gave to the clerical party what they had long been wanting—a logical system, or what may be called by that name, for the defence of patristic theology against the rationalistic conceptions of the Mu'tazilas, the philosophers, and the Fâtimide Imâms. Abu'l Hasan maintained the Sifâtia doctrines, with very slight modifications.

A short summary of his views, taken from Shahristâni, will explain the present mental lethargy of so many Moslems. " He maintained," says our author, " that the attributes of the Deity are eternal and subsistent in His Essence, but they are not simply His Essence, rather they are additional to His Essence ; . . . that God speaks by an eternal word, and wills by an eternal will, for it is evident that God is a Sovereign, and, as a Sovereign, is One to whom it belongs to command and prohibit, so God commands and prohibits ; . . . that His ordering is eternal, subsistent in Him, a quality pertaining to Him ; that the will of God is indivisible, eternal, embracing all things subject to volition, whether determinate actions of His own or actions of His creatures—the latter, so far as created

[1] Al-Ashâ'ri was born at Basra in 260 A.H. (874 A.C.), but passed the greatest part of his life in Bagdad. Up to the fortieth year of his age he was a devoted adherent of the Mu'tazilas. He ascribed his theatrical abjuration of his old beliefs to an admonition he received from the Prophet in a dream during the fasting month of Ramazân.

by Him, not as they are their own actions by *appropriation* ; [1]
. . . that God wills all things morally, good and evil, beneficial
and injurious ; and, as He both knows and wills, that He wills
on the part of His creatures what He knows, and has caused to
be registered in the memorial-book—which fore-knowledge
constitutes His decree, His decisions, and His determination,
therein there is no varying or change ; that an *appropriated*
action means an action which is pre-destined to be done by
created ability, and which takes place under the condition of
created ability." In plainer language, he taught that every
human action emanates from God, or is pre-destined by His
decree, to be performed by a particular person, and this person,
having the capacity of *appropriation* or *acquisitiveness*, does
the act ; the act is primarily God's act, secondarily the man's.
For example, if a man applies himself to write a letter, his
desire to write is the outcome of an eternal decree that he
should write ; then he takes up the pen, it is the will of God
that He should do so ; and so on. When the writing is finished,
it is due to his *acquisitiveness*. Shahristâni very appropriately
observes that, according to Abu'l Hasan, no influence in
respect to origination (of action) pertains to created ability.
This worthy divine further maintained that " God rules as a
Sovereign over His creatures, doing what He wills and determining as He pleases ; so that were He to cause all men to
enter Paradise, there would be no injustice, and if He were to
send them all to hell, there would be no wrong-doing, because
injustice is the ordering in respect to things which do not
come within the sphere of control of the Orderer, or the
inversion of established relations of things, and God is the
Absolute Sovereign, on whose part no injustice is imaginable,
and to whom no wrong can be attributed ; . . . and that nothing
whatever is obligatory upon God by virtue of reason—neither
that which is beneficial, nor that which is most advantageous,
nor gracious assistance . . . and that the ground of (human)
obligation is nothing which constitutes a necessity binding
upon God." . . .

After mentioning the doctrines of Abu'l Hasan, Shahristâni
proceeds to state the views of Abu'l Hasan's principal disciple,

[1] Shahristâni explains this word later.

whose teachings were adopted by a large body of people—Abû Abdullah Mohammed bin Karrâm, " whom we count as one of the Sifâtias." This man maintained that the Divine attributes were distinct from His Essence, that God can be perceived by eyesight, and that He creates human actions from time to time as He wills.

No account of al-Asha'ri's teachings would be complete without a reference to Ibn 'Asâkir's work.[1] Shahristâni in his *résumé* of the Asha'rite doctrines maintains a philosophical and judicial attitude. Ibn 'Asâkir, on the other hand, makes no pretence of holding an even balance between contending schools. To him, as to Asha'ri, the doctrines of the Rationalists are rank heresy; and he denounces their teachings with uncompromising violence. His exposition, however, of al-Asha'ri's emphatic rule that the dogmas of the Faith must be accepted by the orthodox, without questioning, helps us to understand the tendencies which were set in motion at an early stage of Moslem development, and which eventually succeeded in arresting the progress of Moslem nations and paralysing, in the course of centuries, their intellectual energy. All questioning was declared to be an impiety and an unforgivable sin, whilst the spirit of inquiry was held to be a manifestation of the devil. " God," says the Koran, " sees all things "; therefore, it was assumed, He must have eyes, and the believer must accept it *bila kaifa*, without " why or wherefore ";—thus reasoned al-Asha'ri, and thus has reasoned his school through all ages.

Two hundred and fifty years separate al-Asha'ri from his distinguished exponent and apologist. Within this period of time, Islâm had undergone a great change. Until al-Asha'ri started his new school of dogmatic theology, the struggle for ascendancy was confined between Rationalism on one side and Patristicism on the other. Al-Asha'ri supplied the latter with a weapon it had never possessed before. As Ibn 'Asâkir

---

[1] Abil-Kasim Ali bin al-Hasan b. Hibat-ullah, b. Abdullah bin al-Hasan Ali Shafe'i, surnamed Ibn 'Asâkir, famous for his monumental work on the history of Damascus, was born in 499 A.H., died 571 A.H. He was a rigid Shafe'ite and a violent partisan of al-Asha'ri, whom he regarded as a renovator and foremost champion of Islâm. Ibn 'Asâkir's work is called *The Exposure by al-Imâm Hasan al-Asha'ri of Mischievous Untruths.*

remarks, " al-Asha'ri was the first orthodox dialectician,[1] who reasoned with the Rationalists and other heretics according to their own principles of logic." As an attempted compromise between Rationalism and Patristicism, between " orthodoxy " and " heterodoxy," his doctrines found a ready acceptance among the extreme theologians and divines, who saw in his system the means for overthrowing Rationalism from the pinnacle of power and influence which it had attained in the enlightened reigns of al-Mâmûn and his two immediate successors. Rationalism was also favoured by the earlier Buyides, and, under their auspices and encouragement, its influence had become paramount in Mid-Asia. " The power of the Mu'tazila," says Ibn 'Asâkir, " was very great in Irâk until the time of Fenâkhusru " ('Azud-ud-Dowla).[2] In his reign Asha'rism first found favour at Court and gradually spread among all classes. Up to the middle of the fifth century of the Hegira it was often confounded with Mu'tazilaism, which al-Asha'ri had professed until his dramatic secession. His disciples appear even to have been subjected to some persecution at the hands of the sects who claimed the special privilege of orthodoxy.

Under Sultan Tughril, the founder of the Seljukide dynasty, the followers of al-Asha'ri were suspected of unorthodoxy, and had to undergo proscription and exile. The Sultan himself was a follower of Imâm Abû Hanîfa and professed Hanafite orthodoxy. He had given orders for public imprecation on heretics from the pulpits of the mosques. According to Ibn 'Asâkir, his vizier,[3] who was a Mu'tazili, included the Asha'rites in the imprecation, and started a persecution of the

---

[1] *Mutakallim bi'lisan.*

[2] Al-Malik Fenâkhusru reigned as the Mayor of the Palace from 367-372 A.H. Ibn 'Asâkir tells the story of how Fenâkhusru, after attending one of the " Assemblies of the learned " which were held in the house of the Chief Kazi, who was a Mu'tazili, found that there was not a single Asha'rite in their midst. On being told that there was no learned Asha'rite in Bagdad, he pressed the Judge to invite some from outside. It was at his instance, it is stated, that Ibn al-Bakillani, one of the principal disciples of al-Asha'ri, was summoned to Bagdad. To him Fenâkhusru confided the education of his sons. Whether this story be true or not, the period of 'Azud-ud-Dowla's reign fixes the date of the rise of the Star of Asha'rism.

[3] Abû Nasr Mansur Kunduri, surnamed 'Amid ul-Mulk.

most prominent Imâms and doctors among the disciples of al-Asha'ri.

The cloud under which Asha'rism laboured in the reign of Tughril Beg lifted on his death, and with the accession of Alp Arslân and the rise of Nizâm ul-Mulk, " who favoured the adherents of the Sunnat," Asha'rism became the dominant sect. " He recalled the exiles, covered them with honours, opened colleges and schools in their names." Thus one of the most generous patrons of learning among the Moslems unconsciously allied himself to a tendency to which, more largely than any other cause, the sterilisation of the intellectual energies of the Moslems is due.

Ibn 'Asâkir's account of the progress of Asha'rism is enthusiastic. From Irâk it spread into Syria and Egypt under the Ayyubides [1] and Mamelukes ; from Irâk also it was carried into Western Africa by Ibn Tumart,[2] and it took firm root in the *Maghrib* (Morocco). " There remained no other sect in Islâm, excepting some followers of Ibn Hanbal and some partisans of Abû Hanîfa, to compete with the adherents of al-Asha'ri." " Ahmed bin Hanbal and al-Asha'ri were in perfect harmony," says Ibn 'Asâkir, " in their religious opinions and did not differ in any particular, in the fundamental doctrines and in the acceptance of the authority of the Traditions." " This is the reason," he continues, " why the Hanbalites relied from always and at all times on the Asha'rites against the heterodox, as they were the only dialecticians among the orthodox."

To throw into relief the cardinal principles of al-Asha'ri's teachings, Ibn 'Asâkir places in juxtaposition the opinions held by different sects.

After mentioning various other sects, he gives an account, in the words of al-Asha'ri, of the Mu'tazilite doctrines (" in which they have strayed from the right path "). He tells us that the Mu'tazilas repudiate the notion that God can be seen by the corporeal sight, or that the Almighty has any similitude to human beings ; or that there will be a corporeal resurrection on the Day of Account. " They repudiate also," he says,

---

[1] Saladin and his successors.

[2] The founder of the Almohade dynasty in north-west Africa.

" the doctrine of pains and penalties (*'Azâb*) [1] in the grave,"
nor do they believe in the intercession (*Shafâ'at*) of the Prophet ;
they hold that human sins can only be forgiven or remitted by
Divine Mercy, and that neither His mercy nor justice can be
influenced or deflected by human intercession ; they believe
that the Koran is created and revealed to the Prophet
and that the " law has been announced according to human
needs."

After stating the Mu'tazilite doctrines Ibn 'Asâkir proceeds
to give in detail the creed of al-Asha'ri. They are twenty-four
in number, but to show the theological attitude of al-Asha'ri
and his sharp difference with rationalistic Islâm it is sufficient
to refer only to a few. After the confession of Faith, regarding
the unity of God and the messengership of the Prophet in which
all Islâm is agreed, the Asha'rite creed proceeds thus :—

" We declare that Paradise and Hell are true, that the arrival
of the Hour of Judgment is certain, and that without doubt
God will raise the dead from their graves ; that God will appear
to human sight on the Day of Judgment.[2] We declare that the
word of God (*i.e.* the Koran), and every part thereof, is
uncreated : that there is nothing on earth, neither good nor
bad, which does not come into existence but by the will of God :
that nothing, in fact, comes into being unless He wishes. We
believe that God the Almighty knows the acts of His servants
and their ends and consequences, as well as those which do not
come to pass. We believe that human actions owe their
origin to His will and are determined in advance by Him ; that
man has no power to originate or create anything by himself
(*i.e.* without God's help). That man is incapable of obtaining
by himself that which is good for his soul, or avoiding that
which is harmful, except by the will of God."

The Asha'rite creed then goes on thus :—" We believe in
the intercession of the Prophet, and that God will redeem from

---

[1] The meaning of *'Azab* will become clearer later on.

[2] It is believed that on the third day after burial the grave is visited
by two angels named Munkir and Nakir, who raise the dead to life by blows
from their batons, and interrogate him as to his or her past life and record
the answers in a register. They act as a sort of *Juge d'instruction*. This
belief, evidently an offshoot from the Egyptian conceptions, was imbedded
in the folk-lore of the country before the promulgation of Islâm.

the punishment of fire believers who have sinned." "We believe in the Day of Resurrection, we believe in the appearance of the anti-Christ, in the interrogation of the dead by the two angels (Munkir and Nakir). We believe in the Ascension of the Prophet ;[1] we believe that all evil thoughts are inspired by Satan ; we believe that it is sinful to rise in arms against the lawful Imâm."[2]

This summary shows more clearly than Shahristâni's philosophical analysis the attitude of al-Asha'ri towards Moslem development.

In order to meet the Mu'tazilas on their own ground, Abu'l Hasan invented a rival *science of reason*—the real scholastic theology of the Moslems, which, though supposed to be an offshoot of the *'Ilm-ul-kalâm* founded by the Mu'tazilas, is in many essential features different from it. For example, most of the Mu'tazilas were *conceptualists*, whilst the Asha'rî *Mutakallimîn* were either *realists* or modified *nominalists*. The Asha'rîs maintained that a negative quality like ignorance is an actual entity, whilst the Mu'tazilas declared that it was the mere negation of a quality, for example, ignorance was the absence of knowledge. The Asha'rî *Mutakallim* maintained that the Koran was uncreated and eternal ; the Mu'tazilite declared that it represented the words of God revealed to the Prophet from time to time as occasion arose, otherwise there would be no meaning in *nâsikh* and *mansûkh*, for admittedly some of the later verses repealed others which had been uttered before.

Asha'rism thus became the dominant school in the East. When the enlightened Buyides became the mayors of the palace Rationalism again raised its head in Bagdad ; but Asha'rism never lost its hold over the conscience of the masses,

---

[1] The belief in the Ascension of the Prophet is general in Islâm. Whilst the Asha'ri and the patristic sects believe that the Prophet was bodily carried up from earth to heaven, the Rationalists hold that it was a spiritual exaltation, that it represented the uplifting of the soul by stages until it was brought into absolute communion with the Universal Soul.

[2] The orthodox Sunni belief, that once the sacramental oath of allegiance is sworn to the Caliph any rising against him is a religious crime, led all Moslem sovereigns to beg for investiture from the Caliph, however impotent, as it made insurrection against them or their authority on the part of their subjects unlawful.

nor did Mu'tazilaism ever regain its old position of preponderance.   The Buyides were Rationalists ; but the Seljukides, in
spite of their patronage of learning and science, belonged to
the Asha'rî school.   Renan [1] has observed that Islâmism,
having become, by the accident of history, the property of races
given over to fanaticism, such as the Spaniards, the Berbers,
the Persians, the Turks, acquired in their hands the garb of
a rigid and exclusive dogmatism.   " What has happened to
Catholicism in Spain has happened to Islâm, what would have
happened in all Europe if the religious revival which took place
(in Christendom) at the end of the sixteenth and the beginning
of the seventeenth century had stopped all national development."   This observation is absolutely true.   The Persian
always associated an idea of divinity with the person of his
sovereign ; the Turk, the Mongol, the Berber looked upon their
chiefs as the direct descendants of God ; conversion to Islâm
did not detract from their veneration of their kings or princes.
For centuries the Arabs had tried to exorcise the demon of
fanaticism which had been introduced into the hearts of the
Spaniards by the Christian clergy ; they failed, and the moment
the Chancellor al-Mansûr, in order to enlist popular support
in furtherance of his ambitious designs, raised in Spain a cry
against Rationalism, the same crowd which afterwards assisted
with willing hands and gleeful faces at the *auto-da-fé* of heretics,
helped in the burning of philosophical works in the market-place
of Cordova.   The victorious arms of Saladin carried Asha'rîsm
into Egypt.   Whilst Rationalism was thus fighting a losing
battle with its old enemy, the writings of Imâm al-Ghazzâli,
which were directed chiefly against the study of philosophy,
strengthened the hands of Patristicism.   Abu Hâmid Mohammed ibn Mohammed al Ghazzâli [2] was a man of undoubted
talents and purity of character.   He had studied philosophy
and dived into the mysteries of the sciences ; he had even

[1] *Averroes et Averroism*, p. 30.

[2] Was born at Tûs in Khorâsân (the birthplace of Firdousi) in the year
1058 A.C. (450 A.H.) ; died in IIII A.C. (505 of the Hegira).   His most celebrated works are the *Ihya ul-'ulûm* (" the Revival of the Sciences of Religion ") ;
the *Munkiz min-az-zalâl* (" Deliverance from Errors ") ; *Makâsid-ul-falâsifa* (the
" Tendencies of Philosophers ") ; and *Tahâfut-ul-falâsifa* (" Destruction of
Philosophers "), to which Ibn-Rushd wrote a refutation called the *Tahâfut-u-
Tahâfut ul-falâsifa* (" the Destruction of Destruction," etc.) ; see chap. xi.

indulged in free-thought. Suddenly the spirit of earnest longing for a solid rock on which to rest the weary soul, the spirit that has worked similarly upon other minds in later ages, spoke to his heart, and from a philosopher he turned into a mystic. In the *Munkiz*, which appears to have been a discourse delivered either verbally or written to his religious brethren, he describes with some *naïveté* how he hankered for knowledge, and in its search went everywhere, dipped into everything, acquainted himself with every subject ; and how he abandoned the doctrines which had been instilled into him in early life. He says he knew the saying of the Prophet, which declared that every child was born with a knowledge of the truth in nature, and therefore wanted to know what that truth was. Then he describes how he was seized with scepticism, and how he escaped from its consequences by betaking himself into the higher regions of faith, viz. a mystical exaltation. The discourse contains a violent attack on the philosophers, whom he groups under three heads. (1) The *Dahrîs*, who believe in the eternity of matter, and deny the existence of a Creator. (2) The Physicists or naturalists, who believe in the existence of a Creator, but think that the human soul once separated from the body ceases to exist, and that therefore there is no accountability for human actions ; both of them were infidels. (3) The Theists (Plato and Aristotle), " these have completely refuted the doctrines of the first two, and God has saved thereby the true believer from the battle." " But they must be pronounced infidels ; and so also the Moslem philosophers who have followed them, especially Fârâbî and Ibn-Sîna, for their philosophy is so confused that you cannot separate the truth from the false, so as to refute the latter ! From what we can discover of the writings of these two men, knowledge may be divided under three heads ; one group we are bound to pronounce as *infidel*, another as heresy, and about the third we need say nothing ! " And yet with all this simplicity there is considerable practical sense displayed in Ghazzâli's writings. He praises wisdom as far higher than mere belief, and opposes the fanatical dogmatism which rejects all rational inquiry and all knowledge because it is cultivated by his *bêtes noires* the philosophers. He calls this dogmatism the unwise friend of

Islâm. At the same time his precepts on personal independence, on moral discipline, on self-purification, on practical kindness, and on the education of the young, and his denunciation of the immoral and useless lives of the Mullahs of his time, reflect great credit on the goodness of his nature.[1]

From this period there was an unceasing struggle between Rationalism and Patristicism. In the year 1150, under the orders of the Caliph Mustanjid, all the philosophical works of Ibn-Sîna and the copies of the *Rasâil-i-Ikhwân us-Safâ* found in the public and private libraries were consigned to the flames. In 1192 the physician Ar-Rukn Abdus-Salâm was accused of atheism, and the populace and priests proceeded to make a bonfire of his books. The Mullah who presided at this ceremony stood on a chair and delivered a sermon against philosophy. As the books were brought out they were delivered to him, and with a few remarks on their impiety, he threw them into the fire. A disciple of Maimonides was a witness to this strange scene, and has left an account of it. " I saw," says he, " in the hands of this doctor the work of Ibn-ul-Haithem (Al-Hazen) on astronomy. Showing to the people the circle by which the author represented the celestial sphere, the doctor burst forth, ' Misery of miseries, inexpressible disaster ! ' and with these words he threw the book into the flames." But even the influence of Imâm al-Ghazzâli and the temporal power of the sovereigns, some of whom were at heart rationalists, would not have prevented the eventual victory of reason over the dead-weight of authority, had not the Mongol's sword turned the scale. " One Khan, one God : as the Khan's ordinance is immutable, so is God's decree." Could any doctrine be more logical or more irresistible, backed as it was by a million swords ? Rationalism, philosophy, the sciences and arts went down before that avalanche of savagery—never to rise again. The gleams of light which we have seen shining on Western Asia under the successors of Hulâku were the fitful rays of the setting sun. Policy worked with an inborn fanaticism in crushing any endeavour to introduce rationalism and philosophy in the Moslem world. The lawyers were not

[1] See chapter xi, *post.*

only strong, but also the main support of despotism. The result was, as we have already seen, Patristicism took possession of the hearts of large sections of Moslems, and has in course of time become a second nature with them. They can perceive nothing except through the medium of the patristic glasses. The Prophet inculcated the use of reason ; his followers have made its exercise a sin. He preached against anthropolatry and extravagant veneration for human beings ; the Sunnis have canonised the *salaf* and the four jurists ; the Akhbâri Shiahs, their Mujtahids,—and have called any deviation from the course laid down by them—however much that deviation might accord with the Master's own teachings and with reason—a crime. He had said that " ghosts, apparitions, and the like have nothing to do with Islâm." They now believe firmly in them. He impressed on them to go in quest of knowledge to the land of the heathens. They do not take it even when it is offered to them in their own homes.

Under the Safawis, rationalism and philosophy came to life once more—though not in that vigorous shape in which they had flourished under the earlier Abbasides. From the twelfth to the fifteenth century Irân had suffered terribly ; and in the darkness which enshrouded the land during this long period of disaster and trouble, the Shiah Mullahs had assumed the position of the clergy in Christendom to a larger degree than even the Sunni lawyers. They claimed the sole and absolute power of expounding the laws on the ground that they were the representatives of the Fâtimide Imâms. Mulla Sadra, whom I have already mentioned as the reviver of the Usûli doctrines,— the religion of Mohammed as it was understood and accepted by his immediate descendants,—applied himself to revive the study of philosophy and science among his countrymen. It was by no means an easy task, but he worked with tact and judgment. Avicennism came to life again, and, in spite of the political vicissitudes of Irân, the destruction of lives during the Afghan domination, and the establishment of the Kajârs on the throne of Persia, has persistently maintained its hold over many of the cultivated class. One of the best epitomes of Avicennistic philosophy was published in the reign of Shah

Abbas II.,[1] by Abdur Razzâk bin Ali bin al-Hassan al-Lâhîji, under the name of *Gouhar-i-Murâd*, "The Pearl of Desire." It contains a summary of Ibn-Sîna's views, explained and illustrated by references to the opinions of the Caliph Ali and his descendants, and philosophers and physicists like Imâm Fakhr ud-dîn Râzi, Nasîr ud-din Tûsi, Imâm Taftazâni, and others.

Some of Abdur Razzâk's views are extremely interesting. For example, dealing with Mu'tazilaism and Asha'rîsm, he states that " the Mu'tazilas invented the science of *Kalâm* with the object of establishing a harmony between the precepts of religion and the requirements of society, and of explaining by principles of Reason the [Koranic] verses and the traditions which at first sight seem unreasonable (ظاهر الحسب ال) ; whilst their opponents (طائفة مخالف) upheld the literal acceptance [of the verses of the Koran and of the traditions] partly from motives of bigotry and partly from policy ; prohibited all interpretations, and pronounced the interpretations of the Mu'tazilas and all their opinions as heresy (بدعت), and designated the Mu'tazilas heretics (مبتدع), and considered themselves in opposition to them [the Mu'tazilas] as *ahl-i-Sunnat wa-Jamâ'at. . . .* So much so, that many of them have fallen into the sin of thinking God to be a material being, all of them are immersed in that of anthropomorphism.—And this has happened of their shutting the door upon all interpretations; they have construed in their literal acceptation, the verse that ' He is seated on the Throne,' and such like, and the traditions as to رویت (the sight of God) until they derived *tajsim* (corporeality) from one, and *tashbîh* (similarity, or anthropomorphism) from the other. These people had at first no method of reasoning or putting forward of logical arguments ; they relied only on the literal words of the Koran and traditions until the appearance of Abu'l Hasan Asha'rî, who was a prominent disciple of Abû Ali Jubbâi, one of the learned Imâms of the Mu'tazilas. Abu'l Hasan had acquired great knowledge

[1] Of this sovereign it is said that he was as tolerant to all religions as his great ancestor Abbas I. He often declared the principle by which his conduct on this point was regulated : " It is for God, not for me, to judge of men's consciences : and I will never interfere with what belongs to the tribunal of the great Creator and Lord of the Universe."

of logic and argumentation. He abandoned the *Mazhab-i-'itizâl*, and adopted that of the *Ahl-i-Sunnat wa-Jamâ'at* and made great endeavours to advance the cause of this sect, which up to his time had no influence whatsoever. Henceforth it began to be called after him. He invented principles and rules according to the Mu'tazilite models. . . . And as the tyrannical sovereigns found that the doctrines of this *Mazhab* suited their policy,

خلفا و ایمه جور نیز در اغلب بنا بران که قواعد مذهب ایشان موافق مصالح آنان بود

they supported this sect; and so Asha'rïsm spread widely among the *Ahl-i-Islâm*. But, as the doctrines of the Mu'tazilas (قواعداعتزل) were founded on the principles of reason (اصول عقایه), they found acceptance among a large number of the true-hearted people (ادر قوالب حق رفته). And as the Mu'tazilas had studied deeply the philosophical and scientific works, they introduced arguments borrowed from them in the discussion of metaphysical and theological subjects. And when the Asha'rîs became aware of this, as they considered everything which was not contained in the bosom of Islâm a heresy—هر چه در صدر سلام معمول نبوده بدعت دانسته بودند, they at once pronounced the study of philosophy (مطالعه کتب حکمت) to be unlawful and dangerous. It was owing to the endeavours of this sect that philosophy became so unpopular among the *Ahl-i-Islâm* as to affect even the learned of the Mu'tazilas. But the *Asha'rïa* were the originators of this antagonism to philosophy, for, otherwise, it is in truth in no way inconsistent with religion or the mysteries (اسرار) of the Koran and traditions. . . . The prophets and their representatives (اوصیا) have explained the truths of philosophy which are Divine by *tamsîl*, similitudes." . . . "With regard to the freedom of human actions, there are three *Mazhabs*: the first is the doctrine of *Jabr*, and that is the *Mazhab* of the Asha'rïas; they hold that the actions of man are immediately created by God without any exercise of will on the part of human beings—so much so, that if a person lights a fire, the lighting is said to be an act of God." Then after exposing the immorality of this doctrine, the author proceeds to say, " the second *Mazhab*, that of *tafwîz*, was adopted by a few Mu'tazilas, who held that man has absolute power to choose what is right and what is wrong, and

S

do accordingly. The third is the *Mazhab* of the Fâtimide Imâms, and the majority of the philosophers and rationalists who maintain that human actions are the immediate creations of man, but evil and good are pointed out by God." . . .

We cannot help contrasting the present condition of the Church which claims to be orthodox in Christendom with that of the one which advances a similar claim in Islâm. From the fourth century, ever since its foundation, until the revolt of Luther, Catholicism proved itself the mortal enemy of science, philosophy, and learning. It consigned to the flames myriads of beings for heresy ; it trampled out the lispings of free-thought in Southern France : and closed with violence the schools of rational theology. But Catholicism, after the great break of Luther and Calvin, discovered that neither the cultivation of science nor the pursuit of philosophy renders the faithful an unbeliever. It broadened its base and now includes men of the largest minds, scientists, litterateurs, etc. To an outsider it presents a more liberal aspect than even the Reformed Christian Churches. For five centuries Islâm assisted in the free intellectual development of humanity, but a reactionary movement then set in, and all at once the whole stream of human thought was altered. The cultivators of science and philosophy were pronounced to be beyond the pale of Islâm. Is it impossible for the Sunni Church to take a lesson from the Church of Rome ? Is it impossible for her to expand similarly —to become many-sided ? There is nothing in Mohammed's teachings which prevents this. Islâmic Protestantism, in one of its phases,—Mu'tazilaism,—has already paved the way. Why should not the great Sunni Church shake off the old trammels and rise to a new life ?

CHAPTER XI

THE MYSTICAL AND IDEALISTIC SPIRIT IN ISLÂM

هُوَ الْأَوَّلُ وَ الْأُخِرُ وَ الظَّاهِرُ وَالْبَاطِنُ وَ هُوَ بِكُلِّ شَئٍ عَلِيْمٌ

THE mystical philosophy which forms the life and soul of modern Persian literature owes its distinct origin to the esoteric significance attached by an important section of Moslems to the words of the Koran. The elevated feeling of Divine pervasion with which the Prophet often spoke, the depth of fervent and ecstatic rapture which characterised his devotions, constitute the chief basis on which Moslem mysticism is founded. During his lifetime, when the performance of duties was placed before religious speculation, there was little scope for the full development of the contemplative and mystical element in Islâm. This mystical and contemplative element exists in all religions and among every people. And yet it varies with the peculiarities of the individual and the race, and according to their tendency to confound the abstract with the concrete. The Hindu looks on absorption of the finite into the Infinite as the culmination of happiness; and to attain that end he remains immovable in one spot, and resigns himself to complete apathy. The sense of infinity makes it difficult for him to distinguish objectively between the priest and the God, or himself and the God; and eventually between the Deity and the different forms of nature in which He is supposed to be manifested. Gradually this train of contemplation leads to the formal conclusion, as appears from the Bhagavad Gîta, that Creator and creation are identical. We see thus how curiously pantheism, in its extreme manifestation, approaches to fetishism, which preceded every other idea of the Divinity. In its infancy the human mind knows no spiritual sentiment but one of unmixed terror. The primeval forests, which the hand of man has not yet touched, the stupendous mountains looming in the distance, the darkness of the night, with the grim, weird shapes which hover about it, the howling of the wind through the forest tops, all inspire fear and awe in the infant mind of man. He worships every material object he finds more powerful or more awe-striking than himself or his immediate surroundings. Gradually he comes to attach an ideality to all these objects of nature, and thinks these idealities worthy of adoration. In process of time all these separate idealities merge in one universal all-embracing Ideality. Materialistic pantheism is the first step in the rise from fetishism.

Neo-Platonism, itself the child of Eastern thought, had impressed its character on Christianity, and probably given rise to the eucharistic idea. With the exception of Johannes Scotus and Eckhart,[1] the mystics of Europe during the Middle Ages fought only on this ground. Mysticism, properly so called, with its higher yearning after the Infinite, was ushered in by the Moslem doctrine of " inward light."

The idea among the nobler minds in the world of Islâm, that there is a deeper and more inward sense in the words of the Koran, arose not from the wish to escape from the rigour of " texts and dogmas," but from a profound conviction that those words mean more, not less, than the popular expounders supposed them to convey. This conviction, combined with a deep feeling of Divine pervasion,—a feeling originating from and in perfect accordance with the teachings of the Koran and the instructions of the Prophet, led to the development among the Moslems of that contemplative or idealistic philosophy which has received the name of Sûfïsm, and the spread of which, among the Mohammedans, was probably assisted by the prevalence of Neo-Platonic ideas. Imâm al-Ghazzâlî in the East, and Ibn-Tufail in the West, were the two great representatives of mysticism among the Moslems. The former, as we have already seen, dissatisfied with every philosophical system, which based knowledge on experience

[1] 1260-1328 A.C.

or reason, had taken refuge in Sûfîsm.   Al-Ghazzâlî's influence
served greatly to promote the diffusion of Sûfîsm among the
Eastern Moslems, and idealistic philosophy was embraced by
the greatest intellects of the Mohammedan East.   Moulânâ
Jalâl ud-dîn of Rûm (Turkey), whose *Masnavî* [1] is venerated
by the Sûfî; Sanâî, whom Jalâl ud-dîn himself has called his
superior; [2] Farîd ud-dîn Attâr, Shams ud-dîn Hâfiz, Khâkâni,
the moralist Sa'di, the romancer Nizâmî,—all belonged to this
school.

It must not be supposed that al-Ghazzâlî was the first
preacher of " inward light " in Islâm.   Intuitive knowledge of
God (*ta'arruf*) is inherent in the Faith.   The intent (*niyyet*) of
" approach " (*kurbat*) to and communion with Him is the
essential preliminary to true devotion; the " Ascension "
(the *mi'râj*) of the Prophet meant the absolute communion of
the finite with the Infinite.   Not only does God speak to the
hearts of men and women who in earnest sincerity seek divine
help and guidance, but all knowledge is from the Supreme
Intelligence; it comes to the Prophets by direct revelation
(وَحى) and often   " The sacrament of the heart " is
conveyed by Him to His chosen few, " *fi-sirrat'-kalbi*,
فى سِرَّةِ ثلبى , without an intermediary.   This in Islâm is
called '*Ilmi-ladunni*. [3]   It is referred to in the Koran, where
it says, " We taught him [His chosen servant] knowledge from
Ourself." [4]   The same conception of intimate communion with
God occurs in the well-known *hadis*, where the Almighty says,
" My earth and My heaven contain Me not, but the heart of
My faithful servant containeth Me." [5]   And the Divine promise
finds a responsive note in the human heart when it is uplifted

---

[1] One of the apologues of the *Masnavî* on true devotion being the *service
of man*, has been beautifully rendered into English by Leigh Hunt in the lines
beginning—

> " Abou ben Adhem (may his tribe increase)
> Awoke one night from a deep dream of peace," etc.

[2] See Appendix III.   [3] ملم لَدُنِّى

[4] Koran, Sura xviii. v. 65, وَ عَلَّمْنَاهُ مِن لَّدُنَّا عِلْمًا.

[5] See Appendix II.   Also quoted by Dr. Reynold Nicholson of Cambridge
in his *Mystics of Islâm*.   This work, by a scholar whose knowledge of Sûfî
literature is unrivalled in Europe, gives in a small compass a lucid summary
of Persian mysticism.

in prayer : " The Almighty God hears whatever prayers (*lit.* praises) I offer Him. O my Lord, I thank Thee." [1]

The same transcendentalism is to be found in other traditions ; and Ali discourses on the inward light in his sermons ; [2] Fâtima'-t az-Zahra, " our Lady of Light," dwells on it in her preachings ; [3] and it finds ecstatic expression in the prayers of the grandson of Ali, the son of Husain the Martyr. [4] But nowhere in these earliest records of the conception of " Inward Light " is there any ground for the suggestion that either the Prophet or the direct inheritors of his spiritual heritage ever preached the abandonment of the affairs of the world in the pursuit of Truth, or the observance of asceticism which he so strongly reprobated. [5] And that is exactly what has happened in the evolution of Moslem esotericism. In the endeavour to obtain spiritual perfection [6] numbers of Moslems have forgotten the precept that human existence depends on constant exertion. How this has taken place is not without interest.

The mystic cult neither in Christianity nor in Islâm is a new

---

[1] سَمِعَ اللّٰهُ لِمَنْ حَمِدَهُ رَبَّنَا وَلَكَ الْحَمْدُ

[2] The *Nahj-ul-Balâghat*. There are two commentaries on the *Nahj-ul-Balâghat*, one by Ibn Abi'l Hadîd, the other in Persian by Lutf Ullah Kâshâni. The full name of Ibn Abi'l Hadîd is given in the editorial note to the *Sharh* as " Abu Hâmid Abdul Hamîd bin Hibatullah bin Mohammed bin Mohammed bin Husain bin Abi'l Hadîd." He was born at Madâin in the month of Zu'l Hijja 586 A.H. (December 1190 A.C.). He was a Mu'tazili and a Shiah, and those designations are applied to him in the note. He was a jurisconsult of the first rank, profoundly versed (*mutabahhir*) in science and learning, a *mutakallim* (dialectician) and a poet ; and was attached to the Chancellery (the *Diwân*) under the Caliphs Nâsir and Zâhir. Ibn Khallikân (De Slane, vol. iii. p. 543, in the biography of Ziâ-ud-din Ibn ul-Athir) speaks of him as the " jurisconsult Izz-ud-din and a man of letters " ; but does not mention Ibn Abi'l Hadîd's great work, the Commentary on the *Nahj-ul-Balâghat* ; nor the fact that he was a Mu'tazili and a Shiah. Ibn Abi'l Hadîd refutes at the beginning of his work, where he propounds the human duty of thankfulness and worship to the Almighty, the Asha'ri doctrine of the corporeal vision of God on the day of Judgment (*r'uyat ul-Bâri fi'l Âkhirat*).

Ibn Abi'l Hadîd died at Bagdad in A.H. 655 (1257 A.C.), the year before its destruction by the Mongols (Persian Ed., date apparently 1304 A.H.).

[3] *Lum'at-ul-Baiza.*   [4] *Sahîfai Kâmila.*

[5] The Prophet and the early disciples spent " the greater part of the night in devotion ; and their days in transacting the affairs of the people." So did Omar ibn Abdul Azîz, the fifth Ommeyyade Caliph, who deserved the title of saint more than many others.

[6] To become what in Sûfi phraseology is called a " perfect man," " *insâni kâmil.*"

development. It existed in the Roman world and was not
unknown to the Jews. In Aryan India, it practically ran riot
and was cultivated in every form. From India it was transported into Western and Central Asia, where it assumed from
time to time most fantastic shapes. Wherever it was planted
it implied the abandonment of all commerce with the outside
world, the renunciation of family ties and obligations, and the
concentration of the human mind on one object to the exclusion
of all others. This, in fact, represents the essence of the mystic
cult. The call of Jesus was an echo of the world-old teaching
of the Mystic. The Prophet of Islâm, on the other hand,
emphasised the faithful performance of the less impressive
duty, the service of man, as the most acceptable worship to
God. His call was the direct antithesis of the older conceptions.

Unfortunately, the convulsions that followed on the break-
up of the original and true Caliphate with the assassination
of Ali,[1] the sack of Medîna with all its attendant horrors, and
the pagan licence which came into vogue in social life under
the more dissolute Ommeyyade sovereigns of Damascus, drove
many earnest-minded Moslems to take refuge in retirement and
religion. From piety there is only a step to Quietism. Thenceforward the evolution of the mystical cult runs a natural course.
The adoption of the distinctive woollen garment (the *khirka*)
as a mark of penitence and renunciation of the world dates
from early times.[2] The Sûfi theory of spiritual development is
based on complete self-abnegation and absolute absorption in
the contemplation of God. The Sûfi believes that by this
absorption and mental concentration [3] he can attain a far

---

[1] See *ante*, p. 296 ; also *Short History of the Saracens*, pp. 52 and 70.

[2] In Christianity garments made of sackcloth or hair served the same
purpose. The *Khirka* is a sort of gaberdine like a long pillow-case. The Sûfi
derives his name from the woollen garment he wears, the word *sûf* meaning
wool. The term *sûfi* has no connection either with the *ahl-us-Suffa*, the
religious men who were wont to sit and sleep outside the Prophet's mosque
and receive daily their food from him, nor with the *Ikhwân-us-Safâ*, "The
Brethren of Purity."

[3] It is stated that Abû Sa'îd bin Abi'l Khair who also holds a high place
in Sûfi hagiology, kept his mind, like the Hindu yogis, centred on his navel.
An excellent biography of Abû Sa'îd bin Abi'l Khair is given in Dr. Nicholson's
Studies in Islamic Mysticism, published by the Cambridge University Press ;
see also Professor E. G. Browne's *Literary History of Persia*. He is said to
have been a contemporary of Avicenna. He died in 1049.

closer communion with the Divinity and a truer cognition of the Truth. This belief, whilst it no doubt led many pious and devout men and women to consecrate their lives to religion, produced at the same time a rank growth of fantastic ideas.

Ali the Caliph and the Imâms of his House are regarded as having possessed in a superlative degree the " Inward Knowledge." Abû Nasr as-Sarrâj, in his work *al-Luma'* on the philosophy of Sûfîsm,[1] quoting Junaid [2] says, that had Ali not been occupied in so many wars, he would have imparted to the world the vast measure of the *'Ilm-ul-ladunni* [3] with which he was endowed.[4]   And in the *Tazkirat-ul-Awlia*[5] of Farîd-ud-dîn 'Attâr [6] the first place in the list of mystic saints is given to Ja'far as-Sâdik, the sixth apostolical Imâm.   It is worthy of note that in the case of almost every Sûfi saint the line of spiritual descent is traced back to Ali and through him to the Prophet.[7]   A few only trace it to Abû Bakr.

The holy men and women who flourished in the first two centuries were more Quietists than Sûfis.   They had abandoned the world and devoted themselves exclusively to devotion and piety (*zuhd* and *takwa*).   Such were Imâm Hasan al-Basri,[8]

---

[1] *Al-Luma' fi-tasawwuf*; *tasawwuf* is the philosophy of Sûfism.   The *Luma'* of as-Sarrâj has been recently edited with great care and erudition by the learned author of *Studies in Islâmic Mysticism.*   According to Nûr-ud-din Abdur Rahmân Jâmi (*Nafahât-ul-Uns*, Calcutta ed. p. 319) as-Sarrâj occupies an eminent position among the Sûfi saints.   He appears also from Jâmi's account to have been a proficient mathematician, versed in the abstract sciences.   As-Sarrâj died in 378 A.H. (988 A.C.), nearly 100 years before al-Ghazzâlî.

[2] *Al-Luma'*, p. 129.   Junaid was one of the earliest mystics of Islâm ; he died A.H. 297 (A.C. 910).   He is stated to have declared that " the Sûfi system of doctrine is firmly bound with the dogmas of the Faith and the Koran " (Ibn Khallikân).

[3] عَلَّمُ اللّٰدُنِّي

[4] The Indian poet Dabîr calls Ali the " Knower of the mysteries of God," *ramûzdân-i-Khuda.*

[5] *Biography of the Saints.*

[6] See *ante*, p. 396 ; 'Attâr was born in 545 A.H. (1150 A.C.), and is believed to have been killed by the Mongols in 627 A.H. (1229-30 A.C.).

[7] See *post.*

[8] Wâsil bin 'Ata, the founder of Mu'tazilaism, was a pupil of Hasan Basri.   Imâm Hasan Basri died in A.H. 110 (A.C. 728).

Ibrâhim ibn Adham,[1] Ma'rûf Karkhi,[2] Junaid,[3] Râbi'a,[4] the pious lady whose name has become famous in the annals of Islâm, Bâyezid Bistâmi and a host of others.   In the third century when Junaid flourished, Sûfïsm had become a recognised offshoot of Islâmic philosophy, but owing to the scope it afforded to indulgence in undisciplined thought, Sûfïsm began to assume in different minds distinctly non-Islâmic shapes. Abû Nasr as-Sarrâj denounces the erratic tendencies which now emerged from the welter of old ideas and conceptions. Some of the professors of the mystic cult anticipated Johannes Agricola in declaring that perfect knowledge absolved the " knower " from all trammels of the moral law.[5]

As-Sarrâj was the predecessor of al-Ghazzâlî in his endeavour to systematise Sûfïstic philosophy.   In spite of his efforts to shape Sûfïsm into a disciplined channel, it still continued to run in the old gnostic and often antinomian currents.   And yet throughout the five centuries which elapsed between the death of the Prophet and the rise of Al-Ghazzâlî there flourished numbers of men and women revered for their learning, piety and nobleness of character.   One of these was the famous Imâm-ul-Haramain, the master of al-Ghazzâlî.

To Imâm al-Ghazzâli eastern Sûfïsm owes in a large measure its systematisation and most of the colour and beauty in which it is clothed.   His appearance on the stage of the world was well-timed ; for the Sunni Church, owing to causes which I propose to review briefly, needed vitalisation.

[1] Abû Ishâk Ibrâhim ibn Adham ibn Mansûr is spoken of in the *Tazkirat-ul-Awlia* as the son of a prince of Balkh.   His father appears to have been a rich magnate.   He abandoned the world, gave all his riches to the poor and lived a life of piety and devotion.   He is said to have been a disciple of Abû Hanîfa.   He died in 161 A.H.

[2] Ma'rûf Karkhi was the son of a Christian ; he was converted to Islâm by the eighth Apostolical Imâm Ali ar-Rizâ the son of Imâm Musâ.   He was Imâm Riza's disciple.   The Imâm was greatly attached to him and treated him as a son, from which comes the saying " *Ali Mûsi Riza az-wai-raza bûd.*"   Ma'rûf was killed in a riot at the gate of the Imâm's residence in Meshed.

[3] In Junaid's time already convents and congregational lodges had come into existence.

[4] Râbi'a died in the year 160 A.H., and her name is embalmed in the annals of mysticism as one of the holiest of saints.   She had a long line of successors ; the last of them, Bibi Pâkdâman, died in Lahore about the middle or towards the end of the last century.

[5] These Sûfis or *dervishes* in India are called *Be Shara'*—" without law."

Al-Asha'ri died in 320 of the Hegira ; al-Ghazzâlî was born exactly 130 years later, towards the close of the fifth century of the Moslem era, and began his work of revivification when he was forty years of age. The sixth century was the most critical in the history of Islâm. Whilst the faith of Mohammed was involved in a deadly struggle with Christendom which threatened its very existence, an insidious enemy within its own bosom was poisoning its life. Hasan Sabbâh's tenets inculcated implicit and unquestioning obedience to him as the vicegerent of the Fatimide Caliph Nizâr, commonly regarded by the sect as the incarnate Imâm ; he taught that the " path " to Truth led to and through him. His disciples, drugged by *hashîsh*, obtained on awakening a foretaste of the delights he promised them in after-life as the reward for their obedience and unfaltering execution of his orders. Beautiful maidens gathered from every quarter helped in fastening his chains on the neck of his votaries. His emissaries, actuated by varied motives, but all subject to an irresistible driving force, abounded in every city, township and village of Central and Western Asia. Every household contained a concealed member of the dread fraternity. Neither heroic service to the Faith, nor learning, devoutness or nobility of character was a protection against these nihilists of Islâm.[1] The best and noblest of Moslems were struck down by these enemies of society. Their propaganda was not confined among Moslems alone. Jews, Christians, Zoroastrians and Hindus alike became the victims of their insidious methods of proselytism. Both men and women, and even children, were seduced from their faith by alluring hopes of immediate reward from Heaven. To contend against these enemies of Islâm it had become essential to galvanise the conservative forces into fresh vitality. Whilst Asha'rism had hardened into a rigid formalism, among the populace the cult of the mystic had run wild. Every man or woman who found the discipline of the Faith irksome turned

---

[1] Compare the destructive tendencies of Hasan Sabbâh's cult with those of the Illuminati in the eighteenth century. Professor E. G. Browne in his *Literary History of Persia* gives a list of some of the eminent men who fell victims to the daggers of the Isma'îlis. See also the opening chapter in M. Guyard's *Un Grand Maître des Assassins au Temps de Saladin* ; and the life of Hasan Sabbâh by Moulvi Abdul Halîm in Urdu, published in Lucknow.

XI. THE MYSTICAL AND IDEALISTIC SPIRIT 463

to Sûfîsm, to a life independent of rules. Philosophical reasoning brought no immediate relief or consolation to minds in terror from enemies within and without. There was a general relaxation in ethical conceptions and an amazing deterioration in ideals. It was just at this critical period in the life of Islâm that al-Ghazzâlî's call to a mystical life in God, and to the attainment of truth by the individual soul in direct communion with the Almighty, struck a responsive chord in many distracted hearts. It relaxed the tension and gave orthodoxy a new weapon with which to fight the disruptive teachings of Hasan Sabbâh's emissaries.[1]

It is a dispensation of Providence that wherever a religion becomes reduced to formalism cross-currents set in to restore spiritual vitality. The author of *The Forerunners and Rivals of Christianity* enumerates the men, each of whom, according to his light, tried to vitalise the old creed of Palestine. But it was the Prophet of Nazareth who, by his mystical summons to the worship of the Spirit in place of the national God of Israel, infused new life into Judaism.

Al-Ghazzâlî was preceded by other intuitionalists besides the Apostolical Imâms. Immediately before him came as-Sarrâj and al-Kushairi.[2] But al-Ghazzâlî set the coping stone upon their work, and freed the Sunni church from Asha'rite dogmatism.

The story of al-Ghazzâlî's life told by himself, of his trials and tribulations, of his doubts and his hopes, of his final emergence from " darkness into light," is an interesting record of spiritual growth finally ending in Quietism, a form of spiritual relief which brings solace and comfort to many a heart tossed on the ocean of doubt.

Al-Ghazzâlî[3] was born in 450 of the Hegira (1058 A.C.) at

[1] In Professor Goldziher's learned chapter on " Ascetism et Sûfîsm " in *Le Dogme et la loi de l'Islâm*, which I read only after I had sent this chapter to the press, I find that my estimate of the causes which brought forward al-Ghazzâlî is in general accord with the views of that eminent scholar ; compare also the masterly essay of Professor D. B. Macdonald in the *Journal of the American Oriental Society*, vol. xx.

[2] Al-Kushairi (Abu'l Kâsim) died in 465 A.H. (A.C. 1074).

[3] Abâ Hâmid Mohammed al-Ghazzâlî surnamed, says Ibn Khallikân, *Hujjat-ul-Islâm*, " the Proof of Islâm," and *Zain ud-dîn*, " the ornament of Religion."

Tûs,[1] a township in the neighbourhood of Meshed in Khorâsan. He must have been gifted with a peculiarly virile and independent mind, for, as he tells us in the *Munkiz*, he had abandoned in early youth that test of orthodoxy in all creeds called *taklîd* or conformity. To abandon *taklîd* and strike out a path for the exercise of individual judgment in the domain of religious thought has been in all ages and in all creeds regarded by dogmatic theologians as a sin of the first degree. Orthodoxy in the Sunni Church meant conformity with the principles of one or other of the founders of the four schools of law. Ghazzâlî, with an audacity which demands admiration, refused to adhere to any particular dogma without independent examination.[2] But as he always called himself ash-Shâfe'i', he must have conformed more or less to the doctrines of that school. Ibn Khallikân, in fact, says al-Ghazzâlî was a doctor of the Shâfe'i sect. " Towards the close of his life the Shâfe'is had not a doctor to be compared to him." In the twentieth year of his age al-Ghazzâlî proceeded from Tûs to Naishapur, a great centre of learning until its destruction by the Mongols in 1256 A.C. Here he enrolled himself in the Nizâmièh College, which had been founded only a few years before, as a pupil of the *Imâm ul-Haramain* al-Juwaini. Al-Ghazzâlî studied with this saintly Imâm until his death in 478 A.H. (1084 A.C.). Al-Ghazzâlî was then in his twenty-eighth year ; ambitious, energetic, well-versed in all the learning of the Islâmic world, he betook himself to the court of Nizâm-ul-Mulk,[3] the great Vizier of the Seljukide sovereign Malik Shah. Nizâm-ul-Mulk by his munificent patronage of scholarship, science and arts, had gathered round him a brilliant galaxy of savants and learned men. He recognised the worth of the new aspirant for his help and support, and after a short probation in his own

---

[1] Tûs is also the birthplace of Firdousi, the greatest of Persian poets. Meshed, properly Mashhad (mausoleum), is venerated by the Shiahs as the eighth Apostolical Imâm Ali bin Musa ar-Rizâ is buried there.

[2] It is only in recent times that a new sect has grown up among the Moslems of India, which bears the proud name of ' *Ghair Mukallid* ' (" Non-conformists "), see *ante*, p. 353.

[3] Abû Ali al-Hasan, also a native of Tûs. He is the author of the *Siâsat-Nâmèh*, a book on the administration of the commonwealth—" the art of government." The text of this work in the original Persian with a French translation has been published by the late M. Ch. Schefer.

entourage conferred on al-Ghazzâlî a professorial seat in one
of the colleges in Bagdad. Nothing shows so clearly the extraordinary solidarity of the intellectual world of Islâm nor the
link throughout the vast extent of the territories over which
the Seljukide sovereigns in the plenitude of their power held
sway as the manner in which officials of every rank, including
professors and lecturers, were transferred from one centre to
another.

In Bagdad al-Ghazzâlî performed his professorial duties for
six years. His lectures attracted pupils of all classes from
every part of the Empire to hear his discourses on scholastic
theology and logic. Towards the end of 488 A.H. (1095 A.C.)
he was compelled to leave Bagdad in consequence of a severe
nervous breakdown. The very subjects on which he lectured
strengthened his doubts in the teachings of the schoolmen and
divines of his Church. Asha'ri had emerged from his retreat
after a fortnight's contemplation of the comparative virtues
of Rationalism and Patristicism. It took ten years for
al-Ghazzâlî to find the resting-place for his soul. That rest he
found, as he tells us himself, in the Master's words read in the
light of the revelation which the Fashioner of the Universe
vouchsafes to all hearts that seek Him. During his prolonged
wanderings he visited every centre of learning and every
scholastic or religious institution, where he found scholars or
holy men engaged in the pursuit of knowledge, secular or
divine. Al-Ghazzâlî was in Jerusalem just before the crusading storm burst on that devoted city (Sha'bân 492).[1] He
seems to have tarried longest at Damascus, where he lectured
in a corner of the cathedral mosque situated on the west bank
of the river. The cloister he occupied in the mosque is still
called the *Zâvia of Imâm al-Ghazzâlî*. When he returned to
Naishapur after his long wandering, he was forty-eight years
of age, still in the prime of life, worn and scarred, though he
had found what he sought—the knowledge of God and peace
of soul. His great and generous patron, Nizâm-ul-Mulk, had
been assassinated by an Isma'îli *Fidâi*, one of Hasan Sabbâh's
emissaries, in 485 A.H. (1092 A.C.), whilst al-Ghazzâlî was still
lecturing in Bagdad. Malik Shah had died six months after

---

[1] He is said to have visited in his wanderings even Alexandria.

the assassination of his faithful servant, the bulwark of his empire. Sultan Sanjar, one of Malik Shah's sons, now reigned over the shrunken patrimony of Tughril and Alp Arslân, and Fakhr-ul-Mulk, a son of Nizâm-ul-Mulk, held at this time the office of Vizier under Sanjar. As great a patron of learning as his distinguished father, Fakhr-ul-Mulk at once requisitioned the services of Ghazzâlî and appointed him to a high professorial post in the Maimunièh-Nizâmièh College [1] at Naishapur. Here commenced that marvellous activity of a prolific mind which has left its impress on the emotional and mystical side of Islâm.

The *Munkiz-min-az-Zalâl* (" The deliverer from darkness ") [2] was evidently written about this time. In this book, which is not more than a discourse, he divides the " seekers of truth " (*at-tâlibîn*) into three classes or groups (*sinf*). The first group consists of the dogmatic theologians (the *Ashar'ite Mutakal-limîn*). These people base their conceptions on " deductions " (*râi*) and speculation (*nazar*). Their unsatisfactory dogmatism is ruled out in rather a measured criticism. In the second group are included the Bâtinis or Isma'ilias,[3] those who profess to derive their knowledge from a " living Imâm." After an examination of the views of the philosophers, among whom are included the authors of the *Ikhwân-us-Safâ*, " which is no more than a compilation of philosophy," al-Ghazzâlî subjects the teachings of the *Ta'limis*, that is the Isma'ilias, to a merciless criticism and exposes their anti-Islâmic character. To their assertion that they follow a living Imâm, he replies, " There is the Prophet, why should we follow any other leader." [4] And he adds that these misbelieving heretics would not have met with so much success among the people, had their opponents (implying the dogmatists) not been so remiss and feeble in their arguments. In the fourth group

---

[1] The old Nizâmièh College appears to have been extended and enlarged by Fakhr-ul-Mulk, and received the new designation.

[2] مُنْقِذٌ مِنَ الضَّلَال   Printed with Schmölder's *Essai sur les Écoles Philoso-phiques chez les Arabes* ; India Office copy.

[3] See *ante*, note, p. 326.

[4] This is identical in spirit to the famous couplet of Sanâi already quoted, *ante* p. 47.

come the Sûfis, the intuitionalists, people of "vision and manifestation." In other words, they *see* Truth where others find the Divine Essence from reason. According to the historian Ibn-ul-Athîr, who compiled his great work in Mosul not long after al-Ghazzâlî's death, the *Ihya-ul-'Ulum*[1] (" the Revivification of Knowledge ") was written before the Imâm returned to Naishapur. There is sòme difference of opinion on this point ; although by consensus it is by far the most important of his productions. The *Ihya-ul-'Ulum* is an encyclopædic work dealing comprehensively with the philosophy and ethics of Sûfïsm.

Al-Asha'ri had condemned all enquiry into the mysteries of existence. Although equally dogmatic in his denunciation of philosophers and philosophy, of rationalism and its ideals, al-Ghazzâlî gives them a hearing ; appraises their work and finds it wanting, wanting in the capacity to attain the goal to which, according to him, humanity should strive. And what is more, as people of the same *kibleh*[2] he includes them within the pale of Islâm. It is extraordinary that the greatest mystics of the succeeding ages make little reference to him. Jalâl-ud-dîn sings of Attâr and Sanâi but expresses no obligation to al-Ghazzâlî for his transcendentalism. Is

---

[1] اَحْيَاالْعُلُرْمَ وَالدِّيِّ يْنَ   Cairo Ed. İndia Office copy.

A short reference to some of the subjects with which it deals will show its extraordinary range and the industry and intellectual powers of the writer. The book (in vol. i.) opens with a disquisition on the excellence of learning (knowledge)—*fazilat-ul-'Ilm* ; and it is established by proofs furnished by reason and authority (*ash-shawâhîd ul-'aklieh wa'l naklieh*) ; there is a disquisition on the " excellence of Reason " (*Sharaf-ul-'akl*) and the difference between soul (*nafs*) and Reason ('*akl*) ; and *Islâm* and *Imân* (faith). Toleration is extended to all who bow to the same *kibleh* (*i.e.* are followers of Islâm). In vol. ii. he deals with the duties of man to man, of the reciprocal duties of children and parents. He defines here the meaning of *nafs* (the soul) and *rûh* (the spirit), of *kalb* (the heart), and '*akl* (Reason) ; he points out the distinction between intuition (*ilhâm*) and instruction (*ta'allum*). And in this volume he deals with the whole philosophy of Sûfïsm (*tarîk-us-Sufiyeh fi-istikshâf il-Hak wa-tarîk un-nazâir*).

The other two volumes are mainly concerned with the ethics of Islâm ; he condemns pride, anger and vindictiveness, avarice and miserliness ; and commends condescension and humility (*hilm*), forgiveness and mercy, generosity (*sakha*) and kindness. The *Ihya-ul-U'lum* is held in high esteem also among the Shiahs; in the *Bihâr-ul-Anwâr*, in the thesis on Reason and Knowledge it is mentioned as one of the *Isnâds* or " supports."

[2] *Kibleh* is the point to which the Moslem turns his face when offering his orisons, *i.e.* Mecca, or rather the Kaaba.

it because the impetus he gave to emotional Islâm lost its force
in the life and death struggle with the crusading hordes which
lasted for nearly two centuries ? To the Christian onslaught
in Western Asia, followed by the Mongol avalanche which swept
over mid-Asia, destroying in its course every vestige of civilisation and culture, is entirely due the long night that followed
the sack of Bagdad. It is not improbable that the force of
his example and precept became barren in the cataclysm that
overwhelmed Islâm not long after his death. And yet the
faith in communion with the Almighty, with its aspirations
and inwardness, survived in the hearts of the truly earnest
and devout disciples, and the *árif* claimed to have visions
where the philosopher and the rationalist obtained cognition
by reason. The emotional part of al-Ghazzâlî's mystical
philosophy found refuge in the monasteries of the dervishes ;
zâvias, rabâts [1] and *khânkâhs* [2] sprang up on all sides.
Wherever the holy men who claimed a transcendental insight,
an insight beyond the ken of reason, took up their abode,
disciples clustered round them ; they founded orders, and
imparted mystical knowledge to their followers. Many were
sincere and honest, others were impostors. The influence and
teachings of the first, whilst they lasted, were undoubtedly
beneficent ; the influence of the others, with their sundering
tendencies from Islâm, were demoralising.

Al-Ghazzâlî himself did not place his trust in dogmatic
theology (*Kalâm*) and denounces it as opposed to reason,
but the exact sciences, arithmetic, geometry and the connected
branches, are considered by him as absolutely unassailable
and not open to doubt or controversy. At Naishapur he wrote,
among other works, the *Makâsid ul-Falâsifa* (" The Aims of
Philosophy "), and the *Tahâfut-ul-Falâsifa* (" the Destruction
of the Philosophers "), both directed against philosophy and
those who cultivated it, and in both he tries to prove the

[1] From the word *rabât* is derived the word " marabout." In the eleventh
century the Murâbita established a powerful empire in Morocco and Spain ;
see *History of the Saracens*, p. 532.

[2] Meninski defines a khânkâh thus : domus propter Deus extructa in usum
sophorum aut religiosorum ; coenobium. Richardson calls it a monastery or
religious structure built for Eastern Sûfis and dervishes. There is a startling
analogy between those Moslem institutions and the Hindu Muths in southern
India, where also disciples gather for religious instruction.

futility of philosophic reasoning and the unsatisfying character of the teachings of philosophy.

On the assassination of his patron and friend Fakhr-ul-Mulk Ali [1] by an emissary of that arch-enemy of ordered society "the Old Man of the Mountain," Hasan Sabbâh, in the Muharram of 500 A.H. al-Ghazzâlî retired sorrow-stricken to his native city of Tûs, where he had built a *madrassa* for students and a *khânkâh* (monastery) for his disciples. Here he lectured, and here he laboured on his works which have made him a personality in the world of Islâm. The great Sûfi died on Monday the 14th of Jumâdi II. 505 A.H. (18th December 1111).

With him passed away one who, in spite of his mysticism, was endowed with a particularly virile character, the influence of which lasted long after his death.   Imâm al-Ghazzâlî as a follower of Shâfe'i, was bitterly hostile to Imâm Abû Hanîfa, whose encouragement of analogical reasoning and of the exercise of ratiocination [2] he seems to have strongly disapproved.   Whilst on the one hand the mystic Imâm by his Quietism chilled the blood in the veins of the Moslem races and arrested their energies [3] for progress and development, on the other he imparted to Ash'arism an idealism it did not previously possess.

The desire to enforce conformity and repress "heresy" has been the curse of every religious system where ecclesiastics and legists have usurped authority in the church.   Islâm has not escaped from it, though it has been less harsh to "unbelievers" than to its own "innovators," whom orthodoxy designated as *ahl-ul-bida'*.   Men suffering from spiritual exaltation, or whose minds had become unhinged by excessive self-mortification, along with rationalists and reformers, became the victims of persecution.   The story of Mansûr al-Hallâj

---

[1] Fakhr-ul-Mulk was held in such love and esteem by the people, for his wise and beneficent administration of Sanjar's kingdom, that history has named him *Jamâl-ush-Shuhada*, "The Glory of the Martyrs." Husain, the grandson of the Prophet massacred at Kerbela, is called the *Syed ush Shuhada*, "The Chief of the Martyrs."

[2] The followers of Abû Hanîfa were accordingly called *ahl-ur-rai-wa'l-Kyâs*, "people of reasoning and analogy."

[3] Dr. Sachau, the eminent translator of al-Beiruni's *Indika*, says that "were it not for al-Asha'ri and al-Ghazzâli the Arabs would have been a nation of Galileos and Newtons."

is one of the most pitiful in the annals of mysticism.[1] Farîd-
ud-din-'Attar was, like Firdousi, an adherent of the House of
Mohammed ; he was also a Sûfi of the first degree. In the
Mazhar-ul-'Ajâib[2] 'Attar gives an account of his sufferings ;
of his expulsion from the place of his birth (Tûs) ; of the confiscation of his property and goods, and of his subsequent
wanderings. Many of them suffered the penalty of death ;
in the case of others the punishment was posthumous ; their
works were consigned to the flames. Even al-Ghazzâli's
Ihya-ul-'Ulum met with that fate in Cordova, at one time the
home of Saracenic culture.[3] But these repressive methods
did not succeed in stopping the spread of the mystical cult.
Every holy man round whom gathered disciples became a
saint or *wali*. The saints were credited with supernatural
powers ; and although the most noted Sûfis of early times who
rank now as *walis* of the first rank, like Junaid and Bâyezid
Bistami, strongly discountenanced thaumaturgic practices, the
Tazkirat-ul-Awlia, and the *Nafahât-ul-Uns* recount remarkable acts by the saints outside ordinary human experience.
These wonders are called *karâmât*, performed as they are by
virtue of the powers gifted to them by God. In these days
they would probably be attributed to what is called " psychic
influence." Hypnotism and mesmerism, under the name of
tâsir ul-anzâr, and telepathy have long been known in the
East. Some of the acts might be due to unconscious
hypnotism.

Sufïsm travelled speedily from Irâk and Persia into India,
where it found a congenial soil. A large number of Sûfi saints,
both men and women, flourished in Hindustan and the Deccan
and acquired great fame in their lifetime for sanctity and good
work. Their tombs are up to the present day the objects of
pilgrimage to Moslems and, remarkable to note, to Hindus as
well.[4] These saints taught their disciples who congregated in
the colleges or monasteries they established Islâmic theosophy

[1] *Tazkirat-ul-Awlia*, Pt. ii. p. 135.

[2] *Mazhar-ul-'Ajâib* is a title of the Caliph *Ameer ul-Mominîn Ali*.

[3] This happened in the reign of 'Ali bin Yusuf Tâshfin, who died in 1143 A.C.

[4] Lutfullah in his *Qânûni Islâm*, translated by Herklot, gives an account of
most of these *walis*, with the practices and superstitions common among the
Inndia Sûfis.

and Sûfi rules of life.   They, like their successors, were called
sajjâdanashin.[1]   They are, in fact, spiritual preceptors.   In
the West the preceptor is called the *sheikh* ; in India, *pír* or
murshid ; the disciple the *muríd*.   On the death of the *pír* his
successor assumes the privilege of initiating the disciples into the
mysteries of *dervishism* or *Sûfism*.   This privilege of initiation,
of making *muríds*, of imparting to them spiritual knowledge,
is one of the functions which the *sajjâdanashin* performs or is
supposed to perform.   He is the curator of the mausoleum
where his ancestor is buried, and in him is supposed to continue the spiritual line (*silsila*).   The shrines (*dargahs*), which
are to be found all over India, are the tombs of celebrated
dervishes who in their lifetime were regarded as saints.   Some
of these men had established *khânkâhs* where they lived and
where they taught their Sûfi doctrines.   Many did not possess
khânkâhs and when they died their tombs became shrines.
They were mostly Sûfis ; but some were undoubtedly the
disciples of Miân Roushan Bâyezîd,[2] who lived about the
time of Akbar, and who had founded an independent esoteric
brotherhood, in which the chief occupied a peculiarly distinctive
position.   They called themselves dervishes or *fakírs*, on the
hypothesis that they had abjured the world, and were humble
servitors of God ; by their followers they were honoured with
the title of *shah* or king.   Although the Persian word
" dervish " is significantly Moslem in its origin and meaning,
" dervishes " have always existed in Western Asia.   The
minor Prophets of the Hebrews, designated *nabiin*, were
only the prototypes of the modern " dervish."   John the
Baptist, who lost his life for his temerity before Herod's
wife, acted exactly as hundreds of dervishes have done in
later ages, challenging kings and princes in their palaces.   One
of the most celebrated of these Indian *walis* is Shah Nizâm
uddin Awlia, who came from Ghazni and is buried in the
neighbourhood of Delhi, where he lived for many years.   He is
said to have died in 1325.[3]   Khwâja Mu'in ud-din Chishti

---

[1] *Sajjâda* is a prayer mat ; and *nashin* is the person seated on it.

[2] See *ante*, p. 345.   This man should not be confounded with the celebrated
Bâyezid Bistâmi, who died in A.H. 261 (A.C. 874-5).   In the Surâh Bistâmi
is spelt as Bastâmi.

[3] In the reign of Ala-ud-din Khilji, who was his *muríd*.

appears to have preceded Nizâm uddin Awlia into India. He died at Ajmere at the age of 97 in 663 A.H. (1265 A.C.). His mausoleum at Ajmere is the resort of pilgrims, both Moslem and Hindu, from all parts of India.[1]

Another *wali*, Burhân ud-din, is buried in Burhanpur (named after him) in Central India. Shah Kabir Dervish flourished in the reign of Farrukh Siyar in the eighteenth century. He is buried in Sasseram in Behar. One of his descendants is still in charge of his monastery. Ameer Khusru, poet laureate of Ala-ud-din Khilji, the Pathan King of Delhi, is also claimed as a Sûfi saint.[2]

In the West, orders of dervishes sprang up on all sides. One of the most famous and probably the most influential is the *Kâdiria* founded by the celebrated Sunni saint Sheikh Muhi-ud-din Abd ul-Kâdir Ghilani.[3] Another was founded by Moulâna Jalâl ud-din, which is called after his title the *Moulaviya* and has a great reputation for the holy life of its members. The *Nakshbandia* is another powerful order, which has many adherents in India.

But it is given to few to be saints and to still fewer to combine a holy life of concentrated devotion with the discharge of the daily duties of life. To the bulk of humanity the call to abjure the world and to betake ourselves to complete absorption in the contemplation of the Divinity is an inducement to mental lethargy. The responsibility for the present decadence of the Moslem nations must be shared by the formalism of the

---

[1] Mu'in ud-dîn (usually styled among Indian Sûfis *Moulâna Hazrat Sultan ul-Mashâikh*) traced his *silsila* through Ibrâhim Adham, and through Ibrâhim Adham to Hasan Basri, and through him to the Caliph Ali, and through him to the Prophet, *Sarwar-i-Kâinât*, "Chief of the Creation." Mu'in ud-dîn Chisti is the founder of the Chistia order in India. Three hundred years later Sheikh Selim Chishi became the spiritual preceptor of the great Akbar, who named his son and successor Jehangir after his *murshid*.

Moulâna Jalâl ud-din Rûmi traced his *silsila* similarly through Junaid to the 8th Apostolical Imâm Ali son of Musa (ar-Riza), and through him to the Caliph Ali and the Prophet.

[2] See Appendix III.

[3] 'Abdul Kâdir was a descendant of Ali and is credited with the performance of many miracles. He is the patron saint of the Kurds and is held in great veneration among the Sûfis of the Sunni sect in India. He is usually called "*Ghous Âzam.*" According to the authors of *Les Confréries Religieuses Musulmanes* (MM. Depont et Cappolani, vol. i. p. 303) the Kadiria order has a wide influence in the East, which extends to Java and China, and its lodges *Zavias*) are established in Mecca and Medîna. "Abnegation of self," say

Asha'ri and the quietism of the Sûfi.   Mystical teachings like
the following :

> The man who looks on the beggar's bowl as a kingly crown
> And the present world a fleeting bubble,
> He alone traverseth the ocean of Truth ·
> Who looks upon life as a fairy tale.[1]

can have but one result—intellectual paralysis.

I must now return to al-Ghazzâlî's conceptions of Sûfi
theosophy and theosophical life.   He certainly did not claim
any exclusive knowledge of the mysteries of Creation nor
were his doctrines so esoteric as those professed by latter-day
Sûfis.   Like as-Sarrâj he propounded a scheme of life which
he considered formed the true Path (tarîkat) to the ultimate
goal " the attainment of nearness to God," and final peace
in the Beatific Vision.   But as his insistence on the Path
depends on the larger theory of the Cosmos it is necessary to
say something about its essential features.   His enunciation
about all nature and all existence being the direct Creation of
God the Almighty is but an echo of what is told in the Koran.
His theory assumes a broader aspect when he begins to state
his conception of the universe as a whole.   He divides Creation
into two categories, viz. the Visible and the Invisible.   The
Visible world ('âlam-ul-Mulk) is the world of matter ; and
is subject to the law of evolution, to change and growth.   Here
he is in accord with the Rationalists (the Mu'tazilas).

The invisible world, imperceptible to human sense, he divides
into two sub-categories ; first, the 'âlam-ul-jabarût,[2] which
stands between pure matter and pure spirit ; it is not wholly
matter nor wholly spirit but partakes of the character of both.
The forces of nature belong to this category.   Had al-Ghazzâlî
lived in these days he would probably have assigned some of
the discoveries of modern science like the properties of radium

the authors of the Confréries, " to the service of God ; ecstatic mysticism
bordering on hysteria ; philanthropic principles developed to the highest
degree, without distinction of race or creed ; intense charity ; vigorous piety,
humility, pervading all actions, and a gentleness of spirit, have made him
(Abdul Kâdir) the most popular and most revered saint of Islâm."

[1] See Appendix III.

[2] " Jabarût, in the language of the sâlikân [those who strive to attain Truth],"
says the Farhang, " is the sublime realm, the abode of angels and Divine
Attributes " (sifât Ilâkî).

to the '*âlam-ul-jabarût*. His idea of the purely spiritual world, *al-'âlam-ul-malakût*,[1] forms the most interesting part of his theory. The '*âlam-ul-malakût* is the realm of " Ideas." The human soul belongs to this world. It comes as a spark from its original home and on separation from the earthly body, it flies back to the region whence it came.[2]

These divisions are merely al-Ghazzâlî's deductions from the Koran. His abhorrence of analogical reasoning does not prevent him from arriving at the conclusion by the usual process of ratiocination. Neither the theory nor the division was altogether new, for they had been anticipated by al-Fârâbi in his '*Uyûn-ul-Masâil*.[2] According to the Mu'tazilas, the references in the Koran to the " Balance " (*Mizân*) in which human actions are weighed, to the " Pen " (*Kalam*) and Tablet (*Lauh*) with which and on which the decrees of Providence are inscribed, are allegorical. As already mentioned, al-Asha'ri affirms them to be actual, corporeal objects. Imâm al-Ghazzâlî takes another course ; he relegates them to the '*âlam ul-malakût*, the realm of " abstract ideas." It was thus he endeavoured to reconcile Patristicism with his doctrine of " inward light " and its longings for the upward flight of the human soul.

Some of the extreme Sûfis believe that when the final nearness is attained the human soul becomes absorbed in the Divinity. This is called *hulûl* (absorption) and sometimes *ittihâd* (union). But this pantheistic conception is strongly repudiated both by as-Sarrâj and al-Ghazzâlî ; though often the words *wisâl* and *waslat* are used to signify the closeness of the approach to the Divine Essence. Even when the Sûfi talks of *fana-f'il Allâh* (annihilation in God) he does not mean to imply that the human soul becomes merged in the Universal Soul. Al-Ghazzâlî's notion, like that of his great predecessor, is that the individual soul (*rûh*) at the Almighty's bidding emanates from a realm, the '*âlam ul-Malakût*, nearest to the Divine Essence, and on its separation from the corporeal body reverts to its original home ; and that this is the meaning of the Koranic

---

[1] In the *Farhang*, *Malakût* is defined thus : " in the language of the Sûfis, it means the Realm of Ideas " ('*âlami ma'ni*).

[2] See *ante*, p. 426.

declaration " We come from God and unto Him we return." [1]

The Mu'tazili, the Asha'ri and the follower of al-Ghazzâlî do not differ in the essentials ; their difference is due more to the angle from which they look at the dogmas of the Faith. The rationalist holds that a knowledge of God is attainable by Reason. He appeals to Reason because the call of the Koran to the worship of one God is based on Reason. The Asha'ri believes because he is so taught ; the Sûfi believes because, as he says, of " the inward light." According to the Sûfi, the seeker for Truth by intensive " inwardness " and communion with God can rise by successive stages of exaltation to a state when he can actually have a vision of the Divine Essence. The first step for the novitiate is to form the *niyyat* (the resolve or intention) ; then comes *tauba* (penitence and renunciation). He is now on the forward path, this stage is called *mujâhada* (probation or striving). After a prolonged probation the ecstatic soul appears in the Presence still veiled. Hâfiz, in a mood of exaltation, refers to this stage, technically called *Muhâzara*, as *huzûri*, when the soul presents itself in absolute surrender to God and " abandonment of the world and all its vanities." [2] The next is " the uplifting of the veil " (*mukâshafa*), when the veil which curtained off the Unseen is lifted and the God becomes revealed to the worshipper's heart ; the last stage is the Vision (*mushâhada*), when the entranced Soul stands in the presence of Truth itself, and the light falls distinctly on " the human heart."

Even in the primary stage, the psychological effort to concentrate all thought on one object causes the disciple (the *murîd*) to see visions, hear the voices of angels and prophets, and gain from them guidance. Exactly parallel forms of psychological exaltation have appeared in Christianity in all ages. In the phraseology of the Sûfi the effort by which each stage is gained is called (*hâl*) a " state." It is a condition of joy or longing. And when this condition seizes on the

---

[1] اِنَّالِلّٰهِ وَاِنَّااِلَيْهِ رَاجِعُرنَ The pious Moslem pronounces these words whenever he passes a bier or a cemetery.

[2] *Huzûri gar hami khâhi, as-o ghâib mashau Hâfiz*
Matâ mâ-talk, man-tahwâ da'i'd-dunyâ wa amhilha.

" seeker," he falls into ecstasy (*wajd*). The dervishes in their monasteries may be seen working themselves up into a condition of " ecstasy." [1]

The Sûfi holds that the knowledge of God is vouchsafed to him by inward light ; the Rationalist affirms that the cognition comes to him from Reason, a gift of the Creator. Does not the Koran constantly appeal to human reason and human intelligence " to reflect, to consider, to speculate " about God's Creation and the mysteries of nature ? Had the Koran condemned the exercise of reason, would it have exhorted the people to whom it spoke to look at the marvels of nature and draw their own conclusions whether this wonderful world was a creation of accident, or was brought into existence by an all-pervading Intelligence. Religion and Rationalism are correlated and bound together. If we find anything in the Koran which seems superficially to be in conflict with the results of philosophy, we may be sure there is an underlying meaning, which it should be the work of reason to unravel. Ibn Rushd places this proposition with extreme lucidity in his *Fasl-ul-Makâl*.[2] He affirms that there is no disagreement between religion and philosophy ; religion is revelation from God ; philosophy is the product of the human mind. He was thus not far removed from al-Ghazzâlî's plane. For al-Ghazzâlî did not believe like Asha'ri that the earth was flat because it was said in the Koran " God had spread it out as a carpet." He accepts all the revelations of science and the conclusions of mathematicians and astronomers. The stars and planets revolve round the world according to pre-ordained laws. Nature itself contains its own proof of the Power, Benevolence and Intelligence that brought it into existence. He is thus in complete accord with Ibn Sina, Ibn Rushd and the rationalists in general. Examined closely it will be seen that the mind of al-Ghazzâlî, who saved Asha'rism from becoming a hard-crusted formalism, and by joining it to an exalted form of

---

[1] *Zikr* is the name of the function in which the dervishes usually congregate for obtaining the ecstatic condition. There is an excellent description of a *Zikr* in an Egyptian *Závia* by Dr. D. B. Macdonald in his *Aspects of Islam*. In India *Zikrs* are usually held at the celebration of the '*Urs* (anniversary ceremony of the death of the original spiritual preceptor).

[2] See *ante*, p. 427.

emotionalism infused into it fresh vitality, ran really in the same groove as the minds of those masters.

The Senussi confraternity [1] is not a religious order like the Kâderia, but unquestionably, in the civilising and uplifting work it is doing in Northern and Central Africa, it imparts a mystical meaning into the teachings of its *Ikhwân*. They convey to their converts and disciples some of the lessons of " inward knowledge " without detaching them from the world of struggle and advance.

The exalted idealism which breathes in the Prophet's words, in the preachings of the Imâms and in the teachings of the expounders of " inward light," rationalists, philosophers and Sûfis alike, has modelled the lives and inspired the actions of the noblest men in Islâm.   Heroes like 'Imâd-ud-dîn Zangi, rulers like Salâh-ud-din bin Ayyub (the Saladin of European history) have found in it their guiding star.   And poets like Sanâi, 'Attâr and Jalâl ud-dîn have given fervent expression to that universal Divine love, which pervades nature from the lowest type of creation to the highest, and their idylls are regarded by many Moslems with a respect only less than that entertained for the Koran.

But Sûfîsm in the Moslem world, like its counterpart in Christendom, has, in its practical effect, been productive of many mischievous results.   In perfectly well-attuned minds mysticism takes the form of a noble type of idealistic philosophy ;   but the generality of mankind are more likely to unhinge their brains by busying themselves with the mysteries of the Divine Essence and our relations thereto.   Every ignorant and idle specimen of humanity, who, despising real knowledge, abandoned the fields of true philosophy and betook himself to the domains of mysticism, would thus set himself up as one of the *Ahl-i-Ma'rifat*.   And that this actually occurred in the time of Ghazzâlî we see by his bitter complaint that things had come to such a pass that husbandmen were leaving their tillage and claiming the privileges of " the advanced." In fact the greatest objection to vulgar mysticism, whether in Islâm or in Christendom, is that, being in itself no religion, wherever it prevails it unsettles the mind and weakens the

[1] See Appendix III.

foundations of society and paralyses human energy ; it naturally drifts into anthropolatry and naturalistic pantheism.

Yet the benefits conferred by the nobler type of idealistic philosophy are too great to be ignored ; and the Idealism of Averroes developed in Europe the conception of Universal Divinity. Christian Europe owes its outburst of subjective pantheism—and its consequent emancipation from the intense materialism of a mythological creed—to the engrafting of Moslem idealism on the Western mind. It was the influence of Averroistic writings that attracted the attention of reflecting people to the great problem of the connection between the worlds of matter and of mind, and revived the conception of an all-pervading spirit, " which sleeps in the stone, dreams in the animal, and wakes in the man," " the belief that the hidden vital principle which produces the varied forms of organisation is but the thrill of ' the Divine Essence ' that is present in them all."

جان عالم گویمــش گر ربط جان دانم بذن
در دل هر ذره هم پنهان و هم پیداستنی

" I would have said He was the Soul of the Universe if I had known the relation of the human soul to the body, for He is present and hidden in the heart of every atom."

THE END.

APPENDIX I

TRANSLATION OF THE PERSIAN AND ARABIC MOTTOES AT THE HEAD OF THE CHAPTERS

479

He surpassed all the Prophets in constitution and disposition,
Nor any did approach him either in knowledge or nobleness.
Avoid what the Christians assert about their Prophet ;
(But) declare whatever else thou wishest in his praise, and contend
    for it.   -   -   -   -   -   -   -   -   -   -   101

Indeed the Prophet is a light from which guidance is sought,
And a drawn sword out of God's swords. -   -   -   -   -   101

Is it from the remembrance of the neighbours at Zi-Salam
That thou hast mixed tears flowing from the eyes with blood ?   107

When the help of God and victory come and thou seest the
    people entering into the religion of God in troops,
Celebrate the praise of thy Lord, and ask pardon of Him ; for
    He is the Forgiver.   -   -   -   -   -   -   -   -   109

Hold fast, all ye, to the Rock of God
And be not disunited.   -   -   -   -   -   -   -   -   122

Come to Me, do not seek except Me ;
I am the Beneficent ; seek Me thou wilt find Me.
Dost thou remember any night in which thou hast called to Me
    secretly,
And I did not hear thee ?   Then seek Me thou wilt find Me.
When the afflicted one says " dost not Thou seek me " ?
I look towards him ; seek Me, thou wilt find Me.
When My servant disobeys Me, thou wilt find Me
Quick in chastising ; seek Me, thou wilt find Me.   -   -   -   137

Say, unto whom belongeth whatsoever is in heaven and earth ?
Say unto God ; He hath prescribed unto Himself mercy. -   -   159
        (For translation of the other passage, see p. 173.)

The disputes of the seventy-two sects put them all aside,
As they did not see the Truth they took to the path of fiction -   290

He is the Beginning and the End,
The Manifest and the Hidden,
And the knower of all things.   (Koran). -   -   -   -   -   455

APPENDIX II

p. 166 - - - - - - لا صلوا ة ا لا بحضور القلب

Ibid. - - - - - اقرار باللسان و تصديق بالقلب

p. 274 - - من كان له ذمتنا فد مه كدمنا ون يته كد يتنا

ولنجران و حاشيتها جوار الله و ذمّة محمدالنبى رسول الله علىٰ
انفسهم و ملتهم و ارضهم و اموالهم و غائبهم و شاهدهم و عيرهم و
بعشهم و امثلتهم ولا يغيَّر ما كانوا عليه ولا يغيرّ حق من حقوقهم و
امثلتهم لايفتن اسقف من اسقفيته ولا راهب من رهبانيته ولا واقه من
وقاهيته على ماتحت ايدهم من قليل او كثير وليس عليهم رهق ولادم
جاهلية ولا يحشرون ولايعشرون ولايطأ ارضهم جيش p. 273 -

لا يهدم لهم بعية ولا كنية ولا يمنعون من ضرب النوا قبين ولا من
اخراج الصلبان فى يوم عيدهم p. 274 - - - - - -

ما وسعنى ارضى ولا سمائى وكدن
و سعنى قلب عبدى المؤمن التقى النقى
p. 457 - - - - - - الورع -

481

APPENDIX III

Whatever the sins of the Bábís may have been, their punishment, in its barbarous inhumanity, far exceeded their deserts—a punishment borne with sublime fortitude which cannot help evoking the admiration of every heart not steeped in racial or religious fanaticism and which is bearing its natural fruit. The sect, instead of dying out, is increasing in number, and judging from the few *professed* Bábís I have met, actuated with bitter hatred against the Mullahs whom they believe to be the primary cause of their persecution.

The cruelties to which the Bábís were subjected were the acts of an ignorant populace and a frightened governor hounded on by fanatical priests. In China, in our own times, under the eyes of the civilised world, disciplined troops of certain civilised Powers perpetrated the most diabolical and nameless horrors upon unoffending citizens and helpless women and children. Crimes like these destroy one's faith in humanity and progress. (p. 359)

The astronomer Ali Ibn Yunus was a man of versatile talent. " He made astronomy his particular study," says Ibn Khallikân, " but he was well-versed in other sciences and displayed an eminent talent for poetry." (p. 377)

The *Indian Social Reformer* of Bombay (of the 28th of July, 1901), in an appreciative article on " The Liberal Movement in Islâm," drew my attention to certain statements of M. Renan in one of his lectures delivered in March, 1883, at the Sarbonne.[1] In this lecture M. Renan has tried to show that Islâm is opposed to science, and that scientific pursuits came into vogue among the Moslems only when the religion became weakened. " Omar," he says, " did not burn, as we are often told, the library of Alexandria ; that library had, by his time, nearly disappeared. But the principle which he caused to triumph in the world was in a very real sense destructive of learned research and of the varied work of the mind."

The correctness of this somewhat wild and reckless assertion, which, coming from the author of *Averroes and Averroism*, is startling, was at once challenged by the learned Shaikh Jamâl ud-din who was residing at Paris at the time. M. Renan's reply to the Shaikh's criticism is instructive. The learned Frenchman had to qualify his generalisations

---

[1] The lecture is headed " Islâmism and Science," and is printed in a book called *The Poetry of the Celtic Races and Other Studies.*

and to acknowledge that by Islâm he meant the religion of Mohammed as accepted and practised by the ignorant and fanatical sections of the Moslem communities. I will quote here the passage in which he limits his strictures, as it may perhaps be of some help in awakening the Musulmans themselves to a sense of their responsibilities :—" One aspect in which I have appeared unjust to the Shaikh is that I have not sufficiently developed the idea that all revealed religion is forced to show hostility to positive science ; and that, in this respect, Christianity has no reason to boast over Islâm. About that there can be no doubt. Galileo was not treated more kindly by Catholicism than was Averroes by Islâm. Galileo found truth in a Catholic country despite Catholicism, as Averroes nobly philosophised in a Moslem country despite Islâm. If I did not insist more strongly upon this point, it was, to tell the truth, because my opinions on this matter are so well known that there was no need for me to recur to them again before a public conversant with my writings. I have said, sufficiently often to preclude any necessity for repeating it, that the human mind must be detached from all supernatural belief if it desires to labour at its own essential task, which is the construction of positive science. This does not imply any violent destruction or hasty rupture. It does not mean that the Christian should forsake Christianity, or that the Musulman should abandon Islâm. It means that the enlightened parts of Christendom and Islâm should arrive at that state of benevolent indifference in which religious beliefs become inoffensive. This is half accomplished in nearly all Christian countries. Let us hope that the like will be the case for Islâm. Naturally on that day the Shaikh and I will be at one, and ready to applaud heartily. . . . I did not assert that all Musulmans, without distinction of race, are and always will be sunk in ignorance. I said that Islâmism puts great difficulties in the way of science, and unfortunately has succeeded for five or six hundred years in almost suppressing it in the countries under its sway ; and that this is for these countries a cause of extreme weakness. I believe, in point of fact, that the regeneration of the Mohammedan countries will not be the work of Islâm ; it will come to pass through the enfeeblement of Islâm, as indeed the great advance of the countries called Christian commenced with the destruction of the tyrannical church of the Middle Ages. Some persons have seen in my lecture a thought hostile to the individuals who profess the Mohammedan religion. That is by no means true ; Musulmans are themselves the first victims of Islâm. More than once in my Eastern travels I have been in a position to notice how fanaticism proceeds from a small number of dangerous men who keep the others in the practice of religion by terror. To emancipate the Musulman from his religion would be the greatest service that one could render him. In wishing these populations, in which so many good elements exist, a deliverance from the yoke that weighs them down, I do not believe that I have any unkindly thought for them. And, let me say also, since the Shaikh Jamâl ud-dîn desires me to hold the balance equally between different faiths, I should not any the more believe that

I was wishing evil of certain European countries if I expressed a hope that Christianity should have a less dominant influence upon them."

It is a matter of regret that European scholars, generally speaking, should persist in comparing the lowest form of Islâm with the highest form of Christianity. All religions have different phases ; they vary according to the climatic and economic conditions. of the country, the environments and education of the people, their national characteristics and a multitude of other causes. To compare modern idealistic Christianity with a debased form of Islâm is an insult to common sense and intelligence. In this work I have endeavoured to show how Islâm furthered the intellectual movement of the world, how it brought to life a dying world, how it promoted culture and civilisation. It was not the Islâm which is professed to-day by the ignorant bigot, the intriguing self-seeker, but it was nevertheless Islâm—Islâm in its truest, highest and noblest sense. I have tried to show the cause of the blight that has fallen on Moslem nations. It is more than probable that my views will not satisfy the critic of Islâm who has started with a preconceived bias, or who judges of the Faith by its latter-day professors. All the same I venture to assert that my statements are founded on historical facts.   .   .   .   .

One assertion of M. Renan requires a categorical refutation. He has alleged in his lecture " as a very remarkable thing that among the philosophers and learned men called Arabic, there was but one alone, Alkindi, who was of Arabic origin : all the others were Persians, Trans-oxians, Spaniards, natives of Bokhara, of Samarcand, of Cordova, of Seville. Not only were those men not Arabs by blood, but they were in nowise Arabs in mind." The memory of this great French scholar, whose acquaintance I had the privilege of making, deserves every respect. But surely this sweeping observation is very wide of the truth. A glance at the *Wafiât ul-Ayân* (Ibn Khallikân's great Biographical Dictionary), the *Târikh ul-Hukama* and other works of the like nature, will show how utterly unfounded the assertion is. From the genealogy of the eminent men whose lives are contained in these books, it will be seen that a vast number of the great scholars, doctors and savants, although born in places outside Arabia, were Arabs by descent.

Probably M. Renan would not have admitted that Ali (the Caliph) was a philosopher, but his descendants Ja'far as-Sâdik and Ali ar-Rizâ were unquestionably entitled to be included in that designation. And Ja'far as-Sâdik was a scientist besides. Jâbir ibn Haiyyan (Geber), the father of modern chemistry, worked in fact with the materials gathered by Ja'far. It is admitted that Al Kindi, " the Philosopher of the Arabs," was descended from the royal family of Kinda and was an Arab of the Arabs. But it is not known that Yahya ibn Ali Mansûr (see *ante*, p. 374) was a pure Arab. Nor is it known that Ali ibn Yunus (*ante*, p. 377) belonged to the tribe of as-Sadaf—" a great branch," says Ibn Khallikân, " of the tribe of Himyar which settled in Egypt." Al-Jâhiz, Abû Osmân Amr *al-Kinâni al-Laisi*, the celebrated Mutazilite philosopher, who died at Basra in A.H. 255 (868-9 A.C.), was a pure Arab, a member of the tribe of Kinâna. Avenpace (*ante*, p. 428) was a Tujîbite by descent. "Tujîbi pronounced also Tajîbi," says Ibn Khallikân, "means descended from Tujîb the mother of 'Adi and Sa'd, the sons of Ashras ibn us-Sakûn. She herself was the daughter of Saubân bin Sulaim ibn Mazis, and her sons were surnamed after her."

The Avenzoars (*ante*, p. 386) belonged to the Arabian tribe of Iyâz ibn Nizâr, and hence bore the title of al-Iyâzi.

The great grammarian al-Khalîl ibn Ahmed was a member of the tribe of Azd. The Spanish historian and philosopher Ibn Bash-kuwal was a descendant of one of the Medînite Ansâr who had settled in Spain. Mas'ûdi (*ante*, p. 390) was a direct descendant of one of the Prophet's immediate companions and disciples, Ibn Masûd, hence the title; whilst Ibn ul-Athîr was a member of the celebrated tribe of Shaibân.

The political economist and jurisconsult, al-Mâwardi, a native of Basra, was a pure Arab.[1]

The soldier, statesman, philosopher and poet, Osâma was a member of the tribe of Kinâna.

Sharîf al-Murtaza, the author of the *Ghurar wa'd Durar*, one of the greatest scholars of his time, was descended from Imâm Ali ar-Rizâ.

Ibn Tufail (*ante*, pp. 386, 429) was a member of the tribe of Kais, and hence the title of al-Kaisi.

Ibn Khaldûn was descended from an Yemenite family which had settled in Spain. They came from Hazramaut and were therefore called *al-Hazramî*.

I have given only a few names picked out at random, but the curious reader will find numberless instances in the books I have mentioned.[2]

To say that these men were not Arabs and had no Arab blood in them is surely a bold assertion. I might with equal effrontery assert that, because Longfellow, Channing, Emerson, Draper were born in America, they were not Anglo-Saxons.

Ibn Khallikân calls al-Fârâbî "the greatest philosopher of the Moslems," and speaks of him in the following terms :—

ابو نصر محمد بن محمد طرخان بن اوزلغ الفارابي التركي
الحكيم المشهور صاحب التصانيف فى المنطق و الموسيقى و غيرهما
من العلوم و هو اكبر فلاسفة المسلمين لم يكن فيهم من بلغ رتبته
فى فنونه و الرئيس ابو علي ابن سيناء المقدم ذكره بكتبه نخرج
بكلامه و انتفع فى نصانيفه

---

[1] Two of his most important works are the *Ahkâm us-Saltâniyyah* and *as-Siâsat ul-Mudan*, both spoken of highly by Von Hammer.

[2] See also Wüstenfeld's *Geschichte der Arabischer Aerzte*, *Târîkh ul-Islâm* of Zahabî, and Casiri's *Bibliotheca Arabica*.

T

" Abû Nasr Mohammed bin Mohammed bin Turkhân bin Auslagh al-Fârâbî at-Turki (the Turk), a celebrated philosopher, author of many works in logic, music, and other sciences. He was the greatest of philosophers among the Moslems, and no one among them attained a rank equal to his in the sciences. And the *chief* (of philosophers) Abû Ali Ibn Sîna, whom I have mentioned before, derived benefit from his writings "
(p. 382)

Abu'l Kâsim Kinderski was a famous poet and *Avicennistic* philosopher of Persia in the eighteenth century

Hayy ibn Yakzân was translated into English and published in London so long ago as 1686.
(p. 429)

Sanâï has given expression to his admiration for Ibn Sîna and his devotion to philosophy in the following lines :

نخواهم لا جرم نعمت نه در دنیا نه در جنت

همي گویم بهر ساعت چه در سرا چه در صرا

'٥ یارب مر سنائي را صنائی نه تو در حکمت

توان کز وي برشک آید روان بو علی سینا

" I do not seek for any reward in this world or the next.
" Every moment I pray, whether in prosperity or in adversity.
" O my Lord, bestow on Sanâï the proficiency in philosophy and sciences
" Such as would make even the soul of Bû Ali Sîna jealous."

The position of Sanâï in the world of Islâm can be gathered from the following lines of Jalâl ud-dîn Rûmî, revered nowadays by educated Musulmans throughout Asia and Egypt :

عطار روح بود و سنائی دو چشم او

ما از پي سنائی و عطار آمدیم

" 'Attâr was its soul [of the philosophy of mysticism], Sanâï was its eyes ; I only walked in the footsteps of 'Attâr and Sanâï."
(P 457)

The reactionary character of the influence exercised by Abu'l Hasan Ali al-Asha'ri and Ahmed al-Ghazzâli can hardly be over-estimated. It has been happily summed up in a few words by the learned editor of al-Beirûni's *al-Asâr ul-Bâkieh*—" but for al-Asha'ri and al-Ghazzâli the Arabs might have been a nation of Galileos, Keplers and Newtons." By their denunciations of science and philosophy, by their exhortations that besides theology and law no other knowledge was worth acquiring, they did more to stop the progress of the Moslem world than most other Moslem scholiasts. And up to this day their example is held forth as a reason for ignorance and stagnation.

Al-Asha'ri was born at Basra in 883-4 A.C. (270 A.H.), and died at Bagdad; but the year of his death is not certain; it occurred probably some time between 941 and 952 A.C. (300 and 340 A.H.). He was originally a Mu'tazili and publicly taught the rationalistic doctrines. A clever, ambitious man he saw no opportunity of power or influence among the Rationalists; an alliance with the party of retrogression meant fame and tangible reward. He, accordingly, made a public renunciation of his former creed in man's free will and " of his opinion that the Koran was created." This happened on a Friday at the Cathedral mosque of Basra. Whilst seated on his chair lecturing to his pupils, he suddenly sprang up, and cried aloud to the assembled multitude :—" They who know me, know who I am, as for those who do not know me, I shall tell them : I am Ali ibn Isma'îl al-Asha'ri, and I used to hold that the Koran was created, that the eyes (*of men*) shall not see God, and that we ourselves are the authors of our evil deeds ; now I have returned to the truth, I renounce these opinions and I take the engagement to refute the Mu'tazilites and expose their infamy and turpitude." And with the recantation of each doctrine that he formerly professed, he tore off from his person some garment saying, " I repudiate this belief as I repudiate this dress." First went the turban, then the mantle and so on. The effect of this theatrical display was immense among the impressionable inhabitants of Basra, and the fame of al-Asha'ri spread so rapidly among the people that he soon became their recognised leader. Ibn Khallikân calls him " a great upholder of the orthodox doctrines."

. . . .

Upon the death of the last Fâtimide Caliph al-'Azid li-dîn Illâh, Saladin, who was Commander-in-chief and Prime Minister, proclaimed the Abbaside Mustazii and thus restored Egypt to the spiritual sovereignty of Bagdad. Asha'rism henceforth became dominant in that country.

The theological students, who were chiefly the followers of Ibn Hanbal, under the weaker Abbaside Caliphs became a source of great trouble in Bagdad. They constituted themselves into a body of irresponsible censors ; they used forcibly to enter houses, break musical instruments, and commit similar acts of vandalism.

APPENDIX III—*contd.*

ADDITIONAL NOTES

P. 17. The word *Ikra* might be rendered also as "recite."

P. 106. The incident to which reference is made in the footnote at p. 106 has been immortalised by the Persian Poet Sa'di. The poem opens with the following lines, which are difficult to render properly into another language :

کرم کن بجای من ای محترم

که مولای من بود زاهل کرم

P. 264. The following lines evince the estimation in which Meshed is held by the Shiahs

Mash-had afzal tari rui Zamin ast.
Ke án-já núr-i Rabb ul-'álamin ast.

" Mashhad is the most excellent spot on the face of the earth, for there is to be found the light of the Lord of the Creation (God)."

P. 279. *Moslem toleration.*—" In the first century of Arab rule," says Sir Thomas Arnold in his *Preaching of Islâm,* " the various Christian churches enjoyed a toleration and a freedom of religious life, such as had been unknown for generations under the Byzantine Government." And he adds, " In the course of the long struggles with the Byzantine Empire, the Caliphs had had occasion to distrust the loyalty of their Christian subjects, and the treachery of Nikophoros was not improbably one of the reasons for Hárûn's order that the Christians should wear a distinctive dress and give up the good posts they held."

Abû Yusuf's appeal to Hârûn ar-Rashid on behalf of the non-Moslem subjects is noteworthy.

" It is incumbent on the Commander of the Faithful (May God grant thee His aid !) that thou deal gently with those that have a covenant with thy Prophet and thy cousin Mohammed (the peace and blessing of God be upon him), and that thou take care that they be not wronged or ill-treated and that no burden be laid upon them beyond their strength and that no part of their belongings be taken from them beyond what they are in duty bound to pay, for it is related of the Apostle of God (the peace and blessing of God be upon him !) that he said whosoever wrongs a *zimmi* or imposes a burden upon him beyond his strength I shall be his accuser on the Day of Judgment " ; (Arnold).

P. 279. *The Zimmis.*—The following was the charter granted by the Caliph Omar at the capitulation of Jerusalem surrendered in 638 A.H. " In the name of God, the Merciful, the Compassionate. This is the security which Omar the Servant of God, the Commander of the Faithful, grants to the people of Aelia. He grants to all, whether sick or sound, security for their lives, their possessions, their churches and their crosses, and for all that concerns their religion. Their churches shall not be changed into dwelling places nor destroyed, neither shall they nor their appurtenances be in any way diminished, nor the crosses of the inhabitants, nor aught of their possessions, nor shall any constraint be put upon them in the matter of their faith, nor shall anyone of them be harmed" ; *Balâzuri*, p. 132 ; *Kitâb ul-Kharâj*, p. 54 ; Al-Makin, *Historia Saracenica*, p. 11.

Prophet's declaration :—" Whoever wrongs a *Zimmi* and lays on him a burden beyond his strength I shall be his accuser."

" Whoever torments the Zimmis torments me."

Omar's injunction to Osman :—" I commend to your care the Zimmis of the apostle of God ; see that the agreement with them is kept, and they be defended against their enemies, and that no burden is laid on them beyond their strength," Abû Yusuf, p. 71.

In similar terms is Ali's injunction to Mohammed Ibn Abû Bakr, Governor of Egypt in 36 A.H. Tabari, *in loco*. See also *D'Ohsson*, p. 44.

P. 285. In the times of the later Abbaside Caliphs three more *Diwâns* or departments came into existence, viz., the *Diwân-ul-Kazâ* (the Ministry of Justice), the *Diwân ul-'Arz* (the Paymaster General's office), and the *Diwân ul-Tughra*, where the imperial seals were kept and the documents checked.

P. 288. In my former edition of the book I had said as follows :

" The importance which Islâm attaches to the duties of sovereigns towards their subjects, and the manner in which it promotes the freedom and equality of the people and protects them against the oppression of their rulers is shown in a remarkable work by the celebrated publicist Imâm Fakhruddîn Râzi (*i.e.* of Rhages) on " the Reciprocal Rights of Sovereigns and Subjects," edited and enlarged afterwards by Mohammed bin Ali bin Taba Taba, commonly known as Ibn Tiktaka."

This statement represents the view commonly entertained by the Moulvis of India. In his work on the history of Arabic literature (Weimar and Berlin, 1898-1902), Brockelmann apparently entertained the same opinion. And he was not singular among the scholars of Europe on this point. Noel Devergers and apparently de Sacy and several others were in agreement with him. Hartwig Derenbourg, however, strongly challenged this view ; and Brockelmann in his later work (*the Nachträge*, Vol. II. p. 708) altered his opinion. What has influenced me, however, to cut out the attribution of the authorship of the *Tárîkh ud-duwal* to Imam Fakhr ud-dîn Râzi is the fact that in his enumeration of the works of this great scholar Ibn Khallikán does not include the *Tárîkh-ud-duwal*. His omission is by no means conclusive, for he often leaves out important works, as in the case of Ibn Ab'il Hadîd, to whose great commentary on the *Nahj-ul-Balâghat* he does not make the slightest reference. It has, however, been a determining factor in my omission of the passage in the new edition.

I am indebted to Mr. C. A. Storey of the India Office for the following passage from Brockelmann's works bearing on this point :

C. Brockelmann in his *Geschichte der Arabischen Litteratur* (Weimar and Berlin, 1898-1902), Vol. I. p. 506, has the following entry under Fahraddîn Abû 'Abdallâh M. b. 'Omar b. al-Hosain b. al Hatîb ar-Râzî :

" 2. ta'rîh adduwal in 2 Teilen : (*a*) Staatswissenschaft, (*b*) Gesch. der 4 ersten Chalifen, der Bûjiden, Selǵûqen und Fâtimiden, Paris, 895, Auszüge von Jourdain, Fundgruben d. Or., V. 23. D. R. Henzius, Fragmenta Arabica e. Codd. mss. nunc primum ed. (Fachraddini Razii hist. Chal. prim.) Petrop. 1828."

In the *Nachträge* (Vol. II. p. 705) he has the following entry :

" 506, 6, 2. zu streichen, = al Fahrî von b. at Tiqtaqâ."

The entry relating to Ibn al Tiqtaqâ (Vol. II. p. 161) is as follows :

" M. b. 'Ali b. Tabâtabâ b. at Tiqtaqâ, geb. um 660/1261, schrieb 701/1301 während eines Aufenthaltes in Môsul für den dortigen Statthalter Fahraddîn 'Îsâ b. Ibrâhim :
Al k. al Fahrî fî'l âdâb as Sultânija wad duwal al islâmîja, Paris 2441, Fürstenspiegel und Geschichte der islâmischen Reiche von Anfang bis zu Ende des Chalifats, hrsg. v. W. Ahlwardt, Goth. 1860, v. H. Derenbourg, Paris, 1895, Bibl. de l'école des hautes études, fs. 105. Auszug vom Verf. Paris 2442 ; vgl. Cherbonneau JAP. s. 4 t.7.8.9.[2] "

A footnote to this page says :

" [2] Damit identisch ist der *ta'rîh ad duwal*, Bd. I. p. 506 mit Wiederholung eines alten Irrtums dem Fahraddîn ar Râzî zugeschrieben."

P. 288. *Justice.*—In the *Kitâb-ul-Mizân ul-Hikma* (" The Balance of Wisdom "), written in the 12th century, occurs the following definition of justice :—" Justice is the stay of all virtues and the support of all excellences. In order to place justice on the pinnacle of perfection, the Supreme Creator (*al-Bâri Ta'âla*) made himself known to the choicest of His Servants under the name of the Just ; and it was by the light of justice that the world became complete and perfected and was brought to perfect order—to which there is allusion in the words of him on whom there be blessings : " By Justice were the Heavens and the Earth established."

P. 340. Although some Western scholars have doubted the accuracy of the story that Nizâm-ul-Mulk, Omar Khayyâm and Hasan bin Sabbâh were fellow students, the latest biographer of " The Old Man of the Mountain " re-affirms that all three were at one time pupils of Imâm Mûsik ud-dîn (Muwaffak ud-dîn) (?). This new life of Hasan Sabbâh is by the pen of a learned Moulvi of Lucknow (Moulvi Abdul Halîm surnamed *Sharar*), and gives in a short compass an exhaustive and well-balanced summary of Hasan Sabbâh's life and objects, and of the pernicious character of his propaganda.

P. 340. *Hasan Sabbâh.*—Moulvi Abdul Halîm points out how Hasan Sabbâh's followers worked with *hashish* in carrying out their pernicious propaganda ; how they drugged the minds of their proselytes for the furtherance of their designs against the existing order. He also describes the hydra-headed character of the occult doctrine professed by these enemies of society ; how on the destruction of the *Karâmita* the Isma'îlias sprang into existence.

P. 359. *Bâbis.*—The Bâbis, who have now split up into several sections, are to be found chiefly in foreign countries. They are said to abound in the United States ; many of them are settled in Beyrout and not a few in Bombay and Calcutta. The greatest authority in England on Bâbism, Professor E. G. Browne, says that the Babi cult has nothing in common with Sûfism. One fundamental difference between the two cults lies in their mentality ; whilst Sûfism shows great charity towards differing systems, Bâbism is intensely exclusive, not to say fanatical.

P. 400. *Safawi.*—A new theory appears to have been recently started attributing the derivation of the term " Safawi," the designation of the dynasty founded by Shah Isma'il in Persia, to the word *Safi* which forms part of the name of Safi-ud-din, the ancestor of Shah Isma'il ; and not to " Sufi," the title borne by Safi ud-din. To this theory I venture to enter a respectful protest. For several centuries after the foundation of the Persian Empire the Shahs of Persia were styled by European travellers, merchants, and chroniclers " The Grand Sophi," in contradistinction to " The Grand Mogul " and " The Grand Turk." The reason is obvious. Among oriental writers the word " safawi " has always been recognised as derived from Sûfi, just as the other designation of this dynasty, " Musawi," is derived from the Imâm Mûsa al-Kâzim. The Rizawi Syeds trace their descent from Imâm Ali, son of the Imâm Mûsa.

P. 402. *The sack of Bagdad.*—In the following couplet Sa'di has expressed his horror at the terrible scenes he witnessed at the sack of Bagdad :

" It is meet that Heaven should rain tears of blood on earth
    At the destruction that has befallen
    The Empire of Musta'sim, Commander of the Faithful.
O Mohammed ! If in the Day of Judgment you will raise your
    head above the earth
    Raise your head and see the tribulation of the people now."

The effect of the picture drawn by the poet is lost in the translation.

آسـان را حق بود گر خون بباره بر زمین

بر روال ملک مستعصم امیر المؤمنین ؟

ای محمد گر قیامت سر بون آری زخاك :

سر بون آر و قیامت در میان خلق بین

P. 406. *Predestination.*—The following tradition reported by 'Ubayy ibn Ka'b throws considerable light on the view held by the Prophet on the subject of predestination :—" the most prosperous man is he who becomes prosperous by his own exertions ; and the most wretched man is he who becomes wretched by his own actions."

The great Caliph Omar is reported to have inflicted double punishment on a man who was caught in the act of committing an evil deed and had said in exculpation that he was led to do it by the decree of God.

Ameer-ul-Mominin Ali (The Caliph), in answer to one of his men who had fought at Siffin, and had enquired whether it was the decree of God that had led them to Syria, is reported to have said as follows :

" Perhaps you consider predestination to be necessary and the particular decree to be irreversible ; if it were so, then would reward and punishment be vain, and the promise and the threat would be of no account ; and surely blame would not have come from God for the sinner nor praise for the righteous, nor would the righteous be more worthy of the reward of his good deeds than the wicked, nor the wicked be more deserving of the punishment of his sin than the righteous. Such a remark (savours) of the brethren of devils and the worshippers of idols and of the enemies of the Merciful and of those who bear witness to falsehood and of those that are blind to the right in their concerns—such as the fatalists and the Magians of this church. God hath ordained the giving of choice (to men) and forbidden the putting (of them) in fear ; and He hath not laid duties upon men by force, nor sent His Prophets in sport. This is the notion of unbelievers, and woe unto the unbelievers in hell ! " Then asked the old man : " What is this predestination and particular decree which drove us ? " He answered : " The command of God therein and His purpose." Then he repeated (the verse) : " The Lord hath ordained (predestined) that ye worship none but Him, and kindness to your parents."

The second apostolical Imâm's letter to the people of Basra also contains the following passage which is worthy of note : " Whoever makes his Lord responsible for his sin is a transgressor ; God does not make people obey Him against their will, nor force them to sin against their will."

P. 414. *The word Mu'tazila.*—In the *Ghyas-ul-Lughat* and the *Farhang* (Lucknow) the word معتزل is spelt with a *fatha* on the third syllable, which would make it in its English garb *Mu'tazala.* The *Farhang* is the work of three of the most learned Moslem scholars of India, and is the best and most comprehensive lexicon of its kind, a real encyclopædia. In its compilation the authors have used every existing lexicon, among them the *Kashf-ul-Lughât*, the *Surâh* the *Tâj-ul-'Urûs* and a number of others, so that it cannot be said they have decided lightly. In Richardson's Dictionary the word is spelt similarly.

In the *Lisân-ul-'Arab* the word is printed with a *Kesra* under the third syllable, which would make it read *Mu'tazila.* And Western Orientalists have almost entirely adopted this view.

The difference, which to an outsider unacquainted with the Arabic language may sound like a distinction without a difference, arises from the question, did Wâsil bin 'Ata leave the *majlis* of his own accord, or was he asked on account of his disagreement with the Imâm to withdraw ? Ibn Khallikân says he was " expelled." In the first case the active participle would be the right form, and the word would be *mu'tazila* ; in the latter case it would be *mu'tazala.* The Indian Moulvis hold the opinion that he was asked to leave ; in which they are supported by Ibn Khallikân. And yet de Slane, the translator of the *Wafi'ât al-Ayân* transliterates the word as *Mu'tazilite.*

In all my previous works I have followed the *Ghyâs* and the *Farhang*, but in view of the unanimity among Western Orientalists and in order to avoid confusing the reader I have decided in this Edition to range myself with them. This does not, however, alter my adherence to the scholars of my country.

P. 419. *Mu'tazila doctrines.*—" The Mu'tazilas are agreed that the world has a Creator, Eternal, Almighty, Omniscient, Living. He is neither a body nor an accident nor a substance ; He is self-sufficient. One, incomprehensible by sense, Just, All-wise, doth no wrong ; nor purposeth any ; He lays duties on human beings by way of indicating retribution to them. He renders man capable of action, removes hindrance out of the way, and retribution is absolutely necessary ; further, they agree upon the necessity of the sending of a Prophet when a sending is desirable, and that the Prophet must bring a new law or revive one of which no trace is left, or provide some new life to humanity ; and they are agreed that the last of the Prophets is Mohammed ; and that faith is a declaration and knowledge and action. And they agree that man's action is not created in him ; they agree in having friendly feelings towards the Companions of the Prophet, but they disagree about Osmân after the events that he brought about ; most of them, however, have friendly feelings towards him and offer explanations for his conduct. And most of them are agreed about standing aloof from Mu'âwiyâh and 'Amr ibn al-'Âs and they are agreed upon the necessity of enjoining good acts and the forbidding of evil."

P. 472. Ameer Khusru, although he has been accorded a place amongst the *Awlia* (the Sûfi saints), was certainly not a professed Sûfi. Most of the Moslem poets of India bear more than a tinge of mysticism, and have given expression to it in their poetry. I have already mentioned Dabîr (*ante*, p. 460). The three brothers, Anîs, Mûnis, and Uns (*noms de plume* derived from one and the same root), were contemporaries of Dabír and their thoughts run in the same channel. Altâf Husain Khan *Hâli* and Asad ullâh Khan *Ghâlib*, like the unfortunate Bahâdur Shah, the last titular King of Delhi, who was deported by the British to Rangoon after the Mutiny, were "intuitionalists" In one of his finest poems Ghâlib speaks of Bahâdur Shah in these terms :

> Shah-i-roushan dil Bahâdur Shah kehai
> Râz-i-hasti uspeh sar-ta-sar khula.

The King Bahadur Shah of the illumined heart,
He has had opened to him fully the mysteries of existence.

P. 472. *Sennusi.*—The Sennusiya order, if it can be so called, was founded by Mohammed bin Ali as-Sennusi al-Idrisi. He was a descendant of the Prophet through Idris, who had escaped into the Maghrib (West Africa) from the massacre in Medina by Yezid's troops. He was born in a place called Mustaghanem in Algeria in 1787. He appears to have been a man of a particularly virile character. He travelled much in the Islâmic countries which were easy of access, and noted the deterioration in morals which resulted to the Arabs and other Moslems of North Africa from contact with the peoples of the Mediterranean littoral. He also observed how the Moslems had fallen away from the old teachings, and how lethargic and fatalistic they had become. He uplifted them by directing their energies to such industries as conduced to material prosperity and their minds to the duties imposed by their religion.

Sidi Mohammed bin Ali, before his death in 1859, had founded numbers of *zavias* or lodges in the Hijaz and Yemen, in the Libyan Oases, in Cyrenaica and Algeria. And those lodges, in mid-Africa at least, exercised considerable moral influence. In Morocco his disciples, who are usually called Brothers (" Ikhwân "), made little or no progress in consequence of the old established Moulai Tyyib order. Sidi Mohammed was succeeded by his son Mohammed al-Mahdi as the head of the fraternity.

P. 473. I am quoting from memory—

> Kajkol ko tâj khusrawâni sahmjhai
> Aur dunyâ dani ko fâni samjhai
> Dariai Hakikat wahi jawai pair
> Jo Kisai 'umar ko kahâni samjhai.

A postasy.—The punishment for apostasy provided by the ecclesiastical laws of Islâm has recently caused some amount of perturbation among politicians and others in England. " Apostasy " has always from the earliest times been regarded as a capital offence in all the religious and civil systems of the world, as it formed a breach of loyalty to established order. The Romans condemned the early Christians to death because they had set themselves up against the government and the State-religion. The Christians, when they obtained supremacy, followed the Roman example. The Romish Church burnt apostates, heretics, men, women and even children, without mercy all over the globe. The Reformed Churches were not lacking in ardour in the cause of orthodoxy and maintenance of conformity. Apostates were subject to the penalty of death up to very recent times in England. At the present time a person renouncing Christianity is not put to death, but is subject to social and civil ostracism. The Prophet of Islâm never condemned freedom of conscience, but treason to the Commonwealth was punished with death. It was frequently the case that the Meccans made a profession of the faith in order to get into the city of Medina, and after obtaining all the information connected with the security of the little Moslem State returned to Mecca and threw off Islâm. When captured they were condemned to execution. Treason is still in our own days, throughout the world, punishable with death, and no objection can be taken to these executions. The Moslem ecclesiastical law that an apostate must undergo the penalty of death is based on this rule. But women are not punishable with death, they are only imprisoned ; nor is any child subject to that penalty. This is the difference between Islâm and Christianity in the matter of humanity and freedom of conscience. If I am not mistaken, the penalty of death for " apostasy " was abolished in Turkey in the reign of Sultan Selim II. towards the end of the eighteenth century.

APPENDIX IV

For the Genealogical Tables of the Saracenic Caliphs and Sovereigns see my *Short History of the Saracens*. I give here the names of the Ommeyyade Caliphs of Damascus and Spain, of the Abbaside Caliphs of Bagdad and the Fâtimide Caliphs of Cairo, with the dates of their accession to make the text intelligible.

THE RÂSHIDÎN CALIPHS.

		A.H.	A.C.
1.	Abû Bakr	11 =	632
2.	Omar	13 =	634
3.	Osmân	23 =	644
4.	Ali	35 =	656

THE OMMEYYADE SOVEREIGNS OF DAMASCUS.

		A.H.	A.C.
1.	Mu'âwiyah I.	41 =	661
2.	Yezîd	61 =	681
3.	Muâwiyah II.	64 =	683
4.	Merwân I.	65 =	684
5.	Abdul Malik	65 =	685
6.	Walîd I.	86 =	705
7.	Sulaimân	96 =	715
8.	Omar bin Abdul Azîz	99 =	717
9.	Yezîd II.	101 =	720
10.	Hishâm	105 =	724
11.	Walîd II.	125 =	743
12.	Yezîd III.	126 =	744
13.	Ibrâhim	126 =	744
14.	Merwân II.	127 =	745

THE ABBASIDE CALIPHS OF BAGDAD.

		A.H.	A.C.
1.	As-Saffâh, *Abu'l Abbâs* (Abdullah)	132 =	750
2.	Al-Mansûr, *Abû Ja'far*	136 =	754

		A.H.		A.C.
3.	Al-Mahdi (Mohammed) - - - - - -	158	=	775
4.	Al-Hâdi (Mûsa) - - - - - - -	168	=	785
5.	Ar-Rashîd (Hârûn) - - - - - -	170	=	786
6.	Al-Amîn (Mohammed) - - - - - -	193	=	809
7.	Al-Mâmûn (Abdullah) - - - - - -	198	=	813
8.	Al-Mu'tasim b'Illâh (Abû Ishâk Mohammed) -	218	=	833
9.	Al-Wâsik b'Illâh (Abû Jaafar Hârûn) - - -	227	=	842
10.	Al-Mutawakkil 'ala-Illâh (Jaafar) - - - -	232	=	847
11.	Al-Muntasir b'Illâh (Mohammed) - - - -	247	=	861
12.	Al-Mustaîn b'Illâh (Ahmed) - - - - -	248	=	862
13.	Al-Mu'tazz b'Illâh (Mohammed) - - - -	252	=	866
14.	Al-Muhtadi b'Illâh (Mohammed Abû Ishâk) - -	255	=	869
15.	Al-Mu'tamid al'-Allâh (Ahmed, Abû'l Abbâs) -	256	=	870
16.	Al-Mutazid b'Illâh (Ahmed, Abû'l Abbâs) -	279	=	892
17.	Al-Muktafi b'Illâh (Ali, Abu Mohammed) - -	289	=	902
18.	Al-Muktadir b'Illâh (Ja'far, Abû'l Fazl) -	295	=	908
19.	Al-Kâhir b'Illâh (Mohammed, Abû Mansur) - -	320	=	932
20.	Ar-Râzi b'Illâh (Mohammed Abu'l Abbâs) - -	322	=	934
21.	Al-Muttaki b'Illâh (Ibrahim, Abu'l Ishâk) -	329	=	940
22.	Al-Mustakfi b'Illâh (Abdullah, Abu'l Kâsim) -	333	=	944
23.	Al-Muti 'Ullâh (Fazl, Abûl Kâsim) - - -	334	=	946
24.	At-Tâi b'Illâh (Abdul Karim, Abû Bakr) - -	363	=	974
25.	Al-Kâdir b'Illâh (Ahmed, Abu'l Abbas) - -	381	=	991
26.	Al-Kâim biamr Illâh (Abdullah, Abû Jaafar) - -	422	=	1031
27.	Al-Muktadi bi'amr-Illâh (Abdullah, Abu'l Kasim) -	467	=	1075
28.	Al-Mustazhir b'Illâh (Ahmed, Abu'l Abbâs) - -	487	=	1094
29.	Al-Mustarshid b'Illâh (Fazl, Abu'l Mansûr) - -	512	=	1118
30.	Ar-Râshid b'Illâh (Mansûr, Abû Jaafar) -	529	=	1135
31.	Al-Muktafi bi'amr-Illâh (Mohammed, Abû Abdullah)	530	=	1136
32.	Al-Mustanjid b'Illâh (Yusuf, Abu'l Muzaffar) -	555	=	1160
33.	Al-Mustazii bi'amr-Illâh (Hasan, Abû Mohammed)	566	=	1170
34.	An-Nâsir li-dîn-Illâh (Ahmed, Abu'l Abbâs) - -	575	=	1180
35.	Az-Zâhir bi'amr-Illâh (Mohammed, Abû Nasr) -	622	=	1225
36.	Al-Mustansir b'Illâh (Mansûr, Abû Ja'far) -	623	=	1226
37.	Al-Musta'sim b'Illâh (Abdullah, Abû Ahmed) -	640	=	1242

THE FÂTIMIDE CALIPHS OF EGYPT

		A.H.		A.C.
1.	Al-Mahdi, Obaidullah - - - - - -	296	=	908
2.	Al-Kâim bi-amr-Illâh - - - - - -	322	=	934
3.	Al-Mansûr bi-amr-Illâh - - - - - -	334	=	945
4.	Al-Muizz li-dîn-Illâh - - - - - -	341	=	953
5.	Al-Azîz b'Illâh - - - - - - -	365	=	975
6.	Al-Hâkim bi-amr-Illâh - - - - - -	386	=	996
7.	Az-Zâhir l'-azâz-dîn-Illâh - - - - -	411	=	1021
8.	Al-Mustansir b'Illâh - - - - - -	427	=	1036

									A.H.		A.C.
9.	Al-Musta'li b'Illah	-	-	-	-	-	-	-	487	=	1094
10.	Al-'Âmir bi-Ahkam-Illâh	-	-	-	-	-			494	=	1101
11.	Al-Hâfiz li-dîn-Illâh	-	-	-	-	-	-		523	=	1130
12.	Az-Zâfir bi-amr-Illâh	-	-	-	-	-	-		544	=	1149
13.	Al-Fâiz bi-amr-Illâh	-	-	-	-	-	-		549	=	1154
14.	Al-'Âzid-li-dîn-Illâh	-	-	-	-	-	-		555	=	1160

THE OMMEYYADE CALIPHS OF CORDOVA.

138-422, 756-1031 A.C.

					A.H.		A.C.
Abdur Rahmân I. (ad Dâkhil)	-	-	-	-	138	=	756
Hishâm I. (Abu'l Walîd)	-	-	-	-	172	=	788
Hakam I., al-Muntasir	-	-	-	-	180	=	796
Abdur Rahmân II. (al-Ausat)	-	-	-	-	206	=	822
Mohammed I.	-	-	-	-	238	=	852
Munzir	-	-	-	-	273	=	886
Abdullâh	-	-	-	-	275	=	888
An-Nâsir li-dîn-Illâh, Abdur Rahmân III.	-	-	-	300	=	912
Al-Mustansir b'Illâh, Hakam II.	-	-	-	-	350	=	961
Al-Muwayyid b'Illâh, Hishâm II.	-	-	-	366	=	976
Al-Mahdi, Mohammed II.	-	-	-	-	399	=	1009
Al-Musta'in b'Illâh, Sulaimân	-	-	-	-	400	=	1009
Mohammed II (again)	-	-	-	-	400	=	1010
Hishâm II. (again)	-	-	-	-	400	=	1010
Sulaimân (again)	-	-	-	-	403	=	1013
Ali bin Hamûd (An-Nâsir the Idriside)	-	-	-	407	=	1016
Abdur Rahmân IV (al-Murtaza)	-	-	-	-	408	=	1018
Kâsim bin Hamûd (al-Mâmûn)	-	-	-	-	408	=	1018
Yahya bin Ali bin Hamûd (al-Musta'li)	-	-	-	412	=	1021
Kâsim bin Hamûd (again)	-	-	-	-	413	=	1022
Abdur Rahmân V. (al-Mustazhir b'Illâh)	-	-	-	414	=	1023
Mohammed III. (al-Mustakfi b'Illâh)	-	-	-	414	=	1024
Yahya bin Ali bin Hamûd (again)	-	-	-	416	=	1025
Hishâm III. (al-Mu'tazz b'Illâh)	-	-	-	-	418	=	1027

GENERAL INDEX.

N.B.—In the following index the definite article *al* before proper names is disregarded, while the prefix *Banu* or *Bani* (" sons of . . .") before the names of tribes is omitted ; al-Hallâj, *e.g.* should be sought under H, and Banû-Abbâs under A.

The letter *b.* between two names stands for *ibn* (" son of . . ."), and *n* for *note*.

A.

Abbâs, uncle of the Prophet, 6, 7, 9 *n*, 14, 44, 113, 128, 305-6.
Abbâs II., Shah of Persia, 451.
Abbasides (Banû-Abbâs), 276, 283-4, 285, 304, 305, 307-13, 315, 316, 324, 325, 326, 339, 367, 371, 372, 389.
Abdullah, father of the Prophet, 7, 8, 128.
Abdullah Abu'l Abbâs, see Saffâh.
Abdullah Abû Ja'far, see Mansûr (Caliph).
Abdullah b. Abbâs, 237, 274, 296, 306, 363, 436.
Abdullah b. Abû Kuhâfa, see Abu Bakr.
Abdullah b. Ahmed b. Ali al-Beithâr, 386.
Abdullah b. Juda'ân, 13.
Abdullah b. Maimûn al-Kaddâh, 326, 330-5, 336, 337.
Abdullah b. Sa'd b. Surrah, 295.
Abdullah b. Ubayy, 57, 60, 68, 76, 103, 115 *n*.
Abdullah b. Zubair, 7 *n*.
Abd ud-Dâr b. Kosayy, 4, 5.
Abd ul-Halîm *Sharar*, Moulvi, 494.
Abd ul-Kabir, a friend of Ibn-Rushd, 431.
Abd ul-Kâdir Ghilâni, Sheikh, 343 *n*, 369, 472.
Abd ul-Kais, tribe of, lxvi.
Abd ul-Malik b. Merwân, 128, 254, 303 *n*, 355.
Abd ul-Malik II., Caliph, 3 *n*.

Abd(u) Manâf, see Abû Tâlib.
Abd(u) Manâf b. Kosayy, 4, 5 *n*.
Abd ul-Muttalib, grandfather of the Prophet, lxviii, 5, 6, 7, 9, 10, 13, 128.
Abd ur-Rahmân b. 'Auf, 21.
Abd ur-Rahmân al-Hâzini, astronomer, 381.
Abd ur-Rahmân Sûfi, physicist, 376.
Abd ur-Razzâk b. Ali b. Hasan al-Lâhiji, 451, 452.
Abd us-Salâm ar-Rukn, physician, 450.
Abd ush-Shams b. Abd(u) Manâf, 4, 5 *n*.
Abd ush-Shams, surnamed ' Saba,' lxii-lxiii.
Abd ul-'Uzza, see Abû Lahab.
Abelard, 397.
Aben-Bethar, see Abdullah b. Ahmed b. Ali al-Beithâr.
Abraha al-Ashram, lxiii *n*, 7-8.
Abraham, lxiv, lxx, 20.
Abu'l Abbâs, see Saffâh.
Abû Abdullah b. al-Mubârak, 351.
Abû Abdullah Mohammed b. Karrâm, 443.
Abû Abdullah Mohammed b. Sa'îd, poet, 107 *n*.
Abû Ali Mohammed al-Jubbâî, 415, 420, 452.
Abû Bakr, Caliph, 6, 21, 26, 27, 38, 46, 47, 48, 69, 86, 103, 116, 122, 126, 127, 234, 264, 278, 280, 293, 294, 323, 460.

Sylvanus, Constantine, 329.
Sylvester II., Pope, 371 n.
Syria, lx, 5, 11, 15, 77 n, 102, 115, 127, 128, 324, 438, 445.

T.

Tabari, historian, 42, 96, 390-1.
Tabaristân, 322.
Tabûk, expedition of, 104.
Tacitus, 225.
tafwîz, doctrine of, 411-2, 413, 453.
Taghlibites, the, lxvi.
Tahârt, 375.
Tâherides of Khorâsan, 375.
Tâj ud-Dîn, Kâzi of Cairo, 130.
takeyya, practice of, 335-6.
Talha, companion of the Prophet, 296.
Talha, standard bearer of the Koreish, 69 n.
Talmud, the, 222.
Tantarâni, poet, 395.
tashbîh, doctrine of, 412.
Tasso, 254.
tauba, doctrine of, 475.
tauhîd, doctrine of, 417, 423.
tawâf (circumambulation of the Kaaba), 3.
Tay, tribe of, lxvi, lxviii, 106.
Tâyef, lxvi, 10, 41, 98, 104.
Taym, family of, 13.
Taym b. Murra, 6.
Teraphim, the, 140, 151.
Tertullian, St., xxix, 251.
Thakîf, tribe of, 41, 97-8, 99, 105 n.
Thamûd, tribe of, lix, lx, lxx, 25.
Thaur, mount, 47.
Theodora, liii, 330 n.
Thompson, Joseph, African traveller, 266 n.
Thracians, the, 223.
Thumâma b. Uthal, 85.
Tihâma, lvii, lxii, 68.
Timûr, 383.
Titus, xxxvii.
Tlemcen, 375.
Toledo, 392.
Tours, in France, 69, 292.
Treitheism, doctrine of, xlix-l.
Tughlakabad, 131.
Tughril, Sultân, 315 n, 444.
Tulaiha b. Khuwailid, 116.
Turanians, the, xix, xxx.
Tûs, 464, 469.
Tyre, sack of, xxxiv.

U.

'Ukâz, fair of, lviii, 10-11, 12.
Ulugh Beg, Shah Rukh's son, 383.
Umm ul-Fazl, Mâmûn's sister, 255, 312, 345.
Umm ul-Habîb, Mâmûn's daughter, 255, 346.
Umm-Habîba, wife of the Prophet, 235.
Umm-Hakîm, daughter of Abd ul-Muttalib, 7 n.
Umm ul-Jamîl, wife of Abû Lahab, 24.
Uns, Indian poet, 497.
'Unsuri, poet, 380.
Upanishads, the, xxii, xxiii.
Ur, in Chaldæa, xx.
Usûlîs, the, 346-9.
Uzbegs, the, 400, 402.
al-'Uzza, goddess, lxvi, 34, 36, 101.

V.

Valentinian, Emperor, 226.
Valentinians, the, xlvii, lxx, 343.
Vandals, the, 401.
Vasudeva-Krishna, xxiv, xxv.
Vendidad, the, 191.

W.

Wahâbis and Wahâbîsm, 125-6, 353, 356, 357.
Wahb, grandfather of the Prophet, 7.
Wahraz, Marzbân of Yemen, lxiii n.
wajd, a Sûfi term, 476.
Walîd, Caliph, 128, 319 n.
Walîd, Osman's uterine brother, 295.
walîs, the, 470.
Waraka b. Naufal, 15 n, 18, 19.
Wâsil b. 'Atâ al-Ghazzâl, 414-5, 496.
Wâthik, Caliph, 312, 422, 439.
Watwât, poet, 396.
Wellington, Duke of, 80.
wisâl, a Sûfi term, 474.
Wycliffe, 397.

X.

Xerxes, 68.

Y.

Yahya, grandson of Zain ul-'Âbidîn, 308, 322.
Yahya b. Abi Mansûr, astronomer, 374, 484.
Yakhzûm b. Murra, house of, 6.

BIBLIOGRAPHICAL INDEX

Akhlâk Muhsini (Mulla Husain Wâiz).
Akhlâk Nâsiri (Nasîr ud-din Abdur Rahim Ibn Abi Mansûr).
al-Âsâr ul-Bâkièh (Al-Beiruni).
Al-Karrâr (*Life of the Caliph Ali*) (Riza Ali).
Al-Luma' (Abu Nasr as-Sarrâj).
Âtesh Kadeh (Lutf Ali Azar).
Bihâr-ul-Anwâr (Mulla Bâkir Majîsi).
Dabistâni Mazâhib (Mohsini Fâni).
Dîwâni Hâfiz (Shams ud-dîn Hâfiz).
The Durrul-makhtâr.
Fasl-ul-Makâl (Ibn Rushd).
The Fatâwai Âlamgiri.
Fi't Tahkîk ma l'il Hind (Al-Beiruni).
Futûh ul-Buldân (Balazuri).
Ghurar wa'durar (Sharîf al-Murtaza).
Gouhar-i-Murâd (Mulla Abdur Razzâk).
Hadîka (Sanâi).
Hayy ibn Yakzân (Ibn Tufail).
Ihya ul-'Ulum (Imâm al-Ghazzâli).
Ihtijâj ut-Tabrasi (Shaikh at-Tabrasi).
'Ijâz ut-Tanzil (Khalifa Mohammed Hasan).
Insân ul 'Uyûn (al-Halabi).
Jâmi'-ul-Akhbâr.
Jâmi'-ut-Tirmizi (Imâm Tirmizi).
Kashf uz-Zunûn Haji Khalifa).
Kirân us-Sa'dain (Ameer Khusru M. E. 1228 A.H.).
Kitâb ul-Ishtikâk (Ibn Doreid).
Kitâb-ul-Kharâj (Imâm Abû Yusuf).
Kitâb ul-Mustatraf.
Kitâb al-Tawâsin (*The poems of al-Hallâj*) (M. Louis Massignon, Paris, 1913).
Kitâb Ridz al-Jinân (Ashraf Ali Ibn Abdul Wali).
Kitâb ud-duwal al-Fakhri (Ibn Tiktaka, Derenbourg ed. 1877).
Kitâb ul-Tabyin (Ibn Asâkir (pub. Report Congress Orientalists, 1876 ; Vol. II.)).
Lisân ul-Arab (Jamâluddîn bin Mohammed al-Misri).
Luma't-ul Baiza (Sermons of Fâtima't az-Zahra).
Makkari (Umdat ut-Tâlib).
Mâkhaz-'Ulûm (Syed Kerâmat Ali).
Manâkibi Martazawi.
Masnavi (Moulâna Jalâl ud-dîn Rumi).
Milal wa'Nihal (Shahristâni).
Mishkât al-Masâbih.
Mu'jam-ul-Buldân (Yakût).
Munkiz-min azzalâl (Imâm al-Ghazzâli).
Murûj uz-Zahab (Mas'udi).
Nafahât ul-Uns (Nûr-uddîn Jâmi).
Nahaj-ul-Balâghat (Sermons of Ameer ul-Mominin Ali ibn Abi Tâlib).
Nahaj ul-Balâghat (Sharh of Ibn Abi'l Hadid on the).
an-Nujûm uz-Zâhira (Jamâl ud-Din Abu'l Mahâsin Ibn Taghri-bardi).
The Radd ul-Muhtâr.
Sharhi Nahaj ul-Balâghat (Lutfullah Kâshâni).
Siâsatnameh (Nizâm ul-Mulk).
Sîrat ur-Rasûl (Ibn Hishâm).
Sîrat ur-Nabawiyeh wa'l Âsâr ul-Mohammediya (Syed Ahmed Zaini).
Tafsir al-Kasshâf (Imâm Zamakhshari).
Tahhrîj ul-Hedaya (Zail'yi).
Târîkh-ul-Islâm (az-Zahabi).
Tarîkh al-Kâmil (Ibn ul-Athir).
Târîkh ul-Imâm Ibn Khaldun.
Târîkh Wassâf.
Târîkh ul-Khulafâ (Suy'uti).
Târîkh ul-Hukama (Jamâl ud-din Kifti).
Tazkirat-ul-Awlia (Farîd ud-din 'Attâr).
Umdat ut-Tâlib (Makkari).
'Uyûn ul-Masâil (Abû Nasr Fârâbi).
Wafiât ul-'Ayân (Ibn Khallikan).

Etc.

A Literary History of Persia (E. G. Browne).
Ancient History of the East (Lenormant).
Angel-Messiah (de Bunsen).
Arnold's Sermons.
Aspects of Islâm (Duncan Black Macdonald).
Code Rabbinique.
Concubina (du Cange).
Conflict of Religion and Science (Draper).
Culturgeschichte des Orients unter den Caliphen (Von Kremer).
Curiosities of Literature (Disraeli).
Decline and Fall of the Roman Empire (Gibbon).
Ecclesiastical History (Mosheim).
Essay on Islâm (Emmanuel Deutsch).
Essay on Mahommed's Place in the Church (de Bunsen).
Hallam's History of England.
Hindu Religion and Castes (H. H. Wilson).
Hindu Tribes and Castes (Sherring).
Histoire des Arabes (Sédillot).

Histoire des Musulmanes d'Espagne (Dozy).
Histoire des Philosophes et les Théologiens Musulmanes (Gustave Dugat).
History of Ancient Egypt (Rawlinson).
History of Latin Christianity (Milman).
History of Christianity (Milman).
History of Christian Theology in the Apostolic Age (Reuss).
History of Greece (Grote).
History of Rationalism (Lecky).
History of the Jews (Milman).
History of the Doctrine of the Future Life (Alger).
History of the Christian Church (Blunt).
History of the Church of Christ (Milner).
Ibn Khallikân (De Slane's Translation).
Intellectual Development of Europe (Draper).
Islâm under the Arabs (Osborne).
Jewish Literature and Modern Education (Maitland).
Law of Nature and Nations (Pufendorff).
Le Dogme et la Loi de l'Islam (Goldziher).
L'Influence des Croissades sur l'état des Peuples de l'Europe (d'Aillecourt).
Les Confréries Religieuses Musulmanes (Dupont et Coppolani).
Les Ecoles Philosophiques chez les Arabes (Auguste Schmölders).
Les Effects de la Rêligion de Muhammed (Oelsner).
Les Rêligions et les Philosophies dans l'Asie Centrale (Gobineau).
Life of Jesus (Strauss).
Life of Mahomet (Muir).
Life of Mohammed (Bosworth-Smith).
Literature and Dogma (Matthew Arnold).
Manichaeism (Beausobre).
Materials for the Study of the Babi Religion (E. G. Browne).
Mélange de Philosophie Juive et Arabe (Munk).
Oriental Religions (Johnson).
Philosophie und Theologie von Averroes (Müller).
Rêligion des Druzes (de Sacy).
Religions of India (Hopkins).
Roman Society from Nero to Marcus Aurelius (Samuel Dill).
Secret Societies of All Ages (C. W. Hecklethorn).
Selections from the Koran (Stanley Lane-Poole).
Studies in Islamic Mysticism (R. A. Nicholson).
Tableau Général de l'Empire Ottoman (d'Ohsson).
The Forerunners and Rivals of Christianity (Legge).
The Gentile and the Jew (Döllinger).
The Jewish Church (Stanley's Lectures on).
The Moors in Spain (Stanley Lane-Poole).
The Mystics of Islâm (R. A. Nicholson).
The Preaching of Islâm (Arnold).
The Religion of the Tantras (" Arthur Avalon ").
The Upanishads (Tr. Hume).
Un Grand Maître des Assassins au temps de Saladin (M. Stanislas Guyard).
Vie de Jesus (Renan). Etc.